Monetary Statistics of the United States:
Estimates, Sources, Methods

NATIONAL BUREAU OF ECONOMIC RESEARCH
Studies in Business Cycles

1. *Business Cycles: The Problem and Its Setting* WESLEY C. MITCHELL
2. *Measuring Business Cycles* ARTHUR F. BURNS AND WESLEY C. MITCHELL
3. *American Transportation in Prosperity and Depression* THOR HULTGREN
4. *Inventories and Business Cycles, with Special Reference to Manufacturers' Inventories* MOSES ABRAMOVITZ
5. *What Happens during Business Cycles: A Progress Report* WESLEY C. MITCHELL
6. *Personal Income during Business Cycles* DANIEL CREAMER WITH THE ASSISTANCE OF MARTIN BERNSTEIN
7. *Consumption and Business Fluctuations: A Case Study of the Shoe, Leather, Hide Sequence* RUTH P. MACK
8. *International Financial Transactions and Business Cycles* OSKAR MORGENSTERN
9. *Federal Receipts and Expenditures During Business Cycles, 1879–1958* JOHN M. FIRESTONE
10. *Business Cycle Indicators:* Volume I, *Contributions to the Analysis of Current Business Conditions;* Volume II, *Basic Data on Cyclical Indicators* EDITED BY GEOFFREY H. MOORE
11. *Postwar Cycles in Manufacturers' Inventories* THOMAS M. STANBACK, JR.
12. *A Monetary History of the United States, 1867–1960* MILTON FRIEDMAN AND ANNA JACOBSON SCHWARTZ
13. *Determinants and Effects of Changes in the Stock of Money, 1875–1960* PHILLIP CAGAN
14. *Cost, Prices and Profits: Their Cyclical Relations* THOR HULTGREN
15. *Cyclical Fluctuations in the Exports of the United States Since 1879* ILSE MINTZ
16. *Information, Expectations, and Inventory Fluctuation: A Study of Materials Stock on Hand and on Order* RUTH P. MACK
17. *Forecasting and Recognizing Business Cycle Turning Points* RENDIGS FELS AND C. ELTON HINSHAW
18. *The Business Cycle in a Changing World* ARTHUR F. BURNS
19. *Economic Forecasts and Expectations* JACOB MINCER ET AL.
20. *Monetary Statistics of the United States: Estimates, Sources, Methods* MILTON FRIEDMAN AND ANNA JACOBSON SCHWARTZ

Monetary Statistics of the United States

ESTIMATES, SOURCES, METHODS

MILTON FRIEDMAN

ANNA JACOBSON SCHWARTZ

National Bureau of Economic Research

NEW YORK

1970

Distributed by Columbia University Press

NEW YORK AND LONDON

Relation of the Directors to the Work and Publications
of the National Bureau of Economic Research

1. The object of the National Bureau of Economic Research is to ascertain and to present to the public important economic facts and their interpretation in a scientific and impartial manner. The Board of Directors is charged with the responsibility of ensuring that the work of the National Bureau is carried on in strict conformity with this object.

2. The President of the National Bureau shall submit to the Board of Directors, or to its Executive Committee, for their formal adoption all specific proposals for research to be instituted.

3. No research report shall be published until the President shall have submitted to each member of the Board the manuscript proposed for publication, and such information as will, in his opinion and in the opinion of the author, serve to determine the suitability of the report for publication in accordance with the principles of the National Bureau. Each manuscript shall contain a summary drawing attention to the nature and treatment of the problem studied, the character of the data and their utilization in the report, and the main conclusions reached.

4. For each manuscript so submitted, a special committee of the Board shall be appointed by majority agreement of the President and Vice Presidents (or by the Executive Committee in case of inability to decide on the part of the President and Vice Presidents), consisting of three directors selected as nearly as may be one from each general division of the Board. The names of the special manuscript committee shall be stated to each Director when the manuscript is submitted to him. It shall be the duty of each member of the special manuscript committee to read the manuscript. If each member of the manuscript committee signifies his approval within thirty days of the transmittal of the manuscript, the report may be published. If at the end of that period any member of the manuscript committee withholds his approval, the President shall then notify each member of the Board, requesting approval or disapproval of publication, and thirty days additional shall be granted for this purpose. The manuscript shall then not be published unless at least a majority of the entire Board who shall have voted on the proposal within the time fixed for the receipt of votes shall have approved.

5. No manuscript may be published, though approved by each member of the special manuscript committee, until forty-five days have elapsed from the transmittal of the report in manuscript form. The interval is allowed for the receipt of any memorandum of dissent or reservation, together with a brief statement of his reasons, that any member may wish to express; and such memorandum of dissent or reservation shall be published with the manuscript if he so desires. Publication does not, however, imply that each member of the Board has read the manuscript, or that either members of the Board in general or the special committee have passed on its validity in every detail.

6. Publications of the National Bureau issued for informational purposes concerning the work of the Bureau and its staff, or issued to inform the public of activities of Bureau staff, and volumes issued as a result of various conferences involving the National Bureau shall contain a specific disclaimer noting that such publication has not passed through the normal review procedures required in this resolution. The Executive Committee of the Board is charged with review of all such publications from time to time to ensure that they do not take on the character of formal research reports of the National Bureau, requiring formal Board approval.

7. Unless otherwise determined by the Board or exempted by the terms of paragraph 6, a copy of this resolution shall be printed in each National Bureau publication.

*(Resolution adopted October 25, 1926, and revised February 6, 1933,
February 24, 1941, and April 20, 1968)*

Contents

Preface   xix

1. Introduction   1

   1. Our Estimates   3
   2. Coverage of Our Estimates   58
   3. Derivation of Our Estimates   77
   4. Alternative Monetary Totals   79

PART ONE. DEFINITION OF MONEY

Introduction to Part One   89

2. Prior Usage   93

3. A Priori Approaches   104

   1. "Medium of Exchange"   104
      Claims to Money Versus Money   105
      Net Wealth and Neutrality   110
   2. "Liquidity"   126
      Definition of Liquidity   128
      Statistical Counterparts Used   130
      Theoretical Analysis   132
   3. Conclusion on A Priori Approaches   136
   4. Relevant Empirical Considerations   137
      Statistical Considerations   138
      Nominal vs. Real; Demand vs. Supply   138
      Why We Stress Demand   139
      Substitution in Demand   140
      Substitution in Supply   142
      Conclusion   145

4. Basis for Our Choice of Definition   147

   1. Alternatives Considered   147
   2. Commercial Bank Demand and Time Deposits   154
      The Period Before 1914   154
      The Period 1914–29   155
      The Great Contraction   163
      The Period 1933–45   165
      The Postwar Period   167
   3. Comparison of Total Chosen with Broader Totals   171
   4. More Recent Evidence   178

Appendix to Chapter 4. Evidence on Alternative Definitions of
Money   189
   1. Comparison of States with and without Savings Banks   189
   2. Cross-Section Correlations of Deposits and Personal
      Income   193
5. *Conclusion on Definition*   197

PART TWO. EARLIER ESTIMATES

Introduction to Part Two   201

6. *Sources and Accuracy of Basic Data*   205

   1. Sources of Data   205
      Specie   205
      Currency   207
      Banking Statistics   208
   2. Accuracy of the Data   209
      Specie   210
      Banking Statistics   211

7. *Estimates for the Period Before 1867*   214

   1. Nineteenth Century Private Estimates   233
      Samuel Blodget, Jr.   233
      Albert Gallatin   234
      Ezra C. Seaman   235
   2. Official Estimates   237
      William H. Crawford   237
      Successive Secretaries of the Treasury   240
      Official Documents   243
      Federal Deposit Insurance Corporation   250
   3. Twentieth Century Private Estimates   251
      Wesley C. Mitchell   251
      Clark Warburton   251
      J. G. Gurley and E. S. Shaw   253
      George Macesich   254
      Peter Temin   255
   4. Alternative Money Stock Estimates   257

8. *Estimates for the Period Since 1867*   260

   1. Estimates by Kemmerer, Fisher, and Mitchell   262
      Currency Held by the Public   262
      Deposits Held by the Public   263
   2. Estimates by King and Leong   267
   3. Estimates by Currie and Angell   268

4. Estimates by Federal Reserve System   272
Appendix to Chapter 8. Federal Reserve Estimates of Demand and
Time Deposits Before 1914   274
    1. National Banks   275
    2. Nonnational Banks   286
    3. All Commercial Banks   302

9. *Comparison of Earlier Estimates With Our Own*   303

PART THREE. DERIVATION OF OUR ESTIMATES

Introduction to Part Three   313

10. *General Features of Our Estimates*   315

    1. Choice of Date to Begin Monthly Estimates   315
    2. Sources of the Data   316
    3. Classification of Banks   317
    4. Dating and Seasonal Adjustment   318
        Dating   319
        Seasonal Adjustment   320
    5. Interpolation Procedures   321
        Method L   322
        Method R   323
        Method of Estimating Relevant Parameters   326
        Choice of Related Series   327
        Method S   328
    6. Reliability of the Estimates   329
    7. Definitions   331

11. *Annual, Semiannual, and Quarterly Estimates, 1867–1907*   334

    1. Annual Estimates, January 1867–February 1875   335
        Nonnational Commercial Bank Deposits and Vault Cash   335
        All Commercial Bank Deposits, All Bank Vault Cash, and
            Currency Held by the Public   336
        Mutual Savings Bank Deposits   336
    2. Semiannual and Annual Estimates, 1875–95   337
        Nonnational Commercial and Mutual Savings Bank Deposits
            and Vault Cash   337
        All Commercial Bank Deposits, All-Bank Vault Cash, and
            Currency Held by the Public   338
    3. Quarterly Estimates of Currency Held by the Public and Com-
    mercial Bank Deposits, 1867–1907   339

12. *Currency Held by the Public: Call Date and Monthly Estimates* 352

    1. Currency Outside Treasury and Federal Reserve Banks   352

Revisions of Basic Data   353
Seasonal Adjustments   357
Call Date Series   357
2. All-Bank Vault Cash: Call Dates   357
   Problems in Compilation of Nonnational and Mutual Savings
      Bank Data   358
   Report Dates   359
   Seasonal Adjustment of Vault Cash Figures   360
   Shifting Nonidentically Dated Observations to National and
      Member Bank Call Dates   363
   Interpolation of Missing Call Date Figures, by States   364
   Final Call Date Estimates   369
3. All-Bank Vault Cash: Monthly Estimates   370
   Federal Reserve Estimates, 1943 to Date   379
4. Currency Held by the Public: at Call Dates and Monthly   395
5. Reliability of the Estimates   395
Appendix to Chapter 12. Daily and Monthly Seasonal Factors for
Vault Cash   417

13. Deposits at Commercial Banks: Call Dates   423

1. Problems in Compilation of Nonnational Bank Data   423
2. Report Dates   426
3. The Sample of States   427
4. Nonnational Bank Estimates, National Bank Call Dates,
   1907–23   431
5. National Bank Estimates, National Bank Call Dates, 1907–23   451
6. Nonmember Bank Estimates, Member Bank Call Dates,
   1919–46   452
7. Reconciliation of Nonnational and Nonmember Bank Estimates, 1919–23   473
8. Member Bank Estimates, Member Bank Call Dates, 1919–46   474
9. All Commercial Bank Estimates of Demand and Time Deposits Adjusted, National and Member Bank Call Dates, 1907–46 476
10. Reliability of the Call Date Estimates   477

14. Deposits at Commercial Banks: Monthly Estimates   481

1. Deposit Estimates, Monthly, 1907–19   482
2. Deposits at Member Banks, Monthly, 1919–45   498
   Published Figures for All Member Banks, 1923 on   498
   Estimates for All Member Banks, 1919–23   502
3. Deposits at Nonmember Banks, Monthly, 1919–45   503
4. Federal Reserve Monthly Data, 1946 to Date   523
5. Reliability of the Estimates   525

15. *Deposits at Mutual Savings Banks: Call Date and Monthly Estimates*   531

  1. Problems of Compilation   532
  2. Mutual Savings Bank Report Dates   533
  3. Mutual Savings Bank Deposits, by States   534
  4. Scheme of Interpolation at Call Dates and End of Months   536
      Subperiod 1907–23   536
      Subperiod 1924–46   537
  5. Federal Reserve Estimates, 1947 to Date   554
  6. Reliability of the Estimates   556
  Appendix to Chapter 15. Sources of Mutual Savings Bank Deposit Data   558

16. *Deposits with the Postal Savings System*   562

17. *United States Government Balances*   564

  1. Treasury Cash and Government Deposits at Federal Reserve Banks, Call Dates, 1907–46   572
  2. Government Demand Deposits, Call Dates, 1907–46   573
      Problems of Reconciling Treasury and Bank Records   574
      Estimates from Bank Records   577
  3. Government Time Deposits, Call Dates, 1938–46   581
  4. Total Government Deposits at Commercial and Mutual Savings Banks, Monthly, 1907–42   590
  5. Federal Reserve Estimates of Government Deposits, Monthly, December 1942 to Date   593

Indexes   613

Tables

1. Currency, Deposits, and Savings and Loan Shares Held by the Public, and Consolidated Totals, 1867–1968   4
2. Currency and Commercial Bank Deposits Held by the Public and Consolidated Total of Money Stock, Quarterly, 1867–1968   61
3. Average Annual Rates of Growth of Demand and Time Deposits at Member and Nonmember Banks, and Time Deposits as a Fraction of Total Deposits Adjusted, 1915–29   157
4. Average Annual Rates of Growth of Demand and Time Deposits at Three Reserve Classes of Member Banks, June 1919–June 1929   158
5. Interest Rates Earned and Paid By Member Banks and Ratio of Their Time to Demand Deposits Adjusted, 1919–29   160
6. Debits to Deposit Accounts: Ratio to Demand Plus Time Deposits and to Demand Deposits Only, Weekly Reporting Member Banks in and Outside New York City, 1919–29   162
7. Interest Rates Earned and Paid by Member Banks, and Ratio of Their Time to Demand Deposits Adjusted; Debits to Deposit Accounts: Ratio to Demand Plus Time Deposits and to Demand Deposits Only, Weekly Reporting Member Banks, 1929–33   164
8. Interest Rates Earned and Paid by Member Banks and Ratio of Their Time to Demand Deposits Adjusted, 1933–45   166
9. Differential Between Interest Rate Paid on Commercial Bank Time Deposits and on Mutual Savings Bank Deposits, Postal Savings, and Savings and Loan Shares, 1920–29, 1946–66   173
10. Ratio of Time Deposits to Demand Deposits, by States With and Without Mutual Savings Banks, 1915, 1929, 1950   190
11. Correlation Between Per Capita Personal Income and Various Per Capita Monetary Components and Totals, by States, Selected Years, 1929–60   194
12. Mean and Standard Deviation of Natural Logarithms of Per Capita Deposits and Per Capita Personal Income, by States   195
13. Monetary Statistics Before 1867   216
14. Alternative Money Stock Estimates, Selected Dates, 1799–1865   231
15. Classification of Individual Deposits in Banks of the United States at Four Dates, 1896–1909, According to Andrew and the National Monetary Commission   276
16. *All-Bank Statistics* Derivation of Demand and Time Deposits at National Banks in Continental United States, 1896–1913   282
17. Classification of States According to Character of Estimates in *All-Bank Statistics* of Demand and Time Deposits at Nonnational Incorporated Banks, 1896–1913   288
18. Alternative Estimates of Ratio of Time to Total Demand and Time Deposits, Nonnational Commercial Banks, 1896–1913   299

19. Alternative Estimates of Ratio of Time to Total Demand and Time Deposits, All Commercial Banks, 1896–1913   300
20. Currency Held by the Public, Adjusted Deposits, and Related Series, Annually and Semiannually, 1867–1906   340
21. Currency Held by the Public, Adjusted Deposits, and Related Series, Quarterly, 1867–1907   344
22. Classification of States for Call Date Interpolation   366
23. Pairs of States Correlated by Groups; Average Coefficients of Correlation, 1907–44   368
24. Vault Cash at All Banks, at Call Dates, 1907–42   371
25. Vault Cash at All Banks, at End of Month, 1907–42   380
26. Currency in Circulation Outside Treasury and Federal Reserve Banks, All Bank Vault Cash, and Currency Held by the Public, National and Member Bank Call Dates, 1907–42   396
27. Currency in Circulation Outside Treasury and Federal Reserve Banks, All Bank Vault Cash, and Currency Held by the Public, Wednesday Nearest End of Month, 1907–42   402
28. Reported and Interpolated Vault Cash in Various Classes of Banks at Call Dates and End of Month as Percentages of Total Vault Cash, 1907–42   416
29. Intraweekly and Monthly Seasonal Indexes, Vault Cash, Call Date Series   418
30. Combined Intraweekly and Monthly Seasonal Indexes, Vault Cash, Call Date Series   420
31. Percentage of Population in Urban Areas of Sample States Grouped Regionally, 1910–40   428
32. Deposits at All U.S. Commercial Banks, Distinguishing National from Nonnational Banks in New York, Urbanized, and Rural States, National Bank Call Dates, 1907–23   432
33. Deposits at All U.S. Commercial Banks, Distinguishing Member from Nonmember Banks in New York, Urbanized, and Rural States, Member Bank Call Dates, 1919–46   454
34. Reported and Interpolated Deposits in Various Classes of Banks at Call Dates as Percentages of Total Deposits Adjusted, Demand Deposits Less Duplications, and Time Deposits Adjusted, 1907–46   478
35. Deposits Adjusted at All Commercial Banks, May 1907–June 1919   486
36. Adjusted Demand and Time Deposits at Member, Nonmember, and All Commercial Banks, June 1919–December 1945   504
37. Reported and Interpolated Deposits in Various Classes of Banks at End of Month as Percentages of Total Deposits Adjusted, Demand Deposits Adjusted, and Time Deposits Adjusted, 1907–45   528
38. Deposits at Mutual Savings Banks by Groups of States, at End of Month, May 1907–November 1923   538

39. Deposits at Mutual Savings Banks by Groups of States, at End
of Month, December 1923–December 1946   544
40. Reported and Interpolated Deposits at Mutual Savings Banks in
Various States as Percentages of Aggregate Mutual Savings Bank
Deposits, 1907–46   557
41. United States Government Balances, Call Dates, 1907–46   566
42. Derivation of Demand Deposits Less Duplications, Nonmember
Banks, Member Bank Call Dates, 1917–19   579
43. Derivation of United States Government Demand Deposits, at
Call Dates, in Nonnational Banks, 1917–23, and in Nonmember
Banks, 1917–46   582
44. Demand Deposits Less Duplications at Noninsured Nonmember
Banks, June and December 1934–June 1946   589
45. United States Government Time Deposits at All Banks, at Call
Dates, 1938–46   591
46. United States Government Deposits at All Banks, Monthly, 1907–
08, 1917–42   594
47. United States Government Demand Deposits at Nonweekly Reporting Member Banks, at Monthly Dates Nearest Member Bank
Call Dates, 1917–42   606

Charts

1. Currency, Deposits, and Savings and Loan Shares Held by the Public, 1867–1968   *facing*   58
2. Ratio of Time to Total Demand and Time Deposits for Three Groups of States and for All Nonnational Banks, According to *All-Bank Statistics,* 1896–1924   295
3. Ratio of Time to Total Demand and Time Deposits for a Sample of Group I States, 1896–1924   296
4. Comparison of Earlier Annual Estimates of Monetary Totals and NBER Series, 1880–1940   304
5. Comparison of Earlier Monthly Estimates of Monetary Totals and NBER Series, 1914–34   307
6. Money Stock, Quarterly, 1867–1907   351
7. Two Estimates of Commercial Bank Demand and Time Deposits, 1943–45   524
8. Two Estimates of Commercial Bank Demand and Time Deposits, 1919–23   526
9. Two Estimates of Mutual Savings Bank Deposits, 1943–47   555

The writer has found so much difficulty in securing a long series of yearly averages . . . that the results are here presented in the hope that they may be of use to others.

IRVING FISHER

Preface

This is the third of a quintuplet of books based on new estimates of the quantity of money in the United States. *A Monetary History of the United States, 1867–1960,* by the present authors, "traces the changes in the stock of money . . . , examines the factors that accounted for the changes, and analyzes the reflex influence that the stock of money exerted on the course of events." [1] *Determinants and Effects of Changes in the Money Stock, 1875–1960,* by Phillip Cagan, examines the sources of changes in the stock of money and analyzes the cyclical and secular behavior of each of the proximate determinants of the quantity of money: high-powered money, the ratio of deposits at banks to their reserves, and the ratio of the public's holdings of deposits to its holdings of currency.[2]

As stated in those books, our original plan called for one further volume that was to have a dual function: to describe in greater detail than we have heretofore the sources underlying the new estimates and the methods used to construct them; and to present a statistical analysis of the characteristic behavior of the quantity of money in relation to other economic magnitudes as revealed by the new estimates.

As we progressed with the draft of that projected volume, it got out of hand. We finally decided that it would have to be subdivided into three parts: the present book, which presents the statistical estimates, their sources, and methods of estimation; a second, on monetary trends; and a third, on monetary cycles, making five books in all. We promise the reader that this is the end of the process of reproduction by fission.

The change in plan has been enforced by a broadening of the scope of the material covered. In the present book, in addition to the detailed description of sources, methods, and supplementary tables, we have added an examination of the definition of money and a survey of earlier estimates.

In the book on trends, we have added an analysis of data for the United Kingdom, in order to test the results obtained for the United States. In the book on cycles, which is in a less finished state at this

[1] *A Monetary History of the United States, 1867–1960,* Princeton University Press for the National Bureau of Economic Research, 1963, p. 3.

[2] *Determinants and Effects of Changes in the Stock of Money, 1875–1960,* National Bureau of Economic Research, 1965.

writing than the book on trends, we plan to include some comparative data for a number of countries.

We owe thanks to Allan H. Meltzer, Clark Warburton, and Leland B. Yeager for their comments on selected chapters of this book. On some issues their judgments differ from ours. Though they have not persuaded us to shift our stand, we and our readers are in their debt since their criticisms led us to make changes that we believe improve the exposition of our views.

We beg the indulgence of Phillip Cagan and Solomon Fabricant of our staff reading committee who read a draft of monetary statistics when it was still combined with monetary trends. We have taken into account their penetrating comments on the part of the draft from which this volume emerged, and in the next volume we shall reap the benefit of their comments on monetary trends.

We also acknowledge the generous review of our manuscript by Moses Abramovitz, Frank W. Fetter, and Gabriel Hauge, who constituted the reading committee of NBER Directors.

In the derivation of the monetary statistics presented in this volume, we had assistance initially from Edith Hanover, Juanita Johnson, and Phyllis A. Wallace; and at later stages from Nadeschda Bohsack, Antonette Burgar, Martha S. Jones, David Laidler, Marilyn McGirr, Esther D. Reichner, Selma Seligsohn, Hanna Stern, Mark L. Wehle, Gerald I. White, and Tom Teng-pin Yu. We gratefully acknowledge their help.

We are indebted to H. Irving Forman for the charts. Roger J. Kopstein and Gnomi Schrift Gouldin edited this book.

Milton Friedman

Anna Jacobson Schwartz

Monetary Statistics of the United States:
Estimates, Sources, Methods

1

INTRODUCTION

THIS BOOK ATTEMPTS to provide a comprehensive survey of the construction of estimates of the quantity of money in the United States—an activity that dates back almost to the beginnings of the Republic. The survey covers sources, methods of construction, and the end product.

The immediate motivation for this study is to make available such information for the set of estimates that we have constructed for the period 1867–1946 and for the Federal Reserve estimates that can be used to extend our estimates to subsequent years. This chapter gives our final estimates and a brief explanation of their coverage and derivation.

Part I discusses the definition of money in the context of various totals that can be formed from our basic estimates. The problem of definition has received much attention—in our opinion far more than it deserves. So far as we can see, no issue of principle is involved, and no single definition need be "best." The problem is one common in scientific work: how to choose an empirical counterpart to an abstract concept. For us the test is strictly pragmatic: which counterpart is most useful in making predictions about observable phenomena on the basis of the theory one accepts. The answer may well vary with time and place and may differ according to the phenomena to be predicted and also according to the theory accepted. Any answer is necessarily tentative and subject to change as further evidence accumulates.

Our own tentative answer—for the United States, for the period we cover, and for the purpose of predicting changes in prices and in nominal income—is that the most useful definition designates as "money"

the sum of currency outside banks plus all deposits of commercial banks
—demand and time—adjusted to exclude interbank deposits, U.S. government deposits, and items in the process of collection. However, alternative totals, both narrower and broader than this one, seem to us
almost as satisfactory, and for some specific purposes more satisfactory.
To judge from our experience, important substantive conclusions seldom
hinge on which definition is used.

We have considered only alternatives that draw a sharp line between
items classified as "money," and those classified as "near-money" or
"liquid assets" or "assets." We conjecture that if a major improvement
in definition is feasible, it will be arrived at not by the selection of a
better line of this kind but by the more sophisticated device of constructing weighted sums of assets, the weights reflecting the "moneyness" of
the several assets.

Part II summarizes the work of our predecessors. The basic data used
by them and by us to estimate the stock of specie, other currency, and
deposits held by the public were not collected especially for this purpose
but, like most statistical raw material, were largely an unintended by-
product of governmental activities; in the present instance, largely a
by-product of the regulation of banking institutions.

Until recent years, private scholars—from Samuel Blodget in 1806
to ourselves—rather than governmental agencies have used these data
to construct aggregate estimates. The estimates of different scholars, rest-
ing as they had to on the same basic data, have generally been very
similar in level and trends, as our comparison of different estimates
for the period both before and after the Civil War indicates. However,
they have differed in some not unimportant details, and not all changes
have represented improvements. Scholars too can regress as well as
progress.

We have tried in Tables 13 and 14 to present a compendium of the
major statistical estimates of the basic aggregates—currency, deposits,
and their total—covering roughly the seventy-five years before our estimates start.

We are acutely aware from our own work of the defects and gaps in
these estimates. Yet it is probably true that there are few other important
economic magnitudes for which measurements of anything like the same
accuracy and comparability exist for so long a period of time—popula-

tion, a few commodity prices, and interest rates are the only others that come readily to mind.

Part III explains in detail how our estimates were constructed. In the process, we present various subsidiary series and breakdowns of our deposit estimates that are of interest in their own right. These include deposits of Federal Reserve member and nonmember banks monthly; deposits of national and nonnational or Federal Reserve member and nonmember banks at call dates in New York State, other urban states, and the remainder of the states (Tables 32, 33, and 36).

As this brief description indicates, the present book is for the monetary statistician who is interested in basic data on the quantity of money. It provides raw material for analysis but little economic analysis. For the analysis using the raw material, we refer the reader to the other volumes described in the preface.

1. Our Estimates

Our new estimates of the quantity of money are summarized in Table 1 and Chart 1.[1] Table 1 gives estimates of the U.S. public's holdings of U.S. currency (including coin); four classes of U.S. dollar deposits: commercial bank demand deposits, commercial bank time deposits, mutual savings bank deposits, and Postal Savings System deposits; and savings and loan shares.

The currency figures exclude vault cash held by commercial banks and cash in the U.S. Treasury (with some exceptions noted below) and Federal Reserve Banks. These items are regarded as held not by the "public" but by banks and monetary authorities. Similarly, the deposit figures exclude U.S. government deposits and inter-commercial-bank deposits and are adjusted to avoid the double-counting of checks in the

[1] Table 1 is based on the currency and deposit components of Table A-1 in *A Monetary History*. As explained in section 4 of this chapter, columns 1–4 through 1946 differ from those in the earlier table because they have been adjusted to provide a consolidated total in column 9. In addition, from 1947 on we have revised the estimates in the earlier table to incorporate the latest revisions of Federal Reserve data and extended them to 1968.

We omit the notes to the earlier table which comprise a brief summary of the more detailed explanation of the construction of the estimates given in Chapters 10–17, and we do not present the other appendix tables in *A Monetary History*, which give figures on bank reserves, U.S. government balances, the proximate determinants of the money stock (high-powered money, the deposit-reserve ratio, and the deposit-currency ratio), and a number of other items.

TABLE 1

*Currency, Deposits, and Savings and Loan Shares Held by the Public,
and Consolidated Totals, 1867–1968*

Part I. January 1867 – January 1961
(seasonally adjusted, in billions of dollars)

| | Currency Held by the Public | Deposits Adjusted, Commercial Banks | | | Deposits at | | |
| | | | | | Mut. Sav. | Post. Sav. | S & L |
Date	(1)	Demand (2)	Time (3)	Total (4)	Banks (5)	Syst. (6)	Shares (7)
1867							
Jan.	0.59			0.73	0.28		
1868							
Jan.	0.54			0.71	0.32		
1869							
Jan.	0.54			0.74	0.37		
1870							
Jan.	0.52			0.78	0.44		
1871							
Jan.	0.56			0.84	0.52		
1872							
Jan.	0.55			1.04	0.61		
1873							
Feb.	0.56			1.07	0.68		
1874							
Feb.	0.54			1.07	0.74		
1875							
Feb.	0.56			1.15	0.80		
Aug.	0.53			1.18	0.84		
1876							
Feb.	0.53			1.16	0.84		
Aug.	0.52			1.15	0.85		
1877							
Feb.	0.53			1.17	0.84		
Aug.	0.54			1.09	0.82		
1878							
Feb.	0.54			1.05	0.80		
Aug.	0.54			1.03	0.77		
1879							
Feb.	0.53			1.02	0.75		
Aug.	0.58			1.20	0.74		
1880							
Feb.	0.64			1.30	0.79		
Aug.	0.67			1.38	0.83		

M_1[b] (Cols. 1 + 2) (8)	M_2 (Cols. 8 + 3) (9)	Consolidated Totals[a]			
		Duplications Betw. Col. 9 and Cols. 5 + 6 (10)	M_3 (Cols. 9+5 +6 − 10) (11)	Duplications Betw. Cols. 11 and 7 (12)	M_4 (Cols. 11+7 −12) (13)
	1.32	0.01	1.59		
	1.25	0.01	1.56		
	1.28	0.01	1.64		
	1.30	0.01	1.73		
	1.40	0.01	1.91		
	1.59	0.01	2.19		
	1.63	0.01	2.30		
	1.61	0.02	2.33		
	1.71	0.01	2.50		
	1.71	0.02	2.53		
	1.69	0.01	2.52		
	1.67	0.01	2.51		
	1.70	0.01	2.53		
	1.63	0.01	2.44		
	1.59	0.01	2.38		
	1.57	0.01	2.33		
	1.55	0.01	2.29		
	1.78	0.01	2.51		
	1.94	0.01	2.72		
	2.05	0.01	2.87		

(continued)

TABLE 1 (continued)

Date	Currency Held by the Public (1)	Deposits Adjusted, Commercial Banks			Deposits at		S & L Shares (7)
		Demand (2)	Time (3)	Total (4)	Mut. Sav. Banks (5)	Post. Sav. Syst. (6)	
1881							
Feb.	0.73			1.54	0.87		
Aug.	0.81			1.70	0.96		
1882							
June	0.82			1.79	0.95		
1883							
June	0.87			1.96	1.00		
1884							
June	0.85			1.92	1.03		
1885							
June	0.80			2.06	1.07		
1886							
June	0.77			2.33	1.12		
1887							
June	0.81			2.49	1.18		
1888							
June	0.84			2.54	1.24		
1889							
June	0.83			2.72	1.30		
1890							
June	0.90			3.02	1.37		
1891							
June	0.94			3.10	1.43		
1892							
June	0.94			3.54	1.52		
1893							
June	1.00			3.20	1.55		
1894							
June	0.90			3.34	1.57		
1895							
June	0.90			3.60	1.65		
1896							
June	0.85			3.51	1.69		
1897							
June	0.89			3.69	1.78		0.42
1898							
June	1.03			4.22	1.87		0.42

		Consolidated Totals[a]			
M_1[b] (Cols. 1 + 2) (8')	M_2 (Cols. 8 + 3) (9')	Dupli- cations Betw. Col. 9 and Cols. 5 + 6 (10')	M_3 (Cols. 9+5 +6 − 10) (11')	Dupli- cations Betw. Cols. 11 and 7 (12')	M_4 (Cols. 11+7 −12) (13')
	2.27	0.01	3.13		
	2.51	0.01	3.46		
	2.61	0.01	3.55		
	2.83	0.01	3.82		
	2.77	0.01	3.79		
	2.86	0.02	3.91		
	3.10	0.01	4.21		
	3.30	0.01	4.47		
	3.38	0.02	4.60		
	3.55	0.02	4.83		
	3.92	0.02	5.27		
	4.04	0.01	5.4 6		
	4.48	0.02	5.98		
	4.20	0.02	5.73		
	4.24	0.02	5.79		
	4.50	0.02	6.13		
	4.36	0.09	5.96		
	4.58	0.10	6.26	0.02	6.66
	5.25	0.11	7.01	0.03	7.40

(continued)

TABLE 1 (continued)

Date	Currency Held by the Public (1)	Deposits Adjusted, Commercial Banks			Deposits at		S & L Shares (7)
		Demand (2)	Time (3)	Total (4)	Mut. Sav. Banks (5)	Post. Sav. Syst. (6)	
1899							
June	1.08			5.06	2.00		0.41
1900							
June	1.21			5.29	2.13		0.40
1901							
June	1.25			6.21	2.26		0.40
1902							
June	1.30			6.84	2.39		0.40
1903							
June	1.42			7.23	2.50		0.41
1904							
June	1.42			7.70	2.60		0.42
1905							
June	1.49			8.71	2.74		0.43
1906							
June	1.60			9.39	2.91		0.45
1907							
May	1.74			10.06	3.02		
June	1.72			10.04	3.01		
July	1.68			10.06	3.02		
Aug.	1.68			10.02	3.03		
Sept.	1.65			9.87	3.03		
Oct.	1.75			9.66	3.02		
Nov.	1.81			9.50	3.02		
Dec.	1.88			9.31	3.02		0.51
1908							
Jan.	1.91			9.15	3.02		
Feb.	1.84			9.12	3.02		
Mar.	1.78			9.26	3.02		
Apr.	1.77			9.36	3.02		
May	1.73			9.52	3.02		
June	1.74			9.64	3.00		
July	1.73			9.77	3.01		
Aug.	1.69			9.94	3.02		
Sept.	1.70			10.04	3.03		
Oct.	1.72			10.18	3.04		

		Consolidated Totals[a]			
M_1[b] (Cols. 1 + 2) (8)	M_2 (Cols. 8 + 3) (9)	Duplications Betw. Col. 9 and Cols. 5 + 6 (10)	M_3 (Cols. 9+5 +6 − 10) (11)	Duplications Betw. Cols. 11 and 7 (12)	M_4 (Cols. 11+7 −12) (13)
	6.14	0.12	8.02	0.03	8.40
	6.50	0.12	8.51	0.03	8.88
	7.46	0.12	9.60	0.03	9.97
	8.14	0.12	10.41	0.03	10.78
	8.65	0.12	11.03	0.02	11.42
	9.12	0.13	11.59	0.02	11.99
	10.20	0.13	12.81	0.02	13.22
	10.99	0.13	13.77	0.02	14.20
	11.80	0.14	14.68		
	11.76	0.14	14.63		
	11.74	0.14	14.62		
	11.70	0.14	14.59		
	11.52	0.14	14.41		
	11.41	0.15	14.28		
	11.31	0.15	14.18		
	11.19	0.15	14.06	0.02	14.55
	11.06	0.15	13.93		
	10.96	0.15	13.83		
	11.04	0.15	13.91		
	11.13	0.15	14.00		
	11.25	0.16	14.11		
	11.38	0.16	14.22		
	11.50	0.16	14.35		
	11.63	0.16	14.49		
	11.74	0.16	14.61		
	11.90	0.16	15.10		

(continued)

TABLE 1 (continued)

Date	Currency Held by the Public (1)	Deposits Adjusted, Commercial Banks			Deposits at		S & L Shares (7)
		Demand (2)	Time (3)	Total (4)	Mut. Sav. Banks (5)	Post. Sav. Syst. (6)	
1908							
Nov.	1.70			10.36	3.04		
Dec.	1.73			10.41	3.06		0.54
1909							
Jan.	1.70			10.54	3.07		
Feb.	1.70			10.60	3.08		
Mar.	1.69			10.69	3.09		
Apr.	1.70			10.79	3.10		
May	1.70			10.91	3.12		
June	1.70			11.03	3.13		
July	1.69			11.11	3.15		
Aug.	1.71			11.19	3.17		
Sept.	1.73			11.26	3.18		
Oct.	1.72			11.32	3.20		
Nov.	1.72			11.34	3.21		
Dec.	1.73			11.43	3.22		0.58
1910							
Jan.	1.74			11.41	3.24		
Feb.	1.72			11.49	3.25		
Mar.	1.71			11.59	3.26		
Apr.	1.71			11.56	3.28		
May	1.72			11.52	3.30		
June	1.74			11.54	3.29		
July	1.73			11.52	3.30		
Aug.	1.75			11.56	3.32		
Sept.	1.78			11.67	3.33		
Oct.	1.79			11.78	3.34		
Nov.	1.76			11.85	3.35		
Dec.	1.75			11.90	3.36		0.64
1911							
Jan.	1.75			11.96	3.37	c	
Feb.	1.75			12.03	3.38		
Mar.	1.76			12.08	3.39		
Apr.	1.79			12.22	3.40		
May	1.80			12.30	3.41		
June	1.76			12.37	3.43		

M_1[b] (Cols. 1 + 2) (8)	M_2 (Cols. 8 + 3) (9)	Duplications Betw. Col. 9 and Cols. 5 + 6 (10)	M_3 (Cols. 9+5 +6 − 10) (11)	Duplications Betw. Cols. 11 and 7 (12)	M_4 (Cols. 11+7 −12) (13)
			Consolidated Totals[a]		
	12.06	0.16	14.94		
	12.14	0.16	15.04	0.02	15.56
	12.24	0.16	15.15		
	12.30	0.16	15.22		
	12.38	0.16	15.31		
	12.49	0.16	15.43		
	12.61	0.16	15.57		
	12.73	0.16	15.70		
	12.80	0.16	15.79		
	12.90	0.16	15.91		
	12.99	0.16	16.01		
	13.04	0.16	16.08		
	13.06	0.16	16.11		
	13.16	0.16	16.22	0.02	16.78
	13.15	0.16	16.23		
	13.21	0.16	16.30		
	13.30	0.16	16.40		
	13.27	0.16	16.39		
	13.24	0.16	16.38		
	13.28	0.16	16.41		
	13.25	0.16	16.39		
	13.31	0.16	16.47		
	13.45	0.16	16.62		
	13.57	0.16	16.75		
	13.61	0.16	16.80		
	13.65	0.16	16.85	0.02	17.47
	13.71	0.16	16.92		
	13.78	0.16	17.00		
	13.84	0.17	17.06		
	14.01	0.17	17.24		
	14.10	0.17	17.34		
	14.13	0.17	17.39		

(continued)

TABLE 1 (continued)

| Date | Currency Held by the Public (1) | Deposits Adjusted, Commercial Banks | | | Deposits at | | S & L Shares (7) |
		Demand (2)	Time (3)	Total (4)	Mut. Sav. Banks (5)	Post. Sav. Syst. (6)	
1911							
July	1.77			12.44	3.44		
Aug.	1.79			12.42	3.46		
Sept.	1.77			12.53	3.47		
Oct.	1.77			12.68	3.48	0.01	
Nov.	1.76			12.81	3.49	0.01	
Dec.	1.71			12.91	3.50	0.01	0.70
1912							
Jan.	1.72			13.01	3.52	0.01	
Feb.	1.75			13.06	3.53	0.01	
Mar.	1.77			13.15	3.54	0.02	
Apr.	1.80			13.18	3.55	0.02	
May	1.84			13.22	3.56	0.02	
June	1.85			13.34	3.59	0.02	
July	1.84			13.38	3.60	0.02	
Aug.	1.85			13.44	3.61	0.02	
Sept.	1.85			13.48	3.62	0.02	
Oct.	1.87			13.57	3.63	0.03	
Nov.	1.84			13.67	3.64	0.03	
Dec.	1.83			13.69	3.66	0.03	0.78
1913							
Jan.	1.85			13.73	3.67	0.03	
Feb.	1.86			13.80	3.68	0.03	
Mar.	1.85			13.77	3.69	0.03	
Apr.	1.89			13.80	3.70	0.03	
May	1.90			13.74	3.72	0.03	
June	1.90			13.71	3.73	0.03	
July	1.89			13.70	3.74	0.04	
Aug.	1.89			13.83	3.75	0.04	
Sept.	1.91			13.98	3.76	0.04	
Oct.	1.93			14.06	3.77	0.04	
Nov.	1.90			14.10	3.78	0.04	
Dec.	1.89			14.15	3.79	0.04	0.86
1914							
Jan.	1.87			14.21	3.80	0.04	
Feb.	1.89			14.24	3.82	0.04	

		Consolidated Totals[a]			
M_1[b] (Cols. 1 + 2) (8)	M_2 (Cols. 8 + 3) (9)	Dupli- cations Betw. Col. 9 and Cols. 5 + 6 (10)	M_3 (Cols. 9+5 +6 − 10) (11)	Dupli- cations Betw. Cols. 11 and 7 (12)	M_4 (Cols. 11+7 −12) (13)
	14.21	0.17	17.48		
	14.21	0.17	17.50		
	14.30	0.17	17.60		
	14.45	0.17	17.77		
	14.57	0.17	17.90		
	14.62	0.17	17.96	0.03	18.63
	14.73	0.17	18.09		
	14.81	0.17	18.18		
	14.92	0.17	18.31		
	14.98	0.17	18.38		
	15.06	0.17	18.47		
	15.19	0.18	18.62		
	15.22	0.19	18.65		
	15.29	0.19	18.73		
	15.33	0.19	18.78		
	15.44	0.19	18.91		
	15.51	0.19	18.99		
	15.52	0.19	19.02	0.03	19.77
	15.58	0.20	19.08		
	15.66	0.20	19.17		
	15.62	0.20	19.14		
	15.69	0.20	19.22		
	15.64	0.20	19.19		
	15.61	0.20	19.17		
	15.59	0.21	19.16		
	15.72	0.21	19.30		
	15.89	0.21	19.48		
	15.99	0.21	19.59		
	16.00	0.22	19.60		
	16.04	0.22	19.65	0.03	20.48
	16.08	0.22	19.70		
	16.13	0.22	19.77		

(continued)

TABLE 1 (continued)

Date	Currency Held by the Public (1)	Deposits Adjusted, Commercial Banks			Deposits at		S & L Shares (7)
		Demand (2)	Time (3)	Total (4)	Mut. Sav. Banks (5)	Post. Sav. Syst. (6)	
1914							
Mar.	1.87			14.35	3.83	0.04	
Apr.	1.78			14.44	3.84	0.04	
May	1.86			14.56	3.85	0.04	
June	1.85	9.84	4.68	14.52	3.84	0.04	
July	1.84	9.84	4.69	14.53	3.85	0.04	
Aug.	1.93	9.83	4.68	14.51	3.86	0.05	
Sept.	2.09	9.89	4.77	14.66	3.86	0.05	
Oct.	2.10	9.82	4.86	14.68	3.86	0.05	
Nov.	1.91	9.88	4.82	14.70	3.86	0.06	
Dec.	1.90	9.90	4.78	14.68	3.86	0.06	0.93
1915							
Jan.	1.92	9.96	4.83	14.79	3.88	0.06	
Feb.	1.88	10.13	4.86	14.99	3.88	0.06	
Mar.	1.90	10.16	4.92	15.08	3.88	0.06	
Apr.	1.93	10.19	4.95	15.14	3.89	0.06	
May	1.91	10.28	5.06	15.34	3.89	0.06	
June	1.92	10.40	5.08	15.48	3.87	0.07	
July	1.92	10.50	5.10	15.60	3.90	0.07	
Aug.	1.90	10.61	5.13	15.74	3.92	0.07	
Sept.	1.93	10.88	5.25	16.13	3.94	0.07	
Oct.	1.97	11.36	5.41	16.77	3.95	0.07	
Nov.	1.94	11.50	5.50	17.00	3.97	0.07	
Dec.	2.00	11.62	5.65	17.27	3.99	0.07	1.02
1916							
Jan.	2.07	11.85	5.69	17.54	4.01	0.08	
Feb.	2.04	12.08	5.78	17.86	4.04	0.08	
Mar.	2.08	12.12	5.81	17.93	4.06	0.08	
Apr.	2.15	12.23	5.94	18.17	4.08	0.08	
May	2.15	12.33	6.09	18.42	4.10	0.08	
June	2.20	12.38	6.08	18.46	4.10	0.09	
July	2.20	12.52	6.22	18.74	4.14	0.09	
Aug.	2.19	12.78	6.22	19.00	4.17	0.10	
Sept.	2.21	13.00	6.38	19.38	4.20	0.10	
Oct.	2.24	13.21	6.52	19.73	4.23	0.10	
Nov.	2.28	13.41	6.70	20.11	4.25	0.11	

		Consolidated Totals[a]			
M_1[b] (Cols. 1 + 2) (8)	M_2 (Cols. 8 + 3) (9)	Duplications Betw. Col. 9 and Cols. 5 + 6 (10)	M_3 (Cols. 9+5 +6 - 10) (11)	Duplications Betw. Cols. 11 and 7 (12)	M_4 (Cols. 11+7 -12) (13)
	16.22	0.23	19.86		
	16.22	0.23	19.87		
	16.42	0.23	20.08		
11.69	1 6.37	0.23	20.02		
11.68	16.37	0.24	20.02		
11.76	16.44	0.24	20.11		
11.98	16.75	0.24	20.42		
11.92	16.78	0.24	20.45		
11.79	16.61	0.25	20.28		
11.80	16.58	0.25	20.25	0.03	21.15
11.88	16.71	0.25	20.40		
12.01	16.87	0.26	20.55		
12.06	16.98	0.26	20.66		
12.12	17.07	0.26	20.76		
12.19	17.25	0.26	20.94		
12.32	17.40	0.27	21.07		
12.42	17.52	0.27	21.22		
12.51	17.64	0.27	21.36		
12.81	1 8.06	0.28	21.79		
13.33	1 8.74	0.28	22.48		
13.44	18.94	0.29	22.69		
13.62	19.27	0.29	23.04	0.04	24.02
13.92	19.61	0.30	23.40		
14.12	19.90	0.30	23.72		
14.20	20.01	0.30	23.85		
14.38	20.32	0.31	24.17		
14.48	20.57	0.31	24.44		
14.58	20.66	0.32	24.53		
14.72	20.94	0.32	24.85		
14.97	21.19	0.32	25.14		
15.21	21.59	0.33	25.56		
15.45	21.97	0.33	25.97		
15.69	22.39	0.34	26.41		

(continued)

TABLE 1 (continued)

| Date | Currency Held by the Public (1) | Deposits Adjusted, Commercial Banks | | | Deposits at | | S & L Shares (7) |
		Demand (2)	Time (3)	Total (4)	Mut. Sav. Banks (5)	Post. Sav. Syst. (6)	
1916							
Dec.	2.27	13.57	7.00	20.57	4.28	0.11	1.10
1917							
Jan.	2.38	13.84	7.08	20.92	4.29	0.12	
Feb.	2.45	14.01	7.03	21.04	4.30	0.12	
Mar.	2.53	14.13	7.12	21.25	4.31	0.12	
Apr.	2.61	14.20	7.21	21.41	4.32	0.13	
May	2.67	14.36	7.32	21.68	4.33	0.13	
June	2.70	14.41	7.19	21.60	4.34	0.13	
July	2.77	14.67	7.37	22.04	4.35	0.14	
Aug.	2.85	14.78	7.37	22.15	4.36	0.14	
Sept.	2.95	14.58	7.38	21.96	4.37	0.14	
Oct.	2.98	14.35	7.54	21.89	4.36	0.14	
Nov.	3.09	14.43	7.57	22.00	4.36	0.14	
Dec.	3.18	15.36	7.56	22.92	4.36	0.14	1.22
1918							
Jan.	3.12	15.20	7.59	22.79	4.36	0.14	
Feb.	3.28	14.75	7.63	22.38	4.35	0.14	
Mar.	3.35	15.32	7.64	22.96	4.35	0.15	
Apr.	3.41	15.34	7.66	23.00	4.35	0.15	
May	3.45	14.70	7.63	22.33	4.35	0.15	
June	3.55	14.96	7.69	22.65	4.34	0.15	
July	3.72	15.05	7.77	22.82	4.37	0.16	
Aug.	3.91	15.20	7.84	23.04	4.40	0.16	
Sept.	4.05	15.99	7.88	23.87	4.42	0.16	
Oct.	4.13	15.36	7.91	23.27	4.44	0.15	
Nov.	4.11	15.82	8.04	23.86	4.47	0.16	
Dec.	4.12	16.89	8.30	25.19	4.50	0.16	1.32
1919							
Jan.	3.99	16.59	8.48	25.07	4.53	0.17	
Feb.	3.98	16.33	8.63	24.96	4.56	0.17	
Mar.	3.97	17.04	8.73	25.77	4.60	0.17	
Apr.	3.99	17.29	8.81	26.10	4.64	0.18	
May	3.96	17.30	8.90	26.20	4.68	0.17	
June	3.91	17.70	9.07	26.77	4.72	0.17	

		Consolidated Totals[a]			
M_1[b] (Cols. 1 + 2) (8)	M_2 (Cols. 8 + 3) (9)	Duplications Betw. Col. 9 and Cols. 5 + 6 (10)	M_3 (Cols. 9+5 +6 − 10) (11)	Duplications Betw. Cols. 11 and 7 (12)	M_4 (Cols. 11+7 −12) (13)
15.84	22.84	0.34	26.89	0.06	27.93
16.22	23.30	0.34	27.37		
16.46	23.49	0.35	27.56		
16.66	23.78	0.35	27.86		
16.81	24.02	0.36	28.11		
17.03	24.35	0.36	28.45		
17.11	24.30	0.36	28.41		
17.44	24.81	0.36	28.94		
17.63	25.00	0.36	29.14		
17.53	24.91	0.36	29.06		
17.33	24.87	0.36	29.01		
17.52	25.09	0.36	29.23		
18.54	26.10	0.36	30.24	0.06	31.40
18.32	25.91	0.36	30.05		
18.03	25.66	0.36	29.79		
18.67	26.31	0.36	30.45		
18.75	26.41	0.36	30.55		
18.15	25.78	0.36	29.92		
18.51	26.20	0.36	30.33		
18.77	26.54	0.36	30.71		
19.11	26.95	0.36	31.15		
20.04	27.92	0.36	32.14		
19.49	27.40	0.36	31.63		
19.93	27.97	0.36	32.24		
21.01	29.31	0.36	33.61	0.06	34.87
20.58	29.06	0.36	33.40		
20.31	28.94	0.36	33.31		
21.01	29.74	0.36	34.15		
21.28	30.09	0.36	34.55		
21.26	30.16	0.36	34.65		
21.61	30.68	0.36	35.21		

(continued)

TABLE 1 (continued)

| Date | Currency Held by the Public (1) | Deposits Adjusted, Commercial Banks | | | Deposits at | | S & L Shares (7) |
		Demand (2)	Time (3)	Total (4)	Mut. Sav. Banks (5)	Post. Sav. Syst. (6)	
1919							
July	3.98	17.99	9.34	27.33	4.75	0.17	
Aug.	3.99	18.27	9.48	27.75	4.79	0.16	
Sept.	4.03	18.56	9.67	28.23	4.82	0.16	
Oct.	4.08	18.92	10.04	28.96	4.86	0.16	
Nov.	4.15	19.12	10.20	29.32	4.89	0.16	
Dec.	4.24	19.45	10.17	29.62	4.93	0.16	1.47
1920							
Jan.	4.20	19.28	10.49	29.77	4.96	0.16	
Feb.	4.33	19.50	10.66	30.16	4.99	0.16	
Mar.	4.40	19.73	10.87	30.60	5.03	0.16	
Apr.	4.44	19.57	11.01	30.58	5.07	0.16	
May	4.44	19.53	11.10	30.63	5.11	0.16	
June	4.49	19.33	11.24	30.57	5.15	0.16	
July	4.53	19.28	11.24	30.52	5.18	0.16	
Aug.	4.60	19.16	11.34	30.50	5.22	0.16	
Sept.	4.65	19.07	11.37	30.44	5.27	0.16	
Oct.	4.68	18.87	11.38	30.25	5.30	0.16	
Nov.	4.56	18.57	11.41	29.98	5.33	0.16	
Dec.	4.51	18.85	11.46	30.31	5.36	0.16	1.74
1921							
Jan.	4.34	18.35	11.52	29.87	5.39	0.16	
Feb.	4.30	18.18	11.45	29.63	5.41	0.16	
Mar.	4.24	17.72	11.41	29.13	5.43	0.16	
Apr.	4.18	17.45	11.38	28.83	5.45	0.16	
May	4.15	17.43	11.34	28.77	5.47	0.16	
June	4.07	17.09	11.30	28.39	5.49	0.15	
July	4.01	16.92	11.22	28.14	5.50	0.15	
Aug.	3.96	17.03	11.25	28.28	5.52	0.15	
Sept.	3.93	16.82	11.23	28.05	5.53	0.15	
Oct.	3.83	17.04	11.32	28.36	5.54	0.15	
Nov.	3.77	17.15	11.32	28.47	5.56	0.15	
Dec.	3.76	17.10	11.30	28.40	5.57	0.14	1.96
1922							
Jan.	3.64	17.03	11.26	28.29	5.60	0.14	
Feb.	3.64	17.22	11.44	28.66	5.62	0.14	

		Consolidated Totals[a]			
M_1[b] (Cols. 1 + 2) (8)	M_2 (Cols. 8 + 3) (9)	Duplications Betw. Col. 9 and Cols. 5 + 6 (10)	M_3 (Cols. 9+5 +6 − 10) (11)	Duplications Betw. Cols. 11 and 7 (12)	M_4 (Cols. 11+7 −12) (13)
21.97	31.31	0.36	35.87		
22.26	31.74	0.36	36.33		
22.59	32.26	0.35	36.89		
23.00	33.04	0.35	37.71		
23.27	33.47	0.35	38.17		
23.69	33.86	0.35	38.60	0.07	40.00
23.48	33.97	0.35	38.74		
23.83	34.49	0.35	39.29		
24.13	35.00	0.35	39.84		
24.01	35.02	0.35	39.90		
23.97	35.07	0.35	39.99		
23.82	35.06	0.35	40.02		
23.81	35.05	0.34	40.05		
23.76	35.10	0.33	40.15		
23.72	35.09	0.32	40.20		
23.55	34.93	0.32	40.07		
23.13	34.54	0.31	39.72		
23.36	34.82	0.30	40.04	0.06	41.72
22.69	34.21	0.29	39.47		
22.48	33.93	0.28	39.22		
21.96	33.37	0.28	38.68		
21.63	33.01	0.27	38.35		
21.58	32.92	0.26	38.29		
21.16	32.46	0.25	37.85		
20.93	32.15	0.26	37.54		
20.99	32.24	0.26	37.65		
20.75	31.98	0.26	37.40		
20.87	32.19	0.26	37.62		
20.92	32.24	0.26	37.69		
20.86	32.16	0.26	37.61	0.07	39.50
20.67	31.93	0.26	37.41		
20.86	32.30	0.26	37.80		

(continued)

TABLE 1 (continued)

| Date | Currency Held by the Public (1) | Deposits Adjusted, Commercial Banks | | | Deposits at | | S & L Shares (7) |
		Demand (2)	Time (3)	Total (4)	Mut. Sav. Banks (5)	Post. Sav. Syst. (6)	
1922							
Mar.	3.66	17.24	11.54	28.78	5.65	0.14	
Apr.	3.66	17.78	11.69	29.47	5.66	0.14	
May	3.64	17.98	11.78	29.76	5.67	0.14	
June	3.66	18.18	12.07	30.25	5.68	0.14	
July	3.64	18.31	12.33	30.64	5.72	0.14	
Aug.	3.69	18.26	12.52	30.78	5.76	0.14	
Sept.	3.75	18.51	12.50	31.01	5.80	0.13	
Oct.	3.75	18.59	12.66	31.25	5.85	0.13	
Nov.	3.77	18.53	12.70	31.23	5.88	0.13	
Dec.	3.81	19.25	12.91	32.16	5.92	0.13	2.22
1923							
Jan.	3.76	19.16	12.95	32.11	5.97	0.13	
Feb.	3.82	19.19	13.10	32.29	6.01	0.13	
Mar.	3.88	18.73	13.47	32.20	6.06	0.13	
Apr.	3.92	18.98	13.57	32.55	6.10	0.13	
May	3.98	19.05	13.70	32.75	6.15	0.13	
June	4.02	18.85	13.82	32.67	6.19	0.13	
July	4.01	18.84	13.81	32.65	6.23	0.13	
Aug.	4.03	18.78	13.90	32.68	6.27	0.13	
Sept.	4.03	18.92	13.95	32.87	6.31	0.13	
Oct.	3.99	19.05	14.04	33.09	6.34	0.13	
Nov.	4.05	19.03	14.13	33.16	6.37	0.13	
Dec.	4.01	19.16	14.21	33.37	6.40	0.13	2.63
1924							
Jan.	3.92	19.06	14.24	33.30	6.44	0.13	
Feb.	3.98	18.94	14.44	33.38	6.46	0.13	
Mar.	4.01	18.97	14.54	33.51	6.51	0.13	
Apr.	4.00	19.07	14.68	33.75	6.51	0.13	
May	4.02	19.22	14.73	33.95	6.53	0.13	
June	3.97	19.50	14.86	34.36	6.59	0.13	
July	3.94	19.83	15.01	34.84	6.62	0.13	
Aug.	3.93	20.15	15.13	35.28	6.64	0.13	
Sept.	3.88	20.47	15.31	35.78	6.68	0.13	
Oct.	3.93	20.52	15.48	36.00	6.73	0.13	
Nov.	3.95	20.89	15.58	36.47	6.78	0.13	

		Consolidated Totals[a]			
M_1[b] (Cols. 1 + 2) (8)	M_2 (Cols. 8 + 3) (9)	Duplications Betw. Col. 9 and Cols. 5 + 6 (10)	M_3 (Cols. 9+5 +6 − 10) (11)	Duplications Betw. Cols. 11 and 7 (12)	M_4 (Cols. 11+7 −12) (13)
20.90	32.44	0.27	37.96		
21.44	33.13	0.27	38.66		
21.62	33.40	0.27	38.94		
21.84	33.91	0.27	39.46		
21.95	34.28	0.27	39.87		
21.95	34.47	0.27	40.10		
22.26	34.76	0.27	40.42		
22.34	35.00	0.27	40.71		
22.30	35.00	0.27	40.74		
23.06	35.97	0.27	41.75	0.08	43.89
22.92	35.87	0.27	41.70		
23.01	36.11	0.27	41.98		
22.61	36.08	0.28	41.99		
22.90	36.47	0.28	42.42		
23.03	36.73	0.28	42.73		
22.87	36.69	0.28	42.73		
22.85	36.66	0.28	42.74		
22.81	36.71	0.29	42.82		
22.95	36.90	0.29	43.05		
23.04	37.08	0.30	43.25		
23.08	37.21	0.30	43.41		
23.17	37.38	0.31	43.60	0.10	46.13
22.98	37.22	0.31	43.48		
22.92	37.36	0.32	43.63		
22.98	37.52	0.32	43.84		
23.07	37.75	0.33	44.06		
23.24	37.97	0.33	44.30		
23.47	38.33	0.34	44.71		
23.77	38.78	0.34	45.19		
24.08	39.21	0.34	45.64		
24.35	39.66	0.34	46.13		
24.45	39.93	0.34	46.45		
24.84	40.42	0.34	46.99		

(continued)

TABLE 1 (continued)

Date	Currency Held by the Public (1)	Deposits Adjusted, Commercial Banks			Deposits at		S & L Shares (7)
		Demand (2)	Time (3)	Total (4)	Mut. Sav. Banks (5)	Post. Sav. Syst. (6)	
1924							
Dec.	3.94	20.70	15.66	36.36	6.84	0.13	3.15
1925							
Jan.	3.96	21.00	15.81	36.81	6.86	0.13	
Feb.	3.96	21.19	15.94	37.13	6.90	0.13	
Mar.	3.97	21.07	16.07	37.14	6.92	0.13	
Apr.	3.95	21.22	16.13	37.35	6.96	0.13	
May	3.96	21.40	16.29	37.69	6.99	0.13	
June	3.95	21.65	16.43	38.08	7.04	0.13	
July	3.97	21.73	16.50	38.23	7.06	0.13	
Aug.	3.94	22.23	16.61	38.84	7.08	0.13	
Sept.	3.93	22.54	16.74	39.28	7.06	0.13	
Oct.	3.96	22.50	16.85	39.35	7.14	0.13	
Nov.	3.95	22.43	16.96	39.39	7.19	0.13	
Dec.	3.99	22.33	17.04	39.37	7.24	0.13	3.81
1926							
Jan.	3.99	22.35	17.19	39.54	7.23	0.13	
Feb.	4.01	22.43	17.24	39.67	7.29	0.13	
Mar.	3.98	22.36	17.26	39.62	7.32	0.13	
Apr.	4.04	22.07	17.36	39.43	7.34	0.13	
May	4.00	22.37	17.47	39.84	7.38	0.13	
June	4.00	22.31	17.56	39.87	7.43	0.13	
July	4.05	22.04	17.61	39.65	7.46	0.14	
Aug.	4.01	22.19	17.69	39.88	7.50	0.14	
Sept.	4.00	22.13	17.69	39.82	7.55	0.14	
Oct.	4.00	21.92	17.74	39.66	7.59	0.14	
Nov.	3.98	21.98	17.73	39.71	7.69	0.14	
Dec.	4.01	21.68	17.68	39.36	7.70	0.14	4.38
1927							
Jan.	4.02	21.76	17.92	39.68	7.74	0.14	
Feb.	4.02	21.89	18.24	40.13	7.78	0.14	
Mar.	4.04	22.04	18.27	40.31	7.84	0.14	
Apr.	4.04	21.93	18.39	40.32	7.86	0.15	
May	4.01	22.40	18.57	40.97	7.91	0.15	
June	3.98	22.06	18.70	40.76	7.96	0.15	
July	3.99	22.09	18.81	40.90	8.01	0.15	
Aug.	3.93	22.29	18.85	41.14	8.05	0.15	

M_1[b] (Cols. 1 + 2) (8)	M_2 (Cols. 8 + 3) (9)	Duplications Betw. Col. 9 and Cols. 5 + 6 (10)	M_3 (Cols. 9+5 +6 − 10) (11)	Duplications Betw. Cols. 11 and 7 (12)	M_4 (Cols. 11+7 −12) (13)
Consolidated Totals[a]					
24.64	40.30	0.34	46.93	0.11	49.97
24.96	40.77	0.34	47.42		
25.15	41.09	0.34	47.78		
25.04	41.11	0.34	47.82		
25.17	41.30	0.33	48.06		
25.36	41.65	0.33	48.44		
25.60	42.03	0.33	48.87		
25.70	42.20	0.33	49.06		
26.17	42.78	0.33	49.66		
26.47	43.21	0.33	50.07		
26.46	43.31	0.33	50.25		
26.38	43.34	0.33	50.33		
26.32	43.36	0.33	50.40	0.13	54.08
26.34	43.53	0.33	50.56		
26.44	43.68	0.33	50.77		
26.34	43.60	0.33	50.72		
26.11	43.47	0.34	50.60		
26.37	43.84	0.34	51.01		
26.31	43.87	0.34	51.09		
26.09	43.70	0.34	50.96		
26.20	43.89	0.34	51.19		
26.13	43.82	0.34	51.17		
25.92	43.66	0.35	51.04		
25.96	43.69	0.35	51.17		
25.69	43.37	0.35	50.86	0.15	55.09
25.78	43.70	0.35	51.23		
25.91	44.15	0.36	51.71		
26.08	44.35	0.36	51.97		
25.97	44.36	0.36	52.01		
26.41	44.98	0.36	52.68		
26.04	44.74	0.37	52.48		
26.08	44.89	0.36	52.69		
26.22	45.07	0.36	52.91		

(continued)

TABLE 1 (continued)

| Date | Currency Held by the Public (1) | Deposits Adjusted, Commercial Banks | | | Deposits at | | S & L Shares (7) |
		Demand (2)	Time (3)	Total (4)	Mut. Sav. Banks (5)	Post. Sav. Syst. (6)	
1927							
Sept.	3.97	22.10	18.94	41.04	8.11	0.15	
Oct.	3.93	22.24	19.02	41.26	8.17	0.15	
Nov.	3.88	22.76	19.33	42.09	8.24	0.15	
Dec.	3.89	22.09	19.34	41.43	8.29	0.15	5.03
1928							
Jan.	3.85	22.52	19.63	42.15	8.34	0.15	
Feb.	3.83	22.62	19.74	42.36	8.38	0.15	
Mar.	3.90	22.56	20.00	42.56	8.40	0.15	
Apr.	3.91	22.91	20.09	43.00	8.46	0.15	
May	3.90	22.72	20.20	42.92	8.49	0.15	
June	3.95	22.05	20.22	42.27	8.52	0.15	
July	3.91	22.29	20.12	42.41	8.55	0.15	
Aug.	3.93	22.11	20.13	42.24	8.60	0.15	
Sept.	3.90	22.37	20.06	42.43	8.66	0.15	
Oct.	3.85	22.59	20.25	42.84	8.70	0.15	
Nov.	3.94	22.69	20.17	42.86	8.74	0.15	
Dec.	3.86	22.80	20.26	43.06	8.78	0.15	5.76
1929							
Jan.	3.86	22.47	20.20	42.67	8.78	0.15	
Feb.	3.88	22.60	20.16	42.76	8.81	0.15	
Mar.	3.93	22.57	20.05	42.62	8.81	0.15	
Apr.	3.90	22.67	19.89	42.56	8.82	0.15	
May	3.91	22.37	19.87	42.24	8.83	0.15	
June	3.94	22.47	19.86	42.33	8.84	0.15	
July	3.92	22.99	19.85	42.84	8.86	0.16	
Aug.	3.95	22.75	19.94	42.69	8.87	0.16	
Sept.	3.85	22.79	20.04	42.83	8.88	0.16	
Oct.	3.86	24.64	20.02	44.66	8.84	0.16	
Nov.	3.88	21.86	19.67	41.53	8.82	0.16	
Dec.	3.83	22.85	19.57	42.42	8.82	0.16	6.24
1930							
Jan.	3.78	22.15	19.76	41.91	8.86	0.16	
Feb.	3.78	22.42	19.66	42.08	8.91	0.17	
Mar.	3.75	22.86	19.96	42.82	8.96	0.17	
Apr.	3.70	22.50	19.85	42.35	8.99	0.17	
May	3.73	21.88	19.99	41.87	9.02	0.17	

		Consolidated Totals[a]			
M_1 [b] (Cols. 1 + 2) (8)	M_2 (Cols. 8 + 3) (9)	Duplications Betw. Col. 9 and Cols. 5 + 6 (10)	M_3 (Cols. 9+5 +6 − 10) (11)	Duplications Betw. Cols. 11 and 7 (12)	M_4 (Cols. 11+7 −12) (13)
26.07	45.01	0.36	52.91		
26.17	45.19	0.36	53.15		
26.64	45.97	0.36	54.00		
25.98	45.32	0.36	53.40	0.16	58.27
26.37	46.00	0.36	54.13		
26.45	46.19	0.36	54.36		
26.46	46.46	0.36	54.65		
26.82	46.91	0.35	55.17		
26.62	46.82	0.35	55.11		
26.00	46.22	0.35	54.54		
26.20	46.32	0.35	54.67		
26.04	46.17	0.35	54.57		
26.27	46.33	0.35	54.79		
26.44	46.69	0.35	55.19		
26.63	46.80	0.35	55.34		
26.66	46.92	0.35	55.50	0.20	61.06
26.33	46.53	0.35	55.11		
26.48	46.64	0.35	55.25		
26.50	46.55	0.35	55.16		
26.57	46.46	0.34	55.09		
26.28	46.15	0.34	54.79		
26.41	46.27	0.34	54.92		
26.91	46.76	0.35	55.43		
26.70	46.64	0.36	55.31		
26.64	46.68	0.37	55.35		
28.50	48.52	0.37	57.15		
25.74	45.41	0.38	54.01		
26.68	46.25	0.39	54.84	0.17	60.91
25.93	45.69	0.40	54.31		
26.20	45.86	0.40	54.54		
26.61	46.57	0.41	55.29		
26.20	46.05	0.42	54.79		
25.61	45.60	0.43	54.36		

(continued)

TABLE 1 (continued)

Date	Currency Held by the Public (1)	Deposits Adjusted, Commercial Banks			Deposits at		S & L Shares (7)
		Demand (2)	Time (3)	Total (4)	Mut. Sav. Banks (5)	Post. Sav. Syst. (6)	
1930							
June	3.71	21.87	20.16	42.03	9.06	0.18	
July	3.70	21.99	20.10	42.09	9.12	0.18	
Aug.	3.74	21.63	20.21	41.84	9.16	0.19	
Sept.	3.67	21.69	20.23	41.92	9.23	0.19	
Oct.	3.63	21.68	20.27	41.95	9.28	0.19	
Nov.	3.71	21.64	19.93	41.57	9.33	0.20	
Dec.	3.84	21.41	19.36	40.77	9.42	0.24	6.30
1931							
Jan.	3.85	21.05	19.33	40.38	9.53	0.28	
Feb.	3.86	21.21	19.48	40.69	9.60	0.29	
Mar.	3.90	21.22	19.39	40.61	9.66	0.30	
Apr.	3.93	20.68	19.49	40.17	9.75	0.31	
May	3.93	20.33	19.32	39.65	9.82	0.32	
June	4.03	20.24	19.02	39.26	9.86	0.35	
July	4.10	20.09	18.85	38.94	9.90	0.37	
Aug.	4.22	19.60	18.51	38.11	9.94	0.42	
Sept.	4.33	19.44	17.96	37.40	9.98	0.47	
Oct.	4.58	18.53	17.08	35.61	10.01	0.54	
Nov.	4.55	18.21	16.56	34.77	10.02	0.56	
Dec.	4.65	17.65	15.94	33.59	9.97	0.60	5.92
1932							
Jan.	4.94	16.98	15.58	32.56	9.90	0.66	
Feb.	4.87	16.86	15.36	32.22	9.90	0.69	
Mar.	4.79	16.74	15.24	31.98	9.94	0.70	
Apr.	4.80	16.51	15.16	31.67	9.92	0.72	
May	4.80	16.16	15.01	31.17	9.89	0.74	
June	5.01	15.87	14.71	30.58	9.89	0.78	
July	5.10	15.48	14.69	30.17	9.87	0.83	
Aug.	5.04	15.58	14.58	30.16	9.85	0.85	
Sept.	5.00	15.65	14.50	30.15	9.86	0.86	
Oct.	4.92	15.76	14.62	30.38	9.86	0.87	
Nov.	4.90	16.08	14.56	30.64	9.88	0.88	
Dec.	4.89	15.88	14.52	30.40	9.90	0.90	5.33
1933							
Jan.	5.04	16.02	14.38	30.40	9.90	0.94	
Feb.	5.65	14.76	13.50	28.26	9.84	1.00	

		Consolidated Totals[a]			
M_1[b] (Cols. 1 + 2) (8)	M_2 (Cols. 8 + 3) (9)	Duplications Betw. Col. 9 and Cols. 5 + 6 (10)	M_3 (Cols. 9+5 +6 − 10) (11)	Duplications Betw. Cols. 11 and 7 (12)	M_4 (Cols. 11+7 −12) (13)
25.58	45.74	0.44	54.54		
25.69	45.79	0.46	54.63		
25.37	45.58	0.48	54.45		
25.36	45.59	0.50	54.51		
25.31	45.58	0.52	54.53		
25.35	45.28	0.54	54.27		
25.25	44.61	0.56	53.71	0.20	59.81
24.90	44.23	0.59	53.45		
25.07	44.55	0.61	53.83		
25.12	44.51	0.63	53.84		
24.61	44.10	0.65	53.51		
24.26	43.58	0.67	53.05		
24.27	43.29	0.69	52.81		
24.19	43.04	0.73	52.58		
23.82	42.33	0.76	51.93		
23.77	41.73	0.80	51.38		
23.11	40.19	0.83	49.91		
22.76	39.32	0.87	49.03		
22.30	38.24	0.91	47.90	0.17	53.65
21.92	37.50	0.94	47.12		
21.73	37.09	0.98	46.70		
21.53	36.77	1.01	46.40		
21.31	36.47	1.05	46.06		
20.96	35.97	1.08	45.52		
20.88	35.59	1.12	45.14		
20.58	35.27	1.14	44.83		
20.62	35.20	1.17	44.73		
20.65	35.15	1.19	44.68		
20.68	35.30	1.21	44.82		
20.98	35.54	1.24	45.06		
20.77	35.29	1.26	44.83	0.15	50.01
21.06	35.44	1.28	45.00		
20.41	33.91	1.31	43.44		

(continued)

TABLE 1 (continued)

Date	Currency Held by the Public (1)	Deposits Adjusted, Commercial Banks			Deposits at		S & L Shares (7)
		Demand (2)	Time (3)	Total (4)	Mut. Sav. Banks (5)	Post. Sav. Syst. (6)	
1933							
Mar.	5.57	13.91	11.82	25.73	9.74	1.11	
Apr.	5.26	14.20	11.64	25.84	9.69	1.16	
May	5.08	14.79	11.60	26.39	9.62	1.18	
June	5.01	14.64	11.83	26.47	9.59	1.18	
July	4.95	14.57	12.03	26.60	9.56	1.18	
Aug.	4.91	14.64	12.01	26.65	9.53	1.18	
Sept.	4.89	14.72	12.00	26.72	9.53	1.18	
Oct.	4.86	14.90	11.96	26.86	9.52	1.19	
Nov.	4.90	15.11	11.86	26.97	9.52	1.20	
Dec.	4.90	15.33	11.88	27.21	9.53	1.21	4.75
1934							
Jan.	4.55	15.65	12.05	27.70	9.55	1.20	
Feb.	4.57	16.21	12.10	28.31	9.58	1.20	
Mar.	4.61	16.63	12.26	28.89	9.61	1.20	
Apr.	4.61	16.76	12.43	29.19	9.62	1.20	
May	4.62	16.88	12.52	29.40	9.63	1.19	
June	4.64	16.94	12.70	29.64	9.65	1.20	
July	4.66	17.39	12.70	30.09	9.66	1.19	
Aug.	4.68	17.96	12.75	30.71	9.59	1.19	
Sept.	4.68	17.86	12.69	30.55	9.68	1.19	
Oct.	4.64	18.43	12.78	31.21	9.68	1.20	
Nov.	4.72	18.84	12.73	31.57	9.70	1.20	
Dec.	4.61	18.67	12.83	31.50	9.70	1.20	4.46
1935							
Jan.	4.67	19.50	12.90	32.40	9.71	1.20	
Feb.	4.75	20.12	12.90	33.02	9.74	1.20	
Mar.	4.76	20.01	13.02	33.03	9.76	1.20	
Apr.	4.76	20.35	13.23	33.58	9.77	1.20	
May	4.76	20.53	13.22	33.75	9.78	1.20	
June	4.76	20.96	13.24	34.20	9.79	1.20	
July	4.74	21.22	13.23	34.45	9.79	1.19	
Aug.	4.80	22.53	13.21	35.74	9.80	1.19	
Sept.	4.85	22.06	13.31	35.37	9.81	1.19	
Oct.	4.89	22.36	13.36	35.72	9.82	1.19	
Nov.	4.93	22.87	13.39	36.26	9.84	1.20	
Dec.	4.93	22.63	13.60	36.23	9.84	1.20	4.25

		Consolidated Totals[a]			
M_1[b] (Cols. 1 + 2) (8)	M_2 (Cols. 8 + 3) (9)	Duplications Betw. Col. 9 and Cols. 5 + 6 (10)	M_3 (Cols. 9+5 +6 − 10) (11)	Duplications Betw. Cols. 11 and 7 (12)	M_4 (Cols. 11+7 −12) (13)
19.48	31.30	1.33	40.82		
19.46	31.10	1.35	40.60		
19.87	31.47	1.38	40.89		
19.65	31.48	1.40	40.85		
19.52	31.55	1.38	40.91		
19.55	31.56	1.37	40.90		
19.61	31.61	1.35	40.97		
19.76	31.72	1.34	41.09		
20.01	31.87	1.32	41.27		
20.23	32.11	1.30	41.55	0.14	46.16
20.20	32.25	1.29	41.71		
20.78	32.88	1.27	42.39		
21.24	33.50	1.25	43.06		
21.37	33.80	1.24	43.38		
21.50	34.02	1.22	43.62		
21.58	34.28	1.21	43.92		
22.05	34.75	1.18	44.42		
22.64	35.39	1.16	45.01		
22.54	35.23	1.13	44.97		
23.07	35.85	1.11	45.62		
23.56	36.29	1.08	46.11		
23.28	36.11	1.06	45.95	0.17	50.24
24.17	37.07	1.03	46.95		
24.87	37.77	1.01	47.70		
24.77	37.79	0.98	47.77		
25.11	38.34	0.96	48.35		
25.29	38.51	0.93	48.56		
25.72	38.96	0.91	49.04		
25.96	39.19	0.89	49.28		
27.33	40.54	0.88	50.65		
26.91	40.22	0.87	50.35		
27.25	40.61	0.85	50.77		
27.80	41.19	0.84	51.39		
27.56	41.16	0.83	51.37	0.18	55.44

(continued)

TABLE 1 (continued)

Date	Currency Held by the Public (1)	Deposits Adjusted, Commercial Banks			Deposits at		S & L Shares (7)
		Demand (2)	Time (3)	Total (4)	Mut. Sav. Banks (5)	Post. Sav. Syst. (6)	
1936							
Jan.	4.98	22.61	13.60	36.21	9.85	1.20	
Feb.	5.04	23.04	13.63	36.67	9.87	1.21	
Mar.	5.07	23.04	13.63	36.67	9.89	1.21	
Apr.	5.06	23.62	13.89	37.51	9.90	1.21	
May	5.09	24.41	13.87	38.28	9.90	1.21	
June	5.31	24.87	13.91	38.78	9.93	1.23	
July	5.28	25.06	14.03	39.09	9.95	1.24	
Aug.	5.28	24.96	14.11	39.07	9.96	1.25	
Sept.	5.33	25.40	14.19	39.59	9.98	1.25	
Oct.	5.37	25.32	14.23	39.55	9.99	1.25	
Nov.	5.43	25.52	14.20	39.72	10.00	1.25	
Dec.	5.52	25.86	14.30	40.16	10.02	1.26	4.19
1937							
Jan.	5.52	25.61	14.39.	40.00	10.04	1.26	
Feb.	5.54	25.87	14.59	40.46	10.07	1.27	
Mar.	5.53	26.07	14.53	40.60	10.10	1.27	
Apr.	5.57	25.94	14.56	40.50	10.11	1.27	
May	5.55	25.57	14.70	40.27	10.11	1.26	
June	5.56	25.55	14.74	40.29	10.10	1.26	
July	5.60	25.45	14.88	40.33	10.14	1.27	
Aug.	5.67	25.18	14.97	40.15	10.15	1.27	
Sept.	5.66	25.02	15.10	40.12	10.15	1.27	
Oct.	5.64	24.46	15.08	39.54	10.12	1.27	
Nov.	5.63	24.26	15.01	39.27	10.13	1.27	
Dec.	5.58	24.05	15.00	39.05	10.13	1.27	4.08
1938							
Jan.	5.54	24.32	15.06	39.38	10.14	1.27	
Feb.	5.51	24.56	15.12	39.68	10.16	1.27	
Mar.	5.52	24.64	15.02	39.66	10.18	1.26	
Apr.	5.49	24.50	15.03	39.53	10.17	1.27	
May	5.51	24.12	15.00	39.12	10.18	1.25	
June	5.48	24.25	15.04	39.29	10.16	1.25	
July	5.51	24.55	14.95	39.50	10.19	1.25	
Aug.	5.51	25.30	14.99	40.29	10.20	1.25	
Sept.	5.59	25.58	14.92	40.50	10.20	1.24	
Oct.	5.61	25.94	14.94	40.88	10.23	1.25	

		Consolidated Totals[a]			
M_1[b] (Cols. 1 + 2) (8)	M_2 (Cols. 8 + 3) (9)	Duplications Betw. Col. 9 and Cols. 5 + 6 (10)	M_3 (Cols. 9+5 +6 − 10) (11)	Duplications Betw. Cols. 11 and 7 (12)	M_4 (Cols. 11+7 −12) (13)
27.59	41.19	0.81	51.43		
28.08	41.71	0.80	51.99		
28.11	41.74	0.79	52.05		
28.68	42.57	0.77	52.91		
29.50	43.37	0.76	53.72		
30.18	44.09	0.75	54.50		
30.34	44.37	0.74	54.82		
30.24	44.35	0.73	54.83		
30.73	44.92	0.73	55.42		
30.69	44.92	0.72	55.44		
30.95	45.15	0.71	55.69		
31.38	45.68	0.70	56.26	0.22	60.23
31.13	45.52	0.70	56.12		
31.41	46.00	0.69	56.65		
31.60	46.13	0.68	56.82		
31.51	46.07	0.67	56.78		
31.12	45.82	0.67	56.52		
31.11	45.85	0.66	56.55		
31.05	45.93	0.66	56.68		
30.85	45.82	0.66	56.58		
30.68	45.78	0.67	56.53		
30.10	45.18	0.67	55.90		
29.89	44.90	0.67	55.63		
29.63	44.63	0.67	55.36	0.21	59.23
29.86	44.92	0.67	55.66		
30.07	45.19	0.68	55.94		
30.16	45.18	0.68	55.94		
29.99	45.02	0.68	55.78		
29.63	44.63	0.68	55.38		
29.73	44.77	0.69	55.49		
30.06	45.01	0.69	55.76		
30.81	45.80	0.70	56.55		
31.17	46.09	0.70	56.83		
31.55	46.49	0.71	57.26		

(continued)

TABLE 1 (continued)

Date	Currency Held by the Public (1)	Deposits Adjusted, Commercial Banks			Deposits at		S & L Shares (7)
		Demand (2)	Time (3)	Total (4)	Mut. Sav. Banks (5)	Post. Sav. Syst. (6)	
1938							
Nov.	5.64	26.52	14.86	41.38	10.24	1.25	
Dec.	5.66	26.70	14.94	41.64	10.24	1.25	4.08
1939							
Jan.	5.74	26.57	15.00	41.57	10.27	1.26	
Feb.	5.81	26.39	15.02	41.41	10.31	1.26	
Mar.	5.87	26.81	15.06	41.87	10.35	1.26	
Apr.	5.96	27.01	15.13	42.14	10.36	1.26	
May	5.97	27.20	15.11	42.31	10.38	1.26	
June	6.01	27.27	15.16	42.43	10.39	1.26	
July	6.05	28.13	15.18	43.31	10.43	1.26	
Aug.	6.14	28.94	15.19	44.13	10.44	1.27	
Sept.	6.20	29.64	15.15	44.79	10.44	1.26	
Oct.	6.24	30.02	15.22	45.24	10.47	1.27	
Nov.	6.27	30.93	15.18	46.11	10.47	1.27	
Dec.	6.28	30.56	15.29	45.85	10.48	1.28	4.12
1940							
Jan.	6.36	31.03	15.30	46.33	10.52	1.29	
Feb.	6.43	31.49	15.39	46.88	10.56	1.29	
Mar.	6.49	31.98	15.52	47.50	10.60	1.30	
Apr.	6.52	31.80	15.47	47.27	10.61	1.30	
May	6.58	32.53	15.54	48.07	10.60	1.30	
June	6.68	33.04	15.61	48.65	10.58	1.29	
July	6.74	33.45	15.59	49.04	10.58	1.29	
Aug.	6.82	33.52	15.63	49.15	10.58	1.29	
Sept.	6.92	33.93	15.68	49.61	10.59	1.29	
Oct.	7.04	34.49	15.66	50.15	10.60	1.29	
Nov.	7.15	34.98	15.68	50.66	10.61	1.30	
Dec.	7.35	35.52	15.80	51.32	10.62	1.30	4.32
1941							
Jan.	7.48	36.10	15.85	51.95	10.61	1.31	
Feb.	7.64	37.12	15.94	53.06	10.62	1.31	
Mar.	7.78	37.64	15.98	53.62	10.63	1.32	
Apr.	7.91	37.72	16.05	53.77	10.62	1.31	
May	8.05	38.48	16.00	54.48	10.60	1.31	
June	8.25	38.06	15.98	54.04	10.61	1.30	
July	8.47	39.07	15.98	55.05	10.56	1.30	

		Consolidated Totals[a]			
M_1[b] (Cols. 1 + 2) (8)	M_2 (Cols. 8 + 3) (9)	Duplications Betw. Col. 9 and Cols. 5 + 6 (10)	M_3 (Cols. 9+5 +6 − 10) (11)	Duplications Betw. Cols. 11 and 7 (12)	M_4 (Cols. 11+7 −12) (13)
32.16	47.02	0.72	57.79		
32.36	47.30	0.72	58.07	0.22	61.93
32.31	47.31	0.73	58.11		
32.20	47.22	0.74	58.05		
32.68	47.74	0.74	58.61		
32.97	48.10	0.75	58.97		
33.17	48.28	0.75	59.17		
33.28	48.44	0.76	59.33		
34.18	49.36	0.78	60.27		
35.08	50.27	0.80	61.18		
35.84	50.99	0.82	61.87		
36.26	51.48	0.84	62.38		
37.20	52.38	0.87	63.25		
36.84	52.13	0.89	63.00	0.27	66.85
37.39	52.69	0.91	63.59		
37.92	53.31	0.93	64.23		
38.47	53.99	0.95	64.94		
38.32	53.79	0.97	64.73		
39.11	54.65	0.99	65.56		
39.72	55.33	1.01	66.19		
40.19	55.78	1.01	66.64		
40.34	55.97	1.01	66.83		
40.85	56.53	1.01	67.40		
41.53	57.19	1.00	68.08		
42.13	57.81	1.00	68.72		
42.87	58.67	1.00	69.59	0.31	73.60
43.58	59.43	1.00	70.35		
44.76	60.70	1.00	71.63		
45.42	61.40	0.99	72.36		
45.63	61.68	0.99	72.62		
46.53	62.53	0.99	73.45		
46.31	62.29	0.99	73.21		
47.54	63.52	0.97	74.41		

(continued)

TABLE 1 (continued)

| Date | Currency Held by the Public (1) | Deposits Adjusted, Commercial Banks | | | Deposits at | | S & L Shares (7) |
		Demand (2)	Time (3)	Total (4)	Mut. Sav. Banks (5)	Post. Sav. Syst. (6)	
1941							
Aug.	8.67	38.96	16.01	54.97	10.54	1.30	
Sept.	8.81	39.35	16.05	55.40	10.52	1.31	
Oct.	8.95	39.06	16.13	55.19	10.53	1.31	
Nov.	9.18	39.57	16.04	55.61	10.53	1.32	
Dec.	9.62	39.38	15.96	55.34	10.50	1.31	4.68
1942							
Jan.	9.87	40.37	15.72	56.09	10.35	1.30	
Feb.	10.11	40.86	15.60	56.46	10.32	1.30	
Mar.	10.31	41.25	15.47	56.72	10.29	1.30	
Apr.	10.53	42.20	15.52	57.72	10.30	1.30	
May	10.82	42.94	15.53	58.47	10.31	1.30	
June	11.15	42.98	15.64	58.62	10.35	1.31	
July	11.58	44.48	15.73	60.21	10.38	1.32	
Aug.	11.94	45.43	15.89	61.32	10.42	1.34	
Sept.	12.37	46.36	16.01	62.37	10.45	1.35	
Oct.	12.73	48.03	16.16	64.19	10.50	1.37	
Nov.	13.26	48.64	16.21	64.85	10.57	1.39	
Dec.	13.83	49.51	16.28	65.79	10.64	1.41	4.94
1943							
Jan.	14.18	50.93	16.66	67.59	10.70	1.40	
Feb.	14.68	53.18	16.81	69.99	10.77	1.50	
Mar.	14.98	54.88	16.87	71.75	10.83	1.50	
Apr.	15.28	53.71	17.03	70.74	10.90	1.50	
May	15.78	54.01	17.33	71.34	11.00	1.50	
June	15.98	57.56	17.55	75.11	11.10	1.60	
July	16.58	59.74	17.97	77.71	11.22	1.60	
Aug.	16.98	62.98	18.36	81.34	11.32	1.70	
Sept.	17.28	55.33	18.32	73.65	11.35	1.70	
Oct.	17.58	56.17	18.63	74.80	11.45	1.70	
Nov.	18.18	58.97	18.87	77.84	11.59	1.70	
Dec.	18.68	61.79	19.15	80.94	11.71	1.80	5.49
1944							
Jan.	18.98	59.98	19.55	79.53	11.82	1.80	
Feb.	19.28	60.67	19.75	80.42	11.91	1.90	
Mar.	19.68	61.61	20.08	81.69	12.01	1.90	
Apr.	20.18	62.80	20.55	83.35	12.15	1.90	

M_1[b] (Cols. 1 + 2) (8)	M_2 (Cols. 8 + 3) (9)	Duplications Betw. Col. 9 and Cols. 5 + 6 (10)	M_3 (Cols. 9+5 +6 − 10) (11)	Duplications Betw. Cols. 11 and 7 (12)	M_4 (Cols. 11+7 −12) (13)
		Consolidated Totals[a]			
47.63	63.64	0.95	74.53		
48.16	64.21	0.93	75.11		
48.01	64.14	0.92	75.06		
48.75	64.79	0.90	75.74		
49.00	64.96	0.88	75.89	0.34	80.23
50.24	65.96	0.86	76.75		
50.97	66.57	0.84	77.35		
51.56	67.03	0.82	77.80		
52.73	68.25	0.81	79.04		
53.76	69.29	0.79	80.11		
54.13	69.77	0.77	80.66		
56.06	71.79	0.77	82.72		
57.37	73.26	0.76	84.26		
58.73	74.74	0.76	85.78		
60.76	76.92	0.76	88.03		
61.90	78.11	0.75	89.32		
63.34	79.62	0.75	90.92	0.41	95.45
65.11	81.77	0.75	93.12		
67.86	84.67	0.74	96.20		
69.86	86.73	0.74	98.32		
68.99	86.02	0.73	97.69		
69.79	87.12	0.73	98.89		
73.54	91.09	0.73	103.06		
76.32	94.29	0.71	106.40		
79.96	98.32	0.70	110.64		
72.61	90.93	0.68	103.30		
73.75	92.38	0.66	104.87		
77.15	96.02	0.65	108.66		
80.47	99.62	0.63	112.50	0.46	117.53
78.96	98.51	0.62	111.51		
79.95	99.70	0.60	112.91		
81.29	101.37	0.59	114.69		
82.98	103.53	0.57	117.01		

(continued)

TABLE 1 (continued)

Date	Currency Held by the Public (1)	Deposits Adjusted, Commercial Banks			Deposits at		S & L Shares (7)
		Demand (2)	Time (3)	Total (4)	Mut. Sav. Banks (5)	Post. Sav. Syst. (6)	
1944							
May	20.68	64.36	20.99	85.35	12.29	2.00	
June	21.08	62.78	21.25	84.03	12.43	2.00	
July	21.38	63.24	21.69	84.93	12.55	2.10	
Aug.	21.78	65.40	22.19	87.59	12.71	2.10	
Sept.	22.28	66.67	22.74	89.41	12.84	2.20	
Oct.	22.78	68.73	23.51	92.24	13.02	2.20	
Nov.	23.18	70.65	23.75	94.40	13.18	2.30	
Dec.	23.38	67.90	24.22	92.12	13.34	2.30	6.30
1945							
Jan.	23.78	70.55	24.66	95.21	13.50	2.40	
Feb.	24.18	71.70	25.26	96.96	13.67	2.40	
Mar.	24.48	73.29	25.80	99.09	13.83	2.50	
Apr.	24.78	73.80	26.36	100.16	14.04	2.60	
May	24.98	74.23	26.78	101.01	14.19	2.60	
June	25.38	72.68	27.21	99.89	14.37	2.60	
July	25.68	73.99	27.93	101.92	14.54	2.70	
Aug.	25.88	75.03	28.62	103.65	14.73	2.80	
Sept.	26.18	76.19	29.22	105.41	14.88	2.80	
Oct.	26.28	76.86	29.75	106.61	15.04	2.90	
Nov.	26.08	77.65	29.90	107.55	15.19	2.90	
Dec.	26.28	76.76	30.25	107.01	15.34	2.90	7.36
1946							
Jan.	26.28	76.28	30.61	106.89	15.48	3.00	
Feb.	26.29	77.50	31.11	108.61	15.62	3.00	
Mar.	26.39	77.11	31.41	108.52	15.74	3.00	
Apr.	26.49	79.22	31.71	110.93	15.90	3.10	
May	26.49	80.33	32.01	112.34	16.05	3.10	
June	26.79	80.75	32.51	113.26	16.24	3.10	
July	26.59	81.45	32.71	114.16	16.34	3.10	
Aug.	26.59	81.46	32.91	114.37	16.44	3.20	
Sept.	26.49	81.97	33.21	115.18	16.47	3.20	
Oct.	26.49	82.18	33.31	115.49	16.59	3.20	
Nov.	26.49	82.18	33.61	115.79	16.70	3.20	
Dec.	26.39	81.99	33.91	115.90	16.82	3.30	8.55

		Consolidated Totals[a]			
M_1[b] (Cols. 1 + 2) (8)	M_2 (Cols. 8 + 3) (9)	Duplications Betw. Col. 9 and Cols. 5 + 6 (10)	M_3 (Cols. 9+5 +6 – 10) (11)	Duplications Betw. Cols. 11 and 7 (12)	M_4 (Cols. 11+7 –12) (13)
85.04	106.03	0.55	119.77		
83.86	105.11	0.54	119.00		
84.62	106.31	0.54	120.42		
87.18	109.37	0.55	123.63		
88.95	111.69	0.55	126.18		
91.51	115.02	0.55	129.69		
93.83	117.58	0.56	133.62		
91.28	115.50	0.56	130.58	0.41	136.47
94.33	118.99	0.57	134.32		
95.88	121.14	0.57	136.64		
97.77	123.57	0.57	139.33		
98.58	124.94	0.58	141.00		
99.21	125.99	0.58	142.20		
98.06	125.27	0.58	141.66		
99.67	127.60	0.60	144.24		
100.91	129.53	0.61	146.15		
102.37	131.59	0.62	148.65		
103.14	132.89	0.64	150.19		
103.73	133.63	0.65	151.07		
103.04	133.29	0.66	150.87	0.45	157.78
102.56	133.17	0.67	150.98		
103.79	134.90	0.69	152.83		
103.50	134.91	0.70	152.95		
105.71	137.42	0.71	155.71		
106.82	138.83	0.73	157.25		
107.54	140.05	0.74	158.65		
108.04	140.75	0.75	159.44		
108.05	140.96	0.75	159.85		
108.46	141.67	0.76	160.58		
108.67	141.98	0.77	161.00		
108.67	142.28	0.78	161.40		
108.38	142.29	0.78	161.63	0.54	169.64

(continued)

TABLE 1 (continued)

| Date | Currency Held by the Public (1) | Deposits Adjusted, Commercial Banks | | | Deposits at | | S & L Shares (7) |
		Demand (2)	Time (3)	Total (4)	Mut. Sav. Banks (5)	Post. Sav. Syst. (6)	
1947							
Jan.	26.7	82.8	33.3	116.1	16.9	3.3	
Feb.	26.7	83.0	33.5	116.5	17.0	3.3	
Mar.	26.7	83.7	33.6	117.3	17.2	3.4	
Apr.	26.6	84.5	33.7	118.2	17.2	3.4	
May	26.6	85.1	33.8	118.9	17.2	3.4	
June	26.6	85.5	33.9	119.4	17.4	3.4	
July	26.5	85.7	34.0	119.7	17.5	3.4	
Aug.	26.5	86.1	34.4	120.5	17.5	3.4	
Sept.	26.7	86.3	34.7	121.0	17.6	3.4	
Oct.	26.5	86.4	35.0	121.4	17.6	3.4	
Nov.	26.5	86.8	35.2	122.0	17.7	3.4	
Dec.	26.4	86.7	35.4	122.1	17.7	3.4	9.8
1948							
Jan.	26.4	87.0	35.5	122.5	17.8	3.4	
Feb.	26.3	86.8	35.7	122.5	17.9	3.4	
Mar.	26.2	86.4	35.7	122.1	18.0	3.4	
Apr.	26.1	86.3	35.7	122.0	18.0	3.4	
May	26.0	86.0	35.7	121.7	18.0	3.4	
June	26.0	86.0	35.8	121.8	18.1	3.4	
July	26.0	86.2	35.8	122.0	18.2	3.4	
Aug.	26.0	86.2	35.9	122.1	18.2	3.4	
Sept.	26.0	86.2	35.9	122.1	18.2	3.3	
Oct.	26.0	86.1	35.9	122.0	18.3	3.3	
Nov.	26.0	85.9	36.0	121.9	18.3	3.3	
Dec.	25.8	85.8	36.0	121.8	18.4	3.3	11.0
1949							
Jan.	25.7	85.5	36.1	121.6	18.4	3.3	
Feb.	25.7	85.5	36.1	121.6	18.6	3.3	
Mar.	25.7	85.6	36.1	121.7	18.6	3.3	
Apr.	25.7	85.6	36.2	121.8	18.7	3.3	
May	25.7	85.8	36.3	122.1	18.8	3.3	
June	25.6	85.7	36.4	122.1	18.8	3.3	
July	25.5	85.7	36.4	122.1	18.9	3.3	
Aug.	25.5	85.6	36.4	122.0	19.0	3.2	
Sept.	25.3	85.6	36.4	122.0	19.0	3.2	
Oct.	25.3	85.6	36.4	122.0	19.1	3.2	
Nov.	25.2	85.8	36.4	122.2	19.2	3.2	

		Consolidated Totals[a]			
M_1[b] (Cols. 1 + 2) (8)	M_2 (Cols. 8 + 3) (9)	Dupli- cations Betw. Col. 9 and Cols. 5 + 6 (10)	M_3 (Cols. 9+5 +6 − 10) (11)	Dupli- cations Betw. Cols. 11 and 7 (12)	M_4 (Cols. 11+7 −12) (13)
109.5	142.8	0	163.0		
109.7	143.2	0	163.5		
110.3	143.9	0	164.5		
111.1	144.8	0	165.4		
111.7	145.5	0	166.1		
112.1	146.0	0	166.8		
112.2	146.2	0	167.1		
112.6	147.0	0	167.9		
113.0	147.7	0	168.7		
112.9	147.9	0	168.9		
113.3	148.5	0	169.6		
113.1	148.5	0	169.6	0.6	178.8
113.4	148.9	0	170.1		
113.2	148.9	0	170.2		
112.6	148.3	0	169.7		
112.3	148.0	0	169.4		
112.1	147.8	0	169.2		
112.0	147.8	0	169.3		
112.2	148.0	0	169.6		
112.3	148.2	0	169.8		
112.2	148.1	0	169.6		
112.1	148.0	0	169.6		
111.8	147.8	0	169.4		
111.5	147.5	0	169.2	0.7	179.5
111.2	147.3	0	169.0		
111.2	147.3	0	169.2		
111.2	147.3	0	169.2		
111.3	147.5	0	169.5		
111.5	147.8	0	169.9		
111.3	147.7	0	169.8		
111.2	147.6	0	169.8		
111.0	147.4	0	169.6		
110.9	147.3	0	169.5		
110.9	147.3	0	169.6		
111.0	147.4	0	169.8		

(continued)

TABLE 1 (continued)

Date	Currency Held by the Public (1)	Deposits Adjusted, Commercial Banks			Deposits at		S & L Shares (7)
		Demand (2)	Time (3)	Total (4)	Mut. Sav. Banks (5)	Post. Sav. Syst. (6)	
1949							
Dec.	25.1	86.0	36.4	122.4	19.3	3.2	12.5
1950							
Jan.	25.1	86.4	36.4	122.8	19.4	3.2	
Feb.	25.1	86.9	36.6	123.5	19.4	3.2	
Mar.	25.2	87.3	36.6	123.9	19.6	3.2	12.9
Apr.	25.3	88.0	36.7	124.7	19.7	3.2	
May	25.2	88.5	36.9	125.4	19.8	3.1	1:.
June	25.1	89.0	36.9	125.9	19.8	3.1	13.3
July	25.0	89.6	36.8	126.4	19.8	3.0	
Aug.	24.9	90.1	36.7	126.8	19.8	3.0	:.
Sept.	24.9	90.3	36.6	126.9	19.8	3.0	13.5
Oct.	24.9	90.8	36.5	127.3	19.9	3.0	
Nov.	24.9	90.9	36.6	127.5	20.0	3.0	
Dec.	25.0	91.2	36.7	127.9	20.0	2.9	14.0
1951							
Jan.	25.0	91.7	36.7	128.4	20.0	2.9	
Feb.	25.1	92.0	36.6	128.6	20.0	2.9	
Mar.	25.2	92.4	36.6	129.0	20.0	2.8	14.3
Apr.	25.2	92.6	36.7	129.3	20.2	2.8	
May	25.3	92.8	36.8	129.6	20.2	2.8	
June	25.4	93.2	36.9	130.1	20.2	2.8	14.8
July	25.6	93.4	37.2	130.6	20.4	2.8	
Aug.	25.7	93.8	37.4	131.2	20.4	2.8	
Sept.	25.8	94.5	37.7	132.2	20.6	2.7	15.4
Oct.	26.0	95.1	37.8	132.9	20.6	2.7	
Nov.	26.0	96.0	38.0	134.0	20.8	2.7	
Dec.	26.1	96.5	38.2	134.7	20.8	2.7	16.1
1952							
Jan.	26.2	96.9	38.4	135.3	21.0	2.7	
Feb.	26.3	97.3	38.7	136.0	21.0	2.7	
Mar.	26.4	97.5	38.9	136.4	21.2	2.7	16.8
Apr.	26.4	97.6	39.1	136.7	21.4	2.6	
May	26.5	98.0	39.3	137.3	21.5	2.6	
June	26.7	98.4	39.5	137.9	21.6	2.6	17.5
July	26.7	98.6	39.7	138.3	21.8	2.6	
Aug.	26.8	98.9	40.0	138.9	22.0	2.6	

		Consolidated Totals[a]			
M_1 [b] (Cols. 1 + 2) (8)	M_2 (Cols. 8 + 3) (9)	Dupli- cations Betw. Col. 9 and Cols. 5 + 6 (10)	M_3 (Cols. 9+5 +6 − 10) (11)	Dupli- cations Betw. Cols. 11 and 7 (12)	M_4 (Cols. 11+7 −12) (13)
111.2	147.6	0	170.1	0.9	181.7
111.5	147.9	0	170.5		
112.1	148.7	0	171.3		
112.5	149.1	0	171.9	0.9	183.9
113.2	149.9	0	172.8		
113.7	150.6	0	173.5		
114.1	151.0	0	173.9	0.8	186.4
114.6	151.4	0	174.2		
115.0	151.7	0	174.5		
115.2	151.8	0	174.6	0.8	187.3
115.7	152.2	0	175.1		
115.9	152.5	0	175.5		
116.2	152.9	0	175.8	0.8	189.0
116.7	153.4	0	176.3		
117.1	153.7	0	176.6		
117.6	154.2	0	177.0	0.8	190.5
117.8	154.5	0	177.5		
118.2	155.0	0	178.0		
118.6	155.5	0	178.5	0.9	192.4
119.1	156.3	0	179.5		
119.6	157.0	0	180.2		
120.4	158.1	0	181.4	0.9	195.9
121.0	158.8	0	182.1		
122.0	160.0	0	183.5		
122.7	160.9	0	184.4	1.0	199.5
123.1	161.5	0	185.2		
123.6	162.3	0	186.0		
123.8	162.7	0	186.6	1.0	202.4
124.1	163.2	0	187.2		
124.5	163.8	0	187.9		
125.0	164.5	0	188.7	1.1	205.1
125.3	165.0	0	189.4		
125.7	165.7	0	190.3		

(continued)

TABLE 1 (continued)

Date	Currency Held by the Public (1)	Deposits Adjusted, Commercial Banks			Deposits at		S & L Shares (7)
		Demand (2)	Time (3)	Total (4)	Mut. Sav. Banks (5)	Post. Sav. Syst. (6)	
1952							
Sept.	26.9	99.4	40.3	139.7	22.1	2.6	18.3
Oct.	27.0	99.7	40.5	140.2	22.2	2.6	
Nov.	27.2	99.9	40.9	140.8	22.4	2.6	
Dec.	27.3	100.1	41.1	141.2	22.6	2.5	19.1
1953							
Jan.	27.4	99.9	41.4	141.3	22.7	2.5	
Feb.	27.5	99.9	41.6	141.5	22.8	2.5	
Mar.	27.6	100.4	41.9	142.3	23.0	2.5	20.1
Apr.	27.7	100.7	42.1	142.8	23.2	2.5	
May	27.7	100.7	42.4	143.1	23.4	2.5	
June	27.7	100.7	42.6	143.3	23.4	2.4	21.0
July	27.8	100.8	42.9	143.7	23.6	2.4	
Aug.	27.8	100.9	43.2	144.1	23.8	2.4	
Sept.	27.8	100.8	43.5	144.3	23.9	2.4	21.9
Oct.	27.8	100.9	43.9	144.8	24.0	2.4	
Nov.	27.8	100.9	44.2	145.1	24.2	2.4	
Dec.	27.7	101.1	44.5	145.6	24.3	2.4	22.8
1954							
Jan.	27.7	101.3	44.8	146.1	24.5	2.3	
Feb.	27.7	101.5	45.2	146.7	24.6	2.3	
Mar.	27.6	101.6	45.6	147.2	24.8	2.3	23.9
Apr.	27.6	101.0	46.1	147.1	25.0	2.3	
May	27.6	102.1	46.5	148.6	25.1	2.3	
June	27.5	102.3	46.8	149.1	25.2	2.2	24.9
July	27.5	102.8	47.3	150.1	25.4	2.2	
Aug.	27.5	103.2	47.8	151.0	25.5	2.2	
Sept.	27.4	103.5	47.9	151.4	25.7	2.2	26.1
Oct.	27.4	104.1	48.1	152.2	25.8	2.2	
Nov.	27.4	104.7	48.2	152.9	26.0	2.2	
Dec.	27.4	104.9	48.3	153.2	26.2	2.1	27.1
1955							
Jan.	27.4	105.6	48.5	154.1	26.4	2.1	27.4
Feb.	27.5	106.4	48.7	155.1	26.6	2.1	27.9
Mar.	27.5	106.0	48.8	154.8	26.7	2.0	28.3
Apr.	27.5	106.3	49.0	155.3	26.8	2.0	28.7
May	27.6	107.0	49.0	156.0	27.0	2.0	29.0

$M_1{}^b$ (Cols. 1 + 2) (8)	M_2 (Cols. 8 + 3) (9)	Duplications Betw. Col. 9 and Cols. 5 + 6 (10)	M_3 (Cols. 9+5 +6 − 10) (11)	Duplications Betw. Cols. 11 and 7 (12)	M_4 (Cols. 11+7 −12) (13)
		Consolidated Totals[a]			
126.4	166.7	0	191.4	1.1	208.6
126.7	167.2	0	192.0		
127.1	168.0	0	193.0		
127.4	168.5	0	193.6	1.2	211.5
127.3	168.7	0	193.9		
127.4	169.0	0	194.3		
128.0	169.9	0	195.4	1.2	214.3
128.3	170.4	0	196.1		
128.5	170.9	0	196.8		
128.5	171.1	0	196.9	1.2	216.7
128.6	171.5	0	197.5		
128.7	171.9	0	198.1		
128.6	172.1	0	198.4	1.3	219.0
128.7	172.6	0	199.0		
128.7	172.9	0	199.5		
128.8	173.3	0	200.0	1.3	221.5
129.0	173.8	0	200.6		
129.1	174.3	0	201.2		
129.2	174.8	0	201.9	1.6	224.2
128.6	174.7	0	202.0		
129.7	176.2	0	203.6		
129.9	176.7	0	204.1	1.6	227.4
130.3	177.6	0	205.2		
130.7	178.5	0	206.2		
130.9	178.8	0	206.7	1.8	231.0
131.5	179.6	0	207.6		
132.1	180.3	0	208.5		
132.3	180.6	0	208.9	1.8	234.2
133.0	181.5	0	210.0	1.9	235.5
133.9	182.6	0	211.3	1.9	237.3
133.6	182.4	0	211.1	1.9	237.5
133.9	182.9	0	211.7	1.8	238.6
134.6	183.6	0	212.6	1.8	239.8

(continued)

TABLE 1 (continued)

| Date | Currency Held by the Public (1) | Deposits Adjusted, Commercial Banks | | | Deposits at | | S & L Shares (7) |
		Demand (2)	Time (3)	Total (4)	Mut. Sav. Banks (5)	Post. Sav. Syst. (6)	
1955							
June	27.6	106.8	49.2	156.0	27.2	2.0	29.4
July	27.7	107.2	49.3	156.5	27.2	2.0	29.8
Aug.	27.7	107.0	49.3	156.3	27.4	2.0	30.2
Sept.	27.7	107.3	49.6	156.9	27.6	1.9	30.6
Oct.	27.8	107.4	49.7	157.1	27.8	1.9	31.0
Nov.	27.8	107.1	49.9	157.0	27.9	1.9	31.4
Dec.	27.8	107.4	50.0	157.4	28.0	1.9	31.8
1956							
Jan.	27.9	107.7	49.9	157.6	28.2	1.9	32.2
Feb.	27.9	107.7	49.9	157.6	28.4	1.8	32.7
Mar.	27.9	107.8	50.1	157.9	28.4	1.8	33.1
Apr.	27.9	108.1	50.3	158.4	28.6	1.8	33.5
May	27.9	107.9	50.4	158.3	28.8	1.8	33.9
June	27.9	108.1	50.7	158.8	29.0	1.8	34.3
July	28.0	108.0	50.9	158.9	29.0	1.8	34.7
Aug.	28.0	107.8	51.2	159.0	29.2	1.7	35.2
Sept.	28.0	108.2	51.5	159.7	29.4	1.7	35.5
Oct.	28.0	108.2	51.6	159.8	29.6	1.7	35.9
Nov.	28.1	108.4	51.8	160.2	29.7	1.7	36.4
Dec.	28.2	108.7	51.9	160.6	29.9	1.6	36.8
1957							
Jan.	28.2	108.6	52.6	161.2	30.0	1.6	37.1
Feb.	28.2	108.6	53.1	161.7	30.2	1.6	37.5
Mar.	28.2	108.7	53.7	162.4	30.2	1.6	37.9
Apr.	28.2	108.7	54.0	162.7	30.4	1.6	38.3
May	28.2	108.8	54.5	163.3	30.5	1.5	38.7
June	28.3	108.6	54.8	163.4	30.7	1.5	39.1
July	28.3	108.7	55.3	164.0	30.8	1.4	39.5
Aug.	28.3	108.8	55.7	164.5	30.9	1.4	39.8
Sept.	28.3	108.4	56.1	164.5	31.1	1.4	40.2
Oct.	28.3	108.2	56.6	164.8	31.2	1.4	40.6
Nov.	28.3	108.0	57.0	165.0	31.4	1.4	41.0
Dec.	28.3	107.6	57.4	165.0	31.6	1.3	41.5
1958							
Jan.	28.3	107.2	57.6	164.8	31.8	1.3	42.0
Feb.	28.2	107.9	59.2	167.1	32.0	1.3	42.4
Mar.	28.2	108.3	60.5	168.8	32.2	1.3	42.9

M_1 [b] (Cols. 1 + 2) (8)	M_2 (Cols. 8 + 3) (9)	Duplications Betw. Col. 9 and Cols. 5 + 6 (10)	M_3 (Cols. 9+5 +6 − 10) (11)	Duplications Betw. Cols. 11 and 7 (12)	M_4 (Cols. 11+7 −12) (13)
		Consolidated Totals[a]			
134.4	183.6	0	212.8	1.8	240.4
134.8	184.1	0	213.3	1.8	241.3
134.8	184.1	0	213.5	1.8	241.9
135.0	184.6	0	214.1	1.8	242.9
135.2	184.9	0	214.6	1.8	243.8
134.9	184.8	0	214.6	1.9	244.1
135.2	185.2	0	215.1	1.9	245.0
135.5	185.4	0	215.5	1.9	245.8
135.5	185.4	0	215.6	2.0	246.3
135.7	185.8	0	216.0	1.9	247.2
136.0	186.3	0	216.7	1.9	248.3
135.8	186.2	0	216.8	1.9	248.8
136.0	186.7	0	217.5	1.9	249.9
136.0	186.9	0	217.7	1.9	250.5
135.7	186.9	0	217.8	1.9	251.1
136.2	187.7	0	218.8	1.9	252.4
136.3	187.9	0	219.2	1.9	253.2
136.6	188.4	0	219.8	1.9	254.3
136.9	188.8	0	220.3	1.9	255.2
136.9	189.5	0	221.1	1.9	256.3
136.8	189.9	0	221.7	1.9	257.3
136.9	190.6	0	222.4	1.8	258.5
136.9	190.9	0	222.9	1.8	259.4
137.0	191.5	0	223.5	1.8	260.4
136.9	191.7	0	223.9	1.8	261.2
137.0	192.3	0	224.5	1.8	262.2
137.1	192.8	0	225.1	1.8	263.1
136.8	192.9	0	225.4	1.8	263.8
136.5	193.1	0	225.7	1.8	264.5
136.3	193.3	0	226.1	1.8	265.3
135.9	193.3	0	226.2	1.9	265.8
135.5	193.1	0	226.2	2.0	266.2
136.2	195.4	0	228.7	2.1	269.0
136.5	197.0	0	230.5	2.2	271.2

(continued)

TABLE 1 (continued)

Date	Currency Held by the Public (1)	Deposits Adjusted, Commercial Banks			Deposits at		S & L Shares (7)
		Demand (2)	Time (3)	Total (4)	Mut. Sav. Banks (5)	Post. Sav. Syst. (6)	
1958							
Apr.	28.2	108.7	61.5	170.2	32.4	1.2	43.5
May	28.3	109.2	62.3	171.5	32.6	1.2	43.9
June	28.3	110.1	63.2	173.3	32.8	1.2	44.3
July	28.4	110.0	64.0	174.0	32.8	1.2	44.8
Aug.	28.4	110.7	64.6	175.3	33.0	1.2	45.3
Sept.	28.5	111.1	64.8	175.9	33.2	1.2	45.9
Oct.	28.5	111.6	64.9	176.5	33.4	1.2	46.4
Nov.	28.5	112.4	65.2	177.6	33.6	1.2	46.9
Dec.	28.6	112.6	65.4	178.0	33.9	1.1	47.5
1959							
Jan.	28.6	112.9	66.0	178.9	33.9	1.1	48.0
Feb.	28.7	113.2	66.0	179.2	33.8	1.1	48.5
Mar.	28.8	113.7	66.2	179.9	34.0	1.1	49.0
Apr.	28.8	113.9	66.5	180.4	34.2	1.1	49.6
May	29.0	114.2	66.6	180.8	34.4	1.1	50.1
June	29.0	114.3	67.0	181.3	34.4	1.1	50.6
July	29.0	115.1	67.1	182.2	34.4	1.0	51.3
Aug.	29.1	114.5	67.2	181.7	34.5	1.0	51.9
Sept.	29.0	114.3	67.3	181.6	34.7	1.0	52.5
Oct.	29.0	113.9	67.3	181.2	34.7	1.0	53.0
Nov.	28.9	113.8	67.3	181.1	34.8	1.0	53.5
Dec.	28.9	113.1	67.4	180.5	34.9	1.0	54.1
1960							
Jan.	29.0	112.7	67.2	179.9	34.9	0.9	54.6
Feb.	29.0	112.4	66.9	179.3	34.9	0.9	55.1
Mar.	29.0	111.9	67.0	178.9	35.0	0.9	55.7
Apr.	29.0	111.8	67.3	179.1	35.2	0.9	56.3
May	29.0	111.3	67.4	178.7	35.2	0.9	56.8
June	29.0	111.1	67.9	179.0	35.2	0.8	57.4
July	29.0	111.5	68.7	180.2	35.4	0.8	58.1
Aug.	29.0	112.0	69.7	181.7	35.5	0.8	58.8
Sept.	29.0	112.1	70.5	182.6	35.7	0.8	59.4
Oct.	29.0	112.1	71.3	183.4	35.8	0.8	60.2
Nov.	29.0	111.8	72.1	183.9	36.0	0.8	60.9
Dec.	28.9	112.1	72.9	185.0	36.2	0.8	61.6
1961							
Jan.	29.0	112.3	73.6	185.9	36.4	0.8	62.2

		Consolidated Totals[a]			
M_1[b] (Cols. 1 + 2) (8)	M_2 (Cols. 8 + 3) (9)	Duplications Betw. Col. 9 and Cols. 5 + 6 (10)	M_3 (Cols. 9+5 +6 − 10) (11)	Duplications Betw. Cols. 11 and 7 (12)	M_4 (Cols. 11+7 −12) (13)
137.0	198.5	0	232.1	2.4	273.2
137.5	199.8	0	233.6	2.5	275.0
138.4	201.6	0	235.6	2.5	277.4
138.4	202.4	0	236.4	2.5	278.7
139.1	203.7	0	237.9	2.5	280.7
139.5	204.3	0	238.7	2.5	282.1
140.1	205.0	0	239.6	2.5	283.5
140.9	206.1	0	240.9	2.4	285.4
141.1	206.5	0	241.5	2.4	286.6
141.6	207.6	0	242.6	2.3	288.3
142.0	208.0	0	242.9	2.2	289.2
142.5	208.7	0	243.8	2.2	290.6
142.7	209.2	0	244.5	2.1	292.0
143.2	209.8	0	245.3	2.1	293.3
143.4	210.4	0	245.9	2.1	294.4
144.1	211.2	0	246.6	2.1	295.8
143.6	210.8	0	246.3	2.0	296.2
143.3	210.6	0	246.3	2.0	296.8
142.9	210.2	0	245.9	1.9	297.0
142.7	210.0	0	245.8	1.9	297.4
141.9	209.3	0	245.2	1.9	297.4
141.7	208.9	0	244.7	1.9	297.4
141.3	208.2	0	244.0	1.8	297.3
140.9	207.9	0	243.8	1.8	297.7
140.8	208.1	0	244.2	1.8	298.7
140.3	207.7	0	243.8	1.9	298.7
140.1	208.0	0	244.0	2.0	299.4
140.4	209.1	0	245.3	2.1	301.3
140.9	210.6	0	246.9	2.1	303.6
141.1	211.6	0	248.1	2.2	305.3
141.1	212.4	0	249.0	2.3	306.9
140.8	212.9	0	249.7	2.4	308.2
141.1	214.0	0	251.0	2.4	310.2
141.2	214.8	0	252.0	2.5	311.7

(continued)

TABLE 1 (continued)
Part II. February 1961 — December 1968

Date	Currency Held by the Public (1)	Demand (2)	Deposits Adjusted, Commercial Banks			Deposits at		S&L Shares (7)
			Consumer Type Time (3a)	Large Negotiable CD's (3b)	Total (4)	Mut. Sav. Banks (5)	Post. Sav. Syst. (6)	
1961								
Feb.	28.9	112.8	74.7	0.2	187.7	36.6	0.8	62.8
Mar.	28.9	113.1	75.2	0.3	188.6	36.8	0.7	63.6
Apr.	29.0	113.4	75.7	0.5	189.6	36.9	0.7	64.3
May	28.9	113.8	76.5	0.7	191.0	37.0	0.7	64.9
June	28.9	114.0	77.2	0.9	192.1	37.1	0.7	65.5
July	29.0	114.0	77.9	1.2	193.1	37.3	0.7	66.3
Aug.	29.1	114.3	78.5	1.4	194.2	37.5	0.7	67.0
Sept.	29.2	114.7	79.0	1.7	195.4	37.8	0.7	67.8
Oct.	29.3	115.0	79.5	2.0	196.5	37.9	0.7	68.6
Nov.	29.4	115.5	79.9	2.3	197.7	38.1	0.7	69.4
Dec.	29.6	115.9	80.0	2.7	198.6	38.4	0.7	70.3
1962								
Jan.	29.6	115.8	81.1	3.0	199.9	38.5	0.6	70.9
Feb.	29.7	116.1	82.8	3.2	202.1	38.7	0.6	71.4
Mar.	29.8	116.2	84.3	3.3	203.8	39.0	0.6	72.3
Apr.	30.0	116.4	85.2	3.6	205.2	39.2	0.6	73.1
May	30.0	116.1	85.7	3.8	205.6	39.2	0.6	73.7
June	30.1	116.1	86.6	4.0	206.7	39.4	0.6	74.3
July	30.1	115.9	87.5	4.2	207.6	39.8	0.6	75.0
Aug.	30.2	115.8	88.1	4.5	208.4	40.0	0.6	75.8
Sept.	30.3	115.6	88.9	4.8	209.3	40.4	0.6	76.8
Oct.	30.3	116.0	89.9	5.1	211.0	40.7	0.6	77.7
Nov.	30.4	116.4	90.8	5.4	212.6	41.0	0.5	78.6
Dec.	30.6	116.8	92.1	5.7	214.6	41.4	0.5	79.6
1963								
Jan.	30.7	117.4	93.1	5.9	216.4	41.6	0.5	80.4
Feb.	30.9	117.7	94.1	6.2	218.0	41.8	0.5	81.4
Mar.	31.0	117.8	94.9	6.5	219.2	42.1	0.5	82.6
Apr.	31.1	118.2	95.9	6.8	220.9	42.4	0.5	83.6
May	31.3	118.5	96.5	7.1	222.1	42.6	0.5	84.3
June	31.5	118.9	97.3	7.4	223.6	42.9	0.5	85.1
July	31.6	119.4	98.2	7.7	225.3	43.1	0.5	85.9

Consolidated Totals[a]

M_1[b] (Cols. 1 + 2) (8)	$M_2 -$ CD's (Cols. 8 + 3a)[c] (9a)	M_2 (Cols. 8 +3a + 3b) (9b)	Dupli- cations Betw. Col. 9 and Cols. 5 + 6 (10)	M_3 (Cols. 9b+5 +6 - 10) (11)	Dupli- cations Betw. Cols. 11 and 7 (12)	M_4 (Cols. 11+7 -12) (13)
141.7	216.4	216.6	0	254.0	2.6	314.2
142.0	217.2	217.5	0	255.0	2.6	316.0
142.3	218.0	218.5	0	256.1	2.6	317.8
142.7	219.2	219.9	0	257.6	2.7	319.8
143.0	220.2	221.1	0	258.9	2.8	321.6
143.0	220.9	222.1	0	260.1	2.8	323.6
143.3	221.8	223.2	0	261.4	2.9	325.5
143.9	222.9	224.6	0	263.1	2.9	328.0
144.3	223.8	225.8	0	264.4	2.9	330.1
145.0	224.9	227.2	0	266.0	3.0	332.4
145.4	225.4	228.1	0	267.3	3.0	334.6
145.5	226.6	229.6	0	268.7	2.9	336.7
145.8	228.6	231.8	0	271.1	3.0	339.5
146.0	230.3	233.6	0	273.2	3.0	342.5
146.3	231.5	235.1	0	274.9	3.1	344.9
146.1	231.8	235.6	0	275.4	3.1	346.0
146.2	232.8	236.8	0	276.8	3.1	348.0
146.1	233.6	237.8	0	278.2	3.1	350.1
146.0	234.1	238.6	0	279.2	3.2	351.8
145.8	234.7	239.5	0	280.5	3.2	354.1
146.4	236.3	241.4	0	282.7	3.3	357.1
146.9	237.7	243.1	0	284.6	3.3	359.9
147.4	239.5	245.2	0	287.1	3.4	363.3
148.0	241.1	247.0	0	289.1	3.5	366.0
148.6	242.7	248.9	0	291.2	3.6	369.0
148.8	243.7	250.2	0	292.8	3.6	371.8
149.3	245.2	252.0	0	294.9	3.7	374.8
149.8	246.3	253.4	0	296.5	3.6	377.2
150.4	247.7	255.1	0	298.5	3.6	380.0
151.0	249.2	256.9	0	300.5	3.6	382.8

(continued)

TABLE 1 (continued)

Date	Cur-rency Held by the Public (1)	Deposits Adjusted, Commercial Banks				Deposits at		S&L Shares (7)
		Demand (2)	Con-sumer Type Time (3a)	Large Nego-tiable CD's (3b)	Total (4)	Mut. Sav. Banks (5)	Post. Sav. Syst. (6)	
1963								
Aug.	31.8	119.5	99.1	8.1	226.7	43.4	0.5	86.8
Sept.	31.9	119.6	100.0	8.4	228.0	43.6	0.5	87.8
Oct.	32.0	120.3	100.8	8.8	229.9	43.8	0.5	88.8
Nov.	32.3	121.0	101.9	9.2	232.1	44.4	0.5	89.7
Dec.	32.5	120.5	102.8	9.6	232.7	44.6	0.5	90.6
1964								
Jan.	32.6	120.9	103.2	10.2	234.3	44.8	0.4	91.2
Feb.	32.8	121.1	103.8	10.7	235.6	45.2	0.4	91.9
Mar.	32.9	121.2	104.4	10.9	236.5	45.6	0.4	93.0
Apr.	33.1	121.4	105.0	11.2	237.6	45.9	0.4	93.9
May	33.3	121.8	105.6	11.8	239.2	46.2	0.4	94.6
June	33.5	122.1	106.7	12.0	240.8	46.4	0.4	95.3
July	33.6	123.0	107.6	12.1	242.7	46.8	0.4	96.2
Aug.	33.8	123.6	108.4	12.4	244.4	47.2	0.4	97.2
Sept.	33.9	124.2	110.0	12.2	246.4	47.6	0.4	98.4
Oct.	34.0	124.6	111.0	12.5	248.1	48.0	0.4	99.5
Nov.	34.2	125.0	112.1	12.9	250.0	48.4	0.4	100.4
Dec.	34.2	125.1	113.8	12.8	251.7	48.8	0.4	101.3
1965								
Jan.	34.4	125.2	115.2	13.5	253.9	49.2	0.4	101.7
Feb.	34.6	125.4	116.8	14.0	256.2	49.5	0.4	102.1
Mar.	34.7	125.7	117.9	14.2	257.8	49.8	0.4	103.2
Apr.	34.7	126.1	118.9	14.7	259.7	50.0	0.4	103.9
May	34.9	126.0	119.7	15.2	260.9	50.1	0.4	104.2
June	35.0	126.7	120.9	15.5	263.1	50.4	0.4	104.8
July	35.2	127.2	122.1	15.9	265.3	50.7	0.3	105.4
Aug.	35.5	127.6	123.3	16.4	267.3	51.1	0.3	106.1
Sept.	35.7	128.4	125.1	16.3	269.8	51.4	0.3	107.2
Oct.	36.0	129.3	127.0	16.5	272.8	51.7	0.3	108.2
Nov.	36.1	129.6	128.6	16.6	274.8	52.2	0.3	109.0
Dec.	36.3	130.4	130.4	16.3	277.1	52.6	0.3	109.8
1966								
Jan.	36.6	131.4	131.4	16.3	279.1	52.8	0.3	110.0
Feb.	36.7	131.9	132.1	16.6	280.6	52.9	0.3	110.2
Mar.	36.9	132.4	132.9	17.0	282.3	53.2	0.3	111.1
Apr.	37.1	133.5	134.5	17.6	285.6	53.2	0.3	111.4

			Consolidated Totals[a]			
M_1[b] (Cols. 1 + 2) (8)	$M_2 -$ CD's (Cols. 8 + 3a)[c] (9a)	M_2 (Cols. 8 +3a + 3b) (9b)	Dupli-cations Betw. Col. 9 and Cols. 5 + 6 (10)	M_3 (Cols. 9b+5 +6 - 10) (11)	Dupli-cations Betw. Cols. 11 and 7 (12)	M_4 (Cols. 11+7 -12) (13)
151.2	250.3	258.4	0	302.3	3.6	385.5
151.5	251.5	259.9	0	304.0	3.6	388.2
152.3	253.1	261.9	0	306.2	3.6	391.4
153.3	255.2	264.4	0	309.3	3.6	395.4
153.0	255.6	265.2	0	310.3	3.6	397.3
153.5	256.7	266.9	0	312.1	3.6	399.7
153.8	257.6	268.3	0	313.9	3.5	402.3
154.1	258.5	269.4	0	315.4	3.5	404.9
154.5	259.5	270.7	0	317.0	3.5	407.4
155.1	260.7	272.5	0	319.1	3.5	410.2
155.6	262.3	274.3	0	321.1	3.5	412.9
156.6	264.2	276.3	0	323.5	3.5	416.2
157.3	265.7	278.1	0	325.7	3.6	419.3
158.0	268.0	280.2	0	328.2	3.6	423.0
158.5	269.5	282.0	0	330.4	3.6	426.3
159.1	271.2	284.1	0	332.9	3.6	429.7
159.3	273.1	285.9	0	335.1	3.6	432.8
159.6	274.8	288.3	0	337.9	3.6	436.0
160.0	276.8	290.8	0	340.7	3.5	439.3
160.4	278.3	292.5	0	342.7	3.5	442.4
160.8	279.7	294.4	0	344.8	3.4	445.3
160.9	280.6	295.8	0	346.3	3.4	447.1
161.7	282.6	298.1	0	348.9	3.4	450.3
162.4	284.5	300.4	0	351.4	3.4	453.4
163.1	286.4	303.2	0	354.6	3.5	457.2
164.0	289.1	305.4	0	357.1	3.6	460.7
165.2	292.2	308.7	0	360.7	3.6	465.3
165.8	294.4	311.0	0	363.5	3.6	468.9
166.7	297.1	313.4	0	366.3	3.6	472.5
167.9	299.3	315.6	0	368.7	3.4	475.3
168.6	300.7	317.3	0	370.5	3.3	477.4
169.3	302.2	319.2	0	372.7	3.3	480.5
170.6	305.1	322.7	0	376.2	3.1	484.5

(continued)

TABLE 1 (concluded)

Date	Currency Held by the Public (1)	Deposits Adjusted, Commercial Banks				Deposits at		S&L Shares (7)
		Demand (2)	Consumer Type Time (3a)	Large Negotiable CD's (3b)	Total (4)	Mut. Sav. Banks (5)	Post. Sav. Syst. (6)	
1966								
May	37.3	133.0	135.9	17.8	286.7	53.0	0.3	111.2
June	37.4	133.1	136.5	17.8	287.4	53.2	0.2	111.3
July	37.6	132.0	137.8	18.3	288.1	53.4	0.2	111.1
Aug.	37.8	132.1	138.2	18.4	288.7	53.7	0.2	111.2
Sept.	37.9	132.7	139.8	17.5	290.0	54.0	0.2	111.8
Oct.	38.0	132.1	140.7	16.3	289.1	54.3	0.2	112.3
Nov.	38.2	131.9	141.3	15.6	288.8	54.7	0.1	112.7
Dec.	38.3	132.1	143.0	15.5	290.6	55.1	0.1	113.4
1967								
Jan.	38.5	131.7	144.2	16.8	292.7	55.4	0.1	113.7
Feb.	38.7	133.0	145.6	18.4	297.0	55.8	0.1	114.2
Mar.	38.9	134.3	147.2	19.0	300.5	56.2	0.1	115.5
Apr.	39.0	133.7	149.5	18.9	302.1	56.7	0.1	116.7
May	39.1	135.3	151.7	18.8	305.8	57.0	0.1	117.6
June	39.3	136.7	153.6	19.2	309.5	57.5	0.1	118.3
July	39.4	138.1	155.8	19.4	313.3	58.0	0.1	119.3
Aug.	39.5	139.3	156.5	20.4	316.2	58.4	0.1	120.4
Sept.	39.7	139.9	158.6	20.2	318.7	58.8	–	121.7
Oct.	39.9	140.5	160.3	20.0	320.8	59.2	–	122.7
Nov.	40.0	141.1	161.3	20.7	323.1	59.8	–	123.4
Dec.	40.4	141.3	163.0	20.7	325.0	60.1	–	124.0
1968								
Jan.	40.6	142.0	163.5	20.6	326.1	60.5	–	123.9
Feb.	40.7	142.6	164.9	20.9	328.4	60.9	–	124.0
Mar.	41.1	143.2	166.4	20.8	330.4	61.4	–	125.2
Apr.	41.3	143.8	167.7	20.0	331.5	61.6	–	125.9
May	41.6	145.3	168.6	19.6	333.5	61.8	–	126.2
June	41.9	146.3	169.3	19.3	334.9	62.2	–	126.5
July	42.1	147.5	170.5	20.6	338.6	62.4	–	126.9
Aug.	42.4	148.6	171.6	22.2	342.4	62.8	–	127.6
Sept.	42.7	148.8	174.3	22.1	345.2	63.2	–	128.7
Oct.	42.8	149.1	176.4	23.0	348.5	63.6	–	129.7
Nov.	43.2	150.5	178.4	23.7	352.6	64.1	–	130.4
Dec.	43.4	151.4	181.0	23.9	356.3	64.6	–	131.1

Consolidated Totals[a]

M_1[b] (Cols. 1 + 2) (8)	$M_2 -$ CD's (Cols. 8 + 3a)[c] (9a)	M_2 (Cols. 8 +3a + 3b) (9b)	Duplications Betw. Col. 9 and Cols. 5 + 6 (10)	M_3 (Cols. 9b+5 +6 - 10) (11)	Duplications Betw. Cols. 11 and 7 (12)	M_4 Cols. 11+7 -12) (13)
170.3	306.2	324.0	0	377.3	3.1	485.4
170.5	307.0	324.8	0	378.2	3.1	486.4
169.6	307.4	325.7	0	379.3	3.0	487.4
169.9	308.1	326.5	0	380.4	2.9	488.7
170.6	310.4	327.9	0	382.1	2.9	491.0
170.2	310.9	327.2	0	381.7	2.8	491.2
170.1	311.4	327.0	0	381.8	2.9	491.6
170.4	313.4	328.9	0	384.1	3.0	494.5
170.2	314.4	331.2	0	386.7	3.1	497.3
171.8	317.4	335.8	0	391.7	3.2	502.7
173.2	320.4	339.4	0	395.7	3.4	507.8
172.7	322.2	341.1	0	397.9	3.6	511.0
174.4	326.1	344.9	0	402.0	3.5	516.1
176.0	329.6	348.8	0	406.4	3.5	521.2
177.5	333.3	352.7	0	410.8	3.6	526.5
178.8	335.3	355.7	0	414.2	3.5	531.1
179.6	338.2	358.4	0	417.2	3.4	535.5
180.4	340.7	360.7	0	419.9	3.3	539.3
181.2	342.5	363.2	0	423.0	3.2	543.2
181.7	344.7	365.4	0	425.5	3.2	546.3
182.6	346.1	366.7	0	427.2	3.0	548.1
183.3	348.2	369.1	0	430.0	2.9	551.1
184.2	350.6	371.4	0	432.8	2.9	555.1
185.1	352.8	372.8	0	434.4	2.8	557.5
186.8	355.4	375.0	0	436.8	2.7	560.3
188.2	357.5	376.8	0	439.0	2.7	562.8
189.6	360.1	380.7	0	443.1	2.6	567.4
191.0	362.6	384.8	0	447.6	2.6	572.6
191.4	365.7	387.8	0	451.0	2.7	577.0
191.8	368.2	391.2	0	454.8	2.7	581.8
193.6	372.0	395.7	0	459.8	2.8	587.4
194.8	375.8	399.7	0	464.3	2.7	592.7

Notes to Table 1

[a]Sums of unrounded figures.

[b]Not correctly consolidated because that part of currency in commercial bank vaults and of interbank deposits of commercial banks
regarded as held on account of time deposits has been subtracted in
computing cols. 1 and 2. Since any estimates of these amounts are
necessarily arbitrary, we have not tried to correct this error.

[c]Less than five million dollars from Jan. 1911 (start of operations)
through Sept. 1911.

[d]These estimates are not correctly consolidated because that part
of currency in commercial bank vaults and of interbank demand and
time deposits at commercial banks regarded as held on account of
such certificates has been subtracted in computing cols. 1, 2, and 3.
Since any estimates of these amounts are necessarily arbitrary, we
have not tried to correct this error.

Source, by Column
Part I

1. This column was obtained by adding vault cash in mutual
savings banks, 1867—1946, and Postal Savings System currency holdings, 1919—63 (the period with reported data), to the estimates of
currency held by the public in the sources listed below.

Vault cash in mutual savings banks, 1867—1906, is from Table 20,
col. 10; 1907—46, from *All-Bank Statistics*, p. 47, interpolated mon:hly
along a straight line between end-of-June figures. Postal Savings
System currency holdings are from *Statement of Operations*, Board of
Trustees, U.S. Postal Savings System, annual issues, interpolated
along a straight line between end-of-June figures. Sources of the
currency estimates are: *1867—1906*, Table 20, col. 1; *1907—42*,
Table 27, col. 3; *1943—45*, end-of-month data, *Federal Reserve Bulletin*, monthly issues beginning Feb. 1944, seasonally adjusted by us;
1946, end-of-month data, seasonally adjusted by Federal Reserve,
ibid., Feb. 1960, p. 136. *Thereafter*, monthly averages of daily figures,
seasonally adjusted by Federal Reserve, which include currency held
by mutual savings banks, *ibid.*, Oct. 1969, pp. 790—793.

2. This column was obtained by adding bank balances due to
mutual savings banks, 1914—46 (from *All-Bank Statistics*, p. 47,
interpolated monthly along a straight line between end-of-June figures)
to the estimates of demand deposits adjusted in the following sources:
1914—17, Table 35, Part II, col. 4; *1917—19*, Table 35, Part III,
col. 5; *1919—45*, Table 36, col. 3; *1946*, end-of-month data, seasonally
adjusted by Federal Reserve, *Federal Reserve Bulletin*, Feb. 1960,
p. 135. *Thereafter*, monthly averages of daily figures, seasonally
adjusted by Federal Reserve, which include demand balances with

Notes to Table 1 (continued)

commercial banks of mutual savings banks (same sources as for col. 1).

3. This column was obtained by adding bank balances due to the Postal Savings System, 1919—63 (see the source in col. 1 above) to the estimates of time deposits adjusted in the following sources: *1914—17,* Table 35, Part II, col. 8; *1917—19,* Table 35, Part III, col. 9; *1919—45,* Table 30, col. 6, *1946,* Federal Reserve end of month data, seasonally adjusted by us, *Federal Reserve Bulletin,* monthly issues. *Thereafter,* monthly averages of daily figures, seasonally adjusted by Federal Reserve (same sources as for col. 1).

4. This column was obtained, 1896—1914, by adding bank balances due to mutual savings banks (figures before 1896 are unavailable), as described in col. 2 above, to total deposits adjusted in the following sources: *1867—1906,* Table 20, col. 2; *1907—14,* Table 35, Part I, col. 4; *1914—Jan. 1961,* sum of cols. 2 and 3.

5. *Jan. 1867 — Feb. 1875:* Emerson W. Keyes, *A History of Savings Banks in the United States,* New York, 1878, table facing p. 532, sum of all cols. except for Cal., Iowa, Chicago, and Wash., D.C. Deposit figures in latter cols. are for stock savings banks, according to present definition, while cols. used omit deposits of such banks. Data were interpolated on a straight line to the end of each month. *Aug. 1875 — June 1895,* David Fand, "Estimates of Deposits and Vault Cash in the Nonnational Banks in the Post-Civil War Period in the United States" (unpublished Ph.D. dissertation, University of Chicago, 1954), corrected for seasonal variations by us as required: *June 1896 — June 1906, All-Bank Statistics,* p. 48; *1907—23,* Table 38, col. 5; *1923—46,* Table 39, col. 5; *1947—Jan. 1961,* Federal Reserve estimates for last Wed. of month, seasonally adjusted by us, with pairs of the last Wed.-of-month figures averaged to get figures centered at midmonth, *Federal Reserve Bulletin,* monthly issues.

6. The Postal Savings System opened for business January 1911.

   a. Jan. 1911— Oct. 1955: Depositors' balances including principal of outstanding and unclaimed deposits, monthly, from its *Annual Report of Operations,* minus monthly estimates of depositors' balances at banks in the U.S. possessions. The series was seasonally adjusted by us, Jan. 1913 — July 1930.

   b. Nov. 1955 — Jan. 1961: Federal Reserve estimates for last Wed. of month, from *Federal Reserve Bulletin,* monthly issues, without seasonal adjustment.

7. *1896—1919,* Raymond Goldsmith, *A Study of Saving in the United States,* Vol. I, Princeton University Press, 1955, Table J-5, p. 441, col. 2, adjusted to lower level of following segment, 1920—35, obtained from sources listed below: *1920—21, Federal Home Loan Bank Review,* Statistical Supplement, 1947, p. 9, *1922—58* (Dec.

Notes to Table 1 (continued)

figures), *Trends in the Savings and Loan Field, 1958,* Federal Home Loan Bank Board, Washington, Nov. 1959. *1950—54* (Mar., June, Sept. figures), *Selected Balance Sheet Data, All Operating Savings and Loan Associations,* FHLBB, Feb. 1956. *1955—58* (Jan. — Nov. figures), *ibid.,* Dec. issues showing revised figures for year earlier than year of publication. *1959—Jan. 1961, ibid.,* issues showing final revisions.

Quarterly and monthly data were seasonally adjusted by us. The monthly seasonal adjustment factors are as follows:

Jan.	100.4	Apr.	99.8	July	100.0	Oct.	99.5
Feb.	100.2	May	100.0	Aug.	99.8	Nov.	99.3
Mar.	100.0	June	101.1	Sept.	99.5	Dec.	100.3

Beginning 1955, we averaged pairs of the seasonally adjusted end-of-month data to get figures centered at midmonth.

10. Sum of vault cash in and bank balances due to mutual savings banks (through 1946), and currency holdings of and bank balances due to Postal Savings System (for sources, see cols. 1—4 above). Zeros are shown, beginning 1947, because Postal Savings System cash assets were under $50 million.

12. Cash and bank balances of savings and loan associations: *1896—1932* from Raymond Goldsmith, *A Study of Saving,* Vol. I, p. 436, Table J-2, col. 5; *1933—35,* from A. G. Hart, *Debts and Recovery,* Twentieth Century Fund, 1938, p. 303; *1936—49, Trends in the Savings and Loan Field,* 1961, Table 1; *1950—68, Selected Balance Sheet Data, All Operating Savings and Loan Associations.* June estimates were interpolated between Dec. figures, 1896—1906. Quarterly and monthly figures, 1950—68, were seasonally adjusted by Census X-11 method. Beginning 1955, pairs of seasonally adjusted end-of-month figures were averaged to get figures centered at midmonth.

Part II

1—2. See Part I.

3a. Total time deposits, as in Part I, minus col. 3b.

3b. Large negotiable certificates of deposits, beginning Jan. 1964, are reported weekly for weekly reporting member banks — since June 29, 1966, weekly reporting large commercial banks — *(Federal Reserve Bulletin,* Feb. 1965, p. 329, note 9; Mar. 1966, p. 419, note 9; Mar. 1967, pp. 464—465; Mar. 1968, pp. A-92 and A-93; monthly issues thereafter, p. A-29). The weekly figures were averaged monthly by us, and the segment for Jan. 1964—June 1965 was raised to the level of the new series available since that date. We treated the first weekly figure reported (for Jan. 8, 1964), adjusted in level, as a bench-mark figure in addition to annual (Dec.) bench-mark figures available for 1960—62 *(ibid.,* Apr. 1963, p. 460). To obtain monthly estimates beginning Feb. 1961, when a secondary market dealing in large negoti-

Notes to Table 1 (concluded)

able certificates was formed, we interpolated logarithmically along a straight line between the bench-mark dates to the middle of intervening months. From this monthly series, we subtracted an estimate of the amount of large (but not negotiable) certificates outstanding. The estimate was obtained by decumulating along a straight line the amount outstanding on Dec. 31, 1960, the amount declining to zero in Jan. 1962.

4. Sum of cols. 3a and 3b.

5–6. *Federal Reserve Bulletin,* monthly issues; see Part I.

7, 12. *Selected Balance Sheet Data, All Operating Savings and Loan Associations,* FHLBB, issues showing final revisions; see Part I.

10. Zeros are shown because Postal Savings System cash assets were under $50 million.

process of collection.[2] The savings and loan figures are the redeemable value of savings and loan association shares.

For currency and deposits, the estimates in Table 1 are for the period since 1867. They are annual from 1867 through 1874 and 1882 through 1906, semiannual from 1875 through 1881, and monthly from May 1907 through 1968. Through December 1946, the estimates are for the *end* of the month listed in the table; and were constructed by us for the whole period for deposits, through December 1942, for currency. From 1943 through 1946, we use Federal Reserve estimates for currency. After 1946, the estimates of both deposits and currency are those of the Federal Reserve, in the form of monthly averages of daily figures that refer to the *middle* of the month. In part, then, the estimates are of the stock as of the indicated date, and in part they are averages of the stock for a number of dates (at the limit, daily) centered on the indicated date. Where feasible, we have used the averages for a number of dates in order to average out random fluctuations.

For savings and loan shares, the estimates are for the period since 1897 and are all from published sources. They are for one date a year from 1897 through 1949 (end of June 1897 through 1906; end of December, 1907 through 1949), for four dates a year from 1950

[2] We do not show, or use, a total of the public's and government's money combined either before or after the establishment of the Federal Reserve System, because Treasury cash and government deposits are susceptible to change by simple bookkeeping transactions. Statisticians who include government deposits at the Federal Reserve System in the money stock implicitly do not consolidate Federal Reserve operations with the monetary operations of the Treasury. Yet the distinction between the two monetary

through 1954 (end of March, June, September, and December), and centered at the middle of each month from 1955 through 1968.

Current estimates published by the Board of Governors of the Federal Reserve System and by the Federal Home Loan Bank Board monthly can be used to extend the estimates beyond 1968.[3]

In addition to the annual, semiannual, and monthly estimates in Table 1, we give quarterly estimates of currency held by the public and commercial bank deposits in Table 2. The derivation of the quarterly estimates for 1867–1907 is described in Chapter 11, section 3. The quarterly estimates for 1907–68 are averages of the monthly figures in Table 1.

2. Coverage of Our Estimates

The "public" of the United States, ideally defined, excludes the monetary authorities and all banks, whether operated by private individuals, partnerships, corporations, or governments, and includes all other individuals, partnerships, corporations, states, counties, municipalities, and government agencies resident in the United States and its possessions. For the public so defined, we would have liked to determine the total holdings of U.S. currency, the four classes of U.S. dollar deposits listed,

authorities seems a technical one without fundamental economic significance. Given the artificial separation between the two, government money holdings can be whatever the monetary authorities choose to make them. See *A Monetary History,* Appendix B, pp. 776 ff.

[3] See the *Federal Reserve Bulletin* (tables for "Money Supply" and "Banks and the Monetary System") and the monthly FHLBB release ("Table 1, Selected Balance Sheet Data, All Operating Savings and Loan Associations").

The "Money Supply" table shows seasonally adjusted monthly averages of daily figures. The columns headed "Currency component," "Demand deposit component," "Time deposits adjusted," and "Total money supply" provide the basic entries for Table 1, cols. 1–3 and 8.

The "Banks and the Monetary System" table shows seasonally unadjusted last-Wednesday-of-the-month figures for time deposits at mutual savings banks and the Postal Savings System. We apply a seasonal adjustment to the mutual savings bank figures (for the factors, see pp. 552–553, note 4), but the amplitude of the adjustment is small. We use a two-month moving average to get middle-of-month estimates for Table 1, col. 5.

Note that the Postal Savings System was discontinued on April 27, 1966, by the Act of March 28, 1966. No entries for Postal Savings System deposits have been given in the *Federal Reserve Bulletin* table since September 27, 1967.

The FHLBB release shows end-of-month figures. The column headed "Total Savings Capital" corresponds to the column on savings and loan shares in Table 1. For seasonal adjustment factors, see the source notes to the table. We use a two-month moving average of the seasonally adjusted figures to get midmonth estimates.

CHART 1

Currency, Deposits, and Savings and Loan Shares
Held by the Public, 1867–1968

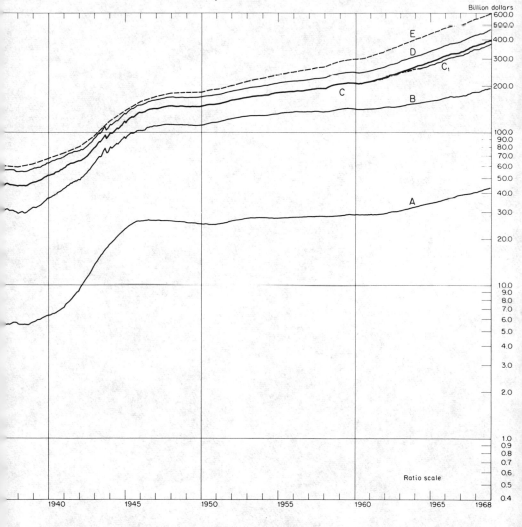

SOURCE: Table 1.

on dollars

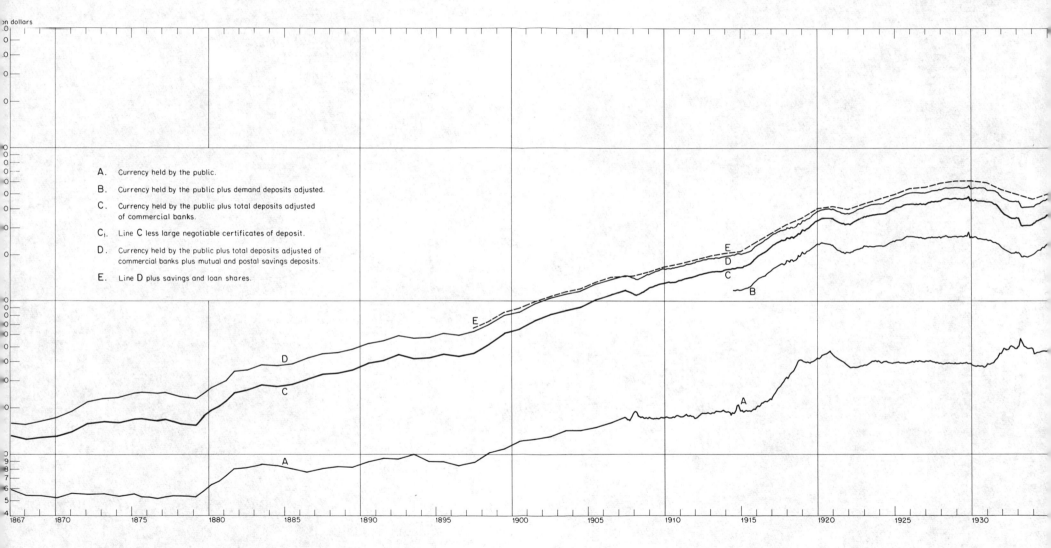

A. Currency held by the public.

B. Currency held by the public plus demand deposits adjusted.

C. Currency held by the public plus total deposits adjusted
    of commercial banks.

C₁. Line C less large negotiable certificates of deposit.

D. Currency held by the public plus total deposits adjusted of
    commercial banks plus mutual and postal savings deposits.

E. Line D plus savings and loan shares.

1867   1870   1875   1880   1885   1890   1895   1900   1905   1910   1915   1920   1925   1930

and savings and loan shares. In practice, we have had to depart from this ideal. The departures are explained by a single circumstance: the basic data we use are reported by the issuers of currency and by the banking institutions whose liabilities are so misleadingly termed "deposits," [4] rather than by the holders of the currency and the deposits. As a consequence, it is often necessary to make the coverage of the data correspond to the geographic location or other characteristics of the issuers of currency or of the banking institutions or correspond to the character of their liabilities, rather than, as we should prefer, to the characteristics of the holders and of their monetary assets.[5]

[4] Misleadingly, because "deposit" connotes the placing of something in safekeeping, as in a 100 per cent reserve banking system. In a fractional reserve system, a "deposit" is a loan of funds to a bank, which uses the excess over the cash reserves it keeps to acquire other assets, i.e., to make loans in its turn. The bank is thus basically a financial intermediary that borrows from one group and lends to another rather than a depositary institution, in any literal sense.

[5] There is also a discrepancy between holder records of deposits and bank ledgers, due to mail float, a factor that our estimates ignore. The mail float refers to the dollar amount of checks which holders of deposits have drawn against their accounts and mailed, but which have not been received or deposited by the payees, and hence are not credited on payees' records. Because of the amount always in transit, bank ledgers record a higher total of deposits than holder records would if holders promptly deducted all checks drawn.

Another important discrepancy results from bank float. When payees receive and deposit the checks, they are entered to their credit on the ledgers of the banks in which the checks are deposited before they are subtracted from the ledgers of the banks on which the checks are drawn. Our deposit figures exclude this bank float, which in recent years has been as high as 16 per cent of demand deposits adjusted. In constructing owner-records of demand deposits for flow-of-funds accounts for years before 1959, the Federal Reserve estimated mail float as equal to bank float, though no empirical evidence existed for the assumed one-to-one relationship. In 1959 it abandoned this technique. Since then, demand deposit figures in the flow-of-funds accounts have differed from demand deposits in its money supply figures only by the estimated amount of business checks sent to other business firms. As Earl Hicks has pointed out, the discrepancy is not a measure of mail float ("Comment: The Float in Flow-of-Funds Accounts," *The Flow-of-Funds Approach to Social Accounting*, Studies in Income and Wealth, Vol. 26, Princeton for NBER, 1962, p. 460).

One consistent accounting concept of the amount of money according to holders' records would deduct mail float as well as bank float. However, it is by no means clear that such an accounting concept would be economically more meaningful than the concept we use—just as it is not entirely clear that deduction of bank float, despite the hoary vintage of the practice, yields an economically more meaningful monetary total. The man who mails a check is fully aware that the corresponding amount will not be debited against his account until the check has reached its destination, has been deposited by the recipient, and has been forwarded to his bank for collection. Whatever accounting practice may call for, he is unlikely to refrain from taking this knowledge into account when pressed for cash. The practice of "kiting" checks, i.e., writing them for a larger sum than the payer currently has to his credit (when there are, in bank jargon, "insufficient funds") but that the payer intends to "cover" before the checks are presented for collection is no less ancient than the practice of deducting "checks in the process of collection" in computing demand deposits adjusted.

The main departures from our ideal are slightly different for currency and for commercial bank deposits. We include as currency held by the U.S. public (1) currency held by both the public of foreign countries and banks in foreign countries,[6] and (2) currency held by U.S. government departments and bureaus outside the Washington, D.C., offices of the Treasury and outside the mint and assay offices of the United States. The currency that is held by the Treasury outside Washington in its role as a monetary authority should be excluded. On the other side, the currency that is held by the Treasury in Washington, D.C., in its role as an operating agency should be included. Hence we do not know whether item 2 makes our currency estimates too large or too small. We exclude from currency held by the U.S. public (3) some items that should be counted as currency but for which we were unable to make estimates, notably private issues during banking panics and travelers' checks. (Travelers' checks issued by reporting banks are included as deposits, but travelers' checks issued by the American Express Company, which is not a bank, are excluded from both currency and deposits.)[7]

We include as deposits held by the U.S. public (1) deposits held by the public of foreign countries at banks located in the continental United States, and (2) since 1947, deposits held by foreign commercial banks at U.S. commercial banks and by foreign governments, central banks,

In the source cited above in this note, Earl Hicks takes the position that owner-records of deposits have no special importance, while the total quantity of money shown as liabilities of the issuers is of the greatest importance. He would use only bank record data and offset the discrepancy between bank-records and owner-records in the sector accounts by the opposite discrepancies in goods receivable or bills payable accounts of the two parties to purchases and sales.

Whatever the verdict on the treatment of owner-records of deposits in the flow-of-funds accounts, the absence of data has made it impossible for us to do anything about mail float, so that in fact, if not also in principle, our position is similar to that of Hicks.

[6] The treatment of foreign branches of U.S. banks varies: before 1920, their holdings of U.S. currency are excluded; after 1920, they are included. U.S. currency holdings of banks in U.S. territories and possessions are excluded through 1946, but included thereafter.

[7] On emergency issues of currency in 1893, 1907, and 1933, see Phillip Cagan, *Determinants and Effects of Changes in the Stock of Money, 1875–1960,* National Bureau of Economic Research, 1965, pp. 139–140.

Travelers' checks issued by the American Express Company are in effect private currency issues subject to no legal requirements with respect to reserves and the like. They are, in fact, issued on a fractional reserve basis. So far as we know, they are the only major monetary issue in the U.S. that is not subject to legal reserve requirements. At the end of 1967 the American Express Company balance sheet showed $647 million in liabilities for travelers' checks, equal to 1½ per cent of currency then held by the public. Leland Yeager argues that travelers' checks are not the equivalent of currency ("Essential Properties of the Medium of Exchange," *Kyklos,* 1968, No. 1, p. 57). For an analysis of his argument, see Chapter 3, section 1.

TABLE 2

Currency and Commercial Bank Deposits Held by the Public and Consolidated Total of Money Stock, Quarterly, 1867–1968

(seasonally adjusted, in billions of dollars)

Part I. 1867–1960

Year and Quarter	Currency Held by the Public (1)	Deposits Adjusted, Commercial Banks			Money Stock, Consolidated Total (5)
		Demand (2)	Time (3)	Total (4)	
1867 I	0.60			0.71	1.31
II	0.59			0.69	1.28
III	0.58			0.69	1.27
IV	0.56			0.70	1.26
1868 I	0.55			0.71	1.26
II	0.54			0.73	1.27
III	0.54			0.75	1.29
IV	0.54			0.73	1.27
1869 I	0.55			0.72	1.27
II	0.56			0.73	1.29
III	0.55			0.74	1.29
IV	0.53			0.76	1.29
1870 I	0.53			0.78	1.31
II	0.54			0.81	1.35
III	0.55			0.81	1.36
IV	0.56			0.83	1.39
1871 I	0.55			0.88	1.43
II	0.53			0.95	1.48
III	0.54			1.00	1.54
IV	0.55			1.02	1.57
1872 I	0.55			1.06	1.61
II	0.54			1.07	1.61
III	0.56			1.06	1.62
IV	0.56			1.05	1.61
1873 I	0.56			1.07	1.63
II	0.55			1.08	1.63
III	0.57			1.08	1.65
IV	0.56			1.03	1.59
1874 I	0.54			1.06	1.60
II	0.54			1.10	1.64
III	0.54			1.13	1.67
IV	0.55			1.14	1.69

(continued)

TABLE 2 (continued)

| Year and Quarter | Currency Held by the Public (1) | Deposits Adjusted, Commercial Banks | | | Money Stock, Consolidated Total (5) |
		Demand (2)	Time (3)	Total (4)	
1875 I	0.56			1.16	1.72
II	0.54			1.18	1.72
III	0.53			1.19	1.72
IV	0.54			1.16	1.70
1876 I	0.53			1.16	1.69
II	0.53			1.15	1.68
III	0.52			1.16	1.68
IV	0.53			1.15	1.68
1877 I	0.53			1.15	1.68
II	0.53			1.14	1.67
III	0.54			1.11	1.65
IV	0.54			1.07	1.61
1878 I	0.54			1.06	1.60
II	0.55			1.03	1.58
III	0.54			1.03	1.57
IV	0.52			1.03	1.55
1879 I	0.54			1.02	1.56
II	0.56			1.05	1.61
III	0.58			1.10	1.68
IV	0.62			1.19	1.81
1880 I	0.65			1.28	1.93
II	0.66			1.32	1.98
III	0.67			1.38	2.05
IV	0.71			1.46	2.17
1881 I	0.74			1.54	2.28
II	0.76			1.64	2.40
III	0.80			1.72	2.52
IV	0.81			1.74	2.55
1882 I	0.83			1.75	2.58
II	0.83			1.77	2.60
III	0.84			1.81	2.65
IV	0.85			1.84	2.69
1883 I	0.88			1.88	2.76
II	0.88			1.92	2.80
III	0.87			1.96	2.83
IV	0.86			1.97	2.83

(continued)

TABLE 2 (continued)

| Year and Quarter | Currency Held by the Public (1) | Deposits Adjusted, Commercial Banks | | | Money Stock, Consolidated Total (5) |
		Demand (2)	Time (3)	Total (4)	
1884 I	0.85			1.99	2.84
II	0.85			1.94	2.79
III	0.84			1.93	2.77
IV	0.83			1.95	2.78
1885 I	0.81			1.99	2.80
II	0.80			2.03	2.83
III	0.79			2.11	2.90
IV	0.78			2.17	2.95
1886 I	0.78			2.26	3.04
II	0.78			2.30	3.08
III	0.79			2.34	3.13
IV	0.79			2.38	3.17
1887 I	0.80			2.45	3.25
II	0.82			2.49	3.31
III	0.84			2.49	3.33
IV	0.85			2.49	3.34
1888 I	0.85			2.52	3.37
II	0.85			2.52	3.37
III	0.85			2.57	3.42
IV	0.86			2.59	3.45
1889 I	0.86			2.65	3.51
II	0.86			2.70	3.56
III	0.88			2.76	3.64
IV	0.88			2.81	3.69
1890 I	0.90			2.90	3.80
II	0.92			2.98	3.90
III	0.93			3.04	3.97
IV	0.96			3.03	3.99
1891 I	0.96			3.05	4.01
II	0.96			3.08	4.04
III	0.95			3.14	4.09
IV	0.96			3.24	4.20
1892 I	0.96			3.37	4.33
II	0.97			3.48	4.45
III	0.97			3.52	4.49
IV	0.96			3.48	4.44

(continued)

TABLE 2 (continued)

| Year and Quarter | Currency Held by the Public (1) | Deposits Adjusted, Commercial Banks | | | Money Stock, Consolidated Total (5) |
		Demand (2)	Time (3)	Total (4)	
1893 I	0.98			3.42	4.40
II	1.00			3.29	4.29
III	1.04			3.14	4.18
IV	0.99			3.18	4.17
1894 I	0.96			3.26	4.22
II	0.92			3.31	4.23
III	0.91			3.39	4.30
IV	0.92			3.44	4.36
1895 I	0.90			3.46	4.36
II	0.91			3.53	4.44
III	0.92			3.58	4.50
IV	0.90			3.53	4.43
1896 I	0.89			3.45	4.34
II	0.86			3.42	4.28
III	0.88			3.48	4.36
IV	0.92			3.50	4.42
1897 I	0.92			3.56	4.48
II	0.90			3.63	4.53
III	0.92			3.77	4.69
IV	0.94			3.92	4.86
1898 I	0.95			4.05	5.00
II	1.02			4.13	5.15
III	1.02			4.30	5.32
IV	1.03			4.52	5.55
1899 I	1.06			4.76	5.82
II	1.09			4.96	6.05
III	1.12			5.10	6.22
IV	1.14			5.14	6.28
1900 I	1.16			5.19	6.35
II	1.19			5.24	6.43
III	1.24			5.46	6.70
IV	1.25			5.69	6.94
1901 I	1.27			5.94	7.21
II	1.26			6.13	7.39
III	1.27			6.30	7.57
IV	1.29			6.46	7.75

(continued)

TABLE 2 (continued)

Year and Quarter	Currency Held by the Public (1)	Deposits Adjusted, Commercial Banks			Money Stock, Consolidated Total (5)
		Demand (2)	Time (3)	Total (4)	
1902 I	1.30			6.65	7.95
II	1.31			6.77	8.08
III	1.35			6.89	8.24
IV	1.38			7.02	8.40
1903 I	1.40			7.14	8.54
II	1.43			7.19	8.62
III	1.43			7.29	8.72
IV	1.44			7.40	8.84
1904 I	1.44			7.52	8.96
II	1.44			7.63	9.07
III	1.44			7.89	9.33
IV	1.45			8.17	9.62
1905 I	1.45			8.43	9.88
II	1.49			8.64	10.13
III	1.50			8.85	10.35
IV	1.54			9.06	10.60
1906 I	1.56			9.18	10.74
II	1.61			9.31	10.92
III	1.65			9.52	11.17
IV	1.69			9.78	11.47
1907 I	1.70			9.96	11.66
II	1.71			10.09	11.80
III	1.67			9.98	11.65
IV	1.81			9.49	11.30
1908 I	1.84			9.18	11.02
II	1.75			9.51	11.26
III	1.71			9.92	11.63
IV	1.72			10.32	12.04
1909 I	1.70			10.61	12.31
II	1.70			10.91	12.61
III	1.71			11.19	12.90
IV	1.72			11.36	13.08
1910 I	1.72			11.50	13.22
II	1.72			11.54	13.26
III	1.75			11.58	13.33
IV	1.77			11.84	13.61

(continued)

TABLE 2 (continued)

Year and Quarter	Currency Held by the Public (1)	Deposits Adjusted, Commercial Banks			Money Stock, Consolidated Total (5)
		Demand (2)	Time (3)	Total (4)	
1911 I	1.75			12.26	14.01
II	1.78			12.30	14.08
III	1.78			12.46	14.24
IV	1.75			12.80	14.55
1912 I	1.75			13.07	14.82
II	1.83			13.25	15.08
III	1.85			13.43	15.28
IV	1.85			13.64	15.49
1913 I	1.85			13.77	15.62
III	1.90			13.75	15.65
III	1.90			13.84	15.74
IV	1.91			14.10	16.01
1914 I	1.88			14.27	16.15
II	1.83			14.51	16.34
III	1.95	9.85	4.71	14.56	16.51
IV	1.97	9.87	4.82	14.69	16.66
1915 I	1.90	10.08	4.87	14.95	16.85
II	1.92	10.29	5.03	15.32	17.24
III	1.92	10.66	5.16	15.82	17.74
IV	1.97	11.49	5.52	17.01	18.98
1916 I	2.06	12.02	5.76	17.78	19.84
II	2.17	12.31	6.04	18.35	20.52
III	2.20	12.77	6.27	19.04	21.24
IV	2.26	13.40	6.74	20.14	22.40
1917 I	2.06	13.99	7.08	21.07	23.13
II	2.17	14.32	7.24	21.56	23.73
III	2.20	14.68	7.37	22.05	24.25
IV	2.26	14.71	7.56	22.27	24.53
1918 I	2.45	15.09	7.62	22.71	25.16
II	2.66	15.00	7.66	22.66	25.32
III	2.86	15.41	7.83	23.24	26.10
IV	3.08	16.02	8.08	24.10	27.18
1919 I	3.98	16.65	8.61	25.26	29.24
II	3.95	17.43	8.93	26.36	30.31
III	4.00	18.27	9.50	27.77	31.77
IV	4.16	19.16	10.14	29.30	33.46

(continued)

TABLE 2 (continued)

| Year and Quarter | Currency Held by the Public (1) | Deposits Adjusted, Commercial Banks | | | Money Stock, Consolidated Total (5) |
		Demand (2)	Time (3)	Total (4)	
1920 I	4.31	19.50	10.67	30.17	34.48
II	4.46	19.48	11.12	30.60	35.06
III	4.59	19.17	11.32	30.49	35.08
IV	4.58	18.76	11.42	30.18	34.76
1921 I	4.29	18.08	11.46	29.54	33.83
II	4.13	17.32	11.34	28.66	32.79
III	3.97	16.92	11.23	28.15	32.12
IV	3.79	17.10	11.31	28.41	32.20
1922 I	3.65	17.16	11.41	28.57	32.22
II	3.65	17.98	11.85	29.83	33.48
III	3.69	18.36	12.45	30.81	34.50
IV	3.78	18.79	12.76	31.55	35.33
1923 I	3.82	19.03	13.17	32.20	36.02
II	3.97	18.96	13.70	32.66	36.63
III	4.02	18.85	13.89	32.74	36.76
IV	4.02	19.08	14.13	33.21	37.23
1924 I	3.97	18.99	14.41	33.40	37.37
II	4.00	19.26	14.76	34.02	38.02
III	3.92	20.15	15.15	35.30	39.22
IV	3.94	20.70	15.57	36.27	40.21
1925 I	3.96	21.09	15.94	37.03	40.99
II	3.95	21.42	16.28	37.70	41.65
III	3.95	22.17	16.62	38.79	42.74
IV	3.97	22.42	16.95	39.37	43.34
1926 I	3.99	22.38	17.23	39.61	43.60
II	4.01	22.25	17.46	39.71	43.72
III	4.02	22.12	17.66	39.78	43.80
IV	4.00	21.86	17.72	39.58	43.58
1927 I	4.03	21.90	18.14	40.04	44.07
II	4.01	22.13	18.55	40.68	44.69
III	3.96	22.16	18.87	41.03	44.99
IV	3.90	22.36	19.23	41.59	45.49
1928 I	3.86	22.57	19.79	42.36	46.22
II	3.92	22.56	20.17	42.73	46.65
III	3.91	22.26	20.10	42.36	46.27
IV	3.88	22.69	20.23	42.92	46.80

(continued)

TABLE 2 (continued)

Year and Quarter	Currency Held by the Public (1)	Deposits Adjusted, Commercial Banks			Money Stock, Consolidated Total (5)
		Demand (2)	Time (3)	Total (4)	
1929 I	3.89	22.55	20.14	42.69	46.58
II	3.92	22.50	19.87	42.37	46.29
III	3.91	22.84	19.94	42.78	46.69
IV	3.86	23.12	19.75	42.87	46.73
1930 I	3.77	22.48	19.79	42.27	46.04
II	3.71	22.08	20.00	42.08	45.79
III	3.70	21.77	20.18	41.95	45.65
IV	3.73	21.58	19.85	41.43	45.16
1931 I	3.87	21.16	19.40	40.56	44.43
II	3.96	20.42	19.28	39.70	43.66
III	4.22	19.71	18.44	38.15	42.37
IV	4.59	18.13	16.53	34.66	39.25
1932 I	4.87	16.86	15.39	32.25	37.12
II	4.87	16.18	14.96	31.14	36.01
III	5.05	15.57	14.59	30.16	35.21
IV	4.90	15.91	14.57	30.48	35.38
1933 I	5.42	14.90	13.23	28.13	33.55
II	5.12	14.54	11.69	26.23	31.35
III	4.92	14.64	12.01	26.65	31.57
IV	4.89	15.11	11.90	27.01	31.90
1934 I	4.58	16.16	12.14	28.30	32.88
II	4.62	16.86	12.55	29.41	34.03
III	4.67	17.74	12.71	30.45	35.12
IV	4.66	18.65	12.78	31.43	36.09
1935 I	4.73	19.88	12.94	32.82	37.55
II	4.76	20.61	13.23	33.84	38.60
III	4.80	21.94	13.25	35.19	39.99
IV	4.92	22.62	13.45	36.07	40.99
1936 I	5.03	22.90	13.62	36.52	41.55
II	5.15	24.30	13.89	38.19	43.34
III	5.30	25.14	14.11	39.25	44.55
IV	5.44	25.57	14.24	39.81	45.25
1937 I	5.53	25.85	14.50	40.35	45.88
II	5.56	25.69	14.67	40.36	45.92
III	5.64	25.22	14.98	40.20	45.84
IV	5.62	24.26	15.03	39.29	44.91

(continued)

TABLE 2 (continued)

| Year and Quarter | Currency Held by the Public (1) | Deposits Adjusted, Commercial Banks | | | Money Stock, Consolidated Total (5) |
		Demand (2)	Time (3)	Total (4)	
1938 I	5.52	24.51	15.07	39.58	45.10
II	5.49	24.29	15.02	39.31	44.80
III	5.54	25.14	14.95	40.09	45.63
IV	5.64	26.39	14.91	41.30	46.94
1939 I	5.81	26.59	15.03	41.62	47.43
II	5.98	27.16	15.13	42.29	48.27
III	6.13	28.90	15.17	44.07	50.20
IV	6.26	30.50	15.23	45.73	51.99
1940 I	6.43	31.50	15.40	46.90	53.33
II	6.59	32.46	15.54	48.00	54.59
III	6.83	33.63	15.63	49.26	56.09
IV	7.18	35.00	15.71	50.71	57.89
1941 I	7.63	36.95	15.92	52.87	60.50
II	8.07	38.09	16.01	54.10	62.17
III	8.65	39.13	16.01	55.14	63.79
IV	9.25	39.34	16.04	55.38	64.63
1942 I	10.10	40.83	15.60	56.43	66.53
II	10.83	42.71	15.56	58.27	69.10
III	11.96	45.42	15.88	61.30	73.26
IV	13.27	48.73	16.22	64.95	78.22
1943 I	14.61	53.00	16.78	69.78	84.39
II	15.68	55.09	17.30	72.39	88.07
III	16.95	59.35	18.22	77.57	94.52
IV	18.15	58.98	18.88	77.86	96.01
1944 I	19.31	60.75	19.79	80.54	99.85
II	20.65	63.31	20.93	84.24	104.89
III	21.81	65.10	22.21	87.31	109.12
IV	23.11	69.09	23.83	92.92	116.03
1945 I	24.15	71.85	25.24	97.09	121.24
II	25.05	73.57	26.78	100.35	125.40
III	25.91	75.07	28.59	103.66	129.57
IV	26.21	77.09	29.97	107.06	133.27
1946 I	26.32	76.96	31.04	108.00	134.32
II	26.59	80.10	32.08	112.18	138.77
III	26.56	81.63	32.94	114.57	141.13
IV	26.46	82.12	33.61	115.73	142.19

(continued)

TABLE 2 (continued)

Year and Quarter	Currency Held by the Public (1)	Deposits Adjusted, Commercial Banks			Money Stock, Consolidated Total (5)
		Demand (2)	Time (3)	Total (4)	
1947 I	26.7	83.2	33.5	116.6	143.3
II	26.6	85.0	33.8	118.8	145.4
III	26.6	86.0	34.4	120.4	147.0
IV	26.5	86.6	35.2	121.8	148.3
1948 I	26.3	86.7	35.6	122.4	148.7
II	26.0	86.1	35.7	121.8	147.9
III	26.0	86.2	35.9	122.1	148.1
IV	25.9	85.9	36.0	121.9	147.8
1949 I	25.7	85.5	36.1	121.6	147.3
II	25.7	85.7	36.3	122.0	147.7
III	25.4	85.6	36.4	122.0	147.4
IV	25.2	85.8	36.4	122.2	147.4
1950 I	25.1	86.9	36.5	123.4	148.6
II	25.2	88.5	36.8	125.3	150.5
III	24.9	90.0	36.7	126.7	151.6
IV	24.9	91.0	36.6	127.6	152.5
1951 I	25.1	92.0	36.6	128.7	153.8
II	25.3	92.9	36.8	129.7	155.0
III	25.7	93.9	37.4	131.3	157.1
IV	26.0	95.9	38.0	133.9	159.9
1952 I	26.3	97.2	38.7	135.9	162.2
II	26.5	98.0	39.3	137.3	163.8
III	26.8	99.0	40.0	139.0	165.8
IV	27.2	99.9	40.8	140.7	167.9
1953 I	27.5	100.1	41.6	141.7	169.2
II	27.7	100.7	42.4	143.1	170.8
III	27.8	100.8	43.2	144.0	171.8
IV	27.8	101.0	44.2	145.2	172.9
1954 I	27.7	101.5	45.2	146.7	174.3
II	27.6	101.8	46.5	148.3	175.9
III	27.5	103.2	47.7	150.8	178.3
IV	27.4	104.6	48.2	152.8	180.2
1955 I	27.5	106.0	48.7	154.7	182.2
II	27.6	106.7	49.1	155.8	183.4
III	27.7	107.2	49.4	156.6	184.3
IV	27.8	107.3	49.9	157.2	185.0

(continued)

TABLE 2 (continued)

Year and Quarter	Currency Held by the Public (1)	Deposits Adjusted, Commercial Banks			Money Stock Consolidated Total (5)
		Demand (2)	Time (3)	Total (4)	
1956 I	27.9	107.7	50.0	157.7	185.5
II	27.9	108.0	50.5	158.5	186.4
III	28.0	108.0	51.2	159.2	187.2
IV	28.1	108.4	51.8	160.2	188.4
1957 I	28.2	108.6	53.1	161.8	190.0
II	28.2	108.7	54.4	163.1	191.4
III	28.3	108.6	55.7	164.3	192.7
IV	28.3	107.9	57.0	164.9	193.2
1958 I	28.2	107.8	59.1	166.9	195.2
II	28.3	109.3	62.3	171.7	200.0
III	28.4	110.6	64.5	175.1	203.5
IV	28.5	112.2	65.2	177.4	205.9
1959 I	28.7	113.3	66.1	179.3	208.1
II	28.9	114.1	66.7	180.8	209.8
III	29.0	114.6	67.2	181.8	210.9
IV	28.9	113.6	67.3	180.9	209.8
1960 I	29.0	112.3	67.0	179.4	208.3
II	29.0	111.4	67.5	178.9	207.9
III	29.0	111.9	69.6	181.5	210.4
IV	29.0	112.0	72.1	184.1	213.1

Part II. 1961–68

Year and Quarter	Currency Held by the Public (1)	Deposits Adjusted, Commercial Banks				Money Stock, Consolidated Total	
		Demand (2)	Consumer Type Time (3a)	Large Negotiable CD's (3b)	Total (4)	Excl. Large Negotiable CD's (5a)	Incl. Large Negotiable CD's (5b)
1961 I	28.9	112.7	75.0	0.2	188.2	216.8	216.3
II	28.9	113.7	76.5	0.7	190.9	219.1	219.8
III	29.1	114.3	78.5	1.4	194.2	221.9	223.3
IV	29.4	115.5	79.8	2.3	197.6	224.7	227.0
1962 I	29.7	116.0	82.7	3.2	201.9	228.5	231.7
II	30.0	116.2	85.8	3.8	205.8	232.0	235.8
III	30.2	115.8	88.2	4.5	208.4	234.1	238.7
IV	30.4	116.4	90.9	5.4	212.7	237.8	243.2

(continued)

TABLE 2 (concluded)

| Year and Quarter | Currency Held by the Public (1) | Deposits Adjusted, Commercial Banks | | | | Money Stock, Consolidated Total | |
		Demand (2)	Con- sumer Type Time (3a)	Large Negoti- able CD's (3b)	Total (4)	Excl. Large Negoti- able CD's (5a)	Incl. Large Negoti- able CD's (5b)
1963 I	30.9	117.6	94.0	6.2	217.9	242.5	248.7
II	31.3	118.5	96.6	7.1	222.2	246.4	253.5
III	31.8	119.5	99.1	8.1	226.7	250.3	258.4
IV	32.3	120.6	101.8	9.2	231.5	254.7	263.8
1964 I	32.8	121.1	103.8	10.6	235.5	257.6	268.2
II	33.3	121.8	105.8	11.7	239.2	260.8	272.5
III	33.8	123.6	108.7	12.2	244.5	266.0	278.2
IV	34.1	124.9	112.3	12.7	249.9	271.3	284.0
1965 I	34.6	125.4	116.6	13.9	256.0	276.6	290.5
II	34.9	126.3	119.8	15.1	261.2	281.0	296.1
III	35.5	127.7	123.5	16.2	267.5	286.7	303.0
IV	36.1	129.8	128.7	16.5	274.9	294.6	311.0
1966 I	36.7	131.9	132.1	16.6	280.7	300.7	317.4
II	37.3	133.2	135.6	17.7	286.6	306.1	323.8
III	37.8	132.3	138.6	18.1	288.9	308.6	326.7
IV	38.2	132.0	141.7	15.8	289.5	311.9	327.7
1967 I	38.7	133.0	145.7	18.1	296.7	317.4	335.5
II	39.1	135.2	151.6	19.0	305.8	326.0	344.9
III	39.5	139.1	157.0	20.0	316.1	335.6	355.6
IV	40.1	141.0	161.5	20.5	323.0	342.6	363.1
1968 I	40.8	142.6	164.9	20.8	328.3	348.3	369.1
II	41.6	145.1	168.5	19.6	333.3	355.2	374.9
III	42.4	148.3	172.1	21.6	342.1	362.8	384.4
IV	43.1	150.3	178.6	23.5	352.5	372.0	395.5

Notes to Table 2 (concluded)

Source, by Column

Part I

1. *1867–1907,* estimates of vault cash in mutual savings banks (Table 20, col. 10) were interpolated along a straight line to middle of Feb., May, Aug., and Nov., and added to quarterly estimates of currency (Table 21, col. 1); *1907–60,* quarterly averages of monthly figures (Table 1, col. 1).

2–3. *1914–60,* quarterly averages of monthly figures (Table 1, cols. 2, 3).

4. *1867–96,* Table 21, col. 2; *1896–1907,* estimates of bank balances due to mutual savings banks (from *All-Bank Statistics,* p. 47) were interpolated quarterly along a straight line to middle of Feb., May, Aug., and Nov., and added to quarterly estimates of deposits (Table 21, col. 2); *1907–60,* quarterly averages of monthly figures (Table 1, col. 4).

5. Sum of cols. 1 and 4.

Part II

1–5b. Quarterly averages of monthly figures (Table 1, cols. 1–4, 9a, and 9b).

and international institutions at Federal Reserve Banks. At the end of 1968, items 1 and 2 combined approximated $10.5 billion exclusive of negotiable certificates of deposit. This is an overestimate of foreign-held U.S. deposits because it includes deposit liabilities to foreigners of institutions not counted as commercial banks in the money stock estimates (principally deposit liabilities to head offices of agencies or branches of foreign banks located in the United States; deposit liabilities to their foreign branches of U.S. domestic banks; and American Express Company deposit liabilities to foreigners). We exclude (3) dollar deposits held by the U.S. public at banks located in U.S. territories and possessions;[8] and (4) dollar deposits held by the U.S. public at foreign banks

[8] Again, the treatment of foreign branches of U.S. banks varies. Before 1920 all their deposits are included, whether held by U.S. residents or foreigners; since 1920, all their deposits are excluded.

not located in the continental United States.[9] We include as deposits (5) some items that should be classified as currency, notably bank-issued travelers' checks.

The same reason for which we were driven to depart from our ideal —the character of the data—makes it impossible for us to assess accurately the quantitative importance of the departures. Some raise, others lower, the level of the estimates, so that we cannot even judge whether their net effect is to make our estimates too high or too low. We can only record our impression, based on occasional scraps of information and on our general knowledge of the financial structure, that, while several are appreciable, none is of major moment and that all together they do not seriously distort our estimates. Hence we shall for the most part disregard the departures and treat our estimates as if they were the magnitudes we wanted.

[9] Foreign banks include the American Express Company which has a banking affiliate abroad at which U.S. corporations hold deposits (see the company's balance sheet).

"Euro-dollars" are only the most recent and perhaps the most publicized example of the class of U.S. dollar deposits that we exclude from our estimates of deposits held by the U.S. public. On estimates of the size of the market in Euro-dollars, see Roy Reierson, *The Euro-Dollar Market,* New York, Bankers Trust Company, 1964, p. 13. At the end of 1968, the Bank for International Settlements estimated there were some $25 billion in Euro-dollars of which U.S. and Canadian residents owned $4.5 billion (*Thirty-ninth Annual Report,* p. 149).

To an unknown extent, the omission of Euro-dollars and similar dollar deposits is offset by the inclusion of U.S. currency held by foreign banks and, since 1947, of their demand deposits at U.S. commercial banks and Federal Reserve Banks. The extent of the offset depends on two factors. The first is the fractional reserves in these forms held by foreign banks in connection with their U.S. dollar deposit liabilities. Though much published commentary presumes that 100 per cent reserves are held for Euro-dollars, this is not the case. Of course, the total of U.S. dollar assets is roughly equal to the total of U.S. dollar liabilities, as for any bank, but only a fraction of the assets are in the form of U.S. dollar currency or demand deposits at U.S. banks. Euro-dollar deposits are "created" in precisely the same way as the U.S. dollar deposits at U.S. banks. The only difference is in the nation having jurisdiction over the bank. Some unpublished estimates by Aryeh Blumberg indicate that the reserve ratio in the early 1960's varied from about 20 to about 30 per cent. The second factor on which the extent of the offset depends is the fraction of the Euro-dollars held by the U.S. public. This appears to be between one-tenth and two-tenths.

If the above two fractions were equal, the two deficiencies of our estimates would precisely offset each other. If the first fraction is larger than the second, our estimates are, on this score alone, in excess of the total we wish to estimate. If the second fraction is larger than the first, the converse is true.

For further discussions of Euro-dollar deposits, see Fred H. Klopstock, "The Euro-Dollar Market: Some Unresolved Issues," *Essays in International Finance,* No. 65, Mar. 1968, International Finance Section, Princeton University, Princeton, N.J.; Joseph G. Kvasnicka, "Eurodollars—An Important Source of Funds for American Banks," *Business Conditions,* Federal Reserve Bank of Chicago, June 1969, pp. 9–20; Jane Sneddon Little, "The Euro-dollar Market: Its Nature and Impact," *New England Economic Review,* Federal Reserve Bank of Boston, May/June 1969; Milton Friedman, "The Euro-Dollar Market, Some First Principles," *Morgan Guaranty Survey,* Oct. 1969.

We consider a financial institution to be a bank if it provides deposit facilities for the public, or if it conducts principally a fiduciary business —in accordance with the definition of banks agreed upon by federal bank supervisory agencies. Of these two classes, fiduciaries are negligible in importance. Banks are classified as either commercial or mutual savings banks. Commercial banks include national banks, incorporated state banks, loan and trust companies, stock savings banks, industrial and Morris Plan banks if they provide deposit facilities, special types of banks of deposit—such as cash depositories and cooperative exchanges in certain states—and unincorporated or private banks. Mutual savings banks include all banks operating under state banking codes applying to mutual savings banks.[10]

By this definition savings and loan associations are not banks. Holders of funds in these institutions are technically shareholders, not depositors, though they may regard such funds as close substitutes for deposits, as we define them. Savings and loan associations are home financing institutions, most of which are mutual in form rather than stock corporations, operating under state or federal charters. The associations invest the funds they accept from shareholders principally in monthly-payment amortized loans for the construction, purchase, or repair and modernization of homes.

The figures in Table 1 are seasonally adjusted throughout. Before 1947 no comparable unadjusted figures are available for currency and deposits. The reason is that some components of these figures were interpolated from corresponding figures for other dates. Such interpolation is generally more accurate if done with seasonally adjusted data.[11] We therefore seasonally adjusted all data before interpolation; hence we have no unadjusted estimates for the interpolated components. "Seasonal" is an incomplete designation of the adjustments made to the data. Some data used in the estimates, vault cash in particular (which had to be subtracted from the stock of currency outside the Treasury and Federal Reserve Banks in order to derive currency held by the public), have a consistent intraweekly movement; that is, the stock on Monday tends to differ systematically from the stock on Tuesday and so on through the week. The data were adjusted for intraweekly movements that

[10] See Federal Deposit Insurance Corporation (FDIC), *Annual Report*, 1956, pp. 88–89.
[11] Milton Friedman, *The Interpolation of Time Series by Related Series*, Technical Paper 16, NBER, 1962, pp. 11, 16, 23.

seemed significant. The adjustment was made in such a way that the figures from 1907 through 1942 can be regarded as being on a Wednesday basis.

For savings and loan shares seasonally unadjusted data are available from the original sources. The quarterly and monthly data were adjusted by us.

For the period 1867 through 1913, Table 1 gives only total deposits at commercial banks, not demand and time deposits separately. The reason is that, until 1914, there is no statistically satisfactory basis for subdividing total commercial bank deposits into demand and time deposits. Before the Federal Reserve System, the reserve requirements of national banks, and of most state banks as well, did not distinguish between demand and time deposits, but applied to their total.[12] The regulatory agencies had no reason to collect separate data on each type of deposits and most did not do so. Hence, only scattered and unsatisfactory data on the division of total deposits are available. The large fraction of total deposits reported as unclassified by all categories of banks in the decade before 1914 and by nonnational or nonmember banks in the two decades after 1914 is one indication of the data problem. As we point out in the appendix to Chapter 8, these data have been used imaginatively by the Federal Reserve to construct separate estimates of demand and time deposits for 1896–1913.[13] However, the Federal Reserve estimates rest on such unsatisfactory basic data and involve so much interpolation and extrapolation of an essentially arbitrary character that, in our view, they are subject to much larger errors than the total deposit series in Table 1.

[12] R. G. Rodkey states that before 1900 only four states imposed differential reserve requirements against demand and time deposits, and that by 1914 only seven additional states had introduced such requirements (*Legal Reserves in American Banking, Michigan Business Studies,* Vol. VI, No. 5, University of Michigan, 1934, pp. 43–44). The eleven states he enumerates and the dates of their statutes are: Maine (1869, 1893); N.H. (1874); Neb. (1889); Iowa (1897); N.C. (1903); Ore. (1907); Penna. (1907); Conn. (1909); Vt. (1910); Utah (1911); Colo. (1913). Rodkey omits from his list: Ohio, which in 1908 imposed the same total requirement against demand and time deposits, but required a smaller percentage in vault for time deposits, and four other states —N.J. (1899); Ariz. (1901); Tex. (1905); Wash. (1907)—which required reserves against demand deposits but made no reference to time deposits. Rodkey apparently considered deposits in those states to be no more differentiated than in states that required reserves simply against deposits.

[13] *All-Bank Statistics, 1896–1955,* Board of Governors of the Federal Reserve System, Washington, D.C., 1959, pp. 31–32, 35–36, 47–48. These estimates supersede earlier ones constructed by the Federal Reserve for 1892–1913 (*Banking and Monetary Statistics,* Board of Governors of the Federal Reserve System, Washington, D.C., 1943, pp. 34–35).

In addition, there is much evidence that the concept of time deposits underlying the pre-1914 data is not comparable with the concept underlying the data for subsequent years. Because the reserve requirements for time and demand deposits were the same, banks had no incentive to distinguish sharply between the two classes, and common concepts that were widely accepted by the banking system failed to develop. Some banks might designate as time deposits what others designated as demand deposits, and the same banks might change the classification from one report date to another. What were called time deposits were frequently transferable by check, and what were called demand deposits frequently paid interest. The importance of this problem of classification is illustrated by the change from 1913 to 1914 in the Federal Reserve estimates of time deposits at national banks. These deposits fell 12 per cent, whereas estimated demand deposits rose by 11 per cent, so that time deposits as a percentage of total deposits fell from 23 to 19 per cent. According to the Federal Reserve, the drop of 12 per cent was "probably because of the . . . changes in classification," resulting from the establishment of the Federal Reserve System.[14] When, after 1914, the distinction between demand and time deposits became important to banks for reserve purposes, the result was not only that better data became available but also that the distinction changed its meaning (see Chapter 4, section 2).

These difficulties in constructing and interpreting estimates of the separate classes of deposits for years before 1914 led us to begin our estimates with that year.

3. Derivation of Our Estimates

As with any compilation of data for a long period, the one summarized in Table 1 is made up of many bits and pieces. This is abundantly evident from the detailed description of the construction of the estimates in Chapters 10–17.[15] Some of these bits and pieces have been around for a long time; others have been fashioned especially for this purpose. For the period from 1867 to 1896, the major new piece is a set of esti-

[14] *All-Bank Statistics*, p. 18.
[15] And from the source notes to Tables A-1, A-2, and A-3 in *A Monetary History*, pp. 722–734, 744–748, 765–768.

mates of deposits and vault cash in nonnational banks made by James K. Kindahl for 1867 to 1875 and by David Fand for 1875 to 1896.[16] Kindahl and Fand exploited a wide variety of evidence, in particular, data on revenue from taxes on bank deposits that were levied during much of the period. We have combined their estimates with the generally available data on deposits and vault cash in national banks and on currency outstanding.

For the period from 1896 to date, our estimates are keyed to the recently revised annual estimates of the Board of Governors of the Federal Reserve System. Though we have modified their annual figures in some instances, the main addition we have made is an estimate of intra-yearly movements for deposits from 1907 through 1946; and for currency from 1907 through 1942, when we shift to Federal Reserve monthly estimates.

The chief new piece of evidence we have used on intrayear movements is a compilation we made for a sample of states from the reports of agencies charged with regulating the state banks. This compilation underlies our vault cash and deposit estimates for nonnational or nonmember banks, the segment of the total that has heretofore been most inadequately covered by the readily available data.

Though our fundamental aim was to produce a deseasonalized monthly total, much of our basic data were for national or member bank call dates. These are the irregularly spaced dates, numbering three to five a year, as of which the Comptroller of the Currency and the Federal Reserve System "called" for reports of condition from national or member banks. Hence, we first constructed deseasonalized call-date totals for each of our basic series: currency outside the Treasury and Federal Reserve Banks, vault cash (subtracted from the preceding series to get currency held by the public), commercial bank deposits to 1914, and commercial bank demand and time deposits thereafter, and mutual savings bank deposits. The vault cash and commercial bank deposit series are sums of the corresponding items for national and nonnational banks (up to 1923), or for member and nonmember banks (beginning in 1919). (For 1919–23 both sets of data were compiled to take advan-

---

[16] See James K. Kindahl, "The Economics of Resumption: the United States," unpublished Ph.D. dissertation, University of Chicago, 1958; and David Fand, "Estimates of Deposits and Vault Cash in the Nonnational Banks in the Post-Civil War Period in the United States," unpublished Ph.D. dissertation, University of Chicago, 1954.

tage of two additional call dates in both 1921 and 1922, when national banks, but not state member banks, reported.)

Except for some fringe details, national and member bank figures required no estimation. The figures for nonnational and nonmember banks are in turn a sum of corresponding items for component groups of banks, the particular groups varying from series to series according to the basic data that happened to be available.

Our call date series, which are given in Tables 32 and 33, and their subdivisions, are of interest in their own right and not simply as a way station to monthly estimates.

The monthly estimates depend only in part on the call date estimates. Some are the sum of published monthly data for member banks (corrected for seasonal movements and conceptual discrepancies between the original series and the series we desired) and estimates for nonmember banks derived from the call date series and various monthly interpolators. Others are the sum of monthly data for a sample of banks that did not coincide with the national or member banks (e.g., clearinghouse city banks; weekly reporting member banks) and estimates for the remaining banks. In all cases, our aim was to use directly whatever monthly data were available, and then fill in the rest by interpolation from our call date series.

The estimates in Table 1 are a highly synthetic product and, as such, cannot be guaranteed accurate in full detail. In particular, great significance should not be attached to isolated month-to-month movements. At the same time, the figures in Table 1 are for the most part based on reasonably direct evidence; the errors and inaccuracies in this part are in the raw data. In addition, such tests as we have been able to make of the estimates, mostly unsystematic comparisons with known qualitative phenomena, have persuaded us that in all but their minor movements, and even in many of these, the data reproduce faithfully the behavior of the quantity of money in the United States for the periods covered.

4. Alternative Monetary Totals

In addition to the figures for currency, different types of deposits, and savings and loan shares, Table 1 gives four totals through January 1961 (M_1, M_2, M_3, M_4), and five totals thereafter, each of which has some claim to be designated *the* money stock. In Part I we discuss the considerations that led us to assign that designation to one of those totals rather than the others. This section discusses some statistical aspects of the construction of these totals.

The narrowest total (M_1) is the sum of currency and demand deposits (column 8), the two items that are commonly described as media of circulation in the sense that they are transferred directly from person to person to discharge debts. However, this total is not available for the period before 1914, for reasons already stated.

The second total (M_2), currency plus all deposits of the public at commercial banks except, after January 1961, large negotiable certificates of deposit (column 9 through January 1961, column 9a, thereafter), is available throughout the period. It is the total that we have designated "money" in our earlier volume and in this one, and that we shall so designate in our subsequent volumes. The component added to the narrower total to get this total is termed "time deposits" through January 1961, and "time deposits other than large negotiable certificates of deposit" thereafter. These terms are something of a misnomer. In practice, these deposits have almost always been available on demand. The only important exceptions are periods during and after banking panics when there have been restrictions on convertibility of deposits into currency. However, such restrictions applied equally to all deposits at commercial banks, whether termed demand or time deposits. The distinction between demand and time deposits at commercial banks, at least since 1933, has typically been that demand deposits were, and time deposits were not, transferable by check.

The large negotiable certificates of deposit (shown separately in column 3b) that are excluded after 1961 are a recent development that have no counterpart earlier. We are inclined to regard them as more nearly comparable to market instruments such as commercial paper than to the items earlier classified as "time deposits." Hence, we regard column 9a as economically more continuous with column 9 for earlier years than column 9b. The economic discontinuity of column 9b is not apparent in the statistical data regularly reported by the Federal Reserve System. The label used for the total added to column 8 to get column 9b, "time deposits at commercial banks," has been kept unchanged despite the inclusion after February 1961 of large negotiable certificates of deposit which hardly existed before (see also Chapter 4, footnote 1).

The total in Table 1 designated M_3 includes not only adjusted time deposits at commercial banks but also adjusted deposits at mutual savings banks and the Postal Savings System (column 11). These deposits too have in fact almost always been available on demand. Their chief difference from time deposits at commercial banks is that they are obligations of institutions that do not also offer checking facilities. They have been included with commercial bank time deposits in some monetary totals, as in *Banking and Monetary Statistics*.[17]

The broadest total in Table 1 (M_4) includes savings and loan shares in addition to the other components (column 13). Savings and loan shares are closely similar to deposits at mutual savings banks and the Postal Savings System and to commercial bank time deposits.

With two exceptions the totals in Table 1 are, in accounting terminology, consolidated totals, rather than simply sums of independently determined components. This does not appear on the surface of the table for the total in columns 9 and 9a, the total we call money, or for the total in column 8, currency plus demand deposits adjusted—the total designated money by the Federal Reserve System and many other economists—or for the total in column 9b: these totals are simply sums of other items—or for 9a, of components of other items—in the table. The reason that their consolidated nature is not evident for columns 9 and 9b is that the components were constructed in such a way as to be correct for those columns and only those columns. The reason it is not evident for columns 8 and 9a is that these totals are the exceptions. They are the only totals that are not fully consolidated.

[17] The rationale for including time deposits was described as follows in *Banking and Monetary Statistics:*

> Time deposits are also sometimes included in measures of money supply, although in general they probably represent savings and not funds intended to be used for current expenditures. The principal reasons for their inclusion in measures of money supply are the following: (1) the distinction between time and demand deposits has been a varying one—during the 1920's time deposits at banks could be and were more freely used for current payments than at other times, while in recent years demand deposits have included for various reasons an increasing amount of savings: (2) time deposits and demand deposits both represent similar bank liabilities and have similar roles in the process of bank credit expansion or contraction (p. 11).

See also *Banking Studies*, Board of Governors of the Federal Reserve System, Washington, D.C., 1941, p. 447.

The reason for consolidation rather than combination can be illustrated with currency. The total given in column 1 is not all currency but only "currency held by the public," where the only institutions regarded as not part of the public are commercial banks and the monetary authorities (the Federal Reserve System and the U.S. Treasury). This total has been computed by subtracting from total currency outstanding the amount held by the monetary authorities to get currency in circulation and by subtracting from currency in circulation the amount of cash in the vaults of commercial banks to get currency held by the public. This subtraction is correct if the currency figure is to be used as a component of money as we define it through January 1961 (the total in column 9), because that total treats the deposit liabilities of commercial banks as monetary assets held by the public. The currency figure should therefore omit the currency that these institutions hold, to avoid double counting —the deposit liabilities that are the counterpart of this currency are already counted once in the monetary total; to count this currency also would include the same item twice.

But for any other definition of money, the currency figures in column 1 are not correct. For "money" defined to exclude all bank deposits, as money was generally defined before the twentieth century and as it is most useful today to define it for some countries, the currency figures in column 1 are too small. Commercial bank vault cash should be added back in. It is held for the public indirectly by the banks. On this view, the excess of deposit liabilities over vault cash is a nonmoney asset of the public, but the vault cash is clearly a monetary asset.

Similarly, the currency figures are too small for money defined to include currency and demand deposits adjusted only. If commercial bank time deposits are not included in the monetary total, then there is no double counting between such time deposits and that part of currency held by the commercial banks that can be regarded as held on account of time deposits; that part of currency should be included in currency held by the public. This monetary total (column 8) in effect treats a commercial bank as a mixed entity, part "bank" and part "public." It is a "bank" with respect to its demand deposit business, part of the "public" with respect to its time deposit business. Hence correct treatment requires in principle separating its accounts into two corresponding parts. We have not done this because any separation seems arbitrary (see footnote 20, below).

On the other hand, the currency figures in column 1 are too large as a component of monetary totals broader than column 9, such as the totals in columns 11 and 13. For the total in column 11, the vault cash in mutual savings banks and the Postal Savings System, as well as in commercial banks, should be subtracted out; so should vault cash of savings and loan associations for the total in column 13. We have achieved this result in constructing the final totals by including the relevant vault cash items in columns 10 and 12, but we have not given alternative currency estimates separately.

Similar considerations apply to interbank deposits. For the total we designate money through January 1961 all deposits of one commercial bank at another commercial bank should be excluded from total commercial bank deposits. Accordingly, they are excluded from the totals in column 4 of the table, interbank demand deposits from column 2 and interbank time deposits from column 3. Such deposits are liabilities of commercial banks to commercial banks and hence cancel out when the books of all commercial banks are consolidated. On the other hand, commercial bank deposits at the Federal Reserve Banks should not be (and are not) subtracted, just as cash in vault is not subtracted: these are assets of banks that are the counterpart of deposit liabilities to the public and involve no double counting. If these items were excluded from columns 2, 3, and 4, they would have to be included in an expanded column 1, which might then be designated: "High-powered money held, directly or indirectly, by the public." The revised columns 2 to 4 would then be designated: "Net fiduciary liabilities of banks held by the public." [18] Similarly, deposits of mutual savings banks and the Postal Savings System at commercial banks should not be (and are not) excluded. These institutions are regarded for this definition of money as part of the public, hence their holdings of currency and commercial bank deposits are part of the public's holdings.[19]

For the narrower monetary total, currency plus demand deposits adjusted alone, this treatment is incorrect. That part of interbank *demand*

[18] The expanded column 1 would be perhaps the closest modern counterpart to nineteenth century definitions of "money." See Chapter 3, section 1.

[19] In principle, any deposits of mutual savings banks, the Postal Savings System, and savings and loan associations at Federal Reserve Banks should be included in the total money stock on a par with either their deposits at commercial banks or their vault cash. We have neglected this refinement because the amount involved is trivial for mutual savings banks and nonexistent for the Postal Savings System and savings and loan associations, since they have held no deposits at Federal Reserve Banks.

deposits held on account of *time* deposits should be included as part of the public's demand deposits, since it does not duplicate any other part of what is regarded as the public's monetary holdings, just as the corresponding part of vault cash should be included as part of the public's currency holdings. Similarly, that part of commercial bank deposits at Federal Reserve Banks regarded as held on account of time deposits should be included as part either of the public's demand deposits or the public's currency. Unfortunately, there is no unambiguous way to construct a correct estimate for currency plus demand deposits adjusted. Any division of commercial bank holdings of currency, deposits at the Federal Reserve Banks, and deposits at other commercial banks into the part held on account of demand deposits and the part held on account of time deposits would necessarily be arbitrary, involving as it does matching specific assets with specific liabilities. Hence, we have accepted the error in the total in preference to an arbitrary allocation.[20] It may be worth noting explicitly that this error is present in the figures regularly published by the Federal Reserve System labeled "money supply." [21] These considerations explain also why we have not tried to

[20] To get some idea of the amounts involved, assume that the same fraction of bank vault cash, deposits at Federal Reserve Banks, and deposits at other commercial banks can be regarded as held on account of time deposits and that this common fraction is equal to the fraction of total required reserves that is required for time deposits. Then the amounts for 1963 (annual averages in billions of dollars) are:

Currency held by the public (Table 1)		31.6
Held by banks on account of time deposits:		
Currency	0.7	
Corrected currency held by the public		32.3
Demand deposits adjusted (Table 1)		119.1
Held by banks on account of time deposits:		
Deposits at F.R. Banks	2.8	
Interbank demand deposits	2.7	
Corrected demand deposits adjusted		124.6
Corrected total of currency and demand deposits		156.9
Currency plus demand deposits (Table 1)		150.6

The error introduced by combining rather than consolidating the accounts is thus over $6 billion or more than 4 per cent.

[21] In the estimates of member bank "reserves available against private demand deposits" that it publishes regularly, the Federal Reserve Bank of St. Louis is faced with the same problem of allocating reserves held by banks to various classes of deposits. (See the bank's releases, "Monetary Trends," monthly, and "U.S. Financial Data," weekly.) The bank proceeds on a different basis than we did in deriving our estimates in the preceding footnote. It assumes that all reserves other than those required by law to be held against time deposits, interbank deposits, and Treasury deposits are "available" for private demand deposits. This is in one sense literally correct. But it would be equally correct to say that all reserves not required by law to be held against private demand deposits, interbank deposits, and Treasury deposits are "available against time deposits" and so on for the other classes of deposits. Consistently

adjust column 9a for the inappropriate exclusion of bank vault cash and deposits at Federal Reserve Banks held on account of large negotiable certificates of deposit.

For the broader totals in columns 11 and 13, "banks" include more than commercial banks and hence the category of interbank deposits must be broadened to include deposits of mutual savings banks and the Postal Savings System at commercial banks and at one another for column 11 and of these and savings and loan associations for column 13 and, in principle, also commercial bank deposits at these institutions. (In fact, commercial banks hold no deposits at these institutions.)

We have not produced alternative estimates of the components for these broader monetary totals. Instead, we give in columns 10 and 12 the total of the additional duplications—both cash and deposits—that must be subtracted from the sum of the stated components in order to get properly consolidated totals. The adjustments required to correct for duplication are mostly minor in amount, but for some dates they are far from trivial. For example, in June 1933, postal savings redeposited in commercial banks and included in total time deposits in column 3, amounted to 9 per cent of those time deposits. This accounts for the large size of the duplications in column 10 for that date.[22]

followed, therefore, this assumption leads to estimates of the reserves available for each class of deposits that sum to more than the total amount of reserves held by member banks.

Such estimates may be useful for some purposes, but not, we believe, for obtaining properly consolidated monetary totals. For that purpose, there is no reason to isolate one class of deposits rather than any other as the residual claimant of reserves in excess of legal requirements. All classes of deposits are jointly determined in the money supply process.

[22] When our estimates were first constructed, we did not fully recognize the problem of consolidation. As it happens, our estimates were constructed in such a way as to be correct for column 11 rather than column 9; i.e., we subtracted vault cash in mutual savings banks along with commercial bank vault cash in computing currency held by the public, and treated the deposits of these institutions at commercial banks as interbank deposits in computing demand and time deposits at commercial banks. We have not thought it worthwhile to redo all the tables in Chapters 11–16 to make them correspond with Table 1. Hence they are still on the original basis.

PART ONE

DEFINITION OF MONEY

Introduction

The four monetary totals in Table 1 are only a selection from a much larger number that could be constructed by: further subdividing the items in Table 1 (for example, currency into commodity and fiduciary currency, or commercial bank deposits into member and non-member bank deposits); grouping the items differently (for example, combining currency and time deposits); or adding other items representing a claim expressed in nominal money value terms (for example, Series E government bonds, brokerage accounts, cash surrender value of life insurance policies, deposits of policyholders at life insurance companies, other federal government securities, local and municipal securities, corporate obligations).

Which of these items should be labeled "money," which "near-money," which "nonmonetary nominal value liquid assets," and which "nonliquid nominal value assets"?

This question has a long background in the literature (Chapter 2), and remains a live issue today, as the continuing discussion in articles and books testifies.[1]

Any answer is bound to be somewhat arbitrary. Hence, it is a tempting approach to try to avoid the question altogether by working only with individual assets. However, that is impossible. The separate items listed in Table 1 are themselves subtotals. Currency is of different kinds and so is each of the categories of deposits, and the differences among the various kinds have at times been of great importance. No subtotal should be used blindly without regard to the elements of which it is composed, but it is impossible to deal only with irreducible elements; there are simply too many of them.

Even if it were possible to work only with individual assets, it would

---

[1] H. A. Latané, "Cash Balances and the Interest Rate—A Pragmatic Approach," *Review of Economics and Statistics,* Nov. 1954, p. 457; J. G. Gurley and E. S. Shaw, "The Growth of Debt and Money in the United States, 1800–1950: A Suggested Interpretation," *Review of Economics and Statistics,* Aug. 1957, p. 250; H. G. Johnson, "Monetary Theory and Policy," *American Economic Review,* June 1962, pp. 351–352; W. T. Newlyn, *Theory of Money,* New York, 1962, Chap. 1, and "The Supply of Money," *Economic Journal,* June 1964, pp. 327–346; B. P. Pesek and T. R. Saving, *Money, Wealth, and Economic Theory,* New York, 1967, pp. 163–254; Leland B. Yeager, "Essential Properties of the Medium of Exchange," *Kyklos,* 1968, No. 1, pp. 45–68.

For an older discussion of the question, see A. P. Andrew, "What Ought to Be Called Money?," *Quarterly Journal of Economics,* Jan. 1899, pp. 219–227. Andrew approaches the question in much the same spirit as we do, though his choice of definition differs from ours.

be undesirable to do so. A distinction between "money" and "other assets" has been found extremely useful for a long time in many contexts. There is nothing that makes this inevitable. The continuum of assets might be so gradual and substitution among various types so easy and frequent that no subtotal would have any particular significance short of, let us say, total nonhuman wealth. It is an empirical generalization that this is not the case: there is a subtotal, labeled "money" for convenience, which it is useful to distinguish because it is related to other economic magnitudes in a fairly regular and stable way, though its particular content may be different from place to place or time to time. This empirical generalization underlies the distinction between price theory and monetary theory—a distinction that has been central in economic analysis for centuries.

Another tempting approach is to try to separate "money" from other assets on the basis of a priori considerations alone. One version, perhaps the most common, takes as the "essential" function of money its use as a "medium of exchange." It therefore tries to determine which assets are used to effect transactions and classifies these and only these as money. This version tends toward a rather narrow definition of money (Chapter 3, section 1). Another version, which has recently received much attention, goes to the opposite extreme. Its proponents regard "liquidity" as the essential feature of money and so see little point in stopping short of a total that includes almost all assets that are both expressed in nominal values and convertible into one another reasonably quickly and at relatively little financial cost (Chapter 3, section 2).

Both the a priori approach and these two specific versions of it seem to us misleading, though highly suggestive (Chapter 3, section 3). The approach is misleading because it puts the cart before the horse. Once we have a "good" definition, it may turn out that it can be described in terms of "medium of exchange" or "liquidity" or some similar general characteristic. The fact that we have a good definition will be evidence on what the "essential" characteristics of money are; we cannot start from the "essential" characteristics and proceed to the definition. The a priori approach is nonetheless suggestive because it implicitly records the tentative hypotheses derived from earlier studies. These studies suggest that it has been found useful to distinguish totals of items that have the characteristics of serving as a medium of exchange or of providing liquidity. These tentative hypotheses narrow the scope of our further investigation and limit the alternatives that it seems most fruitful to explore.

To put the matter differently, the economic theory accepted at any time is in part a systematic summary of the empirical generalizations that have been arrived at by students of economic phenomena. This theory implicitly contains a specification of the empirical counterparts to the concepts in terms of which it is expressed—otherwise it would be pure mathematics. But the specification may be more or less precise, more or less definite. As the theory is refined and improved, it will generally lead to more precise specifications and, conversely, as we find one counterpart or the other to be more useful, it will enable us to refine the theory. It is our judgment that economic theory does not, as yet, give a very precise indication of the appropriate counterpart of the term "money." It simply suggests some of the general characteristics of assets that are likely to be relevant (see Chapter 3, section 1).

As these comments imply, the selection of a specific empirical counterpart to the term money seems to us to be a matter of convenience for a particular purpose, not a matter of principle. Dogmatism is out of place. The selection is to be regarded as an empirical hypothesis asserting that a particular definition will be most convenient for a particular purpose because the magnitude based on that definition bears a more consistent and regular relation to other variables relevant for the purpose than do alternative magnitudes of the same general class (Chapter 3, section 4). It may well be that the specific meaning it is most convenient to attach to the term money differs for different periods, under different institutional arrangements, or for different purposes. It is certainly highly likely that, as our understanding of the relevant phenomena increases, we shall change our views about what definition is most convenient even for a given period and purpose.

The problem is one that is common in scientific work. A preliminary decision—in this case, on the definition of money—must be made. Yet the decision can be made properly only on the basis of the research in which the preliminary decision is to be used. Strictly speaking, the "best" way to define money depends on the conclusions that we reach about how various monetary assets are related to one another and to other economic variables; yet we need to define "money" to proceed with our research. The solution, also common in scientific work, is successive approximations.

Prior research and writing narrow down the choice to a limited number of alternatives if "money" is defined to correspond to a total like those in Table 1. The range of choice is much wider if a more sophisticated approach is adopted whereby different degrees of moneyness are attributed to different assets. We have not ourselves adopted this approach though we conjecture that it is probably the most promising for the future (Chapter 4, section 1).

After considering the alternatives in Table 1, we chose to designate as "money" the sum of currency held by the public plus adjusted deposits of commercial banks, both demand and time (Table 1, column 9). We chose this total in preference to a narrower total including only demand deposits largely on the basis of a historical examination of the meaning of commercial bank demand and time deposits in the United States and of the factors producing alterations in their relative magnitude (Chapter 4, section 2). The decision was reinforced by other evidence bearing on the comparison between the total we use and both narrower and broader totals (Chapter 4, section 3). Further evidence has since become available from our own work and also the work of others. The further evidence partly supports and partly argues against the choice we made (Chapter 4, section 4).

Though the definition we use seems to us clearly the best single choice for the period as a whole, its superiority to any of the other totals is slight, and for some specific periods one of the others may be preferable. We have tried to check many of our results to see whether they depend critically on the specific definition used. Almost always, the answer is that they do not, though some numerical statements would be altered in detail if we had chosen a different definition. In addition, we have analyzed the behavior not only of the total but also of the components of the total, plus the savings deposits and savings and loan shares not included in the definition. We believe, therefore, that the definition we have adopted has served mainly to organize our analysis rather than to determine its content in any important respect (Chapter 5).

2

PRIOR USAGE

THE COMMONEST TYPE of money in the world in the sixteenth and seventeenth centuries and probably also the eighteenth was the Spanish coin of eight reales. Alexander Hamilton took the silver real as the model for the U.S. dollar, to which he assigned the same specie content as the Spanish "pieces of eight" of average abrasion then circulating in the United States. To a lesser extent Spanish gold coins and gold and silver coins of other countries were in use. During these centuries a wide variety of forms of money in addition to metallic money also became familiar. Facilities for transferable deposits had long existed at private banks on the Continent, and later the public banks established in various European countries also issued banknotes and transferred fractional reserve deposits by entries on their books. Before the Bank of England and the Bank of Scotland came into existence as banks of issue, English goldsmith bankers circulated their own notes—promises to pay bearer on order. Endorsed domestic bills of exchange circulated as money in Italy, France, and later England. In France banknotes were issued from 1716 to 1720 in the course of John Law's experiment, and paper money in the form of assignats, from 1789 to 1796, by the revolutionary government. The American Colonies and later the Continental Congress issued bills of credit that were used in making payments.[1]

As a result of this proliferation of means of payment, the term "money" from the eighteenth century on has meant different things to

[1] Alexander Hamilton, "On the Establishment of a Mint" (May 5, 1791), in *Reports of the Secretary of the Treasury of the United States*, Washington, D.C., 1828, Vol. I, pp. 133–156. J. G. van Dillen, *History of the Principal Public Banks*, The Hague, 1934. We are indebted to Earl J. Hamilton for this reference, for suggestions concerning this paragraph, and for his comments on a draft of this chapter. N. S. B. Gras, "Bill of Exchange," and D. R. Dewey, "Bills of Credit," *Encyclopaedia of the Social Sciences*, New York, 1937, Vol. II, pp. 540, 542.

different writers, or even to the same writer in different passages. In the theoretical literature, the term was often used without explicit consideration of its precise empirical counterpart, and this was sometimes true even in policy or in applied writing. However, it is generally possible to infer the meaning a writer attaches to the term money even when he gives no formal definition.

Three definitions of money have coexisted from that time to this: (1) metallic money and the paper money created by governments to meet their own financial requirements; (2) metallic money, government paper money, and bank notes; and (3) metallic money, government paper money, bank money, including deposits, and sometimes bills of exchange. To illustrate the difficulty of classifying views on the definition, those who used a restrictive definition of money tended to accept the real-bills doctrine, but some real-bills adherents did not use a restrictive definition; those who defined money broadly tended to accept the quantity theory, but many quantity theorists adopted the in-between definition. Critics of the bullionist position during the restriction of cash payments by the Bank of England (1797–1821) and writers of the Banking School in the decades thereafter usually used a restrictive definition, while bullionists and writers of the Currency School usually favored the in-between definition.

A further complication exists. Some writers made a distinction between the circulating medium or means of payment and money, and they did not identify the circulating medium—a more comprehensive concept—with money. In classifying such writers, we have referred only to their definition of money. Others, however, apparently used the terms "circulating medium" or "means of payment" as synonyms for money. We cite their definitions of the former term as their definition of money.

Most proponents of the narrowest definition argued that money had to have intrinsic value, that it had to be, or be fully backed by, some commodity that had exchange value independent of its monetary role, ideally, gold or silver. Though these writers have generally been labeled metallists, they also regarded "forced" government issues as money. The reasoning behind this definition had many strands. One strand was the implicit assumption that "money" had to be net wealth.[2] Metallic money and inconvertible government paper money, it was argued, were net wealth, while bank notes and deposits were exactly matched by

[2] This strand has reappeared in the writings of B. P. Pesek and T. R. Saving. See *Money, Wealth, and Economic Theory*, New York, 1967, pp. 235–244.

liabilities to the banks. Another strand was the view that metallic money and inconvertible government paper money were final income to those who acquired them, whereas bank notes and deposits, issued as advances by banks, merely anticipated final income. To repay the advances, an exactly equivalent amount had to be taken from final income. Still another strand was the classification of bank notes and deposits as two out of a host of credit instruments, all of which were interchangeable. To single out bank notes and deposits as playing any special role was condemned as error. It was on this ground that the Banking School opposed as futile the limitation of bank note issues which the Currency School proposed and which was enacted in Great Britain in 1844. The Banking School viewed bank notes and deposits as means of raising the velocity of bank vault cash but not as adding to the quantity of money. In the short run, its members argued, all forms of credit might influence prices,[3] but in the long run only "money" defined as metallic and as inconvertible government paper could influence prices. This was so because the domestic price level could deviate only temporarily from normal equilibrium with the world level of prices determined by the gold standard. Preeminent among such metallists were Cantillon (1730–34), James Mill (1807), Tooke (1834–48), Fullarton (1844), John Stuart Mill (1848), Willis (1925), and Rist (1940).[4]

---

[3] This view is the intellectual antecedent of the contemporary definition of "money" in terms of liquidity. See Chapter 3, section 2, below.

[4] The term "metallist" is a coinage of G. F. Knapp (*The State Theory of Money*, H. M. Lucas and J. Bonar, trans., London, 1924, pp. 212 ff.). He also coined the antonym "chartallist," meaning one who denied that a monetary unit had to be tied to the value of a particular metal. J. A. Schumpeter in adopting Knapp's usage (and incidentally changing chartallist to cartalist), also distinguished between "Theoretical" and "Practical" Metallists (*History of Economic Analysis*, New York, 1954, p. 288). According to him, theoretical metallists affirmed that it is logically essential for money to consist of a commodity or to be convertible into it; practical metallists simply espoused a monetary policy of tying the monetary unit to, and keeping it freely interchangeable with, a given quantity of a commodity. On the basis of Schumpeter's distinction, David Hume would have to be classified as a practical metallist, while the other writers mentioned in this note would have to be classified as theoretical metallists. Hume saw that "institutions of Banks, funds and paper credit . . . render paper equivalent to money, circulate it throughout the whole state, make it supply the place of gold and silver . . ." and that paper money can have the same effects as metallic money, but he was opposed to the permanent and widespread use of paper money because of "the dearness of everything, from plenty of money" (*Essays, Moral, Political and Literary* (1752), London, 1875, Vol. I, pp. 337 and 311).

Richard Cantillon described bankers who issued bank notes as putting money back into circulation after it had been deposited, thus accelerating the circulation of coins left with them, the acceleration being "equivalent to an increase of actual money up to a point" (*Essai sur La Nature du Commerce en Général*, written 1730–34, trans. Henry Higgs, London, 1931, p. 161; see also pp. 141–143, 305).

For James Mill, neither bank notes nor "a common cheque upon a banker" were "money" (Review of Thomas Smith, *Essay on the Theory of Money and Exchange*,

London, 1807, in *Edinburgh Review*, Oct. 1808, p. 52). "We are disposed to give Mr. Smith very considerable praise whether he discovered the distinction, or learned it elsewhere, for having very clearly perceived the difference between the paper which a government may force upon the people, and the paper circulated from banks, which nobody receives but at his pleasure. He has seen, too, that many errors may be traced to the strange inaccuracy of confounding together these two species of paper money" (pp. 50–51).

Thomas Tooke's views embraced virtually all the strands described above. See his *History of Prices*, Vol. IV, London, 1848, pp. 171–183.

John Fullarton held that bank notes and deposits were not money but forms of credit, the total of which was important but uncontrollable (*On the Regulation of Currencies*, London, 1844, pp. 29–36). He wrote:

> Gold and silver coin pass current in exchange for all sorts of commodities, because gold and silver are themselves commodities of value, and furnish the buyer and seller with a convenient equivalent that is universally in demand. Inconvertible government notes, though valueless in themselves, acquire a value in exchange . . . from the conditions annexed to their emission, and by reason of that value are received in exchange for commodities precisely on the same principle as coin. These two descriptions of circulation, therefore, fall naturally under a common head; and the phrase "money" may by a fair analogy be applied equally to the one as the other (p. 36).

Tooke and Fullarton were two leaders of the Banking School. In his discussion of the controversy between the Currency and Banking Schools, Viner leaves the impression that the Banking School adherents defined money more broadly than did the Currency School adherents, when, in fact, they did the opposite (Jacob Viner, *Studies in the Theory of International Trade*, New York, 1937). For example, he writes:

> The banking school . . . pointed out that under a purely metallic currency there existed in addition to specie, and under a mixed currency there existed in addition to specie and paper notes, a large quantity of bank deposits and bills of exchange which, they claimed, were also "currency" and in any case operated on prices in the same manner as did bank notes and specie (p. 222).
>
> It was, as we have seen, the position of the banking school that bank notes and bank deposits were both means of payment and parts of the circulating media, and that, since the proposals of the currency school dealt only with bank notes and left bank deposits free of control, they were bound to operate unsatisfactorily if put into practice (p. 243).

John Stuart Mill stated: "I apprehend that bank notes, bills, or cheques, as such, do not act on prices at all. What does act on prices is Credit, in whatever shape given, and whether it gives rise to any transferable instruments capable of passing into circulation or not" (*Principles of Political Economy*, W. J. Ashley, ed., London, 1909, Book III, Chapters VII–XIII, p. 523).

H. P. Willis wrote of bank notes: "they are spoken of as *currency* or (incorrectly) as money. . . . In fact they are not money . . . and the only difference between an issue of bank notes and the placing of a volume of deposits on the books of a bank is in the form in which bank credit is thus given circulation" (*Banking and Business*, New York, 1925, pp. 96–97, 103).

For Charles Rist, bank notes and deposits are "instruments of circulation," but cannot be considered money, because they are not a standard of value (*History of Monetary and Credit Theory from John Law to the Present Day*, J. Degras, trans., New York, 1940, p. 41). Rist distinguishes between the velocity of circulation of bank vault cash and of the total stock of money within the country, as follows:

> The two phenomena may occur simultaneously, may strengthen each other, cancel out, or act in contrary directions. But they do not arise from the same causes. The second phenomenon is slow and steady in its working, the first displays rapid alternations of growth and decline, corresponding to phases of boom and slump, or to a prolonged rise or fall in prices. It is by far the more important. The second is of interest because, up to a certain point, it can compensate for an inadequate supply of the precious metals (pp. 320–321).

Writers who regarded bank notes as money but excluded deposits usually relied on one of three lines of argument. One was that general acceptability in exchange was an essential characteristic of money. Bank notes, like metallic money and government paper money, had this quality, while checks drawn on bank deposits did not, since they were acceptable only under particular conditions.

A second argument was that the exclusion of deposits and bills of exchange from the definition of money was justified by their much lower velocity of circulation as compared to that of bank notes or coin.

A third argument was that the total of specie and notes, whether issued by banks or by governments, remained a fairly constant proportion of deposits, so that no special notice of deposits was needed in the definition of money. These arguments flourished in the nineteenth century because of the failure to understand the distinction between primary and derivative deposits. Some writers believed that deposits were all primary and not money because their very presence in banks indicated they were not in use as means of payment.

So far as we know, Ricardo was the first writer to discriminate between checks and bank notes, considering the former a money substitute and treating bank notes, inconvertible government issues, and metallic money as indistinguishable components of money. Paper money in his view differed from metallic money only in that it cost less to produce, whereas he regarded the use of checks as restricting the quantity of money and increasing the velocity of its circulation. Ricardo explicitly recognized that the multiplication of claims to money would tend to raise the level of prices that could be supported by any given quantity of money. For a single country on a commodity standard, the effect would be not a higher price level, but a lower quantity of money, the claims on money "driving out" the specie. For the group of countries on a single-commodity standard, the initial effect would be a higher price level, but the long-run effect might also be a smaller quantity of money. The extent to which one or the other of these effects predominated would depend on the production conditions of the monetary commodity. Other economists [5] who defined money in the same way as

[5] Adam Smith is not listed in this group, although he was not a metallist, because he did not specifically discuss the role of bank deposits. He held that bank notes simply displaced an equivalent amount of specie, so that the total of bank notes plus specie did not exceed the amount of specie alone that would have been in circulation in the absence of bank notes (*An Inquiry into the Nature and Causes of the Wealth of Nations*, London, 1776, Modern Library Edition, Edwin Cannan, ed., New York, 1937, pp. 276–277, 284).

Ricardo were Thornton (1802), a contemporary, and Norman of the Currency School (1838–41), McCulloch (1850), Walker (1878), Fisher (1911), Marshall (1887, 1922), and Cannan (1931).[6]

[6] *The Works and Correspondence of David Ricardo,* ed. by Piero Sraffa with the collaboration of M. H. Dobb, Royal Economic Society, 1951, Vol. I, *On the Principles of Political Economy and Taxation* (1817), Chapter XXVII; Vol. III, *The High Price of Bullion, A Proof of the Depreciation of Bank Notes* (1810), pp. 54–55, and *Reply to Mr. Bosanquet's 'Practical Observations on the Report of the Bullion Committee'* (1811), pp. 210–212; Vol. IV, *Proposals for an Economical and Secure Currency* (1816), pp. 54–58.

Henry Thornton, *An Enquiry into the Nature and Effects of the Paper Credit of Great Britain* (1802), reprinted New York, 1939, pp. 55, 134, 271. Thornton noted that bills of exchange were also used in making payments and took the place of money (p. 92).

J. R. McCulloch, *Essays on Interest, Exchange, Coins, Paper Money, and Banks* (1850), republished from the 7th ed. of the *Encyclopedia Britannica,* Philadelphia, 1851, pp. 146–147.

For the views of George Warde Norman (who, incidentally, was the grandfather of Montagu Norman, Governor of the Bank of England, 1920–44), see Great Britain, Parliament, House of Commons, *Report from the Select Committee on Banks of Issue* (1840), pp. 142–143, 199, 204, 206; *Remarks upon Some Prevalent Errors, with Respect to Currency and Banking,* London, 1833, p. 23.

F. A. Walker, *Money,* New York, 1878, pp. 8–17. The page headings read as follows: Bank Notes Are Money (pp. 9–13); Cheques Are Not Money (p. 15); Inconvertible Notes Are Money (p. 17).

Irving Fisher, *The Purchasing Power of Money,* New York, 1911, p. 53. Fisher's views are summarized in the following quotations: "Banks supply two kinds of currency, viz. bank notes—which are money; and bank deposits (or rights to draw)—which are not money. . . . There tends to be a normal ratio of bank deposits (M') to the quantity of money (M); because business convenience dictates that the available currency shall be apportioned between deposits and money in a certain more or less definite, even though elastic ratio. The inclusion of deposit currency does not normally disturb the quantitative relation between money and prices" (pp. 53–54). Fisher, however, recognized that "transition periods," when the normal ratio of deposits to money was disturbed, were the rule and analyzed the consequences of such disturbances.

Allan H. Meltzer has suggested to us that by the term money, Fisher really meant high-powered money. That may be so. Fisher used the term "circulating media" to refer to the total of money, as he then defined it, and bank deposits subject to check. Later Fisher discarded the definition of money which excluded deposits (*100% Money,* New York, 1935).

Alfred Marshall, *Money, Credit, and Commerce,* London, 1922. After noting "the need for elasticity in the use of the term 'money,'" Marshall went on to say that when nothing was implied to the contrary, "'money' is to be taken to be convertible with 'currency' and therefore to consist of all those things which (at any time and place) are generally 'current,' without doubt or special inquiry, as means of purchasing commodities and services and of defraying commercial obligations. Thus in an advanced modern society, it includes all the coin and notes issued by Government. Almost in the same class are the notes issued by banks which are in good repute . . . and therefore we may proceed on the understanding that they are reckoned as money, unless something is said to the contrary" (p. 13). In 1887, testifying before the Royal Commission on the Values of Gold and Silver, Marshall had given essentially the same definition, excluding deposits, "because a cheque requires the receiver to have formed some opinion for himself as to the individual from whom he receives it" (*Official Papers,* London, 1926, p. 35).

Edwin Cannan, *Modern Currency and the Regulation of Its Value,* London, 1931. Cannan is scornful of the practice of

the last forty years . . . of regarding the amount which bankers are bound to pay their customers on demand or at short notice as a mass of "bank-money" or of "credit" which must be added to the total of the currency (of notes and coin)

John Law was probably the first to define money to include bank deposits. "The use of banks has been the best method yet practised for the increase of money," he wrote. He was thinking primarily of bank note issues but was clearly aware of the existence of deposits. Law remarked that the Bank of Amsterdam, which by its constitution was required to maintain a 100 per cent reserve behind its transferable receipts, in fact lent some of the funds on deposit with it. "So far as they lend they add to the money, which brings a profit to the country by employing more people, and extending trade; they add to the money to be lent, whereby it is easier borrowed, and at less use; and the bank has a benefit. But the bank is less sure, and though none suffer by it, or are apprehensive of danger, its credit being good; yet if the whole demands were made, or demands greater than the remaining money, they could not all be satisfied, till the bank had called in what sums were lent." [7]

Law thought that silver should be the monetary standard and that gold should be coined for use in large payments, but should circulate at its market value. He argued that, when properly issued, paper money is more stable in value than gold or silver.[8] He proceeded, therefore, to

whenever variations in the quantity of money are being thought of as influencing prices. . . . The more intelligent of the bank-deposit theorists, as we may for short call those who add bank deposits to currency in considering the effect of quantity of money on prices, cannot be supposed to believe with the populace that the banks are full of bank-notes and coin, but they rely on the rather misleading idea that a credit balance at a bank is "purchasing power" and therefore if the total of such balances increases, aggregate purchasing power in the sense of power to spend money on goods and services is increased. They assume that the additional power, having been once created, will be used, and thus raise prices just as additional currency does.

Cannan goes on to say

Few if any pseudo-economic theories have fared worse than this one did in the third decade of the century. Prices continued to wax and wane with currencies, and to exhibit towards the variation of bank deposits the complete indifference which would have been expected by the nineteenth century innocent who could see no more money in the world when he let his bank have £100 which it lent to somebody else than he saw when he lent that £100 to the other person direct (pp. 88 ff.).

[7] John Law, *Money and Trade Consider'd; With a Proposal for Supplying the Nation with Money,* 2nd ed., Edinburgh, 1720, pp. 30–31.

Though he made no explicit reference to bank deposits, Sir William Petty may also have had in mind the same definition of money as did Law. In his *Quantulumcunque concerning Money* (1682), Petty's answer to "What remedy is there if we have too little Money?" was "We must erect a Bank, which well computed, doth almost double the Effect of our coined Money . . ." (*The Economic Writings of Sir William Petty,* C. H. Hill, ed., reprinted, New York, 1963, Vol. II, p. 446).

[8] Law was expelled from France in 1707 for having proposed to issue there paper money more stable in value than gold or silver (Earl J. Hamilton, "John Law," *International Encyclopedia of the Social Sciences,* New York, 1968, Vol. 9, p. 79). Schumpeter suggests that Law must be classed as a theoretical metallist, on the ground

propose a form of money with extrinsic rather than intrinsic value. In 1705 he suggested that Scotland appoint a public body with powers to issue notes against the security of land. Anybody who was prepared to mortgage his land or sell it to the public body could obtain notes therefor. Nothing came of this proposal, but Law subsequently gained a following in France. In 1716, a royal edict authorized Law to establish the Banque Générale, with the right to issue notes, to receive and transfer deposits payable on demand, to deal in bullion, and to discount commercial paper. Sixteen months later, another royal edict authorized the establishment of the Compagnie d'Occident (later changed to Compagnie des Indes), of which Law was to be the managing director, with a monopoly of the trade with the Louisiana territory and in furs with Canada (later also of the trade with the East Indies, Africa and China and of the right to the profits of the royal mint and collection of royal revenues). In December 1718 the bank was nationalized under the title Banque Royale, with the government assuming responsibility for the note issue. In 1720 the bank was managed by the colonial company and, as Controleur Général, Law was placed in charge of all the public finances and of internal administration. Before its nationalization, Law's bank had been conservatively managed. In fact his reputation as a financial adventurer grew out of his association with the Mississippi Bubble, the name by which his ill-fated System has since been known, not with the Banque Générale.[9]

that he was opposed to debasement of coinage, recognized several physical attributes of silver which made it useful as a medium of exchange (*Money and Trade*, p. 6), and in practice redeemed notes as long as he could (*History of Economic Analysis*, pp. 321–322).

In general, Schumpeter held that, whatever a writer's definition of money, if he regarded convertibility as essential, he was basically a theoretical metallist. We have classified as metallists only those who denied the label money to bank notes and deposits, whether convertible or not, and who applied it exclusively to specie and inconvertible government paper money.

9 As the Banque Générale, 1716–18, it made no significant increase (about 3 per cent) in the currency circulation, but as the Banque Royale its actions were first highly inflationary and then correspondingly deflationary. The bank freely granted loans secured by the shares in the colonial company, initially to float an increase in capital and later to peg the price of the shares in an attempt to dampen the wild speculation that had developed. By May 1720 the bank had increased the note issue to double the specie circulation in 1716 before Law's bank was opened. At Law's behest, action was taken to contain the inflation. A royal edict of May 21 announced a reduction of one-half in the value of bank notes and of five-ninths in the pegged price of the company shares, to be accomplished in successive stages by December 1. Panic ensued and the bank stopped payment for ten days, although the edict was in the meantime repealed. Shares, however, were no longer pegged. The bank resumed payment on June 1, on a restricted basis, and proceeded to contract the note issue by 35 per cent from June to September. Loss of confidence in the notes led to their withdrawal from circulation as of Novem-

After Law, we may add to the roster of those who defined money to include bank deposits (and, in some instances, also more broadly) the names of Steuart (1767), Bollman (1810), Gallatin (1831), MacLeod (1855), Sidgwick (1883), Newcomb (1886), Dunbar (1887), Hawtrey (1913), Robertson (1922), Mitchell (1927), Pigou (1927), Keynes (1930, 1936), and Hansen (1949). Bank deposits were sometimes limited to demand deposits, sometimes not.[10]

ber 1. In January 1721 liquidation of the combined enterprise began. Holders of bank notes and shares realized from 5 to 95 per cent of the nominal value of their claims. See A. M. Davis, "An Historical Study of Law's System," *Quarterly Journal of Economics*, Apr. 1887, pp. 289–318; July 1887, pp. 420–452; and E. J. Hamilton, "Prices and Wages at Paris Under John Law's System," *Quarterly Journal of Economics*, Nov. 1936, pp. 42–70; *idem*, "Prices and Wages in Southern France Under John Law's System," *Economic History Supplement to the Economic Journal*, 1937, pp. 441–461; *idem*, "John Law of Lauriston: Banker, Gamester, Merchant, Chief," *American Economic Review*, May 1967, pp. 273–282.

10 Sir James Steuart, *An Inquiry into the Principles of Political Economy*, London, 1767, Vol. I, pp. 32, 365. Steuart, who was influenced by Law, defined money as follows: "By money, I understand any commodity, which purely in itself is of no material use to man . . . , but which acquires such an estimation from his opinion of it, as to become the universal measure of what is called value, and an adequate equivalent for anything alienable" (p. 32). For internal purposes, "symbolical money," meaning "bank notes, credit in bank, bills . . ." (p. 365), would suffice, but in addition, a country needed gold and silver, "the money of the world," for international payments.

Erick Bollman, *Paragraphs on Banks*, 2nd ed., Philadelphia, 1810, p. 11. Bollman (who gained some notoriety as an agent of Aaron Burr in the western military project for which Burr was tried for treason, and who only subsequently turned to the analysis of the U.S. banking system in several pamphlets) referred to "the quantity of circulating medium afloat in the form of checks, bank notes, or specie" (p. 26; also pp. 35, 80, 86).

Albert Gallatin, *Considerations on the Currency and Banking System of the United States*, Philadelphia, 1831. Gallatin included bank deposits payable on demand in "the currency of the United States. This, it appears to us, embraces not only bank notes, but all demands upon banks payable at sight, and including their drafts and acceptances" (p. 31).

H. D. MacLeod, *The Theory and Practice of Banking*, London, 1855, Vol. 1, p. 37; *The Elements of Political Economy*, London, 1858, pp. 41–42. MacLeod included not only bank deposits and bills of exchange in his definition of "the currency or circulating medium," but all promissory notes, book debts of traders, and private debts between individuals, excluding only stocks and bonds because holders did not expect to receive exactly the sum of money stated on their face.

Henry Sidgwick, *Principles of Political Economy*, London, 1883. Sidgwick described money as coin, bank notes, and "bankers' liabilities . . . not embodied or represented otherwise than by rows of figures in their books" (pp. 233–234).

Simon Newcomb, *Principles of Political Economy*, New York, 1886. Newcomb used the term currency "to designate everything, material or immaterial, which passes from hand to hand as money" (p. 188), and then proposed a method for determining the total volume of currency in dollars:

. . . the total volume of the currency may be obtained in this way: Add up all the coin in the hands of persons, all the legal-tender and bank notes in circulation, and all the bank deposits. The sum is the total volume of the currency. We do not include the coin held by the banks or the treasury as a reserve because this is not in circulation. If we know the total amount of coin in the country, we may find the amount in the hands of individuals by subtracting the bank and treasury reserves from the sum total. We may therefore find the volume by adding up the total

In the past quarter of a century, the definitions of money restricted to coin and inconvertible government issues or to these plus bank notes have lost ground. Some variant of the third class of definition, which includes bank deposits, is now common. The tendency to broaden the total regarded as money has continued under the stimulus of Keynes' emphasis on liquidity preference, which led economists to pay more attention to the asset motive for holding money balances. Since World War II, a number of British and American economists have urged the desirability of using a definition of money, discussed in Chapter 3, that includes not only deposits at commercial and mutual savings banks but also a wide variety of other assets expressed in nominal terms.

Advocates of very broad definitions of money have however remained a minority, probably a declining minority. Recently there has been renewed emphasis on defining money to include only those items generally used as a medium of exchange. The most common usage is

amount of coin, bank-notes, and deposits, and subtracting the reserves held by the banks (pp. 190–191).

C. F. Dunbar, "Deposits as Currency," *Quarterly Journal of Economics*, July 1887. Dunbar deplored the failure to attend to "deposits as a part of the currency" in the public concern over the post-Civil War retirement of greenbacks and the contraction of national bank notes during the decade of the 1880's: "It is a circulating medium in as true a sense and in the same sense as the bank-note, and . . . , like the bank-note, it is created by the bank and for the same purpose" (p. 402).

R. G. Hawtrey, *Good and Bad Trade*, London, 1913. Hawtrey wrote that money is "taken to cover every species of purchasing power available for immediate use, both legal tender money and credit money, whether in the form of coin, notes, or deposits at banks" (p. 3).

D. H. Robertson, *Money*, New York, 1922. Robertson defined money "to denote anything which is widely accepted in payment for goods, or in discharge of other kinds of business obligation" including both "common money," "which is universally acceptable within a given political area," and bank money, "which requires special knowledge, and the making of special arrangements, on the part of the recipient" (pp. 2, 40).

W. C. Mitchell, *Business Cycles*, NBER, 1927. Mitchell abjured the term money, because of the "confusing variety of meanings" attached to it, and substituted the "circulating medium" which included "all the common means of making monetary payments." These are described as "coin and paper money" (p. 117) and as "bank notes, checking deposits, and bills of exchange" on which business depended "to keep the supply of the circulating medium adjusted to its changing pace" (pp. 121–122).

A. C. Pigou, *Industrial Fluctuations*, London, 1927. In *The Veil of Money*, London, 1949, Pigou defined money as the sum of "two divisions, current money and bank money." Current money is his term for currency. "Bank money consists of bank balances —the distinction between balances on current and on deposit account is more formal than real—*plus* overdraft facilities." Pigou remarked that commercial bank note issues could be classed either under current money or under bank money, "convenience favouring the former, logic perhaps the latter" (p. 6).

J. M. Keynes, *Treatise on Money*, New York, 1930; *General Theory of Employment Interest and Money*, New York, 1936, *vide* p. 167, note 1. In both works Keynes defined money as "co-extensive with bank deposits" including time deposits.

Alvin Hansen, *Monetary Theory and Fiscal Policy*, New York, 1949. Hansen gave figures on "money supply—currency plus demand and time deposits" (p. 3).

probably to identify "money" with currency plus demand deposits adjusted (Table 1, col. 8) rather than any other total. However, current practice is itself sufficiently diverse and imprecise that it has become common to attach adjectives such as "narrow" or "broad" or identifying numbers such as 1 and 2 to the term money wherever the precise meaning is important.

Historically, the choice of definition has been made on two different grounds. Some writers have regarded the choice as dictated by a priori considerations which enforced a sharp dividing line between "money" and "nonmoney" assets; others have regarded it as involving no question of principle but simply the need to draw a line "at whatever point is most convenient for handling a particular problem." [11] For the former, one dividing line signified truth, any other dividing line, error; for the latter, the line could be shifted, depending on the nature of the problem under investigation, but once drawn required consistent use of the term money as defined.[12]

[11] J. M. Keynes, *The General Theory*, p. 167, note 1.

[12] Examples of writers who adopted an a priori approach include Tooke, Rist, and Cannan. On the empirical approach, in addition to Keynes, we may cite Marshall: ". . . the need for elasticity in the use of the term 'money' is somewhat greater than in most other economic terms. There are some inquiries in which it may with advantage be used narrowly and others in which a broad use of it is appropriate" (*Money, Credit, and Commerce,* p. 13). D. H. Robertson commented: "It is clearly desirable to arrive at an early understanding of what we mean by money. There is no very general agreement upon this point; but as with so many other economic terms, it does not matter very much what meaning we adopt as long as we stick to it, or at any rate do not change it without being aware that we are doing so" (*Money,* p. 2).

3

A PRIORI APPROACHES

AFTER CENTURIES of consideration in the literature, the best way to define money remains a live issue today. Contemporary writers who have tried to formulate the definition of money on a priori grounds have generally stressed either the "medium of exchange" function (section 1), or the "asset" function of money (section 2). Both the general approach and these two specific versions of it seem to us to provide an unsatisfactory basis for defining money (section 3). We conclude that the definition of money is an issue to be decided, not on grounds of principle as in the a priori approach, but on grounds of usefulness in organizing our knowledge of economic relationships. There is no hard and fast formula for deciding what total to call "money" (section 4).

1. "Medium of Exchange"

Many writers regard it as nearly self-evident that the role of money is to facilitate transactions and hence that money must be defined as currency plus demand deposits. Still others reach the same conclusion less directly, through a sophisticated theoretical analysis of the monetary system. In fact, this conclusion is not a valid implication of two of the recent analyses considered more fully below. These analyses imply rather that money should be defined as equal to high-powered money (currency outside banks plus bank reserves)—the modern counterpart of the early definition of money as coin plus government issues. Convention is stronger than logic!

Claims to Money Versus Money

Just as earlier writers regarded bank notes as claims to money rather than money itself, and argued that debts could not be discharged finally with bank notes but only with the specie that could be obtained for the bank notes, so many current writers argue that time deposits or savings and loan shares or other assets expressed in nominal terms can be used to discharge debts only by being first converted into currency or demand deposits, and hence cannot themselves be regarded as money.[1]

A minor difficulty with this approach is that the apparently simple criterion of whether an item directly serves as a "medium of exchange" turns out, on close examination, to be an uncertain guide to the classification of assets. At first glance, currency clearly seems to satisfy this criterion. Yet U.S. currency includes ten-thousand dollar notes. These can seldom be used directly as means of payment; they must first be converted into smaller denominations.[2] Should they therefore be excluded from the total termed "money"? How about $5,000 bills; $1,000 bills? How do we decide which denominations are media of exchange, which near-money assets? A holder of a demand deposit may not be able to effect transactions with persons he does not know by direct transferal of his check; he may first have to "cash" a check at his bank or with someone who knows him. On the other hand, banks have often been willing to transfer time deposits from party to party, sometimes even by the close equivalent of checks. Many people in the United States, and even more in other countries, pay a part of their bills by converting currency into postal money orders or their equivalent. Are the money orders to be regarded as the medium of exchange, and currency not? Brokerage balances are employed as a means of payment for a large class of transactions, and used cars for still another.[3]

[1] J. W. Angell, *The Behavior of Money*, New York, 1936, pp. 5–10; P. A. Samuelson, *Economics*, 2nd ed., New York, 1951, p. 308; H. A. Latané, "Income Velocity and Interest Rates—A Pragmatic Approach," *Review of Economics and Statistics*, Nov. 1960, p. 447.

[2] See Mark Twain's, "The £1,000,000 Bank-Note," for the classic illustration of the fact that a large denomination note is not a means of payment for the holder, but a near-money asset on the basis of which he can borrow to discharge debts.

On July 14, 1969, the Federal Reserve System and the Treasury Department announced that they would cease issuing currency in denominations over $100.

[3] An interesting modern counterpart in some countries to the "bills of exchange," the small denominations of which were so widely regarded as media of exchange in the nineteenth century literature, is the postdated check. In countries like Israel and the Republic of China (Taiwan), the postdated personal check is a major short-term credit instrument, which is transferred from person to person, each adding his endorsement and

These problems of classification are, in practice, rather minor; the puzzles cited can properly be regarded as exceptions. There would be little dispute that at the present time in the United States, currency, demand deposits, and travelers' checks are the only major items generally used as media of exchange and that the bulk of these items can be regarded as so usable. The significance of the exceptions is the light that they throw on the ambiguity of a "medium of exchange" as a theoretical concept.

The major difficulty with this approach is that it begs the question of whether the "essential" feature of money is its use as a means of payment. A "money" economy is distinguished from a barter economy by the separation of the act of purchase from the act of sale. An individual who has something to exchange does not need to search out the double coincidence of someone who both wants what he has and offers what he wants in exchange. He need only find someone who wants what he has, sell it for general purchasing power, and then separately find someone else who has what he wants and buy it with general purchasing power. In order for the act of purchase to be separated from the act of sale, there must indeed be something that will be generally accepted in payment—this is the feature emphasized in the "medium of exchange" approach. But also, there must be something that can serve as a temporary abode of purchasing power, in which the seller holds the proceeds in the interim between sale and subsequent purchase or from which the buyer can extract the general purchasing power with which he pays for what he buys. This is the feature that is emphasized in the so-called Cambridge cash-balances approach, and that has received increasing attention in modern monetary theory.[4] Both features are necessary to permit the act of purchase to be separated from the act of sale, but the "something" that is generally accepted in payment need not

so improving the "quality" of the check. After several endorsements, it is widely accepted and is used to make payments. In general, the standard analysis for checking deposits is that the "money" or "medium of circulation" is the individual's deposit credit on the books of the banks, not the check, and that the check is simply an order to transfer the deposit. This is clearly not correct for postdated checks of the kind just described. There may be no corresponding deposit credit at the time the check is written or when it circulates; the deposit credit may arise only on the date when the check is payable.

[4] H. G. Johnson, "Monetary Theory and Policy," *American Economic Review*, June 1962, pp. 344–345, 351–352; Milton Friedman, "The Quantity Theory of Money," *International Encyclopedia of the Social Sciences*.

In the *Treatise on Money* (New York, 1930, Vol. I, p. 13), Keynes defined money in language almost identical with that used above. In his view money was "that by delivery of which debt-contracts and price-contracts are *discharged,* and in the shape of which a store of General Purchasing Power is *held*." (His italics.)

coincide with the "something" that serves as a temporary abode of purchasing power; the latter may include the former and more besides.

For a somewhat fanciful illustration, suppose that silver were used as the medium of exchange for all but "money changing" transactions, yet gold, because of its convenience, remained the major constituent of the temporary abode. Of course, there would have to be some "money changers" who would facilitate the conversion of silver into gold.

To illustrate in a less fanciful way: for many a low-income consumer, time or savings deposits may be the major temporary abode, and currency or money orders the chief means of payment. There is some evidence that savings deposits and currency are closer substitutes for one another among some groups and at some times than either is for demand deposits. It is suggestive that individuals are the main holders of both currency and time deposits and business enterprises the main holders of demand deposits.

Of course, we can regard the term "medium of exchange" as referring to both features we have stressed—general acceptability in payment and use as a temporary abode of purchasing power. But then the term is of little use in deciding on an empirical counterpart to "money." Accordingly, we have interpreted "medium of exchange" narrowly as referring solely to general acceptability in payment.

A few numbers show the empirical importance of recognizing the asset as well as the medium of exchange role of whatever is regarded as money—at least for personal as opposed to business balances. Consider the definition of money currently favored by those who emphasize the medium-of-exchange role: currency plus demand deposits. In the United States in 1966, this total was equal to the value of four months' personal disposable income, about one month's in currency and three months' in demand deposits. Roughly two-thirds of the currency and two-fifths of the demand deposits were held by individuals and the rest by businesses. On the average, therefore, individuals held in currency about three weeks' income, in demand deposits about five weeks', or a total amount equal to two months' disposable income. Is it plausible that anything like this large a sum was held for the narrow medium of exchange function of money alone—that is, for mechanical transactions needs?

When money has been an unattractive asset to hold, as in hyperinflation, the quantity held, expressed in terms of income or in real value, has sometimes fallen to less than 1 per cent of its initial value. This quantity represents an estimate of the irreducible minimum necessary for transactions purposes. And even in much more moderate inflations, the quantity held has often fallen to one-half or one-third of its level when prices are stable. Applied to the United States, this experience would imply that, for individuals and businesses combined, roughly one to two days' income is the hard core, as it were, of what might be called transactions balances proper, and one to two months' income is the level of balances that can be maintained for extended periods without serious transactions difficulties.[5]

Another bit of evidence that current balances are much larger than can readily be accounted for by mechanical transactions needs is provided by recent attempts to analyze cash balance holdings on inventory lines—in terms of the difference in timing of income receipts and consumption expenditures. These studies yield estimates of the required amount of cash balances that are of about the same order of magnitude as the actual amount held during inflations. The simplest model assumes that income is received in equal amounts at regular intervals but spent continuously and that only cash balances are used to correct for the lack of synchronization between payments and receipts (i.e., that transactions balances are never temporarily held in a liquid interest-yielding asset). This model makes the individual's cash balances equal to half his regular income receipt, which means that, if he is paid weekly, his cash balances equal half a week's income; if he is paid bi-weekly, they equal a week's income, etc. It would be difficult along these lines to explain cash balances equal to about two months' income. Complications introduced into more sophisticated models may either raise or lower the estimated transactions demand derived from the simple model.[6]

[5] See Phillip Cagan, *Proceedings of a Symposium on Inflation: Its Causes, Consequences and Control,* C. K. Kazanjian Economics Foundation, Inc., 1968, pp. 30–48; *idem,* "The Monetary Dynamics of Hyperinflation," *Studies in the Quantity Theory of Money,* M. Friedman, ed., Chicago, 1956, p. 26; also C. D. Campbell and G. C. Tullock, "Hyperinflation in China," *Journal of Political Economy,* June 1954, pp. 236–245.

[6] See J. W. Angell, "Money, Prices, and Production: Some Fundamental Concepts," *Quarterly Journal of Economics,* Nov. 1933, pp. 39–76; W. J. Baumol, "The Transactions Demand for Cash: An Inventory Theoretic Approach," *Quarterly Journal of Economics,* Nov. 1952, pp. 545–556; James Tobin, "The Interest-Elasticity of Transactions Demand for Cash," *Review of Economics and Statistics,* Aug. 1956, pp. 241–242; R. L. Teigen, "Demand and Supply Functions for Money in the United States: Some Structural Estimates," *Econometrica,* Oct. 1964, pp. 482–485; M. H. Miller and D. Orr, "A Model of the Demand for Money by Firms," *Quarterly Journal of Economics,* Aug. 1966, pp. 413–435; Paul E. Smith, "Probabilistic Demand for Cash Balances and (s,S) Inventory Policies," *Weltwirtschaftliches Archiv,* Band 100, Heft 1, 1968, pp. 72–83.

Still another bit of evidence is the very different ratio of business and personal balances of currency and demand deposits to the transactions effected by each. The asset motive is largely irrelevant for business, hence business holdings per dollar of transactions can be taken as something of an estimate of the amount held for mechanical transactions purposes.

Business holdings of currency and demand deposits are estimated to be roughly equal to personal holdings of these items, or about two months' personal disposable income. Yet business transactions are a substantial multiple of personal transactions—at least triple and perhaps more than triple—because most intermediate transactions are between business enterprises.[7] It follows that at least two-thirds of personal balances of currency and demand deposits alone (i.e., even excluding time deposits) would have to be attributed to asset motives.

The rough estimates underlying this comparison yield business balances of demand deposits that are reasonably consistent in size with the level suggested by the inventory analysis of cash balance needs, but, as noted above, yield personal balances of deposits and currency that are much larger.[8]

[7] For example, in the second quarter of 1968, seasonally adjusted total debits to demand deposits (excluding interbank and U.S. government deposits but including float) in 233 Standard Metropolitan Statistical Areas averaged about $7,700 billion, at an annual rate, and in the 232 areas outside New York City (excluding the large volume of transactions connected with security dealings), about $4,200 billion (*Federal Reserve Bulletin*, Nov. 1968, p. A-15). This last figure must be raised about 20 per cent to say, roughly $5,000 billion, to allow for debits not included in the 232 areas covered by the Federal Reserve estimates. (Dividing bank debits by turnover gives an estimate of average deposits in covered SMSA's for May 1968 of $26 billion for New York City and $99 billion outside New York City. Total seasonally adjusted demand deposits in that month were $144.5 billion, excluding not only interbank and U.S. government deposits, but also float [*ibid.*, p. A-17]. Adding float, which averaged $1.5 billion, yields a demand deposit total of $146 billion. This leaves roughly $20 billion of deposits not covered in the turnover figures, all of which are presumably outside New York City, or just 20 per cent of the deposits in the 232 SMSA's outside New York City.) Even this figure is a substantial underestimate of total transactions, not only because it excludes New York but also because it excludes transactions in currency.

In the second quarter of 1968, personal income in excess of taxes withheld (which involve business, not personal transactions) was about $650 billion, at an annual rate. Personal transactions can roughly be estimated at about double this amount, say, $1,300 billion, consisting of the receipt and then subsequent spending of the income. This is an underestimate since individuals do engage in some intermediate and capital transactions, but it is almost surely much larger as a fraction of total personal transactions than $5,000 billion is of total transactions. Yet taking these figures at face value, business transactions would be $3,700 billion or only a little less than triple personal transactions.

[8] Business demand deposit holdings implied by the preceding estimates (assigning three-fifths of demand deposits to business) would amount to about 8.5 days' transactions effected by check. We have estimated personal balances of currency and demand deposits as roughly two months' personal disposable income and personal transactions

These comments are not intended to deny in any way the importance of a generally accepted "medium" of exchange for the functioning of a money economy. They do not deny that it is in principle possible to define a "medium of exchange" or to identify in practice the assets commonly used as a "medium of exchange." Their purpose is rather to deny that it is self-evident that the term "money" should be restricted to the class of assets so identified. Perhaps that is the most useful definition of "money" for analyzing the behavior of prices and nominal income in a money economy. But to establish that it is requires more than unsupported assertion.

Net Wealth and Neutrality

Recently, several self-consciously formal attempts have been made to settle the proper definition of money by theoretical considerations. Pesek and Saving approach the problem in the course of an examination of the role of wealth in economic theory. They distinguish between "money" as a separate item of net wealth, and "debt," an asset to some and a liability to others. Newlyn, whose approach is adopted and elaborated by Yeager, considers that the key issue is whether a payment is "neutral" in its effect on the asset and interest rate structure. Gramley and Chase discuss the effect of monetary changes on interest rates, thereby implementing the analysis of Newlyn and Yeager.

Net Wealth (Pesek-Saving). Pesek and Saving start with three entirely correct propositions.[9] (1) Commodity money and fiat money are assets to their holders, but in no meaningful sense debts to anyone. Hence they should be included in the consolidated net wealth of the community without any offsetting entries. They are "money" without simultaneously being debt. (2) The charter granted to a commercial bank empowering it to offer deposits convertible into "dominant money" on demand and transferable by check is a valuable privilege if the number of charters is restricted by considerations other than the demand for such charters. This privilege increases the net worth of a bank beyond

as roughly double personal income in excess of withholding. This implies that personal balances of currency and demand deposits amount to a little less than one month's transactions.

The figures for business are expressed in terms of demand deposits only because the residual figure derived in the preceding footnote is based on a total figure covering only transactions effected by debits to demand deposits.

[9] Boris P. Pesek and Thomas R. Saving, *Money, Wealth, and Economic Theory*, New York, 1967, especially pp. 39–254.

any sums invested in setting up the bank. In the special case in which it costs nothing to set up a bank and nothing to run a bank (in particular, if banks are prohibited from paying interest on demand deposits and the prohibition is fully effective), the net worth so created would be precisely equal to the volume of deposits outstanding. An inventory of the wealth of the community will include this net worth as an item of wealth, which can be done, in the special case cited, by including *either* the quantity of deposits *or* the value of the equity in the bank. (3) The services rendered by money do not depend on its "resource content," [10] i.e., on the number of physical units, but on the existence of a stock (plus other variables); "if the quantity of the money resource (the nominal quantity of money) is constant, demand for the service of money will create its own supply at no expenditure of resources but merely through the change in the price of money." [11]

Pesek and Saving argue that these propositions have the following implications: (a) There is a sharp distinction in theory between the activity of banks as "producers" (their term) of deposits transferable by check, which pay no interest, and as financial intermediaries borrowing at one rate of interest and lending at another. (b) Noninterest-bearing deposits transferable by check are, like specie and fiat money, an asset to their holders but a liability to no one, while interest-bearing time deposits are a debt, like a bond. (c) The payment of interest on deposits transferable by check converts them into money-debt, which has the property of losing its moneyness (its capacity to serve as a medium of exchange) as the interest rate paid tends to approach the market interest rate. At the limit, it is entirely debt—in no part money. (d) Hence, theory provides a sharp line of demarcation between "money" and "debt," money consisting of items used as a medium of exchange which are best regarded as assets to their holders but liabilities to no one.

This analysis differs from that of the earlier writers cited primarily by giving greater weight to the net wealth criterion than to the medium of exchange criterion, and by being much more self-consciously formal. While Pesek and Saving have many valid and important things to say on topics other than the definition of money, unfortunately on this issue their analysis seems to us clearly wrong. Like the other writers, they beg a basic question by taking it for granted, albeit by rather subtle

[10] *Ibid.*, p. 170.
[11] *Ibid.*, p. 250.

implication, that the medium of exchange function is the essential function of "money." [12] More important, their conclusions (a to d) are not valid inferences from their propositions 1 to 3.

Consider conclusions a and b, which they believe to be implications of propositions 1 and 2. Suppose that financial intermediation by some institutions that do not have demand liabilities transferable by check, such as insurance companies or savings and loan associations, may be conducted only by chartered enterprises (as is in fact the case) and that the number of charters issued is restricted by considerations other than the demand for such charters. These financial enterprises will, like Pesek's and Saving's "producers" of money, have a net worth in excess of the sums required to establish the enterprise.[13] This net worth will be the capitalized value of the part of the difference between interest received and interest paid that is not required to pay operating expenses. Or to go farther afield, radio and television stations have a net worth in excess of the sums required to establish them, because licenses are limited and granted without charge. The value of these licenses is properly included in the wealth of the community.

In all these cases, the community might be better off if free or freer entry were permitted, even though net wealth as measured might be lower. This is simply an example of a point recognized by Pesek and Saving in a footnote,[14] but thereafter almost completely disregarded. We value items by market price, which corresponds to marginal utility, not average utility; hence, a reduction in scarcity may reduce the total value (in terms of a numeraire or other goods) that we attach to the total quantity. In the extreme, a free good will have an aggregate value of

[12] What they take for granted is that use as a medium of exchange is the sole nonpecuniary service rendered by liquid assets and is the only service to which proposition 3 applies. This is not the case. Liquid assets may also render nonpecuniary services in the form of such satisfactions as pride of possession and a feeling of security, as, for example, in having a reserve for the future. Such nonpecuniary services must obviously be introduced to explain differences in interest rates on assets that they and we alike would regard it as undesirable to call "money." These nonpecuniary services must also be rendered by assets that we do call money. The volume of such services, too, need not depend on the resource content of the assets.

For a fuller discussion of these issues, see Milton Friedman, *The Optimum Quantity of Money and Other Essays,* Chicago, 1969, Chap. 1.

[13] Strictly speaking, two qualifications are necessary: We must suppose that: (1) the granting of a charter cannot be affected by the amount of money spent to persuade the authorities to grant one, otherwise competition will lead to expenditures in this direction equal to the net value of the charter (or we must exclude such sums from consideration); and (2) there exist diseconomies of scale beyond some point, else expansion in the size of the individual enterprise could substitute completely for increase in the number of enterprises.

[14] Pesek and Saving, p. 43, footnote 2.

zero, yet it clearly contributes more to total utility than a lesser amount of it would. This is the classical diamond-water paradox.

Because a bank issuing deposits transferable by check can be regarded as having a net worth equal, in the special case of proposition 2, to the amount of deposits outstanding, it does not follow that these deposits are not a liability of the bank. It simply means that the bank has a valuable charter.[15] And this would also be true for bank notes issued under similar conditions. Fiduciary currency is not the same as fiat currency. Banks are engaged in financial intermediation when they issue promises to pay dominant money bearing no interest that are in excess of the amount of dominant money they hold in their vaults. These promises to pay are properly regarded as debts of the banks.

Assume free entry, and, in the spirit of the Pesek-Saving special assumption, that there is no resource cost involved in setting up or running a bank, but that banks are permitted to pay interest on deposits transferable by check. Competition will then eliminate completely the net worth so far considered. Banks will be driven to pay depositors interest that differs from the interest they earn only because they find it prudent to hold reserves of noninterest-bearing dominant money. Interest paid will differ from interest received by a fraction equal to the ratio of such reserves to total deposits. The deposits may still be available on demand and transferable by check, but since the privilege of issuing deposits is no longer restricted, it will be worth nothing.[16] Pesek and Saving explicitly discuss this case but conclude that if interest payments continue, the result would be that "demand deposits will cease serving as money." [17]

[15] In terms of one of the T accounts (*ibid.*, p. 143, Table 6-1D) Pesek and Saving present, their bank account should be as follows:

Assets		*Liabilities*	
Debt of private sector	1,000	Debt to private sector	1,000
Charter	1,000	Net worth	1,000

Of course, more generally, the two items on each side will not be equal, as they recognize, because of costs.

[16] Pesek and Saving recognize, of course, that in practice there are costs of setting up and running a bank, and that these must be allowed for in a full analysis. However, we agree with them that ignoring these costs is useful in isolating the basic characteristic of money-debt. They discuss the resource costs explicitly and conclude correctly that these convert part of the money-debt into commodity money. The capital facilities required (buildings, machinery, etc.) will enter the bank's balance sheet as assets. These assets will be balanced on the liability side by either debt or net worth (stockholders' equity), which will enter into the net wealth of the community in the same way as the net worth of other enterprises.

[17] *Ibid.*, p. 109.

The source of this remarkable conclusion is the failure of the writers to distinguish, on a rather subtle level, between price and quantity, or alternatively, between marginal and average—a confusion that is greatly fostered by the use of "dollar" (or similar unit) to describe both price and quantity of money. They maintain that "if the interest rate paid on private money-debt is equal to the market rate of interest, then the value of this money-debt as a medium of exchange must have fallen to zero if we are to be in equilibrium on the demand side." [18] This is entirely correct if "value" is interpreted as marginal nonpecuniary services rendered by the money-debt over and above any marginal nonpecuniary services rendered by assets paying the market rate of interest,[19] or, equivalently, as the price in terms of sacrificed interest that must be paid to acquire such services. If deposits transferable by check pay interest equal to the market rate, people will indeed be induced to hold an amount such that, at the margin, an additional dollar will render no additional services in facilitating transactions. The transactions services rendered by demand deposits have become a free good, available without cost to the holders of demand deposits. At this point, Pesek and Saving make an invalid leap, concluding as follows: "As a result, private money-debt has become entirely a bond, and the money supply is once again equal to the supply of dominant money alone so that the price of this dominant money will rise; the general price level will fall." [20] This is a nonsequitur. A zero *price* for the transactions services of demand deposits does not mean that the *quantity* of money in the form of demand deposits is zero. Alternatively, a *zero marginal* yield of transactions services does not mean that the *average* yield is zero.

The actual effect on the general price level will be just the contrary of what Pesek and Saving say it will be. Removal of restrictions on entry and on the payment of interest on deposits transferable by check would make dominant money a less attractive asset, would lead to a smaller real quantity being desired, and hence, to a rise in the general price level for a given nominal amount of dominant money—provided only that the deposits are in fact convertible into dominant money on demand.[21] In a

---

[18] *Ibid.,* p. 118.

[19] As noted above, in footnote 12, they take the provision of a medium of exchange as the only nonpecuniary service rendered by liquid assets, and in their frame of reference would omit the qualification "over and above . . . interest."

[20] *Ibid.,* p. 118.

[21] This is what Pesek and Saving call the instant repurchase clause. Although they put great stress on this clause elsewhere, they do not refer to it in the context of the

hypothetical world in which there were no costs of setting up and running a bank, and in which deposits transferable by check provided precisely the same services as dominant money, there would be no limit to this process short of a price level of infinity in terms of dominant money. In fact, a limit would be set by the differential usefulness of deposits and dominant money for different purposes, as Pesek and Saving recognize.[22]

Another manifestation of the confusion of price and quantity in the Pesek and Saving analysis occurs in their discussion of money-debt as a joint product. Suppose that a dollar of deposits pays interest. It is entirely valid to view this dollar as they do, as providing the joint products of, say, "moneyness" and "interest-payingness," just as a rented house may provide the joint products of, say, protection against the elements and a view. It is entirely valid to regard the cost of holding a dollar of deposits as equal to the "market interest rate," [23] and to divide this cost into two parts, one paid for "interest-payingness" (equal to the interest received on the deposit), the other paid for "moneyness" (equal to the difference between the market interest rate and the interest received). This is comparable to dividing the rent paid for the house into two parts, one paid for shelter (the rent that would have to be paid for a house

quotations cited above. The reason for the omission is that the writers are under the impression that either permitting the payment of interest or not requiring convertibility is sufficient to destroy the moneyness of money-debt.

They argue that unless the instant repurchase clause is legally enforced, bank money will necessarily depreciate. As proof they cite wildcat banking (*ibid.*, p. 116). It is certainly true that there is an incentive to adulterate the product of banks as there is to adulterate any other product, and it is also true that it may be easier to get away with adulteration of bank money than of many other products, for reasons spelled out elsewhere. (See Milton Friedman, *A Program for Monetary Stability*, New York, 1959, pp. 6–8.) But competitive forces will tend to prevent the adulteration of bank money as they do the adulteration of other products—by destroying the repute of firms engaged in the practice and denying them custom. This will be so even if the operation of these competitive forces on bank money may be less rapid or less uniform than on other products. In the absence of any legal requirement for, or legal enforcement of, an instant repurchase clause (except under general legal penalties for fraud), the market will nonetheless tend to the widespread use of such a clause. At the level of abstraction on which Pesek and Saving reason, therefore, they have no need for a legally imposed instant repurchase clause.

Incidentally, by implication they grossly exaggerate the depreciation of bank money that occurred in the era of wildcat banking. As always, it is the departures from the rule that are headline news. The overwhelming bulk of bank money at the time circulated at par or differed from par only by costs of shipment (comparable to gold points).

[22] *Ibid.*, p. 117.

[23] At the level of abstraction of Pesek and Saving, it is also valid to regard this cost as equal simultaneously to the rate of interest that could be earned on a dollar invested in other assets and the rate that would have to be paid to borrow a dollar in order to hold a dollar as deposits.

identical except for the view) and the other paid for the view (the excess
of rent paid over the hypothetical alternative rent).

So far so good. But Pesek and Saving go a step farther. Suppose the
interest received on the deposit is 80 per cent of the market interest rate.
Then, according to them the dollar of money-debt is 20 cents of money
and 80 cents of debt. If the rate received is equal to the market rate,
they hold that the money-debt consists of zero cents of money and one
dollar of debt. This is like saying, in the case of the house, that if the
rent of a house with a view happens to be the same as that of a house
without a view, then there is no view! For a house, it is obvious that
the two products, shelter and view, do not have a common unit of
quantity whose total can be fixed in advance; if there is more of the
one, there does not have to be less of the other. Hence it is easy to see
the distinction between measures of quantity (how much shelter and how
much of a view) and the prices paid for these quantities. It is easy to
see that the fraction of the rental price paid for shelter can vary without
the quantities varying because the relative price of the two products
varies. The price of the view can be zero, so that no part of the rent is
attributed to it, yet there can be a view. The view can be a "free" good,
yet be a good.

The money-debt case is in principle identical, yet it is far less obvious
because the same unit—"dollar"—is used to describe the price paid for
the services of the asset (the rent), the price paid for the asset (capital
value), the quantity of "debt," and the quantity of "money." A "dollar"
of deposits can perfectly well contain a "dollar" of interest-payingness
yet simultaneously contain a "dollar" of moneyness, provided only that
the rental price of a "dollar" of moneyness is zero. We have seen that
the view and shelter are two economic dimensions of the house that
cannot be added directly together, though the values attributable to them
can be. Likewise the "dollar" of moneyness and the "dollar" of interest-
payingness can be two dimensions of the "dollar" of deposits that cannot
be added directly together, though the values attributed to them can be.
And just as the quantity of view may not be capable of being enjoyed
continuously unless combined with the quantity of shelter, as a joint
product, yet have a price of zero, so the quantity of "moneyness" may
not be capable of being available in this form without being combined
with the quantity of "interest-payingness," yet also have a price of zero.

This very fruitful notion of actual assets as joint products is one we shall return to in section 4, below. For the present, the distinction between the prices paid for the separate services of an asset, and the quantities of the different dimensions of the asset, explains why Pesek's and Saving's conclusion c does not follow from their propositions 1, 2, and 3. It suggests also that if interest-paying deposits transferable by check can have a "dollar" of moneyness, then commercial bank time deposits or mutual savings bank deposits, and so on, can have moneyness as one of their components. That is a question of how we choose to define moneyness, not something to be decided a priori.[24]

The tortured analysis of Pesek and Saving reflects their attempt to keep two balls in the air at once. Money is to be simultaneously a "medium of exchange" and an item of "net wealth" and these two categories are to be wholly coincident. To categorize money as a "medium of exchange," they understandably feel driven to include all demand deposits transferable by check. But if the demand deposits paid interest, they would have to be regarded, at least in part, as a liability of the bank that issued them, and hence could not be regarded wholly as an item of "net wealth." Pesek and Saving are therefore driven to insist that the nonpayment—in fact and not merely in form [25]—of interest on demand deposits transferable by check is a necessary condition for demand deposits to be usable as a medium of exchange.

If Pesek and Saving were to carry their "net worth" criterion to its logical conclusion, regarding use as a medium of exchange as a neces-

[24] On an entirely different level, the implicit assumption that the only nonpecuniary services obtained from assets are those that facilitate transactions leads Pesek and Saving to use a model that does not seem to us fruitful for their or our purposes.

The wide range of "market" interest rates and the common observation that an individual may borrow at a far higher rate than he receives on assets he owns, suggest that it is useful to regard assets as yielding a variety of nonpecuniary services. For example, the "market interest rate" which corresponds to zero nonpecuniary services might be 10 per cent, not the 5 per cent yielded currently by long-term government securities. A long-term government bond would then be regarded as producing a joint product with 5 cents per dollar of such a bond being paid for the nonpecuniary services it yields.

With such a model, even treating a dollar of deposits as decomposable into money and debt with quantities necessarily adding to a dollar, as Pesek and Saving do, would lead them to the conclusion that a dollar of interest-paying deposits transferable by check has much moneyness and so may a dollar of interest-paying time deposits.

Even with their model, they are led to recognize that the nonpecuniary services of facilitating transactions are not homogeneous but can be of different kinds (*ibid.*, p. 117), so that in principle there are different kinds of "moneyness."

[25] Though the payment of explicit interest on demand deposits is currently prohibited by law, it is widely recognized that there are numerous indirect devices by which implicit interest is paid on demand deposits. Benjamin Klein, in an unpublished Ph.D. dissertation at the University of Chicago, has investigated the hypothesis that these devices are sufficiently effective to render the legal prohibition essentially nugatory.

sary but not sufficient condition for an item to be regarded as "money," they would be led to define money as equal to "high-powered money." This would include, for the United States, currency in the hands of the public (though not travelers' checks) [26] and the assets of banks held in the form of vault cash or deposits at Federal Reserve Banks. This total consists now, and has consisted for at least a century, of commodity money plus fiat money (i.e., governmentally issued money which has no "backing" except the "faith and credit" of the sovereign), though at times the fiat money has borne the promise to pay a fixed weight of a commodity (gold or silver) on presentation. Total high-powered money can all properly be regarded as assets of some individuals and liabilities of none.

Proceeding along this line, Pesek and Saving would include the value of bank franchises as an item of net worth along with the value of franchises for life insurance companies, savings and loan associations, and radio and TV stations. But this item of net worth would not be "money" because it is not used as a medium of exchange. This would make their treatment logically consistent—and, incidentally, align them with the early writers who treated only specie plus government note issues as money, excluding both the bank notes that then circulated and bank deposits.

Neutrality (Newlyn and Yeager). W. T. Newlyn, in a book and a subsequent article in the *Economic Journal*,[27] offers an analytical basis for defining money that we find more attractive than Pesek's and Saving's, yet still unsatisfactory. Because it can be considered an a priori approach, we discuss Newlyn's analysis in this section even though Newlyn himself, and Leland Yeager, who builds on Newlyn's analysis, both take the same view as we do, that the definition of money is "an analytic convention, and as such, should be made on the basis of analytic efficiency," rather than something that can be settled on wholly a priori grounds.[28]

---

[26] The treatment of American Express travelers' checks by Pesek and Saving is illustrative of their ambivalence. Because these seem obviously a medium of exchange, they treat them as money, though as "money-goods" like demand deposits, not "entirely money" like currency (Pesek and Saving, p. 190). Yet, so far as we know, there is no restriction on entry into the business of issuing travelers' checks and no legal prohibition on the payment of interest on them. In practice, of course, American Express charges rather than pays, so that interest is negative, but this does not alter the principle.

[27] *Theory of Money*, New York, 1962, and "The Supply of Money and Its Control," *Economic Journal*, June 1964, pp. 327–346.

[28] Newlyn, *Theory of Money*, p. 6. Newlyn here cites a footnote reference to a passage in *The General Theory of Employment, Interest and Money* (New York, 1936,

Newlyn starts out with the usual textbook statement that "anything is money which functions as a medium of exchange." [29] He then proceeds to distinguish in an original fashion between "the status of assets as determined by law or convention" and the "way in which they actually function." [30] By status, he asserts, only demand deposits at commercial banks in the United Kingdom (called "current accounts") are used as means of payment. Time deposits (called "deposit accounts") must be converted into demand deposits or currency to serve as a medium of exchange. He designates as *quasi-money* by status "those assets which, although indistinguishable from money as assets, do not function generally as a medium of exchange." [31]

However, "the significant [functional] characteristic of a means of payment is that ownership of it by an individual automatically increases or decreases as a result of any difference between the individual's payments and receipts, without altering its aggregate and without having any effect in the market for loans." By this criterion, he says, the total of deposits in the United Kingdom, demand and time, must be classified as money because "the banks in the United Kingdom do not make any significant distinction between the two types of deposits, with the result that time deposits can be drawn upon to make a payment without either altering the total of deposits or having any effect in the market for loans." [32]

In his subsequent article, Newlyn discusses these distinctions at greater length, and states the definition to which he is led somewhat more formally: "We classify as money those assets which can be drawn upon by their owners so as to produce an increase in aggregate expenditure without causing either a decrease in their aggregate or an increase in demand relative to supply in the market for loans. *Mutatis mutandis* for a decrease in expenditure." [33] He describes the second characteristic—not affecting the loan market—as "neutrality."

p. 167, note 1), in which Keynes states that no question of principle is involved in distinguishing "money" from "nonmoney assets." The line separating them may be drawn "at whatever point is most convenient for handling a particular problem."

[29] *Theory of Money*, p. 2.
[30] *Ibid.*, pp. 8–9.
[31] *Ibid.*, p. 6.
[32] *Ibid.*, p. 9.
[33] "The Supply of Money and Its Control," p. 339.

In order for this definition to have the empirical content Newlyn associates with it, some qualifying phrase like "on any of a wide variety of goods and services" must be understood to follow "aggregate expenditure." Otherwise, used cars traded in towards the purchase of other cars would satisfy these conditions fully—the total of used cars is unchanged, only the ownership shifts, and there is no necessary effect on the loan

Newlyn cites currency as the most obvious case of an asset satisfying his functional criterion: "currency . . . changes hands physically in making a payment, and this involves no repercussion in the economy whatever." [34] As noted, he asserts that this is true also of total commercial bank deposits. He adds, "it is satisfied by no other asset." [35]

To illustrate why it is not satisfied by other assets, Newlyn considers a "withdrawal of deposits from institutions such as building societies" (the U.K. counterpart of U.S. savings and loan associations). Such a withdrawal "will be effected by cheques drawn by these institutions on their banks in favor of their depositors. The latter will draw on the proceeds of these cheques to make payment to their creditors. As a result of these transactions bank deposits will have been redistributed, but will be unaltered in total; on the other hand quasi-money will have been reduced so that the total of quasi-money and deposits will also have been reduced. This combination of assets does not therefore satisfy the requirement that its total should be unaffected by a payment made in any of its components. Moreover, the building societies or finance houses will need to replenish their bank balances. This they may do by curtailing their lending or by selling securities; in either case the effect will be to add to the demand pressure in the market for loans." [36]

Unfortunately for this extremely appealing approach, the distinction Newlyn draws between building society deposits and other quasi-money, on the one hand, and deposits and currency, on the other, is not a logical implication of his functional criterion for money. Rather the distinction is a reflection of different unstated assumptions for payments effected by drawing on the different categories of assets. For currency and for deposits, Newlyn implicitly assumes that the recipient wishes to hold the sum transferred in the same kind of asset as that on which the payer drew: that if the payment was made by drawing on currency, the recipient wishes to hold currency; if made by drawing on deposits, the recipient wishes to hold deposits. Make the same assumption for savings and loan deposits, and they too will satisfy Newlyn's criterion. Let the purchaser

market. The same would be true for other durable goods for which it is customary to trade in used items of the same kind.

This is intended not as a criticism, only as an amplification. Newlyn would describe such transactions, we suspect, as a residuum of barter, and would note that he is implicitly referring to a "money" economy in which such transactions can be neglected.

[34] *Ibid.*, p. 335.
[35] *Ibid.*, p. 339.
[36] *Theory of Money*, p. 9.

transfer to the seller the building society's check on a commercial bank and the seller redeposit the check in a building society and both the total of quasi-money and deposits and the loan market will be unaffected.

On the other hand, suppose that the purchaser pays the seller by a check drawn on his own demand deposit at a commercial bank, but that the seller chooses to hold the proceeds in currency and so "cashes" rather than "deposits" the check. The transaction is then nonneutral in precisely the same sense as the withdrawal from the building society. The bank on which the check is drawn, and banks as a whole, to use Newlyn's words, "will need to replenish their [reserve] balances. This they may do by curtailing their lending or by selling securities; in either case the effect will be to add to the demand pressure in the market for loans." Whether the total of currency and deposits under these circumstances will be different than otherwise depends on the point at which the analysis is stopped. If it is stopped before banks have started adjusting to their depleted reserves, the total will be the same. If, as seems more consistent with Newlyn's approach, it is stopped only after the full repercussions on the financial sector of the particular payment, then this total will be less.

Leland Yeager, in his expansion of Newlyn's analysis, recognizes this problem. Indeed, on these grounds he excludes from his definition of money for the United States both time deposits at commercial banks and travelers' checks, the former because—in contrast with the United Kingdom—reserve requirements are different for time and demand deposits, and hence banks do not regard the two classes as the same; and the latter because the issuer of travelers' checks does not hold 100 per cent cash reserves.[37]

He notes that "when demand deposits are cashed in for currency, the drain on reserves limits banks' assets and deposits." But he regards this qualification as "minor" because "if the authorities that create 'high-powered dollars' and the banks, taken together, want to expand the money supply, they can do so. . . . By providing enough reserves to support them, the monetary authorities can maintain any desired amount of demand deposits in existence."[38] He therefore defines money for the United States as currency and demand deposits.

But this lets the cat out of the bag. Clearly, the monetary authorities

37 "Essential Properties of the Medium of Exchange," *Kyklos,* 1968, No. 1, p. 57.
38 *Ibid.,* p. 50, note 8.

and the banks, acting together, can as readily "maintain any desired amount" of total commercial bank deposits "in existence" as of demand deposits alone. If they wish to, they can render "neutral" the conversion of savings and loan shares into currency or demand deposits by absorbing the assets that are the counterpart of the savings and loan liability and creating the currency desired or the reserves required to support the demand deposits desired. Once we permit this escape valve, the "neutrality" criterion loses both its appeal and its definiteness. Strictly speaking, only high-powered money has the characteristic that it "can be drawn upon . . . to produce an increase in aggregate expenditure without . . . a decrease in [the] aggregate of that sort of asset in existence." Similarly, high-powered money is "neutral" in Newlyn's sense, though it requires a somewhat strained interpretation of some ordinary transactions to be able to interpret it as such.

To illustrate, let someone make an expenditure by drawing on a demand deposit. If we are testing Newlyn's criterion on "high-powered money" only, we shall have to interpret this as a joint drawing on two assets: the now quasi-money consisting of (1) the excess of the deposit over its pro rata share of bank-held high-powered money and (2) high-powered money itself. The part of the payment financed by the quasi-money will not be neutral unless the recipient happens to wish to hold it in the same form, which he can do only by redepositing it, along with the high-powered money part, in a bank. For the purchaser to pay in full in high-powered money, he will have to transfer currency. To get the currency by simply drawing down his demand deposit will be a non-neutral transaction (like withdrawing a savings and loan account in Newlyn's example). The only way he could get the cash in a "neutral" way would be by a joint transaction in which he (a) drew down his deposits by an amount such that the high-powered money part was sufficient to make the desired payment, (b) received this part in currency, and (c) used the balance to purchase an asset from the banking system (which could mean repaying a loan). This would provide him with high-powered money without affecting the loan market, since the reserve position of the banking system would not be disturbed by his transactions. If the recipient holds the proceeds in currency, that is clearly "neutral" in Newlyn's sense. If he chooses to hold the proceeds in deposits, that is not simply a money-changing transaction (with high-powered money as the definition of money); it is partly the purchase of a quasi-money asset (nonhigh-powered part of his deposits) and so should not be neutral. In order for him to convert the whole of his currency receipt into a corresponding high-powered money asset at a bank, he would have to deposit a sum such that the high-powered money part corresponded to the currency deposited and to finance the rest of his deposit by borrowing from, or selling an asset to, a bank.

We therefore conclude that if Newlyn's criterion is consistently adhered to, money must be regarded as that part of the medium of exchange the nominal amount of which is outside the control of the actions of the public.[39] Accordingly, it is the same total of high-powered money that must be regarded as money on Pesek's and Saving's net wealth criterion.

Market Equilibrium (Gramley-Chase). Gramley and Chase, in a highly formal analysis of monetary adjustments in the shortest of short periods (Marshall's market equilibrium contrasted with his short-run and long-run equilibria), discuss the definition of money only incidentally.[40] Yet their analysis qualifies for consideration along with the analyses of Pesek and Saving, Newlyn, and Yeager because, like the

[39] Yeager also argues that "asset preferences work asymmetrically. Because of them, a constant supply of actual money can restrain the expansion of near-moneys. But there is no such restraint the other way around: not even some sort of ceiling on near-moneys could keep the monetary authorities from creating as much money as they wished. In the absence of a ceiling, near-moneys tend to gear themselves to the money supply" (*ibid.,* p. 53). In our view there is no such asymmetry. In the absence of a ceiling, let the monetary authorities choose a given quantity of specified near-moneys as their objective. To attain this objective, they would have to let money "gear itself" to the supply of near-moneys (i.e., they would have to let the quantity of high-powered money be whatever is necessary for the quantity of money to be the amount desired, given the specified quantity of near-moneys), so that "a constant supply" of near-moneys "can restrain the expansion" of money.

Yeager goes on, "To dramatize the asymmetry, . . . let us suppose that some official ban on the expansion of near-moneys thwarts this gearing. As the quantity of money expanded beyond what people initially wanted to hold, competition for the fixed supply of near-moneys would drive their yields low enough to keep people indifferent at the margin between them and money. But nothing would keep prices or incomes from rising until people desired to hold all the new money" (pp. 53–54). We might also suppose, however, an "official ban on the expansion" of the nominal quantity of money, coupled with an official desire to expand the quantity of near-moneys beyond the level initially consistent with the quantity of money. To achieve this desire the authorities would raise the yields offered on near-moneys to whatever extent is necessary to induce the public to hold additional near-moneys. This would lower the nominal quantity of money desired at prior prices. But nothing would keep prices or nominal incomes from rising to keep people "indifferent at the margin between" money and near-moneys.

The real asymmetry, if there be any, is on the side of supply, which again means that Yeager's analysis leads to high-powered money, not currency plus demand deposits, as the relevant total.

[40] Lyle E. Gramley and Samuel B. Chase, Jr., "Time Deposits in Monetary Analysis," *Federal Reserve Bulletin,* Oct. 1965, pp. 1380–1404.

others, Gramley and Chase believe that far-reaching substantive conclusions about monetary analysis can be derived from rather simple abstract considerations and, like Newlyn and Yeager,[41] they put great stress on whether the decisions of the public can or do affect monetary totals.[42] That "the stock of money" is "an exogenous variable set by central bank policy," they regard as one of the "time-honored doctrines of traditional monetary analysis." They contrast this "more conventional view" with the "new view" that "open market operations alter the stock of money balances if, and only if, they alter the quantity of money *demanded* by the public." [43]

In their model—and also in the "more conventional view"—only high-powered money is a strictly exogenous variable in the sense that the amount outstanding cannot be altered by transactions among the public or between the public and banks other than the central bank (or monetary authority). The "more conventional view" nonetheless—and correctly—treats the quantity of money (defined more broadly than high-powered money) as, for all practical purposes, "an exogenous variable set by central bank policy" because it accepts the empirical hypothesis that a change in high-powered money will produce private reactions that will rapidly alter the quantity of money *demanded* by the public in a predictable way. Far from incorporating a "new view" in any substantive sense, the Gramley-Chase analysis involves the elaborate spelling out of one minor component of the adjustment process envisaged by the "more conventional view"—the component that consists of the *initial* readjustment of portfolios abstracting both from subsequent portfolio readjustments and from any effects of the initial and subsequent readjustments on spending for current services or on the production of capital goods, or on incomes and prices. As in any Marshallian market equilibrium which holds constant quantities (other than a quantity change that has

[41] Yeager, we should note, explicitly criticizes Gramley and Chase ("Essential Properties of the Medium of Exchange," p. 49, note 7).

[42] In this respect they follow James Tobin, "Commercial Banks as Creators of 'Money'" in *Banking and Monetary Studies,* Deane Carson, ed., Homewood, Ill., 1963, pp. 408–419. Tobin presents a lucid exposition of commercial banks as financial intermediaries with which we agree fully and which we find most illuminating. His analysis, like that of Pesek and Saving, Newlyn, Yeager, and as we shall note, Gramley and Chase, demonstrates that emphasis on supply considerations leads to a distinction between high-powered money and other assets but not between any broader total and other assets. Unlike Gramley and Chase, Tobin explicitly eschews drawing any far-reaching conclusions for policy and analysis from his qualitative analysis.

[43] "Time Deposits in Monetary Analysis," p. 1390.

initiated the adjustment), prices (in this case, interest rates) take the brunt of the adjustment, moving much more than the amount required to clear markets in the short run, let alone the long run.

If Gramley and Chase were to let more items out of the pound of *ceteris paribus,* they would find that the adjustments to open market operations would spread in such a way as to reduce the direct impact on interest rates and increase the effect on the quantity of money. Accordingly, they would find less reason to distinguish between the alleged "new view" and the "more conventional view." Even on the level of portfolio adjustment alone, still abstracting from effects on spending, income, and prices, the particular securities initially affected by an open market operation (the securities purchased and sold by the central bank plus, under the Gramley-Chase assumptions, bank assets) are only part of the whole structure of assets.

Let the central bank make an open market purchase of a particular category of securities. To induce holders of the securities to sell, it will have to raise the price (i.e., lower the yield). This will induce some holders to part with securities, accepting money in return. Gramley and Chase stop their analysis at this point—treating the seller of securities as if he were in equilibrium with respect to his asset structure. But this is only the first reaction. The seller of the securities accepted money not as a permanent abode of his wealth to replace the securities sold but— as for all other purchases and sales in a money economy—a temporary abode, pending the opportunity to buy alternative assets. As he attempts to buy other assets, he raises their prices, spreading the effect on interest rates but at the same time moderating the effect on the initial assets considered.

As the prices of existing assets are bid up, it becomes more advantageous to produce rather than to buy such assets, to rent service flows rather than buy existing sources of services. This spreads the effect to spending, income, and prices, further moderating initial interest rate effects.

It is instructive to have the initial component of this adjustment process spelled out in detail, as Gramley and Chase have done. But it is scarcely justifiable, to say the least, to leap as they do from the wholly abstract analysis of this minor component to substantive conclusions about the process as a whole—to express judgments, as it were, about a man's physiognomy, character, and familial relations on the basis of a microscopic examination of his finger tips.[44]

2. "Liquidity"

We turn now to a view that is at the opposite end of a continuum. The view of "liquidity" as the essential characteristic of money has been stressed in the United States largely as a result of the pioneering work on financial intermediaries by Gurley and Shaw. They argued that the liabilities of nonbank financial intermediaries are close substitutes for currency and commercial bank deposits, that such liabilities may be expected to grow secularly relative to currency and bank deposits and, in the course of cyclical fluctuations, to change in the opposite direction thereby frustrating attempts by monetary authorities to affect the economy by controlling the quantity of currency and bank deposits.[45] This view, put forward tentatively by Gurley and Shaw, was asserted—almost

[44] To illustrate: They state correctly that "central bank actions do not affect the actual money stock except as they lead to a change in desired money balances. The effect of these actions on money income occurs not because the money stock has been altered, but because financial variables through which the central bank alters the desired stock of money also affect the public's decisions to purchase goods and services" (*ibid.*, p. 1403). (Equivalent: The rabbit was killed not because the hunter pressed the trigger but because the bullet hit it.)

From this they conclude, "Whether financial markets ever behaved in such a way as to permit . . . changes in the money stock [to be interpreted as an appropriate indicator of monetary policy conducted through conventional means] is debatable, but there is little doubt that such a simple rule for appraisal of central bank operations is no longer appropriate" (p. 1403).

This may or may not be true, but it cannot be inferred from a theoretical analysis alone, let alone from one that omits what many analysts would consider the most important aspects of the adjustment process. It requires some empirical evidence, none of which is presented or even adverted to by Gramley and Chase.

[45] John G. Gurley and Edward S. Shaw, "Financial Aspects of Economic Development," *American Economic Review*, Sept. 1955, pp. 515–538; "Financial Intermediaries and the Savings-Investment Process," *Journal of Finance*, May 1956, pp. 257–276; "The Growth of Debt and Money in the United States, 1800–1950: A Suggested Interpretation," *Review of Economics and Statistics*, Aug. 1957, pp. 250–262; *Money in a Theory of Finance*, Washington, D.C., 1960.

Gurley and Shaw themselves do not regard their analysis as requiring, or even suggesting, that "money" be defined as the sum of all liquid assets. Rather they view it as contributing to an understanding of the relation between money and other economic magnitudes, however money is defined. In another context, Gurley has experimented with defining money as the weighted sum of different categories of assets. (See *Liquidity and Financial Institutions in the Postwar Period*, Study Paper No. 14, U.S. Congress, Joint Economic Committee, Study of Employment, Growth, and Price Levels, Washington, D.C., 1960, pp. 7–8.) In a discussion of policy, Shaw has defined money as equal to currency plus demand deposits adjusted ("Money Supply and Stable Economic Growth," *United States Monetary Policy*, New York, American Assembly, 1958, pp. 49–71).

without qualification—in the *Report* by the Radcliffe Committee on the Working of the Monetary System: ". . . monetary action works upon total demand by altering the liquidity position of financial institutions and of firms and people desiring to spend on real resources; the supply of money itself is not the critical factor." [46] "We must," wrote Sayers, one of the chief authors of the *Radcliffe Report,* "put, in the place conventionally occupied by 'the supply of money,' " a "wide concept of liquid assets" as "the monetary quantity influencing total effective demand for goods and services." Just as, in the course of the nineteenth century, notes became, as Keynes pointed out, the "small change" of bank money, so "in an important sense, bank deposits have already become the small change of the system. . . . 'Commercial banks' shade into industrial banks, savings banks and building societies, and these into a host of other financial intermediaries; the liabilities of these are close substitutes for each other, so that a clamping down on one group will not create such an abrupt scarcity of liquidity as will have a worthwhile impact on the pressure of total demand." [47]

Sayers and others who take the same view may be right. As noted earlier, there is a priori no reason why a fairly narrowly defined subtotal of liquid assets should have any special importance. With this version, as with the version stressing the strict medium of exchange function, the issue is an empirical one to be settled by an appeal to the facts. Sayers recognizes this, yet neither he nor other proponents of the broad "liquidity" approach have offered more than the most casual empirical observations to support their assertions—in Sayers' case frequently expressed in an unqualified manner as what we "must" do—even when the assertions run counter to the judgment of many economists over a long period.

Several studies have been made in recent years to test various aspects of the Gurley-Shaw and Radcliffe Committee empirical conjectures; in particular, to investigate whether the liabilities of financial intermediaries do in fact behave in such a way as to offset the movements in currency and commercial bank deposits over the cycle; and to estimate the degree of substitutability among various liquid assets. No tested conclusion has

---

[46] *Radcliffe Report,* Cmnd. 827, 1959, para. 397 (d).

[47] R. S. Sayers, "Monetary Thought and Policy in England," *Economic Journal,* Dec. 1960, pp. 712, 721–724. The reference to Keynes is to *A Treatise on Money,* Vol. I, p. 40. These conclusions are sharply criticized by Newlyn in both *Theory of Money* and "The Supply of Money and Its Control," as well as by Roy Harrod, "Is the Money Supply Important?" *Westminster Bank Review,* Nov. 1959, pp. 3–7.

yet emerged from these studies. It is perhaps fair to say that, taken as a whole, the evidence is adverse to the Gurley-Shaw thesis that the movements in the liabilities of financial intermediaries severely hinder the effectiveness of monetary policies.[48] In regard to substitutability, all of the studies show that various assets are substitutes for one another to some degree, as is to be expected. Estimates of the degree of substitutability differ, but the major difference among authors is less in the numerical size of the elasticities they find, than in the adjectives they use to describe the size. The same numerical elasticity is described by one author as showing that the assets are "close" substitutes, by another that they are "weak" or "distant" substitutes.[49] This ambiguity reflects the absence of any clear purpose in terms of which to judge the size of the elasticity.

Definition of Liquidity

In discussing the medium-of-exchange criterion, we noted that it offered an uncertain guide to the classification of assets into those that serve as a medium of exchange and those that do not. This difficulty is

[48] See Carl F. Christ, "Interest Rates and 'Portfolio Selection' Among Liquid Assets in the U.S.," *Measurement in Economics: Studies in Mathematical Economics and Econometrics,* in Memory of Yehuda Grunfeld, 1963, pp. 201–218; Edgar L. Feige, *The Demand for Liquid Assets: A Temporal Cross-Section Analysis,* Englewood Cliffs, N.J., 1964, pp. 24 ff.; Allan H. Meltzer, "The Demand for Money: The Evidence from the Time Series," *Journal of Political Economy,* June 1963, pp. 227, 230. Meltzer's finding that the growth of financial intermediaries produced primarily a wealth effect and not a substitution effect was challenged by T. J. Courchene and H. T. Shapiro on the grounds that (1) his regression procedure was not a useful method to measure the extent of the substitution effect, with respect to interest rates, between the various monetary variables, and (2) his conclusion was not based on relevant evidence. Additional evidence that they presented, however, supported Meltzer's conclusion ("The Demand for Money: A Note from the Time Series," *Journal of Political Economy,* Oct. 1964, pp. 498–500). Tong Hun Lee reported findings adverse to the Gurley-Shaw thesis in "Income, Wealth, and the Demand for Money: Some Evidence from Cross-Section Data," *Journal of the American Statistical Association,* Sept. 1964, pp. 746–762, and findings favorable to the thesis in "Substitutability of Non-Bank Intermediary Liabilities for Money," *Journal of Finance,* Sept. 1966, pp. 448–452. David Fand concludes that the Gurley-Shaw effect is "an assumption rather than a proposition derived from empirical evidence" ("Some Implications of Money Supply Analysis," *American Economic Review,* May 1967, p. 392).

See also F. P. R. Brechling and R. G. Lipsey, "Trade Credit and Monetary Policy," *Economic Journal,* Dec. 1963, pp. 618–641. They find that trade credit is "at least a very strong potential frustrator of monetary policy." W. H. White disputes this conclusion, arguing that if proper allowance is made for bias in the data cited in support, "trade credit yields a completely negligible offset to monetary policy in all years" ("Trade Credit and Monetary Policy: A Reconciliation," *Economic Journal,* Dec. 1964, p. 944). A rejoinder appeared in the March 1966 issue of the same periodical (pp. 165–167), a mimeographed reply by White in May 1967, and a further mimeographed analysis by Brechling and Lipsey in June 1967. See also Chapter 4, footnote 5.

[49] See Chapter 4, pp. 181–184.

minor for the medium-of-exchange criterion. The corresponding difficulty is major for the "liquidity" criterion.

Attempts to define "liquidity" precisely have failed to produce anything like a consensus. Consequently, the term is usually used without precise definition, different writers stressing different characteristics of assets. Whatever common content there is to the notion of "liquidity" at the present stage of development is multidimensional and does not provide an unambiguous way to classify assets by degree of liquidity, let alone to draw a line between assets that can be termed "nonliquid" and those "liquid" assets whose total value Sayers and others would put in "the place conventionally occupied by 'the supply of money.' " [50]

One dimension often stressed in discussions of "liquidity" is the ability to sell an asset on demand (more precisely, within a specified time interval) for a nominal sum fixed in advance (i.e., to convert the asset into a fixed nominal number of units of "money").[51] By this measure, Series E U.S. government bonds and cash surrender values of life insurance policies are almost perfectly liquid. So also are time deposits and savings and loan shares, given that banks and savings and loan associations in practice honor requests for conversion on demand. These assets would not be liquid by this measure if the banks and associations exercised their legal right to require extended notice before conversion. Marketable U.S. government securities, corporate bonds, commercial paper, and corporate equities are nonliquid (or less liquid than the other items) by this measure.

Another dimension frequently stressed in discussions of liquidity is the degree of perfection of the market in the asset as manifested in the ready salability of the asset at a well-defined market price. This dimension can be measured by the difference between the price at which the asset can be purchased and the price at which it can be sold at any particular time (more precisely, within a specified time interval). In other words, the dimension can be measured by the range between the

[50] See Arthur L. Broida, "Liquidity as a Variable in Monetary Analysis," unpublished Ph.D. dissertation, University of Chicago, 1963; also J. R. Hicks, "Liquidity," *Economic Journal,* Dec. 1962, pp. 787–802, and *Critical Essays in Monetary Theory,* New York, 1967, essays 1–3 on the "Two Triads."

[51] When this approach is taken, it is with the implicit qualification that the nominal sum fixed in advance is equal to or close to the sum paid for the asset or to its "value" calculated in some nonmarket way (e.g., initial amount paid plus accumulated interest). Otherwise, puts and calls, for example, would convert equities into perfectly liquid assets by this definition.

"bid" and "ask" prices, both including any brokerage charges.[52] By this measure, most marketable U.S. securities are highly liquid assets, typically more liquid, for example, than savings and loan shares, the withdrawal of which may involve a loss of accumulated interest amounting to a larger fraction of the sum withdrawn than the bid-and-asked range on, say, Treasury bills of the same amount. Similarly, by this measure, equity stocks or corporate bonds traded on major stock exchanges are clearly highly liquid assets, much more so, for example, than holdings of British or Japanese currency by a U.S. citizen.

This discussion is not intended to be exhaustive.[53] It is intended only to suggest that the use of the term "liquidity" conceals more conceptual problems than it resolves.

Statistical Counterparts Used

Diversity characterizes not only the dimensions of liquidity stressed in conceptual discussions but also the statistical counterparts to liquid assets used in empirical studies.[54] In the United States, surveys of consumer finances, including ownership of liquid assets, have been conducted for the Board of Governors of the Federal Reserve System from 1946 on. Prior to 1957, the surveys treated as liquid assets demand deposits, savings deposits, shares in savings and loan associations and credit unions, U.S. savings bonds, and marketable U.S. government securities. Thereafter, marketable government securities were dropped from the definition of liquid assets (currency holdings have never been obtained).[55] In addition, the Federal Reserve constructed annual estimates

[52] Note that the bid-and-asked range will typically be a function of the period of time allowed to sell the asset. Therefore by this measure asset A may be more liquid than asset B if a day is specified as the time interval, while B may be more liquid than A if a month is specified as the time interval.

[53] Broida's dissertation ("Liquidity as a Variable in Monetary Analysis") indicates what a major undertaking that involves.

[54] In the United Kingdom, the Radcliffe Committee did not agree upon a concept of liquidity, much less develop a statistical measure of it. In a survey of liquid assets of nonfarm families in Canada conducted by the Dominion Bureau of Statistics, liquid assets are defined to include current accounts, savings accounts, other deposits, and all bond holdings, whether obligations of the Government of Canada, other public authorities, or corporations (*Income, Liquid Assets and Indebtedness of Non-Farm Families in Canada, 1955*, Reference Paper No. 80, Dominion Bureau of Statistics, 1958).

[55] See *Federal Reserve Bulletin*, Mar. 1959, p. 251. The same definition of liquid assets was used in the survey of financial characteristics of consumers, conducted for the Board of Governors, in 1962 (*ibid.*, Mar. 1964, p. 290), and in a Survey Research Center study (*Consumer Behavior of Individual Families Over Two and Three Years*, R. F. Kosobud and J. N. Morgan, eds., Monograph 36, Institute for Social Research, University of Michigan, 1964, pp. 76–78).
Data based on the earlier definition of liquid assets, including government securities,

of liquid asset holdings of individuals and businesses, 1939–54, in which liquid assets were defined as currency, demand deposits, time deposits, savings and loan shares, and U.S. government securities.[56] More recently, the Federal Reserve has published estimates of the public's holdings of "selected" liquid assets, restricting the coverage of government securities included to U.S. savings bonds and short-term government securities.[57] It has also published a chart of liquid asset holdings, defined as above, except that U.S. savings bonds are excluded.[58]

SEC quarterly estimates of savings of individuals in the U.S. have been used to derive quarterly estimates of liquid assets.[59] Through 1957, the SEC estimates included a subtotal labeled "total liquid saving," which changed in composition, becoming less inclusive over the period it was shown.[60] The flow-of-funds accounting system has since superseded the SEC individual savings data as the source of quarterly estimates of liquid assets, but users must still decide for themselves which items to include in the total.[61]

were used by Mordechai E. Kreinin, "Analysis of Liquid Asset Ownership," *Review of Economics and Statistics,* Feb. 1961, p. 76, and by Harold W. Guthrie, "Consumer Propensities to Hold Liquid Assets," *Journal of the American Statistical Association,* Sept. 1960. Guthrie commented: "Currency and the cash surrender value of life insurance policies, although liquid in the economic sense, are not included in the surveys for technical reasons" (p. 470).

[56] Klein and Goldberger's econometric model of the U.S. (L. R. Klein and A. S. Goldberger, *An Econometric Model of the United States, 1929–1952,* Amsterdam, 1955) relied on these Federal Reserve liquid asset estimates.

[57] S. H. Axilrod, "Liquidity and Public Policy," *Federal Reserve Bulletin,* Oct. 1961, p. 1168.

[58] D. H. Brill, "Recent Changes in Liquidity," *Federal Reserve Bulletin,* June 1963. The author notes: ". . . any operational definition must be somewhat arbitrary. Given the availability and quality of data, attempts at further refinement in measurement are not likely to add substantially to understanding and insight" (p. 757).

[59] Zellner used SEC bench mark estimates of currency, deposits, savings and loan shares, and U.S. savings bonds to obtain quarterly estimates by cumulating individual quarterly saving or dissaving in these forms, 1947 I–1955 I (Arnold Zellner, "The Short-Run Consumption Function," *Econometrica,* Oct. 1957, p. 559). Griliches *et al.* replaced Zellner's estimates beginning 1952 I and extended them through 1961 II, substituting flow-of-funds data described in the text. With one minor exception (the exclusion of individuals' business liquid assets, which Zellner had included), there is no difference in definition of the estimates in the two segments (Z. Griliches, G. S. Maddala, R. Lucas, and N. Wallace, "Notes on Estimated Quarterly Consumption Functions," *Econometrica,* July 1962, pp. 491–500). Zellner adopted the series as revised by Griliches in subsequent work (A. Zellner, D. S. Huang, and L. C. Chau, "Further Analysis of the Short-Run Consumption Function," *Econometrica,* July 1965, pp. 571–581).

[60] When the subtotal included the change in currency and bank deposits, savings and loan shares, private insurance, securities, mortgage debt, and consumer and other debt, it was used as a measure of change in liquid assets by Morris Cohen, "Liquid Assets and the Consumption Function," *Review of Economics and Statistics,* May 1954, p. 210.

[61] A definition including currency, demand deposits, and fixed-value redeemable claims (savings deposits, savings and loan shares, U.S. savings bonds) is used by D. B. Suits, in "The Determinants of Consumer Expenditure: A Review of Present Knowl-

Data on liquid asset holdings have been obtained from sources other than the regularly reported ones thus far listed, and the definitions used have varied with the user. Liquid asset holdings of a sample of home-buyers were defined as "lender-confirmed bank deposits, stocks, and bonds." [62] Business holdings of liquid assets are frequently defined as cash and marketable securities, or as cash and government obligations.[63]

In short, numerous statistical measures of liquid assets that include a very wide variety of items in various combinations have been used. Indeed, almost the only broad class of assets that has uniformly been excluded is physical capital. And the differences among the various totals used have been far from trivial. The dollar value of a fairly comprehensive total can easily be double that of a fairly restrictive total.[64]

Theoretical Analysis

This diversity in usage reflects in part the absence of an explicit, consistent application of the theoretical approach under discussion. Let us, therefore, tentatively accept the empirical judgments that we believe are implicit in the "liquidity" approach and see whether we can specify more precisely the monetary total that this approach recommends. The key empirical judgments, we believe, are as follows: (1) The critical distinction to holders of wealth is not between *nominal* and *real* assets

edge," in *Impacts of Monetary Policy,* Commission on Money and Credit, Englewood Cliffs, N.J., 1963, pp. 1–57; and D. B. Suits and G. R. Sparks, "Consumption Regressions with Quarterly Data," *The Brookings Quarterly Econometric Model of the United States.* J. S. Duesenberry *et al.* (ed.), Chicago, 1965, pp. 210, 222.

[62] D. B. Rathbun, "Liquid Assets: A Neglected Factor in the Formulation of Housing Finance Policies," *Journal of Finance,* Dec. 1952, p. 547.

[63] Two studies in which the first definition is used are: F. E. Norton, "Some Cross-Sectional Explorations in Investment Behavior," *Southern Economic Journal,* Jan. 1956, p. 332 (the author lists ten different liquidity variables of which liquid assets is one); Yehuda Grunfeld, "The Determinants of Corporate Investment," unpublished Ph.D. dissertation, University of Chicago, 1958. Two examples of the use of the second definition are M. Cohen and M. R. Gainsbrugh, "Capital Appropriations: Durables Spark Recovery," *The Conference Board Business Record,* June 1959, p. 263; E. Kuh and J. R. Meyer, "Investment, Liquidity, and Monetary Policy," in *Impacts of Monetary Policy,* p. 353.

[64] For example, on June 29, 1960, the value of separate categories of financial assets held by the public was as follows (in billions of dollars):

1. Currency	28.3	7. Cash surrender value of life insurance policies (policy reserves)	98.5
2. Demand deposits	107.8		
3. Commercial bank time deposits	67.4	8. Short-term marketable U.S. government securities	42.0
4. Mutual savings bank deposits	35.4		
5. Savings and loan shares	58.3	9. Other U.S. government securities	59.6
6. U.S. savings bonds	47.5	10. State and local securities	52.2
		11. Private marketable bonds	161.3

The sum of items 1 to 6, which would be a fairly restrictive definition, is $345 billion; the sum of items 1 to 11, a fairly comprehensive total, is $758 billion.

but between short-dated and long-dated assets, whether nominal or real (more fundamentally, assets with "low" and "high" capital risk).[65] (2) There exists a set of relative returns on short-dated assets at which the public is largely indifferent to the composition of its portfolio of such assets and issuers of such securities are largely indifferent to the composition of their liabilities. As a result, relative quantities can fluctuate considerably with little fluctuation in relative yields (a partial liquidity trap). (3) The public desires to hold a fairly constant total amount of such assets relative to its spending,[66] or, alternatively, shifts in the ratio of such assets to all other assets produce changes in the level of interest rates on such assets, both absolutely and relative to the rates on other assets, which have significant effects on spending for current resource services.

This discussion is in terms of "assets" but clearly its logic requires that "debts" be treated as "negative" assets. This has in fact been suggested by some writers.[67] If the total is to include short-dated assets (as assets with little capital risk), it should also include short-dated debts (with equally little capital risk), since an asset that matures at the same date as a debt provides no net purchasing power to the holder of the asset. Similarly, the logic of the approach suggests treating the translations in parentheses in the preceding sentence not as translations but as additional conditions. The empirical judgment is that most short-dated assets and liabilities have little capital risk—because changes in interest rates have little effect on their present value—and hence that a total of short-dated assets and liabilities can be used as an approximation to the total of assets and liabilities subject to little capital risk. But it might be better to use the low capital risk criterion directly, to allow for types of

[65] See Axel Leijonhufvud, *On Keynesian Economics and the Economics of Keynes: A Study in Monetary Theory*, New York, 1968, pp. 146–149, for a persuasive argument that when Keynes distinguished between "money" and "bonds" in *The General Theory*, he intended this distinction rather than the distinction that has been used by later writers between money, interpreted as noninterest-bearing assets, and all other assets of whatever period.

As for real vs. nominal, note that the view under discussion has been supported largely by economists who follow Keynes' practice of treating the price level as rigid and who therefore tend to treat real and nominal magnitudes as synonymous.

[66] This proposition is less clear than the other two. However, it is necessary if any total is to have significance. In particular, it would be strongly denied by those economists who regard a full liquidity trap as empirically important. But they would deny significance to any total short of total wealth and perhaps even to that.

[67] Albert G. Hart, *Money, Debt, and Economic Activity*, New York, 1948, p. 134; and "Uses of National Wealth Estimates and the Structure of Claims," *Studies in Income and Wealth*, Vol. 12, New York, NBER, 1950, pp. 86–87.

risk other than changes in interest rates. For example, short-term personal loans stated in nominal value may have considerable capital risk; inventories are a real asset that may have considerable capital risk, not because of changes in interest rates or in the general price level but because of changes in relative prices. It is on this ground that followers of this approach would exclude most real assets—even the short-dated, a category in which inventories can be classified.

A central notion in this approach is the distinction between "financial intermediaries" and the rest of the public. This distinction plays the same role as the distinction between "banks" and the nonbank public in more conventional definitions of money.[68] Just as, in our measures of "money," we exclude vault cash and interbank deposits, so, in measuring the liquidity total, we must exclude short-dated assets held by financial intermediaries and not subtract their short-dated debts.[69] Unless this is done, the subtraction of short-dated debts would involve the cancellation of the corresponding short-dated assets, since one person's or institution's liability is some other person's or institution's asset. For example, consider trade credit, which is one of the items that has been extensively discussed. Trade credit is a short-term liability of some firms and a short-term asset of others. If neither set of firms is treated as financial intermediaries, the assets and liabilities will cancel. In order to avoid cancellation, one would have to treat the firms owing the liabilities as financial intermediaries, which seems very strained usage indeed.[70] The same considerations apply to short-term commercial paper.

The notion "short-dated" is also rather arbitrary—is it to be taken to mean one day, one week, one month, three months? This could be handled in principle by constructing a series of estimates, $L(m)$, where m is the maturity regarded as separating short-dated from long-dated assets and liabilities.

[68] See Joseph M. Burns, "The Saving-Investment Process in a Theory of Finance," unpublished Ph.D. dissertation, University of Chicago, 1967, for a discussion of the meaning and role of financial intermediation.

[69] To the best of our knowledge, all liquid asset totals actually constructed have neglected this caveat and so have introduced double-counting—e.g., currency and commercial bank deposits have been added to liabilities of savings and loan associations without subtracting currency and commercial bank deposits held by associations.

[70] Of course, theoretically there is no necessity for a dollar of debt to have negative "liquidity" equal in absolute value to the positive "liquidity" of a dollar of assets. This point is essentially the same as the one we have referred to in suggesting the possibility that money might be defined as a weighted aggregate of selected assets. A corresponding variant of the liquidity approach would be to weight assets differently from liabilities.

If we neglect capital risks other than those arising from changing interest rates (i.e., neglect risks from default, changing relative prices, etc.), and let m approach infinity, then $L(m)$ would approach total national wealth, equal, after consolidation, to real wealth plus high-powered money, if individuals are regarded as treating the obligation to pay taxes to finance interest payments on government debt as a liability. If individuals do not regard this obligation as a liability, then net government debt would be added to real wealth and high-powered money.

This limiting process makes it clear that this approach stresses the division of total wealth into two parts—one that asset holders regard as subject to control over short periods and that they try and are able to keep in a fairly consistent relation with their spending, the other that asset holders regard as not subject to control except over longer periods and that they are willing to let vary considerably relative to spending. Rates of interest can vary considerably between the two parts of wealth but, within each part, different rates are fairly fixed in relation to one another. Changes between the two sets of rates of interest are the major channel through which policies altering the total of the liquid assets are believed to affect economic activity.[71]

This approach is an appropriate theoretical counterpart to an analysis of changes in income and expenditures along Keynesian lines. That analysis takes the price level as an institutional datum and therefore minimizes the distinction between nominal and real magnitudes. It takes interest rates as essentially the only market variable that reconciles the structure of assets supplied with the structure demanded.[72]

The usefulness of the approach is, of course, an empirical, not a theoretical, question. On this, there is much assertion but little hard evidence.

[71] See Radcliffe Committee; Sayers; Gramley and Chase; and Tobin, *oper. cit.*

[72] It is instructive that economists who adopt this general view typically write as if the monetary authorities could determine the real and not merely the nominal quantity of high-powered money. For example, William C. Brainard and James Tobin in setting up a financial model to illustrate pitfalls in the building of such models use "the replacement value of . . . physical assets . . . as the numeraire of the system," yet regard "the supply of reserves" as "one of the quantities the central bank directly controls" ("Pitfalls in Financial Model-Building," *American Economic Review*, May 1968, pp. 101–102). If the nominal level of prices is regarded as an endogenous variable, this is clearly wrong. Hence the writers must be assuming this nominal level of prices to be fixed outside their system.

Keynes' "wage unit" serves the same role in his analysis and leads him and his followers also to treat the monetary authorities as directly controlling real and not nominal variables.

3. Conclusion on A Priori Approaches

A key difference between the two theoretical approaches considered in
this chapter is that the medium-of-exchange approach stresses conditions of supply and the liquidity approach stresses conditions of demand.
With each the aim is to determine a total that can be regarded as both
homogeneous and economically significant—according to the first approach, because the public cannot affect the aggregate amount of the
total; according to the second approach, because the public is largely
indifferent to the internal composition of the total, yet concerned about
its size relative to other assets and to the level of spending.

The approach stressing the medium-of-exchange function of money
has the virtue of possessing a fairly clear empirical counterpart. Ad-
mittedly, there is some ambiguity in the specific assets that serve as
literal media of exchange; and the assets that serve this function will
differ from time to time and place to place. But for any one time and
place the ambiguity is likely to be confined to a narrow range. For the
United States at present, most observers would agree that currency, demand deposits, and American Express travelers' checks should for the
most part be regarded as media of exchange and that no other substantial items should be.

However, it turns out that when the approach is developed more
formally and systematically, its empirical counterpart, while clear, is
different from that assigned to it by its proponents. High-powered money,
not currency plus demand deposits, is the total that has the autonomy
and the "net worth" or "neutrality" quality suggested as relevant criteria.

Even at first sight the "liquidity" approach does not have a reasonably clear empirical counterpart. It is frequently treated as providing at
least a reasonably unambiguous way of ordering assets. But even this
impression derives primarily from the failure to specify in any precise
way the meaning of liquidity. Any attempt to do so demonstrates that
there are different dimensions of the general concept that provide very
different orderings of assets. Statistical totals used to approximate the
concept have varied widely in composition.

This variation partly reflects a failure to apply consistently the central theoretical approach, which calls for considering both assets and

liabilities and stressing the capital risk involved in reducing assets or adding to liabilities to finance current spending.

We consider the prominence that the medium-of-exchange approach assigns to the distinction between nominal and real assets to be valid, but we regard the approach as an unsatisfactory basis for defining money for two reasons: first, as is pointed out in section 4, we have been led to stress conditions of demand rather than of supply in defining "money"; second, we see no compelling reason to regard the literal medium-of-exchange function as the "essential" function of the items we wish to call "money."

We consider the stress that the liquidity approach assigns to conditions of demand to be valid, but we do not accept the basic empirical judgments underlying the versions of it that have been most prominent in the theoretical literature—especially the judgment that the price level is to be regarded as primarily an institutional datum.

We conclude that the definition of money is to be sought for not on grounds of principle but on grounds of usefulness in organizing our knowledge of economic relationships. "Money" is that to which we choose to assign a number by specified operations; it is not something in existence to be discovered, like the American continent; it is a tentative scientific construct to be invented, like "length" or "temperature" or "force" in physics.

4. Relevant Empirical Considerations

We warn the reader that, as so often occurs in scientific work, the section that follows was written after the event, and is an attempt ex post to systematize what we did. We cannot claim that it guided us explicitly in our initial choice.

It is much easier to see why a priori considerations cannot decide the proper empirical counterpart to the concept "money" than it is to state at all comprehensively the considerations that are relevant. These depend in part on the availability of data for a sufficiently long period and for fine enough time units; in part on the developing theory in accordance with which we interpret the empirical data; and in part on the difficulties and problems that have arisen in analyzing experience with the help of the theory and in improving the theory with the help of experience.

Statistical Considerations

Little of a general nature can be said about the purely statistical considerations, even though they play a major role in determining the definition of money (see Chapter 4). Data are almost always a by-product of reports made for business reasons or to satisfy regulatory agencies. This means that the data almost always refer to the institutions that specialize in the issuance of "money" or claims (governments, banks, other financial institutions), not to the holders of claims. The issuance of money or claims is the main or major activity of the issuers; the holding of such assets is but one of many activities of the holders. Hence the issuers are concentrated and lend themselves to reporting and regulation; the holders are dispersed and their information on holdings of claims is imbedded in reports on their major activities. That is why most sets of monetary statistics are based on reports of issuers, not of holders. A further corollary, relevant to the problem of definition, is that the inevitable element of statistical arbitrariness is minimized for any magnitudes that reflect the condition of an issuing institution as a whole and do not require a separation of major accounts into categories that have or have had no relevance to its business operations or to regulatory agencies. For our purposes, the main example of this is that there is less arbitrariness in estimating the total deposits of commercial banks in excess of their high-powered money holdings than in estimating demand and time deposits separately in excess of the high-powered money holdings relevant to each category of deposits (see Chapter 1, section 4).

Nominal vs. Real; Demand vs. Supply

The key proposition of monetary theory that seems to us relevant to the definition of money is the distinction between the "nominal" and the "real" quantity of money, a distinction which underlies the determination of the "price level." This distinction is of crucial importance because of the associated empirical generalization that the nominal quantity of money is determined primarily by conditions of supply (production conditions for specie, institutional and legal arrangements for fiat money and fiduciary money), while the real quantity of money is determined primarily by conditions of demand (the balances that holders of money wish to hold—given their circumstances, the level of prices, and the market costs of and returns to holding money).

Our aim is to formulate an empirical definition of money that will facilitate, as far as possible, the separation and analysis of the forces of demand and supply for the country or countries and period or periods being studied. Or to express the same point in a forward-looking context, a definition that will enable us most readily and accurately to predict the consequences for important economic variables of a change in the conditions of demand for or supply of money. The economic variables that we regard as important for this purpose are nominal and real income, prices, and interest rates.

Why We Stress Demand

Our purpose was primarily the analysis of monetary experience in the United States over a long period. Our historical studies convinced us that conditions of supply had changed fairly drastically over the period, so that there was little hope of getting a single fairly simple supply function of nominal money that would hold for the period as a whole.[73] It was not clear that this was true to anywhere near the same extent for conditions of demand. Hence, we were led to put primary emphasis on demand and to seek a definition of money that could be regarded as having as nearly as possible the same meaning to the holders of money balances over the entire period of our study.

Since we began our studies, we have been impressed that this consideration is of much wider relevance. Among different countries, and in any one country over time, conditions of supply of nominal assets of the class generally regarded as money or near-money differ widely. On the other hand, our own work and the work of other scholars suggests that conditions of demand are much less variable and that most of the differences among countries or periods in the real quantities of such nominal assets can be explained by differences in a small number of key variables. These findings have reinforced our belief that it is desirable to emphasize the conditions of demand in defining money.

To express the same point in more specific terms: the desideratum is a monetary total whose real value (measured as the ratio of the total to a price index or as a ratio to a measure of total income or transactions,

[73] The words "fairly simple" are included in this sentence because there is always a stable function for anything, if the number of variables included can be indefinitely large.

i.e., as the inverse of a velocity) bears a relatively stable relation (as between the different time periods or geographical areas under study) to a small number of variables that theoretical considerations lead us to believe affect the real quantity of money demanded—in particular, real wealth or income and the cost of holding money as measured by interest rates and the rate of change in prices. This desideratum recommends the consolidation into a single total of different monetary items, the relative size of which is likely either to be more heavily influenced by conditions of supply than by conditions of demand or to have little effect on the total amount that demanders wish to hold.

Substitution in Demand

The clearest illustration is presented by items that are near-perfect substitutes to holders of money balances. In the United States, for example, holders of money balances have seldom paid any attention to whether the notes in their pockets were U.S. Treasury notes of 1890, or greenbacks, or national bank notes, or Federal Reserve notes, or Federal Reserve Bank notes, or, before the 1960's, silver certificates, or, between 1879 and 1933, gold certificates. These items were near-perfect substitutes to the bulk of holders the bulk of the time—though the necessity to insert some qualifying dates indicates that this statement is very much a matter of time and place and not to be taken for granted without substantive knowledge.[74] Because these items were near-perfect substitutes, holders of money did not react to a shift in the proportions in which they were available. They were willing passively to accept them in whatever proportions they were issued. Knowledge of the proportions does not enable us to predict anything about the behavior of the holders of notes that we cannot predict simply from knowledge of the total. To explain the proportions we must look to conditions of supply, and we can largely end the analysis at that point without having to take into account any repercussions on the side of demand.[75]

[74] Another example: national bank notes did not satisfy legal reserve requirements for national banks, hence were not at all perfect substitutes for "legal tender" to those banks.

[75] Again this is a place-time limited generalization that has its exceptions. For example, the conditions of issuance of U.S. Treasury notes of 1890 were such as to produce fears of indefinite multiplication that might force the nation off the gold standard; hence the conditions of issuance induced expectations that affected the quantity of money demanded.

More generally, the limitations imposed on issuance of notes in the form of reserve requirements, asset backing, quantity limits, etc., attest the power of the possible reflex influence on demand.

The extent of substitutability in demand is much harder to determine on the basis of casual empiricism for monetary items other than currency. It is customary to proceed next to deposits transferable by check (we shall follow current usage and use "demand deposits" as a synonym, though, as explained in Chapter 8, this is not literally correct) and to regard such deposits as clearly the "nearest" thing to currency and the next candidate for inclusion in a total to be called "money."

Initially, we accepted the customary view. As a result, the systematic empirical tests—summarized in Chapter 4—that we made to choose among different monetary totals did not even consider totals that excluded demand deposits but included other categories of deposits. As our research has proceeded, we have become more and more dubious that we did the right thing, and if we were starting anew we might well follow a different course.

The most important single distinction on the side of demand is probably between business and personal holdings of money—even though there exists no sound statistical basis for separate estimates. However, we do know that until the recent development of large negotiable time certificates of deposit, businesses held negligible amounts as time deposits at commercial banks, mutual savings banks, or savings and loan associations; that they held much larger amounts as demand deposits than as currency; and that very probably business balances account for the bulk of demand deposits but for less than half of currency. For business firms, the customary view seems entirely valid: demand deposits are close substitutes in demand for currency as a medium of exchange.

The situation is very different for individuals (ultimate wealth-holders). It appears that more individuals have time deposit accounts (at commercial banks or other institutions) than have demand deposit accounts; and clearly individuals hold a far larger total amount as time deposits than as demand deposits.[76] For them, the relationship between

[76] For decades the number of time and savings deposit accounts has persistently exceeded the number of demand deposit accounts (see FDIC, *Annual Report,* 1964, p. 78). For at least five reasons, however, the difference in numbers of accounts is not a reliable indication of the difference in number of individuals owning time but not demand deposits. (1) Each time certificate of deposit is a separate account in the statistics, and holders of certificates may hold several. (2) A husband and wife may have a joint checking account but separate savings accounts. (3) Individuals are more likely to divide their savings than their checking deposits between two or more banks or between two or more accounts in the same bank, each account having different "rights" or "capacities." (4) Businesses have many of the demand accounts; until recently, few of the time accounts. (5) It is common practice for businesses to divide their checking

currency and time deposits may well be closer than between currency and demand deposits. That relationship itself is probably very much like the mixture of substitutability and complementarity that characterizes the relationship between small and large denominations of currency. Currency is the primary immediate medium of exchange, time deposits are probably the primary temporary abode of purchasing power. We hasten to add that the validity of this observation is particularly dependent on time and place. It has little relevance to countries at an early stage of financial development or to countries experiencing substantial inflation that impose a limit on the interest rate that may be paid on time deposits. In the first set of countries, no widely used institutions for time deposits have developed; in the second set, time deposits tend to disappear.

However, for countries like the United States and those in Western Europe, Japan, and a few others, in the mid-twentieth century, demand deposits alone may be a good index of business balances of "money," and currency plus some categories of time deposits may be a good index of the balances of ultimate wealth-holders.

Though we have not ourselves followed this route, these speculations suggest that casual observation may be an uncertain guide to the substitutability of items on the side of demand. For individuals, time deposits may well be closer substitutes for currency than demand deposits are. Any general statement about any category of deposits as a whole, then, requires aggregating in some fashion the different substitution relationships for business firms and individuals.

Substitution in Supply

Near-perfect substitutability of different assets in demand, while a sufficient condition for combining them, is not a necessary condition. We can illustrate with different denominations of notes. A twenty-dollar bill and twenty one-dollar bills are not at all perfect substitutes for one another to the holder of money balances. On the contrary, bills of differ-

accounts between a number of banks. Items 1 to 3 bias the figures in one direction; items 4 and 5 in the other.

There is no way of knowing the net effect of these five items. However, in view of the sizable excess of the number of time accounts, it is plausible that many individuals own time but not checking accounts. It is almost certain that at least technically there are more holders of time than demand accounts because of the large number of minors with savings accounts (often established and maintained by a parent).

We are indebted to Clark Warburton for the foregoing comments.

ent denominations are in considerable measure complementary commodities. Holders of notes are not indifferent to the composition of their balances by denomination. Yet it seems obvious that we can treat the total amount of currency notes as a single magnitude on the side of demand—without paying much attention to its distribution by denomination. The reason is that there is near-perfect elasticity of substitution of different denominations in supply at fixed rates of exchange, and hence holders of money can readily adjust the composition of their currency balances with little or no further side effects.[77] Near-perfect substitution in supply *at fixed rates of exchange* can be a substitute for near-perfect substitution in demand.

Recent experience with coins in the United States is an interesting, if trivial, illustration. For a few years in the 1960's there was a coin "shortage," i.e., the mints were not producing a large enough volume to enable holders of money to have the desired ratio of coins to notes—a ratio that apparently had risen for a number of reasons ranging from the spread of coin-operated vending machines to the "hoarding" of Kennedy half-dollars. The result was that the difference between coins and notes became a meaningful one. Some enterprising individuals collected coins and sold them to business firms with a special need for them at a premium that is said to have ranged up to 5 per cent.[78] At that time, coins and notes were not homogeneous on the side of demand; the total value of the two together in note units was greater, and in coin units less, than the sum of their nominal values because of the market premium on the coins. And the total nominal value demanded was different than it would have been in the absence of the premium.[79] But this is so special a phenomenon that we have little hesitancy in general in combining notes and coins into a single total we call currency, not because they are near-

[77] Again, this does not mean that the denominations available are necessarily irrelevant. A common phenomenon in countries that have experienced much inflation is that the largest denomination available is inconveniently small in terms of real purchasing power, yet the issuers of currency are hesitant to issue larger denominations for fear that this will be interpreted as a harbinger of further inflation by the sensitized population. In these cases, the inconvenience of the denominations available has the effect of reducing the usefulness of currency and so of reducing the real quantity that people wish to hold.

[78] See *The Wall Street Journal*, Apr. 23 and June 8, 1964.

[79] A more important example of the same phenomenon was the premium on gold coin and currency from 1862 to 1879 and, more recently, the premium on silver certificates. The latter may suggest why it is not possible to say whether the effect of a market premium on one type of money is to decrease (as the premium on coin probably did) or to increase (as the premium on silver certificates probably did) the total nominal value demanded.

perfect substitutes in demand—indeed, they have perhaps an even greater element of complementarity than notes of different denomination—but because they have been near-perfect substitutes in supply.

It is interesting to note that complementarity in demand (provided there are fixed rates of exchange and near-perfect substitutability in supply) is a substitute for substitutability in demand. Suppose holders of currency insisted on holding different denominations in rigidly strict proportions, say, four one-dollar bills, one five-dollar bill, and one ten-dollar bill for every twenty-dollar bill. Then, so far as currency alone is concerned, it would not matter whether we treated only one-dollar bills as our monetary total or any other subset of denominations or all denominations. We shall find this point of some importance when we consider deposits.

The relation between currency and deposits on the side of supply is somewhat clearer than on the side of demand. For any given business firm or individual at any given time, there is near-perfect substitutability in supply between currency and those deposits that are readily available to it or him. However, every firm or individual will not have the same kinds of deposits available. Some firms or individuals may be located in a place that is remote from a commercial bank—though for many decades now, few have been. For such firms or individuals deposits at a commercial bank would not be a close substitute in supply for currency. Firms or individuals located in one of the eighteen states with mutual savings banks may regard a mutual savings deposit as a close substitute in supply for currency or for a deposit at a commercial bank. Firms or individuals located in one of the thirty-two states without mutual savings banks clearly will not.[80]

For the United States as a whole for the period we cover, different categories of commercial bank deposits have clearly been near-perfect substitutes in supply for most firms and individuals most of the time. If one category of commercial bank deposits was available, so were other categories. This reinforces the statistical considerations that recommend the treatment of commercial bank deposits as a single total. Further, commercial bank deposits have been close substitutes in supply for currency for most firms and individuals most of the time. In many localities this has been true also of mutual savings deposits and, more

---

[80] Banking by mail is, of course, a device that strengthens substitutability in supply when depositors are far from a bank.

recently, of savings and loan association shares. It has been true to a lesser extent, however, which is why we have tended to treat commercial bank time deposits as an item distinct from time and savings deposits at other financial institutions.

Though at each point in time, commercial bank demand and time deposits have been near-perfect substitutes for one another in supply, the terms on which they could be substituted have varied because of changes in the advantage to commercial banks of having deposits in the one form or the other. Thus the ratio of demand to time deposits—like, for example, the ratio of national bank notes to silver certificates (though to a lesser extent)—has been much influenced by conditions of supply, probably more so than by conditions of demand. This point is discussed in detail in Chapter 4, and constitutes a major reason why we chose the definition of money we did.

Our further research has impressed on us that this phenomenon has much wider relevance. Governments have a strong proclivity for "regulating" or "tinkering" with the conditions on which deposits are offered. In many a country, currency has retained much the same meaning to holders over time (although of course the cost of holding currency may have changed drastically because, for example, of changes in the rate of change in prices), whereas the meaning of different categories of bank deposits has altered as banks have reacted to government regulations and interventions. The result is that there have been sharp changes in the ratios of different kinds of deposits to one another and to currency, deriving very largely from changing conditions of supply. To put it in the joint product terms introduced earlier in our discussion of the views of Pesek and Saving, the degree of "moneyness" of different categories of deposits has varied frequently and erratically. Accordingly, in studying monetary conditions in some of the above countries, we have found it preferable to return to earlier definitions of "money" as currency (or high-powered money) solely and to omit all deposits. The rationalization is that currency may be a better index from the side of demand of a total that is homogeneous over time than is the sum of currency and deposits, the "moneyness" of which changes frequently.

Conclusion

The empirical considerations that have guided us can be summarized as follows: Statistical considerations recommend avoiding, where possible, the subdivision of liabilities of individual institutions. Historical considerations recommend stressing homogeneity in demand rather than autonomy in supply. Theoretical considerations recommend combining items that are *either* near-perfect substitutes in demand *or* near-perfect substitutes in supply at fixed rates of exchange even though they may be complementary in demand.

What degree of substitutability in demand or supply is sufficient to justify treating it as "near perfect" cannot be decided by casual empiricism or qualitative considerations. These can guide investigation into alternative possibilities, but the final test is how well any definition works in enabling "us most readily and accurately to predict the consequences for important economic variables of a change in the conditions of demand for or supply of money."

4

BASIS FOR OUR CHOICE
OF DEFINITION

WE SELECTED a specific empirical counterpart to the term money after considering a limited number of alternatives corresponding to the totals in Table 1. One alternative that we did not consider nonetheless seems to us a promising line of approach. It involves regarding assets as joint products with different degrees of "moneyness" and defining the quantity of money as the weighted sum of the aggregate value of all assets, the weights varying with the degree of "moneyness" (section 1). After considering the alternatives, we chose the sum of currency held by the public plus adjusted deposits of commercial banks, both demand and time. We chose this total in preference to a narrower total including only currency and demand deposits, largely on the basis of a historical review of the meaning of commercial bank demand and time deposits in the United States and of the factors that produced changes in their relative magnitude (section 2). We chose this total in preference to broader totals on the basis of other evidence which also supported its superiority to the narrower total (section 3 and the appendix to this chapter). Further evidence that has become available since we made our choice partly supports and partly argues against it (section 4).

1. Alternatives Considered

The common procedure, and the one that we have followed, is to define money by classifying some assets as "money," and others as nonmoney assets. The quantity of money is then equal to the aggregate value of the assets it is decided to treat as money. In practice, for any given country and period, only a small number of distinct asset categories deserve serious consideration for designation as "money," in the light of prior research and writing and the availability of data. As already noted, each such category could in principle be further subdivided, so that there is implied in listing categories an initial decision to neglect the differences among the items within the categories. For the United States, this limited set includes (in current terminology):

1. Currency (including coins and, in principle though not in practice, American Express travelers' checks)
2. Demand deposits adjusted at commercial banks
3. Time deposits at commercial banks (including the few stock savings banks in existence), which, since 1961, should be subdivided into (a) large negotiable certificates of deposits and (b) other time deposits [1]
4. Deposits at mutual savings banks and at the Postal Savings System
5. Savings and loan shares
6. Cash surrender value of life insurance policies (i.e., the stated amount which is available on demand by terminating a life insurance policy)

[1] For the bulk of the period we cover it is correct to treat commercial bank time deposits as a single item, as we have done. However, the extensive development of large negotiable certificates of deposit since 1961 makes it currently desirable to divide this category into two parts: large certificates of deposit and other time deposits (see the division of col. 3, Table 1, beginning Feb. 1961). The large certificates of deposit are held primarily by firms and may be more like demand deposits or Treasury bills; the other time deposits are held primarily by individuals and are comparable to the category as a whole before 1961.

If not held to maturity, certificates are indistinguishable from other short-term money market instruments like Treasury bills and commercial paper. On the other hand, the practice of tailoring maturities to suit the needs of the persons or firms to which they are issued may make the certificates closer in practice to demand deposits than are other short-term money market instruments. We have no information on the extent of tailoring of maturities, but we know that a secondary market in certificates is in existence. Pending further information, our present inclination is to regard them as more nearly comparable to Treasury bills and commercial paper than to demand deposits.

Recent experience has reinforced the desirability of separating out the large negotiable certificates of deposit. In late 1968, market interest rates rose above the maximum rates that banks are permitted to pay on certificates of deposit under Regulation Q. The result was a rapid runoff of recorded certificates of deposit. However, this so-called "disintermediation" was largely formal. Banks found ways to pay higher rates by various devices that involved substituting other liabilities for recorded certificates of deposit. The most important device was to substitute certificates of deposit issued by overseas branches for certificates of deposit issued by head offices, the counterpart in the head offices' books being "due to branches." From Jan. 1, to July 30, 1969, certificates of deposit liabilities of U.S. banks declined $9.3 billion; and U.S. banks' indebtedness to own branches rose $8.6 billion.

7. Series E government savings bonds (i.e., those government bonds that are redeemable on demand for amounts stated in advance).

The distinctive characteristics of these seven items that make it plausible that they may be close substitutes in demand to their owners are as follows: (a) each has a "face" value stated in nominal monetary units and this "face" value is close to the nominal amount for which the asset can be acquired (the buying price) and is also close to the nominal amount that can be realized for the asset (the selling price); (b) in practice, despite the use of the word "time" in item 3 and the formal notice time required for items 4 and 5,[2] the assets can be sold within so short a period that all can be described as available on demand; (c) using the asset to finance purchases does not automatically involve incurring a matching liability. As far as we know, the only sizable sets of assets other than those listed that share these characteristics are balances at stockbrokers and policy dividends left at interest with life insurance companies (the return to policy-holders of part of the payments they have made on participating policies and annuity contracts). Perhaps these additional items should have been included in the list. Their omission simply reflects faithfulness to the literature.

It has often been argued that this list should also include "overdraft" facilities at banks or established lines of credit at banks or "borrowing power" on listed stocks and bonds and life insurance policies, or, more recently, borrowing power on credit cards. These items do share many of the characteristics of the seven listed—they are ways in which purchasing power can be acquired on demand at terms specified in advance. But they all differ in one important respect: acquiring purchasing power automatically involves assuming a matching specific liability. Realizing any of the seven items listed converts one asset into another; if the sum realized is spent in ways that do not add to assets or reduce liabilities, the result is a decline in net worth, but not in a form that involves specific obligations to make future payments. Drawing on a line of credit involves simultaneously adding in the first instance to assets and to liabilities; it means assuming obligations to make future payments.

Put differently, the sum of the seven items listed (plus the two omitted), adjusted for double-counting, can be regarded as approximately the theoretical concept $L(m)$, defined in Chapter 3 (pp. 134–

[2] No formal notice was required for Postal Savings System deposits. Though interest bearing, they were subject to withdrawal on demand.

135), as m tends toward zero, provided only that we limit $L(m)$ to refer solely to assets expressed in nominal values. The one apparent difference is that $L(m)$ is defined as the excess of assets over liabilities. However, for m approaching zero, demand obligations of nonbanks or, more generally, nonfinancial intermediaries, are the only ones that should be deducted. We can regard the omission of overdraft facilities, established lines of credit, and "borrowing power" on securities, life insurance policies, and credit cards as justified because the obligations established through their exercise would cancel the assets obtained—though this is not strictly valid since the maturity of the obligations is different from the maturity of the assets acquired. The only other major demand obligation over the period we cover has been call loans on stocks. In the late 1920's and early 1930's—the only time when such call loans were of considerable magnitude—most of the loans were made by nonbanks. These would have to be treated as assets as well as liabilities and would cancel each other. Such loans by banks were appreciable (ranging as high as 5 per cent of total commercial bank deposits) during those few years but not for most of the period we cover.

It may be that our neglect of overdraft facilities, lines of credit, "borrowing power," credit cards, and call loans is not the most useful procedure. That is an empirical question, on which unfortunately we have no evidence. In the absence of such evidence, we have followed the common practice in the literature of calling attention to such items and then subsequently ignoring them. More systematic attention to them would be highly desirable.

Each of the seven items listed is defined by the class or classes of institutions issuing the asset, although for currency this involves stretching the term "institutions" to include not only governments and banks but also gold or silver mines. This is a consequence of a point made earlier: the data are available mostly as a by-product of reports made for business reasons or to satisfy regulatory agencies. As noted earlier, it would be highly desirable to have data for classes of holders—particularly for individuals and business enterprises separately—but no such data exist that are anywhere nearly as comprehensive and accurate as the data for classes of issuers.

The seven categories listed can in principle be combined into 127 different combinations of one or more items. In choosing a definition we have in fact considered only four combinations:

I: (1) plus (2)
II: (1) plus (2) plus (3)
III: (1) plus (2) plus (3) plus (4)
IV: (1) plus (2) plus (3) plus (4) plus (5)

These four totals are shown in Table 1, suitably adjusted for double-counting. If we were starting over again, we would now consider also, for reasons stated above, these four combinations less item 2, and item 2 separately, with the idea of having two monetary totals, one approximating the balances of ultimate wealth-holders, and a second, the balances of business firms.

In extending these combinations beyond January 1961, we have also distinguished in Table 1 two variants of II, IIa, excluding large negotiable time certificates of deposit; IIb, including them.[3] In making this distinction—which had no significance at the time we chose our definition of money—we were naturally faced with the problem of which total to regard as continuous with the earlier total II. As noted, we have decided that IIa is and hence designate that total "money."

We restricted our attention to the four combinations listed, partly for practical reasons, partly because they seemed much the most likely candidates in light of earlier research and writing. The main practical reasons were the availability of comparable data for a long period and the fact that the main original data underlying our new estimates were for banks.

The restriction of our attention to these four combinations seems a less serious limitation to us than our acceptance of the common procedure of taking the quantity of money as equal to the aggregate value of the assets it is decided to treat as money. This procedure is a very special case of the more general approach discussed earlier. In brief, the general approach consists of regarding each asset as a joint product having different degrees of "moneyness," and defining the quantity of money as the weighted sum of the aggregate value of all assets, the weights for individual assets varying from zero to unity with a weight of unity assigned to that asset or assets regarded as having the largest quantity of "moneyness" per dollar of aggregate value. The procedure we have followed implies that all weights are either zero or unity.

---

[3] See footnote 1, above. Statistics on large negotiable time certificates of deposits began to be regularly reported weekly beginning June 1964. Weekly figures for earlier months of that year are given in a summary table for 1964 (see *Federal Reserve Bulletin*, Feb. 1965, p. 329). We constructed estimates beginning February 1961.

The more general approach has been suggested frequently but experimented with only occasionally.[4] We conjecture that this approach deserves and will get much more attention than it has so far received. The chief problem with it is how to assign the weights and whether the weights assigned by a particular method will be relatively stable for different periods or places or highly erratic. So far there is only the barest beginning of an answer.[5]

Pesek and Saving implicitly suggest that the weight be defined by (or be proportional to) the ratio to the "market rate" of interest of the difference between the "market rate" and the rate paid on the asset in question. In application, the term "market rate" would be susceptible to different interpretations. In the spirit of their analysis, presumably it should be the rate on an asset like Treasury bills. If service charges on demand deposits are treated as negative interest paid, this method would currently assign a higher amount of "moneyness" (i.e., a higher weight) to demand deposits than to currency and on many occasions a negative

[4] J. G. Gurley, *Liquidity and Financial Institutions in the Postwar Period*, Study Paper No. 14, U.S. Congress, Joint Economic Committee, Study of Employment, Growth, and Price Levels, Washington, D.C., 1960, pp. 7–8; E. J. Kane, "Money as a Weighted Aggregate," *Zeitschrift für Nationalökonomie*, No. 3, Sept. 1964, pp. 222–243; J. L. Ford and T. Stark, *Long and Short Term Interest Rates*, New York, 1967, pp. 1–3.

[5] Roy Elliott, in an unpublished dissertation, "Savings Deposits as Money" (University of Chicago, 1964), considered a special case in which he assigned a weight of unity to currency plus demand deposits, of w to time deposits (defined as our items 3 and 4), and of zero to all other items. He estimated w by finding the value that gave the highest correlation between the weighted sum and income among states, and income plus various interest rates among time units for the country as a whole. His estimates of w varied widely, both those from cross-section data for different years (.26 for 1929, .35 for 1937, .65 for 1954) and those from time-series data for different periods.

A similar procedure has been used for time-series data by Richard H. Timberlake, Jr., and James Fortson, "Time Deposits in the Definition of Money," *American Economic Review*, Mar. 1967, pp. 190–194, and by G. S. Laumas, "The Degree of Moneyness of Savings Deposits," *American Economic Review*, June 1968, pp. 501–503. From annual data, 1897–1965, Timberlake and Fortson conclude that only for the 1930's should time deposits be included at all. From quarterly post-World War II data, Laumas concludes that commercial bank time deposits should have a weight of .69; these plus mutual and Postal Savings System deposits, an average weight of .48; and these plus savings and loan shares, an average weight of .32.

V. Karuppan Chetty, "On Measuring the Nearness of Near-Moneys," *American Economic Review*, June 1969, pp. 270–281, followed a somewhat more indirect procedure. To get an adjusted stock of money he estimated indifference curves for various combinations of different assets by calculating the hypothetical amount of currency plus demand deposits which would be equivalent in utility to the actual amount of currency plus demand deposits and, say, commercial bank time deposits (i.e., he calculated one intercept of an indifference curve). His statistical findings imply that if the weight of currency plus demand deposits is taken to be unity, the weights of commercial bank time deposits, mutual savings deposits, and savings and loan shares are all very close to unity. However, his estimates are solely for the postwar period and are dominated by trends during that period and so cannot be considered reliable. The approach nonetheless has much appeal.

weight to mutual savings deposits or savings and loan shares. We have doubts about the theoretical validity of this approach for reasons noted in Chapter 3, section 1, above. However, as Elliott shows in his dissertation, the rates of interest paid on assets should enter into the determination of the weights, though perhaps in a somewhat different way.

Robert Noble has done much experimentation in the Workshop in Money and Banking at the University of Chicago with the assignment of weights by the use of factor analysis. These experiments are unpublished because they were uniformly unsuccessful, in the sense that the results do not appear reasonable when applied to special cases for which the correct answer seems clear in advance (e.g., different kinds of currency).

From time to time, there have been vague suggestions that the elasticity of substitution can be used to assign weights. Recently, V. K. Chetty has worked out a procedure for assigning weights that is a logical application of this idea. As yet, however, the procedure is in a very early stage.[6]

In choosing among the four combinations listed, we in effect proceeded in two stages. First, we decided to regard commercial bank deposits as an aggregate rather than as separated into demand and time components; in other words we combined items 2 and 3 instead of keeping them separate. Second, we compared combinations II, III, and IV. That is, in essence, we first chose between I and II, then among II, III, and IV, though in making the tests to choose among the latter, we included combination I as a further check on our initial decision.

This procedure was forced on us by purely statistical considerations. The most important was that, for reasons explained in the appendix to Chapter 8, we do not believe it is possible to get a reasonably accurate statistical breakdown of commercial bank deposits between demand and time deposits before 1914. After 1914 it is possible, and we present a breakdown in Table 1. Hence, if we had decided that it was preferable to use combination I instead of II after 1914, we would have had either to engage in further statistical attempts to get a satisfactory breakdown before 1914, or to reconcile ourselves to the use of two monetary totals, one before and one after 1914. A much less important statistical consideration is that the use of total commercial bank deposits makes it un-

6 See footnote 5, above.

necessary to divide high-powered money held by banks into the parts considered as separately related to demand and time deposits in order to eliminate double-counting correctly (see Chapter 1, section 4).

These statistical considerations, especially the first, were clearly strong arguments in favor of combination II instead of I, since it is a great advantage to be able to use a single concept for the whole period under investigation. Had all other considerations been equal or even slightly in favor of combination I, the statistical considerations would have tipped the scales. However, we decided, on the basis of the material presented in the next section, that other considerations also argued in favor of treating all commercial bank deposits as a single total. In section 3, we indicate the evidence that led us to choose combination II instead of III or IV.

2. Commercial Bank Demand and Time Deposits

The issue discussed in this section is whether the total of demand-plus-time deposits at commercial banks is a more homogeneous magnitude to holders of deposits over the period we cover than demand deposits alone. The total will be more homogeneous if changes in the proportions in which it is divided can be regarded either as a result predominantly of changes in conditions of supply with little reflex influence through demand (similar, for example, to changes in the ratio of silver certificates to national bank notes) or as reflecting near-perfect substitutability in supply (similar, for example, to different denominations of notes). Demand deposits alone will be more homogeneous if changes in the division of a given total produced, let us say, by changes in conditions of supply, exert a substantial reflex influence through demand, because holders of demand deposits seek to restore their former real value and can do so only by changing income flows, not by simply converting one type of deposit into another at unchanged terms. In that case demand and time deposits would be more nearly analogous to, say, currency and equity stocks than to national bank notes and silver certificates or to different denominations of currency.

The Period Before 1914

For the period before 1914, there can be little question about the answer: the total is more homogeneous than its parts. Precisely for this reason data on the division of the total between demand and time deposits are hard to come by. As we have noted, banks had little reason to be concerned about the relative size of demand and time deposits, since reserve requirements for the two were the same. Their incentive was to make their deposits as a whole attractive to customers by tailoring them to their needs. Bank supervisory agencies had little reason to insist on uniform classification and did not do so. What one bank called time deposits, another might call demand deposits. So-called time deposits were often transferable by check. So-called demand deposits often paid interest. The situation was clearly analogous to that of different denominations of currency: the various kinds of deposits offered by the same institutions (commercial banks) displayed near-perfect elasticity of substitution in supply; the actual proportions were determined by the requirements of depositors. The only difference from the example of denominations of currency is that the rates of exchange were not rigidly fixed, since banks paid different rates of interest on different kinds of deposits to offset differences in other costs, and these rates changed relative to one another from time to time.

The Period 1914–29

Since 1914, the situation has been very different and the correct answer is much less clear. The division between demand deposits and time deposits has been important to banks themselves for reserve purposes, and supervisory agencies have had reason to insist on a uniform classification of deposits. The importance of the distinction to banks has meant that conditions of supply have played a much more important role in determining the form of the deposits. The importance of the distinction to supervisory agencies has meant that there has undoubtedly been a more stable and systematic connection between the words used to describe the deposits and their formal characteristics. However, it is very likely that this has gone along with a good deal less stability over either space or time in the economic significance of the distinction. The relative costs to banks of supplying the two kinds of liabilities have differed greatly among groups of banks at any one time and for any one group of banks over time. As a result, banks have had, to a varying degree at different times, incentives to enhance or reduce the relative attractiveness of time deposits to their depositors, and they have done so at least in part by changing the characteristics of deposits labeled as "time" so as to make them either more like or less like deposits labeled "demand."

The introduction in the Federal Reserve Act of lower reserve requirements for time deposits than for demand deposits gave member banks an incentive to persuade their depositors to hold time deposits rather than demand deposits. Nonmember banks initially had no such incentive, though as time went by some states altered their laws to match the federal law.[7] The differential impact on the two classes of banks is dramatically reflected in the figures (see Table 3). From June 1919 to June 1929, demand deposits grew at only a slightly higher rate at member than at nonmember banks, while time deposits grew over three times as rapidly. From June 1919 to June 1929, time deposits rose from 34 to 47 per cent of the sum of time deposits and adjusted demand deposits at all commercial banks. For member banks alone, they rose from 26 per cent to 44 per cent; for nonmember banks, from 48 per cent only to 51 per cent.[8] As the table shows, almost the whole of the relative growth in time deposits occurred after 1919, although the change in reserve requirements occurred in 1914. The reason, presumably, is that banks were not under reserve pressure until discount rates were raised sharply in 1920.[9]

The changed reserve requirements did not affect all classes of member banks equally. For time deposits the reserve requirement was the same for all, but for demand deposits it was 13 per cent for banks in central reserve cities, 10 per cent for banks in reserve cities, and 7 per cent for country banks. Hence the differential varied sharply. As Table 4 shows, the differential incentive clearly had the expected effect: there is a definite tendency for the spread between the rates of growth of time and demand deposits to widen as the reserve differential widens.

[7] See Cagan, *Determinants and Effects of Changes in the Stock of Money*, NBER, 1965, Table 20, p. 186. This table shows the average of state reserve requirements weighted by the demand or time deposits of the commercial banks subject to them in each state at ten different dates from 1909 to 1950. It does not indicate the number of states with a different reserve requirement for demand and time deposits, at any date, nor the growth in that number over time.

[8] It should be noted explicitly that these figures are for changing groups of banks. Not only did some banks go out of business and others start, but many banks shifted from nonmember to member status. Such shifts might bias the results. For example, if banks which shifted had a high ratio of time to demand deposits, it would be arithmetically possible for the ratio for all member banks to rise even though every bank separately had a constant ratio. However, the shift in the ratio of time deposits is so large, and deposits in banks shifting so small, that it seems most unlikely that data for a stable group of member banks would differ much from those in Table 3.

[9] See *A Monetary History*, p. 209.

TABLE 3

*Average Annual Rates of Growth of Demand and Time Deposits
at Member and Nonmember Banks, and Time Deposits as a Fraction of
Total Deposits Adjusted,*[a] *1915-29*

(per cent)

Period and Class of Deposit	Class of Banks		
	Member	Nonmember	Total
	Average Annual Rates of Growth		
June 1915–June 1919			
Adjusted Demand	22.3	0.2	13.4
Time	29.4	6.6	14.8
June 1919–June 1929			
Adjusted Demand	2.9	2.0	2.6
Time	11.2	3.4	7.8
June 1915–June 1929			
Adjusted Demand	8.4	1.5	5.7
Time	16.4	4.3	9.8
	Time as Fraction of Total Deposits Adjusted[a]		
June 1915	20.7	41.6	33.0
June 1919	25.7	48.0	34.2
June 1929	44.4	51.4	46.6

[a]Other than interbank and U.S. government deposits.

Source: All banks, from *All-Bank Statistics,* pp. 36, 60; member
banks, from *Banking and Monetary Statistics,* p. 73; nonmember banks,
by subtraction.

TABLE 4

Average Annual Rates of Growth of Demand and Time Deposits
at Three Reserve Classes of Member Banks, June 1919–June 1929
(per cent)

Reserve Class of Member Banks	Rate of Growth		Spread Between Rates of Growth of Demand and Time Deposits	Percentage Point Difference Between Reserve Requirements on Demand and Time Deposits
	Demand Deposits Adjusted	Time Deposits		
Central reserve city	3.0	17.0	14.0	10
Reserve city	3.7	14.1	10.4	7
Country	2.0	9.1	7.1	4

Source: *Banking and Monetary Statistics,* pp. 81, 87, 93, 99.

The devices by which the banks affected the ratio of time to demand deposits were fairly straightforward. As we noted in *A Monetary History,* "banks increased the differential between interest paid on the two kinds of deposits and offered services in connection with time deposits designed to assimilate them to demand deposits." [10]

How great an inducement did member banks have to offer their depositors to achieve such a dramatic shift in the proportion of time to demand deposits? Were depositors largely passive and easily induced to switch or were they highly resistant? Unfortunately, data on rates of interest paid by member banks on various classes of deposits are available only beginning 1927, and for insured nonmember banks only beginning 1934, so a precise answer is impossible. However, the data available are sufficient to permit an unambiguous answer.

The average rate paid by all member banks on all deposits is available from 1919 on (Table 5). It varied only from 1.81 to 2.06 per cent from 1919 to 1929 despite a rise in the ratio of time to demand deposits ad-

[10] *A Monetary History,* p. 276. See *ibid.,* pp. 276–277, for evidence from Federal Reserve documents about the tendency and about Federal Reserve concern.

justed from .35 to .80, and despite a rate of interest on time deposits at the end of the period that was nearly three times as high as on demand deposits. The variations in the average rate paid are clearly related to variations in the rate earned on assets. However, if allowance is made for the rate of interest earned, the general trend over the period is upward; interest earned is lower in 1927–29 than in 1919–21, but interest paid is higher. Clearly, then, there was a rise in the average rate paid that can be interpreted as the inducement offered to depositors to shift from demand to time deposits.

The rise in average rate paid was sharpest from 1919 to 1921, when the ratio of time deposits to demand deposits adjusted also rose most rapidly. But the rise in those years as well as over the period as a whole was so moderate that it does little violence to the facts to describe the figures as showing a constant average rate of return to depositors over the period on the whole of their deposits.

The relatively constant average rate presumably conceals a widened differential between separate rates paid on time and on demand deposits —the rate must have risen on time deposits and fallen on demand deposits, with the rise in the rate on time deposits adding more to interest payments than the fall in the rate on demand deposits subtracted. But even this shift could not have been large. At the extreme, both rates could have been 1.81 in 1919, and the rate on time deposits could have risen to 3.41 by 1929 and on demand deposits fallen to 1.23. But this is a drastic overstatement since we know that rates were considerably higher on time deposits than on demand deposits in 1919. Another indication of the mildness of the shift is provided by applying the 1929 rates to the amounts of deposits of each class in each year. The hypothetical average rate thus obtained differs only slightly from the actual rate (Table 5, column 6) and rises only slightly more.

These rates of return summarize the pecuniary return that depositors received and show that it was roughly constant per dollar of total deposits. However, a major return from bank deposits is nonpecuniary— the transfer of funds. The expenses incurred for this purpose explain why banks pay a lower rate on deposits transferable by check than on other deposits, and the value of the services explains why depositors are willing to accept a lower rate. One measure of the quantity of nonpecuniary services rendered is the volume of debits to bank accounts per dollar of deposits ("turnover"). Unfortunately, we have accurate

TABLE 5

Interest Rates Earned and Paid by Member Banks and Ratio of Their Time to Demand Deposits Adjusted, 1919–29

| Year | Interest Rate Earned on Loans and Investments (1) | Interest Rate Paid on | | | | Hypothetical Average Rate on All Deposits Based on 1929 Rates on Different Classes of Deposits (6) | Ratio of Time to Demand Deposits Adjusted (7) |
		All Deposits (2)	Demand Deposits (3)	Time Deposits (4)	Interbank Deposits (5)		
1919	5.68	1.81				1.73	.35
1920	6.29	1.86				1.81	.43
1921	6.32	2.01				1.88	.51
1922	5.84	2.05				1.91	.54
1923	5.69	2.01				1.95	.61
1924	5.52	2.00				1.97	.64
1925	5.45	1.99				1.99	.66
1926	5.50	2.00				2.00	.70
1927	5.24	2.03	1.19	3.37	2.00	2.04	.75
1928	5.40	2.06	1.23	3.36	1.83	2.07	.81
1929	5.70	2.05	1.23	3.41	1.77	2.06	.80

data only for weekly reporting member banks, not for all member banks. Table 6 summarizes turnover figures for the former, separated into banks in New York—where financial transactions make the turnover much higher than elsewhere—and in 100 other leading cities. For each category of banks the table gives turnover calculated in two ways: per dollar of demand plus time deposits and per dollar of demand deposits only.

The figures show an initial sharp drop in turnover. Undoubtedly this is a reflection of the shift from the inflationary boom of 1919–20 to the sharp contraction of 1920–21—since turnover typically varies cyclically. Thereafter all the turnover figures tend to rise. But the striking fact for our purposes is that they rise much more drastically when calculated per dollar of demand deposits alone than per dollar of total deposits—indeed, for banks outside New York City and for total deposits turnover can be described as having remained roughly constant from 1921 to 1929.

If we view deposits as an aggregate, these figures lend themselves to the interpretation that depositors received roughly the same return in both interest received and nonpecuniary services received per dollar of total deposits. What happened was simply that the mix from which they received this return varied, more of the interest coming from deposits labeled time deposits and less from the deposits labeled demand deposits.

Notes to Table 5

Source, by Column

1. *Banking and Monetary Statistics,* pp. 72 (loans and investments) and 262 (earnings). Earnings, 1919–26, include profits on securities sold and interest on interbank balances. Earnings were divided by annual average of total loans and investments at Dec. to Dec. call dates inclusive, each Dec. weighted one-half and other call dates unity.

2–5. *Banking and Monetary Statistics,* pp. 73 (classes of deposits) and 262 (interest paid). Rates were computed by dividing interest paid by annual average of relevant deposits; annual average computed as described above for earnings.

6. Rate of interest paid in 1929 on each class of deposits (cols. 3, 4, and 5) was applied to the actual annual average of demand, time, and interbank deposits, 1919–28. The sum of the hypothetical amounts paid in each year was then divided by the sum of the three classes of actual deposits.

7. Computed from deposit figures, *ibid,* p. 73.

TABLE 6

Debits to Deposit Accounts: Ratio to Demand Plus Time
Deposits and to Demand Deposits Only, Weekly Reporting
Member Banks in and Outside New York City, 1919–29

(annual turnover rate)

| Year | New York | | Outside New York | |
	Demand Plus Time Deposits	Demand Deposits	Demand Plus Time Deposits	Demand Deposits
1919	56.7	59.9	28.4	36.1
1920	56.0	60.0	26.9	37.3
1921	51.4	54.9	22.3	32.3
1922	55.3	61.8	21.3	31.1
1923	56.1	65.5	21.7	32.6
1924	56.8	66.5	20.8	31.8
1925	60.8	71.9	21.3	33.4
1926	65.2	77.8	21.3	34.3
1927	70.4	85.3	21.5	35.7
1928	85.3	106.3	22.1	37.6
1929	99.5	124.4	23.8	40.5

Source: *Banking and Monetary Statistics,* p. 254.

The labeling of the ingredients was changed, but the combined package was much the same. And only a minor increase in total return was required to induce the customers to buy the new mix, suggesting that they had no strong preference about the proportions.

For the period 1914–29 it seems nearly crystal clear that the total of commercial bank deposits is a more homogeneous category to holders and more continuous with the corresponding total in earlier years than demand deposits alone.

This conclusion is reinforced by the cyclical behavior of total deposits. Their pattern during the 1920's seems entirely consistent with the pattern of the corresponding total during earlier years.[11]

[11] See also R. T. Selden, "Monetary Velocity in the United States," in Milton Friedman, ed., *Studies in the Quantity Theory of Money,* Chicago, 1956, p. 237. The conclusion is reinforced also by the behavior of velocity. The velocity of currency plus demand deposits alone rose during the 1920's. The velocity of currency plus total commercial bank deposits fell slowly, continuing the trend of earlier decades, again suggesting that this monetary total was homogeneous over time.

The Great Contraction

During the Great Contraction, time and demand deposits at commercial banks fell by roughly the same percentage—over one-third—so that the percentage distribution between them remained unchanged. Mutual savings deposits, on the other hand, actually rose—the relatively low failure rate of mutual savings banks made them an attractive haven for funds. Commercial banks were under fairly steady reserve pressure, certainly until they started to accumulate reserves in excess of legal requirements in late 1932, so that they continued to have an incentive to expand time deposits relative to demand deposits. They did not succeed in doing so, either because they had already largely exhausted the worthwhile possibilities in this direction by 1929, or because the declining interest rates and the rising bank failure rates made their task so much more difficult that the best they could do was to stay in the same place.

Interest rates earned by member banks on their loans and securities fell drastically—from 5.70 per cent in 1929 to 4.06 in 1933—and so did rates of interest paid depositors—from 2.05 per cent on all deposits to 1.07 per cent (Table 7). The decline in the rate paid was smaller in absolute size than in the rate earned, the difference reflecting the pressure on other costs and on profits, for the most part the latter. Rates paid fell on both demand and time deposits, on time deposits from 3.41 per cent in 1929 to 2.74 in 1933, on demand deposits from 1.23 per cent in 1929 to 0.28 in 1933. The decline was slightly greater for demand deposits, so that the differential rose a trifle. Service charges on demand deposits—for which there are no data for this period—may have been imposed or may have risen. But this could hardly have affected significantly the main point—that the relative conditions of supply of time and demand deposits at commercial banks did not change appreciably during 1929–33.

Turnover fell drastically both for demand plus time deposits and for demand deposits only (Table 7)—a reflection of the business contraction and the associated decrease in velocity—whether measured for currency plus demand deposits or for currency plus total commercial bank deposits.

All in all, on the main issue of this section, these considerations suggest that the conclusion reached for 1914–29 holds for 1929–33 as well, except that for the Great Contraction not only the total of time and de-

TABLE 7

Interest Rates Earned and Paid by Member Banks, and Ratio of Their Time to Demand Deposits Adjusted;
Debits to Deposit Accounts: Ratio to Demand Plus Time Deposits and to Demand
Deposits Only, Weekly Reporting Member Banks, 1929–33

| Year | Interest Rate Earned on Loans and Investments (1) | Interest Rate Paid on | | | | Ratio of Time to Demand Deposits Adjusted (6) | Annual Turnover Rate, New York | | Annual Turnover Rate, Outside New York | |
		All Deposits (2)	Demand Deposits (3)	Interbank Deposits (4)	Time Deposits (5)		Demand Plus Time Deposits (7)	Demand Deposits (8)	Demand Plus Time Deposits (9)	Demand Deposits (10)
1929	5.70	2.05	1.23	1.77	3.41	.80	99.5	124.4	23.8	40.5
1930	5.15	2.03	1.17	1.63	3.41	.83	61.3	77.0	19.8	33.8
1931	4.62	1.67	.79	1.18	3.09	.83	45.0	54.7	16.4	28.6
1932	4.62	1.52	.64	1.01	3.01	.79	31.7	37.6	13.6	23.9
1933	4.06	1.07	.28	.40	2.74	.68	29.7	34.8	13.5	22.4

Source: Cols. 1–6, same as for Table 5; cols. 7–10, same as for Table 6.

mand deposits at commercial banks, but each component separately, was a homogeneous magnitude.

On an issue to be considered later, the rise in mutual savings deposits raises the possibility that, for this period, commercial bank deposits plus mutual savings deposits may be more continuous with the corresponding total before 1929 than are commercial bank deposits alone.

The Period 1933–45

After the Great Contraction, a number of developments, all on the supply side, affected, for the rest of the 1930's, the significance of the division between demand and time deposits at commercial banks: the emergence of large excess reserves, the prohibition of the payment of interest on demand deposits, and the imposition of a maximum rate that could be paid on time deposits.

The emergence of large reserves in excess of legal requirements after 1932 presumably reduced the importance to banks of the differential reserve requirement for demand and time deposits. However, banks accumulated excess reserves, we believe, primarily because their experience from 1929 to 1933 led them to regard the Federal Reserve as an undependable source of funds to meet unexpected drains; and so they felt the need to provide their own "prudential" reserves by accumulating cash in excess of required reserves.[12] Hence they still had an incentive to reduce required reserves, and therefore the differential requirements remained important to them. The rises in reserve requirements imposed in 1936 and 1937 and only partly rescinded in 1938 raised requirements against both demand and time deposits by roughly the same percentage. This had the effect of increasing the absolute differential between them.

The large excess reserves were almost surely the most important factor on the side of supply from 1932 to 1940, and they appear to have had the effect one might expect: time deposits at commercial banks fell sharply relative to demand deposits adjusted, from three-quarters of demand deposits to less than one-half. However, there is no very close connection between the size of the excess reserves in different groups of banks and the extent of the decline in time deposits. Hence, we cannot be sure that the decrease in time deposits was related to the increase in excess reserves. After 1940, excess reserves fell to negligible

[12] *A Monetary History*, pp. 449–462.

TABLE 8

Interest Rates Earned and Paid by Member Banks and Ratio of
Their Time to Demand Deposits Adjusted, 1933–45

Year	Interest Rate			Differential Between Demand and Time Deposit Rates (4)	Ratio of Time to Demand Deposits Adjusted (5)
	Earned on Loans and Investments (1)	Paid on Time Deposits (2)	Paid on Demand Deposits (service charges treated as negative interest) (3)		
1933	4.06	2.74	.14	2.60	.68
1934	3.76	2.55	−.09	2.64	.63
1935	3.35	2.02	−.13	2.15	.56
1936	3.19	1.70	−.14	1.84	.52
1937	3.18	1.58	−.17	1.75	.52
1938	3.15	1.51	−.21	1.72	.54
1939	3.07	1.39	−.21	1.60	.48
1940	2.96	1.25	−.20	1.45	.43
1941	2.66	1.14	−.18	1.32	.38
1942	2.50	1.05	−.16	1.21	.33
1943	1.88	.88	−.12	1.10	.29
1944	1.87	.87	−.12	.99	.31
1945	1.20	.86	−.11	.97	.35

Source: Cols. 1–3 and 5: through 1941, same as for Table 5; thereafter, *Member Bank Call Report,* Board of Governors of the Federal
Reserve System, is the source of loans and investments and deposits,
and *Supplement to Banking and Monetary Statistics, Section 6, Bank
Income,* Board of Governors of the Federal Reserve System, Dec. 1966,
p. 6, is the source of income earned on loans and investments and service charges on deposits. Beginning 1942, "other charges on loans"
are shown separately and were included with other income earned on
loans and investments in calculating the rate of interest shown in col.
1. Col. 4: col. 2 minus col. 3.

levels and have remained small since. Whatever effect this factor might
have had in the 1930's, it was of no importance thereafter.

The prohibition of the payment of interest on demand deposits enacted in the Banking Acts of 1933 and 1935 might be expected to have
mixed effects. Because banks were protected from price competition in
respect of demand deposits but not time deposits, the banks became
more eager to attract demand deposits. By the same token, the prohibi-

tion made it more difficult for banks to attract demand deposits, since they could offer only nonpecuniary inducements, and a widening of the difference in pecuniary returns would make the two categories more distinct for depositors. For the 1930's, none of these effects was of appreciable significance. Market rates of interest were so low that commercial banks offered low rates on time deposits and, even without the legal prohibition, would have paid negligible interest on demand deposits. The legally fixed ceiling was, as it were, above the market price.

This is shown clearly in Table 8, which gives the rates of interest earned and paid by member banks, 1933–45. This is the first period for which service charges on demand deposits are quantitatively significant, as well as the first for which separate data on them are available. Service charges have been subtracted from interest paid on demand deposits—of which there was a small and declining amount reported through 1937—to give the net yield on demand deposits. From 1934 on, this net yield was negative.

In order to achieve the reduction in time deposits that banks appear to have desired after 1933 because of their large excess reserves, they had to induce depositors to alter the proportions and, as Table 8 shows, they did so. The differential in favor of time deposits, which was 2.60 percentage points in 1933, fell to 1.32 by 1941. Again, depositors appear to have been very sensitive to the terms offered. A decline in the differential by about one percentage point was accompanied by a decline in the ratio of time to demand deposits adjusted from two-thirds to two-fifths.

The downward trend in the differential continued throughout the war years, though the ratio of time to demand deposits adjusted fell through 1943 only and then rose to 1945, nearly reversing the earlier wartime decline. This reversal probably reflects a shift in public preferences as total liquid asset holdings rose and as the low level of rates on time deposits was accepted as part of a structure of interest rates expected to persist.

The Postwar Period

Prohibition of the payment of interest on demand deposits became more important after World War II, when rising market interest rates produced rises in the rates paid on time deposits. In the absence of the prohibition, the rising market rates would have raised the rates paid on demand deposits. Instead, the banks were driven to devising indirect means of paying interest on demand deposits, mostly through offering a variety of additional services. One device they used was to facilitate the substitutability of demand and time deposits—this time not primarily to reduce required reserves, but in order to pay interest on what, from the depositors' point of view, were the equivalent of demand deposits, just as in the 1920's they had done the same thing to enhance the attractiveness of time deposits. This offset to some extent, perhaps to a major extent, the dramatic widening of the differential between the pecuniary returns to time and demand deposits from 0.93 percentage points in 1946 to 4.63 percentage points in 1966.[13]

Frequently, the offset is explicit. The posted schedule of bank service charges consists of a stated charge for each item handled, less an allowance at a stated rate for each dollar of average or minimum ledger balance (or average less reserves). In a recent year the stated rate in a sample of banks ranged from 1.20 to 3.00 per cent per annum on regu-

---

[13] The additional services vary widely: from making loans at favorable rates to holders of demand deposits (one reason for "compensating balances" on loans is to facilitate this form of recompensing holders of demand deposits) to providing advice on investments or, in other areas, to pushing the sales of items produced by holders of demand deposits to other borrowers, and to still other devices so varied as to defy organized description. See Albert H. Cox, Jr., *Regulation of Interest Rates on Bank Deposits,* Michigan Business Studies, Vol. XVII, No. 4, University of Michigan, 1966, p. 127.

The only component of these services that can be easily measured, even in principle, is that of check clearing and the like rendered specifically in connection with demand deposits. In a study of eighty small and medium-size member banks by the Federal Reserve Bank of Boston for 1959, total operating expenses of demand deposits were estimated at 2.31 per cent of demand deposits (Paul M. Horvitz, "A Close Look at Bank Earnings," *New England Business Review,* Federal Reserve Bank of Boston, Aug. 1959). No comparable figure is given for service charges on demand deposits, but for all member banks it was 0.38 per cent.

To derive from these figures an estimate of the contribution to the offset from these services, we need to know (a) the corresponding figure for time deposits; (b) the corresponding figures for both demand and time deposits in 1946; and (c) the change in service charges on demand deposits. The increase in the gap between the costs per dollar for demand and time deposits from 1946 to 1966 would be a measure of the increase in differential services on demand deposits; the excess of this increase over (c) would be a measure of the increase in uncompensated differential services. For all member banks, (c) is 0.28 per cent, so allowance for additional service charges is a minor factor. Unfortunately, we do not have figures for (a) and (b). On the extreme assumption that all were zero the maximum offset would be about 2 percentage points. The actual offset must be much less. Hence, if the figures for New England are reasonably representative for the United States as a whole, and if increased services offset a large part of the indirect interest differential, they have taken forms other than services directly allocable to the conduct of checking accounts.

Instead of trying to explain the change in the differential return from 1946 to 1966, we can use these figures to explain the absolute gap of 4.63 percentage points in 1966. The maximum contribution of direct operating costs to this gap would be 2.31 less service charges, or about 2 percentage points. This overestimates the contribution by the operating cost per dollar of time deposits.

lar checking and 1.50 to 4.50 per cent per annum on business checking accounts.[14]

Another factor that assumed importance only after the war was the maximum that the monetary authorities were authorized by the Banking Acts of 1933 and of 1935 to impose on the rates that commercial banks could pay on time deposits. The ceiling first imposed was meaningless for some years because it was well above the rates that banks were induced to pay by market considerations. However, as interest rates in general rose, the ceiling became effective, the rate of growth of commercial bank time deposits slowed down drastically, and pressure developed to raise the ceiling. When the ceiling was raised (on January 1, 1957), there was initially a sharp spurt in commercial bank time deposits. As interest rates rose further, this cycle was repeated sporadically, the ceiling being lifted again on January 1, 1962, July 17, 1963, November 4, 1964, and December 6, 1965, partly lowered on July 20, 1966, and again on September 26, 1966, and raised for selected classes on April 19, 1968, and January 21, 1970.[15] Each rise followed a period of a slow rate of growth of commercial bank time deposits and ushered in a period of unusually rapid growth. The legal regulation of the rate thus clearly contributed to erratic behavior of time deposits relative to demand deposits.

Both the extraordinarily rapid growth of time deposits relative to demand deposits from 1946 to 1967, as the differential interest paid widened so dramatically, and the sensitivity of the time-demand deposit ratio to the ceiling interest rate are further testimony to the willingness of holders of deposits to change their form in response to rather modest

[14] See O. S. Pugh and O. G. Wood, Jr., "Bank Service Charges in the South," *National Banking Review*, Dec. 1966, pp. 177–178; also, A. F. Jung, "Commercial Bank Charges in New York and Ontario," *ibid.*, Mar. 1965, p. 400.

[15] In December 1965, the ceiling was raised only on time certificates of deposits of all maturities, the ceiling on returns to regular savings deposits remaining unchanged. On July 20, 1966, the ceiling on multiple-maturity time certificates was reduced, and on Sept. 26, 1966, the ceiling on single-maturity certificates less than $100,000 was also reduced. On Apr. 19, 1968, single-maturity certificates of over $100,000 were further subdivided by maturity, and the rates on maturities of sixty days and over raised. On Jan. 21, 1970, the ceiling was raised on savings deposits and eight classes of time certificates of deposit. The only classes on which the ceiling was not changed were multiple-maturity certificates of less than ninety days and up-to-one-year single-maturity certificates of less than $100,000.

Since November 1964 ceiling rates applicable to time certificates of deposit have been higher than those applicable to savings deposits, except for certificates of less than ninety days (from November 1964 to December 1965 and, for multiple-maturity certificates of this maturity, again since July 1966), to which the same ceiling rate as on savings deposits applied.

incentives. The postwar changes in the ratio of time to demand deposits were larger than those that occurred earlier, but only because the changes in the incentive were also larger.

The erratic changes on the side of supply, in particular those produced by the discontinuous changes in ceiling interest rates, have made the changes in the ratio of time deposits to demand deposits more erratic as well. Undoubtedly, this means that both total deposits and demand deposits alone are less homogeneous magnitudes over time than they used to be, that both are cruder approximations to a concept that had unchanging significance to a holder of deposits. However, the continuity of the behavior of the ratio toward the forces affecting it, the major role of changes affecting conditions of supply, and the sensitivity of the response all suggest that, for the postwar as for the prewar period, total commercial bank deposits is the less imperfect of the two magnitudes.

One change that occurred toward the end of the period considered and that was referred to earlier very likely justifies a slight modification of that conclusion for the future. That change occurred in the composition of time and savings deposits held by individuals, partnerships, and corporations at commercial banks. At the end of 1960, savings deposits (which may be held only by individuals and certain nonprofit organizations and are usually evidenced by a passbook) accounted for nearly nine-tenths of total time and savings deposits held by the public at member banks; by mid-1967, the proportion had dropped to three-fifths. The remainder was about equally divided between consumer-type time deposits (savings certificates, savings bonds, other nonnegotiable certificates of deposit, and negotiable certificates in denominations of less than $100,000), other time deposits (held mainly by business firms and other large investors in the form of marketable instruments—generally $100,000 and over—at rates competitive with other money market instruments), and open account time deposits (evidenced by a written contract specifying terms and conditions and tailored to the needs of the depositor). A large secondary market has developed in negotiable certificates of deposit. Other time deposits held by business firms and other large investors have been growing rapidly since 1961, though they are still a minor part of total time and savings deposits held by individuals, partnerships, and corporations. They are more analogous to money market instruments than to household time deposits.

It seems likely that total commercial bank deposits less large certificates of deposit and possibly less large, open account time deposits will prove more homogeneous with the earlier total of commercial bank deposits than will the total itself. This is the reason we have given the two subtotals for the period since January 1961 in Table 1.

3. Comparison of Total Chosen with Broader Totals

The evidence presented in the preceding section argues strongly that monetary total II (currency held by the public plus all commercial bank deposits adjusted) was a more homogeneous magnitude to holders in the United States, both for the century 1867–1968 as a whole and for distinctive short periods within the century, than monetary total I (currency held by the public plus demand deposits adjusted). But that evidence gives no guidance in the choice between monetary total II and broader totals: total III, which adds deposits at mutual savings banks and the Postal Savings System, and total IV, which adds also savings and loan shares.

Total III shares with total II the practical advantage that it is available on a comparable basis for the whole period since 1867. Total IV shares with total I the disadvantage that it is available for only part of the period. However, the disadvantage of total IV on this score is much less serious. Our estimates go back further, to 1897 instead of 1914, and when they start, the total amount of savings and loan shares is only 6.7 per cent of total III, so that even fairly crude estimates for earlier years would serve to yield a conceptually homogeneous and statistically reliable total for the whole period. This consideration therefore played no role in our choice of II in preference to III and IV.

Deposits at mutual savings banks, postal savings, and savings and loan shares have clearly been assets with a different mixture of pecuniary and nonpecuniary returns than time deposits at commercial banks. During the 1920's and again in the postwar period, at least until 1962, the rate of interest paid on mutual savings deposits was about 1 percentage point higher than the rate paid on commercial bank time deposits, and the rate paid on savings and loan shares, $1\frac{1}{4}$ to $1\frac{1}{2}$ percentage points higher (Table 9).

Because the rate paid on postal savings was held constant at 2 per cent, the differential between that rate and the rate on commercial bank time deposits is a mirror reflection of the latter, ranging, in the years covered in Table 9, from a high of 1.16 in 1946 to a low of -2.03 in 1966. The differentials between the rate on postal savings and on mutual savings deposits and savings and loan shares show a similar pattern. Postal savings have responded sensitively to these differentials: from 1900 to 1929, when the differential was negative, they never exceeded $150 million or about 1 per cent of commercial bank time deposits. They rose rapidly during the Great Contraction; reached a peak of $3.4 billion in 1947, a year after the highest differential recorded in Table 9; and then declined rapidly to $300 million in April 1966, when the Postal Savings System was discontinued. Never large relative to the other items, these deposits seem most nearly comparable in their characteristics to mutual savings deposits, with which we have tended to combine them.

The differentials between the rates paid on mutual savings deposits and savings and loan shares and the rate paid on commercial bank time deposits are about the same size or smaller than the differential between the rates paid on commercial bank time and demand deposits. Given our willingness to combine commercial bank time and demand deposits, we cannot regard these differentials as disqualifying the broader total from consideration.

However, the former differentials are in some respects more significant than the differential between the rates on commercial bank time and demand deposits. In the first place, the differential for commercial bank deposits is clearly overstated by the costs of the services rendered without charge in transferring and accounting for demand deposits. If all service charges were made explicitly and separately, and explicit interest on demand deposits replaced services rendered without charge, the differential between rates paid on time and demand deposits would be drastically reduced, possibly to a very small level.[16] In the second place, because commercial bank demand and time deposits are at the same institutions, explicit or implicit arrangements are possible whereby an individual holds both at the same institution, and it is mutually recognized that what matters is primarily the total in both accounts, the mix being determined to facilitate the bank's accommodation to legal reserve requirements.

Given the general tendency for rates of return on debt instruments to rise, at least for some range, with term to maturity—i.e., for there to

[16] See footnotes 13 and 14, above.

TABLE 9

Differential Between Interest Rate Paid on Commercial Bank Time Deposits and on Mutual Savings Bank Deposits, Postal Savings, and Savings and Loan Shares, 1920–29, 1946–66

Year	Interest Rate Paid On				Excess Over Rate Paid on Commercial Bank Time Deposits		
	Member or Insured Commercial Bank Time Deposits (1)	Mutual Savings Deposits (2)	Postal Savings Deposits[a] (3)	Savings and Loan Shares[b] (4)	Mutual Savings Deposits (5)	Postal Savings Deposits (6)	Savings and Loan Shares (7)
1920		3.85	2.00				
1921		3.95	2.00				
1922		3.95	2.00				
1923		4.04	2.00				
1924		4.06	2.00				
1925		4.09	2.00				
1926		4.19	2.00				
1927	3.37	4.21	2.00		0.84	-1.27	
1928	3.36	4.31	2.00		0.95	-1.26	
1929	3.41	4.48	2.00		1.07	-1.41	
1946	0.84	1.57	2.00	2.36	0.73	1.16	1.52
1947	0.87	1.62	2.00	2.38	0.75	1.13	1.51
1948	0.90	1.66	2.00	2.43	0.76	1.10	1.53
1949	0.91	1.82	2.00	2.51	0.91	1.09	1.60

(continued)

173

TABLE 9 (concluded)

| | Interest Rate Paid On | | | | Excess Over Rate Paid on Commercial Bank Time Deposits | | |
| | Member or Insured Commercial Bank Time Deposits | Mutual Savings Deposits | Postal Savings Deposits[a] | Savings and Loan Shares[b] | Mutual Savings Deposits | Postal Savings Deposits | Savings and Loan Shares |
Year	(1)	(2)	(4)	(5)	(5)	(6)	(7)
1950	0.94	1.90	2.00	2.52	0.96	1.06	1.58
1951	1.03	1.96	2.00	2.58	0.93	0.97	1.55
1952	1.15	2.31	2.00	2.69	1.16	0.85	1.54
1953	1.24	2.40	2.00	2.81	1.16	0.76	1.57
1954	1.32	2.50	2.00	2.87	1.18	0.68	1.55
1955	1.37	2.64	2.00	2.93	1.27	0.63	1.56
1956	1.58	2.77	2.00	3.02	1.19	0.42	1.44
1957	2.08	2.94	2.00	3.26	0.86	-0.08	1.18
1958	2.21	3.07	2.00	3.37	0.86	-0.21	1.16
1959	2.36	3.19	2.00	3.53	0.83	-0.36	1.17
1960	2.56	3.47	2.00	3.85	0.91	-0.56	1.29
1961	2.68	3.55	2.00	3.91	0.87	-0.68	1.23
1962	3.12	3.85	2.00	4.06	0.73	-1.12	0.94
1963	3.28	3.96	2.00	4.16	0.68	-1.28	0.88
1964	3.41	4.06	2.00	4.17	0.65	-1.41	0.76
1965	3.68	4.11	2.00	4.21	0.43	-1.68	0.53
1966	4.03	4.50	2.00	4.34	0.47	-2.03	0.31

exist liquidity premiums [17]—the higher rates on mutual savings deposits and the still higher rates on savings and loan shares suggest that they are held for longer term contingencies than the time deposits at commercial banks—that if they are a temporary abode of purchasing power, the "temporary" is of longer duration than for commercial bank time deposits.

Another factor differentiating these savings deposits from commercial bank time deposits is the difference in geographical spread.

Mutual savings banks have operated in only eighteen states. If deposits at such banks are a very close substitute for time deposits at commercial banks, their exclusion would impart a geographical bias to the total. On the other hand, if they are not a close substitute, their

[17] R. A. Kessel, *The Cyclical Behavior of the Term Structure of Interest Rates,* Occasional Paper 91, NBER, 1965, pp. 44–58.

Notes to Table 9

[a]Deposits were limited to a maximum of $2,500 per depositor.

[b]Data on actual dividends paid by savings and loan associations during the 1920's are not available. However, the figure mentioned in the text is supported by a survey by states, as of 1924, conducted by the American Bankers Association. Information was obtained from 42 states on the nominal rate of interest paid by the associations compared to that by banks on savings deposits *(Building and Loan Associations: A Survey,* American Bankers Association, New York, n.d.).

Source, by Column

1. *1920–29* (member bank), Table 5, col. 4. *1946–66* (insured commercial bank), FDIC, *Annual Report,* 1953–66; annual interest on deposits divided by average time deposits, Dec., June, Dec.

2. *1920–29,* Raymond Goldsmith, *A Study of Savings in the United States,* Princeton, 1955, Vol. I, pp. 413, 425; estimated annual U.S. dividends paid divided by two-year average of year-end mutual savings deposits. *1946–60, Mutual Savings Banking,* National Association of Mutual Savings Banks, prepared for Commission on Money and Credit, Englewood Cliffs, N.J. 1962, p. 87. *1961–66, Mutual Savings Banking, National Fact Book,* NAMSB, May 1967, p. 29.

3. Act of June 25, 1910, as amended 39 U.S.C. 5201–5224.

4. *1946–66, Savings and Loan Fact Book,* 1967, U.S. Savings and Loan League, pp. 58, 66; annual dividends on shares divided by two-year average of year-end value of savings and loan shares outstanding.

5. Col. 1 minus col. 2.

6. Col. 1 minus col. 3.

7. Col. 1 minus col. 4.

inclusion would impart such a bias. To determine which is the case, we computed for individual states and particular years (1915, 1929, 1950) the ratios of mutual savings bank deposits to demand deposits (call this M) and of commercial bank time deposits to demand deposits (call this T)—with only the latter, of course, having any significance in states without mutual savings banks. It was expected that T would tend to be less in mutual savings bank states than in others, but $M + T$ greater, and that whether mutual savings deposits should be combined with commercial bank time deposits would be indicated by just where in this range the value of T fell for states not having mutual savings banks. To our surprise, T itself, and therefore a fortiori $M + T$, turned out to be larger in mutual savings bank states than in others.[18] This test, therefore, did not give the reasonably direct answer that had been anticipated. Comparison of different mutual savings states showed some evidence of substitutability between the two types of deposits. However, both the evidence and the indicated degree of substitutability were weak. So far as this evidence goes, it probably argues for excluding mutual savings deposits (section 1 of appendix to this chapter).

Savings and loan associations are present in all states. However, savings and loan shares are somewhat more concentrated geographically than commercial bank time deposits. In December 1966 the four states with the largest amounts of savings and loan shares (California, Illinois, Ohio, and New York) accounted for 41 per cent of the aggregate of such shares, whereas the four states with the largest amounts of commercial bank time deposits (New York, California, Illinois, and Pennsylvania) accounted for 35 per cent of the aggregate of these deposits. Hence, savings and loan shares raise somewhat the same problem of geographical bias as mutual savings bank deposits.

These general considerations, though suggestive, offer a most uncertain guide. We therefore supplemented them with a number of more systematic and comprehensive tests designed to provide a quantitative criterion. In these tests we included total I as well as broader totals to check our earlier conclusions.

---

[18] After the event, we rationalized our results by noting that states with mutual savings banks tend to be located in the older and more developed regions of the United States. Residents of those states probably have larger accumulated capital and liquid assets than residents of states without mutual savings banks. This is supported by the evidence that such states tend to have lower interest rates than other states and to be exporters of capital.

The general idea of these tests was to determine which total was likely to yield the most stable demand function involving a small number of variables. It is generally agreed that a scale variable—income, total transactions, wealth, or a similar aggregate—is the most important single variable affecting the quantity of money demanded.[19] Hence we made our tests by relating differences in the various totals for various years or spatial units to corresponding differences in income. We checked also the relation between the individual components of a total and income to assure that the items combined are substitutes, as shown by a higher correlation for the total than for the individual components.

One such test was applied to data for 1929–58 for the United States in connection with a study of the relative stability of income velocity and the multiplier.[20] In that study a criterion was developed for choosing among alternative definitions along the lines just described.[21] The conclusion was that total II satisfied the criterion best.

Another test was applied to data for individual states in selected years. Since there are no data on currency holdings, by states, this test had to be restricted to deposits only.

Deposits per capita in the various states were correlated with income per capita for each of the selected years (1929, 1935, 1940, 1950, 1955, 1960). The details are given in section 2 of the appendix to this chapter. The correlation between income and demand deposits alone is decidedly lower in each year than between income and either total commercial bank deposits or commercial bank deposits plus mutual savings deposits, or the latter total plus savings and loan shares, confirming the conclusion reached in section 2, above. For 1929, 1935, and 1940 the correlations are highest for income and total commercial bank deposits, though the correlations for income and the next broader total, including mutual savings deposits, are not much lower. For 1950, 1955, and 1960, the correlations are highest for the broadest total, including savings and loan shares, though again, the correlations are not

[19] We note that the concept of "most important variable" is itself a complex one.

[20] Milton Friedman and David Meiselman, "The Relative Stability of Monetary Velocity and the Investment Multiplier in the United States, 1897–1958," *Stabilization Policies*, prepared for Commission on Money and Credit, Englewood Cliffs, N.J., 1963, pp. 182–183 and 242–244.

[21] The criterion was that the correlation between the total called money and national income be higher than between each of the individual components of the total and national income. Note that this is *not* the same as saying that the best total is the one that has the highest correlation with national income, though in practice it turned out that this condition was also satisfied.

much lower for income and the next narrower total, including mutual savings deposits. The correlation between each class of deposits and income is considerably lower than that between the monetary totals in which each is included and income, suggesting that the three deposit items and savings and loan shares are substitutes.

This test alone suggests that the best definition of money until World War II includes both demand deposits adjusted and commercial bank time deposits, and after World War II includes, in addition, mutual saving deposits and saving and loan shares.[22]

Though this evidence was not completely unmixed, it clearly confirmed our conclusion that total II was preferable to total I, and on the whole seemed to favor II over III and IV. Hence, we settled on II as the total to which we would apply the term "money" without additional modifiers.

Evidence from cyclical behavior, though also somewhat mixed, reinforced our decision to keep mutual savings deposits separate. For some individual cycles—notably in the World War I cycle, the 1929–33 contraction, and the 1933–38 cycle—mutual and postal savings deposits behave very differently from commercial bank time deposits, which move in close harmony with demand deposits. However, in other cycles —notably in 1924–27, 1945–49, and 1949–54—savings deposits move in close harmony with commercial bank time deposits, whereas the latter move quite differently from demand deposits.

4. More Recent Evidence

We made our decision about how to define money early in the course of our research, roughly a decade ago at the present writing (1968). Since then, additional evidence bearing on the problem has become

---

[22] In his 1964 dissertation, "Savings Deposits as Money," Roy Elliott correlated data for per capita deposits and per capita income in the various states in 1929, 1937, and 1954, using per capita demand deposits in one set of correlations, and per capita total deposits, including time deposits at commercial banks, mutual savings banks, and the Postal Savings System, in the other. The r^2's between the logarithms of per capita income and per capita demand deposits in 1929, 1937, and 1954 are .82, .76, and .49; and between per capita income and per capita total deposits in the same years, .85, .87, and .80. To test whether mutual savings differed from other savings, Elliott, working with 1929 and 1954 data, added a dummy variable of unity for eleven states with mutual savings banks and of zero for all other states in his sample. He concluded on the basis of the test that mutual savings and other savings did not differ significantly.

available, from our own work as well as the work of others. In addition, the question of the best definition has received much more explicit attention than it had earlier—partly in response to our work, partly as a by-product of the tremendous increase in the amount of research on monetary questions.

This additional light that has been shed on the question of definition has forced us to reexamine and spell out in much greater detail than we did initially the considerations that seem to us relevant to the choice. But we have not undertaken a thorough reexamination of the question. Though some of the additional evidence, like some that we considered, argues for a different total, nothing that has come to light seemed to us sufficient to compel a reexamination of our choice. Hence we cannot say for certain, though we believe it highly likely, that if we were to face the question anew at the present time, we would come out with the same answer.

Insofar as the new evidence is adverse to our conclusion, or insofar as the scholars interpreting the evidence believe that it is, the conflict is primarily on the point on which we feel most secure: namely, our decision to treat commercial bank deposits as a single total and hence to choose total II in preference to I. And none of this new evidence seems to us anything like so conclusive as that summarized in section 2, above.

We would find it easier to be persuaded that, at least for the period after World War II, total III or IV is preferable to II. But hardly any of the additional evidence bears on this question.

In the rest of this section, we list with only brief comment the additional material that has come to our attention.

1. In studying the relation between the variability of the rate of change in money and of the rate of change in net national product, we made computations for 1915–60 for both totals I and II. The correlations were consistently higher—though not by much—for total II.[23]

2. In exploring the possibility of defining money as a weighted sum of different asset totals, Roy Elliott estimated the weight that should be assigned to savings deposits in combining demand deposits and savings deposits. His calculations are for savings deposits defined to include not only commercial bank time deposits but also deposits at mutual savings

[23] See M. Friedman and A. J. Schwartz, "Money and Business Cycles," *Review of Economics and Statistics*, Feb. 1963 Supplement, p. 45, footnote 16.

banks and the Postal Savings System. He estimated the weight of savings deposits in a total where currency and demand deposits had a weight of unity as .26 in 1929, .35 in 1937, and .65 in 1954. The implications of Elliott's work are mixed. The first two results argue for the narrow total of currency plus demand deposits; the final result, for a broader total. Unfortunately, Elliott did not make any corresponding estimate for commercial bank time deposits alone.[24] The differences among the years are consistent with our conclusion that narrower totals may be indicated for the pre-World War II period than for the postwar period.

More recently, related calculations have been made by Timberlake and Fortson, and by Laumas.[25] Timberlake and Fortson interpret their results as favoring total I. Laumas' results indicate that commercial bank time deposits alone should be given a weight of .69 and other time deposits decidedly lower weights. Thus his results favor total II.

3. In a recent study of cross-sectional state data for the United States for the eleven-year period 1949–59 Edgar L. Feige argues for the narrow definition, since he finds demand and time deposits at commercial banks to be weak substitutes, with a declining degree of substitutability over time.[26] However valid the evidence in Feige's study for the period since 1949, it may not be valid for earlier periods, especially the 1920's. Equally important, because of the nature of his data, Feige had no evidence on currency holdings.

In a review of Feige's book Donald Hester criticized Feige's results on statistical grounds that do not appear to us persuasive.[27] Tong Hun

[24] See footnote 22, above.

[25] See footnote 5, above.

[26] *The Demand for Liquid Assets: A Temporal Cross-Section Analysis,* Englewood Cliffs, N.J., 1964, pp. 25, 29, 37, 43.

[27] Donald Hester, Review of *The Demand for Liquid Assets, Journal of Political Economy,* Aug. 1966, pp. 409–410. Hester argues that there is simultaneous equation bias because (1) income and (2) rates of return on various categories of deposits are endogenous variables whereas Feige assumes them exogenous. This criticism might be valid if Feige had constructed his regressions from aggregate data for the United States, though even then some quantitative evidence would be required to show that the bias is important.

However, Feige's basic unit of analysis is the state, not the nation. Even though nominal income in the nation can be regarded as the endogenous resultant of an exogenously determined money supply, the distribution of the total money supply among the states in any year can be regarded as an endogenously determined resultant of an exogenously determined distribution of income among the states. And, for any single year, that is what Feige's regressions examine. At most this criticism has merit for Feige's pooled regressions in which temporal variation is given scope to affect his results. However, his results for the pooled regressions are roughly the same as for the average results for individual years, suggesting that any bias on this score is minor.

Lee has published a more extensive criticism of Feige's results, involving additional computations from both Feige's and other data. We consider this in the next item, because Lee considers that his results besides contradicting those of Feige also contradict our definition.

4. Lee concludes from his own calculations that "nonbank intermediary liabilities"—by which he means deposits at mutual savings banks and savings and loan shares—"are close substitutes for money" whether money is defined as equal to our total I or our total II. He also concludes that his results "contradict" the "supposition" that "time deposits are close or more perfect substitutes for demand deposits, but other nonbank intermediary liabilities are not substitutable for demand and time deposits," which he takes to be the basis for our choice of total II over total I. "It is difficult," he says, "to reconcile their reasoning especially where savings and loan shares appear to be better substitutes for demand deposits than do time deposits." [28]

Lee does not himself indicate which definition of money he believes his estimates to favor, but we interpret him as implicitly endorsing total IV.

He explains the difference between his own results and the results obtained by Feige as the consequence of what he regards as "an excessive use of dummy variables" by Feige.[29] Feige uses these variables to allow for special circumstances of particular states or regions, such as states that permit establishment of mutual savings banks and those that do not and states that contain the main financial centers of each of four regions and those that do not. As evidence that the use of dummy variables is excessive, Lee cites multicollinearity between them and other independent variables. This does suggest a real problem with the statistical stability of Feige's estimates. However, it certainly does not mean that if the special features Feige seeks to control are present, as they clearly are, correct results can be obtained by neglecting them, as Lee

The same considerations apply to rates of return. For the nation as a whole, as Hester notes, it would be surprising if supply were perfectly elastic at an exogenously determined interest rate. But, surely, that is precisely what one would expect on theoretical grounds to be true for individual states in a national financial market—just as horizontal supply curves for individual consumers of a product are entirely consistent with an inelastic supply curve for the industry as a whole.

28 Tong Hun Lee, "Substitutability of Non-Bank Intermediary Liabilities for Money: The Empirical Evidence," *Journal of Finance*, Sept. 1966, pp. 441–457, quotations from p. 455.

29 *Ibid.*, p. 453.

does in a regression using Feige's data (though not in one using Consumer Survey data).

In part the difference between Lee and Feige is purely verbal. At one point Lee interprets elasticities of one category of deposits with respect to the return on another (cross-elasticities, for short) of $-.75$ and $-.31$ as "consistent with the substitution hypothesis of Gurley and Shaw," despite seven other cross-elasticities in the same set of regressions ranging from $-.28$ to $+.12$ with four negative and three positive.[30] Feige interprets cross-elasticities of $-.55$ and $-.28$, in a comparable set of regressions, in which the seven other cross-elasticities range from $-.13$ to $+.30$ also with four negative, as indicating little substitutability and as inconsistent with the Gurley-Shaw hypothesis. Clearly the difference in the words used is vastly greater than in the statistical results.

The value of $-.75$ cited above is the largest cross-elasticity Lee finds for aggregate data. In his principal regressions for 1934–64, his cross-elasticities vary from $-.28$ to $-.58$.[31] By most standards these would be designated inelastic responses, not interpreted as exhibiting in the words of Lee, "strong support of the Gurley-Shaw hypothesis that non-bank intermediary liabilities are a close substitute for money." Lee has succumbed to the widespread confusion between statistical and economic significance.[32]

But the difference is not only verbal. In some calculations, Lee gets results that are strikingly different from Feige's.

The outstanding example is Lee's conclusion, quoted above, that "savings and loan shares appear to be better substitutes for demand deposits than do time deposits," and also better substitutes for time

[30] *Ibid.*, p. 455, where Lee comments on Feige's regressions without dummy variables in Table 3 on p. 454.

[31] From much experience, we are suspicious of this regression, which is for the period 1934–64, excluding 1942–45. In such regressions, we have found that the results are overly influenced by the difference between the period 1934–41 and 1946–64, i.e., the prewar and postwar periods. The difference between the averages for these periods provides only one degree of freedom of the twenty-one or twenty-two that Lee has; yet it may account for the bulk of his correlation and dominate the regression coefficients. Before interpreting these results as he does, we would have to check the consistency of behavior within the prewar and postwar periods separately with the difference between the averages for the two periods.

[32] The confusion is well illustrated by a possibly apocryphal story concerning an early experience of Egon Pearson. On the basis of a statistical examination of the results of two techniques, he is reported to have told some textile manufacturers for whom the study was done that the difference between the two techniques was significant. One of the manufacturers is said to have responded, "Young man, you tell us what the difference is, and we will tell you if it is significant."

deposits than are mutual savings bank deposits. He finds further in the set of calculations yielding these results (a recalculation of Feige's regressions without dummy variables) that demand deposits display nearly as elastic a response to the yield on savings and loan shares as to their own yield, and time deposits a much more elastic response than to their own yield. Lee gets these results for data covering the deposits of all holders of money. For such aggregates, the results are hard to accept. Over half of demand deposits are held by business enterprises. These hold next to no savings and loan shares or mutual savings bank deposits but have held nonnegligible time deposits.

Lee also presents regressions using household data from the Survey of Consumer Finances. For these, which presumably cover only household demand deposits, high cross-elasticities for demand deposits and savings and loan shares are less implausible, and in fact Lee finds much higher cross-elasticities than for the aggregate data. But these regressions also yield results that seem highly implausible, to put it mildly, on internal grounds. For example, according to the regressions, a one percentage point decline in the yield on demand deposits (i.e., a one percentage point rise in service charges expressed as a ratio to deposits) will reduce the representative household's demand deposits by $660 and raise its holdings of time and mutual savings bank deposits (treated as one variable) by $441 and of savings and loan shares by $510. That is, it will raise the total of the two categories of nondemand deposits by 50 per cent *more* than it will reduce the holdings of demand deposits.

For time and mutual savings bank deposits there is no such contradiction. A one percentage point decline in their yield will, according to Lee's regressions, reduce them by $588 and also reduce demand deposits by $88 while raising savings and loan shares by $101. This may be a plausible result.

But for savings and loan shares, the results are again clearly most implausible. A one percentage point decline in their yield will, according to Lee's regressions, reduce them by $262 but will raise demand deposits by $227 and time and mutual savings bank deposits by $706 or the two together by more than three and one-half times the reduction in savings and loan shares.

There is clearly something fundamentally wrong with interpreting these regressions as satisfactory demand functions. Yet they are the only ones Lee presents that display high absolute cross-elasticities (-1.6

for demand deposits and -2.9 for time and mutual savings bank deposits with respect to the yield on savings and loan shares).

We conclude that Lee has grossly overstated the economic significance of his calculations and the conflict between them and both Feige's and our own findings.

In a later study, he has correlated per capita M_1 and M_2, in real terms, with permanent per capita real income, various interest rate differentials, and the lagged dependent variable. He uses annual data for the United States for 1951–65 and interprets the results as demand equations.[33] Lee concludes that "savings and loan shares are the closest money substitutes among alternative types of assets."

This conclusion is not a valid inference from Lee's results because they confound own-elasticity and cross-elasticity. Lee measures only the response to the *difference* between the yield on the money total considered and the yield on the other assets, not the response to each yield separately.

In an unpublished paper, Feige has recalculated Lee's regressions, separating out the (negative) yield on demand deposits from the yields on other assets. For two of Lee's regressions, which gave estimates of $-.63$ and $-.66$ for the elasticity of the response of M_1 to the difference between the yield on M_1 and on savings and loan shares, Feige estimates an own-elasticity of demand for M_1 with respect to the yield on demand deposits of $-.20$ (the same in both regressions) and a cross-elasticity with respect to the yield on savings and loan shares of $-.30$ and $-.19$ —hardly impressively high cross-elasticities. For all of the thirty-six regressions Feige replicated, the own-yield absorbs most of the response that is associated with the differentials used by Lee and that he erroneously attributed to cross-elasticities.[34]

[33] "Alternative Interest Rates and the Demand for Money: The Empirical Evidence," *American Economic Review,* Dec. 1967, pp. 1168–1179. The interest rate differentials he uses are between the yields on M_1 or M_2 and (a) on savings and loan shares, (b) on four-to-six month commercial paper, (c) on twenty-year corporate bonds, (d) on common shares (dividend yield), and (e) for M_1, on commercial bank time deposits.

[34] Since this was written, two comments on Lee's December 1967 *American Economic Review* article and a reply by him have been published (Harvey Galper, "Alternative Interest Rates and the Demand for Money: Comment," and Michael J. Hamburger, the identical title, *American Economic Review,* June 1969, pp. 401–412; Lee's reply is *ibid.,* pp. 412–418). None of these items has any additional evidence on the relative merits of M_1 and M_2, since all deal solely with regressions for M_1. All are restricted to time series data for 1951–65. None acknowledges explicitly how slender a basis this is for any far-reaching inferences—fifteen annual or sixty highly serially correlated quarterly observations, submitted to literally dozens of multiple regressions, of which only a sample are reported (twenty-eight based on annual data, and twelve based on quarterly

5. In research on the demand for money, Karl Brunner and Allan H. Meltzer experimented with two alternative definitions of money: the narrow total of currency plus demand deposits, which they designate M_1, and the broader total we term money, which they designate M_2. They concluded, "Our results seem to suggest clearly that currency plus demand deposits is the more appropriate definition. More inclusive definitions of money appear to mix the effects of general and relative changes in interest rates and to obscure a part of the wealth-adjustment process." [35] We do not ourselves regard the evidence presented by Brunner and Meltzer as giving anywhere nearly so clear a verdict.

Brunner and Meltzer describe four sets of comparisons between two definitions of money.[36] They assert that three sets of comparisons (1, 3, and 4 of footnote 36) favor M_1, in the sense of yielding smaller percentage errors of estimate for M_1 than for M_2, and that one set of comparisons (2 of footnote 36) favors M_2.

For one set favoring each definition (1 and 2), the figures Brunner and Meltzer cite clearly justify their assertions. However, the differences in the set favoring M_2 should receive much greater weight, since the

data), and with some reported regressions based on the fifteen annual observations containing seven independent variables, leaving at best only seven degrees of freedom! To add to the difficulty, the series have strong trends, so that the effective number of degrees of freedom is surely still smaller. Any conclusions based on such extensive manipulation of so slender a body of data must be regarded as exceedingly tentative hypotheses until tested with independent evidence. Yet the several authors show no recognition that this is the case. Galper mainly simply repeats Lee's earlier calculations but with quarterly data. His main contribution is the construction of a quarterly series of advertised interest rates on savings and loan shares by interpolation of semiannual data. Given the strong trends in the data, it is not surprising that the quarterly data give about the same results as the annual data. Hamburger separates own-elasticity from cross-elasticity and finds that this reduces appreciably the calculated elasticity attributed to savings and loan shares. He also introduces a variety of different interest rates and concludes that there is a wide variety of different assets that are equally good substitutes for M_1. Lee disputes Hamburger's results largely on statistical grounds, but, as in the difference between him and Feige, his reported regressions differ less from Hamburger's numerically than do the words he uses to describe them. In the nineteen multiple regressions of annual and quarterly data that he reports, the highest estimated cross-elasticity with respect to the rate on savings and loan shares is $-.48$—and this in a regression that combines own- and cross-elasticity. The highest separate cross-elasticity is $-.33$. Yet he describes these results as substantiating "the substitution hypothesis of Gurley and Shaw . . . indicating that the nonbank intermediary liabilities are close substitutes for money" (p. 417)!

[35] Karl Brunner and Allan H. Meltzer, "Predicting Velocity: Implications for Theory and Policy," *Journal of Finance,* May 1963, p. 350.

[36] (1) Between equations K3 and K4, fitted alternatively, using M_1 (the narrow definition) and M_2 (our definition); (2) between equation F2, in which M_2 is used, and equation F3, in which M_1 is used; (3) between equations W1, W2, W3, and W4, in which M_1 and M_2 are used alternatively; and (4) between equation WF2, in which M_2 is used, and equation WF3, in which M_1 is used.

equations in that set give decidedly lower percentage errors than the equations in the other and hence provide more information. For one set (3), Brunner and Meltzer do not give figures on percentage errors for both definitions, so we cannot judge their assertion. For one set which they regard as favoring M_1 (4), their assertion is not justified by the data they present.[37]

We conclude that the evidence is by no means "clear," though if we accept as correct their interpretation of the set (3) that we cannot judge independently, it weights the scales somewhat in favor of M_1.

6. On the basis of a comparison of growth rates of money, defined narrowly and also as we do, and of the turning points of business cycles since June 1914, the St. Louis Federal Reserve Bank has concluded that the relationship is somewhat more reliable for the narrow definition. The rate of change of time deposits did not fall before the business cycle peaks of 1920, 1923, 1937, 1953, and 1957, nor rise before business cycle troughs in 1921, 1924, 1933, and 1949. According to the St. Louis study, the reason that rates of change in money *broadly defined* lead turns in business, by much the same time spans as do the rates of change in money *narrowly defined,* is that movements of the broader definition are dominated by movements of the narrow definition. "Adding time deposits to money does not appear to fashion a variable which is more closely related to business cycle peaks and troughs but simply creates the possibility of obscuring the relationship between monetary action and economic activity. In view of the rapid growth of time deposits relative to demand deposits, the relationship between changes in the growth rate of money plus time deposits and cyclical turning points may be less in the future than in the past." [38]

7. In a paper dealing mostly with other issues, David Laidler incidentally compared the stability of demand functions for both total I and total II, using U.S. data for 1920–60. He concluded that "the

[37] They give two measures of predictive performance for the whole thirty-nine-year period covered (1910–40 and 1951–58): mean absolute percentage error, and root mean square absolute per cent error. They also give the first measure for four subperiods. For the period as a whole, the mean absolute errors are 4.6 per cent for equation WF2 and 4.2 per cent for equation WF3: the root mean square errors are 4.4 per cent and 5.0 per cent. Thus the two measures differ in direction. Moreover, equation WF2 has the smaller mean error for two of the four subperiods; equation WF3 for the other two. This appears to be rather a standoff and does not seem to us to justify the authors' assertion that "a comparison of WF2 shows that . . . demand functions for money defined as M_1 are subject to smaller errors of prediction than those in which money is defined as M_2" (*ibid.,* p. 339).

[38] "Money Supply and Time Deposits, 1914–1964," Federal Reserve Bank of St. Louis *Review,* Sept. 1964, p. 8.

stability of the demand function for money is improved by including time deposits in the definition of money." [39]

8. In a recent study William Gibson, using U.S. data, 1947–66, computed thirty-two pairs of comparable equations expressing interest rates (or first differences of interest rates) as a function of current and prior monetary magnitudes (levels, first, or second differences), the two equations in a pair differing only in that one used M_1 as the monetary total, the other M_2. Of the thirty-two pairs, the correlation coefficient was higher for M_1 in ten, for M_2 in twenty-one, and the same for M_1 and M_2 in one. [40]

9. George Kaufman has extended the Friedman-Meiselman correlations described in section 3 above. [41] He correlated quarter-to-quarter first differences of gross national product and alternative monetary totals for 1953–66 and two subperiods. This interval covers eight years subsequent to those covered in the Friedman-Meiselman correlations, though it drops some of the earlier years. In his computations for leads —ranging from money leading by four quarters to money lagging by two quarters—as well as in his synchronous observations, Kaufman covered a wider variety of monetary totals than Friedman-Meiselman.

By the criterion described in footnote 21 above, Kaufman's correlations show M_2 to be preferable to M_1 when the monetary observation leads the GNP observation by either two or three quarters, for both 1953–66 as a whole and for each of the subperiods 1953–59 and 1960–66. They show M_1 to be preferable for synchronous observations for the period as a whole but only the first of the subperiods. For leads of two and three quarters for the period as a whole and for the first subperiod, and for leads of one and three quarters for the second subperiod, totals broader than M_2 are preferable to M_2, though by very narrow margins. [42] Kaufman himself concludes:

[39] David Laidler, "Some Evidence on the Demand for Money," *Journal of Political Economy,* Feb. 1966, pp. 55–68; quotation from p. 55.

[40] "The Effects of Money on Interest Rates," unpublished Ph.D. dissertation, University of Chicago, 1967.

[41] "More on an Empirical Definition of Money," *American Economic Review,* Mar. 1969, pp. 78–87.

[42] For the period as a whole, the broader totals that are preferable are our totals III and IV, and his M_4 equal to our IV plus U.S. government savings bonds (Kaufman excludes postal savings deposits for his counterpart to our totals III and IV, including them in his M_4; we have neglected this minor difference between his definitions and ours). For a lead of three quarters, the correlation for our total II (M_2) is .36, for M_4, .40; for a lead of two quarters, the corresponding correlations are .44 and .46. Kaufman also computes a still broader total, equal to his M_4 plus U.S. government marketable securities maturing within one year. Generally this is decidedly inferior to the other totals except for leads of one and two quarters for the second subperiod.

. . . defining money according to the dual criteria established by F[ried-man]-M[eiselman] involves not only tests of alternative groupings of financial assets but also tests of alternative definitions over a number of lead-lag relationships with respect to income. Different components show different correlations as they are associated with income in preceding, concurrent, and later periods. A definition that includes demand and time deposits at commercial banks [our II = M_2] appears best at explaining income two or more quarters later. Demand deposits and currency are best at explaining income observed concurrently and one quarter later. Currency alone is the money supply concept most highly correlated with income in earlier periods. . . . [I]nclusion of savings-type deposits beyond time deposits at commercial banks . . . adds relatively little explanatory power to the definition of money. . . . [T]he evidence is generally consistent with the conclusions of F-M that an important and relatively stable relationship exists between money and income in succeeding periods, although the precise characteristic of the relationship varies with the definition of money. Only when money is defined to include currency alone is support provided for a theory relating money to earlier observations of income.[43]

10. V. Karuppan Chetty (see footnote 5 above) has estimated from postwar data the weights that should be assigned to commercial bank time deposits, mutual savings deposits, and savings and loan shares in constructing a monetary aggregate as a weighted sum of components (see footnote 5 above for a brief description of his procedure). He arbitrarily assigned a weight of unity to currency plus adjusted demand deposits and estimated the weights for the other components as unity for commercial bank time deposits, 0.88 for mutual savings deposits, and 0.615 for savings and loan shares.

These results confirm our own, both in indicating that total commercial bank deposits should be included in the monetary aggregate rather than only demand deposits and that, for the postwar period, a still broader aggregate may be better yet.

However, while we believe that this approach is extremely promising, we have serious reservations about how much confidence can be placed in Chetty's specific results for two reasons. First, they are derived entirely from post-World War II data which are dominated by trends. Second, on a purely theoretical level, we believe his formulation has the defect that it makes the results depend on a strictly arbitrary choice of the time unit used in stating interest rates (see footnote 2 of Chetty's article).

[43] *Ibid.,* pp. 86–87.

Appendix to Chapter 4
EVIDENCE ON ALTERNATIVE DEFINITIONS OF MONEY

This appendix presents the evidence summarized in section 3.

1. Comparison of States with and without Savings Banks

Mutual savings banks are in existence in only a minority of the states. A comparison of states with and without mutual savings banks should shed some light on the treatment of deposits in such banks. If these deposits are regarded by their holders as essentially equivalent to— that is, as nearly perfect substitutes for—commercial bank time deposits, the total of the two in states with mutual savings banks should be comparable with commercial bank time deposits alone in other states. On the other hand, if they are regarded as very different from commercial bank time deposits and as substitutes rather for other assets such as government bonds, then commercial bank time deposits alone should be comparable for states with and without mutual savings banks. Given the differences among states in population, per capita income, and economic structure, however, the absolute amount of deposits in different states can hardly be meaningfully compared; some scale adjustment is needed. For our scale adjustment we expressed the various types of time deposits as a ratio to demand deposits; it would be preferable to use currency plus demand deposits, but, unfortunately, no data are available on the distribution of currency among the states.

These ratios are given in Table 10 for 1915, 1929, and 1950. The results were surprising to us. We had expected that the ratio of commercial bank time deposits alone to demand deposits (call this T) in states without mutual savings banks would be between the corresponding ratio for states with mutual savings banks and the ratio of commercial bank plus mutual savings deposits to demand deposits (call this $M + T$) in such states. What we had hoped for from the numerical evidence was an indication of whether T for states without mutual savings banks was closer to the one extreme or the other. In fact, in each of the three years for which the ratios were computed, the value of T alone in states with mutual savings banks tends to be higher than the value of T in states without mutual savings banks! The average ratio of commercial

TABLE 10

Ratio of Time Deposits to Demand Deposits, by States With and Without Mutual Savings Banks, 1915, 1929, 1950

T = Time deposits in commercial banks/demand deposits; M+T = deposits in commercial banks plus mutual savings bank deposits/demand deposits

States Without Mutual Savings Banks	States With Mutual Savings Banks	1915		1929		1950	
		T	M+T	T	M+T	T	M+T
Ala.		.346		.830		.316	
Ariz.		.377		.724		.318	
Ark.		.241		.609		.170	
Calif.		1.208		1.670		.886	
Colo.		.592		.742		.282	
	Conn.	.211	2.902	.797	2.689	.415	1.756
	Del.	.303	.898	.508	.835	.270	.529
D.C.		.358		.698		.271	
Fla.		.520		.787		.256	
Ga.		.613		.943		.295	
Idaho		.349		.691		.362	
Ill.		.650		.774		.427	
	Ind.	.395	.447	.913	.969	.443	.462
Iowa		1.419		1.501		.344	
Kan.		.332		.386		.128	
Ky.		.414		.998		.211	
La.		.521		.534		.240	

(continued)

TABLE 10 (continued)

States Without Mutual Savings Banks	States With Mutual Savings Banks	1915 T	1915 M+T	1929 T	1929 M+T	1950 T	1950 M+T
	Maine	1.694	4.315	2.551	3.973	.842	1.861
	Md.	.441	1.174	1.072	1.767	.442	.822
	Mass.	.114	1.604	.614	2.447	.266	1.437
Mich.		1.167		1.276		.783	
	Minn.	1.007	1.137	1.259	1.459	.553	.658
Miss.		.481		.899		.248	
Mo.		.460		.614		.267	
Mont.		.601		.977		.253	
Nebr.		.602		.758		.152	
Nev.		.604		1.146		.578	
	N.H.	.769	5.425	1.572	5.817	.831	2.910
	N.J.	.629	1.023	1.283	1.582	.878	1.114
N.M.		.432		.398		.165	
	N.Y.	.138	.675	.356	.922	.191	.744
N.C.		.492		.956		.385	
N.D.		1.337		1.256		.448	
	Ohio	.773	.904	1.208	1.303	.646	.704

(continued)

191

TABLE 10 (concluded)

States Without Mutual Savings Banks	States With Mutual Savings Banks	1915		1929		1950	
		T	M+T	T	M+T	T	M+T
Okla.		.183		.412		.962	
Ore.a	Ore.	.480		.891		.439	.458
	Penna.	.475	.675	1.077	1.278	.515	.688
	R.I.	.713	1.675	1.462	2.730	.775	1.464
S.C.		.952		1.248		.174	
S.D.		1.106		.913		.241	
Tenn.		.500		.859		.387	
Tex.		.127		.309		.131	
Utah		.961		1.320		.576	
	Vt.	3.361	7.053	3.795	7.005	1.748	2.709
Va.		.595		1.224		.587	
Wash.a	Wash.	.743		.676	.906	.433	.597
W. Va.a		.842	.864	.975		.434	
	Wisc.	1.224	1.237	1.454	1.477	.826	.835
Wyo.		.702		.781		.254	
	Average	.620	2.000	.882	2.326	.360	1.162
Average		.818		1.287		.617	

aNo mutual savings banks in operation in Oregon, 1915 and 1929, in Washington, 1915, and in West Virginia, 1929 and 1950.

Source: *All-Bank Statistics, 1896–1955*.

bank time deposits to demand deposits in the states with mutual savings banks is .82, 1.29, and .62 for 1915, 1929, and 1950, respectively, and only .62, .88, and .36 in the other states. A glance at the figures in Table 10 shows that this is not an accident produced by one or two extreme values. Apparently there is some relationship between the presence of mutual savings banks and a high preference for time deposits whether in such banks or in others. As we suggest in the text, the fact that mutual savings banks are mostly in older and more highly developed areas may produce such a relationship.

Examination of the ratios for neighboring and reasonably similar states does not resolve the difficulty or give any clear indication of the status of mutual savings deposits. The ratios are closer together for New York and New Jersey, and for New Hampshire and Vermont, when mutual savings deposits are included than when they are excluded; on the other hand, they are closer together for Ohio and Indiana, Maryland and Virginia, when mutual savings deposits are excluded.

It is hard to know how to interpret these data. They clearly raise more questions than they answer. For our purpose, it seems perhaps more reasonable to regard the data as an argument for excluding mutual savings bank deposits than for including them. In either treatment, states with mutual savings banks make a heavier contribution to time than to demand deposits. The inclusion of mutual savings deposits makes this difference greater than their exclusion.

2. Cross-Section Correlations of Deposits and Personal Income

We can use the state-by-state data in still another way by correlating various deposit items and totals with personal income, all the variables being expressed per capita to eliminate the effect of population differences. Table 11 shows, for six selected years (1929, 1935, 1940, 1950, 1955, and 1960), correlation coefficients between personal income and demand deposits, commercial bank time deposits, mutual savings deposits, and two subtotals: (1) demand deposit plus commercial bank time deposits and (2) total 1 plus mutual savings deposits. In addition, for 1950, 1955, and 1960, Table 11 gives correlation coefficients between personal income and savings and loan shares and (3), total 2 plus savings and loan shares.

One striking uniformity is that the correlations with individual deposit components are all lower than, or (in one case only) equal to,

TABLE 11

Correlation Between Per Capita Personal Income and Various Per Capita Monetary Components and Totals, by States, Selected Years, 1929–60

Year	Demand Deposits (D) (1)	Commercial Bank Time Deposits (CT) (2)	Mutual Savings Bank Deposits (MSB) (3)	Savings and Loan Shares (S&L) (4)	Total 1 D+CT (5)	Total 2 D+CT+ MSB (6)	Total 3 D+CT+MSB+ S&L (7)
1929	.91	.81	.40		.93	.91	
1935	.87	.82	.50		.92	.88	
1940	.88	.82	.44		.94	.91	
1950	.77	.75	.10	.62	.9067	.9106	.9189
1955	.69	.71	.24	.54	.82	.88	.90
1960	.65	.61	.18	.38	.75	.8089	.8107

Source: (a) Per capita personal income, by states: *Personal Income by States Since 1929*, U. S. Department of Commerce, OBE, Washington, 1956, pp. 142–143; *Statistical Abstract of the U. S.*, 1962, p. 319.
(b) Demand, time, mutual savings deposits: *All-Bank Statistics, 1896–1955*; *Assets, Liabilities, and Capital Accounts, Commercial and Mutual Savings Banks*, Report on Call No. 53, FDIC.
(c) Savings and loan shares: *Trends in the Savings and Loan Field*, FHLBB, 1950, 1951, 1955, 1956, 1960, 1961.
(d) Population: *Current Population Reports, Population Estimates*, U. S. Bureau of the Census, Series P–25, No. 139, June 27, 1956; *Statistical Abstract of the U. S.*, 1962, p. 9.

194

TABLE 12

Mean and Standard Deviation of Natural Logarithms of Per Capita Deposits and Per Capita Personal Income, by States

Year	Demand Deposits D	Commercial Bank Time Deposits CT	Mutual Savings Bank Deposits MSB	Savings and Loan Shares S&L	D+CT	D+CT+ MSB	D+CT+ MSB+S&L	Personal Income PI
1929	4.8578 (0.4846)	4.7698 (0.6307)	4.2867 (1.5312)		5.5340 (0.5093)	5.6344 (0.6151)		6.3687 (0.3766)
1935	4.5974 (0.5019)	4.2573 (0.6912)	3.9001 (2.0370)		5.1677 (0.5374)	5.2907 (0.6790)		6.0106 (0.3703)
1940	4.9632 (0.5076)	4.4039 (0.6692)	4.2036 (1.7863)		5.4447 (0.5231)	5.5596 (0.6416)		6.2438 (0.3727)
1950	6.1509 (0.3792)	5.1467 (0.6259)	4.6431 (1.5698)	4.2361 (0.6032)	6.4974 (0.3703)	6.5840 (0.4161)	6.6851 (0.4156)	7.2151 (0.2524)
1955	6.2990 (0.3468)	5.3795 (0.5328)	4.8723 (1.5484)	4.9206 (0.5517)	6.6600 (0.3370)	6.7533 (0.3853)	6.9165 (0.3767)	7.4311 (0.2282)
1960	6.3238 (0.3082)	5.6906 (0.4519)	4.8605 (1.8605)	5.4631 (0.5694)	6.7682 (0.3016)	6.8649 (0.3543)	7.1074 (0.3469)	7.6237 (0.2165)

Note: The first entry for each year is the mean. The second entry, in parentheses, is the standard deviation.
Source: Same as for Table 11.

the correlations with totals of the components. So far as this goes, it suggests that the components are in some measure substitutes and that one of the broader totals is preferable as a concept of money to demand deposits alone. As among the totals for 1929, 1935, and 1940 the correlations are highest for the sum of demand deposits and commercial bank time deposits. For 1950, 1955, and 1960, the correlations are highest for the total that also includes mutual savings bank deposits and savings and loan shares. This supports for the pre-World War II period the total we have used, but a broader total for the post-World War II period.

The correlations for the components are roughly the same for the first three years in the table but appreciably lower for 1950, 1955, and 1960 than for the earlier years. There is a similar difference for total 1, commercial bank deposits. For total 2, which adds mutual savings deposits, only the correlation for 1960 is appreciably lower than the others. One possible explanation for these differences is the lower relative variability of personal income among states in the final three years than in the earlier three years (Table 12). The logarithmic standard deviations of personal income, in natural logarithms (these can be regarded as estimates of the coefficients of variation of the original observations), are .38, .37, .37, .25, .22, and .22 in the six years. Such a decline means that there is less of a systematic difference in personal income among states to produce systematic differences in deposits; hence the variation in deposit holdings *attributable* to income differences will tend to be smaller. Unless the other variables affecting deposit holding have also become more uniform among states, the effect is to reduce the fraction of the variation accounted for by income, and hence the correlation coefficient. For total 2, this effect appears to have been overcome, at least to some extent, by the emergence of a closer connection between that deposit total and personal income.

5

CONCLUSION ON DEFINITION

ON A STRICTLY ABSTRACT LEVEL, it makes no difference how money is defined. Different definitions can be accommodated by changing the equations that simultaneously determine the equilibrium values of the variables. If, for example, money is defined simply as currency, variables describing the terms on which demand deposits, time deposits, etc., can be acquired will enter the demand function for money (equal to currency). If money is defined to include demand deposits, some of these variables will instead enter the function defining the fraction of money (equal to currency plus demand deposits) demanded in the form of currency.

More generally, the notion of a "stable" demand function, which has played so large a role in our examination of the empirical magnitude that it is best to term "money," is meaningless unless something is specified about the variables included in the function. The "instability" of a particular function can always be interpreted as the result of omitting some relevant variables. The existence of a stable function for anything can never be contradicted if the number of variables included is permitted to be indefinitely large. Implicitly, therefore, the term "stability" used in empirical discussions always means "relative" stability of a function of a "small number of variables." And the terms in quotation marks are not capable of specification on a strictly abstract level.

In empirical work, it makes a great deal of difference how money is defined. The reason is the costs involved—intellectual even more than computational—in handling a large number of variables. The chief goal in empirical work is to find a way of organizing experience so that it yields "simple" yet highly dependable relationships. And one of the major devices that has proved successful in achieving this goal has been the use of carefully chosen, "right" levels of aggregation of different items, as in such a construct as "money," "income," "consumption," etc.; of different decision units, as in aggregates for households versus business enterprises; or of different geographical or political areas, as in aggregates for nations.

This choice, as we have emphasized, is one that cannot be made by any single set of hard and fast rules. It is a question of judgment on the basis of criteria that are inevitably incomplete and often unformulated. The test of the choice is in the results, that is, in the usefulness of the definitions selected in uncovering dependable and reproducible empirical regularities. The test of our own decision is to be found in the use we have made of our definition of money in the other books of this set (see *Preface*).

While it makes a great deal of difference empirically how money is defined, the unimportance of definitions on an abstract level also has an empirical counterpart. The purpose of a definition is to facilitate organizing the data in a useful way, not to prejudge conclusions. With the definition we have selected—currency held by the public plus all adjusted deposits at commercial banks, demand and time—the behavior of commercial bank deposits relative to currency, or of time deposits relative to demand deposits, becomes a question of the relative composition of the money stock, and we have analyzed it as such. The behavior of savings deposits and of savings and loan shares becomes a question of the behavior of these "near-moneys" relative to the total we have labeled money, and we have analyzed it as such.

We have not carried out parallel analyses in all cases for alternative definitions—that would negate the empirical usefulness of selecting one definition. But wherever there was reason to suspect that a particular conclusion might be especially sensitive to the definition used, we have tried to ascertain whether it is. As a result, we believe, as stated in the introduction to this part, that the definition we have adopted has served mainly to organize our analysis rather than to determine its content.

PART TWO

EARLIER ESTIMATES

Introduction

The construction of comprehensive time series for the United States of the stock of currency or deposits or their sum dates back more than a century and a half—almost to the founding of the Republic. Generally, the final estimates have involved a division of labor between private individuals and official agencies, the individuals constructing the final estimates from basic statistics collected by agencies. This division of labor has never been complete. Official agencies have from time to time, and especially in recent years, constructed comprehensive estimates, and private individuals have contributed to the collection of basic statistics by criticizing official compilations, rearranging and adding to them, and stimulating additional collections of data.[1]

Throughout the period, the monetary estimates, and even more the basic data used in constructing the estimates, have often been by-products of other interests. Currency and banking problems have occasioned public concern and governmental action since Colonial times and still do so today—witness the recent changes in both coins and paper money and the recurring Congressional consideration of the regulation of banks and financial intermediaries. Unquestionably governmental regulatory agencies and legislatures have been the most important sources of data for the monetary estimates—though the data used in constructing the monetary estimates have been only a small part of the total collected by these branches of government.

Until after World War I, neither official agencies nor private individuals combined, as a regular practice, currency and deposits into a single total designated "money."[2] At first the reason was that only currency—and, initially, only specie—was regarded as "money." Bank notes were initially treated simply as "claims" to money, and deposits continued to be

---

[1] The reason private initiative was limited in collecting monetary data was explained by W. M. Gouge (*A Short History of the Paper Money and Banking in the United States,* Philadelphia, 1833, Part II): "To collect and arrange the accounts of five or six hundred Banks which are, or which have been, scattered through twenty-four States and two or three Territories would be no easy task" (p. 221). Gouge was critical of the accuracy of existing banking figures and of monetary estimates (pp. 219–226).

[2] Amasa Walker was one (though not the only) exception. As part of his description of the "mixed currency" system of the United States, he published sums of bank notes outstanding and gross bank deposits, excluding interbank but including Treasury deposits, 1834–59, using the state bank figures in the Treasury annual reports (*The Science of Wealth: A Manual of Political Economy,* Boston, 1866, p. 161). These reports are discussed in Chapter 7.

so treated even after bank notes were accorded the status of money proper.

By the end of the nineteenth century, the reason was slightly different. E. W. Kemmerer, Irving Fisher, and others, while still not treating deposits as "money," in their development of the quantity equation subdivided transactions into those effected by currency (MV) and those effected by check ($M'V'$). To test or fill in this equation, they constructed estimates from which a single total of currency and deposits might have been obtained. However, they were interested mostly in the components, and other investigators followed their lead.

The recognition of the need to separate money held by the public from money held by banks was also crucial to the development of U.S. monetary statistics. Even the earliest bank statements in the United States distinguished the deposits of the nonbanking public from the deposits of banks. However, the parallel distinction between currency held by the public and currency in banks was not usually made until a much later date, even though some early students recognized its importance. Typically, the sum of currency held by the public and banks— total bank notes outstanding reported by the issuing banks—was given as the amount in circulation.[3] The focus of interest was the banks—

[3] On this point, two illustrations may be cited. The first is a remark of Secretary of the Treasury Crawford concerning one set of his own estimates of bank note circulation in 1819 (he made alternative ones) in "Report on Currency Made to the House of Representatives of the United States, 24th February, 1820," in *Reports of the Secretary of the Treasury of the United States,* Vol. II, Washington, 1837:

It is probable, however, that this estimate is too high; as, according to the general practice of banks, all notes issued are considered in circulation, which are not in the possession of the bank by which they were issued. A reasonable deduction being made from the notes supposed to be in circulation, but which are, in fact, in the possession of other banks, it is probable that the actual circulation . . . is less, at this time, than . . . (p. 482).

Despite this insight, Crawford's estimates for 1813 and 1815 were limited to bank notes outstanding, and in tabulations (arranged by other investigators, not by him), of his estimates for these two years and for 1819, his estimate of bank notes held by the public in 1819 was ignored.

The second illustration is in Albert Gallatin, *Considerations on the Currency and Banking,* Philadelphia, 1831: ". . . the notes of other banks on hand, form no part of the circulation, and ought, when considering the banking system as a whole, to be deducted from the amount of the notes in circulation" (p. 41).

Though Gallatin estimated bank note circulation in 1829 "if the notes of other banks on hand are deducted" instead of following the "usual mode of computing" (p. 54), the estimates associated with his name for 1810, 1814, 1815, and 1829 (in his account shown as the beginning of the following years) are for notes outstanding. See U.S. Bureau of the Census, *Historical Statistics of the United States, Colonial Times to 1957, 1960* [*Historical Statistics, 1960*], p. 623, Series X-3.

On the other hand, a table in a Treasury Department document of 1834 distinguishes "All paper issued and in the country" and "All specie in the country" from amounts whether their resources were adequate to their demand liabilities, regardless of the identity of the holders—rather than the public, which chose to hold part of its money in the form of currency. Early statistical practice ignored the cancellation—when the accounts of all banks are consolidated—of bank notes held as an asset by some banks against the corresponding liability of other banks.

The concept of currency held by the public did not become firmly established until it was rediscovered early in this century. On the other hand, from the start of banking operations in the United States there was widespread recognition that some specie in the banks duplicated bank notes outstanding, which were promises to pay specie, and that other specie in banks, which the banks regarded as a reserve for deposits, duplicated some deposits of the public, and hence that specie in banks should be omitted to avoid double-counting. The concept of bank float as duplications in the deposit accounts arising from checks credited to the drawee but not yet debited to the drawer was first developed in this century.

Because 1867 marks the year our own estimates begin, the estimates for the period before 1867 are discussed separately (Chapter 7) from those for the post-Civil War period (Chapter 8). Chapter 9 compares the various earlier estimates with our own. The general contours of all the estimates are similar, but there are numerous differences in detailed movements that would be capable of significantly altering conclusions, especially about cyclical timing and behavior.

Before turning to a detailed examination of the earlier estimates, we discuss in Chapter 6 some common features of the basic data.

"Not circulating"—"Paper in other banks" and "Specie in banks"—and shows the remainder as "Circulations" of "Paper" (private and state bank notes and "national and U. States bank notes," separately) and "Specie" (gold and silver, separately), in selected years 1775–1834, with estimates for whatever items are available (23d Cong., 2nd sess., H. Rept. 27, p. 63). Ezra Seaman in *Essays on the Progress of Nations,* Detroit, 1846, estimated bank notes held by the public after commenting as follows on official statistics for all banks in selected years 1811–45:

> The table exhibits the whole amount of notes issued and outstanding of all banks, without deducting the amount of notes held by the banks respectively, which were issued by other banks; on making this deduction, the nett circulation . . . was but . . . . [B]y deducting the amount of specie in the vaults of the banks from the nett circulation of the same, at any period stated in the table, any one can ascertain the increase of our circulating medium by reason of bank paper (pp. 243–244).

6

SOURCES AND ACCURACY
OF BASIC DATA

DATA FOR SPECIE (gold and silver), currency, and deposits—both their totals and their distributions among the Treasury, the banks, and the public—come typically from different sources. The reasons are both statistical and institutional.

1. Sources of Data

Specie

Official yearly compilations of the U.S. monetary gold stock and the stock of silver begin only with June 30, 1873, the first date for which the Director of the Mint made estimates. That year was chosen as the start of the series because it was believed the stocks at the time could be accurately estimated. Gold was at a high premium. Nearly all the gold coin in the country was either in the Treasury or the banks. Silver dollar coinage had been discontinued in 1873 and few, if any, dollars of the old series were believed to be in circulation. Silver bullion in the Treasury was known. Subsidiary silver coinage circulated mainly on the Pacific coast.

Annual gold stock and subsidiary silver coin estimates, 1860–72, keyed to the Director of the Mint's 1873 estimates, were published by the Treasury in 1922. The figures were described as "only estimates" since the records are not complete for the early years.[1] The Treasury

[1] The 1860–72 estimates, which were first given in the 1922 Treasury annual report (p. 524), are described in the 1928 annual report (p. 551, footnote 1). In Treasury

and Director of Mint figures from 1860 on are the official U.S. gold stock series.

For dates before 1860 the only available official information is the amount of specie minted by the federal government and, beginning October 1820, annual exports and imports of the precious metals, at first for gold and silver combined and then, beginning 1825, separately for gold and silver. Estimates of the gold stock were made from time to time before the Civil War by official or private investigators. The estimates usually assumed a known stock at some date to serve as a base for subsequent calculations. To this, annual net imports were added, sometimes with corrections for unreported imports and exports and withdrawals into the arts.

The annual reporting of total specie in the Treasury began in 1879 (for gold, annual reporting began in 1876, for silver dollars and subsidiary silver, in 1878) and reporting on a current monthly basis began in 1887, with back figures monthly to June 1878. It is possible to derive estimated Treasury specie holdings annually back to 1860 (estimates for 1862–63, however, are lacking) by subtracting the amounts outside the Treasury from the stock, as shown in tables in the 1928 annual re-

publications, 1896–1921, the combined specie stock was shown unchanged at $25 million from 1862 to 1875.

The subsidiary coin estimates for 1873–77 in the Director of the Mint's 1887 report were revised in the 1922 Treasury annual report.

Through 1933 we define the stock of silver as consisting solely of silver dollars, whether held by the public, banks, the Treasury, or the mints. We exclude both subsidiary silver and silver bullion held by the Treasury and the mints through 1933. The coinage of standard silver dollars began in 1878, under the Act of Feb. 28, 1878. The 1873–77 figures for the silver stock in the Director of the Mint's report included silver bullion in the Treasury. These figures were reprinted in the 1922 Treasury annual report (no earlier figures were given).

The exclusion until 1933 of silver bullion from the monetary silver stock until coined was in line with the practice of the U.S. Treasury in its monthly *Circulation Statement*, 1887–1933. Upon the passage of the Silver Purchase Act of 1933, this practice was discontinued and silver bullion was included in the silver stock shown in the *Circulation Statement*. The rationale was that prompt additions to silver certificates were made by the Treasury upon the acquisition of silver bullion. We have followed Treasury practice for the years since 1933. Subsidiary silver, however, has been in a separate category throughout. Gold bullion in the Treasury has always been included in the monetary gold stock. The different treatment of silver bullion before and after 1933 does not affect the final estimates of specie held by the public but only the amount recorded as held by the Treasury.

A. P. Andrew's figures for the stock of standard dollars, 1878–1909, include the bullion in the Treasury at cost value (*Statistics for the United States, 1867–1909*, National Monetary Commission, 1910, S. Doc. 570, 61st Cong., 2nd sess., p. 156). For March 1887–June 1890, Andrew's figures for silver outside the Treasury apparently include an estimate of silver bullion held by banks and the public, which we never include in our stock series.

port of the Treasury. The description of the early specie stock figures as "only estimates" applies also to the amounts in Treasury.

None of the contemporary estimates of the pre-Civil War gold stock referred to specie in the Treasury: only specie in banks and in circulation. In Chapter 7, we examine the evidence on whether the Treasury held any specie before the Civil War.[2]

Data on the amount of specie in banks could be obtained as a by product of the accumulation of banking statistics, but in the absence of estimates of the total stock and of amounts in the Treasury, no reliable estimates of the amount held by the public could be made.

Currency

Until the Civil War, most currency was issued by state banks. During the War of 1812, the Treasury issued interest-bearing notes that to some extent circulated as currency and that were widely used as bank reserves.[3] From 1791 to 1811 the First Bank of the United States and from 1816 to 1836 the Second Bank of the United States issued currency as well. Civil War currency issues—national bank notes, U.S. notes, other U.S. currency, and fractional currency—transformed the composition of the currency. After the Civil War, state bank notes were driven out of circulation; therefore the Civil War marks a watershed in data on currency: earlier the data came primarily from state banking authorities, later from the federal authorities responsible for the various types of national currency.

Before 1860, as indicated earlier, the Treasury reported only its money balance, not the form in which it was held, so that there is no direct information on the Treasury's currency holdings. In Chapter 7, we discuss the indirect evidence bearing on this question. From 1860

---

[2] There are two official versions of Treasury specie holdings before 1860, one shown in the Comptroller's annual report for 1894 and described as prepared by the Loan and Currency Division of the Treasury, and the other shown in the Treasury's annual report for 1906. The Comptroller's table, which shows specie in the Treasury—at decade intervals 1800–30, thereafter annually—is based on the yearly reported figures on money "balance in the Treasury," which were never designated as "specie in the Treasury." The table in the Treasury annual report, which bears the title "Balance in the Treasury," classifies the total from 1789 on into amounts in Treasury offices and amounts in depositary banks. If one reconciles the two official versions by assuming that the Comptroller's table mistakenly designates the Treasury's total balance as specie, it must still be determined whether the amounts in Treasury offices, as given in the Treasury table, were in fact held in specie.

[3] Interest-bearing Treasury notes were also issued in 1837–42, 1846, and 1857–60. They were receivable for all public dues but were not a legal tender. When issued in small denominations, as in 1840, the notes apparently served as currency.

on, the sources of information on the Treasury's holdings of currency are the same as those discussed above for its specie holdings.

Throughout, banking statistics—their coverage is discussed in the paragraphs that follow—provide information on the amount of currency held by banks. Information is generally more readily available for the stock of currency than for the stock of specie. Therefore the residual holdings of the public can be estimated with greater reliability for currency than for specie, even when Treasury holdings of currency are not known with certainty.

Banking Statistics

Of course, deposits were throughout a liability of banks, but the extent of reporting by different kinds of banks varied enormously. Private banks, that is, banks operating without a state or federal charter, reported little data, in many instances, none at all. These banks were important until quite recently. Banks chartered by states have sometimes been required to report to state banking authorities, sometimes not. Before the Civil War, the Second Bank of the United States reported data for each year of its existence, the First Bank reported virtually none, even though, like its successor, the First Bank was at times an important issuer of deposits held by the public as well as of notes. Fortunately, data for the First Bank, discovered in its manuscript records, have been made available to us and are presented in Table 13. For the period 1833–62, the Secretary of the Treasury, in compliance with a resolution of the House of Representatives passed in July 1832, compiled and published such banking statistics as he obtained in response to his annual call for information from the state banks.

With the establishment of the National Banking System figures for the national banks were published for several dates a year in the annual reports of the Comptroller of the Currency. To comply with an act of February 19, 1873, the Comptroller also began to publish balance sheets of nonnational banks for which he received reports from state banking authorities. Initially a relatively small and changing sample of nonnational banks was included. In part this incompleteness was due to the fact that not all nonnational banks were required by the states to submit reports. In 1887, the Comptroller began to obtain by correspondence information from banks not required to report. During the course of the following decades, the coverage gradually increased.

In 1910, the National Monetary Commission, which had been engaged in a searching investigation into monetary and banking systems throughout the world, issued a series of publications that comprised a major addition to the statistical record. A survey of the condition of virtually all U.S. banks in 1909 was the outcome of one of the commission's special inquiries. The commission also published special compilations of data already available (but not all previously published) in official reports, notably A. P. Andrew's *Statistics for the United States, 1867–1909* and the findings of special studies it sponsored and published, notably George E. Barnett's *State Banks and Trust Companies Since the Passage of the National Bank Act,* Edwin W. Kemmerer's *Seasonal Variations in the Relative Demand for Money and Capital in the United States,* and David Kinley's *Use of Credit Instruments in Payments in the United States.*

The Comptroller's reports, the reports of state banking authorities, and the National Monetary Commission studies are the main sources of banknote and deposit statistics for the five decades before the establishment of the Federal Reserve System. For the period 1863–95, when the Comptroller's coverage of nonnational banks is inadequate, data on assessments and also receipts of taxes levied by the federal government upon bank deposits until 1883 provide additional and more comprehensive information on deposits.

Since 1914, data are available for members of the Federal Reserve System, and since 1934, for banks insured by the FDIC. In addition, since 1947, the FDIC has compiled a comprehensive semiannual all-bank series.

Since banks have usually distinguished interbank from other deposits, and since Treasury deposits at banks are known, the distribution of total reported deposits among holders is less difficult to determine than the distribution of the stock of specie and currency. However, the adjustment of deposits held by the public for float presents problems, which are discussed in Chapters 7 and 8.

2. Accuracy of the Data

As in other fields, federal regulation, whatever may be its other returns or costs, has produced one gain: a probable improvement in the quantity and generally in the quality of statistical data. For earlier periods, the quality of the specie figures must be assessed separately from that of the banking statistics.

Specie

The specie estimates before 1873 are subject to large errors.[4] After 1873, the official annual gold stock figures as revised by the Director of the Mint in 1907 are satisfactory.[5] The only change we deemed necessary in the series (apart from adjusting the unrevised monthly stock, 1878–1907, to the level of the revised annual series) was the restoration of $287 million to the gold stock figures that the Federal Reserve arbitrarily excluded, 1914–33.[6]

[4] Accompanying a table in the *Annual Report on the Finances,* 1854, p. 281, giving "estimates of the amount of gold and silver in the United States at different periods," is a list of eight reasons the amount cannot be "indisputably" known:

1. Lack of data on specie imports and exports before 1821
2. Concealment of transactions in bullion by merchants, and failure of custom-houses to report specie brought in by immigrants
3. Lack of data on silver brought in overland from Mexico
4. Lack of data on annual loss on coin by abrasion
5. Failure of census returns showing consumption of precious metals in manufactures, in gold and silverware, and in plating and gilding to distinguish old materials worked over from use of new bullion
6. Unreliability of mint returns as guide to coin in circulation—because foreign coins for many years constituted a major fraction of metallic currency, and mints in many years fabricated coins chiefly for export
7. Variability in the public's preference for bank notes over specie from year to year and from section to section of the country
8. "As the banks make their returns on different days, or different hours of the same day, the same pieces of gold and silver may figure successively in the accounts of several banks. In this way one million may be made to appear as two millions, and five millions as ten or fifteen millions. It is said that in old times the banks used to lend their specie to one another, in order that each might in its turn make a good show to the legislature. It is even said that with this object, specie in one city used to be placed temporarily to the credit of banks in other cities. When the quantity of specie in the country was small, the temptation to resort to such contrivances was greater than it is at present."

[5] Director of the Mint, *Annual Report,* 1907, p. 87. The Treasury Department official series of the gold stock suffers a break in its continuity on June 30, 1907, when it shifts to the lower level of the Director of the Mint's revised series. The official series has not been revised to put the figures for 1873–1906 on a comparable basis with later figures. The discontinuity also exists in the figures for gold outside the Treasury ("in circulation," in official jargon). See, for example, *Banking and Monetary Statistics,* Board of Governors of the Federal Reserve System, Washington, D.C., 1943, p. 408, and *Historical Statistics of the United States, Colonial Times to 1957,* Bureau of the Census, 1960, p. 649, Series X-285. A footnote in the latter source and some text discussion on p. 645 do, however, alert the reader to the discontinuity. It also exists in official series of the total currency stock and the currency outside the Treasury.

[6] It did so to allow for a supposed overestimate of the gold stock inferred, in our opinion erroneously, from the discrepancy between the recorded gold stock outside the Treasury and banks and the amount of gold turned in by the public in 1933 and 1934 when the private holding of gold was made illegal (see our *Monetary History,* pp. 463–464, footnote 45).

Estimates of specie held by banks before 1863 are probably also questionable,[7] as are estimates of specie held by the Treasury before the terminal years of the greenback period, except for 1847–61, when, on the basis of the evidence in Chapter 7, we may assume that all of the Treasury's money balance was held in specie. Hence estimates of specie held by the public for corresponding periods are not reliable. The reliability of estimates of specie held by banks after 1863 is best considered in the context of the banking statistics in general.

Banking Statistics

Investigators, including ourselves, who have not been content simply to use sums of unrefined reported data, particularly for the period before 1947, have had certain common problems in constructing acceptable estimates of aggregate monetary totals from the banking statistics: incompleteness of coverage, ambiguity of reported data, inaccuracy of reported data, and divergent dating of the data. These problems are considered in detail in Chapter 8 in connection with our description of the various estimates for the period since 1867, but a few advance comments may help put the later details in perspective.

The officially reported banking statistics that form the major single source of data for all estimates (except possibly the very earliest) have always been, and remain today, incomplete in their coverage, although today the gaps are miniscule. Every investigator has been plagued by the problem of nonreporting banks and has had to resort to additional information to estimate (at the very least) their number and often to arbitrary assumptions in order to allow for them in his estimates. For banks that did not report regularly to public authorities, records of the Bureau of Internal Revenue are useful for the periods 1864–83 and 1900–02, when taxes were levied on both deposits and capital of banks or on capital alone. Information on nonreporting banks has also been obtained for these and other periods from privately compiled directories of banks, special studies of the National Monetary Commission, publications of state finance or tax departments in instances where banks were subject to state taxes, studies made by individual students of banking, and records of the nonreporting banks themselves.

The nature of the incompleteness is dual: First, many banks—state banks particularly in early decades and private banks throughout—

[7] See item 8 of footnote 4, above.

reported regularly to no government authority. Second, many of the reports to state authorities were not included in the compilations of the federal government. Yet it was these compilations, not the original sources, that perforce were used by most investigators. For example, in constructing our own estimates, we started to supplement the national bank compilation by using all available state reports, but the labor involved was so great that we had to compromise on a sample. Comprehensive coverage of all banks, at annual dates, did not become available until 1959, when the Federal Reserve System published its compilation of these reports in *All-Bank Statistics,*[8] and even this compilation goes back only to 1896.

Even for reporting banks, the data have often been incomplete and ambiguous. The information requested by state or federal authorities depended on their regulatory purposes and varied from time to time along with these purposes and with the interests of the officials in charge of the agencies. A major factor in the ambiguity of the aggregate estimates was the changing and incomplete system of classification whereby deposits were variously classed as individual, i.e., deposits of the nonbank public, as opposed to interbank, and individual deposits were broken down into demand and time deposits.

The accuracy of the reported data is affected also by "window dressing." Before the Civil War, the dates at which banks were required to report to state banking authorities were generally specified in the state laws imposing the requirement. Knowing these dates, banks were able to adjust their balance sheets to appear in the most favorable light in the official report. National banks initially had the same opportunity to "window-dress." Under the National Banking Act of February 1863 they were required to make quarterly reports of their condition on the first Monday of January, April, July, and October. To eliminate window dressing the law was amended in March 1869: report dates were no longer stipulated in the act; thenceforth the Comptroller would "call" for the reports without advance notice. From 1870 to 1913, there were five calls annually, at dates which varied erratically from year to year. Similarly, state banking authorities designated for banks under their jurisdiction call dates which might or might not coincide with those chosen by the Comptroller and which might or might not afford an

---

8 *All-Bank Statistics, United States, 1896–1955,* Board of Governors of the Federal Reserve System, Washington, D.C., 1959.

opportunity for window dressing. No investigator, including ourselves, has adjusted for possible window dressing.

The measures taken to prevent window dressing introduced a different source of error. Banking statistics show a sizable intraweekly movement—deposits are converted into currency for payroll purposes at the end of a week and the currency returns to banks in the early part of the week as pay is spent—as well as sizable seasonal movements. Hence, the varying dates of call, especially because they fell on different days of the week, introduced an appreciably erratic element in the currency figures. In addition, the report dates for nonnational banks, before and after the Civil War, often differed from state to state.

All estimates earlier than ours for the period before 1914 are annual. The general procedure for years up to 1863 was to use an arbitrarily chosen date like January 1 and to sum all the state data "closest to" that date, no matter how distant the individual report dates were in fact, and to describe the estimates as applying to January 1 of each year. For years after 1863 the general procedure was simply to use the national bank call date closest to June 30 along with a cluster of dates for nonnational banks close to June 30 and to describe the estimates as applying to June 30 of each year.

As the foregoing comments on the basic data and their accuracy indicate, monetary estimates of a crude sort can be constructed by ignoring the shortcomings of the data. More refined estimates require adjustment of the basic data. We shall trace the gradual introduction of refinements in the construction of monetary estimates in the next two chapters which review the work of our predecessors.

7

ESTIMATES FOR THE PERIOD
BEFORE 1867

THE ESTIMATES for the period before 1867 are sometimes limited to the stock of specie, currency, or deposits or to the amounts held by the banks or the Treasury rather than the amounts held by the public. Moreover the available estimates are not continuous over the whole period and are very fragmentary and varied in coverage. Therefore a given author may provide estimates for a selected few of a dozen different monetary items and only for selected years in the eight decades covered. The successive subsections of this chapter are therefore somewhat discontinuous. In each we try to explain how the particular author derived his estimates on the basis of his own approach. To help the reader thread his way through this maze, left-hand italic headings listed under the author's name identify the period and the monetary categories in the subsection devoted to each author.

The chapter is organized according to the authors of the estimates. The latter are classified as either private or official. The earliest private estimates deserving mention were published by Samuel Blodget in 1806. These covered both currency and deposits. Later (1846), Ezra Seaman estimated bank note currency outstanding and the stock of specie in selected years. Beginning in the 1830's, estimates of one monetary total or another for specific years may be found in contemporary periodicals, like Hazard's *Commercial Register,* Gouge's *Journal of Banking,* Hunt's *Merchants Magazine,* and Homan's *Bankers' Almanac* (section 1).

The earliest official estimates were made by Secretary of the Treasury W. H. Crawford in 1820. Subsequent secretaries of the Treasury published fairly regularly, during the period 1834–63, annual balance sheet data for reporting banks and occasional tables summarizing the private or official estimates of the stock of specie for whatever dates such estimates were available. Since then estimates of currency held by the Treasury before 1867 have been published by government agencies. The most recent estimates in official reports are those of total bank deposits in 1864–66 prepared by the FDIC (section 2). Private estimates made in this century include currency issues during Civil War years, by Wesley C. Mitchell (1903), and the money stock, in selected years between 1799 and 1865, by Clark Warburton (1949 and 1961), John G. Gurley and Edward S. Shaw (1957), George Macesich (1958 and 1968), and Peter Temin (1969) (section 3).

Table 13 summarizes the estimates that we have been able to find for years before 1867 of the stock of specie, bank notes, Treasury currency issues, and bank deposits, and of the distribution of these items among the Treasury, the banks, and the public. Estimates dated originally as of the first of January are dated in the table as of the thirty-first of the preceding December; similarly, estimates dated originally as of the first of other months are dated in the table as of the end of the months preceding. Table 14 combines the components in Table 13 into alternative estimates of the money stock for those years before 1867— mainly those beginning 1833—for which all the components are available.

Differences in the level and direction of movement of the alternative money stock estimates are discussed in the fourth and final section. These differences arise even though neither nineteenth nor twentieth century investigators attempted to improve the accuracy and coverage of the basic banking data reported from 1833 on. However, they have sometimes interpreted the meaning of items on the balance sheets differently or have used different estimates of specie in the Treasury and of Treasury balances in banks. As a result, while there is general agreement on estimates of currency held by the public from 1833 on, there are some differences in estimates of the specie holdings of the public and of adjusted deposits.

TABLE 13

Monetary Statistics Before 1867
(millions of dollars)

End of Year (Unless Otherwise Indicated)	SPECIE						Gov't. Currency Issues (6)	BANK NOTES		
			Held by Banks					Outstanding		
	Stock (1)	Held by Treas. (2)	State (3)	Bank of U.S. (3a)	Total (4)	Held by Public (5)		State (7)	Bank of U.S. (7a)	Tot (8'
1775						4.0– 9.5	5.0			
1776							9.0			
Apr. 1778							30.0			
June 1778							45.0			
Feb. 1779							115.0			
Sept. 1779							200.0			
1784								2.0		2
1790	9.0– 19.0				3.0	7.0– 16.0		2.5		2.
1791	16.0									9.
1792	18.0			1.0	5.0	12.0			1.7	11.
Mar. 1793				0.8					1.5	
June 1793				1.1					1.5	
1793	20.0			1.2					2.0	11.
Mar. 1794				1.2					2.2	
July 1794				1.9					3.1	
1794	21.5									11.
Jan. 1795				0.7					3.7	
Apr. 1795				0.6					3.3	
Sept. 1795				1.1					3.6	
1795	19.0			1.4					3.7	11.
Mar. 1796				1.2					3.9	
June 1796				1.1					3.6	
1796	16.5			1.6					3.4	10.
Mar. 1797				1.3					3.3	
June 1797				1.9					3.0	
Sept. 1797				2.4					2.9	
1797	16.0			2.7					3.1	10
Mar. 1798				2.6					3.3	
June 1798				2.9					3.6	
Sept. 1798				3.2					3.9	
1798	14.0			3.1					4.1	9
Mar. 1799				2.4					4.6	
Sept. 1799				3.5					4.2	
1799	17.0			4.0					4.3	10

	BANK NOTES				DEPOSITS					
	Held by Banks			Held by Public	Total Excluding Interbank			Treas. Bals. at Depositary Banks	Float	Adj. Dep.
d by eas. 9)	State (10)	Bank of U.S. (10a)	Total (11)	(12)	State Banks (13)	Bank of U.S. (13a)	Total (14)	(15)	(16)	(17)
				5.0						
				3.0				0.6		
								1.0		
				7.0	1.7			0.8		
					1.6					
					1.6					
					1.9			0.8		
					2.5					
					3.3					
								1.2		
					2.6					
					2.3					
					2.7					
					2.5			0.5		
					2.6					
					2.5					
					2.3			0.9		
					2.5					
					2.7					
					2.8					
					3.7			1.0		
					3.5					
					3.5					
					3.6					
					4.2			0.6		
					4.0					
					4.2					
				(17.0)– (18.0)	4.4		10.0– 13.0	2.2		

(continued)

TABLE 13 (continued)

End of Year (Unless Otherwise Indicated)	SPECIE Stock (1)	Held by Treas. (2)	Held by Banks State (3)	Bank of U.S. (3a)	Total (4)	Held by Public (5)	Gov't. Currency Issues (6)	BANK NOTES Outstanding State (7)	Bank of U.S. (7a)	T (
Apr. 1800				4.1					4.8	
Sept. 1800				5.7					5.5	
1800	17.5	1.5								1●
1801	17.0									1
1802	16.5									1●
1803	16.0									1
1804	17.5– 29.5				12.0	17.5				1●
1805	18.0									1.
1806	18.5									1'
1807	20.0									1●
1808	38.0				24.0	14.0			4.5	
1809										
1810	28.0– 33.0	3.0	9.6	5.8	15.4	15.0		22.7	5.4	2●
1811										
1812							2.8			
Sept. 1813			28.0		28.0	8.0		62.0– 70.0		6● 7●
1813							4.9			
1814	17.0– 24.0		10.0– 17.0		10.0– 17.0	7.0	10.6	45.5		4●
Sept. 1815	24.0		16.5		16.5	7.5		99.0– 110.0		9● 11●
1815	26.5		19.0		19.0	7.5	17.6	68.0		6●
1816				1.7			3.4		1.9	
1817				2.5					8.3	
1818				2.7					6.6	
Sept. 1819	20.0– 29.5				15.5– 21.5	4.5– 8.0				4● 5●
1819	25.0		16.7	3.1– 3.4	19.5– 20.1	4.9– 5.2		40.6	3.6– 4.2	4●
Sept. 1820	25.0									
1820	24.3– 41.0	2.0		7.6	21.0	1.3– 18.0			4.6	
1821	39.0			4.8	24.0	15.0			5.6	
1822	32.0			4.4	13.0	19.0			4.4	
1823	31.0			5.8	18.0	13.0			4.6	

		BANK NOTES					DEPOSITS			
		Held by Banks		Held by Public	Total Excluding Interbank			Treas. Bals. at Depositary Banks	Float	Adj. Dep.
1 by as.)	State (10)	Bank of U.S. (10a)	Total (11)	(12)	State Banks (13)	Bank of U.S. (13a)	Total (14)	(15)	(16)	(17)
						5.0				
						5.2				
5								2.6		
								3.3		
								5.0		
								4.8		
				13.0				4.0		
								4.0		
								4.5		
								9.6		
				22.75				9.9		
				(40.0)			25.0–	3.8		
							27.0			
0		0.4				7.8		2.7		
								3.5		
								3.9		
	10.0		10.0	52.0	18.0		18.0			
								5.2		
								1.7		
	5.5		5.5	40.0						
				110.0						
								13.1		
		0.6				11.2		22.0		
		1.8				12.3		15.0		
		1.9				5.8		1.5		
			10.0	40.5						
		1.4		(47.0)	31.2	4.7–	37.0–	2.1		
						6.6	40.0			
●		0.7				7.9		1.2		
		0.9				8.1		1.7		
		0.8				7.6		4.2		
		0.7				13.7		9.4		

(continued)

TABLE 13 (continued)

End of Year (Unless Otherwise Indicated)	SPECIE						Gov't. Currency Issues (6)	BANK NOTES		
		Held by Banks				Held by Public (5)		Outstanding		
	Stock (1)	Held by Treas. (2)	State (3)	Bank of U.S. (3a)	Total (4)			State (7)	Bank of U.S. (7a)	T
Sept. 1824	16.0									
1824	32.0			6.7	21.0	11.0			6.1	
1825	29.0			4.0	18.0	11.0			9.5	
1826	32.0			6.5	19.0	13.0			8.5	
1827	32.0			6.2	18.0	14.0			9.9	
Sept. 1828	16.0									
1828	31.0			6.1	18.0	13.0			11.9	
1829	31.0–		14.9	7.2–	20.0–	8.5–		48.3	12.9–	6
	33.0			7.6	22.7	13.0			13.0	
1830	32.0			10.8	15.0–	8.0		60.7	16.3	7
					24.0					
1831	30.4			7.0	22.0	8.4		70.1	21.4	9
1832	30.6			9.0	23.0	7.6		74.0	17.5	9
1833	29.2–		15.0	10.0	25.2–	4.0–			19.2	94
	42.7				27.0	15.8				
Sept. 1834	45.0									
1834	51.0–		19.3	15.7	43.9	7.0–			17.3	103
	55.0					20.0				
1835	65.0–			8.4	40.0	25			23.1	14C
	73.4									
1836	73.0	0.7		2.6	37.9	(35)			11.4	149
Sept. 1837	62.8									
1837	87.5	1.0		3.8	35.2	(52)			6.8	116
Sept. 1838	75.0									
1838	87.0	1.3		4.2	45.1	(42)			6.0	135
Sept. 1839	70.7									
1839	83.0	0.7		1.5	33.1	(50)			6.7	107
1840	70.0–	1.4	34.8		34.8	(35–		107.3		107
	80.0					45)				
1841	80.0	0.2	28.4		28.4	(52)		83.7		83
Sept. 1842	62.2									

| | | BANK NOTES | | | | DEPOSITS | | | | |
| | | Held by Banks | | | Total Excluding Interbank | | | Treas. Bals. at Depositary | | |
d by eas.)	State (10)	Bank of U.S. (10a)	Total (11)	Held by Public (12)	State Banks (13)	Bank of U.S. (13a)	Total (14)	Banks (15)	Float (10)	Adj. Dep. (17)
		1.1				12.0		1.9		
		1.1				11.2		5.3		
		1.1				14.3		6.3		
		1.4				14.5		6.6		
		1.3				17.1		6.0		
	7.5-	1.5	9.0-	53.5-	40.8	14.8-	61.0-	4.4		
	14.5		16.0	(65.0)		16.0	65.0			
	8.5	1.5	10.0	67.0		17.3		4.8		
		2.2				22.8		3.1		
		2.3		76.3-	(30.0)	20.3	(50.3)	0.9		
				86.0						
		2.0	22.2	72.7		10.8	75.7	10.7	1.5	63.5
		1.5	21.1	82.6		11.8	83.1	7.9	3.1	72.2
		1.7	32.1	108.2		5.1	115.1	25.7	4.8	84.6
7		1.2	36.5	112.0-		2.3	127.4	45.1	5.4	77.0
				112.7						
0		0.9	25.0	90.1-		2.6	84.7	5.8	0.9	78.0
				91.2						
3		1.8	27.4	106.5-		6.8	90.2-	5.4	3.6	81.3-
				107.8			111.0			102.0
				(171.0)						
7		1.4	20.8	85.5-		3.3	75.7-	4.0	3.6	68.1-
				86.2			79.0			71.4
				(153.0)						
4	25.6		25.6	80.2-	64.9		64.9	0.3	3.2	61.4
				81.6						
2	19.4		19.4	64.1-	62.4		62.4	0.2	3.1	59.1
				64.3						

(continued)

TABLE 13 (concluded)

End of Year (Unless Otherwise Indicated)	SPECIE						Gov't. Currency Issues (6)	BANK NOTES Outstanding		
	Stock (1)	Held by Treas. (2)	Held by Banks			Held by Public (5)				
			State (3)	(3a)	Total (4)			State (7)	(7a)	T
1842	90.0	0.4	33.5		33.5	(56)		58.6		
June 1843		0.7								
1843	100.0	0.6	49.9		49.9	(50)		75.2		
June 1844		0.4								
1844	96.0	0.6	44.2		44.2	(52)		89.6		
June 1845	76.3	0.7								
1845	97.0	0.7	42.0		42.0	54.2		105.6		1
June 1846		0.8								
1846	120.0	2.8	35.1		35.1	82.1		105.5		1
June 1847		5.4								
1847	112.0	3.1	46.4		46.4	62.5		128.5		1
June 1848		0.8								
1848	120.0	2.0	43.6		43.6	74.4		114.7		1
June 1849		3.2								
1849	154.0	5.3	45.4		45.4	103.3		131.4		1
June 1850		7.4								
1850	186.0	9.6	48.7		48.7	127.7		155.2		1
June 1851		12.1								
1851	204.0	13.5	48.4		48.4	142.1		171.7		1
June 1852		15.1								
1852	236.0	18.7	47.1		47.1	170.2		188.2		1
June 1853		22.3								
1853	241.0	21.3	59.4		59.4	160.3		204.7		2
June 1854		20.3								
1854	250.0	19.5	53.9		53.9	176.6		187.0		1
June 1855		19.5								
1855	250.0	19.9	59.3		59.3	170.8		195.7		1
June 1856		20.3								
1856	260.0	19.1	58.3		58.3	182.5		214.8		2
June 1857		18.2								
1857	260.0	11.8	74.4		74.4	173.8		155.2		1
June 1858		6.7								
1858	250.0	5.8	104.5		104.5	139.6		193.3		1

	BANK NOTES				DEPOSITS					
	Held by Banks			Held by Public (12)	Total Excluding Interbank			Treas. Bals. at Depositary Banks (15)	Float (16)	Adj. Dep. (17)
by as.)	State (10)	(10a)	Total (11)		State Banks (13)	(13a)	Total (14)			
4	13.3		13.3	44.9–45.3	56.2		56.2	1.7	6.6	47.9
7								10.5		
6	11.7		11.7	62.9–63.5	84.6		84.6	9.4	6.7	68.4
4								8.2		
6	12.0		12.0	77.0–77.6	88.0		88.0	7.8	6.8	73.4
,7								7.4		
7	12.9		12.9	91.9–92.6	96.9		96.9	8.2	8.4	80.4
.8								8.9		
8	13.1		13.1	92.4	91.8		91.8		13.8	78.0
	16.4		16.4	112.1	103.2		103.2		10.5	92.7
	12.7		12.7	102.0– (189.0)	91.2– 127.0		91.2– 127.0		8.7	82.5– 118.3
	16.3		16.3	115.1– (234.0)	109.6– 129.0		109.6– 129.0		11.6	98.0– 117.4
	17.2		17.2	138.0	110.0		110.0		15.3	94.7
	23.8		23.8	147.9	137.3		137.3		18.8	118.5
	30.4		30.4	157.8	145.6		145.6		22.2	123.4
	22.7		22.7	182.0	188.2		188.2		25.6	162.6
	23.4		23.4	163.6	190.4		190.4		21.9	168.5
	24.8		24.8	170.9	212.7		212.7		19.9	192.8
	28.1		28.1	186.7	230.4		230.4		25.1	205.3
	22.4		22.4	132.8	185.9		185.9		15.4	170.6
	18.9		18.9	174.4– (334.0)	259.6– 388.0		259.6– 388.0		26.8	232.8– 361.2

(continued)

Earlier Estimates

TABLE 13 (concluded)

End of Year (Unless Otherwise Indicated)	SPECIE							BANK NOTES Outstanding	
	Stock (1)	Held by Treas. (2)	Held by Banks State (3)	Nat'l. (3a)	Total (4)	Held by Public (5)	Gov't. Currency Issues (6)	State (7)	Nat'l. (7a)
June 1859		4.7							
1859	237.0	4.3	83.6		83.6	149.1		207.1	
June 1860	235.0	3.9–6.7				(150)			
1860			87.7		87.7			202.0	
June 1861	286.0	2.0–3.6				(185)			
1861			102.1		102.1			183.8	
June 1862	296.0	18.3–?				(195.0)	(149.7)		
1862			101.2		101.2			238.7	
June 1863	271.0	8.4–?	50.8		50.8	(220.0)	417.2	163.4	
June 1864	213.0	19.3					639.4	179.2	31.2
Nov. 1864									
June 1865	198.5	41.2		9.4			692.6	142.9	146.1
Nov. 1865									
June 1866	176.0	47.5		12.6			590.6	20.0	281.5
Nov. 1866									

Notes to Table 13

[a]Government currency issues held by Treasury.

[b]National bank notes held by national banks.

[c]From 1864, national bank float.

[d]U.S. notes and fractional currency held by national banks.

[e]Government currency issues and national bank notes held by Treasury.

REFERENCES

(cited by number in source notes that follow)

1. Blodget, Samuel, Jr., *Economica,* Washington, D.C., 1806, pp. 66–67, 160.

2a. Comptroller of the Currency. *Annual Report,* 1876, pp. xciv–xcv.

2b. *Idem. Annual Report,* 1913, pp. 308–311.

	BANK NOTES				DEPOSITS					
	Held by Banks			Held by Public	Total Excluding Interbank			Treas. Bals. at Depository Banks	Float	Adj. Dep.
by s.	State (10)	Nat'l. (10a)	Total (11)	(12)	State Banks (13)	Nat'l. (13a)	Total (14)	(15)	(16)	(17)
	25.5		25.5	181.6–	253.8–		253.8–		19.3	234.5–
				351.0	257.2		257.2			237.9
	21.9		21.9	180.1	254.0		254.0		29.3	224.7
.8[a]	25.3		25.3	158.5	296.3		296.3		27.8	268.5
	58.2		58.2	306.4	393.7		393.7		46.2	347.5
.5[a]				501.1						
.9[a]		5.3[b]	808.6			119.4		40.0–?	5.1[c]	
					393.5					
.4[a]		21.7[b]	736.1			456.4	482.0	24.1–	41.3	
		168.4[d]	(853.0)		165.0			58.0		
.8[e]		17.9[b]	592.0			572.4		34.1–	96.1	
		201.4[d]			230.4			39.1		

Notes to Table 13 (continued)

2c. *Idem. Annual Report,* 1920, Vol. 2, p. 847.

2d. *Idem. Annual Report,* 1931, p. 1018.

3. Crawford, W. H. (Secretary of the Treasury). "Report" in *Reports of the Secretary of the Treasury,* Vol. II, Washington, D.C., 1837, p. 482.

4. Dewey, Davis R. *Financial History of the United States,* New York, 1920 (7th ed.), p. 137.

5. Federal Deposit Insurance Corporation. *Annual Report,* 1934, p. 103.

6. Gallatin, Albert. *Considerations on the Currency and Banking System of the United States,* Philadelphia, 1831.

7. Gurley, J. G. and Shaw, E. S. "The Growth of Debt and Money in the United States, 1800–1950: A Suggested Interpretation," *Review of Economics and Statistics,* Aug. 1957, p. 258.

8. *Historical Statistics of the United States, Colonial Times to 1957,* Bureau of the Census, Washington, D.C., 1960.

9. Holdsworth, J. T. and Dewey, D. R. *The First and Second Banks of the United States,* National Monetary Commission, Washington, D.C., 1910, 61st Cong., 2nd sess., Sen. Doc. 571, p. 112.

Notes to Table 13 (continued)

10. House Report 27, 23rd Cong., 2nd sess., p. 63.

11. *Information Respecting U.S. Bonds, Paper Currency and Coin, Production of Precious Metals,* etc., U.S. Treasury Department, Division of Loans and Currency, Washington, D.C., 1915 ed., p. 45.

12. Macesich, George. Unpublished estimates, 1833—59, in ''Money Stock and its Components in the United States, Nearest January 1, 1834—1860,'' memorandum, 1968.

13. New York State Bank Commissioners. *Report,* 1833, p. 12.

14. Seaman, Ezra C. *Progress of Nations,* Detroit, 1846, pp. 243—248.

15a. Secretary of the Treasury. *Annual Report,* 1854, p. 280.

15b. *Idem. Annual Report,* 1856, pp. 434—435.

15c. *Idem. Annual Report,* 1915, pp. 374—375.

15d. *Idem. Annual Report,* 1928, pp. 522, 554.

16. Temin. Peter. *The Jacksonian Economy,* New York, 1969, pp. 71, 159, 186—187.

17a. Warburton, Clark. ''The Secular Trend in Monetary Velocity,'' *Quarterly Journal of Economics,* Feb. 1949, pp. 76—77 (reprinted in Clark Warburton, *Depression, Inflation and Monetary Policy,* Baltimore, 1966, p. 200).

17b. Warburton, Clark. Unpublished estimates, 1833—44, in ''Specie and the Stock of Money, 1834—1845,'' memorandum, Feb. 1961.

17c. Prepared by Clark Warburton from consolidated balance sheets of the First Bank of the United States at Philadelphia and its offices (Boston, New York, Baltimore, Charleston, and — for Sept. 1800 entry only — Norfolk), compiled by James O. Wettereau. Actual reporting dates are spread over a range of days varying from two days to two-and-one-half months. The end of month closest to the mean date was used by us for the entries.

Source, by Column

(Numbers in brackets refer to preceding references)

1. *1790—1805:* [1]; 1790 and 1804 upper limits are sums of cols. 3, 4, and 5. *1806—07:* [15b], attributed to Blodget. *1808:* sum of cols. 3, 4, and 5. *1810:* lower limit [10], attributed to Gallatin (shown one year later in source, but shifted to end of 1810, to which estimate refers); upper limit is sum of cols. 2, 4, and 5. *1814—15:* 1815 is sum of cols. 4 and 5; 1814 lower limit is sum of lower limit of cols. 4 and 5; 1814 upper limit is sum of upper limit of cols. 3 and 5. *1815 Sept.:* [15a], attributed to Crawford. *1819 Sept.:* upper limit [10], attributed to Crawford; lower limit [3]. *1819 Dec., 1820 Sept., 1824 Sept., 1828 Sept., 1834 Sept., 1837—39 Sept., 1842 Sept., 1845 June:* [14]. *1820:* lower limit [11]; upper limit [16]. *1821—28 Dec.:* [16]. *1829—30:* [10]; 1829 upper limit attributed to Gallatin (shown one year later in source but shifted to end of 1829); 1830 attributed to Senator Sandford. For

Notes to Table 13 (continued)

1830 [11] shows 32.1, which presumably also refers to 1829. *1831—58:*
[11] (shown one year later in source). Stock does not include Treasury
specie holdings. In [15b], which is source of [11] for this period,
1838 figure is attributed to Hazard's *Commercial Register,* 1840
figure to Gouge's *Journal of Banking,* 1843 figure to *Hunt's Merchants
Magazine.* In [15b] 250 is shown in 1853. 1833, lower limit, sum of
lower limits of cols. 4-5; upper limit [10]. Figure in [11], 41.0, falls
between upper and lower limits. Figure in [17b] for total specie stock,
39.0, is Woodbury's estimate *(Report on the Finances,* 1836, III, p.
696). With the 1833 figure serving as a base, subsequent years were
derived in [17b] by adding net imports of gold and silver for years
ending Sept. 30. The following are the estimates:

1834	54.8	1840	86.6
1835	61.5	1841	81.6
1836	70.6	1842	80.6
1837	75.1	1843	101.5
1838	89.3	1844	100.0
1839	86.1		

The final figure agrees with that given in *Hunt's Merchants Magazine*
for Dec. 1844. 1834, lower limit [11]; upper limit [10]. 1840, lower
and upper limits shown in [15b]. *1859:* [12], estimated from June 1860
figure and net gold flows, 1859—60. *1860:* [11, p. 46]. *1861—66:*
[15d], sum of gold and subsidiary silver stock.

2. *1800, 1810, 1820:* [11]. Annual figures from 1830 on in this
source, described as specie in Treasury, are actually the total balance of the Treasury (on an unrevised basis), whether held in specie,
bank notes, or on deposit at banks. *1836—63:* [15c]. Figures are the
amounts (on a revised basis) not on deposit at banks. For 1847—61
they are presumably only specie. For 1836—46 the Treasury may have
held bank notes as well as specie. Since there is no basis for distributing the total, the figures for this period are also shown in col. 9.
For 1862—63 the figures may include Treasury holdings of U.S. currency. Only midyear figures are reported from 1843 on. End-of-year
entries, shown in [12], 1843—59 are based on the change in holdings
between June dates, adjusted for fluctuations in reported quarterly
receipts. *1860—66:* [15d], difference between figures on stock and
amounts outside Treasury (on an unrevised basis). For 1860—61 these
figures for gold only are shown as upper limits. For 1862—63 no data
on specie outside Treasury are given, hence the question marks re-
placing the upper limits. For 1864—66 figures are sums of gold and
subsidiary silver. For 1866 cover for gold certificates was deducted
from Treasury holdings of gold.

3. *1810, 1814* (upper limit), *1815, 1819, 1829:* [6, pp. 45, 49, 53].
1813 Sept., 1815 Sept., [3]. *1814* (lower limit), *1833—34:* [10], minus

Notes to Table 13 (continued)

col. 3a. [3]. *1851:* [12], estimated from specie holdings in state banks of Mass., Pa., and N. Y. *1840–50, 1852–62:* [2a]. *1863:* [2c], attributed to Homan's *Bankers' Almanac.*

3a. *1792–1800:* [17c]. *1810:* [9]. *1819* lower limit, *1829* lower limit: [6, pp. 49, 53]. *1816–18, 1819* upper limit – *1828, 1829* upper limit – *1839:* [8, p. 623, Series X-12]. *1865–66:* [2b], call date nearest June 30. For 1864, national bank specie holdings are combined with notes of other banks.

4. *1790, 1792, 1804, 1808, 1819, 1829* upper limit, *1830* lower limit: [10]. *1813 Sept., 1815 Sept., 1819 Sept.* lower and upper limits: [3, pp. 482–483]. *1815, 1819* lower limit: [6]. *1819* upper limit: cols. 3 plus 3a. *1820–28, 1829* lower limit, *1830* upper limit, *1831–32, 1833* upper limit: [16]. *1833* lower limit, *1851:* [12]. Estimated from specie holdings in state banks of Mass., Pa., and N. Y. Figure for 1833 shown in [10] as 30.7. *1834–50, 1852–62:* [2a]. Figure for 1834 in [16] is 44. *1863:* [2c].

5. *1775, 1790, 1792, 1804, 1808, 1810* (shown one year later in source), *1813 Sept., 1814, 1815* (shown one year later in source), *1829* lower limit, *1830, 1833* lower limit, *1834* upper limit: [10]. For 1829 an upper limit of 10.0 and for 1833, of 12.0 are given. *1815 Sept., 1819 Sept.* lower limit: [3]. *1819:* col. 1 minus col. 4 (upper and lower limits). *1820:* col. 1 (lower and upper limits) minus the sum of cols. 2 and 4. *1821–28, 1831–32:* col. 1 minus col. 4. *1829:* col. 1 (upper limit) minus col. 4 (lower limit). *1830:* col. 1 minus col. 4 (upper limit). *1833:* col. 1 (intermediate figure of 41.0) minus col. 4 (upper limit) falls between upper and lower limits. *1834* lower limit: col. 1 (lower limit) minus col. 4. *1833* upper limit – *1859:* [12]. Shown in parentheses when Treasury specie holdings may be included in the estimates. 1840, col. 1 (lower limit) minus col. 2 and col. 4; col. 1 (upper limit), minus col. 2 and col. 4. *1860–63:* col. 1 minus col. 4, rounded. Shown in parentheses because Treasury specie holdings are probably included in residual amounts shown.

6. *1775:* [10], authorized issues. *1776, 1778–79:* [6, pp. 25–26], authorized issues. *1812–16:* [4], amounts outstanding. *1862–66:* [15d], stock of U.S. notes, fractional currency, and other U.S. currency. W. C. Mitchell *(A History of the Greenbacks,* Chicago, 1903, p. 179) included estimates (not shown here) of interest-bearing and non-interest-bearing government obligations that served as currency at times during the period.

7. *1784, 1790:* [1]. *1810, 1814–15, 1819, 1829:* [6, pp. 45, 49, 53]. *1813 Sept.* upper and lower limits, *1815 Sept.* upper and lower limits: [3]. *1830:* [10], minus col. 7a. *1831–32:* [11] (dated one year later in source), minus col. 7a. *1840–50, 1853–62:* [2a] (dated one year later in source). *1851–52:* [12]. *1863:* [2c], attributed to Homan's *Bankers' Almanac. 1864–66:* [15d].

Notes to Table 13 (continued)

7a. *1792–1800:* [17c]. *1808, 1810:* [9]. *1816–18, 1819* lower limit, *1820–28, 1829,* lower limit, *1830–39:* [8, p. 623, Series X-14]. *1819* and *1829* upper limit: [6, pp. 45, 49]. *1864–66:* [2b], call date nearest June 30.

8. *1784, 1790–1805:* [1]. *1806–07:* [15b], attributed to Blodget. *1810, 1864–66:* sum of cols. 7 and 7a. *1813 Sept.* upper and lower limits, *1815 Sept.* upper and lower limits: [3]. *1814–15, 1819, 1829:* [6, pp. 45, 49, 53]. *1819 Sept.* upper and lower limits: [3]. *1830:* [10]. *1831–32:* [11] (dated one year later in source). *1833–50, 1853–62:* [2a] (dated one year later in source). *1851–52:* [12]. *1863:* [2c], attributed to Homan's *Bankers' Almanac.*

9. *1800, 1810, 1820, 1836–46:* see col. 2. *1862–66:* [15d], sums of difference between figures on stock and amounts outside Treasury for U.S. notes and fractional currency, plus national bank notes in 1866.

10. *1813 Sept., 1814, 1829* upper limit – *30:* [10], minus col. 10a, 1829–30. *1829* lower limit: [6], minus col. 10a. *1840–50, 1852–62:* [2a] (dated one year later in source). *1851:* [12].

10a. *1810:* [9]. 1816–39: [8, p. 623, Series X-11]. *1864–66:* [2b], call date nearest June 30.

11. *1813 Sept., 1814, 1819, Sept., 1829* upper limit – *1830:* [10]. *1829* lower limit: [6]. *1833–50, 1852–62:* [2a] (dated one year later in source). *1851:* [12].

12. *1775, 1790, 1792, 1804, 1808, 1813 Sept., 1832* lower limit: [10]. *1799* (upper limit) – *1829, 1838–58* (1839–59 in source, but re-dated at author's suggestion), decade intervals (shown in parentheses): [17a], sum of specie and bank notes held by public. *1799* (lower limit) – *1859,* decade intervals (dated one year later in source), and *1865* (shown in parentheses): [7], sum of specie and bank notes held by public. *1814, 1830, 1860–61:* col. 8 minus col. 11. *1815 Sept., 1819 Sept.:* [3]. *1829* (without parentheses): [6, p. 54]. *1832* upper limit: [13]. *1833–59:* [12]. Lower limit, 1836–45, excludes col. 9 in addition to col. 11 from col. 8. Upper limit for those years assigns amounts in col. 9 to col. 2. *1862–66:* sum of cols. 6 and 8 minus cols. 9 and 11. Entry for 1862 is too low, since it is based on midyear data for government issues and end-of-year data for bank issues. Entry for 1863 is too high, since it does not include deduction for bank notes and government currency issues held by banks.

13. *1813 Sept.:* [3, p. 489] *1819, 1829:* [6, pp. 49, 53]. *1832:* [13], amount held by the public. *1840–50, 1852–62:* [2a] (dated one year later in source). *1848–58* upper limits (one year later in source): [17a]. *1849–59* upper limits (one year later in source): [7, col. 4]. *1851:* [12], by straight-line interpolation. *1864–66:* [5], described in source as averages for years ending May 31, 1865–67. It is uncertain whether interbank deposits are excluded. Bank balance sheets for that period listed amounts due to banks separately but in preparing

Notes to Table 13 (concluded)

the deposit estimates, Warburton did not ascertain whether the tax on deposits, from which the estimates are derived, applied to amounts due to banks.

13a. *1792—1800:* [17c], excluding U.S. government deposits. *1810:* [9]. *1819, 1829* lower limits: [6, pp. 49, 53]. *1816—39:* [8, p. 623, Series X-15]. *1864—66:* [2b], call date nearest June 30. Individual and other deposits plus (1865—66) U.S. deposits.

14. *1799—1809* lower limits, *1819—29, 1838—58* upper limits (one year later in source), decade intervals: [17a]. *1799—1809* upper limits, *1819—29* lower limits, *1839—59* upper limits (one year later in source), decade intervals, *1865 June:* [7, col. 4]. *1813 Sept.:* [3, p. 489]. *1832:* sum of cols. 13 and 13a. *1851:* [12], by straight-line interpolation. *1833—50, 1852—62:* [2a] (dated one year later in the source).

15. *1790—1846, 1864—66* lower limit: [15c]. Source also shows data for Dec. 1789 and other quarterly dates, 1790—93. Only midyear figures are reported from 1843 on. End-of-year entries, 1843—45, shown in [12], are straight-line interpolations. *1865—66* upper limit: [2b], call date nearest June 30. National banks do not show U.S. deposits as a separate item in 1864, hence the question mark in that year to replace the upper limit. The difference in dating between Treasury and bank records in 1865—66 may account for the difference in reported U.S. deposits. However, even when identically dated, there are usually differences between the amounts shown in the two sets of accounts because they are not in fact fully synchronized.

For 1792—1800, [17c] gives U.S. deposits at the First Bank of the United States, as follows (in millions of dollars):

1792	*1796*	*1799*
Dec. 1.0	Mar. 0.4	Mar. 0.5
1793	June 0.7	Sept. 2.3
Mar. 1.2	Dec. 1.5	Dec. 3.0
June 0.6	*1797*	*1800*
Dec. 1.4	Mar. 0.9	Apr. 2.2
1794	June 1.6	Sept. 4.7
Mar. 0.8	Sept. 2.2	
July 0.5	Dec. 2.0	
1795	*1798*	
Jan. 0.5	Mar. 1.5	
Apr. 0.9	June 1.7	
Sept. 0.7	Sept. 1.1	
Dec. 0.5	Dec. 1.0	

16. *1834—50, 1853—62:* [2a, specie funds] (dated one year later in source). *1833, 1851—52:* [12]. Entry for 1833 is figure in [2a] minus entry in col. 4 (lower limit). Other years by straight-line interpolation. *1864—66:* [2b, checks and other cash items], call date nearest June 30.

17. *1833—62:* col. 14 minus col. 15 (through 1845), and minus col. 16.

TABLE 14

Alternative Money Stock Estimates, Selected Dates, 1799–1865
(millions of dollars)

Year	Warburton (1)	Gurley and Shaw (2)	Macesich (3)	Temin (4)	Miscellaneous (5)
1799	28	30			
1809	65	67			
1813					78
1819	87	84			
1820				85	
1821				96	
1822				81	
1823				88	
1824				88	
1825				106	
1826				108	
1827				101	
1828				114	
1829	130	126		105	
1830				114	
1831				155	
1832				150	134–144
1833	149		152	168	
1834	168		162	172	
1835	218		218	246	
1836	227		224	276	
1837	209		220	232	
1838	236 282[a]		230	240	
1839	210	232	204	215	

(continued)

TABLE 14 (concluded)

Year	Warburton (1)	Gurley and Shaw (2)	Macesich (3)	Temin (4)	Miscellaneous (5)
1840	192		187	186	
1841	175		175	174	
1842	146		149	158	
1843	191		182	194	
1844	205		202	214	
1845			227	241	
1846			252	267	
1847			267	281	
1848	316		259	267	
1849		344	316	329	
1850			379	399	
1851			408	n.a.	
1852			451	451	
1853			505	546	
1854			509	539	
1855			534	565	
1856			574	611	
1857			477	498	
1858	722		547	569	
1859		605	566		
1865		1,335			

Note: Numbers in brackets refer to references following Table 13.
[a]Decade entry.

Source, by Column

1. [17a] for decade.entries, 1839-59 dated one year later in source;
[17b] for annual entries, 1833-44, dated one year later in source. Warburton accounts for the difference between the 1838 decade and annual
estimates as follows: (a) the erroneous inclusion in the decade estimate of $14 million deposits at savings banks and double counting of
$7 million deposits at the Bank of the United States; (b) the inclusion
in the decade estimate of $5 million in U.S. Treasury balances at

Notes to Table 14 (concluded)

depositary banks that are deducted from the annual estimate; (c) the failure to deduct $27 million banknotes held by other banks from the stock of banknotes in the decade estimate; (d) a decade estimate of the stock of specie outside the Treasury (for the figures, see Table 13, cols. 1 and 2) $3 million lower than the annual estimate (for the revised stock figure constructed by Warburton, see the source notes to Table 13, col. 1, under 1833); (e) the erroneous double deduction from the decade specie stock estimate of $4 million specie held by the Bank of the United States.

    2. [7].
    3. [12].
    4. [16].
    5. Table 13. Sum of cols. 5, 12, and 14, for dates (a) when there are entries for these cols., and (b) when only one other estimate is shown in Table 14.

1. Nineteenth Century Private Estimates

SAMUEL BLODGET, JR. (1806)
1774, 1784, 1790–1805:

Specie Stock
Bank Notes Outstanding

The earliest monetary estimates that we have been able to uncover are contained in a statistical manual published by Samuel Blodget, Jr., in 1806. A table in the manual gives the amount of the "metallic medium" and of "bank notes in circulation" in the United States in 1774, 1784, and each year from 1790 through 1804. These two columns of figures were republished several times during the course of the century in various government documents. Figures for 1805 are given in the text of the manual. For years through 1805 the manual lists forty-seven banks in the several states and gives for each bank the amount of its capital and the date of its establishment; it also enumerates twenty-one additional banks known to be in existence, for which information on capital was unavailable.[1]

---

[1] Samuel Blodget, Jr., *Economica*, Washington, 1806, printed for author, pp. 66–67, 159–160; reprinted, Washington, 1810, with additional appendix material, p. 235. For Blodget's figures in later sources, see H. Exec. Doc. 65, 24th Cong., 2nd sess., 1837, Vol. 2, p. 216 (which includes the following note: "In Blodget's Economica is given the following table, many of the amounts in which are probably conjectural, but which may prove interesting to some"); *Annual Report* of the Secretary of the Treasury, 1856, p. 434; *Annual Report* of the Comptroller of the Currency, 1876, p. xxxix.

Blodget's estimates of the specie stock (the "metallic medium") were apparently based on his conjectures about the amount of the authorized capital of banks and the amount stockholders actually paid in specie. A bank's authorized capital was usually paid in by its stockholders in installments. The first installment was generally paid in specie. Later installments might be paid by a loan from the bank collateraled by the stockholders' renewable notes, by the stock of the bank itself, or by other securities. Blodget implicitly assumed first, that bank capital paid in coin accounted for all the specie in the country; and second, that the specie, once paid in, was not thereafter immobilized in banks. As for his estimates of bank notes outstanding ("bank notes in circulation"), they were based on conjectures about the ratio of notes to total capital paid in. He assumed the ratio to be one-third. Thus he explained his estimates for 1805 as follows:

The entire capitals of the preceding institutions, when all is paid in, will be near fifty millions. They, however, at present do not reach forty-five, and if in some instances renewable notes are received with deposits of the *original stock of the bank, and other sufficient securities,* as substitutes for the final payments by instalments *after the first . . . the facilities* created by all these banks do not give to the specie medium an additional circulation of *facile money* more than one-third on the real amount; thus with eighteen million of specie, we may have thirty-three millions.[2]

ALBERT GALLATIN (1831)
Selected Years, 1810–29:

Bank Notes Outstanding
Bank Notes Held by Public
Specie Stock
Specie Held by Banks
Specie Held by Public
Total Bank Deposits

The most consistent early estimates were published in 1831 by Albert Gallatin, who had been Secretary of the Treasury from 1801 to 1814, but was then a private citizen. Gallatin gave the number, capital, circulation outstanding, and specie of banks reporting to authorities in each state at end of the years 1810, 1814, 1815, 1819, and 1829 (also deposits for 1819 and 1829, and loans for 1829). For those years he also

2 *Economica*, p. 160 [italics in original].

provided the number and capital of banks in each state which did not report to authorities. For the Second Bank of the United States he listed eight balance sheet items for each year from 1819 through 1829, and for three of the years he added these figures to those for state banks ("ascertained" for reporting banks, estimated for nonreporting banks) to get national totals. In addition, for 1829 he compared "two modes of computing" the circulation of all banks, one showing notes outstanding, the other, "if the bank notes of other banks on hand are deducted." To each estimate of bank notes he added an estimate of $10 million dollars of silver coins held by the public. ("It is well known that gold has been altogether excluded by the mint regulations.") This estimate he derived by assuming that specie held by the public was about one-seventh of bank notes outstanding, the fraction, according to Gallatin, of silver coinage to note circulation in England. Finally, he showed the result "if deposits are included" with each sum of bank notes and silver coins. Deposits are the gross liabilities of the state banks and the Bank of the United States.[3] Since Gallatin gave estimates of specie in banks and specie held by the public in 1829, Table 13 shows the sum as the stock of specie, though Gallatin does not refer to this item.

EZRA C. SEAMAN (1846)
Selected Years, 1814–45:

Specie Stock
Specie Held by Banks
Specie Held by Public
Bank Notes Outstanding
Bank Notes Held by Public

Another early set of estimates by a private individual, Ezra C. Seaman, was published in 1846. Seaman's point of departure was a table "taken

---

[3] Albert Gallatin, *Considerations on the Currency and Banking System of the United States,* Philadelphia, 1831, pp. 45, 49, 53–54, 101–103, 106. Additional tables include data for reporting banks in seven of the principal cities combined, and in the remainder of the country in 1829 (p. 52); a list of the individual banks and the capital of each, classified by states, in operation on Jan. 1, 1830 (pp. 97–100); a list of the individual banks and the capital of each, classified by states, which had failed or discontinued business from January 1811 to January 1830 (pp. 103–105); the discount on bank notes from 1814 through 1817—during which convertibility of deposits was restricted—in each of three cities (p. 106).

The table in the Treasury document of 1834 referred to above (Introduction to Part Two, footnote 3) shows, in addition to Gallatin's estimate of the specie stock in 1829 described in the text, an estimate by him of the specie stock in 1810. The latter estimate

from official reports and extracts," in which he reprinted Gallatin's estimates of bank capital, circulation outstanding, specie, and deposits, for
the five selected years over the period 1810–29, referred to above. He
then continued with the data the Secretary of the Treasury collected
from state banks beginning 1833 (to be described more fully in section
2, below), showing figures for the same items in selected years, 1833–44.
The official figures for circulation, Seaman commented, were unsatisfactory. Accordingly, he computed "nett circulation," deducting notes
held by banks from notes outstanding, to arrive at notes held by the
public. He next estimated the U.S. specie stock, starting with a base
figure at the end of September 1820 (assumed to be the same as the
1819 end-of-year stock, which was in turn assumed to be $3 million
greater than the end-of-1814 stock, since specie in banks was then
almost $3 million greater than at the earlier date). To the base figure,
Seaman made the following adjustments: he added (a) recorded imports of gold and silver and (b) estimated unrecorded amounts brought
in by emigrants, and deducted (c) recorded exports and (d) estimated
amounts "made into plate, utensils, jewelry and ornaments, over and
above old metal worked over, and the produce of the mines of the
United States" during the periods 1820–24, 1824–28, 1828–34, 1834–
37, 1837–38, 1838–42, and 1842–45. Except for the final period which
began October 1, 1842, and ended June 30, 1845, the periods began
October 1 and ended September 30, corresponding to the dating of
foreign trade statistics during the years Seaman covered. For June 30,
1845, Seaman deducted specie in banks from his estimate of the stock
on that date and added the residual to his "nett circulation" estimate at
end of 1844 to obtain aggregate coin and bank notes held by the public.
Converting to a per capita basis, Seaman concluded the average circulation was too low in the United States.[4]

is omitted in a later version of the table in *Annual Report on the Finances*, 1856, p. 434.
The 1856 *Annual Report* table and a similar table, starting 1815, in the 1854 *Annual
Report* (p. 280), however, attribute to Gallatin an 1815 estimate of the specie stock
which is not given in the Treasury document. We have been unable to locate the source
of either the 1810 or 1815 specie stock estimates in Gallatin's writings.
   Gallatin's 1831 volume was a reprint, with additions and corrections, of an article
originally prepared for *American Quarterly Review*, Dec. 1830, pp. 441–528. Though
Gallatin was writing to advocate bimetallism, Nicholas Biddle, of the Bank of the United
States, was so pleased with the article's support of a national bank that he had the reprint issued and widely distributed at the bank's expense in his efforts to win friends for
its recharter (see Raymond Walters, Jr., *Albert Gallatin*, New York, 1957, pp. 357–359).
   [4] Ezra C. Seaman, *Progress of Nations*, pp. 243–248. W. M. Gouge also obtained "nett
circulation" for 1834–41 (see *The Journal of Banking*, June 8, 1842, pp. 385–386).

As indicated earlier, in addition to the estimates described above, estimates of one monetary total or another—usually the specie stock or bank notes outstanding—were given from time to time beginning in the 1830's in contemporary periodicals. These estimates are included in Table 13, as are also hitherto unpublished figures of the bank note issues, individual deposits, and specie holdings of the First Bank of the United States on one to four dates annually, 1792–1800. These figures were prepared by Clark Warburton from consolidated balance sheets of the Bank of the United States at Philadelphia and its offices, compiled by James O. Wettereau.[5]

2. Official Estimates

SECRETARY OF THE TREASURY WILLIAM H. CRAWFORD (1820)
Selected Years, 1813–19:

Specie Stock
Specie Held by Banks
Specie Held by Public
Bank Notes Outstanding
Bank Notes Held by Public

The first official U.S. monetary estimates were prepared by Secretary of the Treasury Crawford in response to a House resolution of March 1, 1819, directing him to transmit to Congress a statement of the condition of the Second Bank of the United States and of the chartered banks in the several states and the District of Columbia, and "to report such measures as, in his opinion, may be expedient to procure and retain a sufficient quantity of gold and silver coin in the United States, or to supply a circulating medium in place of specie . . ." Crawford's report contained in an appendix a statement for the head office of the Bank of the United States and each of its branches as of various dates in September 1819 and a consolidated balance sheet dated October 1; the authorized bank capital by states in each year from 1814 through 1817; a balance sheet showing the condition of the banks in each state, district, or territory, "as far as the same was known at the Treasury Department, in the year 1819"; and data on capital, circulation, specie,

---

[5] We are indebted to Warburton for making these figures available to us.

and discounts of a sample of sixteen banks in eight states and the District of Columbia on September 30, 1813, 1815, and 1819. From these data Crawford constructed estimates of various balance sheet items for all banks, which he presented in the text of his report. For some items he gave alternate estimates. Crawford's estimates were presented in tabular form by later investigators and reprinted in government documents.[6]

In the text of his report Crawford discussed the data shown in the appendix tables. The balance sheet for all banks for which the Treasury had information in 1819, he concluded, was imperfect. The capital they reported in 1819 was one-quarter smaller in amount than that shown in 1817 in another appendix table, although more banks were in operation at the later date.[7] Accordingly, Crawford assumed that the capital and specie of the banks in 1819 was 25 per cent greater than the appendix table showed. To the specie estimate Crawford added the amount of specie held by the Bank of the United States and an estimate of specie held by the public to get the total specie stock. ("There are no means of ascertaining, with any degree of precision, the amount of specie in circulation; it is probable, however, that it does not exceed $4,500,000.") To revise the appendix table figure on bank note circulation, he raised the combined figure for the state banks and the Bank of the United States not by 25 per cent but by 28 per cent, which he then reduced to allow for "notes supposed to be in circulation, but which are, in fact, in the possession of other banks." [8]

[6] Crawford's original report was reprinted in *Reports of the Secretary of the Treasury of the United States*, Vol. II, Washington, 1837, pp. 481–525; in H. Doc. 15, 28th Cong., 1st sess., 1843, pp. 733–774; and in S. Exec. Doc. 58, 45th Cong., 3d sess., 1879, pp. 502–553. His estimates in tabular form are shown in Comptroller of the Currency, *Annual Report*, 1876, pp. xxix–xxxi, and appear as entries in tables on the circulation of notes or specie in H. Rept. 27, 23rd Cong., 2nd sess., p. 63; *Annual Report on the Finances*, 1854, p. 280; 1856, pp. 434–435.

[7] Crawford decided that the appendix table on authorized bank capital in each of the four years beginning 1814 was probably correct. The figures in the table were derived from taxes paid by banks on their annual dividends to their stockholders. Under the Act of August 2, 1813, taxes were levied either upon note issues of incorporated and unincorporated banks or upon their annual dividends to stockholders, and apparently the banks chose to pay the latter tax. Crawford argued that even if the banks understated the dividend rate they paid and accordingly the amount of their capital, the lower figure was probably a closer approximation to the paid-in capital than the capital figure that would have been derived if the higher actual dividend rate had been used. The reason was that capital was rarely paid in specie after the first installment. Later installments were usually paid with promissory notes of the stockholders. If payment was made in specie or bank notes, a compensating loan was extended to the stockholders by the bank as a permanent accommodation.

[8] Crawford's estimate of notes outstanding is $46 million. He does not give the figure after deducting notes held by banks, but combines the residual with his estimate of

Crawford prepared an alternate set of estimates for 1819 as well as an initial set for 1813 and 1815 based on the appendix table giving figures for a sample of sixteen banks (all of which held Treasury deposits). He applied to the 1819 estimate of capital, described above, the ratios of specie and circulation of the sample of sixteen banks in that year. The resulting estimates were considerably higher than the specie and circulation estimates he first presented. For 1813 Crawford needed an estimate of capital in all banks. He assumed the authorized capital figure for 1814 (in the appendix table covering each of the four years 1814–17) was $15 million greater than in 1813, and then applied the sample ratios in the later year to derive estimates of the specie held by the banks and their circulation of bank notes in the earlier. The estimates for 1815 were based on the authorized capital of the banks and the sample ratios in that year.

For 1813 Crawford also gave an estimate of the amount of specie outside banks, which, combined with the estimate of bank notes outstanding, is usually shown as the upper limit of the estimate for that year. To the estimate of notes outstanding Crawford added an estimate of individual deposits to approximate the "liability of the banks for specie." Incidentally, he also gave an estimate of bank notes held by the public in 1813.

Concerning the initial 1815 estimate of circulation, Crawford wrote:

The banks, upon whose situation that estimate is founded, were established at a period when the practice of dispensing with the payment of those portions of their capital falling due after they went into operation had not been generally introduced. Some of them did not suspend specie payments during the general suspension. The rest were among the first to resume them, and have continued them to the present time. It cannot be expected that banks, which went into operation during the war, and after the general suspension had occurred, were conducted with an equal degree of prudence and circumspection.[9]

He therefore raised the initial estimate "for the excess of issues beyond the estimate" and then reduced it to omit notes held by banks. This amount is usually shown as the upper limit of the 1815 estimate, al-

specie in circulation. He estimates "the actual circulation, both of paper and specie," as less than $45 million. This estimate is usually cited as the lower limit and the alternate estimate of $53 million, described in the text, as the upper limit. The latter estimate does not, however, exclude notes held by banks nor does it include an estimate of specie outside banks.

[9] *Reports of the Secretary of the Treasury*, p. 485.

though it is not actually comparable to the initial estimate which is given as the lower limit, since no deduction from that estimate for notes held by banks was made by Crawford or others.

SUCCESSIVE SECRETARIES OF THE TREASURY (1833–63)
1833–62:

Bank Monetary Assets
Bank Monetary Liabilities

The general public interest in the operation of banks led to a House resolution of July 10, 1832, directing the Secretary of the Treasury to lay before the House of Representatives:

at the next and each successive session of Congress, copies of such statements or returns, showing the capital, circulation, discounts, specie, deposits, and condition of the different State banks and banking companies, as may have been communicated to the Legislatures, Governors or other officers of the several States, within the year, and made public; and where such statements cannot be obtained, such other authentic information as will best supply the deficiency; . . .

Prior to the resolution the Treasury had collected systematically, but published only intermittently and only for certain dates, statements of condition from depositary banks, banks in the District of Columbia chartered by the Congress, and the First and Second Banks of the United States.[10] Some states required some or all banks to report, others did not.[11] In response to the resolution, Secretary Louis MacLane made his first report in February 1833, and successive secretaries made reports each year thereafter until 1863, except for 1834 and 1842–45. In his letter accompanying the report made in December 1863, Secretary

[10] Secretary Crawford referred to the "destruction or loss of the returns made to the Treasury" by depositary banks before 1816 (*Reports of the Secretary of the Treasury,* p. 482). The condition of the principal banks in the District on Jan. 1, 1816, 1819, and 1822, is given in American State Papers, *Finance,* Vol. III, pp. 101, 303, 304, 795–797. Monthly data for the Second Bank are given in 23rd Cong., 2nd sess., Sen. Doc. 117, pp. 204–224.

[11] Continuous data are available for all banks in Mass. semiannually beginning 1803; in R.I. annually beginning 1809; and for individual reporting banks with no aggregate statement, in Penna., Va., N.Y., and N.J. annually beginning 1809. J. Van Fenstermaker recently collected statements of condition of reporting chartered banks in twenty-nine states for whatever years data were available during the period 1819–37. He recast the original statements to fit a uniform balance sheet of his selection. He gives the balance sheet for individual states—of which ten had some reporting banks in each of the years covered, two had reports in only one year, and the rest, reports for varying fractions of the years covered—and for the aggregate of states. In addition he shows annual totals of the number of chartered and of reporting banks. Private banks are not covered in the compilations. See J. Van Fenstermaker, *The Development of American Commercial Bank-*

Salmon P. Chase suggested the "expediency of rescinding the resolution of July 10, 1832," in view of the action of Congress in March 1863 which required banks to report their capital and deposits semiannually for internal revenue purposes. These returns, Chase believed, would make it unnecessary to compile estimates from statements or returns required under state laws.

The reports made between 1833 and 1863 varied greatly in the number and detail of the state reports included and in the extent to which the Secretary prepared independent compilations instead of merely reprinting existing state documents. For single years the reports sometimes covered the banks in a given state more adequately than the published state documents. This happened in cases where some of the banks in operation in a state were not required to report their condition to any authority, and the Secretary on his own initiative obtained statements from them to supplement the published state returns. Every now and then a report also included retrospective figures and summary tables in which the returns for individual states were shown in a uniform way and aggregated. Frequently these summaries included data for more states than were represented in the original report for a given year. Thus the report for 1835 gave statements of condition for the banks in only thirteen states. In the summary table published by the Secretary in 1841, however, returns for twenty states were given for 1835. In addition to the subtotal for all reporting banks for a given year the summary tables included an estimated subtotal for nonreporting banks.[12] For 1852, how-

_____

ing, *1782–1837*, Kent, Ohio, 1965. Earlier, Smith and Cole compiled aggregate annual figures, 1830–45, for the banks of Mass., R.I., N.Y., and Penna. (W. B. Smith and A. H. Cole, *Fluctuations in American Business*, Cambridge, Mass., 1935, p. 75).

[12] Clark Warburton notes in a private communication to the authors that the summary data including estimates for nonreporting banks are not necessarily comprehensive. He bases this judgment on a table of banking data by years for the period 1834–41 in *The Journal of Banking* (Philadelphia, June 8, 1842, p. 386), published by William M. Gouge during the year July 1841–June 1842. For 1834–39 Gouge's table agrees with the Treasury summaries. For 1840 and 1841, however, the figures for all items exceed those in the Treasury summaries. Gouge described the table as follows: "All the columns, except those for 1840 and 1841, have been taken from the tables which were compiled by us while in the Treasury Department. The columns for 1840 and 1841, have been prepared, partly from materials collected in the Treasury Department, and partly from others elsewhere obtained. All the estimates for 1841, have been founded on returns in previous years, the cases of some three or four banks only excepted" (p. 385).

More generally, Warburton believes that the coverage of the Secretary of the Treasury's banking figures was less complete in the 1840's and 1850's than in the 1830's. The number of banks not required to report to State officials increased subsequent to the expiration of the charter of the Second Bank of the United States in 1836, when agitation against chartered banks led to a rapid development of private banks and the spread of "free banks." See Clark Warburton, *Depression, Inflation, and Monetary Policy, Selected Papers, 1945–1953*, Baltimore, 1966, p. 201, note f.

ever, no returns were published and for 1853, only incomplete ones with no estimate for nonreporting banks.

The uniform summary table for each state and the aggregate table for the United States include the following items:

Assets	Liabilities
1. Loans and Discounts	9. Capital
2. Stock	10. Circulation
3. Real Estate	11. Deposits
4. Other Investments	12. Due to Other Banks
5. Due by Other Banks	13. Other Liabilities
6. Notes of Other Banks	
7. Specie Funds	
8. Specie	

For monetary estimates the items of crucial significance are those numbered 5 through 8 and 10 through 12. There is some question about the reliability of the Secretary's classification of entries under these items. In comparing the summary data shown for New York, 1834–43, with the original state bank report figures we noted various inconsistencies in the Secretary's practice. Cash items, which should have been classified as specie funds, were included with discounts in one year. Deposits of the canal commissioners were sometimes shown as deposits, sometimes as other liabilities.

The chief problem raised by the aggregate series is its dating. For each state the summary table showed the condition of the banks for whichever call dates the Secretary obtained information, sometimes for all the dates in one year at which the banks reported, sometimes for only one of the report dates in a given year followed by a different report date the following year and a third report date the succeeding year. When only single report dates for each state are given, they are distributed throughout the year. Nevertheless, the Secretary described the aggregate as compiled from returns "on or about January 1."

Smith and Cole rejected the Secretary's compilations in their study of U.S. business cycles before 1860 because they considered them misleading.[13] Recently, however, George Macesich reached the opposite conclusion regarding the series. He found the coverage of banks to be fairly

[13] *Fluctuations in American Business, 1790–1860*, p. 116.

complete and argued that differences in reporting dates of the individual states included "act like a haphazard moving average to blur the turning points," which in any event cannot be precisely determined from annual data.[14]

OFFICIAL DOCUMENTS (1843–1928)
 Selected Years, 1790–1866.

 Specie Stock
 Specie in Treasury
 Currency Held by Treasury
 Treasury Deposits at Banks
 Currency Outside Treasury

As mentioned above, systematic official reporting of the stock of specie did not begin until the decade after the Civil War. A few pre-Civil War Congressional documents brought together whatever fugitive estimates of the stock their compilers gleaned from a variety of sources.[15] The

[14] George Macesich, "Sources of Monetary Disturbances in the United States, 1834–45," *Journal of Economic History,* Sept. 1960, p. 428. Macesich used as his source of the Secretary's compilations, Comptroller of the Currency, *Annual Report,* 1876, pp. xciv–xcv, where the annual aggregates are reprinted. The Comptroller also reprinted the state-by-state compilations (pp. xciv–cxxi), and most of the historical compilations referred to above (pp. xxxix–xliv). The aggregate series in the 1876 report is also reprinted in Comptroller of the Currency, *Annual Report,* 1920, Vol. 2, p. 847, and 1931, p. 1018. In the 1931 reprinting, the Comptroller gave figures for 1852 omitted in the Secretary's original compilation and in later reprintings. The 1852 figures show the number of banks in that year as the average of five years, 1847–51, and the individual asset and liability items as the average of ten years, 1854–63. Some of the original group of thirteen items, with 1852 figures as estimated by the Comptroller, are also reprinted in U.S. Bureau of the Census, *Historical Statistics of the United States, Colonial Times to 1957,* Washington, D.C., 1960 [*Historical Statistics, 1960*], pp. 624–625, Series X-22, X-25, X-29, X-34, X-39-40.

The banking statistics for 1834–63 have been reprinted in the sources listed above usually with no indication that they refer to January 1 of each year. Also, in the official Treasury table of currency in circulation by kind, 1860 to date, the figures for state bank notes outstanding, which are actually as of Jan. 1, 1860–63, are shown as June 30 data (see *U.S. Statistical Abstract, 1878,* pp. 14–15—this was the source Wesley C. Mitchell used for his table, described in footnote 29, below, and so he was not aware that he combined January 1 and June 30 currency estimates; *Banking and Monetary Statistics,* p. 408; and *Historical Statistics, 1960,* p. 649, Series X-290).

[15] See 23rd Cong., 2nd sess., H. Rept. 27, p. 63, covering selected years from 1775 to 1834; *Annual Report on the Finances,* 1854, p. 280, also 1856, pp. 434–435, the former covering selected years from 1816 to 1854, the latter, from 1790 to 1855.

The latter figures were essentially those reprinted as the "estimated specie in the United States" in a Treasury circular that gave figures for 1800, 1810, 1820, and 1830, and yearly figures thereafter through 1859 (U.S. Treasury Department, *Information Respecting United States Bonds, Paper Currency and Coin, Production of Precious Metals, Etc.,* Washington, 1896, reprinted and extended 1897, 1900, 1904, 1908, 1910, 1912, 1915).

The same series also appeared in the Comptroller of the Currency's annual reports (1894, p. 173; 1896, p. 544; 1916, Vol. II, p. 44; and 1920, Vol. II, p. 49). No state-estimates include some by Blodget, Gallatin, and Crawford (described earlier in this chapter) as well as some others, either not specifically attributed or else attributed without identification of the source. Clark Warburton has traced to their sources some of the estimates of specie stock collected in Treasury documents of 1854 and 1856 (cited in footnote 15) and has found that the reprinted estimates agree only in part with the original figures.[16] In Table 13, we show the reprinted specie stock estimates and in the source notes to the table give corrections by Warburton.

For years beginning 1860, the specie stock was given in the Treasury circular and the Comptroller's annual report referred to in footnote 15. The stock from 1862 to 1875 was shown as an unchanging $25 million. The estimates beginning 1860 were revised in the 1922 annual report of the Treasury, which showed gold coin and bullion separately from silver.[17] Table 13 shows the revised gold stock estimates for 1860–66. No silver is included, since according to the estimates the only silver in the country during those years was subsidiary silver.

Official reporting of gold in the Treasury also did not begin until after the Civil War, a few years after reports of the stock were initiated. For earlier years there are conflicting figures concerning the Treasury's specie holdings.

ment about the source of the series was published, and it is not known where the figures for total specie were obtained for years not shown in the 1856 Treasury annual report. In one instance the later reprinting does not precisely reproduce the 1856 series (for Jan. 1, 1841, a range is shown in the earlier source, but only the upper limit appears in the later one). Also the figures shown for Jan. 1, 1834, and 1835, which do not appear in the earlier source, do not agree with Secretary of the Treasury Woodbury's estimates for those dates in the finance reports.

[16] Thus for four years—1836, 1837, 1838, and 1840—the specie stock estimates are attributed to Secretary of the Treasury Levi Woodbury. The original estimates compare as follows with the reprinted figures:

Date of Original Estimate (1)	Size of Estimate (millions of dollars) (2)	Date of Reprinted Figure (3)	Size of Reprinted Figure (millions of dollars) (4)
1/1/1836	63	1/1/1836	65
12/1/1836	73	1/1/1837	73
12/1/1837	about 80		
12/1/1838	85–90	1/1/1838	87½

Warburton was unable to find the source of the estimate for 1840 attributed to Woodbury. He conjectures that the figure attributed to Hazard's *Commercial Register* for Jan. 1, 1839, is probably also an average, with the fraction omitted, of Woodbury's range for December 1839.

The estimate attributed to Hunt as of Jan. 1, 1844, appears to refer in fact to December 1844 (see Hunt's *Merchants Magazine*, Dec. 1844, p. 551).

[17] Secretary of the Treasury, *Annual Report*, 1922, p. 524; also 1928, p. 552.

Beginning 1801 every annual report of the Treasury (referred to below as the finance reports) gave the balance to its credit, before 1814
usually as of October 1, from 1814 through 1843 usually as of January
1, and thereafter through the Civil War, as of July 1.[18] The form in
which the balance was held—specie, state bank notes, or deposits at
banks—was not mentioned.

In 1894 a table in the Comptroller's annual report, described as prepared by the Loan and Currency Division of the Treasury Department,
classified as specie in the Treasury the entire Treasury balance at annual
dates, 1830–59, as shown in the finance reports, except for January 1,
1836, 1837, and 1838. For those dates, an unchanging amount of $5
million was shown, footnoted, "Specie in Treasury estimated." The table
also included figures for 1800, 1810, and 1820, which were smaller than
the reported Treasury balance, and the same footnote as for 1836–38
applied.[19] The table was subsequently reprinted in a Treasury circular
of 1896, which was republished periodically through 1915, and in *Historical Statistics, 1960.*[20]

In 1906, however, a table in the Treasury annual report classified the
balance beginning 1789 as partly in the Treasury (except 1793–1835,
when no balance in Treasury offices is shown) and partly in depositary
banks (except 1847–63, when the Independent Treasury Act prohibited
the deposit of public moneys in banks).[21] If this table is correct, there
were no cash balances in the Treasury before 1836 (except for negligible

[18] A retrospective table in a Congressional document of 1843 showed "the balances
of money in the treasury" from Mar. 4, 1789, to Dec. 31, 1791, and annually thereafter
to 1842 (28th Cong., 1st Sess., H. Doc. 15, p. 1019). The table did not show in what
form the balances were held.

[19] U.S. Comptroller of the Currency, *Annual Report,* 1894, p. 173; reprinted, 1896,
p. 544; 1916, Vol. II, p. 44; and 1920, Vol. II, p. 49.

[20] *Information Respecting United States Bonds . . . , Etc.* The table in *Historical
Statistics, 1960,* p. 647, Series X-282, is labeled "Currency held in Treasury." A footnote, however, states that prior to 1860 it consists of specie only. The date of the series
is given as of June 30 although the figures before 1844 actually refer to Jan. 1.

[21] Secretary of the Treasury, *Annual Report,* 1906, pp. 196–197, reprinted and extended 1915, p. 374.
A note accompanying the table indicates that the statement is based on "warrants
paid by the Treasurer of the United States to Dec. 31, 1821, and by warrants issued
after that date." This means that the figures are on an unrevised basis through 1821,
reflecting what the Treasury knew about its accounts on the date of report, and on a
revised basis thereafter, reflecting the final state of the accounts after all transactions
as of that date have been recorded. On some dates before 1822 common to both the
finance reports and the 1906 annual report, the total balance shown in both sources is
identical; thereafter the two sources differ, because the finance report continues on an
unrevised basis. The table in the 1894 Comptroller's report and in the Treasury circular
also shows the figures (reported as specie in Treasury, though actually the total balance)
on an unrevised basis.

amounts on June 30, 1791, and December 31, 1792), and therefore it is only with the period after 1836 that we need be concerned. Before attempting to determine the composition of Treasury cash, we shall review the conditions under which the Treasury held its balances in various subperiods.

In the period from August 1846, when the second Independent Treasury Act was passed, until 1862, when greenbacks were first issued we know that only specie and Treasury notes, which were presumably retired on receipt, were made receivable for public dues. For those years, the presumption is that the Treasury balance was held wholly in specie. So it is for the period 1836–46 that the composition of the Treasury balance is in question.

Before the establishment of the Independent Treasury System in 1846, the Treasury balance was in the care of thousands of collectors of public moneys—postmasters, customhouse collectors, commissioners of internal revenue, officers of land offices, marshals, clerks of court—not physically in the possession of the Treasury Department in Washington or its outposts: the mints, customhouses, subtreasuries. In the words of a Congressional committee report, collectors ". . . always had . . . the absolute control, for a time, of the whole of our revenue. . . ." [22] But so far as Treasury records show, the Treasury's balance before 1836 was never held by the collectors in the forms of currency paid to them but was always on deposit in banks. Similarly, disbursing officers, in paying out warrants issued by the Treasury, never held balances of money but always drew on banks.

The Constitution says nothing about where the public money should be kept. The Act of September 2, 1789, which established the Treasury Department, provided that "it shall be the duty of the Treasurer to receive and keep the monies of the United States," but did not designate where. From the start, the Secretary of the Treasury selected the banks in which collecting and disbursing officers kept Treasury balances. An Act of March 30, 1809, however, empowered the President of the United States to designate the banks in which disbursing officers were to keep public moneys. The Secretary continued to select depositaries for collectors. Until its charter expired, the First Bank of the United States was

[22] Report of Committee of Ways and Means, 25th Cong., 2nd sess., H. Rept. 634, Mar. 5, 1838, p. 7.

one such depositary. The charter of the Second Bank provided that public moneys should be kept in the bank or its branches, unless the Secretary of the Treasury should otherwise direct. Under this authority the Treasury kept its balance in the Second Bank until September 1833, although state banks continued to be used as depositaries for limited purposes. At that time the collectors were instructed to cease depositing in the Bank and to deposit exclusively in state banks, including those selected for use earlier and additional ones the Secretary designated. The increase in the number of depositary banks led to the enactment of the Deposit Act of June 23, 1836, which was designed to bring the banks under the supervision of the Secretary. (The act also provided for the distribution of the surplus Treasury balance in excess of $5 million among the states, on their pledge to return it on demand of the Secretary. For this reason, some sources continued to show Treasury balances after 1837, including the surplus that had been distributed among the states.) During the life of the first Independent Treasury, 1840–41, and until the second Independent Treasury was enacted, state banks continued to be employed as depositaries.

It is not clear why Treasury records show Treasury cash separate from balances in depositary banks beginning December 1836. Financial history would suggest a later date for the establishment of Treasury cash accounts—after convertibility was restricted in May 1837. Treasury circulars then notified collectors of customs and other public money to keep the public revenue in their own hands until further notice from the department. If the amounts held exceeded a specified sum, they were authorized to deposit in a specie-paying bank or in one that would agree to return the same kind of money as deposited.

Before 1836 all forms of currency were receivable for public dues, despite the Act of July 31, 1789, which required all duties to be paid in gold and silver only, since Hamilton construed the act to sanction payment also in notes of the two banks then in operation. Notes of the First Bank of the United States were made receivable for public dues in its charter of 1791. Payment for public lands "in money" was specified in an act of 1796. In 1812 Treasury notes were made receivable. A joint Congressional resolution of April 30, 1816, expanded the list of acceptable forms of payment for all duties, taxes, or debts payable to the United States to include the legal tender of the United States, Treasury notes, notes of the Second Bank of the United States, and notes of banks payable on demand in the legal currency of the United States.[23] This resolution was still in effect on July 11, 1836, when the Treasury Department issued the Specie Circular, directing receivers of money for public lands to accept payment only in specie. Other public dues were payable in currency other than specie. An indication of the composition of the Treasury's receipts is given by the provision of the short-lived first Independent Treasury Act of July 4, 1840, directing that one-quarter of all government dues in that year be paid in specie, and an additional one-quarter in each successive year until June 30, 1843, after which only specie was to be receivable. The act was repealed August 13, 1841.

The legislative record suggests that Treasury cash balances before 1846 were at least partly, and perhaps entirely, held in state bank notes. It seems unlikely that they were held wholly in specie.

The Comptroller's annual reports of 1894, 1896, and 1916 (see footnote 19) and the Treasury circular of 1896 (see footnote 15) gave annual figures beginning 1860 on the sum of "coin, bullion, and paper money in Treasury." [24] Tables in the 1928 annual report of the Treasury showing the stock of currency and the amounts outside the Treasury, by kind beginning 1860, make it possible to break down the total shown as held by the Treasury in its circular.[25] In 1860–61 the breakdown shows that the Treasury held only specie. For 1862–63 there is no estimate of specie outside the Treasury nor of amounts in the Treasury. Currency in the Treasury, according to this source, was in greenbacks only in 1862 and in greenbacks and fractional currency in 1863. For the remainder of the greenback period, the sum reported in the circular shows the Treasury as holding only these issues and (beginning 1866) national bank notes. According to the 1928 report, however, the Treasury's gold and subsidiary silver holdings are known beginning 1864, and those

[23] In 1816, when the banks restricted convertibility, the Treasury had four types of accounts with each depository bank: (1) a general cash account, consisting of local currency; (2) a special deposit account of bank notes issued by banks other than the depositary; (3) an account of small interest-bearing Treasury notes; and (4) an account of small noninterest-bearing Treasury notes. (See American State Papers, *Finance*, Vol. III, p. 131.)

[24] The sources cited initially showed the total in the Treasury including the cover for currency outside the Treasury, e.g., gold cover for gold certificates. In the 1915 edition of the circular and the 1916 Comptroller's annual report only the unduplicated sum held in the Treasury was given.

[25] Secretary of the Treasury, *Annual Report*, 1928, pp. 552–554.

amounts have been added in this source to the Treasury cash figures exclusive of its metallic holdings given in the Treasury circular.[26]

Finally, total currency in the Treasury beginning 1860, according to the 1928 annual report, does not agree with the amounts shown as balance in the Treasury in the 1906 and 1915 annual reports. The reason, we believe, is that the 1928 source gives estimates of specie in the Treasury during the Civil War years that are not included in the 1906 and 1915 sources. In addition, the 1928 source gives the figures on an unrevised basis before 1890, while the 1906 and 1915 sources show the figures on a revised basis from 1822 on.

The Treasury circular referred to in footnote 15 above also gives series labeled "Money in circulation" for 1800, 1810, 1820, and 1830, and yearly thereafter through 1859, and "Circulation" for midyears beginning 1860. Both these series purport to be currency outside the Treasury. They were derived for years before 1860 by subtracting the defective series of "Specie in Treasury," described above, from the sum of "Estimated bank notes outstanding" and "Estimated specie in United States"; and for years after 1860 by subtracting unduplicated Treasury coin, bullion, and currency holdings from the stock of coin including bullion in the Treasury plus the stock of U.S. notes and bank notes. The series since 1860 in the Treasury circular has been superseded by the revised figures in the 1928 Treasury annual report. The series before 1860 has not been revised, however, despite its shortcomings and has been widely reprinted.[27]

Since currency outside the Treasury is a residual, the series before 1860 reflects the defects of both the minuend and the subtrahend. The minuend is based on two components: bank notes outstanding and the specie stock. For 1800 the estimate of bank notes outstanding is Blodget's; for 1810, 1820, and 1830 the estimates are Gallatin's for end-of-years 1810, 1819, and 1829. The 1830–33 estimates, identical for 1832 and 1833, are unidentified. For 1834–59 they are January 1 estimates from the Secretary of the Treasury's report on the condition of the state banks. The specie stock estimates in the Treasury circular have been

---

[26] The 1928 report series is reprinted in *Historical Statistics, 1960,* p. 647, Series X-282 (beginning 1860).

[27] In addition to the Comptroller's annual reports listed in footnote 14, see *Statistical Abstract of the United States,* Dept. of Commerce, 1942, p. 277, and *Historical Statistics, 1960,* p. 647, Series X-284.

described earlier in this subsection. The figure shown for 1800 is Blodget's estimate; for 1810, 1820, and 1830 the figures, dated as just indicated for bank notes, are estimates attributed to Gallatin; thereafter they are as shown in the Treasury annual report for 1856, without attribution and with estimates for years not shown in that source included apparently as round amounts to complete the series.

The subtrahend used to obtain currency outside the Treasury is labeled "Specie in Treasury" but, as noted above, from 1830 on, 1836–38 excepted, the figures are drawn from the annual finance reports which gave the Treasury's total balance, whether held in specie, bank notes, or bank deposits. Before the Independent Treasury System was adopted in 1846, the figures overestimate not only Treasury specie holdings but Treasury currency as well, hence they underestimate the residual currency outside the Treasury. From 1846 on, with the Independent Treasury System in operation, the amounts shown may be valid estimates of specie in Treasury if, as seems likely, the Treasury then held no bank notes or bank deposits. For 1800, 1810, 1820, and 1836–38, if the estimates actually refer to specie in the Treasury, they underestimate total currency in the Treasury, hence overestimate residual currency outside the Treasury. Finally, there is a problem in the dating of the "Specie in Treasury" series. It is a January 1 series before 1844, thereafter a July 1 series, and both segments are subtracted from January 1 estimates of the specie stock and bank notes outstanding.

FEDERAL DEPOSIT INSURANCE CORPORATION (1934)
1864–66:

Total Bank Deposits

The final estimate in official reports to be noted here is that for deposits in 1864–66, constructed by the FDIC. Deposits at nonnational banks were estimated from receipts of the tax of one-half of one per cent per year levied upon bank deposits by the federal government, 1863–83, adjusted by an assumed ratio of actual deposits to the estimate from tax collections. The estimates were dated as averages of the year ending May 31. For national banks, yearly averages of deposits reported on call dates were computed.[28]

[28] U.S. Federal Deposit Insurance Corporation, *Annual Report*, 1934, pp. 89, 103. (The estimates were prepared by Clark Warburton.)

3. Twentieth Century Private Estimates

WESLEY C. MITCHELL (1903)
  1860–66:

  Specie Stock
  Bank Notes Outstanding
  Treasury Currency Outstanding
  Government Obligations Used as Currency
  Currency Held by Treasury

In his monumental *History of the Greenbacks,* Wesley C. Mitchell devoted a chapter to a discussion of the "circulating medium." In it he reviewed specie, bank notes, and four kinds of government obligations that were in use as currency at one time or another in each of the seven years 1860–66, and then gave estimates of the components of these obligations without aggregating them yearly. He noted: "To cast up the totals of the above table would be not only useless, but positively misleading, because several of the items are mere guesses, and in the case of others where the amounts are reasonably certain, not all of the sums set down were in use at any time as currency." [29] The amounts shown are apparently outstanding issues as reported in various official sources then available to Mitchell (some of these have since been superseded). In addition, the table showed the aggregate coin, bullion, and paper money in the Treasury. The chief distinction of the table was that it displayed the various kinds of government obligations—interest-bearing and noninterest-bearing, legal tender and not legal tender—that were pressed into use as currency during the war in addition to coin and the conventional bank issues.

CLARK WARBURTON (1949)
  1799–1859, by Decades:

  Money Stock

Using in the main published sources, Clark Warburton constructed estimates at decade intervals, 1799–1859, of total deposits and currency,

---

[29] Wesley C. Mitchell, *History of the Greenbacks,* Chicago, 1903, pp. 141–181. The table is on p. 179; the quotation comes from p. 181.

excluding vault cash and interbank deposits.[30] He gave three components: currency outside Treasury, specie held by banks, and bank deposits excluding interbank. Though well aware of flaws in the original
series (as his footnote comments indicate), Warburton made no attempt
to correct them. He dated as of the preceding year published decade
figures for 1800–30, and thereafter when annual data became available,
used the published figures for 1839, 1849, and 1859. For 1839, he
failed to realize that the Treasury tabulation for state banks included
the Second Bank of the United States, and added the figures for that
bank. For 1839, 1849, and 1859, he added deposits in savings banks,
since these were not included in the Treasury tabulations.

The dating and other problems concerning the published figures for
currency outside the Treasury before 1860, which Warburton used,
have been noted above. To obtain currency held by the public, it is,
however, necessary to deduct from currency outside the Treasury—
regardless of the shortcomings of the published figures—both bank
notes held by other banks and specie in banks. Warburton, however,
apparently overlooked the item of notes held by other banks and deducted only specie in banks.

For specie in banks he used Gallatin's end-of-year estimates for 1810,
1819, and 1829, for 1809, 1819, and 1829, and January 1 estimates
of specie in banks from the Secretary of the Treasury's reports on the
state banks for 1839, 1849, 1859.[31] For 1799 he estimated specie in
banks as one-half the stock of specie, as in Gallatin's 1810 estimate. For
bank deposits excluding interbank Warburton used Gallatin's end-of-
year estimates for 1819 and 1829 and January 1 estimates from the
Secretary of the Treasury's reports for 1839, 1849, and 1859.[32] His
1799 and 1809 estimates Warburton described as "based largely on data

[30] Clark Warburton, "The Secular Trend in Monetary Velocity," *Quarterly Journal
of Economics,* Feb. 1949, pp. 76–77; reprinted in his *Depression, Inflation, and Monetary
Policy,* pp. 200–201.

J. P. Wernette (*Financing Full Employment,* Cambridge, Mass., 1945, p. 36) pre-
ceded Warburton in presenting decennial estimates, 1800–60, of total money. He combined currency outside the Treasury, as given in the Treasury circular (see pp. 244–245
above for the defects of this series) and bank deposits as given in the Secretary of the
Treasury's reports for 1840–60 and as estimated by Wernette, 1800–30, from the 1840
and 1850 ratios between deposits and currency outside Treasury. He did not deduct
bank vault cash although he excluded interbank deposits. His actual source was
Statistical Abstract of the United States, 1942, pp. 277 and 291.

[31] As reprinted in Comptroller of the Currency, *Annual Report,* 1876, pp. xl and xlv.
Gallatin's estimates are dated 1811, 1820, and 1830 in this source. For 1839 Warburton's
figure includes specie held by the Second Bank of the United States.

[32] His source is shown in the preceding footnote.

for circulation and the amount of deposits relative to circulation for later years." Warburton did not exclude Treasury deposits at banks or correct for float.

Warburton's estimates for January 1, 1839–59 are redated in Tables 13 and 14 as end of year, 1838–58.

J. G. GURLEY AND E. S. SHAW (1957)
1800–60 by Decades. 1865:

Money Stock

Gurley and Shaw prepared estimates of the money stock at ten-year intervals, 1800–60, and at five-year intervals thereafter.[33] The decade estimates are dated one year earlier in Tables 13 and 14. Like Warburton they relied on published sources. Their results differ from his principally because they used the series of U.S. government deposits at banks, which they added to estimates of deposits held by the public, 1800–30 and 1865 (the government had negligible deposits, 1840, and no funds on deposit, 1850 and 1860), to obtain money supply figures inclusive of Treasury deposits but exclusive of Treasury currency holdings. Gurley and Shaw also show more components than Warburton does, reprinting the published money in circulation, i.e., currency outside Treasury; money in banks through 1860, vault cash plus cash items in 1865; the residual currency outside banks; and private deposits, U.S. government deposits, and total deposits.

Gurley and Shaw's estimates of currency held by the public, 1800–60, share the defects noted above for Warburton's: the underlying figures, with the possible exception of those for 1850 and 1860, are not in fact amounts outside the Treasury, and the amount subtracted as held by banks is too small through 1860, since bank notes held by banks should be deducted in addition to specie in banks. For 1865 it is doubtful that the amount subtracted, which does include notes of other banks held by national banks, is reliable as an all-bank estimate, a point explored further below.[34]

With one exception, Gurley and Shaw estimated deposits in the same

33 J. G. Gurley and E. S. Shaw, "The Growth of Debt and Money in the United States, 1899–1950: A Suggested Interpretation," *Review of Economics and Statistics,* Aug. 1957, p. 258.
34 Gurley and Shaw describe the 1865 figure of cash in banks as including some cash items. It is not true of the national bank figure, and the nonnational bank figure is not so described in the source they used (see the following footnote).

way that Warburton did, i.e., for 1800 and 1810, when no published estimates are available, they assumed total deposits were approximately 50 per cent of their estimated currency outside Treasury; for 1820, 1830, 1850, and 1860 they used the January 1 estimates from the Secretary of the Treasury's reports on the condition of the state banks. They differed from Warburton in assuming the estimates for 1820–60 referred to deposits held by the public, rather than total deposits. To get total deposits, therefore, they added the published Treasury series of the Treasury balance in banks; for 1800 and 1810 they deducted the Treasury balance in banks to get deposits held by the public. Gurley and Shaw do not indicate why they believed the published 1820–60 figures were estimates of deposits held by the public. The sources do not so describe them. Like Warburton they did not correct for float.

The underlying figures that Gurley and Shaw used for 1865 were first given in the 1931 report of the Comptroller of the Currency.[35] He combined the midyear call date figures for national banks with estimates for nonnational banks described as obtained by "using as basis the previous 10 years, 1854 to 1863, inclusive." Gurley and Shaw used the estimate in the Comptroller's report for cash in banks and a refinement of the total deposit estimate that excluded interbank and U.S. deposits.[36] The Comptroller's estimates in 1931 understated the extent of nonnational banking. One indication available to Gurley and Shaw was the 1934 FDIC estimate of total deposits at nonnational banks, 1864–66. The FDIC estimates are $165 and $230 million, respectively, for years ending May 31, 1865, and 1866. The Comptroller's estimate for 1865 is $75 million; for 1866, $64 million.

GEORGE MACESICH (1958, 1968)
1834–60:

Money Stock

On the basis of published official sources, described in section 2, above, George Macesich constructed annual money stock estimates for 1834–45, which he presented in his 1958 dissertation and in a journal article.[37] He has since revised his estimates and extended them to 1860

---

[35] Page 1023.

[36] As given in *Statistical Abstract of the United States,* 1942, pp. 291–293.

[37] George Macesich, "Monetary Disturbances in the United States, 1834–45," unpublished Ph.D. dissertation, University of Chicago, June 1958; see footnote 14, above, for the journal article.

Macesich's published money stock estimates were reprinted by J. G. Williamson and has kindly made the series available to us. His revisions include the omission of specie funds from the estimate of specie in banks, the use of specie funds as the measure of float, and the substitution for the 1896 Treasury circular series he originally used of the "Balance in Treasury" series (from the 1906 and 1915 Treasury annual reports), with an adjustment of the July 1 figures from 1844 and thereafter to convert them to January 1 figures.

PETER TEMIN (1969)
1820–58:

Specie Stock
Specie in Banks
Money Stock

For a study of the Jacksonian economy, Temin constructed annual estimates of the stock of specie, specie in banks, and the money stock, 1820–58.[38] For 1833–37 he also computed the ratio of the banks' specie holdings to their net obligations measured as the sum of notes outstanding, the deposits of the public and the U.S. government, and amounts due other banks, minus notes of other banks in vault and amounts due from other banks. The money stock is the sum of net bank obligations and specie outside banks.

The specie stock series Temin used for 1829–58 was the published series for this item in the Treasury circular and the Comptroller of the

(*American Growth and Balance of Payments, 1820–1913,* Chapel Hill, 1964, p. 277), who attributed the figures to Moses Abramovitz, except for 1835 which he described as "corrected by George Macesich." The figures for 1834–45, however, are the published Macesich estimates; those for 1846–60 are his unpublished estimates, constructed like the published ones. The sources that Williamson cites as having been used by Abramovitz in constructing the money supply estimates are inaccurate. The series for specie in banks that Williamson gives is, however, correct whereas Macesich's published series is not. T. D. Willett ("International Specie Flows and American Monetary Stability, 1834–1860," *Journal of Economic History,* March 1968, p. 50) reproduces the money supply figures as given by Williamson (though he attributes them to Macesich-Abramovitz) and also the correct specie in banks. For 1839 there is an error in transcription in the series on specie in banks which also appears in the chart of the series.

Clark Warburton's dissatisfaction with Macesich's published estimates led him in 1961 to prepare alternative money stock estimates for dates at or near the beginning of the year for 1834–45. He has kindly made available to us his unpublished table, and we show his money stock estimates in Table 14, after shifting his dates to the end of the preceding year. For Jan. 1, 1839, he has provided us with a comparison of his annual estimate with his earlier decade estimate for that date.

[38] Peter Temin, *The Jacksonian Economy,* New York, 1969. For the same years he also gives the reserve ratio and the ratio of specie outside banks to the money stock. He gives the specie and money stock estimates, 1830–44, in his "The Economic Consequences of the Bank War," *Journal of Political Economy,* Mar.–Apr. 1968, p. 268.

Currency annual report (cited in footnote 15), redated as of the end of the preceding year. He then extrapolated the 1829 published figure backward to 1820 by adding to it the annual net international specie inflow, with no adjustment for difference in calendar year coverage of the base year and October 1–September 30 coverage of the international flow figures. As a check on the reliability of the published series, he compared it with a series he constructed from 1829 forward in the same way that he extrapolated the series backward to 1820, including after 1848 the annual output of domestic gold mines as well as net specie inflows. He concluded that the movements in the published series conformed well to those in the constructed series, though the levels of the two series diverged markedly over time. In 1829 they had a common value; by 1858 the constructed estimate was 50 per cent higher than the published.

For 1820–34 Temin obtained estimates of specie in state banks by "blowing up" the sample aggregate presented by Van Fenstermaker.[39] To these estimates he added specie in the Bank of the United States. For 1835–58 he used the Secretary of the Treasury's compilations of state banking data, which, as noted above, omit returns for 1851 (January 1, 1852).

Temin derived his series of net bank obligations from the same sources as his specie in banks series. Since he was interested in a regional breakdown, he included in net bank obligations, by geographical areas, the net excess of due to overdue from banks. For the banking system as a whole, he assumed interbank obligations would cancel. This is not true of the aggregate state bank data in the Secretary of the Treasury's compilations, or of current aggregate banking data that, unlike antebellum statistics, are complete in coverage and free of reporting errors. In practice, aggregate figures of due to and due from banks disagree essentially because the two sets of accounts are not synchronous, e.g., what is recorded on Bank A's books on a given date as due from Bank B is not yet recorded on Bank B's books as due to Bank A. In the aggregate state bank data, due from banks exceeded due to banks—in some years by as much as $10 million—in twenty-one of the twenty-nine years covered; in the remainder, due to banks exceeded due from banks—usually by much smaller margins. Accordingly, Temin's deposit estimates in

---

[39] In *The Development of American Commercial Banking, 1782–1837.* In each year, Temin divided the sample totals by the fraction of all chartered banks included to obtain estimates for all state chartered banks.

most years understate the aggregate holdings of the public and U.S. government. His estimates of their note holdings follow conventional practice in deducting notes held by other banks from notes outstanding. To obtain his final money stock estimates, he added specie outside banks—a residual—to net bank obligations.

Temin treats the federal government as a member of the public because he believes that its power to create money was limited in the antebellum period and hence that its decisions regarding its money holdings were based on the same considerations that guided other money holders. This decision incidentally made it unnecessary for him to choose among the conflicting published series the one correctly representing the amount of Treasury balances and their composition.

4. Alternative Money Stock Estimates

The estimates of specie, bank notes, Treasury currency issues, and bank deposits, discussed above, are shown in Table 13.[40] In addition, as an initial bench mark the table gives the outstanding nominal issues of Continental currency, 1775–79.[41] An effort has been made to date the

[40] Annual data (1837–49, 1857–58) on Treasury one-year note issues, authorized by Congress to finance federal deficits, sometimes interest-bearing, sometimes not, came to our attention too late for inclusion in Table 13. See Richard H. Timberlake, Jr., "The Independent Treasury and Monetary Policy Before the Civil War," *Southern Economic Journal,* Oct. 1960, p. 96. The note issues, which served both as bank reserves and currency, were as follows (in millions of dollars):

End of Year		End of Year	
1837	3.0	1845	0.6
1838	7.8	1846	15.5
1839	1.0	1847	14.7
1840	2.6	1848	3.6
1841	7.4	1849	0.7
1842	10.1		
1843	2.3	1857	19.8
1844	0.8	1858	14.7

[41] The Continental bills of credit depreciated as the quantity issued multiplied, until they became virtually worthless in transactions. They ceased to circulate as money by the Act of May 31, 1781. Provision for their redemption in specie was first made in 1790, at the rate of $1 in specie for $100 in bills, if presented before September 1791. Later this redemption period was extended to 1797.

The separate colonies had issued bills of credit before the Revolution. They continued to do so as states during and after the Revolution. State currency issues circulated at a discount and were ultimately refunded into various state or federal obligations.

Three banks began operations during the 1780's. When the federal government was established in 1789, the U.S. money stock consisted of the notes issued by, and the deposits at, these banks, and of foreign coins.

estimates as of the end of month to which they refer, but since the original sources are not invariably definite, we cannot be sure that the month to which an estimate is attributed is the true month. The table shows (on two lines) the lower and upper ranges of alternative estimates for a given date where no clear basis exists for preference between them. Where an intelligent choice can be made, the table shows only the estimates that in our judgment are to be preferred. Thus we reject the series described as "Specie in Treasury" because it is actually the finance report total balance of the Treasury, and we do not show this in Table 13. Similarly the currency figures we show, beginning 1860, are the revised estimates the Treasury published in 1928 rather than the original ones it published in 1896.

Table 13 gives the available estimates for various monetary categories including the distribution among the Treasury, the banks, and the public of outstanding amounts of specie, currency, and deposits. Table 14 is limited to estimates of the public's holdings of money—the sum of the components held by the public, shown in Table 13—though the definition of the "public" varies. The four main continuous estimates for selected years in the period before 1867—by Warburton, Gurley and Shaw, Macesich, and Temin—are each given in separate columns. A fifth column shows the remaining miscellaneous estimates, which in some years are sums of components referring to different months.[42]

For Warburton and Macesich, the public *excludes* the U.S. Treasury; for Gurley and Shaw and Temin, the public *includes* the U.S. Treasury. Macesich corrects for float by deducting specie funds—as cash items in process of collection were designated in the antebellum period; the others do not. Though based on common sources in the period for which they overlap, in all but three years, Temin's estimates exceed Macesich's by amounts ranging from $8 million to $52 million. The differences exist because (a) Temin includes and Macesich excludes U.S. Treasury cash and deposits at banks; (b) Temin overlooks float, which Macesich deducts; (c) in years when due from banks exceeds due to banks, Temin's estimates are lower than Macesich's on this score; in the six

[42] David A. Martin gives five-year moving averages, centered annually 1790–1850, for a column designated total money supply, which is the sum of total bank note supply and total specie supply ("Bimetallism in the United States before 1850," *Journal of Political Economy*, May/June 1968, pp. 440–441). His column obviously does not correspond to the money stock totals given in Table 14. It is a sum of bank notes outstanding and the specie stock, the underlying figures coming from published official sources referred to in this chapter.

years when due to banks exceeds due from banks, Temin's estimates on this score are higher than Macesich's. Thus, both items a and b serve to raise the level of Temin's estimates, but their combined effect is partially offset when due from banks exceeds due to banks; in other years, item c raises the level of Temin's estimates still further. An excess of due from banks over due to banks lowers the level of Temin's estimates below that of Macesich's only in years when the sum of items a and b is small.

In view of the tenuous character of the underlying figures the estimates in Table 14 must be viewed as at best suggestive, rather than definitive. The strong upward trend in the U.S. money stock before 1867 is displayed by the four principal sets of estimates. They suggest roughly a ninetyfold increase in the nominal money stock over the eight decades ending 1867. Individual decade estimates, however, differ in regard to the size of short-term growth, e.g., contrast the 1838–48 Warburton and 1839–49 Gurley and Shaw results. The annual Macesich and Temin estimates suggest that the long-term growth was far from smooth. The peaks and troughs in those estimates are clearly related to cyclical peaks and troughs in U.S. business. The early estimates, fragile as they may be, show no obvious discontinuity with the money stock estimates for the century after 1867.

8

ESTIMATES FOR THE PERIOD
SINCE 1867

FOR THE PERIOD after the Civil War, numerous private individuals used the official compilations of currency and deposit data or rearranged and added to them in various ways.[1] However, only three constructed estimates for the period before World War I that are sufficiently close to our own to justify detailed attention: Edwin W. Kemmerer, who constructed estimates of currency held by the public, 1879–1904; Irving Fisher, who constructed estimates of currency held by the public and deposits, 1896–1909; and Wesley C. Mitchell, who revised and extended Fisher's estimates to cover the period 1890–1911. All these were annual (see section 1, below).

The establishment of the Federal Reserve System produced new

---

[1] See, for example, M. L. Muhleman, *The Money of the United States,* New York, 1894, where annual figures, 1873–93, are given for the stock of currency, by kinds, in and outside the Treasury; for the "supply of retail money" (the sum of small-denomination notes, silver coin, and gold coin held by the public) in aggregate and per capita; and for total deposits at national and state banks (pp. 42–43, 56, 59). See also *idem, Monetary Systems of the World,* New York, 1896, an enlarged edition of the previous work, extending the earlier tables to 1895–96 and including a table of the stock of U.S. currency in and outside the Treasury, decennially, 1800–30, and annually, 1831–61, as shown in the Comptroller of the Currency, *Annual Report,* 1896, p. 544. Muhleman prepared or verified the tables at the end of each chapter in A. B. Hepburn, *History of Coinage and Currency in the United States and the Perennial Contest for Sound Money,* New York, 1903. The same tabular material appears in a revised and enlarged version, *A History of Currency in the United States,* New York, 1915, but Muhleman is not acknowledged as he was in the earlier volume.

Muhleman's impact on the development of monetary statistics in the U.S. came with the publication of his criticism of the official gold stock estimates for years beginning 1873 (see his "Stock of Gold in the United States," *Political Science Quarterly,* Mar. 1901, p. 96). This criticism influenced the Director of the Mint in 1907 to correct the error in the estimate that had been accumulating since 1873 (see Chapter 6, footnote 5, above). Muhleman's own earlier revisions of the gold stock were superseded by the Director of the Mint's new series. His estimates of gold coin held by the public was the only significant new trail blazed by Muhleman in his statistical work.

banking and monetary data. W. I. King was perhaps the first scholar to use these to construct currency and deposit estimates. He combined them with data for earlier years to produce annual estimates for the years 1881–1920. He also used them to make the first estimates on a monthly basis—for 1914–20.

Mitchell published annual estimates for 1919–26 of deposits subject to check that had been constructed by Carl Snyder of the Federal Reserve Bank of New York; and Y. S. Leong made detailed monthly, call date, and annual estimates for the years 1914–29 (section 2).

King, Mitchell, and Leong followed earlier practice in stressing the components, not their total. The first estimates stressing the total quantity of money came after the Great Contraction. They were constructed by Lauchlin Currie and James W. Angell. Both considered explicitly the question of how to define money, constructed estimates for alternative variants, and in other ways went considerably farther than earlier scholars (see section 3).

Although the Federal Reserve became a major source of basic data immediately after it began operations, it did not itself publish a historical series on the aggregate quantity of money until 1941.[2] These estimates were superseded in 1943 by the annual series the Board published in 1943 in *Banking and Monetary Statistics*. That series in turn was revised and extended in 1959 in *All-Bank Statistics, 1896–1955*. The annual series in *All-Bank Statistics*, as continued, as well as new monthly and weekly series developed since and published currently have become the standard coin of the field of monetary economics (section 4). We adopted the annual series in *All-Bank Statistics* as the backbone of our own estimates for the period for which they overlap, with one important exception. That exception is the Federal Reserve's estimated subdivision of total commercial bank deposits into demand and time deposits before 1914.[3] We present in the appendix to this chapter the evidence that persuaded us that that subdivision is subject to an intolerably large margin of error—much larger than the margin of error in our

[2] Board of Governors of the Federal Reserve System, *Banking Studies*, Baltimore, 1941, p. 447. This was an annual series of bank deposits and currency beginning 1890, combining Angell's estimates for 1890–1918 with the Board's own estimates, 1919–40, "from reports of condition of all banks in the United States" (p. 447).

[3] H. A. Latané was mistaken when he wrote (in reference to *Banking and Monetary Statistics*), "The demand deposit estimates before 1914 are based on bank call date data and are published by the Federal Reserve Board . . ." ("Income Velocity and Interest Rates—A Pragmatic Approach," *Review of Economics and Statistics*, Nov. 1960, p. 447).

estimates of total deposits before 1914 or of demand and time deposits separately thereafter.

1. Estimates by Kemmerer, Fisher, and Mitchell

Currency Held by the Public

E. W. Kemmerer was the first scholar to construct estimates of currency held by the public in the period since 1867. He made annual estimates, 1879–1904, simply by rearranging official figures. His base was currency outside the Treasury as reported by the Treasury. From this total he subtracted amounts in national banks and in nonnational banks, as reported by the Comptroller of the Currency. He did not adjust the reported figures for nonreporting banks or for other possible sources of error, and he made no attempt to estimate deposits.[4] As we noted in discussing the estimates before 1867, Crawford, Gallatin, and Seaman had earlier recognized the significance of the concept of currency in the possession of the public. No one continued their estimates of that item. Decades later, the concept had to be rediscovered. After Kemmerer, its acceptance was secure. His estimates served as the starting point of the estimates made successively since, beginning with Irving Fisher's, which have refined the base and the subtrahend.

Fisher's estimates were for a briefer period, ending five years later, 1896–1909. He improved on Kemmerer's currency estimates in two ways.[5] First, he corrected the Treasury figures on the stock of currency for revisions in the estimated gold stock for 1906 and earlier years made by the Director of the Mint in his 1907 annual report.[6] Second, he estimated vault cash in nonnational banks that did not report to the Comptroller of the Currency. In computing currency in the hands of the public, he subtracted this amount as well as reported vault cash, and currency held by the Treasury.

Fisher based his estimate of nonreported vault cash on estimates published by the Comptroller for 1900 and 1902–09 of the number and aggregate deposits of nonreporting banks—all of which, of course, were

---

[4] E. W. Kemmerer, *Money and Credit Instruments in their Relation to General Prices,* New York, 1907, pp. 98–100. Kemmerer estimated check transactions ($M'V'$) but not deposits and their velocity separately.

[5] Irving Fisher, *Purchasing Power of Money,* New York, 1911, pp. 432, 435.

[6] See Chapter 6, footnote 5, above.

nonnational. Fisher extrapolated and interpolated these deposit estimates to obtain a continuous series for 1896–1909; he then estimated
vault cash in nonreporting banks by multiplying the estimated deposits
by the ratio of vault cash to deposits in reporting banks, i.e., he assumed
that the two classes of banks held the same amount of vault cash per
dollar of deposits.

Mitchell made two further changes. First, he corrected bank vault
cash for reporting banks by subtracting "cash items" included in the
published figures for nonnational banks.[7] These "cash items" represent
checks in the process of collection rather than specie or bank notes of
other banks. Second, he used a different method of estimating vault cash
in nonreporting banks. His method involved assuming that nonreporting
banks were on the average identical with private banks that reported
rather than with all banks that reported. This approximation was suggested by the estimated size of nonreporting banks which was closest to
that for private banks. He therefore estimated vault cash in nonreporting
banks by multiplying the average vault cash per reporting private bank
by the estimated number of nonreporting banks. This number, in turn,
he derived from a set of annual figures in the National Monetary Commission publication by Barnett, referred to above.[8]

Deposits Held by the Public

The deposit component that both Fisher and Mitchell estimated was
"individual deposits subject to check." The term "individual" referred
to all holders of deposits other than banks and the U.S. government.
That is, it corresponded to what we now term individuals, partnerships,
corporations, states, counties, and municipalities. "Deposits subject to
check" is a component of demand deposits as currently defined but does
not exhaust that class of deposits.[9] Mitchell wrote that, until publication

[7] W. C. Mitchell, *Business Cycles,* Berkeley, 1913, pp. 315–316, 318–322.

[8] George E. Barnett, *State Banks and Trust Companies Since the Passage of the
National Bank Act,* National Monetary Commission, 1911, S. Doc. 587, 659, 61st
Cong., 3rd sess. Barnett's estimates improved upon the Comptroller's but in turn needed
correction for double-counting of some banks, 1900–08. Mitchell therefore revised them.

[9] See *All-Bank Statistics,* p. 88, for a list of components of demand deposits (other
than interbank and U.S. government deposits). The principal components in addition
to deposits subject to check are letters of credit and travelers' checks, sold for cash
and outstanding; certified, cashiers', and treasurers' checks; dividends unpaid; demand
certificates of deposit; time certificates of deposit payable within thirty days; and deposits
subject to withdrawal within thirty days.

Note also the Comptroller of the Currency's statement that even if national banks
establish a savings department and pay interest on deposits, "Deposits in commercial
banks are presumed to be subject to demand" (*Annual Report,* 1912, p. 11).

of the National Monetary Commission's 1909 data for all banks, it had been customary "to assume that the volume of deposit currency available for business use is best represented by the individual deposits of the commercial banks." [10] The 1909 data, however, classified individual deposits for the first time as (1) subject to check; (2) savings deposits or deposits in interest or savings department; (3) demand certificates of deposit; (4) time deposits, including time certificates of deposits; (5) certified checks; (6) cashiers', treasurers', or secretaries' checks outstanding; (7) deposits not classified. [11]

The revelation that only a fraction of individual deposits was subject to check had a marked impact on economists. At the time, a number of them were trying to test the quantity theory of money in transactions form statistically by substituting values for MV, $M'V'$, and T in the equation of exchange and then comparing the calculated with the actual price level. Kemmerer had made such a test by multiplying his currency estimates (M) by 47, which he assumed to be the average velocity of circulation of currency, and adding an independent estimate of $M'V'$, obtained by multiplying bank clearings by 2.86, on the assumption that clearings were 35 per cent of "total check circulation." Fisher estimated each of the five magnitudes separately, confining his estimate of M' to item 1 of the classification of individual deposits.

The same magnitudes interested Mitchell for the purpose of determining their behavior during business cycles—not for testing the quantity theory. Like Fisher, however, he estimated M' as deposits subject to check, describing items 2 to 6 of individual deposits as "deposits . . . made on conditions which precluded their free use as deposit currency." His segregation of item 1 from the other items is understandable in light of his emphasis on transactions. However, he proceeded not only to segregate the remaining items but to ignore them completely, even though he gave figures on deposits at savings banks (the sum of mutual and stock savings bank time deposits) and analyzed their cyclical behavior, noting that in depression years "people seem to put into the savings banks funds which they would have kept in hand or in checking deposits if trade had remained active." [12] Clearly, there is a hiatus in his analysis.

[10] *Business Cycles,* 1913, p. 318.
[11] *Special Report from the Banks of the United States,* National Monetary Commission, 1910, S. Doc. 225, 61st Cong., 2nd sess.
[12] *Business Cycles,* pp. 318, 390, 393.

In order to get earlier data comparable to those for 1909, Fisher asked A. Piatt Andrew to furnish breakdowns for a sample of earlier years. Andrew complied for 1896, 1899, and 1906. For each year, he subdivided individual deposits into the seven classes of deposits listed above for six classes of banks (national, state, stock savings, mutual savings, loan and trust, private).[13] As we shall see later, these breakdowns, despite the extensive use that has been made of them, are of questionable accuracy (see below, appendix to this chapter).[14]

Fisher used Andrew's data for the three years plus the data for 1909 as bench-mark data, adjusting them to get the concept he wanted. He made two main adjustments. First, he added estimated deposits subject to check of nonreporting banks—using the 1896–1909 annual series that he constructed from the Comptroller's estimates for 1900 and 1902–09 (to which we referred above, in discussing Fisher's estimate of nonreporting bank vault cash). Second, he subtracted clearinghouse exchanges (estimated by raising clearinghouse exchanges of national banks by 25 per cent to allow for those of nonnational banks). Fisher ignored cash items, which national banks also reported, and which, following current usage, would be combined with clearinghouse exchanges to estimate float.[15]

To interpolate between the four bench-mark dates, Fisher constructed what he termed "corrected individual deposits." To individual deposits at all national and reporting nonnational banks, as shown in the Comptroller's annual reports, Fisher added the Comptroller's estimate of indi-

---

[13] A. P. Andrew, *Statistics for the United States, 1867–1909*, National Monetary Commission, 1910, S. Doc. 570, 61st Cong., 2nd sess., p. 151.

[14] Fisher wrote that "deposits subject to check" were regularly reported by individual banks to the Comptroller of the Currency, but that the published figures in the 1860's omitted the category and lumped all individual deposits together. Subsequent reports simply followed the precedent established. Writing in 1910, Fisher noted that the Comptroller intended in the future to separate in his reports the item of deposits subject to check (Irving Fisher, *Purchasing Power of Money*, pp. 440–441). If national banks regularly reported deposits subject to check as a separate item, it is puzzling that at call dates, 1910–14, when the Comptroller began to show separately national bank demand certificates of deposit, time certificates of deposit, certified and cashiers' checks—all components of individual deposits—he nevertheless combined deposits subject to check and savings deposits—also components of individual deposits. The reason may well be the "lack of uniformity" in bank reports of their savings or interest-bearing accounts, a condition to which he referred in his 1912 annual report (p. 11) (see further discussion in appendix to this chapter).

[15] Clearinghouse exchanges represented checks on other banks in the process of collection through clearinghouses, i.e., part of what we now term bank float. Fisher was the first monetary statistician to note that a part of deposits corresponding to bank float is counted doubly—as having been credited to the drawee but not yet debited to the drawer (*Purchasing Power of Money*, pp. 436–437).

vidual deposits at nonreporting banks, described above. From the total, he deducted clearinghouse exchanges (as reported for national banks, multiplied by five-fourths) and a number of other items to obtain "corrected individual deposits." [16]

For each of the bench-mark years (1896, 1899, 1906, and 1909) Fisher computed the ratio of estimated individual deposits subject to check to the corresponding "corrected individual deposits." For intervening years he estimated corresponding ratios by straight-line interpolation and estimated individual deposits subject to check by multiplying "corrected individual deposits" by the estimated ratios.

Mitchell had essentially the same basic data as Fisher, except that he also had breakdowns of individual deposits for 1910 and 1911 provided by the Comptroller, and he used roughly the same procedure, but with some variations. First, for both the bench-mark and other years he estimated deposits for nonreporting banks by multiplying average deposits per private reporting bank by the estimated number of nonreporting banks, described above. Second, he adjusted the 1896, 1899, and 1906 published deposits subject to check of five classes of non-national banks by deducting $20 million time deposits "in proportion to their quotas of deposits subject to check," and he adjusted the 1909 and 1910 figures by adding to each class of banks a fraction of much larger amounts reported as "deposits not classified," dividing the amounts "proportionately between the deposits which are and the deposits which are not subject to check." [17] Third, he interpolated before deducting float, making that deduction the last step in his estimate.[18] And fourth, he interpolated separately for each class of banks (except mutual savings banks, which he excluded) the ratio of deposits subject to check to individual deposits. For 1890–95, he used the 1896 ratio for each class of banks and for the remaining years he interpolated along a straight line between the bench-mark years.[19]

---

[16] For 1896–1908 he deducted amounts he assumed were interbank deposits misclassified as individual deposits at national banks, though he subsequently decided that no deduction was needed in 1900 and that the 1896–99 revisions were excessive. He also deducted individual deposits at mutual savings banks—inadvertently using the wrong figures—and at stock savings banks, though the latter are classified as commercial banks.

[17] *Business Cycles,* p. 319.

[18] Mitchell estimated clearinghouse exchanges for all banks as Fisher did, except that he divided the national bank item by .797 instead of by .80 to allow for non-national banks.

[19] In addition, Mitchell did not follow Fisher in correcting for misclassification of interbank deposits of national banks. He decided the correction was not needed.

2. Estimates by King and Leong

For nearly two decades after the pioneer estimates by Fisher and Mitchell, only one set of estimates was published, namely, Mitchell's presentation of Snyder's estimates.[20] Beginning 1929, however, four different ones appeared within a seven-year period. The first was by King, who constructed annual estimates of currency held by the public and deposits subject to check for the period 1881–1920, and monthly estimates for six and a half years, 1914–20, including and excluding Treasury cash and government deposits at commercial banks and Federal Reserve Banks.[21] King did not explain how he derived his estimates.[22] The second of the post-World War I estimates was by Leong, who published monthly, call-date, and annual estimates for the period 1914–26, with considerable detail on sources and methods.[23]

For his annual estimates, Leong extended Mitchell's 1900–11 estimates to 1926, using essentially the same method of construction. With "deposits not classified," he followed the procedure Mitchell used for 1909 and 1910, allocating them for each class of reporting banks, 1912–26, between deposits that are and are not subject to check, according to the distribution of classified deposits.[24] Like Mitchell, he estimated vault

[20] In *Business Cycles,* National Bureau of Economic Research, 1927, p. 126.

[21] W. I. King, "Is Our Currency Elastic?" *Interlocking Chart Series,* No. 4, Special Service II), No. 23, Sept. 21, 1920 (Bankers Statistics Corporation, New York, pp. 9–10).

[22] Leong, however, examined King's worksheets and found that his method of estimating currency and deposits annually was similar to Fisher's (*Journal of Political Economy,* Oct. 1929, pp. 587–589; Apr. 1930, pp. 167–168). King's currency estimates are virtually identical with Fisher's during the period for which they overlap, but his deposit estimates are somewhat higher. Assuming that time deposits, open account, at national banks were subject to check, King included them in deposits subject to check, while Fisher did not. In addition, King assumed that the fraction of deposits not classified in nonnational banks that was subject to check was higher than Fisher did.

King's monthly series (of bank vault cash and deposits subject to check) were derived by a double interpolation: a call-date series was first estimated on the basis of national bank data, and a monthly series was interpolated along a straight line between the call date estimates. The vault cash monthly estimates and monthly data on currency in the Treasury and Federal Reserve Banks were deducted from monthly Treasury data on the stock of currency.

[23] Y. S. Leong, "Money in Circulation in the United States," *Journal of Political Economy,* Apr. 1930, pp. 171, 178, 184–187; "An Estimate of the Volume of Deposit Currency in the United States," *ibid.,* Oct. 1929, pp. 596, 599, 603.

[24] Currie criticized this procedure, noting that "practically all the unclassified deposits are in country [member] state banks and trust companies" (*The Supply and Control of Money,* p. 25). He also noted that up to 1926, unclassified deposits of national banks in the Comptroller's reports were classed as demand deposits in Federal Reserve reports. Had Leong used member-nonmember, rather than national-nonnational bank data, he could have avoided the problem of unclassified deposits.

cash and deposits subject to check in nonreporting banks by multiplying the corresponding per bank figure for reporting private banks by the estimated number of nonreporting banks, using the Comptroller's estimates of the number of such banks to continue the Barnett series Mitchell used. However, he carried this procedure farther than Mitchell had, using it also to estimate clearinghouse exchanges of nonreporting banks.

Leong constructed a call date series by using data for national banks to interpolate the annual estimates. He constructed his monthly series for 1914–17 by interpolating along a straight line between the call date estimates; and for 1918–26 by using data for weekly reporting member banks to interpolate the call date estimates.[25] Leong regretted that he was driven to use a demand deposit series for weekly reporting member banks to interpolate deposits subject to check. He used it, nevertheless, because he found "surprising" agreement between the weekly reporting series and the all-bank estimates, "despite the incomparability" of the two classes of deposits.

3. Estimates by Currie and Angell

The estimates of King and Leong were published at the start of the Great Contraction; those of Currie and Angell were published after it had ended.[26] The Great Contraction was a watershed in the construction of estimates of money. Thereafter, the sum of deposits and currency, not merely the separate components of the quantity of money, was the focus of interest.

Currie estimated the quantity of money annually, 1921–33, using reports of the Federal Reserve System for member banks as well as the Comptroller's reports for national and nonnational banks on which his predecessors had relied. He was the first investigator to broaden the coverage of demand deposits subject to check. Earlier investigators had

25 His method of interpolation in constructing his call date estimates is equivalent to multiplying the relevant values on a straight-line trend between the annual estimates (treated as end-of-June values) by the relatives to a similar trend of the series used as interpolator, though both his description and his actual computational procedure are more complex. Similarly, in constructing his monthly estimates for 1918–26, he used this procedure to interpolate between the call date estimates.

26 L. Currie, *The Supply and Control of Money in the United States,* Cambridge, Mass., 1935, 2nd ed. rev., p. 33 (1st ed., 1934); J. W. Angell, *The Behavior of Money,* New York, 1936, pp. 175, 178–179.

limited it to the item, "individual deposits subject to check." In addition, Currie included in his total cash letters of credit, certified checks, demand certificates of deposits, and U.S. government deposits. His concept of demand deposits is closer to ours than to that of earlier investigators, but we have followed them rather than him in excluding U.S. government deposits. Currie designated his concept "adjusted demand deposits" to distinguish it from "net demand deposits"—the total subject to reserve requirements, which included some interbank deposits and excluded U.S. government deposits. From his adjusted demand deposit total, Currie also deducted float, but for him "adjusted" referred primarily to the exclusion of interbank and the inclusion of U.S. government deposits rather than the exclusion of float. However, when the Federal Reserve System adopted the term in November 1935, "adjusted demand deposits" was given the meaning now in current use, namely, demand deposits held by the public adjusted for items in the process of collection.[27]

Currie retrogressed by comparison with earlier investigators by making no allowance for nonreporting banks. For currency held by the public, he used the Comptroller of the Currency's estimates directly, except that he subtracted $287 million from each annual estimate to correct for gold supposedly lost, destroyed, or exported without record (see Chapter 6, footnote 6, above).

For adjusted demand deposits Currie combined figures for member banks, as reported at June call dates by the Federal Reserve, with figures for nonmember banks taken as the excess of the Comptroller's estimates for nonnational banks over Federal Reserve estimates for state member banks. His chief statistical problems for nonmember banks were how to distribute unclassified deposits and how to estimate float. He did both mainly by adopting a device similar to that used by Mitchell for estimating nonreporting figures: he treated nonmember banks as comparable to country state member banks.[28]

[27] Currie, *The Supply and Control of Money*, p. 13; *Federal Reserve Bulletin*, Nov. 1935, p. 714.

[28] For 1929, gross deposits at nonmember commercial banks other than stock savings banks were fully classified as either time or demand; for 1921–28, a substantial amount of deposits was listed as "unclassified" and for 1930–33, a small amount. Currie extrapolated the ratio of time to gross deposits at nonmember banks in 1929 to earlier years, by assuming that it had changed at the same rate as the corresponding ratio at country state member banks for which data are available in Federal Reserve reports. He then multiplied gross deposits of nonmember banks by the extrapolated ratios and

Angell constructed two variants of the quantity of money, one designated total money, the other circulating money, annually for 1890–1934.
Total money is comparable to our next-to-the-most inclusive series
(Table 1, column 11), except that total money includes U.S. government deposits at commercial banks and Federal Reserve Banks, which
our series excludes, and excludes dividends unpaid and deposits in the
Postal Savings System, which our series includes. Circulating money
equals total money minus time deposits, demand certificates of deposit,
and time certificates of deposits; it is comparable to our narrowest series
(Table 1, column 8), except again that it includes U.S. government demand deposits, which our series excludes, and excludes demand certificates of deposit and dividends unpaid, which our series includes.
In addition, Angell constructed monthly series of currency held by the
public and of circulating deposits, 1919–34.

Like Currie, Angell retrogressed by comparison with earlier investigators by making no allowance in his annual and monthly estimates for
either vault cash or deposits at nonreporting banks. His annual series of
currency held by the public was derived by precisely the method used
by Kemmerer, that of simply subtracting vault cash in reporting banks
and in Federal Reserve Banks and Treasury cash from the official series
of the total stock of currency.[29] Angell did not adjust the stock of currency, 1890–1906, for the discontinuity introduced by the revised level
of the gold stock component beginning 1907, and he did not make any
adjustment for vault cash in nonreporting banks.

For his annual series of total deposits Angell simply accepted the
Comptroller's figures on deposits minus float of national and nonnational

subtracted the resulting time deposit series from gross deposits to get demand deposits.
For 1930–33, unclassified deposits at nonmember banks were distributed between demand and time deposits in the same proportions as classified deposits.

Float at nonmember commercial banks other than stock savings banks was estimated
by multiplying their estimated gross demand deposits by the ratios of the float of country state member banks to their gross demand deposits.

For stock and mutual savings banks Currie interpolated on a straight line between
reported figures of gross demand deposits in 1921, 1923, and 1927, when unclassified
deposits were small. For 1928–33, he used reported gross demand deposits of these
banks. He estimated float by multiplying gross demand deposits by the ratio of float to
gross demand deposits at country state member banks.

Angell challenged two assumptions implicit in Currie's procedure: (a) deposits are
similarly defined in Federal Reserve and Comptroller of Currency reports; (b) the
average nonmember bank resembles the average country state member bank. Angell,
however, presents no evidence to support these challenges (*The Behavior of Money*,
p. 177).

[29] The reporting bank series agrees with the series in Mitchell's and Fisher's books,
1890–1900. For 1901–11 it is $5–$13 million larger; the reason is not known to us.

banks reporting (including mutual savings banks), except that he substituted U.S. government deposits in member banks, 1917–30, for the unaccountably smaller all-bank figures in the Comptroller's reports. Angell notes that his deductions for float are incomplete, since, unlike Currie, he took no account of items in process of collection at Federal Reserve Banks.

For his annual series of circulating deposits, Angell used Mitchell's estimates of deposits subject to check for 1890–1908. For later years he used the figures on various categories of deposits reported by the Comptroller, simply distributing unclassified deposits among the various categories of individual deposits in the same proportions as classified deposits in each class of reporting banks.

For his monthly estimates of currency held by the public, Angell estimated vault cash in member banks by interpolating [30] between reported call date figures on the basis of the monthly series of currency outside the Treasury, and in nonmember banks by straight-line interpolation between reported June data.

His monthly estimates of circulating deposits are the sum of adjusted demand deposits at member and nonmember banks, of U.S. government deposits, and of deposits by foreign banks and others at Federal Reserve Banks. Adjusted demand deposits at member banks were obtained monthly by interpolating between reported figures for call dates on the basis of reported net demand deposits.[31] Adjusted demand deposits at nonmember banks are straight-line interpolations between estimates for June dates. A monthly series of U.S. government deposits at member banks was calculated separately by raising deposits at weekly reporting member banks to allow for deposits at other banks.[32] Government deposits at nonmember banks were ignored. Figures on U.S. government deposits at Federal Reserve Banks and deposits at Federal Reserve Banks by foreign banks and others are, of course, readily available monthly in Federal Reserve publications.

[30] The method of interpolation is not stated.

[31] Member bank net demand deposits are first available for months beginning April 1923. Angell does not state what series was used as the monthly interpolator for earlier dates. The method of interpolation is not stated.

[32] The ratio of member bank call date figures (taken as end-of-month dates) to weekly reporting member bank figures for the week nearest the corresponding end of month was computed, and averaged "over long periods of time." The average ratio used was changed in 1930. The weekly reporting member bank figures at end of months were then multiplied by the average ratio to obtain estimated U.S. government deposits at member banks.

4. Estimates by Federal Reserve System

The Federal Reserve System did not publish comprehensive estimates of the total quantity of money in the United States until 1941, when an annual series of bank deposits and currency, 1890–1940, appeared in *Banking Studies*. This was something of a patchwork job, combining some of Angell's estimates with Board estimates.[33]

The System made a much more significant contribution in 1943, when it published *Banking and Monetary Statistics,* an invaluable compendium of historical data on a variety of monetary topics.[34] That volume contained estimates of currency outside banks; demand deposits adjusted; time deposits at commercial banks, at mutual savings banks, and in the Postal Savings System; U.S. government deposits; and various totals of deposits and currency, for end-of-June dates, 1892–1922, and end-of-June and end-of-December dates, 1923–41. In February 1944, the System began publication in the *Federal Reserve Bulletin* of comparable end-of-month data to provide series continuing those in *Banking and Monetary Statistics,* giving semiannual estimates for 1942 and monthly estimates from January 1943. In March 1947, the Federal Reserve shifted the dating of its monthly estimates to last-Wednesday-of-the-month and has continued to publish the series in the *Federal Reserve Bulletin* on that basis to date. In October 1960, it introduced new semimonthly series of currency outside banks, demand deposits adjusted,

[33] *Banking Studies,* p. 447. Adjusted demand deposits and total time deposits, including commercial bank time, mutual savings bank, and Postal Savings System deposits, are Angell's figures, 1890–1918; thereafter, the Board's own estimates "from reports of condition of all banks in the United States" (p. 447). The currency figures were obtained by deducting bank vault cash, for which no details of construction are given, from the Board's revision of Treasury published figures of money in circulation. The revision involved deducting on a cumulative basis, 1880–97, $6.6 million of gold coin; 1898–1913, $10.5 million; and annually, 1914–33, $287 million, in full. Aggregates are given of total deposits, including U.S. government deposits, and of total deposits and currency.

[34] See p. 261. The series on currency outside banks and deposits held by the public at various classes of banks shown in this source (pp. 34–35) were superseded by the revised annual series at these banks shown in *All-Bank Statistics,* pp. 31–32, 35–36, 47–48. *All-Banks Statistics* (p. 60) compares the revised series of total deposits at all banks, at commercial banks, and at mutual savings banks, and that of demand deposits adjusted with the corresponding series in *Banking and Monetary Statistics* from 1896 on,. but does not give a revised series of currency outside banks. Since *All-Bank Statistics* gives revised figures for commercial bank vault cash, it follows that currency outside banks shown in *Banking and Monetary Statistics* must be superseded. Nevertheless, *Historical Statistics, 1960,* which was published after *All-Bank Statistics* and refers to it in the Banking part of Chapter X on Banking and Finance, ignores it in the part on Money Supply and Gold in the same chapter, and gives only the superseded *Banking and Monetary Statistics* series for deposits adjusted and currency outside banks, 1892–1941 (p. 646, Series 266–274).

and the total, based on averages of daily figures, giving data back to 1947. In August 1962, it revised slightly the three series of semimonthly averages of daily figures and added a fourth series, time deposits at commercial banks, giving data back to 1947 for all four. At that time it also started publishing the same four series weekly, giving data back to 1959. All the series so far cited are unadjusted for seasonal movements.

The System first began regular publication of seasonally adjusted figures in the March 1955 *Bulletin*. For each month back to 1947, seasonally adjusted estimates were given of currency outside banks, demand deposits adjusted, and their sum derived from the last-Wednesday-of-the-month estimates. These estimates have periodically been revised, mostly because of revisions in the seasonal adjustment. At the same time as it started publishing semimonthly averages of daily figures in 1960, the Federal Reserve started publishing seasonally adjusted figures, giving comparable figures back to 1947 and unadjusted weekly averages of daily figures for the current year. In 1962, when it first published time deposits at commercial banks, it also gave seasonally adjusted monthly averages of daily figures as well as revised seasonally adjusted figures for the other three series, again back to 1947, and corresponding unadjusted weekly averages of daily figures back to 1959. In June 1964 the System published revisions of the four series back to 1955 and monthly as well as semimonthly averages back to 1947. In July 1965 it published a new monthly seasonal correction back to 1959, and for the first time gave seasonally adjusted weekly averages of daily figures. In August 1967 it published revisions of both the monthly and the weekly averages back to 1959, in June 1968, further revisions of the monthly and weekly averages back to 1963, and in October 1969, the complete monthly and weekly record beginning 1947, incorporating the latest bench-mark and seasonal revisions.[35]

In 1959 the System published *All-Bank Statistics, 1896–1955,* which gives revised annual figures for the historical series originally published in *Banking and Monetary Statistics,* omitting the initial years there covered and extending the series to 1955. Its main contribution is a set of detailed estimates of deposits by state, as well as of other balance sheet

---

[35] For the period since 1945 we have made no commercial bank estimates of our own but have used the Federal Reserve's—for 1946, at end of month; thereafter, seasonally adjusted monthly averages of daily figures in the latest revision available (see Chapter 14, section 4). For the period since 1947 we have made no mutual savings bank estimates but have used the Federal Reserve's—last-Wednesday-of-the-month, seasonally adjusted by ourselves and centered at midmonth by a two-month moving average (see Chapter 15, section 5).

items by classes of banks in operation. The estimates provide more complete coverage of banks than previously available and for all practical purposes eliminate, for the period they cover, the problem of non-reporting banks that in the past plagued estimators of monetary totals. In addition, the principal balance sheet items are presented on a standard basis, although the detailed classification of items in the original bank reports varies widely. This enforced uniformity means that a good deal of estimation was required to cast the actual data into the desired form. For the period 1896–1946 we keyed our estimates to these annual estimates with a few minor exceptions stemming from adjustments and a single major one. The major exception is our rejection of the Federal Reserve annual estimates of the division of total commercial bank deposits between demand and time deposits for 1896–1913.

These estimates of demand and time deposits seem to us subject to such a wide margin of error as to be unacceptable, and we know of no data that would enable us to improve them significantly. Accordingly, for the period before 1914 we constructed estimates only of total deposits held by the public at commercial banks. The statistical problem reflects an economic fact of life discussed at some length in Chapter 4 (section 2)—the distinction between demand and time deposits had little economic meaning before 1914, and whatever meaning it did have does not correspond to the meaning it later came to have.

In view of the widespread use that has been made of the Federal Reserve demand deposit estimates for earlier years by other scholars, and the attention that has been devoted to the question of whether money should be defined to include or exclude time deposits, it seems desirable to explain fully the basis of our misgivings about the accuracy of the Federal Reserve estimates of demand deposits for 1896–1913. Accordingly, in the appendix to this chapter, we examine in detail the Federal Reserve estimates.

Appendix to Chapter 8
FEDERAL RESERVE ESTIMATES OF DEMAND AND
TIME DEPOSITS BEFORE 1914

Our misgivings about these estimates derive both from the inadequacy of the basic data available on the subdivision of deposits and from the rather arbitrary character of the extensive interpolation and extrapolation that have been required to derive the final estimates from the basic data. As noted in Chapter 4, these misgivings about statistical accuracy are reinforced by our doubts about the conceptual comparability of even accurate data on time deposits before and after 1914.

The basic data available to the Federal Reserve when it constructed the estimates published in *Banking and Monetary Statistics* were those used by Mitchell and Fisher and already described above: (1) the special survey made by the National Monetary Commission for the call date of April 28, 1909, which for the first time gave comprehensive evidence on demand and time deposits separately; (2) the corresponding figures compiled by A. P. Andrew for 1896, 1899, and 1906; and (3) the Comptroller of the Currency's annual reports for 1910–13, which for one date a year gave estimates for a breakdown similar to, but not quite as detailed as, the 1909 breakdown.

In the process of compiling *All-Bank Statistics,* the Federal Reserve accumulated a fourth body of data for nonnational banks, primarily from the reports of the banking authorities in the several states. Though it continued to use Andrew's 1896, 1899, and 1906 estimates for national banks, it discarded them entirely for nonnational banks. For some states, it substituted estimates based on its own compilations for 1896–1908. For the remaining states, it substituted estimates derived by extrapolating back its own estimates for later years.

Because of the very different methods and sources used for national and nonnational banks, it is advisable to consider each class of banks separately.

1. National Banks

Table 15 summarizes the 1909 survey and Andrew's estimates for both national banks and the five other classes of banks distinguished. Although for years other than 1909 only the data for national banks are used in the Federal Reserve final estimates, all the data are presented to permit relevant comparisons.

The form sent to all banks by the National Monetary Commission, requesting a report of condition on April 28, 1909, explicitly asked information for some forty-odd resource and liability items. Of these the form took all but one as self-explanatory. The exception was item 3 in Table 15, savings deposits or deposits in interest or savings department, which the form defined as follows: "Saving deposits may be defined as

TABLE 15

Classification of Individual Deposits in Banks of the United States at Four Dates, 1896–1909,
According to Andrew and the National Monetary Commission

Class of Banks	Year	Total (millions of dollars) (1)	Individual Deposits Subject to Check (2)	Savings Deposits or Deposits in Interest or Savings Dept. (3)	Demand Certificates of Deposit (4)	Time Deposits, including Time Certificates of Deposit (5)	Certified Checks (6)	Cashier's, Treasurer's, or Secretary's Checks Outstanding (7)	Deposits Not Classified (8)	Per Cent of Classified Deposits That Would Currently be Subgrouped as: Demand (2+4 +6+7) (9)	Time (3+5) (10)
National	1896	1,668.4	85.2	0	8.7	4.1	1.2	0.8	a	95.9	4.1
	1899	2,522.2	85.3	a	7.2	3.5	2.7	1.3	0	96.5	3.5
	1906	4,055.9	78.9	0.1	9.0	7.0	3.7	1.3	0	92.9	7.1
	1909	4,826.1	72.8	7.8	7.8	7.6	2.4	1.5	0	84.5	15.4
State	1896	715.8	80.0	8.3	0.5	11.1	0.1	a	0	80.6	19.4
	1899	1,099.0	78.9	8.5	1.8	10.7	0.1	0.1	0	80.9	19.2
	1906	2,528.2	73.3	10.3	2.2	13.8	0.1	0.3	0	75.9	24.1
	1909	2,467.0	57.1	18.3	4.8	16.8	1.7	0.4	1.0	64.0	35.1
Stock savings	1896	175.2	0.8	99.2	0	0	0	0	0	0.8	99.2
	1899	201.3	1.6	98.3	a	0.1	a	a	0	1.6	98.4
	1906	353.7	12.6	84.7	0.6	1.9	a	0.1	0	13.3	86.6
	1909	568.8	17.7	64.4	1.7	15.7	0.1	0.2	0.2	19.7	80.1

(continued)

TABLE 15 (concluded)

Class of Banks	Year	Total (millions of dollars) (1)	Reported Individual Deposit Components as Per Cent of Total							Per Cent of Classified Deposits That Would Currently be Subgrouped as:	
			Individual Deposits Subject to Check (2)	Savings Deposits or Deposits in Interest or Savings Dept. (3)	Demand Certificates of Deposit (4)	Time Deposits, including Time Certificates of Deposit (5)	Certified Checks (6)	Cashier's, Treasurer's, or Secretary's Check Outstanding (7)	Deposits Not Classified (8)	Demand (2+4+6+7) (9)	Time (3+5) (10)
Private	1896	65.5	94.4	0	0.8	4.8	0	a	0	95.2	4.8
	1899	74.1	88.4	0.2	1.1	10.3	a	a	0	89.5	10.5
	1906	102.9	84.1	6.6	0.9	8.2	0.1	0.1	0	85.2	14.8
	1909	193.3	52.9	8.0	13.6	22.0	0.3	0.1	3.1	66.9	30.0
Loan and trust	1896	605.6	91.0	5.4	0.3	2.9	0.2	0.1	a	91.6	8.3
	1899	1,148.6	89.0	5.0	0.2	5.3	0.2	0.2	a	89.6	10.3
	1906	2,333.4	75.0	12.4	1.7	9.7	0.6	0.4	0.2	77.7	22.1
	1909	2,835.8	64.4	20.3	3.2	10.6	0.6	0.4	0.5	68.6	30.9
Mutual savings	1896	1,739.8	0	100.0	0	0	0	0	0	0	100.0
	1899	2,025.4	0	100.0	0	0	0	0	0	0	100.0
	1906	2,999.1	0	100.0	0	0	0	0	0	0	100.0
	1909	3,144.6	0.1	99.9	a	a	0	a	a	0.1	99.9

a Less than one-tenth of one per cent.
Source: A. P. Andrew, *Statistics for the United States, 1867–1909*, p. 151; *Special Report from the Banks of the United States*, National Monetary Commission, 1910.

277

deposits (*a*) which may be withdrawn only on presentation of the pass book, or other similar form of receipts which permits successive deposits or withdrawals to be entered thereon; or (*b*) which at the option of the company may be withdrawn only at the expiration of a stated period after notice of intention to withdraw has been given; or (*c*) upon which no interest is allowed until the funds have remained on deposit for at least three months."

The reason it was necessary to define savings deposits is explained by the Comptroller of the Currency: [36]

Beginning with the call of November 27, 1908, an effort was made to ascertain the extent to which so-called "savings deposits" are held by national banks, in view of the fact that a number of associations conduct savings departments and others carry deposits classed as "savings accounts," although not in a special department [*Annual Report, 1909,* pp. 166–167]. It further appears that in savings deposits are included both time and demand certificates. The question as to what should be reported as savings deposits has been the occasion of considerable correspondence, but the conclusion was reached that it was a question to be determined by the bank upon the advice that "all deposits accepted with the understanding between the officers of the bank and the depositors that they were savings deposits" should be so reported. The same question was raised in connection with the preparation of blanks for use by the National Monetary Commission in obtaining returns from the banks under date of April 28, 1909. The schedule provided for reporting deposits included the item "savings deposits," and the latter were characterized by the commission as . . .

The explanation suggests that savings deposits were not classified as such on the books of the individual banks. Nevertheless, in response to the National Monetary Commission's request, the reporting banks entered their deposit liabilities under one or another of the rubrics on the form. There was no place on the form for item 7, deposits not classified, and only a negligible fraction (three-tenths of one per cent of all deposits at all banks) was shown as unclassified in the final computation.

We have no detailed information on how Andrew constructed the totals for 1896, 1899, and 1906—only the general statement in a footnote to his table: "Statistics for national banks are compiled from statements made to the Comptroller of the Currency for date nearest June 30 of the years indicated; statistics for banks other than national are compiled from the annual reports of state bank superintendents and are

[36] *Annual Report,* 1910, p. 7.

necessarily for varying dates, in some instances it being found necessary to use figures for a date near the close of the year in order to obtain the proper classification of deposits." There is, however, evidence that, for national banks, the pre-1909 reports by individual banks contained information on only five or six of the seven categories of deposits in Table 15, "savings deposits" and perhaps "not classified" being excluded; that the category later designated savings deposits was included with either deposits subject to check or certificates of deposit; and that from the November 1908 call date on, while the standard report submitted by national banks continued to give only the fivefold classification, the national banks were asked to submit a supplementary report on their savings deposits. This evidence is from the 1910 and later annual reports of the Comptroller.[37]

Andrew's figures in Table 15 for national banks are consistent with this evidence. His figures for categories 3 to 6 seem plausible by comparison with those for 1909. His figures for savings deposits do not. He shows no such deposits for 1896; a negligible amount for 1899; an amount equal to one-tenth of one per cent of individual deposits for 1906, and then a sudden jump to 7.8 per cent of individual deposits for 1909. It seems clear that this jump was primarily a change in what was reported, not in the amount of savings deposits of national banks. The only mystery is where he got the trivial amounts he recorded for 1899 and 1906.

Doubts about the accuracy of Andrew's figures on savings deposits of national banks are confirmed by a comparison of his estimates for other classes of banks with the 1909 National Monetary Commission figures. For every class of banks except mutual savings banks, there are

[37] Comptroller of the Currency, *Annual Report*, 1910, p. 7; 1911, p. 28; 1912, p. 11. For the first supplementary report on savings deposits, beginning with the November 1908 call date, see the 1909 volume, pp. 166–167.

When the Comptroller (*Annual Report*, 1910) published for the first time a classification of individual deposits of national banks into these five categories (for the call dates in March, June, and September 1910), he introduced the breakdown as follows: "Prior to March 29, 1910, while the individual deposits were classified in the reports made by the banks, the details were not incorporated in the abstracts. The expressed interest in this feature of the report was an inducement to the publication of the information in detail . . ." (p. 7).

At a later point, the same report gives a consolidated statement of deposits at national banks and six classes of nonnational banks for a midyear date. This table repeats the fivefold classification of national bank deposits, though it contains for other banks a sixth class, savings deposits. In the column for national banks, there is no entry on the line for savings deposits, but instead a footnote stating that savings deposits of a specified amount were "included with individual deposits, demand or time certificates of deposit" (p. 792).

differences in the amount reported as savings deposits that seem much too large to be explained by anything other than reporting error.[38] The Federal Reserve was wise to reject Andrew's figures for nonnational banks; it was unwise, in our opinion, to continue to use his figures for national banks without at least making some adjustment in his obviously incorrect figures for savings deposits.

The Comptroller's deposit breakdowns for national banks for 1910–13 vary in form from year to year and even for different dates for the same year. For each year, there are two sets of figures, one for all call dates in the year; a second, for a midyear date only, as part of a table for all banks, nonnational as well as national. The first set shows, in all four years, only a fivefold division of individual deposits, namely, into the same items 2, 4, 5, 6, and 7 of Table 15. For 1910 and 1911 the second set of figures is virtually identical with the first for the mid-year call date. However, an attached footnote, referring to the 1910 total, specifies, "$580,889,677.65 savings deposits included with individual deposits, demand or time certificates of deposit." [39] No estimate is given of the fraction of savings deposits included in deposits subject to check and in certificates of deposit.[40] For 1912 and 1913 the second

[38] For example, in 1896 New York State banks, which held 29 per cent of total individual deposits at all state banks, did not segregate demand from time deposits in their reports to the state banking superintendent; neither did New York loan and trust companies, which held one-half of total individual deposits at all loan and trust companies.

Presumably, Andrew included all these deposits in his category, "deposits subject to check," since he states that "in a number of States where banks were not required to classify deposits in their reports of condition, such unclassified deposits are included with 'deposits subject to check' in the above compilation." Yet a footnote to the category "individual deposits subject to check" for all banks, which supposedly specifies the estimated time deposits in these unclassified deposits erroneously included with deposits subject to check, shows an insignificant amount—less than one per cent of total individual deposits subject to check. This comment applies equally to the 1899 and 1906 breakdowns for New York and for other large states, like Ohio and California.

Andrew's table records more nonnational banks and a larger total of deposits in each of the three years than does the Comptroller in his annual reports. The largest difference in number is 3.1 per cent for 1906, and in deposits is 7.1 per cent for 1899. These discrepancies are not surprising since the Comptroller's figures for nonnational banks, as mentioned above, were seriously incomplete. The figures in *All-Bank Statistics,* in fact, are substantially higher than Andrew's—for 1896, the number of nonnational banks it records is 42.2 per cent higher and total deposits, 9.1 per cent higher. For 1909, *All-Bank Statistics* records 8 per cent more banks in operation than the National Monetary Commission survey, and 3.1 per cent more deposits.

[39] Comptroller of the Currency, *Annual Report,* 1910, p. 792; for the corresponding footnote in 1911, see the *Annual Report,* p. 791. In the second set of figures, 1910–12, demand and time certificates of deposit are not separately distinguished; in 1913, they are.

[40] So painstaking an investigator as Wesley Mitchell nevertheless showed the deposits subject to check of national banks in 1910 and 1911 inclusive of the savings deposit

set of figures differs from the first, savings deposits being shown separately, with deposits subject to check and certificates of deposit together reduced by the corresponding amount.

There is much evidence that the Comptroller regarded the figures on savings deposits with great suspicion and sought to improve reports of them. In 1911, for example, he sent a questionnaire to the 7,301 national banks about their practices with respect to receiving savings deposits, "In view of the questionable accuracy of statistics presented in relation to this subject." [41] Of 6,813 respondents, 3,502 stated that they received savings deposits. About two-thirds of the banks operated the savings department as a separate division, but virtually all that received savings deposits did not maintain a room for savings deposits separate from the commercial department. A total of 810 banks stated that deposits in the savings department were subject to withdrawal by check, and 2,329 stated that presentation of the passbook was required. The two categories together totaled 363 banks fewer than the number of banks stating that they received savings deposits. No question was asked on what fraction of deposits in savings accounts was subject to check.

The following year the Comptroller again commented on the problems of classifying savings deposits:

During the past two years especial attention has been given to the work of obtaining returns from national banks in relation to the volume of their savings accounts and the number of participants therein. In an appreciable percentage of banks paying more than nominal rates of interest on deposits, there is a lack of uniformity in the characterization of savings or interest bearing accounts. That this condition exists is evident from the examination of the reports of various banks from date to date, as discrepancies occur in the volume of savings accounts and the number of savings depositors which would not appear if there was a complete segregation of accounts of this character from other deposits. Notwithstanding this fact, it is evident that national banks and commercial banks generally are competing to a certain extent with the savings banks, and the reports show a steady increase in deposits of this character in national banks.

There is nothing in the Federal law authorizing the establishment of a savings department by national banks, but as the right to pay interest on

figures, and with no footnote indicating that he had used the Comptroller's figure unadjusted. The reason for Mitchell's oversight is apparently that he used the midyear call date figures in the annual reports and did not refer to the midyear national bank breakdowns, where the presence of savings deposits in the deposits subject to check figures is indicated. See *Business Cycles,* 1913, pp. 318, 320, and Comptroller of the Currency, *Annual Report,* 1910, p. 792; 1911, p. 737.

[41] *Annual Report,* 1911, p. 28.

deposits is recognized, the position of the office is that the question of the conduct of a savings or interest department is a matter for the determination of the directors of each bank. Deposits in commercial banks are presumed to be subject to demand, but whether such institutions have the right to enter into a different arrangement with their customers is a matter for determination by the courts.[42]

Table 16 shows how the Federal Reserve constructed its estimates of demand and time deposits at national banks for 1896–1913.[43] The fig-

[42] *Annual Report,* 1912, p. 11.

[43] The Federal Reserve gives these estimates in *All-Bank Statistics* on a state-by-state basis as well as in aggregate. For 1909–13 the data for the separate states are taken from the same sources as the aggregate in the table. For 1896–1908, total time deposits were allocated among the states in the same proportions as for 1909.

Notes to Table 16

[a]Redeposited postal savings, which are not shown, are 0.3 per cent of total deposits (Comptroller of Currency, *Annual Report,* 1913, table showing abstracts of reports of condition of national banks, dollar figure expressed as percentage of sum of cols. 5 and 6).

Source, by Column

1. Comptroller of the Currency, *Annual Report,* 1896–1913, table showing abstracts of reports of condition of national banks, excluding banks in the Possessions.

2. *Italicized* figures are percentages of col. 6 to sum of cols. 5 and 6, from unrounded figures. Other figures are Federal Reserve interpolations. Note that the base in col. 1 includes dividends unpaid; hence the discrepancies between the percentages shown here and those in the final col. of Table 15 for national banks.

3. Figures underlying Table 15, col. 3, for national banks, and Comptroller of the Currency, *Annual Report,* 1910–13, table showing amounts of savings deposits at national banks, expressed as percentages of col. 1.

4. Figures underlying Table 15, col. 5, for national banks, and Comptroller of the Currency, *Annual Report,* 1910–13, table showing classification of individual deposits at national banks, at call date closest to midyear, expressed as percentages of col. 1.

5. *All-Bank Statistics,* p. 40. Col. 1, plus redeposited postal savings, minus col. 6.

6. *Ibid.* 1897–98, 1900–05, 1907–08 are products of col. 1 times col. 2. 1896, 1899, 1906, and 1909–12 are sums of figures underlying cols. 3 and 4. 1913 is the sum of figures underlying cols. 3, 4, and redeposited postal savings deposits.

7. The average rate of growth of the savings deposit percentage, 1910–13, shown in col. 3, was extrapolated backwards.

8. Sum of unrounded figures in col. 4 and col. 7.

TABLE 16

All-Bank Statistics Derivation of Demand and Time Deposits at National Banks in Continental United States, 1896–1913

Date Close to Midyear	Individual Deposits and Dividends Unpaid (millions of dollars) (1)	Time Deposits as Percentage of Total Deposits (2)	Percentage of Total Deposits in		Deposits Other than U.S. and Interbank (millions of dollars)		Estimates of Percentage of Total Deposits in	
			Savings Deposits (3)	Time Certificates of Deposit (4)	Demand (5)	Time (6)	Savings Deposits (7)	All Time Deposits (8)
1896	1,671	4.1	0.0	4.1	1,603	68	3.9	8.0
1897	1,772	4.1			1,700	73		
1898	2,026	4.1	0.0		1,943	83		
1899	2,530	3.4		3.4	2,443	87	4.8	8.3
1900	2,460	4.0			2,361	98		
1901	2,944	4.5			2,811	132		
1902	3,100	5.0			2,945	155		
1903	3,201	5.5			3,026	176		
1904	3,312	6.0			3,113	199		
1905	3,784	6.5			3,538	246		
1906	4,056	7.1	0.1	7.0	3,766	290	8.1	15.2
1907	4,322	10.0			3,890	432		
1908	4,376	12.0			3,850	525		
1909	4,825	15.4	7.8	7.6	4,082	743	10.2	17.8
1910	5,300	19.1	11.0	8.2	4,286	1,014		
1911	5,477	19.8	11.6	8.2	4,394	1,084		
1912	5,825	20.8	12.3	8.5	4,611	1,214		
1913a	5,952	22.7	13.9	8.8	4,603	1,368		

ures in column 2 for 1896, 1899, and 1906 are from Andrew; and those for 1909, from the National Monetary Commission survey (see Table 15). For 1910–12 the Comptroller's figure for savings deposits from the supplementary report of national banks (also in the footnote to his all-bank table) was added to the figure for time certificates of deposit in the table classifying national bank individual deposits, and the sum was expressed as a percentage of individual deposits plus dividends unpaid. For 1913, the same procedure was followed except that redeposited postal savings deposits (from the regular condition statement) were counted also as time deposits. For the remaining ten of the eighteen years in the table, the figures in column 2 are interpolated, for 1897 and 1898 by being set at the same value as for 1896, for the remaining years apparently by straight-line interpolation.[44] For these ten years, there is no independent evidence whatever on the division between demand and time deposits. Hence we shall not discuss them further. The method of interpolation is, of course, arbitrary, but it is not clear that it is worse than alternative methods.[45]

For 1910 and 1911 there is some double counting involved in adding reported savings deposits and time certificates of deposit, since the footnote containing the savings deposit figures notes that some part is included in the table entry for time certificates of deposit. However, it is clear from the figures for 1912 and 1913, when both deposits subject to check and time certificates of deposit are reported—both exclusive and inclusive of savings deposits—that the great bulk of the savings deposits were reported by banks as deposits subject to check. Hence the error on this account is minor.[46]

[44] The description of the procedure for 1899–1909 in *All-Bank Statistics* is as follows: "In 1899 the reported ratio was 3.4 per cent, and in 1909 it was 15.4 per cent; the reported ratio for 1906, at 7.1 per cent, is somewhat less than halfway between the two. For 1907 and 1908, ratios that were interpolated between ratios for 1906 and 1909 were used" (p. 18).

The reason for "apparently" in the sentence to which this footnote is attached is that the ratio for 1908 by straight-line interpolation would be 12.7 rather than the 12.0 shown.

Possibly the results for 1908 are due to an error in computation. To obtain the figures shown in columns 5 and 6 for that year, column 1 must be multiplied by 12.007. If this ratio was inadvertently used for 12.7, there may be no question of principle involved.

[45] About the only way to get evidence on this point would be to examine similar ratios for later periods for which they are available on a continuous basis and to try alternative methods of interpolation on them.

[46] As for the inclusion of postal savings redeposited in national banks, beginning 1913 (and in nonnational banks at subsequent dates), the desirable procedure depends on the monetary total under construction (see Chapter 1, section 4). For a broad total in-

A more serious problem with these estimates is in the savings deposit component of estimated time deposits. The estimates for time certificates of deposit seem like a reasonably continuous series, and there is no reason to doubt that they were reported explicitly throughout and that the category had the same meaning throughout. As we have seen, the situation is very different for savings deposits. For 1896, 1899, and 1906 negligible amounts are recorded not because there were no savings deposits but because there are no data. But even for 1909, the internal evidence of the table reinforces our knowledge about the source of the data in suggesting that the figure entered is much too low. This was the first time information was requested on savings deposits, and it would be astounding if the result were not an understatement. The table shows a rise of over 40 per cent from 1909 to 1910 in the percentage of deposits classified as savings deposits. The greater part of this rise must surely be a statistical artifact. Despite a sharp upward trend from 1910 to 1913 in this percentage, the largest year-to-year rise is 15 per cent, and it seems likely that this trend, too, partly reflects the continued effect of improved reporting—note that the upward trend in the percentage of deposits classified as time certificates of deposit is only half as large as in the percentage of deposits classified as savings deposits.

We conclude that the percentage of deposits recorded as time deposits in column 2 of Table 16 is drastically understated for 1896, 1899, and 1906, seriously understated for 1909, and probably understated for 1910–13 as well. In order to give some idea of the possible magnitude of the error, column 7 of Table 16 gives rough alternative estimates for the savings deposit percentage for 1896, 1899, 1906, and 1909 that were constructed by extrapolating backwards the corresponding percentage for 1910 on the basis of the average recorded rate of growth of the percentage from 1910 to 1913. Since, as noted, we believe this rate of growth is itself exaggerated by statistical error, the alternative estimates probably still fall short of the correct magnitude. Column 8 adds these estimates to the recorded percentage for time certificates of deposit to give alternative estimates of the time deposit percentage. The indicated error is clearly of major magnitude: the alternative estimate is double

cluding postal savings deposits, the Federal Reserve would have been better advised to follow the procedure of *Banking and Monetary Statistics* (p. 35) in which postal savings redeposited in banks were excluded from commercial bank time deposits. In any event, for 1913 the effect of this treatment of postal savings redeposited is small—they amounted to a little over one per cent of estimated commercial bank time deposits.

or more than double the Federal Reserve estimate for 1896, 1899, and 1906 and 15 per cent higher than the Federal Reserve estimate for 1909. Of course, the relative error is smaller when expressed as a percentage of estimated demand deposits, but even then it is sizable—over 5 per cent of Federal Reserve estimated deposits for the earlier years. To avoid misunderstanding, we emphasize that we have no confidence in our alternative estimates except as a way to indicate the order of magnitude of the error in the Federal Reserve estimates.

2. Nonnational Banks

The Federal Reserve estimates of demand and time deposits at nonnational banks in the United States in *All-Bank Statistics* are sums of state-by-state estimates. Before 1909 the state estimates are a brand-new set of figures, compiled either from reports of state banking authorities or estimated by interpolation or extrapolation from later data. Andrew's estimates for 1896, 1899, and 1906, as noted above, were for the total United States without state-by-state detail. The Comptroller's annual reports, on the other hand, which gave figures for each class of nonnational banks in a state, did not differentiate demand and time components of individual deposits. For 1909 the state figures are mainly taken from the National Monetary Commission survey. For 1910 the Comptroller's annual report gave U.S. totals for various classes of nonnational banks that differentiated demand from time deposits, but gave no state-by-state detail. The Federal Reserve's figures for that year were either obtained from state banking reports or interpolated between the 1909 National Monetary Commission figures and the 1911 figures in the Comptroller's annual report. For 1911–13 the Federal Reserve used primarily state-by-state figures given by the Comptroller in his annual reports.

Table 17, based on the descriptions in *All-Bank Statistics* of the procedures followed in deriving the estimates for each state, classifies the states into three groups.[47] For a group of seventeen states—with aggre-

[47] Table 17 does not summarize the procedures for deriving estimates for unincorporated banks in the eighteen states where a separate balance sheet was compiled for that class of banks. These were states where either most U.S. private banking was concentrated or where most private banks did not report to state banking authorities. The descriptive section in *All-Bank Statistics* for each of the remaining thirty states includes the following sentence: "A separate balance sheet was not compiled for unincorporated banks because adequate data were reported, either separately or in combination with data for other State commercial banks, in the reports of the Comptroller of the Cur-

gate average time deposits of about one-third of the United States non-national bank estimates, 1896–1914—demand and time deposits were reported separately for all or most years before 1914 in state bank reports.[48] For a second group of twenty-three states and the District of Columbia, with about the same aggregate time deposits, the ratio for each state of time to demand-plus-time deposits, 1896–1908, was mostly extrapolated from its own ratio for later years. For a third group of eight states, with the remaining third of aggregate time deposits, the ratio of time to demand-plus-time deposits, 1896–1908, was derived by first extrapolating a trend value of the ratio for each state to 1896, then interpolating between that extrapolated value and the first observed value on the basis of the ratio for nonnational banks in a Group-I state assumed to be similar. In all, five states in Group I were used in this interpolation process.

For the thirteen years 1896 through 1908, therefore, direct evidence on the division of deposits between demand and time deposits is avail-

rency or the State banking department" (pp. 96, 128 . . . 1101. Only in the District of Columbia were no private banks in operation, 1896–1955.).

The data for private banks are described as "the least accurate component of the revised all-bank series—because they were compiled largely from unofficial sources" (p. 22). On the other hand, "two-thirds of the total assets of all private banks in the revised series in 1898 and nearly all in 1933" (p. 726) are accounted for by two large New York private banks, previously nonreporting, one of which made available to the Board of Governors annual balance sheet statements for the period 1896–1933; the other, for all but four years—1896–97, 1929–30. For the large number of private banks remaining, many of which never reported but whose existence was recorded in bankers' directories, balance sheets were constructed from estimated capital accounts (though private banks, of course, have no capital stock), estimated ratios of capital accounts to total assets, and estimated percentage distributions of assets and liabilities. For these conjectural balance sheets, *All-Bank Statistics* does not, in most cases, explicitly state how the demand and time deposit breakdowns were constructed. For a few states, however, this source notes that the 1909 National Monetary Commission percentage breakdowns for reporting private banks were applied to total deposit estimates, 1896–1908. It is puzzling, in view of the Federal Reserve's reliance on the 1909 data, that no time deposits are shown for Minnesota unincorporated banks (p. 560). According to the National Monetary Commission survey, time deposits accounted for three-fifths of the total deposits of this state's reporting private banks.

The deposits of private banks as a percentage of nonnational commercial bank deposits, judging from the revised series, were not insignificant in 1896, but their relative importance dwindled rapidly thereafter. In 1896, the percentages for demand and time deposits, respectively, were nineteen and nearly fourteen; in 1908, eight and nearly five; in 1913, six and nearly four.

[48] Of the seventeen, only four—Me. (from 1893), Mont. (1874), Neb. (1889), and Vt. (1910)—imposed differential reserve requirements for part or all of the period. On the economic significance of the reported breakdowns for banks of the remaining thirteen states without different reserve requirements for demand and time deposits, see above, pp. 154–155.

Reports of states which imposed differential reserve requirements did not necessarily classify deposits as demand or time. Iowa, for example, enacted differential reserve requirements in 1897, but no breakdowns are available through 1908.

TABLE 17

Classification of States According to Character of Estimates in All-Bank Statistics
of Demand and Time Deposits at Nonnational Incorporated Banks,[a] 1896–1913

Group I. All or Most Data Reported

State	1896–1913 Average Per Cent of Nonnational Commercial Bank Time Deposits	Years Not Reported 1896–1913	Adjustments of Reported Data and Method of Estimation in Years Not Reported
Florida	0.1	1910	Ratios for December call dates used; average of ratios for 1909 and 1911 used.
Illinois	10.9		
Indiana	1.5	1896–97, 1906	Ratios for October call dates used; average of ratios for preceding and succeeding years used.
Kansas	0.5		
Maine	0.6		Ratios for fall call dates used.
Massachusetts	0.5		Ratios for October call dates used.
Michigan	6.8		
Missouri	3.2		Ratios for fall call dates used.

Montana	0.3	1899, 1901, 1903	Average of ratios for preceding and succeeding years used.
Nebraska	0.8	1896–97, 1900	Ratio for 1898 and average of ratios for 1899 and 1901 used.
			Ratios for November call dates used 1902, 1908.
New Hampshire	0.6		Reports of various dates adjusted to approximate June 30.
Rhode Island	2.1	1908–10	Average of ratios for 1907 and 1911 used.
South Dakota	0.6	1896	Ratio for 1897 used.
Vermont	1.0		
Washington	0.9	1908	Average of ratios for 1907 and 1909 used.
West Virginia	0.9	1901, 1910	Average of ratios for preceding and succeeding years used; ratios for fall call dates used, 1902–08.
Wisconsin	2.9	1906	Average of ratios for preceding and succeeding years used; ratios for fall call dates used, 1898–1903.
Total	34.2		

(continued)

TABLE 17 (continued)

Group II. 1896–1908 Estimated by interpolating Data for Same State or Extrapolating Later Data for Same State

State	1896–1913 Average Per Cent of Nonnational Commercial Bank Time Deposits	Years Not Reported 1896–1913	Method of Estimation in Years Not Reported	Class of Banks
Alabama	0.3	1896–1908	Ratios for 1911–23 extrapolated.	
		1910	Average of ratios for 1909 and 1911 used.	
Arizona	0.1	1896–1908	Ratios for 1911–15 extrapolated.	
Connecticut	0.3	1896–1901	Average of adjusted ratios (fall call dates used), 1902–07.	Loan and trust
Delaware	b	1896–1908	Ratios for 1909–16 extrapolated.	Loan and trust
		1910	Average of ratios for 1909 and 1911 used.	Loan and trust and state
District of Columbia	0.2	1902–08	Interpolation between 1901 and 1909 ratios.	
		1910	Average of ratios for 1909 and 1911 used.	
		1912	Average of ratios for 1911 and 1913 used.	Stock savings
		1896–1908, 1910	Average ratio of 1909 and 1911 used.	Loan and trust
Georgia	0.9	1896–1908	Ratios for 1909–25 extrapolated.	
		1910	Average of ratios for 1909 and 1911 used.	

290

State	Value	Years	Ratio method	Class
Idaho	0.1	1896–1905, 1907–08, 1910	Ratios for 1906, 1909, 1911–24 extrapolated.	
Louisiana	0.8	1896–1903	Ratio for 1904 used.	
Maryland	0.6	1896–1908	Ratios for 1909–24 extrapolated.	Each class estimated separately
Minnesota	1.9	1896–1908	Ratio for 1909 used.	Loan and trust
		1910	Average of ratios for 1909 and 1911 used	State
		1896–97, 1901–02	Ratios for 1898 and average of ratios for 1900 and 1903 used.	
Mississippi	0.3	1896–1908	Ratio for 1909 used.	
Nevada	0.1	1896–1908	Ratios for 1909–24 extrapolated.	
New Jersey	3.2	1896, 1900	Ratio for 1897 and average of ratios for 1899 and 1901 used.	Loan and Trust
		1896–1906	Average of 1907–09 ratios used.	State
New Mexico	b	1896–1908	Ratios for 1909–17, 1920–24 extrapolated.	
New York	10.3	1896–1908	Ratios for 1909–27 extrapolated.	Loan and trust
		1896–1908	Ratio for 1909 used.	State
		1910	Average of ratios for 1909 and 1911 used.	Loan and trust and state separately

291

(continued)

TABLE 17 (continued)

State	1896–1913 Average Per Cent of Nonnational Commercial Bank Time Deposits	Years Not Reported 1896–1913	Method of Estimation in Years Not Reported	Class of Banks
North Carolina	0.4	1896–1908	Ratios for 1909–24 extrapolated.	
North Dakota	0.4	1896–1903, 1906, 1908	Ratio for 1909 used.	
Oklahoma	0.1	1896–99, 1903, 1907–08	Ratios for 1900, for 1902 and for 1909, used.	
Oregon	0.5	1896–1908	Ratios for 1909–24 extrapolated.	
		1910	Average of ratios for 1909 and 1911 used.	
Pennsylvania	10.6	1899–1908	Interpolation of average of ratios for 1896–98 and for 1909, 1911, and 1912.	Loan and trust and state separately
		1910	Average of ratios for 1909 and 1911.	
South Carolina	0.8	1896–1905	Ratios for 1906–24 extrapolated.	
Texas	0.1	1896–1906	Ratio for 1907 used.	
Utah	0.5	1896–1908	Ratios for 1909–22 extrapolated.	
Wyoming	0.1	1896–1904, 1906–08	Ratios for 1905, 1909–24 extrapolated.	
Total	32.6			

(continued)

TABLE 17 (concluded)

Group III. 1896–1908 Estimated by Movements of a Related Series

State	1896–1913 Average Per Cent of Nonnational Commercial Bank Time Deposits	Years Not Reported	Related Series	Period of Correlation of Related Series and Series Interpolated	Other Estimation
Arkansas	0.2	1896–1908	Missouri	1909–24	
California	14.6	1896–1905	Washington	1906–24	
Colorado	0.5	1896–1907	Nebraska	1908–20	1910 based on average of 1909–11 ratios
Iowa	7.8	1896–1908	Missouri	Not stated.[c]	1910 based on average of 1909–11 ratios
Kentucky	0.8	1896–1908	Missouri	1909–24	1910 based on average of 1909–11 ratios
Ohio	8.3	1896–1908	Michigan	Not stated.	1910 based on average of 1909–11 ratios
Tennessee	0.5	1896–1908	Missouri	Not stated.	
Virginia	0.7	1896–1908	West Virginia	1909–24	1910 based on average of 1909–11 ratios
Total	33.4				

able for only one-third of time deposits. For the remaining two-thirds, the Federal Reserve breakdown is based primarily on a hypothetical reconstruction.

How reliable are the breakdowns in the state banking reports for the seventeen states in Group I? For some states the quality of the data is excellent. The classification of deposits is detailed, clear, and consistent over time. Michigan and Illinois are illustrations. For other states the deposit classifications are ambiguous or deposits are not classified uniformly for different classes of nonnational commercial banks (whose report dates may also differ). Wisconsin, Indiana, and Washington are illustrations. The classification of deposits in state banks differs from that in loan and trust companies and each classification is ambiguous about certain deposit items. The most troublesome item is certificates of deposit. Many state reports that differentiate other deposit items do not separate certificates of deposit into demand and time. New Hampshire, Rhode Island, and South Dakota are illustrations. Even if certificates are classified as demand or time, there are sometimes large annual swings in the percentages of the total that each type of certificate is reported as constituting. Washington is an illustration.

Unfortunately, from 1909 on, the data used by the Federal Reserve for these seventeen states are sometimes less accurate than those available from the state reports. For 1911–13, for example, the Comptroller's annual reports, on which the Federal Reserve relied in many instances, did not classify certificates of deposit into demand and time certificates. As a result, Federal Reserve ratios show abrupt swings for a number of

---

Notes to Table 17

Note: Detail of per cent of nonnational commercial bank time deposits may not add to 100.0, because of rounding.

[a]See Chap. 8, footnote 47.

[b]Less than five-hundredths of 1 per cent.

[c]No breakdowns were available for 1915–25 for Iowa, so correlations with the Missouri data could not have been based on this period, but description of estimating procedure is vague.

Source: *All-Bank Statistics,* pp. 99, 114, 130, 146, 163, 185, 216, 239, 254, 271, 293, 308, 329, 361, 382, 398, 415, 430, 455, 485, 515, 538, 568, 584, 600, 620, 637, 652, 677, 707, 723, 757, 772, 789, 822, 838, 863, 894, 918–919, 935, 950, 965–966, 989, 1004, 1023, 1049–1050, 1078, 1103–1104, 1129.

states for which state bank reports are excellent and would have raised
no problems of classification. Illinois and West Virginia are examples.
Rhode Island certificates of deposit were classified by the Federal Reserve mainly as time deposits, 1911–13, and mainly as demand deposits
thereafter, because of a change in the Comptroller's presentation.

The ratio of time deposits to the sum of demand and time deposits for
Group-I states is plotted in Chart 2. The series is fairly smooth, though
there seems to be a jump after 1910 that may well reflect the shift in the
basic data relied on. There is every reason to believe that for nonnational

CHART 2

Ratio of Time to Total Demand and Time Deposits for Three Groups of
States and for All Nonnational Banks, According to *All-Bank Statistics,*
1896–1924

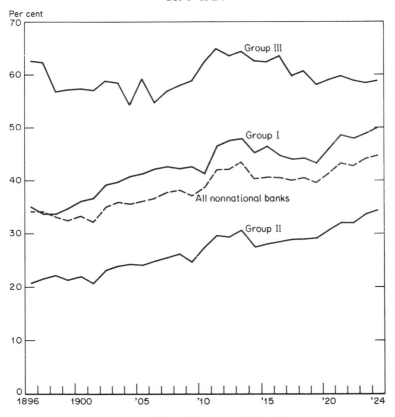

SOURCE: *All-Bank Statistics, 1896–1955.*

as for national banks the increased emphasis by the Comptroller on figures on savings deposits produced an improvement in reporting that
accounts for some of the jump. For individual states there is much more
pronounced discontinuity (see Chart 3). Discontinuities in the figures
at a sample of dates for which we have examined the underlying data

CHART 3

Ratio of Time to Total Demand and Time Deposits
for a Sample of Group I States, 1896–1924

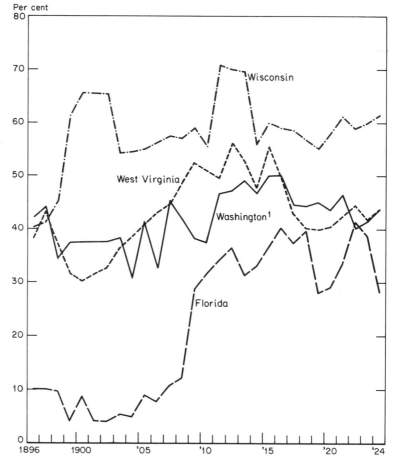

SOURCE: *All-Bank Statistics, 1896–1955.*
[1] Incorporated banks.

clearly occurred because of apparently arbitrary shifts in the classification of some items.

Of the five states in Group I that were used in making estimates for Group-III states, Washington, in particular, has ratios with erratic annual movements. This state accounted for less than one per cent of nonnational bank time deposits, but the movements in its ratios were magnified in importance when they were used to estimate California time deposits, which are nearly 15 per cent of nonnational bank time deposits, according to the Federal Reserve estimates.

For Group-II states, three methods of getting estimates for 1896–1908 were used. For fourteen states the trend of reported data for years after 1909 was extrapolated backwards, presumably by computing a least squares straight-line trend from the percentages for later years.[49] For nine states the ratio for either a single later year or for an average of later years was applied to the earlier years.[50] For the District of Columbia (stock savings banks) and Pennsylvania, ratios were interpolated along a straight line between data for early and late years.

The resulting estimates of the ratio of time to total deposits for Group-II states as an aggregate are shown in Chart 2. As is enforced by the method of estimation, the pre-1909 figures display a common straight-line trend with later figures. We see no way to determine whether this also corresponds to reality.

For the Group-III states in Table 17, a procedure designated "interpolating technique no. 2" was used. This is an adaptation of a technique suggested by Milton Friedman.[51] It involves estimating the relatives to trend for the series to be interpolated from corresponding relatives for a related series, in this case a nearby state, "for which changes could be assumed to be most nearly similar to those for states with incomplete data." The estimate is based on the correlation between the two sets of relatives for a period when both are available. In order to apply the

[49] It is not entirely clear from the descriptions in *All-Bank Statistics* how the extrapolation was performed. We have included Utah in this category, even though the description (*ibid.*, p. 989) is somewhat puzzling.

[50] New York is included with the subgroup of fourteen states because the trend of the ratios for its loan and trust companies was estimated as for the other states. It could also have been included with the subgroup of nine states because the trend of the ratios for its state banks was estimated as for those other states. The District of Columbia (loan and trust companies) could also have been counted as one of the states in the latter subgroup.

[51] *The Interpolation of Time Series by Related Series*, NBER Technical Paper 16, 1962.

technique, trend values are required for the Group-III states. Presumably these were obtained by extrapolation from data for later years. However, there is no explicit statement to this effect in *All-Bank Statistics*. More important, the ratios used do not seem, at least for some Group-III states, to have the same trend for the earlier years, for which they were supposedly estimated in this way, as for the later years for which they are based on reported data. Hence, we are not at all confident that we understand precisely the procedure followed.[52]

Great emphasis apparently was placed on the geographic proximity of a state with reported figures to the state for which it served as interpolator. The Missouri data were used as the related series for estimates of four geographically adjacent states (Arkansas, Iowa, Kentucky, and Tennessee). Washington, Nebraska, Michigan, and West Virginia were each used once as the related series in estimating figures for a nearby state.[53]

The final ratios for Group III, as might be expected from the method of estimation, are highly erratic before 1909 (Chart 2). After 1910 they show a decided downward trend, in sharp contrast with the Group-II states.

Table 18 shows the *All-Bank Statistics* final estimates of the ratio of time deposits to total deposits for all nonnational banks. For comparison it also shows the earlier Federal Reserve estimates[54] and for selected

[52] A general description of the interpolation technique is given in *All-Bank Statistics*, p. 20. A numerical illustration of technique no. 2 is given on pp. 92–94.

[53] In general, the descriptions of procedures for each state given in *All-Bank Statistics* are rather meager despite the mammoth size of the volume. There is a considerable gap between what can be gleaned from the descriptions and what needs to be known for an intelligent assessment of the estimates. For three states (Iowa, Ohio, and Tenn.) the source does not state the later period for which the related series and the series interpolated for earlier years were correlated. In no case are the correlation coefficients presented. No indication is given of possible tests of related series other than the one used. In fact, it is not clear whether the distinction between states in Groups II and III is a systematic one indicating that only after all possible related series were rejected were the procedures used for Group-II states adopted. In the absence of such information, the reader of *All-Bank Statistics* is in no position to judge whether the interpolators were wisely chosen and well matched with the states requiring interpolation.

[54] *Banking and Monetary Statistics* devotes one sentence to the derivation of the estimates before 1914: "From 1892 through 1913, figures are based on unpublished estimates of demand and time deposits, exclusive of interbank deposits, at all domestic banks, made by the Board's staff from a variety of sources, including compilations of the National Monetary Commission and the Comptroller of the Currency" (p. 11). The nonnational bank component of the all commercial bank series in that source was derived by us by deducting "other demand" and "other time" deposits at national banks, given in *All-Bank Statistics*. We do not know that precisely these figures for national banks were used in the *Banking and Monetary Statistics* series for

TABLE 18

Alternative Estimates of Ratio of Time to Total Demand and Time Deposits, Nonnational Commercial Banks, 1896–1913

(per cent)

Year	Andrew; National Monetary Commission; Comptroller (1)	Banking and Monetary Statistics (2)	All-Bank Statistics (3)	Alternative Ratio (4)
1896	23.5	27.3	34.2	33.7
1897		29.7	34.1	32.3
1898		24.7	33.1	32.3
1899	21.2	24.9	32.4	33.3
1900		27.6	33.3	34.7
1901		27.8	32.1	35.2
1902		27.1	35.0	37.7
1903		27.5	35.8	38.2
1904		28.4	35.5	39.3
1905		29.5	36.1	39.5
1906	27.2	29.6	36.6	40.6
1907		31.9	37.7	40.8
1908		35.0	38.1	40.5
1909	37.4	39.7	37.0	40.8
1910	38.8[a]	39.8	38.7	39.7
1911		40.0	42.0	42.1
1912		40.5	42.0	43.1
1913		41.6	43.4	43.4

[a]Excluding unclassified deposits.

Source, by Column

1. Same as for Table 15; *Annual Report* of the Comptroller of the Currency, 1910, p. 792. No entries for 1911–13 are given, because we do not know how to distribute reported certificates of deposit between demand and time accounts.

2. *Banking and Monetary Statistics,* p. 34, minus *All-Bank Statistics,* p. 40 (national banks, "other demand" and "other time" deposits).

3. *Ibid.,* p. 44 (state commercial banks, "other demand" and "other time" deposits).

4. See text, Chap. 8, Appendix, section 2.

TABLE 19

Alternative Estimates of Ratio of Time to Total Demand and
Time Deposits, All Commercial Banks, 1896–1913
(per cent)

Year	Andrew; National Monetary Commission; Comptroller (1)	*Banking and Monetary Statistics* (2)	*All-Bank Statistics* (3)	Alternative Ratio (4)
1896	13.5	15.8	20.8	22.5
1897		16.5	20.8	21.7
1898		14.3	20.0	21.6
1899	12.3	13.6	19.8	22.8
1900		16.6	21.1	24.5
1901		16.9	21.4	26.1
1902		17.2	23.1	27.6
1903		17.8	24.0	28.4
1904		18.7	24.0	29.4
1905		19.6	25.0	30.4
1906	18.5	19.9	25.8	31.8
1907		22.6	27.5	32.1
1908		24.7	28.0	31.6
1909	27.6	29.0	29.2	32.6
1910		30.6	32.3	32.8
1911		31.2	33.8	33.9
1912		32.0	34.2	34.9
1913		33.5	36.0	35.9

Source, by Column

1. Same as for Table 18. No entries for 1910–13 are given, because the Comptroller does not indicate the fraction of time certificates of deposits for national banks to be added to savings deposits he reports at those banks (see text, Chap. 8, Appendix, section 3, nor the classification of certificates of deposit at nonnational banks, 1911–13.

years the estimates by Andrew, the National Monetary Commission, and the Comptroller. The effect of the revision has been to raise substantially for the earlier years the fraction of nonnational bank deposits classified as time deposits. For comparative purposes we have also included an alternative estimate of our own that (a) is linked to the *All-Bank Statistics* 1913 figure, (b) adjusts for the jump in the ratio from 1909 to 1911, and (c) uses for 1896–1913 only the data for Group I—the one group of states for which there are reasonably reliable data for the whole period.[55] As for our national bank estimates, we have no confidence in these alternative estimates except as an indicator of the margin of error in those of the Federal Reserve, though they do seem to us no more arbitrary or inaccurate than the Federal Reserve's estimates.

The four sets of estimates differ by sizable amounts: for some of the earlier years the largest is nearly 60 per cent greater than the smallest. The difference between the Federal Reserve final estimates and our alternative one is as much as 11 per cent in some years.

all banks, but they cannot be significantly different from the figures actually used. The residual nonnational bank figures for demand deposits bear the full adjustment for float at all commercial banks, hence the annual percentage that time deposits are of this total (Table 18) is somewhat higher than the true percentage would be. Andrew's estimates are of course unadjusted for float, as are the *All-Bank Statistics* estimates for nonnational banks.

[55] We accomplished (b) by extrapolating the 1911–13 change recorded for Group-I states back to 1909 and then multiplying the original figures for Group-I states, 1896–1910, by the ratio of the extrapolated value for 1909 to the original value for 1909. This new series for Group I, 1896–1913, was then expressed as relative to the value for 1913 and the results multiplied by 43.4, the *All-Bank Statistics* figure for 1913.

Notes to Table 19 (concluded)

2. Page 34.

3. Pages 36 ("other time" deposits) and 60 (demand deposits adjusted).

4. Based on sums of estimated demand and time deposits at national and nonnational banks. Total deposits at national banks (Table 16, col. 1) were multiplied by ratios of time to total deposits (Table 16, col. 8, 1896–1909, with straight-line interpolations of the ratios for intervening years; col. 2, 1910–13). Demand deposits at national banks are residuals, from which cash items (*All-Bank Statistics*, p. 39) were subtracted. Total deposits at nonnational banks (*ibid.*, p. 44) were multiplied by ratios of time to total deposits (Table 18, col. 4). Demand deposits at nonnational banks are residuals, from which cash items (*All-Bank Statistics*, p. 43) were subtracted.

3. All Commercial Banks

Table 19 gives four sets of estimates of the time deposit ratio for all commercial banks. It is clear that the margin of uncertainty in these estimates is very large indeed—far larger, in our opinion, than that which attaches to the estimates of total deposits or any of the other totals in our Table 1. As the preceding discussion emphasizes, for national banks the ratio for ten of the eighteen years is entirely a constructed one, based on no direct evidence whatsoever. The same is true of about two-thirds of estimated time deposits at nonnational banks for most of the years. In view especially of the uncertain economic meaning of the distinction between demand and time deposits before 1914, this seems to us much too small and uncertain a base on which to erect anything that could be described as a structure of economic analysis.

9

COMPARISON OF EARLIER ESTIMATES
WITH OUR OWN

CHARTS 4 and 5 plot various earlier estimates and those of our own estimates most nearly comparable to them. We include in the charts the 1941 Federal Reserve estimates but not the latest ones, since our estimates differ from the latter only where the two do not overlap (i.e., for the earlier period, and for the finer time units for which we constructed estimates).

Panel A of Chart 4, in which the various annual series are plotted, demonstrates that the series are all very much alike in the level of their broader movements. This result is assured by the common rapid upward trend plus the comparable broader components, e.g., currency outside Treasury, national bank deposits, and national bank vault cash. Closer examination reveals that this general similarity conceals numerous differences in detail. For example, Angell's circulating money reaches a trough in 1922, our comparable total in 1921; his series rises steadily from 1922 to 1929, ours, to 1926, after which it declines for two years before rising in 1929 to a level only a trifle above that in 1926. Interestingly, Angell's total money and our comparable concept show the opposite difference in timing in the late 1920's; his reaches a peak in 1928, ours in 1929. Panel B of the chart, which shows year-to-year rates of change, brings out more clearly these differences in detail.

As might be expected, the differences among the various estimates show up more clearly for the monthly estimates plotted in Chart 5. These are all for currency plus demand deposits, since there are no other monthly estimates comparable to ours for broader totals before 1943. The several series give considerably different evidence on cyclical

CHART 4

Comparison of Earlier Annual Estimates of Monetary
Totals and NBER Series, 1880–1940

Panel A. Level of Nine Estimates

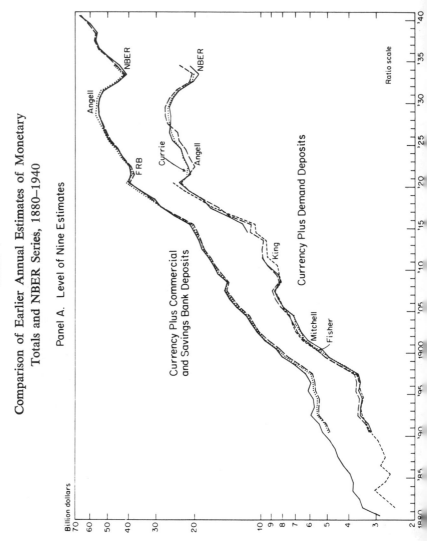

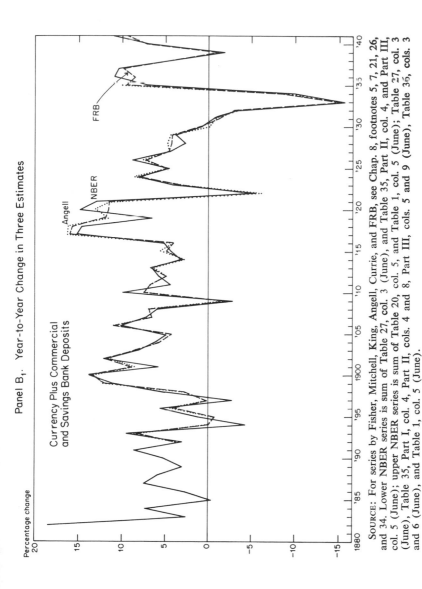

Panel B₁. Year-to-Year Change in Three Estimates

SOURCE: For series by Fisher, Mitchell, King, Angell, Currie, and FRB, see Chap. 8, footnotes 5, 7, 21, 26, and 34. Lower NBER series is sum of Table 27, col. 3 (June), and Table 35, Part II, col. 4, and Part III, col. 5 (June); upper NBER series is sum of Table 20, col. 5, and Table 1, col. 5 (June); Table 27, col. 3 (June), Table 35, Part I, col. 4, Part II, cols. 4 and 8, Part III, cols. 5 and 9 (June), Table 36, cols. 3 and 6 (June), and Table 1, col. 5 (June).

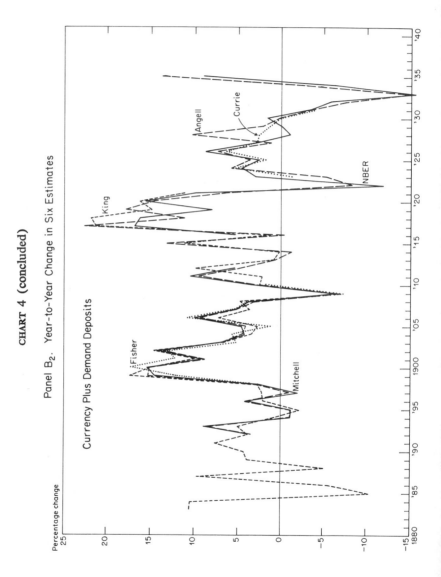

CHART 4 (concluded)

Panel B₂. Year-to-Year Change in Six Estimates

Comparison of Earlier Monthly Estimates of Monetary
Totals and NBER Series, 1914–34

Panel A.   Level of Four Estimates

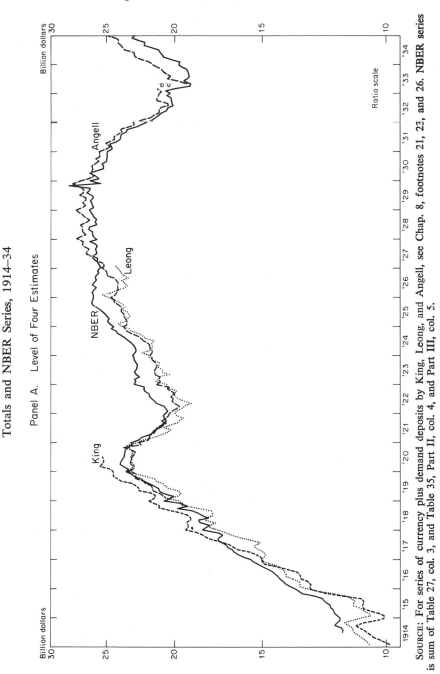

SOURCE: For series of currency plus demand deposits by King, Leong, and Angell, see Chap. 8, footnotes 21, 22, and 26. NBER series is sum of Table 27, col. 3, and Table 35, Part II, col. 4, and Part III, col. 5.

CHART 5 (concluded)

Panel B.   Month-to-Month Change in Four Estimates

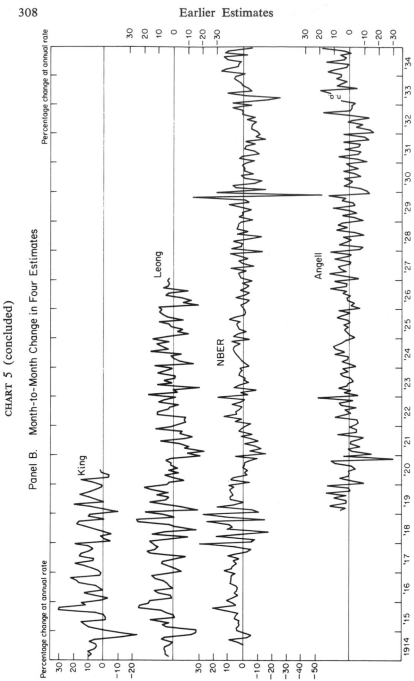

timing. For example, our series has a clearly marked specific cycle peak in March 1920; Angell's and Leong's has a double peak, the first in December 1919 or January 1920, the second, and appreciably higher, in October or November 1920. Our series reaches a specific cycle trough in either September 1921 or January 1922, Angell's in March 1922, and Leong's in April 1922. The biggest difference is for the period 1925 to 1929, when our series shows a decline from September 1925 to December 1926 and then a mild rise until the sudden jump in October 1929, reflecting the action taken by the New York Federal Reserve Bank in response to the stock market crash; whereas Angell's series rises through most of 1926 to the end of 1927 and then, like ours, is roughly horizontal to late 1929. For some reason, the stock market effect is reflected in Angell's series in November rather than October 1929.

PART THREE

DERIVATION OF OUR ESTIMATES

Introduction

Chapter 1 described the scope and coverage of our estimates and outlined in very summary form how they were derived. The eight chapters of this part fill in the details and in addition give supplementary statistical series that, though by products of the derivation of our estimates, are of interest in their own right.

Chapter 10 sets the stage by explaining why we chose the particular date at which we shifted from semiannual and annual estimates to monthly estimates (section 1), supplementing the comments in Chapter 1 on the sources of our basic data (section 2), discussing some of the general statistical methods employed in making the estimates (sections 3, 4, and 5), and commenting on the reliability of the estimates (section 6). It ends with a list of definitions of terms used in the remaining chapters (section 7).

Chapter 11 explains the construction of the semiannual, annual, and quarterly estimates covering the period 1867–1907. The remaining chapters of this part all deal with the monthly estimates from 1907 on. As explained in Chapter 1, most of these were constructed in two stages, of which the first was the preparation of a call date series which was then usually used to construct the monthly estimates.

This procedure was reversed for total currency outside the Treasury and Federal Reserve Banks (Chapter 12, section 1). In this case, we started with a monthly series which we then converted into a call date series to match the independently derived call date series for bank vault cash (section 2). The difference between these two series is our call date series of currency held by the public. The difference between the initial monthly series for currency in circulation and a monthly vault cash series derived from the call date series (Chapter 12, section 3) is our monthly series of currency held by the public (Chapter 12, section 4).

Commercial bank deposits required more extensive estimating than any other component of our series (except possibly vault cash). We first estimated these deposits (as well as those at mutual savings banks and the Postal Savings System) inclusive of U.S. government deposits, and then subtracted separately estimated U.S. government deposits

(Chapter 17). Chapter 13 explains the derivation of the call date estimates of commercial bank deposits and Chapter 14, of the monthly estimates; Chapter 15 explains the derivation of both call date and monthly estimates of mutual savings bank deposits; and Chapter 16, of postal savings.

10

GENERAL FEATURES OF OUR ESTIMATES

1. Choice of Date to Begin Monthly Estimates

FOR BOTH ECONOMIC and statistical reasons we chose to begin our monthly estimates with May 1907. It seemed desirable to have monthly figures for as long a period as possible before the Federal Reserve System was in operation. However, the data at midyear and call dates become less and less satisfactory the further one pushes back before April 28, 1909, the date of the first comprehensive balance sheet of nonnational banks by states, compiled by the National Monetary Commission.[1] By starting with 1907, we avoided placing much reliance on the earlier unreliable data, yet were able to cover two pre-World War I reference cycles, making possible at least some comparison of the detailed cyclical pattern of the money stock before and after the inauguration of the Federal Reserve System.

To avoid duplicating the current estimates that have been published in the *Federal Reserve Bulletin* for monthly dates beginning December 1942, our estimates end in 1946 for mutual savings bank deposits,

---

[1] Oddly enough, for these early years data for monthly interpolation, in the weekly city clearinghouse returns for that sample of banks, are superior to the state returns available at less regular intervals for larger samples. The balance sheet data reported by many states before 1909 present difficulties that weaken the reliability of call date bench marks compared to later years. These defects are largely corrected in the revised annual series of the Federal Reserve for the United States as a whole in *All-Bank Statistics, United States, 1896–1955*, Board of Governors of the Federal Reserve System, Washington, D.C., 1959. But the Federal Reserve series still does not overcome a basic shortcoming of the individual state data: the lack of consistency in dating of annual returns in the earlier years. The aggregate is a sum of returns dated "on or about June 30." The spread of dating about June 30 widens, and the number of states departing from the most common date increases, the earlier the year.

1945 for commercial bank deposits, and 1942 for currency held by the public. The corresponding Federal Reserve monthly series, seasonally adjusted, have been used to continue our series. Although our series are not constructed in the same way as those of the Federal Reserve, the two seem reasonably consistent during the period in which they overlap. The levels are similar at the dates when the shift from our estimates to the Federal Reserve series is made. The series therefore give a continuous monthly record of changes in the money stock from May 1907 to date.

2. Sources of the Data

We took most of the raw data, reported annually, at call dates, monthly, or weekly, from printed sources, principally the annual reports of the Comptroller of the Currency, the Federal Reserve Board, and individual state banking departments; the *Federal Reserve Bulletin; Banking and Monetary Statistics; All-Bank Statistics;* call reports of national, member, and insured banks; clearinghouse returns of member (and certain nonmember) banks shown in various sources including A. P. Andrew's "Statistics of Banks and Banking in the United States" (Part II of *Statistics for the United States, 1867–1909*) and the *Commercial and Financial Chronicle.* We also used unpublished data provided by various state banking departments.

The bank balance sheet information in these sources varies in pertinent detail. In general, federal reports are superior to state reports, although some state reports are more satisfactory sources of nonnational bank information for some years than are the Comptroller of the Currency's compilations.

Until comparatively recent years bank vault cash, demand deposits adjusted, and time deposits adjusted were not itemized as such on most bank balance sheets. They must be compiled by addition (or subtraction) of components listed separately. Special problems exist where no breakdowns are given: the asset side of the balance sheet may show vault cash combined with amounts due from banks or items in the process of collection; there may be no separate entry of items constituting "float"; the liability side may show demand and time deposits as a total or combined with amounts due to banks. Usually U.S. government deposits are not classified apart from those of the public. Our treatment of these problems is discussed in subsequent chapters. Our object was to make our final series as comprehensive as their defined content and to rid them of all extraneous elements. Some estimation was required to achieve this result.

Our annual series after 1896, except for mutual savings bank deposits and vault cash, are Federal Reserve constructions representing the most complete information available. These data are based on an enumeration of banks. It is conceivable that some institutions that should be considered banks may have been overlooked; it is most unlikely that any nonbanking institutions were included. Despite the vagaries of bank reports, deposits of the enumerated banks are not likely to be significantly over- or underestimated when data for other balance sheet items are simultaneously compiled or estimated.

Our call date figures, which conform in definition to the annual series, represent a considerable, though varying, proportion of the total universe. Some of the monthly data, however, differ in content from the call date series for which they served as interpolators. The use of these conceptually different data to estimate inter-call date movements does not introduce any appreciable error since (a) we first ascertained that these related data correlate well with our call date figures; and (b) the levels of our bench-mark series are accurate within the limits of our performance.

3. Classification of Banks

The basic sources of data determine the classification of banks that we have used. Prior to 1914 the obvious classification is into national and nonnational banks. Data for the national banks are excellent, homogeneous, and readily available from the reports of the Comptroller of the Currency. Data for nonnational banks must be gleaned from reports of state supervisory agencies or from the irregular and variable reports made to the Comptroller in response to his request. This division between national and nonnational banks is relevant for our deposit estimates and affects not only them, but also our estimates of bank vault cash and hence of currency in the hands of the public.

For the period since 1914 an additional classification is possible — into banks that are members of the Federal Reserve System and banks that are nonmembers. Since member banks include all national banks plus some other banks as well, we have preferred to use this classification wherever possible. However, satisfactory data are available for member banks only from June 1919 on. Hence we have been able to use only the national-nonnational division up to that date. We have carried our estimates for this division beyond that date to 1922 because for 1919–22 national banks reported at two more call dates each year than member banks did.

Even after 1922, however, we have had to use both classifications to some extent, since data on nonmember banks are not directly available. Each state receives reports from banks under its jurisdiction, and these reports usually do not separate member from nonmember banks. As a result, we generally derive estimates for nonmember banks as the difference between totals for nonnational banks and corresponding figures for state member banks taken from Federal Reserve reports. This frequently raises problems of comparability, and care was always required to assure that our estimation was carried through in such a way as to use the independent information for state member banks, since it is easy and tempting to follow procedures that in effect discard this information.

The nonnational banks are further classified into various groups in various states: commercial banks, loan and trust companies, stock savings banks, mutual savings banks; and incorporated banks and private banks; and so on. It is with these classifications, often varying in number and meaning from state to state, that we have had to work in processing data for individual states. In combining data for different states, however, we have tried to keep distinct only two categories, commercial banks and mutual savings banks (see definitions in section 7 of this chapter). In addition, of course, we have kept separate savings and loan associations, which are not regarded as banks.

4. Dating and Seasonal Adjustment

Our final series were not constructed in one continuous operation from the initial to the terminal dates. In accordance with the data available different procedures were followed in different time periods. Because a variety of devices was adopted—as will be seen from the detailed chapters—it is extremely difficult to summarize our methods adequately. We discuss in this and the next section a few aspects of our procedure that have general relevance and that supplement the brief description of our methods in Chapter 1.

Dating

Our raw data include time series in different time units: annual, call date, monthly, and weekly series. Most of the annual figures are for "June" dates. These are the dates of the figures published in the *Annual Report* of the Comptroller of the Currency. In a few instances these fall in April, May, or July. In all other cases they lie somewhere in June, usually toward the end of the month. The annual and call date series refer to single dates. Some of our monthly and weekly series are averages of daily figures, while others refer to single dates.

Particular attention was paid to the dating of the series utilized in making the monthly estimates of vault cash and currency because there is a consistent daily as well as monthly seasonal characterizing these data. Elimination of the double seasonal affecting these items (see the next part of this section) made it possible to adjust to a common set of dates all reported figures, whatever their original dating, and to use them in constructing the final series.

Intraweekly variability presented no problem for deposit data, since the size of this daily movement is small relative to the monthly seasonal.[2] The questions with respect to dating were: (a) How distant from the most common date at midyear or at call dates could the report of a group of banks be dated and still be considered eligible for inclusion in the total? (b) What adjustments should be made if the dating of a potential monthly interpolator or monthly component differed from the call date or annual series to be interpolated? (c) What adjustment should be made if the dating of potential monthly interpolators or monthly components changed from time to time? The specific answers to these problems are detailed in the succeeding chapters. Here we simply note that the prevailing end-of-month dating of the monthly interpolators led us to produce estimates dated in the same way, though beginning 1947 (for currency and commercial bank deposits) we have shifted to the current Federal Reserve series of monthly averages of daily figures and have centered at midmonth other Federal Reserve data available only for single dates near the end of the month.

---

[2] See Chapter 13, footnotes 6 and 7.

Seasonal Adjustment

The daily and monthly variability of the vault cash and currency data has been mentioned as a compelling reason for seasonal adjustment of these items before their employment in making estimates. Our views on interpolation procedures, which are explained briefly below, also emphasize the importance of deseasonalizing data before interpolation. We therefore examined all our data—on vault cash, currency, and deposits—for evidence of seasonality and eliminated it whenever this seemed necessary.

We measured seasonal variations principally by the method of averaging ratios to a twelve-month moving total. Although our preference is for long seasonal periods, which permit random movements of a series to cancel one another, some of the series from which we eliminated the seasonal were available for brief periods only.

Since many of our series were in call date form, we had to adapt monthly seasonal analysis to the requirements of data reported irregularly during the course of a year.

For the vault cash and currency series, characterized by daily as well as monthly movements, we estimated simultaneously daily and monthly seasonal factors. Our procedure involved the following steps:

(1) The data to be used in estimating the seasonals were expressed as relative deviations from a trend.

(2) The deviations from the trend were cross-classified by the day of the week and the month of the year.

(3) The entries in each day-month cell were averaged.

(4) A multiple regression was computed from these averages, each weighted by the corresponding number of observations, relating the average value to a set of dummy variables representing the days of the week and the months of the year (i.e., a variable which is unity for Monday and zero for other days, another which is unity for Tuesday and zero for other days, and so on; a variable which is unity for January and zero for other months, another which is unity for February and zero for other months, and so on).

(5) The daily seasonal indexes are then given by the differences between the regression coefficients for the separate days and their average value.

(6) The monthly seasonal indexes are given by the differences between the regression coefficients for the separate months of the year and their average value.

The monthly and daily indexes can be combined to yield factors for January for each day of the week, for February for each day of the week, and so on (see the appendix to Chapter 12).

5. Interpolation Procedures

Interpolation to fill in gaps plays an important role in most estimates of comprehensive economic data. It plays a particularly important role in our monthly estimates because of the lack of uniformity of dates for which basic data are available: call dates that are deliberately varied from year to year and that may differ between national and other banks, between nonnational banks in one state and nonnational banks in another, and even between different groups of nonnational banks in the same state (e.g., loan and trust companies and other commercial banks; mutual savings banks and commercial banks). We thus had the choice of discarding most of the available data or of using interpolation devices, not only to fill in gaps, but also to shift dates so as to obtain components that could be added.

The problem of interpolation was so pervasive that a fresh analysis of the general problem of interpolation was undertaken by one of us and the development of a new method of interpolation emerged as a by-product. We refer the reader to the separate publication reporting that analysis[3] for a systematic discussion of interpolation procedures. We limit ourselves here to describing and naming the specific methods that we used, in order to be able to refer to them by name in subsequent chapters and so avoid tedious repetition.

The general idea of interpolation is that the value of a series, say X, is required for dates for which there are no direct observations but that are intermediate between dates for which there are observations. A subclass of interpolation procedures, which cover all those we actually used, is comprised by procedures that use information on X for only one preceding and one subsequent date (say dates t_0 and t_2) to estimate a value for a date for which a value is required, say t_1.[4]

---

[3] Milton Friedman, *The Interpolation of Time Series by Related Series,* New York, NBER, Technical Paper 16, 1962 (reprinted from *Journal of the American Statistical Association,* Dec. 1962, pp. 727–757).

[4] There may of course be several different dates for which a value is required between a particular pair of known values at t_0 and t_2.

Method L

The interpolated value of X at time t_1, say X_1^*, may be estimated solely from its values at times t_0 and t_2, say X_0 and X_2. This is the method of *Linear Interpolation,* which we shall call *Method L*.[5] The general formula is

$$X_1^* = X_0 + \frac{t_1 - t_0}{t_2 - t_0} (X_2 - X_0) \tag{1}$$

$$= \frac{t_2 - t_1}{t_2 - t_0} X_0 + \frac{t_1 - t_0}{t_2 - t_0} X_2 \tag{2}$$

or a weighted average of X_0 and X_2. As long as only the two known values of X are used, this method is perfectly general — a wide variety of particular forms being generated by appropriate transformations of the observations. For example, if X is in dollars, this is linear interpolation of dollar amounts; if X is the logarithm of dollar amounts, this is linear interpolation of the logarithms or logarithmic interpolation of the dollar amounts, and so on for other transformations. We shall refer to X_1^* sometimes as the interpolated value, sometimes as the *trend value* of X, where by *trend* we mean no more than a straight line connecting two successive values of X.

For many actual economic time series we may have information about the movement of X between t_0 and t_2 that is provided not by X_0 and X_2 only but by the date t_1. This information comes from the knowledge that series X is subject to a recurrent seasonal movement that we may be able to estimate from known data for other periods or other series. In such cases, Method L alone is inefficient. The better procedure is to eliminate the known or estimated seasonal and then apply Method L to the deseasonalized values of X_0 and X_2. If the value desired is a seasonally uncorrected value, the seasonal should then be added back.[6]

We followed this procedure throughout, deseasonalizing the original data, as noted in section 4 above, before applying any interpolation method. We accepted a deseasonalized series as our end-product and, therefore, did not add a seasonal back in. Unless otherwise stated, therefore, all series used in interpolation procedures will be assumed to be free from seasonal.

[5] In Technical Paper 16, this method was called Method M_0. We have changed the designation here for mnemonic reasons.
[6] See Technical Paper 16, section IV, pp. 22–23.

Method R

Generally we should like to do better than linear interpolation. In order to do so, we must have additional information that can tell us something about how X changes relative to its trend between t_0 and t_2. The most obvious source of such information is the movement of another series that we have reason to believe is related to X — in the sense that the two move together   and the value of which is known at t_0, t_1, and t_2. Let Y designate a hypothetical example of such a series. (We shall discuss later our method of choosing a related series.) Clearly, the more closely the movements of Y are related to the movements of X, the more useful Y will be for interpolation. If the relation is small or negligible, the use of a related series may simply introduce a random component without improving the accuracy of the interpolated value. Under such circumstances, we have preferred to use Method L.

Given a related series, we have five known observations: X_0, X_2, Y_0, Y_1, Y_2. We want to use the final three to improve the estimate by Method L of X_1. Let Y_1^* be a trend value for Y at time t_1, comparable to X_1^* for X. Let

$$u = \frac{X_1 - X_1^*}{X_1^*}, \tag{3}$$

$$v = \frac{Y_1 - Y_1^*}{Y_1^*}, \tag{4}$$

i.e., the percentage deviations of X and Y from their trend values at time t_1.[7] Then a special case of interpolation by related series, and the only one we used, is to estimate u from v. If we knew the correlation of u and v (ρ_{uv}) and the standard deviations of u and v (σ_u and σ_v), and if we could assume that the means of u and v are both zero (which is what our advance deseasonalization is intended to help assure), the correct estimate would clearly be as follows:

$$\text{Estimate of } u = \rho_{uv} \frac{\sigma_u}{\sigma_v} \cdot v = \beta \cdot v. \tag{5}$$

Needless to say, we cannot know ρ, or the σ's. We have, however, made empirical estimates of them, say r_{uv}, s_u, and s_v, and, maintaining

[7] In some ways it is more elegant to define u and v as simply equal to $X_1 - X_1^*$ and $Y_1 - Y_1^*$, which would make them percentage deviations if X and Y were logarithms of the original observations. The formulas above mix logarithmic and arithmetic operations. However, there is no logical fallacy involved in mixing the operations, the quantitative difference is negligible for most of our series, and the procedure described is slightly simpler computationally. At any rate, it is the procedure we used. See Technical Paper 16, pp. 4–5.

the assumption that the means of u and v are zero, have formed the estimate

$$u^* = r_{uv} \frac{s_u}{s_v} \cdot v = b \cdot v, \tag{6}$$

which gives us an estimate of X_1,

$$X_1^{**} = X_1^*(1 + u^*). \tag{7}$$

Note that Method L can be regarded as a special case of Method R for $b = 0$.

We may distinguish three special cases according to the estimates used for b and for v.

(i) *Method R_1*.[8] We find (or believe or assume) that ρ_{uv} is close to unity and that $\sigma_u = \sigma_v$; i.e., Y is a very near simulacrum of X. In that case, we take

$$u^* = v. \tag{8}$$

This is perhaps the method of interpolation that is most widely used in actual statistical work, although any evidence that ρ_{uv} is close to unity and σ_u is close to σ_v is almost invariably absent. When these assumptions are not satisfied, this method may easily yield an interpolated value that is less rather than more reliable than Method L.[9]

(ii) *Method R_2*.[10] We make statistical estimates of ρ_{uv}, σ_u, σ_v for a single related series Y, compute from these a value of b as an estimate of β, and use equation 6 directly.

(iii) *Method R_3*.[11] This is a variant that arises when there are a number of related series that seem equally good, but not all of which are available for all the dates for which we propose to make estimates. This situation arose in our work in the form of a group of states (e.g., New England states) which, when tested, revealed reasonably homogeneous behavior. For each date and state in the group for which we need to interpolate we should like to use the information for as many other states in the group as possible.

Let $v_1, v_2, \ldots, v_n$ designate the relative deviations from trend for the n states for which information is known and u, as usual, the value it is desired to estimate. In general, the optimum way to estimate u

---

[8] Designated M_1 in Technical Paper 16.
[9] See Technical Paper 16, section II, pp. 9–14.
[10] Designated M_b in Technical Paper 16.
[11] This would also be designated M_b in the notation of Technical Paper 16, since it differs from R_2 only in the way b is estimated.

would be from a multiple regression of u on $v_1, \ldots, v_n$. But this requires much more information than is available, and the gap cannot be easily filled by estimation. A special case, in which the multiple regression reduces to a much simpler expression, is obtained by assuming that, while the v's may have different standard deviations (σ_{v_i} for the "true" but unknown value, s_{v_i} for an estimate), the correlation between any v_i and any other and also between any v_i and u is the same. Designate this common correlation coefficient by ρ for the "true" value, and r for an estimate of it.

Each v_i separately gives an estimate of u, and under our assumptions the estimates are equally good (because the variance of the estimate is $\sigma_u^2(1 - \rho^2)$, and ρ is assumed the same for all the uv correlations). However, the mean or sum of these separate estimates of u will be a still better estimator. Let

$$v' = \frac{1}{n}\left(\frac{v_1}{\sigma_{v_1}} + \frac{v_2}{\sigma_{v_2}} + \cdots + \frac{v_n}{\sigma_{v_n}}\right)\sigma_u \qquad (9)$$

be the estimator, constructed as the mean of the separate estimates, except that the common correlation coefficient is omitted.[12] The standard deviation of v' is then given by [13]

$$\sigma_{v'} = \frac{\sigma_u}{n}\sqrt{n[1 + (n - 1)\rho]}, \qquad (10)$$

and the correlation between u and v' by [14]

$$\rho_{uv'} = \rho\frac{\sigma_u}{\sigma_{v'}} = \rho\left(\frac{n}{1 + (n - 1)\rho}\right)^{1/2}, \qquad (11)$$

---

[12] For this mean to be the optimum estimator requires the further assumption that, aside from the common component used to estimate u, the different v's are independent.

[13] Proof: From (9)

$$\sigma_{v'}^2 = \frac{\sigma_u^2}{n^2}\left[\sum_{i=1}^{n}\frac{\sigma_{v_i}^2}{\sigma_{v_i}^2} + \sum_{i=1}^{n}\sum_{\substack{j=1 \\ i \neq j}}^{n}\rho_{v_iv_j}\right]$$

$$= \frac{\sigma_u^2}{n^2}[n + n(n - 1)\rho].$$

[14] Proof: Treat u's and v's as having zero means; then

$$\rho_{uv'} = \frac{Euv'}{\sigma_u\sigma_{v'}} = \frac{1}{\sigma_u\sigma_{v'}} \cdot \frac{\sigma_u}{n}\left[\frac{Euv_1}{\sigma_{v_1}} + \frac{Euv_2}{\sigma_{v_2}} + \cdots + \frac{Euv_n}{\sigma_{v_n}}\right]$$

$$= \frac{1}{n\sigma_{v'}}[\rho\sigma_u + \rho\sigma_u \ldots] = \frac{n\sigma_u}{n\sigma_{v'}} \cdot \rho = \frac{\sigma_u}{\sigma_{v'}} \cdot \rho.$$

hence the estimate of u from v' by Method R_3 is

$$u^* = \left(\rho\, \frac{\sigma_u}{\sigma_{v'}} \right) \frac{\sigma_u}{\sigma_{v'}} \cdot v', \tag{12}$$

or, substituting for $\sigma_{v'}$ its value from (10) and for ρ its estimate r,

$$u^* = \frac{nr}{1 + (n-1)r} \cdot v'. \tag{13}$$

In many applications of Method R_3 we have assumed that the standard deviations are the same for the different states, both the states entering into v' and the state to which the u refers. In that special case, equation 13 still holds but v' becomes simply the mean of the v's.

It may be worth noting that Method R_3, when it is applicable, is a very effective way of combining a number of pieces of information, each of which separately is fairly unreliable. For example, suppose ρ is 0.5, which means that a particular v_i would reduce the variance of the estimate of u by one-quarter. For $n = 6$, $\rho_{uv'}$ will be .72, which would reduce the variance of u by one-half.

Method of Estimating Relevant Parameters

Given a series Y to be used as the related series in Method R, we need to estimate the value of b to use. This problem is difficult because it cannot be estimated from the correlation between X and Y and their standard deviations at dates at which both X and Y are available but only from the correlation between u and v and their standard deviations, and both u and v are never available. We have therefore had to use a number of surrogates for u and v.

1. DIFFERENT TIME PERIODS. Sometimes both X and Y are known for the same time intervals for which interpolation is required but for a different period.[15] In that case, we have constructed u's and v's for the two series for the period for which both are available and used the correlation and regression coefficient between them as estimates for the period when X is not available.

---

[15] For example, before 1934, bank records for nonmember banks do not segregate U.S. government deposits from other deposits. However, beginning 1934, FDIC reports show this segregation for insured nonmember banks at semiannual dates. See Chapter 17 for a description of the way in which we used the relationships for the period after 1934 to estimate those for the period before.

2. DIFFERENT GEOGRAPHIC UNITS. The most extensive example of the use of different units is in connection with Method R_3. For example, we know mutual savings deposits in all relevant states for a June date each year but for only some states for inter-June dates. For those stretches of dates and states for which we have the requisite information we computed v's by expressing the inter-June values as relative deviations from trend values on a linear trend connecting two successive June values. We then correlated these v's for different states and computed their standard deviations. To estimate the common ρ that is required for Method R_3 we averaged the r's for the states that we regard as in the same group.[16]

3. DIFFERENT SERIES. Sometimes we have used the relation between two different series. For example, we used the relation between demand deposits less duplications (see section 7, below, for the definition) in *member* banks in one set of states and another set to estimate the value of b for interpolating demand deposits less duplications in *nonmember* banks in one of these sets of states from known values for nonmember banks in other states.

4. DIFFERENT TIME INTERVALS. This has been perhaps our most frequent recourse. For example, we have two series at June dates, and only one at inter-June dates. To estimate the b to use we have constructed u's and v's by treating Junes separated by two years as corresponding to the dates t_0 and t_2 and the intermediate June as corresponding to t_1. We have then estimated the correlations and standard deviations for these hypothetical u's and v's and regarded them as applying to the inter-June dates.

Choice of Related Series

Generally we have tested alternative series as possible interpolators. We have estimated r_{uv} for each by one of the methods just listed, the same method of course for all of the alternatives considered. We have selected the series which gave the highest r as the best of the alternatives.

---

[16] The average was constructed by first converting the r's to Fisher's Z [$Z = \frac{1}{2}$ $\{\log_e (1 + r) - \log_e (1 - r)\}$, averaging the Z's, and then transforming back to r.

If that r was very high and the standard deviations of u and v seemed reasonably close, we have used Method R_1. If that r was very low and we were not in a position to use Method R_3, we have preferred to use Method L. We did not have a single numerical criterion for this choice, but it is probably fair to say that we tended to prefer Method L to Method R_2 if the indicated correlation was less than 0.5. One of the findings that surprised us most was how difficult it is to obtain a related series giving a correlation as high as 0.5. The contrary impression of statistical workers, reflected in their widespread use of Method R_1, derives, we believe, from their tendency to judge the correlation by looking at X and Y for dates when both are known rather than looking at counterparts to u and v.

Method S

Step Method Interpolation, which we shall designate *Method S,* is a device for interpolating by steps between values of X known at times t_0 and t_1 to obtain desired values of X at intervening time units. Under this method, if an even number of time units intervenes between t_0 and t_1, the value of X at t_0 is carried forward halfway and the value for X at t_1 is carried backward halfway. If the number of time units intervening between t_0 and t_1 is odd, all but the center unit are assigned the nearer of the two known values and the center one is made the average of the two known values.

An example of the one use we made of Method S in this volume is given in Chapter 11, where we applied it to convert a call date series into a monthly series. We proceeded as follows. The number of days intervening between a given call date and the following one was divided in half. This half-way date usually fell in the month following the given call date. The number of days in the month up to this half-way date was then expressed as a fraction of the total number of days in that month, the balance as 1.00 minus that fraction. For example, there are call dates on January 7 and April 1, 1867. The midpoint date is February 17.5, 1867. Since there are twenty-eight days in the month, 17.5 represents 0.625, the balance of 10.5 days, 0.375. The value for February was then taken to be 0.625 of the January call date figure plus 0.375 of the April call date figure. The months for which no figures were derived as just described were assigned the value of the nearest call date. In the above example, the value for March was the call date figure for April.

6. Reliability of the Estimates

Errors in our estimates arise from two major sources: errors in the original data underlying the estimates; and the interpolation and other devices that we have adopted to fill in gaps and correct other defects of coverage in the original data. One indication of the seriousness of the second source of error for our final call date and monthly estimates is the fraction of the final total derived from original data by interpolation according to Method L and according to Method R. Thus at the end of each of the following chapters, we give a summary table reporting the average fractions of each component of our estimates in these categories. These tables, a by-product of our estimates, provide a convenient summary of their structure, and the reader may find it helpful to consult them first, as a guide to the detailed explanation in the body of each chapter.

The fraction shown as interpolated is a substantial overestimate since it applies not to every date but only to those dates for which interpolation is required. For example, there are generally five or six call dates a year before 1923 (four, thereafter). Hence, in proceeding from call date to monthly estimates, additional information is required for roughly every other month before 1923 and for two months in each quarter thereafter. When this additional information is derived by interpolation, we have recorded the corresponding percentage of the estimate as interpolated in the reliability tables. The only offset to this overstatement is that our bench-mark data for June dates from 1896 on are treated as embodying no interpolation, whereas they may at times have involved some. But this is surely a minor offset.

As this remark indicates, the figures with the least error are almost surely the estimates for June each year. The maximum error is in the estimated change from one time unit to another between June dates. Our methods of interpolation have a bias in this respect. Undoubtedly they smooth the pattern of change during the year, so that the amplitude of actual inter-June movements is larger than of our estimated movements. This bias is in the absolute magnitude (absolute deviation or standard deviation) of the movements. Our methods have been designed to avoid as far as possible any bias in the algebraic average value of the

inter-June movements (this is assured by our consistent use of deviations from June-to-June trends as the magnitude to be estimated). The
bias in amplitude is a price that must be paid to minimize the fraction
of the reported amplitude that is spurious; the bias is a result of our
ignorance. For example, straight-line interpolation, on which we rely
when our information on movements between dates for which we have
evidence is inadequate, reduces the amplitude of reported figures around
the trend between the dates for which we have estimates to zero, which
is surely less than the actual amplitude.

It is difficult to say much that is illuminating about the first source of
error—the errors in the original data underlying the estimates. Several
things are clear, however. First, the final estimates are almost always the
sum of a very large number of components, since the basic data are generally for individual banks, summed into totals for all national banks
or all member banks, or all banks in a particular state and then summed
over states. This means that there is much room for the law of large
numbers to operate: the error in the total in relative terms must be very
much smaller than any errors in the individual components that have a
measure of statistical independence. Second, many of the errors in the
individual components are independent; for example, simple reporting
errors by individual banks, or classification errors by authorities in different states. Third, the reporting units that have compiled the data
have done so for their own business purposes and hence have a strong
interest in making them accurate. Indeed, the reason we are so skeptical
of the breakdown of deposits between demand and time deposits before
1914 is precisely that this condition does not hold for these data prior
to that year.

These three factors together lead us to believe that the aggregate
figures have negligible residual errors arising simply from error in record-
ing or reporting the figures summed. The significant errors in the aggregate reported figures must arise from errors that are not subject to cancellation: incompleteness of coverage of either reporting units or items
reported, misclassifications for our purpose common to many units reporting (e.g., inclusion of items in process of collection with vault cash),
errors in printing of final aggregates we have used, etc. Needless to say,
an effort has been made to eliminate any known sources of error of this
kind. But some unquestionably remain.

The nature of this source of error suggests that it affects the level of the estimates much more than the year-to-year, call-date-to-call-date, or month-to-month movements, since errors of this type are likely to have high serial correlation.

7. Definitions

These definitions are for our vault cash and currency estimates through 1942 and our deposit estimates through 1945, as originally constructed by us. In combining the estimates to obtain the consolidated monetary totals shown in Chapter 1, the definitions listed below were altered to make them applicable to the coverage of each consolidated total. For example, in Part Three we treat mutual savings bank vault cash as a component of bank vault cash and do not include it in currency held by the public. In Chapter 1, however, for the consolidated monetary totals restricted to commercial banks (Table 1, columns 8 and 9), mutual savings banks are treated as part of the public, and hence their vault cash is included in the public's currency holdings. For the consolidated monetary total covering commercial banks, mutual savings banks, and the Postal Savings System, vault cash holdings of all three types of institutions are excluded from the public's currency holdings (Table 1, column 11). The reader should also consult Chapter 1 for variations in the definitions listed below in years subsequent to 1945 covered by Federal Reserve estimates.

The public includes individuals, business firms other than banks, municipalities, states, and federal government agencies other than the Treasury Department in Washington, D.C., and the mints and assay offices in the country. For currency estimates the U.S. public includes the public and banks in foreign countries that own U.S. currency. For deposit estimates the U.S. public includes the public of foreign countries with deposits at banks located in the continental United States. Banks in the U.S. possessions and mutual savings banks in the United States are treated as banks, not as part of the public, for the currency estimates, but as part of the public for deposit estimates.

Government refers to the Treasury Department in Washington, D.C., and the mints and assay offices in the country as well as other departments, bureaus, and officials of the United States. It does not include government corporations and credit agencies.

All banks include all commercial and mutual savings banks.

Commercial banks include banks operating under commercial bank, trust company, or stock savings bank charters; cash depositories; private banks engaged in deposit banking; and Morris Plan and industrial banks operating under general banking codes. Beginning in 1920 foreign branches of commercial banks are excluded.

Mutual savings banks include all savings banks organized without stock, managed by a board of trustees, with earnings distributed among depositors as dividends (usually limited by law to a prescribed maximum), and surplus carried to the guaranty fund.

National banks are commercial banks incorporated under federal law operating under the supervision of the United States Comptroller of the Currency. All national banks in the continental United States are required by law to be members of the Federal Reserve System and of the Federal Deposit Insurance Corporation.

Nonnational banks are commercial banks chartered under state laws and subject to state supervision, and unincorporated (private) banks. Since the start of the Federal Reserve System, nonnational banks include member and nonmember commercial banks without national charters.

Member banks of the Federal Reserve System include national banks in the continental United States and state member banks.

State member banks are commercial banks chartered under state laws —together with a few mutual savings banks—that have been admitted to membership in the Federal Reserve System upon complying with certain prescribed conditions. All state member banks are required to be members of the FDIC and are subject to both federal and state supervision.

Nonmember banks are commercial banks that are not members of the Federal Reserve System. They include *insured nonmember banks,* which have been admitted to Federal deposit insurance upon meeting certain prescribed conditions, and *noninsured nonmember banks.*

General depositaries of government funds, formerly national banks only, now include insured domestic banks and insular territorial and foreign banks in which agents of the federal government deposit funds collected.

Special depositaries of government funds include qualified incorporated banks or trust companies and occasionally mutual savings banks or dealers in government securities, authorized by the Secretary of the Treasury to purchase government securities for their own or their customers' accounts and make payment by crediting the amount of the subscription to special government accounts.

Currency in circulation comprises currency held by the public and bank vault cash. It excludes currency held by the Treasury and, since 1914, by Federal Reserve Banks.

Currency held by the public comprises all kinds of publicly held bank, Federal Reserve Bank, or Treasury issues of coin or paper money, plus any such currency that has been carried abroad, lost, or destroyed.

Bank vault cash excludes the reporting national banks' *own* bank notes and includes all other kinds of U.S. currency, metallic and paper, issued by all banks, Federal Reserve Banks, and the Treasury—whether or not considered part of legal reserves—either held on the premises of member and nonmember banks or in transit to or from Federal Reserve Banks. It includes cash held by all commercial banks in the United States and its possessions and also in all mutual savings banks.

Government balances include government deposits at Federal Reserve Banks and their branches and at commercial and mutual savings banks and Treasury cash.

Treasury cash includes currency assets of the Treasury Department in Washington, D.C., and the mints and assay offices in the country, exclusive of the reserve held against gold and silver certificates, cash held for Federal Reserve Banks, and the gold redemption fund for Federal Reserve notes.

Total deposits adjusted is the sum of demand deposits adjusted and time deposits adjusted at commercial banks.

Demand deposits adjusted include all demand deposit items at commercial banks, except interbank demand deposits and U.S. government demand deposits, less cash items in process of collection.

Time deposits adjusted include all time deposit items at commercial banks except interbank time deposits, postal savings redeposited in banks, and U.S. government time deposits. (For a list of demand and time deposit items and cash items in process of collection, see *All-Bank Statistics, 1896–1955*, pp. 87–88.)

Demand deposits less duplications include all demand deposit items at commercial banks except interbank demand deposits and cash items in process of collection.

11

ANNUAL, SEMIANNUAL, AND QUARTERLY ESTIMATES, 1867–1907

TABLE 1 gives annual estimates from 1867 through 1874 and 1882 through 1906 and semiannual estimates from 1875 through 1881. The figures are totals of reported national bank data and estimates for non-national banks. The annual nonnational commercial bank estimates, January 1867–February 1875, were constructed by James K. Kindahl. The mutual savings bank estimates for those years were constructed by us. The semiannual and annual nonnational commercial and mutual savings bank estimates for August 1875 to June 1895 were constructed by David Fand.[1] The annual figures, 1896–1906, in Table 1 are sums of national bank data and nonnational commercial bank and mutual savings bank estimates constructed by the Federal Reserve.[2]

Section 1 describes Kindahl's estimates, the national bank data from the Comptroller of the Currency's annual reports that we combined with them, and mutual savings bank estimates we constructed. Fand's estimates, and the corresponding national bank figures are described in section 2. Finally, section 3 gives a new series of quarterly estimates that we interpolated between the annual and semiannual figures of currency and commercial bank deposits held by the public in Table 1, 1867–1907.

[1] James K. Kindahl, "The Period of the Resumption in the United States, 1865–1879," unpublished Ph.D. dissertation, University of Chicago, 1958, and David Fand, "Estimates of Deposits and Vault Cash in the Nonnational Banks in the Post-Civil War Period in the United States," unpublished Ph.D. dissertation, University of Chicago, 1954.

[2] *All-Bank Statistics, United States, 1896–1955,* Board of Governors of the Federal Reserve System, Washington, D.C., 1959.

1. Annual Estimates, January 1867–February 1875

Nonnational Commercial Bank Deposits and Vault Cash

Kindahl's basic source for estimating nonnational bank deposits is the voluminous bank tax assessment lists, by internal revenue districts, in the National Archives. The lists show the amount of taxes levied on the average deposits at each bank under a Civil War tax statute. Kindahl drew a random sample of internal revenue districts outside New York City. For each district in the sample he included all listed banks that reported average deposits in January 1868, 1870, and 1872 and in the six months ending May 31, 1874, 1875, and 1876. Capital stock savings banks were kept separate from all other commercial banks in the sample. Kindahl multiplied the simple mean of the deposits of all banks of each class in the sample at each date by the number of corresponding banks in the sample area corrected for estimated nonreporting banks. Estimated deposits in the sample area were then converted into an estimate for all banks of each class by multiplying by the ratio of the total number of banks other than New York City banks listed in bank almanacs to the number of banks in the sample. New York City deposits for each class of banks were estimated separately and added to the estimates for banks outside New York City.

In order to correct for understatement of true deposits and for deposits which were taxed but are not considered a part of the money stock, i.e., float and interbank deposits, Kindahl applied to his estimated totals for stock savings and other commercial banks at the sample dates the ratio of Fand's estimate of deposits to his own estimate at the date in 1876 when the two overlapped. Fand's estimate, described in section 2 of this chapter, is corrected for understatement of deposits and refers to deposits held by the public less float.

For years not covered by his samples (1869 and 1871), Kindahl interpolated by Method R_1, using as the related series published tax receipts reported by the Commissioner of Internal Revenue. For 1873 he used Method L, because reported tax receipts for 1873 are faulty. For 1867 he multiplied reported tax receipts by the ratio of deposits to tax receipts for 1868.

The deposit estimates served as the base for the vault cash estimates.

Kindahl divided his deposit estimates by the average of the ratios of Fand's estimates of deposits to vault cash for 1875–79.

All Commercial Bank Deposits, All Bank Vault Cash, and Currency Held by the Public

We treated Kindahl's estimates as dated at the end of January for 1867–72, and the end of February for 1873–75, and added to his deposit estimates adjusted national bank deposits at call dates closest to the end of those months. For this period adjusted deposits of national banks are the sums of individual deposits and dividends unpaid, less checks and other cash items and clearinghouse exchanges.

To Kindahl's nonnational bank vault cash estimates we added national bank and estimated mutual savings bank vault cash. National bank vault cash is a sum of national bank notes of other banks, state bank notes (1867–68), fractional currency, specie, legal tender and compound interest notes, 3 per cent certificates, and U.S. certificates of deposit.[3] To estimate mutual savings bank vault cash, we first expressed vault cash and deposits in the mutual savings banks of New York and Massachusetts [4] in 1876 as percentages of Fand's vault cash and deposit estimates for all mutual savings banks in that year. We divided the vault cash percentage by the deposit percentage to obtain a factor by which we reduced corresponding percentages for deposits, 1867–75. The resulting estimates of the percentage of total mutual savings bank vault cash in the mutual savings banks of the two states ranged between 53 and 59 per cent. The reciprocal of these percentages multiplied by the reported figures for vault cash in the two states constitutes our estimates of vault cash in all mutual savings banks.

Currency held by the public is the difference between estimated currency outside the Treasury and vault cash in all banks. The derivation of currency outside the Treasury is described in Chapter 12, section 1.

Mutual Savings Bank Deposits

Published end-of-year figures of deposits at savings banks by states and sometimes by cities are available for this period.[5] We omitted data

[3] For a description of these currency issues, see A Monetary History, p. 25.

[4] See New York State Banking Department, Annual Report Relative to Savings Banks and Trust Companies, and Massachusetts Savings Bank Commissioners, Annual Report.

[5] Emerson W. Keyes, A History of Savings Banks in the United States, New York, 1878, table facing p. 532.

for stock savings banks—in California; Iowa; Chicago; and Washington, D.C.—and interpolated by Method L sums of deposits at mutual savings banks in the remaining states to the end-of-month dates in Table 1.

2. Semiannual and Annual Estimates, 1875–95

Nonnational Commercial and Mutual Savings Bank
Deposits and Vault Cash

Fand's basic source for his semiannual estimates is the same as Kindahl's, the assessment data. However, he did not have to go back to the original lists because the data were published for these years—but not for earlier years—in the annual reports of the Commissioner of Internal Revenue. There are no data for years after 1882 because the taxes on bank capital and deposits were eliminated. For his annual estimates Fand also used the Comptroller of the Currency's annual compilations of nonnational bank balance sheet data. The provisional estimates Fand constructed from the data in each source were then reworked to reconcile them with each other during the years in which they overlapped and with the Federal Reserve estimates available beginning 1896. His final estimates include breakdowns for five classes of banks: incorporated state commercial banks, trust companies, private banks, capital stock savings banks, and mutual savings banks, in four regions: New England, Middle States, South, and West.

The initial semiannual provisional estimates for 1875–82 were based on average deposits at stock and mutual savings banks and average taxable deposits at all other commercial banks. "Average taxable deposits" was defined as total deposits less clearinghouse exchanges. Since Fand wanted to measure individual deposits less float, he needed an estimate of interbank balances and cash items to deduct from taxable deposits. For his estimate he used nonnational bank balance sheet data in the Comptroller's reports. He assumed that no correction was necessary for the savings bank data.

He next estimated that, as a reflection of the combined influence of underreporting and understatement of tax liabilities, incorporated commercial bank assessed deposits were understated by 5 per cent and private bank assessed deposits by 10 per cent. The savings bank data again seemed to him free of those defects. Fand then constructed provisional vault cash estimates from the corrected assessed deposit data and the average deposit data, using the ratio of vault cash to deposits for each class of banks in the Comptroller's balance sheet data.

The initial, annual provisional estimates of deposits less float and vault cash in the nonnational banks, 1882–96, were derived from the Comptroller's data. Fand assumed that the major estimating errors in this source were restricted to the omission of data from excluded states. For 1882 he also constructed annual estimates from the data of the Commissioner of Internal Revenue and observed differences between the two sets of estimates for the year that varied from region to region and from one class of banks to another. Since the Comptroller's data beginning 1887 are generally regarded as more reliable than for earlier years, Fand also extrapolated the 1887–96 trends backwards to 1882 to construct estimates to link up with the semiannual estimates ending in 1881. He used varied procedures in revising the estimates for different classes of banks and for different regions, 1882–86, in accordance with his interpretation of the character of the defects in the Comptroller's data.

For 1896 Fand compared the estimates derived from the Comptroller's data with the estimates in *All-Bank Statistics*. To achieve consistency with the levels of the latter, he raised or lowered his provisional semiannual and annual estimates, by region and by class of banks, 1875–95, by the ratios of the provisional to the Federal Reserve estimates in 1896.

All Commercial Bank Deposits, All-Bank Vault Cash, and Currency Held by the Public

Fand's semiannual estimates were dated end of February and end of August, his annual estimates, June 30. As for the earlier period, we obtained adjusted deposits at national banks at call dates closest to the end of those months. For the semiannual dates we made a rough seasonal correction of the national bank deposit figures, lowering the February and raising the August levels. We simultaneously adjusted national bank vault cash at all call dates, 1874–1917, for daily and monthly seasonal changes (see Chapter 12, section 2, for a description of the adjustment). The seasonally adjusted call date figures were then interpolated to monthly figures by Method S (see Chapter 10, section 5, for a description of monthly interpolation of call date figures by the step method). The monthly national bank vault cash figures at the dates in Table 1 were added to the nonnational commercial and mutual savings bank vault cash estimates and the total subtracted from currency outside the Treasury. First the published data for currency outside the Treasury, available at June 30 dates before 1878 and monthly beginning June 30, 1878, were corrected for discontinuities (see Chapter 12, section 1, for a description of these corrections) and then the end-of-June data before 1878, shifted by Method L to the semiannual dates 1875–78. A rough seasonal correction was applied to residual currency held by the public, August 1878–August 1881.

Table 20 shows the national and nonnational deposit and vault cash estimates and their totals for the period 1867–95, discussed above, and also the Federal Reserve annual estimates, 1896–1906. For a description of the Federal Reserve nonnational bank estimates, the reader is referred to Chapter 8. The Federal Reserve June nonnational bank deposit estimates were seasonally adjusted by us. The national bank deposit data for 1896–1906 in Table 20 are from the Comptroller of the Currency at call dates closest to June 30. We corrected the national bank call date vault cash data for daily and monthly seasonals, as described above, and then interpolated to June dates where necessary, by Method S.

3. Quarterly Estimates of Currency Held by the Public and Commercial Bank Deposits, 1867–1907

It was feasible to construct quarterly estimates for 1867–1907 to supplement the annual and semiannual estimates shown in Table 1 because for national banks adjusted deposits and vault cash are available at call dates for the whole of the period, and data for currency outside the Treasury are available monthly from June 1878 on. The quarterly estimates are dated end of February, May, August, and November. However, they are not identical with the underlying estimates in Table 1 for February and August before 1882 or for May 1907, the initial monthly date in Table 1. The reason for the small differences is that the quarterly estimates are a mixture of quarterly averages of monthly estimates and straight-line interpolations.

We converted deseasonalized national bank call date figures to quar-

TABLE 20

Currency Held by the Public, Adjusted Deposits, and Related Series, Annually and Semiannually, 1867–1906

(seasonally adjusted, in billions of dollars)

Date	Currency Held by the Public[a] (1)	Adjusted Deposits			Money Stock[a] (5)	Currency Outside Treasury (6)	Vault Cash			
		All Commercial Banks[a] (2)	National Banks (3)	Non-national Banks (4)			All Banks (7)	National Banks (8)	Non-national Banks (9)	Mutual Savings Banks (10)
1867 Jan.	.585	.729	.457	.271	1.314	.852	.267	.227	.033	.007
1868 Jan.	.531	.713	.425	.288	1.244	.775	.244	.202	.035	.007
1869 Jan.	.529	.735	.426	.310	1.264	.761	.232	.187	.038	.007
1870 Jan.	.510	.779	.437	.342	1.289	.758	.248	.198	.042	.008
1871 Jan.	.546	.844	.420	.424	1.390	.776	.230	.168	.052	.010
1872 Jan.	.542	1.041	.470	.571	1.583	.782	.240	.160	.069	.011
1873 Feb.	.552	1.070	.515	.556	1.622	.783	.231	.153	.067	.011
1874 Feb.	.526	1.066	.524	.542	1.592	.801	.275	.195	.064	.016
1875 Feb.	.544	1.151	.556	.594	1.695	.783	.239	.154	.070	.014
Aug.	.510	1.185	.578	.607	1.695	.767	.257	.167	.074	.015
1876 Feb.	.516	1.158	.556	.602	1.674	.758	.242	.156	.071	.015
Aug.	.506	1.152	.553	.599	1.658	.751	.245	.160	.071	.015
1877 Feb.	.514	1.166	.574	.592	1.680	.757	.243	.158	.071	.014
Aug.	.525	1.092	.531	.561	1.617	.759	.234	.150	.071	.013
1878 Feb.	.526	1.053	.530	.523	1.579	.763	.237	.155	.069	.012
Aug.	.529	1.026	.527	.499	1.555	.767	.238	.152	.074	.012
1879 Feb.	.520	1.023	.530	.493	1.543	.752	.232	.152	.069	.011
Aug.	.574	1.201	.684	.517	1.775	.815	.241	.157	.076	.008

1880 Feb.	.624	1.295	.687	.608	1.919	.897	.273	.174	.086	.012
Aug.	.662	1.380	.729	.651	2.042	.972	.310	.198	.099	.013
1881 Feb.	.714	1.545	.793	.752	2.259	1.005	.291	.184	.096	.012
Aug.	.797	1.702	.854	.848	2.499	1.113	.316	.208	.096	.012
1882 June	.807	1.787	.894	.893	2.594	1.124	.317	.208	.097	.012
1883	.856	1.955	.943	1.012	2.811	1.184	.328	.223	.094	.012
1884	.842	1.922	.900	1.025	2.764	1.189	.347	.216	.120	.011
1885	.780	2.057	.982	1.075	2.837	1.233	.453	.292	.146	.015
1886	.753	2.330	1.059	1.271	3.083	1.195	.442	.265	.163	.014
1887	.793	2.486	1.142	1.344	3.279	1.257	.464	.278	.174	.012
1888	.821	2.541	1.209	1.332	3.362	1.309	.488	.298	.175	.015
1889	.819	2.724	1.330	1.394	3.543	1.318	.499	.314	.170	.016
1890	.888	3.020	1.422	1.598	3.908	1.366	.478	.297	.166	.015
1891	.921	3.098	1.443	1.655	4.019	1.433	.512	.325	.173	.014
1892	.929	3.541	1.650	1.891	4.470	1.529	.600	.382	.202	.016
1893	.985	3.203	1.436	1.767	4.188	1.514	.529	.308	.204	.017
1894	.883	3.341	1.602	1.739	4.224	1.569	.686	.460	.208	.018
1895	.881	3.596	1.642	1.954	4.477	1.502	.621	.392	.211	.018
1896	.832	3.434	1.582	1.852	4.266	1.399	.567	.360	.189	.018
1897	.873	3.609	1.671	1.938	4.482	1.524	.651	.433	.201	.017
1898	1.017	4.120	1.914	2.206	5.137	1.721	.704	.482	.206	.017
1899	1.068	4.966	2.301	2.665	6.034	1.806	.738	.503	.218	.017
1900	1.191	5.187	2.279	2.908	6.378	1.954	.763	.520	.225	.018
1901	1.232	6.104	2.617	3.487	7.336	2.070	.838	.560	.261	.017
1902	1.280	6.729	2.831	3.898	8.009	2.143	.863	.585	.262	.016
1903	1.399	7.123	2.952	4.171	8.522	2.257	.858	.561	.281	.016
1904	1.404	7.580	3.140	4.440	8.984	2.406	1.002	.661	.324	.017
1905	1.476	8.596	3.488	5.108	10.072	2.470	.994	.656	.321	.017
1906	1.586	9.278	3.711	5.567	10.864	2.628	1.042	.672	.354	.016

terly figures by averaging the monthly figures interpolated by Method S
between the call dates and interpolated the nonnational bank annual or
semiannual estimates by Method L to the quarterly dates listed. The
seasonal adjustment of the national bank call date figures for adjusted
deposits was for monthly movements alone, for vault cash the adjustment was for daily and monthly movements. We also interpolated currency outside the Treasury, after correction for discontinuities, by

---

Notes to Table 20 (concluded)

[a]For the reason that these columns differ from the columns with the
corresponding headings in Table 1, see the source notes to Table 1,
cols. 1, 3, and 4.

Source, by Column

1. Col. 6 minus col. 7.
2. Col. 3 plus col. 4, sum of unrounded figures.
3. U. S. Comptroller of the Currency, *Annual Report,* 1918, Vol.
2, pp. 248–269; call dates closest to end of months listed. Sums of
individual deposits and dividends unpaid, less checks and other cash
items and clearinghouse exchanges, 1875–81, were seasonally adjusted by us.
4. *Jan. 1867–Feb. 1875,* James K. Kindahl, "The Period of the
Resumption in the United States, 1865–1879," unpublished Ph.D.
dissertation, University of Chicago, 1958. *Aug. 1875–June 1895,*
David Fand, "Estimates of Deposits and Vault Cash in the Nonnational
Banks in the Post–Civil War Period in the United States," unpublished Ph.D. dissertation, University of Chicago, 1954. Seasonally adjusted by us, 1875–81. *June 1896–June 1906, All-Bank Statistics,
United States, 1896–1955,* Board of Governors of the Federal Reserve
System, Washington, D.C., 1959, pp. 43–44; sums of "other demand"
and "other time" deposits, less cash items in process of collection,
were seasonally adjusted by us.
5. Col. 1 plus col. 2.
6. See Chap. 12, section 1, for the derivation of this column.
7. Col. 8 plus col. 9 plus col. 10.
8. Same as for col. 3. Sums of national bank notes of other banks,
state bank notes (1867–68), specie, and U. S. currency issues. For
1874–1906, original call date figures were corrected for intraweekly
and monthly seasonal changes; seasonally adjusted call date figures
were then interpolated by the step method to monthly figures listed
in this table.
9. Same as for col. 4, except that the *All-Bank Statistics,* p. 43,
series is "currency and coin."
10. *Jan. 1867–Feb. 1875,* estimated by us (see Chap. 11, section 1);
thereafter, same as for col. 4, except that the *All-Bank Statistics,*
p. 47, series is "currency and coin."

Method L before 1878. Thereafter, we averaged the seasonally adjusted monthly data for each quarter.

Table 21 shows the quarterly estimates for adjusted deposits and vault cash for national, nonnational, and mutual savings banks and the estimates of currency held by the public derived by subtracting vault cash at all banks from currency outside the Treasury. It also shows the money stock totals obtained by summing currency held by the public and adjusted deposits. The estimates are charted in Chart 6.

For deposits, direct evidence on quarter-to-quarter movements within a year is available only for national banks; for other banks such movements are simply assumed to be steady. However, national banks throughout this period accounted for roughly half of all deposits, so the quarter-to-quarter variability, while no doubt understated, nonetheless has a very large component that is based on reported, not constructed, evidence.

For currency, the only component the movements of which are primarily constructed is vault cash in nonnational banks. This generally amounts to less than a third of total vault cash, while vault cash amounts to less than a third of total currency outside the Treasury. Hence the bulk of the recorded quarterly movements in currency held by the public is based on reported data.

TABLE 21

Currency Held by the Public, Adjusted Deposits, and Related Series, Quarterly, 1867–1907

(seasonally adjusted, in billions of dollars)

Year and Quarter	Currency Held by the Public[a] (1)	Adjusted Deposits			Money Stock[a] (5)	Currency Outside Treasury (6)	Vault Cash		
		All Commercial Banks[a] (2)	National Banks (3)	Nonnational Banks (4)			All Banks (7)	National Banks (8)	Nonnational and Mutual Savings Banks (9)
1867 I	.590	.710	.438	.272	1.300	.846	.256	.216	.040
II	.582	.694	.417	.277	1.276	.826	.244	.204	.040
III	.570	.692	.411	.281	1.262	.807	.237	.196	.041
IV	.548	.699	.414	.285	1.247	.788	.240	.199	.041
1868 I	.540	.710	.420	.290	1.250	.774	.234	.193	.041
II	.536	.733	.438	.295	1.269	.770	.234	.192	.042
III	.530	.748	.447	.301	1.278	.767	.237	.194	.043
IV	.529	.734	.428	.306	1.263	.763	.234	.190	.044
1869 I	.543	.721	.408	.313	1.264	.761	.218	.173	.045
II	.554	.727	.406	.321	1.281	.760	.206	.159	.047
III	.541	.739	.410	.329	1.280	.759	.218	.170	.048
IV	.525	.765	.428	.337	1.290	.759	.234	.185	.049
1870 I	.521	.784	.435	.349	1.305	.759	.238	.187	.051
II	.530	.811	.442	.369	1.341	.764	.234	.180	.054
III	.541	.813	.423	.390	1.354	.768	.227	.170	.057
IV	.547	.827	.417	.410	1.374	.773	.226	.166	.060

344

1871 I	.539	.884	.448	.436	1.423	.776	.237	.174	.063
II	.523	.951	.478	.473	1.474	.778	.255	.187	.068
III	.530	1.000	.490	.510	1.530	.779	.249	.177	.072
IV	.537	1.025	.479	.546	1.562	.781	.244	.167	.077
1872 I	.539	1.062	.492	.570	1.601	.782	.243	.163	.080
II	.534	1.074	.508	.566	1.608	.782	.248	.169	.079
III	.547	1.062	.499	.563	1.609	.783	.236	.158	.078
IV	.547	1.054	.495	.559	1.601	.783	.236	.158	.078
1873 I	.550	1.070	.514	.556	1.620	.783	.233	.156	.077
II	.543	1.078	.526	.552	1.621	.787	.244	.166	.078
III	.556	1.076	.527	.549	1.632	.792	.236	.157	.079
IV	.541	1.032	.486	.546	1.573	.797	.256	.177	.079
1874 I	.528	1.063	.521	.542	1.591	.801	.273	.193	.080
II	.520	1.100	.545	.555	1.620	.797	.277	.196	.081
III	.530	1.126	.558	.568	1.656	.792	.262	.180	.082
IV	.537	1.143	.562	.581	1.680	.787	.250	.167	.083
1875 I	.541	1.158	.564	.594	1.699	.783	.242	.158	.084
II	.522	1.177	.577	.600	1.699	.775	.253	.166	.087
III	.511	1.192	.585	.607	1.703	.767	.256	.166	.090
IV	.527	1.159	.554	.605	1.686	.763	.236	.148	.088
1876 I	.519	1.158	.556	.602	1.677	.758	.239	.153	.086
II	.511	1.153	.553	.600	1.664	.754	.243	.157	.086
III	.505	1.156	.557	.599	1.661	.751	.246	.161	.085
IV	.515	1.150	.555	.595	1.665	.754	.239	.154	.085
1877 I	.513	1.154	.562	.592	1.667	.757	.244	.159	.085
II	.513	1.135	.559	.576	1.648	.758	.245	.160	.085
III	.525	1.107	.546	.561	1.632	.759	.234	.150	.084
IV	.528	1.074	.532	.542	1.602	.761	.233	.150	.083
1878 I	.527	1.055	.532	.523	1.582	.763	.236	.154	.082
II	.534	1.034	.523	.511	1.568	.771	.237	.153	.084
III	.526	1.028	.529	.499	1.554	.765	.239	.153	.086
IV	.513	1.031	.535	.496	1.544	.753	.240	.157	.083

(continued)

TABLE 21 (continued)

Year and Quarter	Currency Held by the Public^a (1)	Adjusted Deposits			Money Stock^a (5)	Currency Outside Treasury (6)	Vault Cash		
		All Commercial Banks^a (2)	National Banks (3)	Nonnational Banks (4)			All Banks (7)	National Banks (8)	Nonnational and Mutual Savings Banks (9)
1879 I	.532	1.025	.532	.493	1.557	.764	.232	.152	.080
II	.550	1.051	.546	.505	1.601	.780	.230	.148	.082
III	.576	1.102	.585	.517	1.678	.817	.241	.157	.084
IV	.606	1.193	.630	.563	1.799	.864	.258	.167	.091
1880 I	.635	1.284	.676	.608	1.919	.907	.272	.174	.098
II	.647	1.323	.693	.630	1.970	.937	.290	.185	.105
III	.660	1.382	.731	.651	2.042	.970	.310	.198	.112
IV	.697	1.460	.759	.701	2.157	1.005	.308	.198	.110
1881 I	.728	1.542	.790	.752	2.270	1.028	.300	.192	.108
II	.750	1.645	.845	.800	2.395	1.072	.322	.214	.108
III	.787	1.723	.875	.848	2.510	1.104	.317	.208	.109
IV	.802	1.735	.873	.862	2.537	1.121	.319	.210	.109
1882 I	.821	1.753	.878	.875	2.574	1.134	.313	.204	.109
II	.822	1.772	.884	.888	2.594	1.138	.316	.207	.109
III	.827	1.813	.900	.913	2.640	1.142	.315	.206	.109
IV	.835	1.845	.902	.943	2.680	1.155	.320	.212	.108
1883 I	.870	1.875	.903	.972	2.745	1.175	.305	.198	.107
II	.872	1.925	.923	1.002	2.797	1.191	.319	.213	.106
III	.862	1.957	.943	1.014	2.819	1.193	.331	.221	.110
IV	.845	1.971	.955	1.016	2.816	1.193	.348	.232	.116

1884 I	.838	1.991	.972	1.019	2.829	1.196	.358	.235	.123
II	.838	1.945	.924	1.021	2.783	1.189	.351	.222	.129
III	.834	1.931	.900	1.031	2.765	1.212	.378	.242	.136
IV	.816	1.946	.902	1.044	2.762	1.222	.406	.263	.143
1885 I	.798	1.993	.936	1.057	2.791	1.230	.432	.281	.151
II	.789	2.034	.963	1.071	2.823	1.240	.451	.292	.159
III	.778	2.106	.998	1.108	2.884	1.239	.461	.297	.164
IV	.770	2.167	1.010	1.157	2.937	1.220	.450	.282	.168
1886 I	.767	2.255	1.049	1.206	3.005	1.216	.445	.273	.172
II	.767	2.305	1.050	1.255	3.072	1.212	.440	.264	.176
III	.775	2.335	1.052	1.283	3.110	1.207	.432	.253	.179
IV	.780	2.381	1.080	1.301	3.161	1.229	.449	.268	.181
1887 I	.792	2.454	1.134	1.320	3.246	1.247	.455	.272	.183
II	.802	2.490	1.152	1.338	3.292	1.264	.462	.277	.185
III	.824	2.488	1.146	1.342	3.312	1.285	.461	.274	.187
IV	.839	2.490	1.151	1.339	3.329	1.299	.460	.272	.188
1888 I	.835	2.516	1.180	1.336	3.351	1.305	.470	.281	.189
II	.831	2.521	1.188	1.333	3.352	1.316	.485	.294	.191
III	.833	2.567	1.225	1.342	3.400	1.323	.490	.300	.190
IV	.844	2.593	1.235	1.358	3.437	1.330	.486	.297	.189
1889 I	.839	2.651	1.278	1.373	3.490	1.335	.496	.308	.188
II	.841	2.698	1.309	1.389	3.539	1.343	.502	.316	.186
III	.860	2.755	1.327	1.428	3.615	1.347	.487	.302	.185
IV	.868	2.806	1.327	1.479	3.674	1.346	.478	.294	.184
1890 I	.882	2.903	1.373	1.530	3.785	1.361	.479	.296	.183
II	.901	2.979	1.398	1.581	3.880	1.378	.477	.296	.181
III	.915	3.042	1.434	1.608	3.957	1.407	.492	.310	.182
IV	.944	3.028	1.406	1.622	3.972	1.433	.489	.306	.183
1891 I	.947	3.050	1.414	1.636	3.997	1.450	.503	.318	.185
II	.943	3.080	1.430	1.650	4.023	1.454	.511	.324	.187
III	.938	3.145	1.451	1.694	4.083	1.459	.521	.329	.192
IV	.949	3.236	1.483	1.753	4.185	1.490	.541	.341	.200

(continued)

TABLE 21 (continued)

Year and Quarter	Currency Held by the Public[a] (1)	Adjusted Deposits			Money Stock[a] (5)	Currency Outside Treasury (6)	Vault Cash		
		All Commercial Banks[a] (2)	National Banks (3)	Nonnational Banks (4)			All Banks (7)	National Banks (8)	Nonnational and Mutual Savings Banks (9)
1892 I	.946	3.367	1.555	1.812	4.313	1.525	.579	.371	.208
II	.950	3.480	1.609	1.871	4.430	1.547	.597	.382	.215
III	.951	3.521	1.651	1.870	4.472	1.540	.589	.371	.218
IV	.948	3.482	1.643	1.839	4.430	1.522	.574	.355	.219
1893 I	.961	3.418	1.610	1.808	4.379	1.520	.559	.339	.220
II	.988	3.293	1.516	1.777	4.281	1.531	.543	.322	.221
III	1.021	3.141	1.379	1.762	4.162	1.592	.571	.349	.222
IV	.973	3.177	1.422	1.755	4.150	1.620	.647	.424	.223
1894 I	.941	3.256	1.508	1.748	4.197	1.615	.674	.450	.224
II	.905	3.307	1.566	1.741	4.212	1.595	.690	.464	.226
III	.895	3.392	1.617	1.775	4.287	1.568	.673	.447	.226
IV	.898	3.444	1.615	1.829	4.342	1.532	.634	.407	.227
1895 I	.879	3.463	1.581	1.882	4.342	1.493	.614	.386	.228
II	.894	3.528	1.592	1.936	4.422	1.511	.617	.388	.229
III	.901	3.577	1.640	1.937	4.478	1.512	.611	.386	.225
IV	.879	3.534	1.623	1.911	4.413	1.471	.592	.372	.220
1896 I	.873	3.448	1.562	1.886	4.321	1.447	.574	.360	.214
II	.846	3.422	1.562	1.860	4.268	1.417	.571	.362	.209
III	.866	3.408	1.542	1.866	4.274	1.444	.578	.369	.209
IV	.900	3.426	1.538	1.888	4.326	1.509	.609	.397	.212

1897 I	.908	3.487	1.578	1.909	4.395	1.552	.644	.430	.214
II	.887	3.550	1.619	1.931	4.437	1.537	.650	.433	.217
III	.903	3.684	1.701	1.983	4.587	1.556	.653	.434	.219
IV	.923	3.831	1.781	2.050	4.754	1.581	.658	.438	.220
1898 I	.931	3.955	1.838	2.117	4.886	1.614	.683	.462	.221
II	1.000	4.038	1.854	2.184	5.038	1.703	.703	.480	.223
III	1.002	4.201	1.918	2.283	5.203	1.698	.696	.471	.225
IV	1.013	4.421	2.024	2.397	5.434	1.741	.728	.500	.228
1899 I	1.044	4.662	2.150	2.512	5.706	1.790	.746	.515	.231
II	1.071	4.861	2.234	2.627	5.932	1.812	.741	.507	.234
III	1.099	4.998	2.293	2.705	6.097	1.826	.727	.491	.236
IV	1.118	5.042	2.276	2.766	6.160	1.835	.717	.479	.238
1900 I	1.140	5.091	2.264	2.827	6.231	1.874	.734	.494	.240
II	1.172	5.138	2.250	2.888	6.310	1.937	.765	.523	.242
III	1.219	5.361	2.356	3.005	6.580	2.001	.782	.533	.249
IV	1.236	5.583	2.434	3.149	6.819	2.042	.806	.548	.258
1901 I	1.256	5.832	2.538	3.294	7.088	2.080	.824	.558	.266
II	1.247	6.027	2.588	3.439	7.274	2.083	.836	.531	.275
III	1.253	6.198	2.642	3.556	7.451	2.108	.855	.577	.278
IV	1.271	6.356	2.698	3.658	7.627	2.127	.856	.578	.278
1902 I	1.283	6.541	2.780	3.761	7.824	2.140	.857	.579	.278
II	1.297	6.664	2.800	3.864	7.961	2.153	.856	.578	.278
III	1.332	6.785	2.841	3.944	8.117	2.173	.841	.530	.281
IV	1.364	6.916	2.904	4.012	8.280	2.223	.859	.573	.286
1903 I	1.380	7.029	2.949	4.080	8.409	2.241	.861	.570	.291
II	1.416	7.082	2.934	4.148	8.498	2.275	.859	.534	.295
III	1.418	7.188	2.972	4.216	8.606	2.292	.874	.570	.304
IV	1.422	7.293	3.010	4.283	8.715	2.325	.903	.538	.315
1904 I	1.423	7.412	3.062	4.350	8.835	2.388	.965	.639	.326
II	1.418	7.518	3.100	4.418	8.936	2.417	.999	.632	.337
III	1.428	7.769	3.218	4.551	9.197	2.452	1.024	.633	.341
IV	1.433	8.053	3.335	4.718	9.486	2.452	1.019	.679	.340

(continued)

TABLE 21 (concluded)

Year and Quarter	Currency Held by the Public[a] (1)	Adjusted Deposits			Money Stock[a] (5)	Currency Outside Treasury (6)	Vault Cash		
		All Commercial Banks[a] (2)	National Banks (3)	Nonnational Banks (4)			All Banks (7)	National Banks (8)	Nonnational and Mutual Savings Banks (9)
1905 I	1.437	8.310	3.425	4.885	9.747	2.454	1.017	.678	.339
II	1.471	8.520	3.468	5.052	9.991	2.475	1.004	.666	.338
III	1.483	8.733	3.548	5.185	10.216	2.509	1.026	.683	.343
IV	1.528	8.939	3.640	5.299	10.467	2.535	1.007	.656	.351
1906 I	1.546	9.068	3.654	5.414	10.614	2.573	1.027	.668	.359
II	1.591	9.193	3.664	5.529	10.784	2.626	1.035	.668	.367
III	1.630	9.408	3.769	5.639	11.038	2.674	1.044	.663	.381
IV	1.671	9.660	3.913	5.747	11.331	2.745	1.074	.678	.396
1907 I	1.676	9.844	3.989	5.855	11.520	2.790	1.114	.702	.412
II	1.693	9.967	4.004	5.963	11.660	2.826	1.133	.705	.428

[a]For the reason that these columns differ from the columns with the corresponding headings in Table 2, see the source notes to Table 2, cols. 1 and 4.

Source: See Table 20 and text, Chap. 11, section 3.

CHART 6

Money Stock, Quarterly, 1867–1907

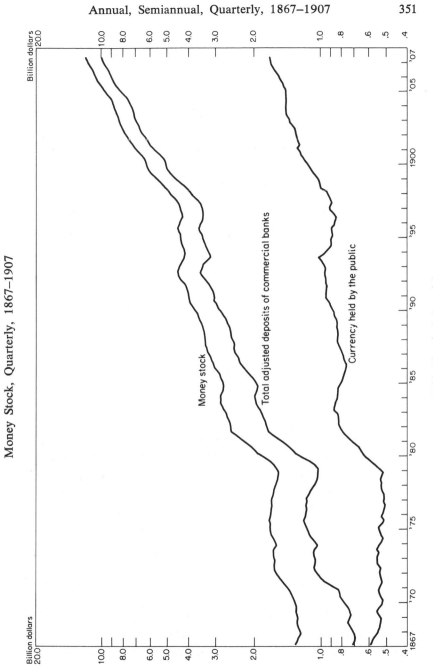

SOURCE: Table 21, cols. 1, 2, and 5.

12

CURRENCY HELD BY THE PUBLIC: CALL DATE AND MONTHLY ESTIMATES

CURRENCY HELD by the public is the difference between currency in circulation (i.e., outside the Treasury and, beginning November 1914, also outside Federal Reserve Banks) and bank vault cash.

The first section below describes our revisions of the published figures for currency outside the Treasury and Federal Reserve Banks. It covers the period 1867–1942. For 1867–1906 we deducted from the revised annual or semiannual currency-in-circulation series, vault cash estimates that other investigators had constructed (described in Chapter 11). For 1907–42 we deducted from the revised monthly or interpolated call date series of currency in circulation, vault cash estimates at call dates (section 2) and at dates nearest the end of month (section 3) that we had constructed. From 1943 on we shift to Federal Reserve estimates. Section 4 describes the residual series of currency held by the public and section 5 evaluates the reliability of the estimates.

1. Currency Outside Treasury and Federal Reserve Banks

The published figures for currency outside the Treasury and Federal Reserve Banks are themselves the difference between the amount of each kind of currency outstanding and the amount in the Treasury and, beginning November 1914, the amount in Federal Reserve Banks. The primary sources of those figures are the "Reports of the Treasurer" in the Secretary of the Treasury's annual reports and the monthly *Circulation Statement of United States Money*. The kinds of currency included in the stock are:

1. Gold coin, gold bullion, and gold certificates issued by the Secretary of the Treasury in return for the deposit of gold
2. Standard silver dollars and silver certificates issued by the Secretary of the Treasury in return for the deposit of silver dollars
3. Fractional or subsidiary silver coin
4. Treasury notes of 1890; in process of retirement and cancellation after March 1900
5. United States notes ("greenbacks"); a permanent issue of $346.7 million
6. National bank notes, issued by national banks on the security of United States interest-bearing registered bonds until 1935; since then in process of retirement and cancellation
7. Federal Reserve notes, issued by Federal Reserve Banks since 1932 on the security of government bonds (earlier, secured by the pledge of collateral consisting of eligible paper, member bank promissory notes, gold and gold certificates)
8. Federal Reserve Bank notes, issued by Federal Reserve Banks in 1916–17, 1918–20, 1933, and 1942, against U.S. bonds (The Reserve Banks extinguished their liability while the notes were still in circulation by the deposit of lawful money with the United States Treasurer)
9. Minor coin.

Revisions of Basic Data

We made adjustments in the published data for selected kinds of currency either outstanding or outside the Treasury and Federal Reserve Banks.

1. GOLD COIN AND BULLION. January 1867–February 1878: Gold outside the Treasury was corrected for gold presumed lost as estimated by us, 1866–72, and by the Director of the Mint, 1873–78.[1] August 1878–May 1907: Gold outside the Treasury was obtained by subtracting the

---

[1] *Banking and Monetary Statistics*, Board of Governors of the Federal Reserve System, Washington, D.C., 1943, p. 408; Director of the Mint, *Annual Report*, 1887, p. 86; 1907, pp. 87 and 92.

amount in the Treasury from corrected figures for the stock.[2] Correction for the amount of gold presumed lost is an interpolation by Method L of the Director of the Mint's June estimates, 1878–79, and of his December estimates, 1879–1907.[3] June 1907–December 1913: The reported figures for the stock of gold minus the amount in the Treasury were used.[4] January 1914–December 1933: Since January 30, 1934, there has been no circulation of gold coin, and the monetary gold stock has included only gold held by the Treasury exclusive of relatively small amounts held since April 1934 in the active portion of the Gold Stabilization Fund. As of January 31, 1934, the estimated amount of gold outside the Treasury and Federal Reserve Banks was $287 million, even though all holders had been legally required to turn in any gold in their possession. The Federal Reserve concluded that in the course of time this amount of coin had been lost, destroyed, or exported without record and so not only excluded it from the monetary gold stock and from currency held by the public and all banks from then on, but also revised the figures prior to January 31, 1934, and subsequent to 1913 by subtracting this $287 million.[5] As a result of this revision, the published figures for the period before 1914 are not continuous with the revised figures beginning 1914. In *A Monetary History,* we concluded that the bulk of the $287 million recorded on January 1934 was retained illegally in private possession.[6] We therefore restored to the estimated gold stock and gold circulation the $287 million which the Federal Reserve subtracted for 1914–33. Since gold coin has not been a component of the money stock since January 31, 1934, we excluded the $287 million since that date.

2. FRACTIONAL CURRENCY. All fractional currency outstanding was to have been returned to the Treasury for retirement by the end of 1878. We assumed that all but $1 million recorded as still outstanding June 30, 1878, had been lost, and we distributed the loss by Method L over the period 1863–78, the amounts being deducted from the published

---

[2] The uncorrected gold stock is in "Report of the Treasurer," Secretary of the Treasury, *Annual Report,* 1898, pp. 109 ff.; 1903, pp. 205 ff.; 1909, pp. 190 ff. Gold in the Treasury is from *ibid.,* 1898, pp. 59 ff.; 1903, p. 173; 1909, pp. 190 ff.

[3] See footnote 1, above.

[4] "Report of the Treasurer," Secretary of the Treasury, *Annual Report,* 1909, pp. 190 ff.; 1915, pp. 339 ff.

[5] *Banking and Monetary Statistics,* pp. 409–412.

[6] Pages 463–464, note 45.

figures.[7] Fractional currency was assumed to have been $1 million in August 1878 and zero thereafter (it is not shown in the published monthly data beginning June 1878).

3. SUBSIDIARY SILVER COIN. In June 1910 the Director of the Mint deducted $9,700 thousand from the estimate of the stock of subsidiary silver coin at that date to adjust for an overestimate "for the fiscal years 1881–1910." [8] He made no attempt to apportion this amount over the years during which the error was accumulating. We assumed that the amount of the error was distributed over the months during the period 1881–1910 in a straight-line fashion, and accordingly we corrected by Method L the published figures for the stock and amount of subsidiary silver coin outside the Treasury.

4. NATIONAL BANK NOTES. In deriving currency outside the Treasury and Federal Reserve Banks, we tried to avoid inconsistencies between it and the vault cash data which constitute a component. On their balance sheets national banks reported bank notes of other national banks in their vaults as an asset; they did not report their own notes on hand (if shown as an asset this item would have been exactly offset as a liability). Published monthly figures for national bank notes outstanding and outside the Treasury and Federal Reserve Banks, however, include notes of issuing banks on hand.

Another component of national bank notes outstanding and in circulation not included in vault cash was national bank notes in transit. This item is equal to the difference between the amount of national bank notes issuers received from the Comptroller of the Currency—the amount shown on the banks' books—and the amount secured by the deposit of U.S. bonds—the amount shown on the Treasury's books.[9]

We therefore subtracted from published figures of national bank notes

---

[7] *Banking and Monetary Statistics,* p. 408.

[8] "Report of the Director of the Mint," in Secretary of the Treasury, *Annual Report,* 1910, p. 290.

[9] The Treasury's figures on national bank notes outstanding as liabilities of national banks were based on its record of "U.S. bonds deposited by national banks to secure the circulation of national bank notes." (The figures for national bank notes outstanding shown in the *Circulation Statement* were a sum of national bank notes secured by U.S. bonds—national bank liabilities—and national bank notes for which lawful money was on deposit with the U.S. Treasury—a Treasury liability. The latter, representing notes of closed banks and banks reducing their circulation, are not involved in the adjustment described in this paragraph.)

in circulation [10] estimates of national bank notes in vaults of issuing banks and in transit. Directly reported data on notes in vaults of issuing banks and in transit are available only for call dates, 1907–28.[11] For other periods we estimated the aggregate of the items by subtracting national bank figures of their note liability from Treasury figures of national bank note circulation secured by U.S. bonds. For 1866–69, when the record of national bank note circulation secured by U.S. bonds is lacking, we substituted for it the data on national bank notes outstanding.[12] After June 1935, when national bank notes were converted into a Treasury obligation and provisions were made for their retirement, no adjustment of the published figures of national bank notes in circulation is needed.

5. MINOR COIN. Figures for minor coin have been reported in the *Circulation Statement* since December 31, 1927. Monthly estimates back to 1914 were prepared by the Federal Reserve, and end-of-June figures beginning 1900 by the Secretary of Treasury.[13] We interpolated monthly

[10] Jan. 1867–Feb. 1878: Interpolation by Method L between June data, from *Banking and Monetary Statistics*, p. 408; Aug. 1878–Feb. 1887: Total outstanding monthly, from *Annual Report*, Comptroller of the Currency, 1891, p. 125, minus amount in Treasury, monthly, from "Report of the Treasurer," 1898, p. 44; Mar. 1887–Dec. 1913: Monthly *Circulation Statement of U.S. Money;* Jan. 1914–June 1935: *Banking and Monetary Statistics*, pp. 409–412.

[11] The banks supplied this information in a memorandum note accompanying their balance sheet returns. See the annual reports of the U.S. Comptroller of the Currency for a table on circulating notes of national banks received from the Comptroller, on hand, and outstanding.

[12] National bank notes in transit and in vaults of issuing banks were estimated as follows:

Jan. 1867–June 1906: For the call date nearest the end of each of the months in Table 1, national bank note liabilities from *Annual Report*, Comptroller of the Currency, 1916, Vol. II, pp. 329–355, were subtracted from (a) 1866–69: National bank notes outstanding from A. P. Andrew, *Statistics for the United States, 1867–1909* (National Monetary Commission, 1910, S. Doc. 570, 61st Cong., 2nd sess.), p. 43; and (b) 1870–1906: Circulation of national bank notes secured by U.S. bonds, from *Annual Report*, Comptroller of the Currency, 1891, Vol. I, p. 125; 1904, Vol. I, pp. 99–101; 1908, pp. 124–129.

May 1907–June 1928: Notes in vaults of issuing banks were interpolated monthly by Method L between call date figures for circulating notes of national banks received from the Comptroller and on hand. Notes in transit were interpolated monthly by Method L between mid- and end-of-year estimates obtained by deducting national bank call date figures of national bank notes received from the Comptroller from circulation of national bank notes secured by U.S. bonds (*ibid.*, 1918, Vol. II, pp. 19–21; 1924, pp. 158–160; 1928, pp. 222–223).

July 1928–June 1935: Notes in vaults of issuing banks and in transit were interpolated monthly by Method L between mid- and end-of-year estimates obtained by deducting national bank call date figures for national bank note liabilities from circulation of national bank notes secured by U.S. bonds (*ibid.*, 1931, pp. 178–179; 1935, pp. 183–184).

[13] *Banking and Monetary Statistics*, pp. 408–409 for June estimates; pp. 409–413 for monthly figures through 1941.

by Method L between the midyear figures from 1907 to 1914 and added the estimates of minor coin back to 1900 to the published figures of currency outside the Treasury. We did not extend the estimates of minor coin before 1900.

Seasonal Adjustments

Our series for currency outside the Treasury and Federal Reserve banks was seasonally adjusted in two stages. This series varies not only with the month of the year but also with the day of the week on which the last day of the month falls. We therefore estimated both daily and monthly seasonal factors by the method described in Chapter 10, section 4. We corrected the end-of-month data by the appropriate index.

We next computed percentage changes from one month to the next for this corrected series, which we then plotted. Repetitive movements appeared, May 1907–December 1913, June 1924–June 1932, and June 1935–June 1941, indicating that further seasonal correction was required. We eliminated residual seasonality by the method of ratios to moving averages. The final monthly series, whose dating was determined by the vault cash series (section 3, below), is given in Table 27, column 1.

Call Date Series

A call date series for 1907–42 was interpolated by Method L between the corrected end-of-month series of currency outside the Treasury and Federal Reserve Banks. It is given in Table 26, column 1.

2. All-Bank Vault Cash: Call Dates

The first step toward monthly estimates was the construction of a call date series for vault cash in all banks. For 1907–23 we summed estimates for national, nonnational, and mutual savings banks; for the overlapping period 1919–42 estimates for member, nonmember, and mutual savings banks.

The national bank estimates are from the reports of the Comptroller of the Currency, the member bank estimates from the reports of the Federal Reserve System. The nonnational, nonmember, and mutual savings bank estimates are based on data assembled by us from the reports of state supervisory agencies in the forty-eight states, the District of Columbia, and the possessions. We collected whatever data on vault cash in all banks were available for each state in such reports, whether or not they were for dates identical with national and member bank call dates. We corrected these data, state by state, for daily and monthly seasonals and shifted nonidentically dated observations to the closest national and member bank call date by interpolating between two observations, using Method L. No observation had to be shifted more than two months. The remaining gaps at inter-June call dates were filled in, state by state, by interpolation Method R_3.

The final call date estimates are the sums for all states of the estimates for mutual savings and nonnational or nonmember banks plus the deseasonalized data for national or member banks.

Problems in Compilation of Nonnational and Mutual Savings Bank Data

In general we used as our basic source of nonnational and mutual savings bank data by states, the reports of the various state banking departments. In addition we used the annual (recently semiannual) returns published by the Comptroller of the Currency. The Comptroller's reports served both as a check on data in state reports and as a source for certain years when the latter were unavailable or unsatisfactory.

Vault cash is shown in various ways on consolidated balance sheets of the different states. It is broken down according to kinds of currency —distinguishing legal tender or currency eligible for reserve computation from other currency—or as a single item. When shown broken down, the components of vault cash were summed. Certain states, however, did not at all times report "cash on hand" separately from "cash items," "due from banks," or other asset categories. If vault cash represented the major component, rough estimates at call dates, excluding the extraneous component, were made on the basis of available information for the breakdown. If vault cash was the minor component, the call date figures were discarded.

For 1933–35, when certain states included unlicensed banks in their returns, estimates of vault cash in these institutions were deducted at call dates on the basis of the Comptroller of the Currency's June data which exclude unlicensed banks.

The reported figures in published sources, 1907–35, understated vault cash in all nonnational banks inasmuch as nonreporting banks, usually private banks, also held cash. Before 1919 the main nonreporting private banks were located in New York. We used annual Federal Reserve figures for vault cash in New York private banks—which include nonreporting banks [14]—to supplement the report date returns, 1907–19. For nonreporting banks in other states, 1907–42, and in New York, 1919–42, we added an aggregate estimate from the same source to our call date series for all reporting banks.

From 1919 on, for our member-nonmember bank estimates, we converted the nonnational estimates into nonmember estimates by subtracting state member bank figures, state by state. [15]

Report Dates

The dating of the reports of nonnational and mutual savings banks presents a problem. Most of the states require their banks to submit condition reports for several dates each year; the remaining states, once a year only. The states requiring more than one condition report annually generally designate the same call dates as those that are designated by the Comptroller of the Currency for national banks and by Federal Reserve authorities for state member banks. Some state banking departments, however, designate call dates that have no apparent relation to those designated by federal agencies. Even those states that usually use federal call dates have occasionally ignored one of them or, from time to time, have designated a call date of their own choosing. For any given national or member bank call date, therefore, there may be condition reports for nonnational and mutual savings banks that are differently dated by several days or by as much as several weeks; and there may be no reports from banks in some states.

Various classes of commercial banks, i.e., so-called "state" banks, loan and trust companies, stock savings banks, unincorporated banks, as well as mutual savings banks, were in operation in individual states. State supervision of these different types of institutions did not begin

[14] *All Bank Statistics, United States, 1896–1955*, p. 747.

[15] State member bank figures by states were compiled from the Federal Reserve Board, *Member Bank Call Report*, through March 1929; thereafter they were derived as residuals. Member bank figures are from the same source, minus national bank figures in the U.S. Comptroller of the Currency, *Abstract of Reports of Condition of National Banks*.

at the same time, and their respective operations were governed by different sections of the banking code. Consequently, the frequency of report dates for different classes of banks within a given state may vary, and the dates of call for the several classes of banks are not necessarily coincident.

As was shown in an earlier study of vault cash,[16] discrepancies in the dating of the components of all bank vault cash create difficulties because of the marked daily seasonal in the data. While information on the character of this intraweekly movement is at present limited, the movement unmistakably indicates that disregard of even small differences in dating between an interpolator and the universe or between components of an aggregate of vault cash will result in gross inaccuracies.[17] Experiments that we made along lines described in the next section showed that the daily seasonal was of about the same order of magnitude as the monthly seasonal. The solution adopted in Technical Paper No. 4 (see footnote 16) was to use only nonnational bank call date figures that were dated identically with national and member bank call dates in estimating all bank vault cash. Information from nonidentically dated call date figures was thereby sacrificed.

Our present approach to the problem of discrepant dating of vault cash figures represents an attempt (a) to correct for both the daily and the monthly seasonal movements characterizing the data, and (b) to use all call date figures of vault cash, whether or not dated identically with national and member bank call dates.

Seasonal Adjustment of Vault Cash Figures

Our preliminary tests convinced us that failure to estimate and eliminate the intraweekly seasonal would yield a poor monthly seasonal correction and make it appear that the monthly seasonal was changing when it was not. Accordingly, we used the method described in Chapter 10, section 4, to estimate simultaneously daily and monthly seasonal indexes for each of the following groups and periods. (1) National

---

[16] A. J. Schwartz and E. Oliver, *Currency Held by the Public, the Banks and the Treasury, Monthly, December 1917–December 1944.* National Bureau of Economic Research, Technical Paper 4, 1947 (hereafter referred to as Technical Paper 4).

[17] Technical Paper 4 (p. 17, note 6) mentions the intraweekly patterns of currency demands of all banks in the New York Reserve district (1926) and in the Minneapolis Reserve District (1927) and daily figures of vault cash holdings of all member banks by districts and reserve classes (June 1930).

banks, 1874–1917; (2) National banks, 1917–49; (3) State member banks, 1919–44; (4) New York State banks and trust companies, 1897–1917; (5) Nonnational and mutual savings banks outside New York, 1907–17; (6) Nonmember and mutual savings banks, 1919–44; (7) Nonnational and mutual savings banks, 1919–44—obtained by combining the indexes for (3) and (6). Computation of these indexes, which are given in Tables 29 and 30 in the appendix to this chapter, raised special problems for some of these groups.

National banks and state member banks (groups 1, 2, and 3). For these groups we had continuous series of vault cash at call dates and so could apply the general procedure directly. We divided the national bank series into two segments, before 1917 and 1917 and later, because vault cash changed its status in 1917. Prior to that date, vault cash satisfied legal reserve requirements; thereafter (until December 1, 1959), member banks could count only deposits at Federal Reserve Banks as meeting legal reserve requirements.

New York state banks (group 4). While New York state banks and loan and trust companies—the chief nonnational banks in the state—reported four times annually, 1907–17, the report dates seldom coincided with national bank call dates. Vault cash in these New York banks, moreover, averaged approximately two-fifths of vault cash in all nonnational banks during this period. Because of the unique dating pattern of the New York returns and the banks' special position in the reserve structure of the banking system, we computed separate daily and monthly seasonal indexes for New York for this period. For 1917–19 we used for New York the indexes for group 7.

Nonnational and nonmember banks (groups 5 and 6). For these banks, the available series were discontinuous. The number of states reporting vault cash varies from call date to call date and the call dates vary from state to state. One possibility would be to compute separate indexes for each of the forty-eight states, the District of Columbia, and the possessions, using all observations available for each unit. However, we rejected this procedure as too time-consuming and unnecessarily detailed. Instead we constructed hypothetical continuous nonnational (1907–17) and nonmember (1919–44) call date series of vault cash, using only identically dated observations. The sole purpose of these series was to estimate daily and monthly seasonal indexes.[18] Only reported vault cash figures, no estimates, were used.[19]

In one respect the construction of the hypothetical call date series differed for 1907–17, when nonnational bank data were used, from that for 1919–44, when nonmember bank data were used. In the earlier period, for the purpose of economizing time, the series was constructed from identically dated figures for the sixteen states with the largest number of inter-June observations; in the later period, it was constructed from all identically dated observations for all states.[20]

The basic table giving all identically dated observations has many gaps for individual states, that is, dates without figures intermediate between dates with figures. If there was at least one inter-June observation for a given state for a given year, the gaps in that year for that state were filled in by interpolation Method R_1, using as the related series the sum of reported data for the largest common sample of states reporting for the date of the gap and for the closest dates preceding and following the gap at which there were observations for the state in question.

For each call date, the reported and filled in observations were summed, the sums being computed for two totals at dates at which the number of states changed. For example, Oregon was first included on August 22, 1907. The sum at this date was obtained excluding Oregon (to make the total comparable with the preceding call date) and in-

[18] The decision to proceed along these lines involved the assumption that the intra-weekly and monthly seasonals were approximately the same for the whole of the periods 1907–17 and 1919–44, and for all the states. Here we shall anticipate one of our findings: the assumption of a uniform seasonal for all the states is contrary to fact. We made an adjustment (described below) to correct for differential seasonal movements by regions. We have no direct evidence from our series to support or oppose the assumption of unchanging seasonal movements within the periods treated separately. See Technical Paper 4 (p. 17, note 6), however, for an indication of instability of intra-weekly indexes, 1921–27. There can be no doubt that a change in the seasonal behavior of vault cash resulted from the change in its status in June 1917, when the requirement went into effect that member banks carry all their legal reserves with Federal Reserve Banks.

[19] Thus, certain June data shown in the Comptroller's *Annual Report* were not used in estimating seasonal variations because footnotes indicated the figures were estimates. These data were, however, corrected by the seasonal indexes derived and used subsequently in obtaining vault cash totals at call dates.

[20] Table B-10 of Technical Paper 4 (p. 51) shows the basic data for nonnational banks for part of the period; lines 1, 3–15, 22, and 25 constituted our sample. Table B-4, *ibid.* (pp. 36–37), shows some of the basic data for nonmember banks. For the states shown additions were made of identically dated figures that were not included in the table because the method of interpolation used in Technical Paper 4 required reports for at least two consecutive call dates for a given state. In addition, available identically dated figures for the states not shown in the table were added.

cluding Oregon (to make the total comparable with the following call date). The resulting discontinuous series of segments was linked together, starting with the segment with the largest representation of states. The ratio of its value at an overlapping call date to the corresponding value for the preceding or succeeding segment was used to raise the level of the connecting segment. This linking was continued backward and forward to yield a continuous artificial series.

The interpolation of gaps and the linking procedure were simply devices to provide a continuous series that would facilitate computation of the daily and monthly seasonals. They affect our final results only insofar as they affect the daily and monthly seasonals that we used.

The hypothetical continuous series had no observations for several of the twelve months for nonmember banks, hence did not provide seasonal factors for those months. We interpolated seasonal factors by Method R_1, using as the related series the seasonal indexes for vault cash in weekly reporting member banks.

Nonnational and mutual savings banks, 1919–44 (group 7). We constructed the daily and monthly seasonal indexes for this period as a weighted average of the corresponding seasonals for nonmember and state member banks, weighting each by the estimated fraction of all nonnational bank vault cash held by the corresponding banks.

The state member bank and nonmember bank series did not yield a seasonal factor for every month, since there were three calendar months for which there were no reported figures. For nonnational banks, 1917–42, we needed seasonal factors for these months. We interpolated them by Method R_1, using the seasonal for vault cash in weekly reporting member banks as the related series.

Shifting Nonidentically Dated Observations
to National and Member Bank Call Dates

The daily and monthly seasonal indexes derived as just described were applied to all observations, by classes of banks and by states. The resulting nonnational and nonmember observations were partly for dates identical with national and member bank call dates, partly for nonidentical dates. To get observations for all series at the same date, we shifted each nonidentically dated figure to the closest call date, which was never more than two months distant.

We shifted nonnational bank observations, 1907–19, by interpolating by Method L between the two nonidentically dated observations closest to the relevant call date, or between one nonidentically dated observation and a preceding or following identically dated observation.

For 1919–44, nonidentically dated nonnational bank observations had not only to be shifted to call dates, but also to be converted into estimates for nonmember banks. Had we estimated the identically dated figures for nonnational banks as we did for 1907–19 and then subtracted adjusted state member bank data at the call dates to get residual estimates for nonmember banks, we would have wasted the information provided by the call date state member bank data. Instead, for each state with nonidentically dated observations we (a) computed the ratio of nonmember to nonnational bank vault cash for whatever dates identically dated figures were available; (b) plotted the ratios as a time series and smoothed the points by a freehand curve; (c) read off from the chart an estimated ratio at the nonidentical date; (d) applied this ratio to the nonnational bank figure at the nonidentical date. We then shifted the resultant estimates for nonmember banks to the closest call date by the method described in the preceding paragraph for nonnational bank estimates.

Interpolation of Missing Call Date Figures, by States

Having seasonally adjusted all identically and nonidentically dated figures and shifted the latter to call dates, we had observations for fifty political units (the forty-eight states, the District of Columbia, and the possessions. Hereafter we use "states" to refer to these fifty units, including the D.C. and the possessions). For some states, moreover, we had separate observations for different classes of banks for different numbers of call dates (e.g., incorporated and unincorporated banks, or commercial and mutual savings banks, or combinations of subclasses). The major component with the most inter-June observations was usually the series for incorporated banks or one of its subclasses (e.g., loan and trust companies or so-called state banks). We proceeded to construct a single vault cash series for each state, interpolating by Method L for missing minor components only for those dates at which there was an observation for the major component. When the minor component was reported on a call date on which the major component was not, this observation was used, if needed, in interpolating the minor component to the nearest date or dates for which the major component was available. No other use was made of it.

The missing call date observations were then interpolated state by state by Method R_3, using as the related series for each state, observations for selected other states. In order to use this method we had (a) to decide what "other" states should be used for each state and (b) to estimate the necessary parameters.

For both purposes we first converted all our available inter-June observations into relative deviations from inter-June trends—i.e., values of v as defined by equation 4 of Chapter 10—and then computed from these v's standard deviations and correlation coefficients separately for 1907–19 and 1919–44. We computed standard deviations for 1907–19 for all units that had at least eighteen observations during that period, and for 1919–44, for all that had at least twenty-three observations during that period. We also computed correlation coefficients for a limited number of states selected at random.[21]

Our initial hypothesis was that vault cash behavior would vary systematically with the size of the banking system within each state and hence that the best states to use to interpolate a given state would be states of roughly the same size. The results did not bear out this hypothesis. When we classified the states into three categories, small, medium, and large, the correlation coefficients between the v's for two states did not tend to be systematically higher when the states were in the same category than when the states were in different categories.

There did, on the other hand, appear to be systematic differences according to the geographical location of the states—partly, we conjecture, because of regional differences in seasonal patterns not corrected by the uniform countrywide seasonal we used, partly for other reasons. Accordingly, for 1919–44, we classified the states into the three groups shown in Table 22: Group I, states with mutual savings banks, which are mostly in the Midwest and the Northeast; Group II, other states not in the South and Southeast; Group III, other states in the South and Southeast. For 1907–19, we further subdivided Group I into Group Ia, New York State alone; Group Ib, the rest of the Group I states.

[21] We should note that this work was done about 1953, when the speed and availability of computers were not what they are at present. Were we doing this analysis today, we would no doubt routinely calculate correlations for all 1,225 possible pairs of states.

TABLE 22

Classification of States for Call Date Interpolation

States with Mutual Savings Banks	States with No Mutual Savings Banks	
	States Outside South and Southeast	States in South and Southeast
Group I	Group II	Group III
Connecticut	Arizona	Alabama
Delaware	California	Arkansas
Indiana	Colorado	District of Columbia
Maine	Idaho	Florida
Maryland	Illinois	Georgia
Massachusetts	Iowa	Kentucky
Minnesota	Kansas	Louisiana
New Hampshire	Michigan	Mississippi
New Jersey	Missouri	North Carolina
New York (1919–44)[a]	Montana	South Carolina
Ohio	Nebraska	Tennessee
Pennsylvania	Nevada	Texas
Rhode Island	New Mexico	Virginia
Vermont	North Dakota	West Virginia
Washington	Oklahoma	
	Oregon	
	U. S. Possessions	
	South Dakota	
	Utah	
	Wisconsin[b]	
	Wyoming	

[a]For 1907–19, New York by itself constituted a subgroup, Ia, and the rest of Group I states, a subgroup, Ib.

[b]Wisconsin was classified with states with no mutual savings banks because vault cash in its mutual savings banks was 1 per cent or less of the total in its nonnational or nonmember banks.

The differential seasonal is reflected in mean values of v that differ from zero, as shown by the following tabulation:

MEAN VALUE OF v TIMES 100

	1907–19	1919–44
Group I	+0.26 (excluding N.Y.)	+2.48 (including N.Y.)
Group II	−1.89	+0.87
Group III	−10.34	−10.55

To allow for this systematic effect, we modified Method R_3 by introducing a constant term, estimating u by

$$u^* = \bar{v} + b(v - \bar{v}),$$

where $\bar{v}$ is the mean value for the relevant group of states in the above tabulation.

Table 23 cross-classifies the pairs of states for which we computed correlation coefficients by the groups in which the states fall and gives the average correlation coefficient for each cell. These results and the individual correlation coefficients underlying them are roughly, but far from fully, consistent with the hypothesis that states in the same group are more like one another than states in different groups. Nonetheless, we proceeded on that basis, using for any state the other states in each group to interpolate missing observations.

For New York nonnational banks, 1907–19, we had reported observations, seasonally adjusted, either identically or nonidentically dated and shifted to national bank call dates, for every call date during the period except May 21, 1919. For this date we interpolated by Method L between the preceding and following seasonally adjusted call-date observations.

To apply Method R_3 we needed to estimate not only the correlation coefficient, for which we used the averages in Table 23, but also the standard deviations for individual states or at least the ratios among them. The computed standard deviations of the v's for individual states are subject to such large sampling variability that we hesitated to use them separately as estimates for the "true" standard deviations. We experimented therefore with relating the size of the standard deviations

TABLE 23

Pairs of States Correlated by Groups; Average Coefficients of Correlation, 1907–44

1907–19

Both Group I	Groups I, II	Both Group II	Groups I, III	Groups II, III	Both Group III
Wash./Mass.	Wis./Wash.	Calif./Wis.	Wash./D.C.	Wis./La.	N.C./La.
N.J./Wash.	Nev./Ind.	Ill./Wis.	Conn./La.	Calif./La.	Va./Miss.
Md./N.J.	Nev./Conn.	Utah/Wis.	N.J./Va.	Utah/La.	N.C./Miss.
	N.D./Ind.	Ill./Calif.	Ind./Miss.	Colo./D.C.	S.C./Ala.
		Utah/Calif.		N.D./Va.	
		Utah/Ill.		Ill./S.C.	
Av. r +.558	+.490	+.265	+.540	+.017	+.440

1919–44

Both Group I	Groups I, II	Both Group II	Groups I, III	Groups II, III	Both Group III
Wash./Mass.	Wis./Wash.	Calif./Wis.	Md./Ga.	Wis./La.	La./N.C.
Conn./Del.	Wis./Del.	Ill./Wis.	N.Y./Tenn.	Calif./La.	Miss./Va.
N.J./Wash.	Calif./Del.	Utah/Wis.	Wash./D.C.	Utah/La.	N.C./Ala.
Del./Ohio	Nev./N.Y.	Ill./Calif.		Calif./D.C.	S.C./Ala.
	Ill./Del.	Utah/Calif.		N.D./Va.	
	Utah/Del.	Ill./Utah		Ill./Ala.	
+.154	+.199	+.352	+.119	+.087	+.441

to the average size of vault cash, on the hypothesis that the larger the size of vault cash, the greater the cancellation of independent errors, and hence the smaller the relative variability that might be expected in the observations (the standard deviation of the v's is analogous to the coefficient of variation of the original observations, hence is a measure of relative variability). The relation is generally in the correct direction, but it is so small and loose that with all groups, 1907–19, and with Groups I and III, 1919–44, we treated the standard deviations for different states in each group as equal to one another. For Group II, 1919–44, we used estimates derived from the relation between the standard deviations and the average size of vault cash.[22]

Final Call Date Estimates

This interpolation procedure meant that for each call date we had either an original or an estimated seasonally adjusted observation on vault cash in reporting nonnational or nonmember banks for each of the fifty states. The entries were summed to get vault cash in all reporting nonnational and mutual savings banks at national bank call dates, 1907–19, and in all reporting nonmember and mutual savings banks at

[22] For 1919–44, the standard deviations for Group I showed the highest correlation with the vault cash figures. However, the negative slope was so slight that it did not lead to widely different estimates of the standard deviation for different sizes of vault cash. For the state with the smallest vault cash the standard deviation was less than twice that for the state with the very largest.

For Group II, there was no significant relation between the size of vault cash and the standard deviation for average vault cash larger than $2,000; there was, however, a significant negative slope for average vault cash of $2,000 and under. A freehand line was drawn to fit this relation. We read off from the chart a value for the standard deviation corresponding to the size of vault cash beginning at $300, and rising by steps of $100 to $2,000 (all dollar figures in thousands). For average vault cash above this amount we used an unchanging standard deviation. The standard deviations used for states in this group are:

.933	.990	1.034	1.273	1.697	2.042	3.589
Wisconsin	South Dakota	North Dakota	Montana	Idaho	Wyoming	New Mexico
Illinois		Arizona		Nevada	Utah	
Michigan						
Iowa						
Nebraska						
Colorado						
Oregon						
California						
Missouri						
Kansas						
Oklahoma						
Possessions						

For Group III there was not enough variation among states in average vault cash to determine its effect on the size of the standard deviation.

national and member bank call dates, 1919–42. Table 24 shows the summations (column 1), estimates for nonreporting banks (column 2), for national or member banks (column 3), and the totals for all banks (column 4).

Member bank figures, mostly available directly in seasonally unadjusted form in the published sources, are a sum of seasonally adjusted national and state member bank data. The only special problem was that for 1919–22 observations were not available for state member banks at national bank call dates that were not also state member bank call dates. For these dates we interpolated estimates by Method L between the deseasonalized state member bank figures.

3. All-Bank Vault Cash: Monthly Estimates

The monthly vault cash series, 1907–17, is a sum of deseasonalized monthly data for clearinghouse banks in seven cities accounting for from one-third to one-half of all bank vault cash; the residual data for reporting banks—clearinghouse banks not included and nonclearinghouse banks—interpolated by Method L between the call date figures; and estimates for nonreporting banks interpolated by Method L between June dates. For 1917–42 the all-bank series is a total of deseasonalized monthly data for weekly reporting member banks; the residual data for nonweekly reporting member banks and the estimates for reporting nonmember and mutual savings banks, both interpolated by Method L between call dates; and estimates for nonreporting nonmember banks interpolated by Method L between June dates. Beginning 1943 we present monthly estimates derived as the difference between currency outside Treasury and Federal Reserve Banks and estimates of currency outside all banks published in the *Federal Reserve Bulletin*. We seasonally adjusted this residual series.

1907–17. During this period vault cash data are available weekly from clearinghouses in selected cities including Chicago, New Orleans, St. Louis, and San Francisco, 1907–08; Philadelphia, 1907–14; Boston, 1907–16; and New York, 1907–17.[23] For New York, the clearinghouse

---

[23] The sources are as follows: A. P. Andrew, "Statistics of Banks and Banking in the United States," *Statistics for the United States, 1867–1909*, pp. 149–150 (Chicago); E. W. Kemmerer, *Seasonal Variation in the Relative Demand for Money and Capital in the United States*, pp. 269, 274, 275 (St. Louis, New Orleans, San Francisco); *The American Banker*, monthly issues (Philadelphia); Boston Clearing House Association, *Statement*

TABLE 24

Vault Cash at All Banks, at Call Dates, 1907–42
(seasonally adjusted, in millions of dollars)

Part I. Nonnational, Mutual Savings, and National Banks, National Bank Call Dates, 1907–1919

National Bank Call Date	Vault Cash		All National Banks (3)	All Banks (4)
	All Nonnational and Mutual Savings Banks			
	Reporting (1)	Nonreporting (2)		
1907				
May 20	412	11	698	1121
Aug. 22	416	11	736	1163
Dec. 3	471	10	736	1216
1908				
Feb. 14	454	10	795	1259
May 14	483	9	894	1386
July 15	490	9	855	1354
Sept. 23	510	9	926	1445
Nov. 27	492	9	923	1424
1909				
Feb. 5	535	8	866	1409
Apr. 28	519	8	902	1429
June 23	551	8	896	1455
Sept. 1	551	8	881	1440
Nov. 16	560	9	886	1454
1910				
Jan. 31	557	9	843	1409
Mar. 29	563	10	896	1469
June 30	595	10	848	1453
Sept. 1	568	10	897	1476
Nov. 10	561	10	851	1422
1911				
Jan. 17	571	10	924	1504
Mar. 7	561	10	956	1527
June 7	573	10	941	1524
Sept. 1	558	10	946	1514
Dec. 5	588	9	953	1551
1912				
Feb. 20	586	9	1002	1597
Apr. 18	573	8	976	1556
June 14	558	8	959	1524

(continued)

TABLE 24 (continued)

National Bank Call Date	Vault Cash		All National Banks (3)	All Banks (4)
	All Nonnational and Mutual Savings Banks			
	Reporting (1)	Nonreporting (2)		
1912				
Sept. 4	575	8	931	1514
Nov. 26	584	9	949	1542
1913				
Feb. 4	597	9	948	1554
Apr. 4	566	10	953	1529
June 4	588	10	913	1511
Aug. 9	586	9	973	1568
Oct. 21	603	9	933	1545
1914				
Jan. 13	611	8	1052	1671
Mar. 4	593	7	995	1595
June 30	639	7	1006	1652
Sept. 12	646	7	1005	1658
Oct. 31	607	7	1025	1639
Dec. 31	599	8	741	1348
1915				
Mar. 4	583	8	779	1370
May 1	579	8	801	1388
June 23	613	8	825	1446
Sept. 2	631	8	908	1547
Nov. 10	637	8	891	1536
Dec. 31	639	8	893	1540
1916				
Mar. 7	675	7	904	1585
May 1	659	7	844	1510
June 30	655	7	805	1467
Sept. 12	721	7	851	1579
Nov. 17	686	7	895	1588
Dec. 27	730	7	873	1610
1917				
Mar. 5	764	6	895	1666
May 1	774	6	842	1622
June 30	752	6	724	1482
Sept. 11	641	6	477	1124
Nov. 20	624	6	483	1113
Dec. 31	596	6	490	1092

(continued)

TABLE 24 (continued)

National Bank Call Date	Vault Cash			
	All Nonnational and Mutual Savings Banks		All National Banks	All Banks
	Reporting (1)	Nonreporting (2)	(3)	(4)
1918				
Mar. 4	589	6	468	1064
May 10	583	6	479	1068
June 29	536	6	430	972
Aug. 31	494	6	405	904
Nov. 1	533	5	472	1010
Dec. 31	542	5	465	1012
1919				
Mar. 4	530	5	437	971
May 12	570	4	443	1016
June 30	556	4	432	992

Part II. Nonmember, Mutual Savings, and Member Banks, Member Bank Call Dates, 1919–42

Member Bank Call Date	Vault Cash			
	All Nonmember and Mutual Savings Banks		All Member Banks	All Banks
	Reporting (1)	Nonreporting (2)	(3)	(4)
1919				
June 30	418	6	567	992
Sept. 12	402	6	624	1032
Nov. 17	451	6	609	1066
Dec. 31	424	7	610	1040
1920				
Feb. 28	426	7	599	1032
May 4	445	7	588	1040
June 30	431	7	601	1039
Sept. 8	404	6	616	1026
Nov. 15	378	6	611	995
Dec. 29	408	5	604	1016
1921				
Feb. 21	392	5	578	975
Apr. 28	383	5	553	941
June 30	370	4	532	907
Sept. 6	334	4	493	831
Dec. 31	358	4	483	845

(continued)

TABLE 24 (continued)

Member Bank Call Date	Vault Cash		All Member Banks (3)	All Banks (4)
	All Nonmember and Mutual Savings Banks			
	Reporting (1)	Nonreporting (2)		
1922				
Mar. 10	362	4	516	882
May 5	364	4	490	858
June 30	366	4	498	868
Sept. 15	353	4	508	866
Dec. 29	389	4	547	940
1923				
Apr. 3	386	4	502	892
June 30	378	4	478	860
Sept. 14	382	4	541	927
Dec. 31	405	4	518	927
1924				
Mar. 31	400	4	499	903
June 30	398	4	508	910
Oct. 10	406	4	550	960
Dec. 31	404	4	531	939
1925				
Apr. 6	406	4	528	939
June 30	407	4	508	919
Sept. 28	418	4	516	938
Dec. 31	431	4	528	963
1926				
Apr. 12	430	4	546	979
June 30	422	4	517	942
Dec. 31	407	3	509	919
1927				
Mar. 23	401	3	521	925
June 30	414	3	540	958
Oct. 10	411	3	530	944
Dec. 31	411	3	529	943
1928				
Feb. 28	406	3	522	931
June 30	395	3	501	899
Oct. 3	404	3	490	896
Dec. 31	414	3	521	938
1929				
Mar. 27	393	3	500	896
June 29	383	3	484	869
Oct. 4	392	3	520	916
Dec. 31	374	2	498	874

(continued)

TABLE 24 (continued)

Member Bank Call Date	Vault Cash		All Member Banks (3)	All Banks (4)
	All Nonmember and Mutual Savings Banks			
	Reporting (1)	Nonreporting (2)		
1930				
Mar. 27	364	2	501	867
June 30	355	2	490	848
Sept. 24	348	2	445	795
Dec. 31	353	2	528	883
1931				
Mar. 25	338	2	448	788
June 30	340	2	504	846
Sept. 29	336	2	525	863
Dec. 31	334	1	482	816
1932				
June 30	303	1	482	786
Sept. 30	273	1	426	700
Dec. 31	283	1	429	712
1933				
June 30	266	1	435	702
Oct. 25	246	1	430	677
Dec. 30	261	1	477	739
1934				
Mar. 5	255	1	504	760
June 30	251	0	530	780
Oct. 17	251	0	529	780
Dec. 31	260	0	563	823
1935				
Mar. 4	261	0	554	816
June 29	260	0	602	862
Nov. 1	266	1	577	844
Dec. 31	276	1	593	870
1936				
Mar. 4	284	1	619	905
June 30	298	1	694	993
Dec. 31	304	1	644	948
1937				
Mar. 31	325	1	643	969
June 30	323	1	611	935
Dec. 31	308	1	577	886
1938				
Mar. 7	321	1	627	949
June 30	335	1	719	1055
Sept. 28	336	1	733	1070
Dec. 31	332	1	756	1089

(continued)

TABLE 24 (concluded)

Member Bank Call Date	All Nonmember and Mutual Savings Banks		All Member Banks (3)	All Banks (4)
	Reporting (1)	Nonreporting (2)		
1939				
Mar. 29	338	1	754	1093
June 30	339	1	767	1106
Oct. 2	339	1	763	1103
Dec. 30	341	1	853	1195
1940				
Mar. 26	362	1	838	1201
June 29	372	1	886	1259
Dec. 31	370	1	886	1257
1941				
Apr. 4	397	1	902	1300
June 30	408	1	1014	1423
Sept. 24	404	1	1007	1413
Dec. 31	394	1	969	1364
1942				
Apr. 4	400	1	994	1395
June 30	410	1	1002	1413
Dec. 31	408	1	946	1356

Source, by Column

Part I

1. The original data were obtained at report dates from the reports of state banking departments and at midyear dates from *Annual Report* of the Comptroller of the Currency. For New York State, June data for vault cash in New York private banks — which include nonreporting banks — from *All-Bank Statistics,* p. 747, were used. For seasonal adjustment and interpolation, see text, Chap. 12, section 2.

2. Vault cash in nonreporting private banks in Mass., N.J., Penna., Md., Va., Ga., Tex., Ohio, Ill., Mich., Minn., Iowa, Mont., and Wash. was obtained at June dates from *All-Bank Statistics* and interpolated by Method L to national bank call dates.

3. Vault cash in national banks, from Comptroller of the Currency, *Annual Report,* was adjusted simultaneously for the daily and for the monthly seasonal in two periods, 1874–1917, 1917–49.

4. Sum of cols. 1, 2, and 3.

reported data not only for banks that were members of the clearing-house, but also, from May 1907 to September 1907, for nonmember banks using it and from February 1908 to December 1917, for all New York City banks not in the clearinghouse.[24]

These data are described variously as the sum of specie and legal tender, or cash reserves, or total money holdings, or lawful money. All these data are presented in the form of weekly averages. We dated them as of Wednesday, the midpoint of the week, selecting the Wednesday date nearest the end of the month. Because they were weekly averages, the data did not require correction for the daily seasonal present in vault cash dated as of a given day, but they did require correction for the monthly seasonal. New York we corrected by itself, the data for the remaining six cities, as a group.

Neither the data for New York nor for the other six cities were continuous, 1907–17. For New York we made a continuous hypothetical series of the three segments by raising the level of the less inclusive segment to that of the more inclusive segments. This hypothetical series was used to estimate seasonal factors that were applied to the discontinuous data. Similarly, for the six-city series a hypothetical total was constructed to compute seasonal factors to apply to the data for individual cities.

of the Associated Banks of Boston, as Returned to the Clearing House, weekly issues (Boston); Commercial and Financial Chronicle, weekly issues (New York, Boston, and Philadelphia).

24 For the distinction between nonmembers using the clearinghouse and banks not in the clearinghouse, see J. G. Cannon, Clearing Houses, pp. 150–156.

Notes to Table 24 (concluded)

Part II

1. See text, Chap. 12, section 2.
2. Same as for Part I, col. 2.
3. Sum of vault cash in national banks from Comptroller of the of the Currency, Annual Report, adjusted simultaneously for the daily and for the monthly seasonal, 1917–49, and in state member banks, from Member Bank Call Report through Mar. 1929; thereafter obtained as a residual by subtracting national bank figures from member bank figures from ibid., also adjusted simultaneously for daily and monthly seasonal. At national bank call dates that were not also state member bank call dates, 1919–22, state member bank figures are interpolations by Method L between closest deseasonalized state member bank figures.
4. Sum of cols. 1, 2, and 3.

At each Wednesday date nearest the end of month we summed the deseasonalized figures for New York and for those of the six cities for which data were available. We did not view this discontinuous monthly series as a potential monthly interpolator of the call date figures. Instead we accepted the monthly data as a component of the total and estimated the residual from call date estimates by interpolation using Method L.

In order to obtain a call date series to be interpolated in this way, it was first necessary to compile the seven-city summation at call dates. For call dates that did not fall on a Wednesday, an estimate was inter- polated by Method L between the deseasonalized Wednesday figures for those of the seven cities for which data were available for weeks immediately preceding and following the call date. This estimate was then subtracted from the call date figure for all reporting banks. If the composition of the seven-city total changed from one call date to the next, the totals were put on the same basis in order to obtain compara- ble residuals. For example, on August 22, 1907, data are available for New York City nonmembers of the clearinghouse as well as members. On the next call date, December 3, 1907, data are available for mem- bers only. The seven-city total at both call dates was therefore obtained with nonmembers excluded and was subtracted from our call date series. The residual was then interpolated to obtain monthly estimates. How- ever, our monthly seven-city totals for August and September 1907 in- cluded New York City nonmembers, consequently the residuals in these two months were too large by the amount of vault cash in these banks. At end of August and September we therefore deducted vault cash in New York City clearinghouse nonmembers.

The final monthly estimates of vault cash, 1907–17, are given in column 4 of Table 25, Part I.

1917–42. Weekly reporting member bank figures are available be- ginning December 1917. These are Friday figures through April 1921, Wednesday figures thereafter. We compiled Friday and Wednesday figures nearest the end of month and adjusted them for the day of the week, on the basis of the daily seasonal indexes we had computed for national and state member bank data.[25] We then made a correction for monthly seasonal in the conventional way.

---

[25] These daily seasonals were weighted by the percentage of the total constituted by vault cash in the component classes of banks and then averaged.

This procedure of course assumes that the distribution of weekly reporting member

We tested vault cash in weekly reporting member banks as a possible interpolator of vault cash in nonweekly reporting member banks and in nonmember banks. The test was made on the call date level, that is, the weekly reporting data were obtained in call date form and deviations from intercall trends correlated with corresponding deviations for the other series. All test correlations were low. When seasonal and movements between alternate call dates have been taken out, apparently only random movements are left in the figures. We also tested currency outside Treasury and Reserve Banks minus vault cash in weekly reporting member banks as a possible interpolator of nonweekly reporting member and nonmember bank data. Again the correlations were low.

We therefore interpolated monthly figures by Method L between the call date figures for nonweekly reporting banks and added these estimates to the weekly reporting member bank figures and to monthly estimates for nonreporting banks to obtain all bank vault cash, monthly. Table 25, Part II, presents the breakdowns and the totals for Friday nearest the end of the month, 1918–19; Part III, for Friday nearest the end of the month, 1919–21, and for Wednesday nearest the end of the month, 1921–42. Beginning August 1, 1919, separate figures are shown for nonweekly reporting member and nonmember banks.

Federal Reserve Estimates, 1943 to Date

It is possible to derive all-bank estimates for 1943–46 by subtracting Federal Reserve published estimates of currency outside all banks [26] from Treasury figures of currency outside the Treasury and Federal Reserve Banks. The estimates of currency outside all banks for these four years are end-of-month figures, so we used data for currency outside the Treasury and Federal Reserve Banks that were similarly dated in order to derive the residual vault cash.

The Federal Reserve System has published monthly estimates of commercial bank vault cash for the period 1947–60,[27] and has made available to us unpublished estimates for 1960–68. For the period since 1947 the Federal Reserve figures are monthly averages of daily figures.

banks between national and state member banks is the same as that of all member banks. If the data on weekly reporting members were broken down by supervisory jurisdiction, the weights for the indexes would more properly be the percentage of vault cash in weekly reporting member banks contributed by national banks and the percentage contributed by state member banks.

[26] *Federal Reserve Bulletin,* monthly issues beginning Feb. 1944.

[27] *Ibid.,* Oct. 1960, pp. 1116–1121. Semimonthly estimates are given.

TABLE 25

Vault Cash at All Banks, at End of Month, 1907–42
(seasonally adjusted, in millions of dollars)

Part I. Clearinghouse Banks of Selected Cities and Other Banks
Wednesdays, 1907–17

Wednesday Nearest End of Month	Clearing-house Banks of Selected Cities (1)	All Other Reporting Banks (2)	All Nonreporting Banks (3)	All Banks (4)
1907				
May 29	493	622	11	1126
July 3	462	645	11	1118
July 31	486	664	11	1161
Sept. 28	469	685	11	1164
Oct. 2	459	715	10	1184
Oct. 30	394	751	10	1155
Nov. 27	420	775	10	1205
1908				
Jan. 1	436	762	10	1208
Jan. 29	446	743	10	1200
Feb. 26	584	687	10	1281
Apr. 1	618	700	9	1328
Apr. 29	645	711	9	1365
June 3	650	694	9	1353
July 1	691	662	9	1362
July 29	723	654	9	1385
Sept. 2	745	675	9	1429
Sept. 30	732	681	9	1423
Oct. 28	742	656	9	1406
Dec. 2	782	629	9	1420
Dec. 30	602	781	8	1391
1909				
Feb. 3	610	795	8	1413
Mar. 3	598	803	8	1409
Mar. 31	600	810	8	1419
Apr. 28	603	818	8	1429
June 2	617	818	8	1443
June 30	628	819	8	1456
July 28	635	819	8	1463
Sept. 1	613	820	9	1442
Sept. 29	601	834	9	1444
Nov. 3	571	852	9	1432

(continued)

TABLE 25 (continued)

Wednesday Nearest End of Month	Clearing-house Banks of Selected Cities (1)	All Other Reporting Banks (2)	All Nonreporting Banks (3)	All Banks (4)
1909				
Dec. 1	575	853	9	1437
Dec. 28	575	844	9	1429
1910				
Feb. 2	566	836	9	1410
Mar. 2	565	864	9	1438
Mar. 30	566	892	10	1469
Apr. 27	538	894	10	1442
June 1	548	896	10	1453
June 29	548	897	10	1455
Aug. 3	582	884	10	1476
Aug. 31	594	874	10	1478
Sept. 28	576	867	10	1453
Nov. 2	555	858	10	1423
Nov. 30	592	871	10	1473
Dec. 28	583	891	10	1484
1911				
Feb. 1	596	901	10	1506
Mar. 1	617	904	10	1530
Mar. 29	614	899	10	1523
May 3	600	890	10	1500
May 31	628	884	10	1522
June 28	645	885	10	1539
Aug. 2	610	889	10	1509
Aug. 30	614	893	10	1517
Sept. 27	616	902	9	1527
Nov. 1	612	914	9	1536
Nov. 29	628	924	9	1561
1912				
Jan. 3	665	927	9	1600
Jan. 31	675	927	9	1610
Feb. 28	658	926	9	1592
Apr. 3	635	921	8	1564
May 1	632	907	8	1547
May 29	640	883	8	1531
July 3	619	874	8	1501
July 31	636	882	8	1525
Aug. 28	626	889	8	1523
Oct. 2	604	900	9	1514

(continued)

TABLE 25 (continued)

Wednesday Nearest End of Month	Clearing-house Banks of Selected Cities (1)	All Other Reporting Banks (2)	All Nonreporting Banks (3)	All Banks (4)
1912				
Oct. 30	600	910	9	1518
Nov. 27	612	919	9	1540
1913				
Jan. 1	627	930	9	1566
Jan. 29	615	939	9	1562
Feb. 26	602	935	9	1546
Apr. 2	593	926	10	1528
Apr. 30	598	913	10	1522
May 28	604	900	10	1514
July 2	603	921	10	1534
July 30	612	945	10	1567
Sept. 3	599	944	9	1552
Oct. 1	611	933	9	1553
Oct. 29	604	930	9	1544
Dec. 3	619	949	9	1576
Dec. 31	634	964	8	1606
1914				
Jan. 28	660	956	8	1624
Feb. 25	676	930	8	1613
Apr. 1	679	943	8	1630
Apr. 29	694	963	7	1664
June 3	690	989	7	1686
June 30	637	1008	7	1652
July 29	610	1037	7	1654
Sept. 2	522	1101	7	1630
Sept. 30	577	1078	7	1662
Oct. 28	608	1027	7	1642
Dec. 2	545	900	7	1452
Dec. 30	439	904	8	1351
1915				
Jan. 27	430	911	8	1349
Mar. 3	438	924	8	1370
Mar. 31	468	910	8	1385
Apr. 28	487	894	8	1390
June 2	511	907	8	1426
June 30	512	921	8	1441
July 28	514	942	8	1464
Sept. 1	569	967	8	1544

(continued)

TABLE 25 (continued)

Wednesday Nearest End of Month	Clearing- house Banks of Selected Cities (1)	All Other Reporting Banks (2)	All Nonreporting Banks (3)	All Banks (4)
1915				
Sept. 29	599	944	8	1551
Nov. 3	624	912	8	1544
Dec. 1	656	907	8	1572
Dec. 28	619	910	7	1536
1916				
Feb. 2	594	953	7	1554
Mar. 1	582	990	7	1579
Mar. 29	563	988	7	1558
May 3	529	972	7	1507
May 31	494	960	7	1461
June 28	525	949	7	1482
Aug. 2	505	1005	7	1518
Aug. 30	531	1053	7	1591
Sept. 27	535	1066	7	1608
Nov. 1	567	1045	7	1619
Nov. 29	498	1063	7	1567
1917				
Jan. 3	575	1065	6	1646
Jan. 31	586	1069	6	1661
Feb. 28	607	1073	6	1686
Mar. 28	563	1092	6	1660
May 2	493	1119	6	1618
May 30	514	1112	6	1632
June 27	332	1087	6	1425
Aug. 1	288	987	6	1281
Aug. 29	262	907	6	1175
Oct. 3	236	873	6	1115
Oct. 31	222	878	6	1106
Nov. 28	227	878	6	1111
1918				
Jan. 2	220	867	6	1093

(continued)

TABLE 25 (continued)

Part II. Weekly Reporting Member Banks and All Other Banks,
Fridays, 1918–19

Friday Nearest End of Month	Weekly Reporting Member Banks (1)	All Other Reporting Banks (2)	All Nonreporting Banks (3)	All Banks (4)
1918				
Feb. 1	390	689	6	1085
Mar. 1	389	669	6	1064
Mar. 29	400	661	6	1067
May 3	406	654	6	1066
May 31	381	626	6	1013
June 28	374	592	6	972
Aug. 2	380	549	6	935
Aug. 30	384	515	6	905
Sept. 27	381	561	5	947
Nov. 1	383	622	5	1010
Nov. 29	389	621	5	1015
1919				
Jan. 3	385	618	5	1008
Jan. 31	384	608	5	997
Feb. 28	365	597	4	966
Mar. 28	382	606	4	992
May 2	376	621	4	1001
May 29	366	623	4	993
June 27	373	619	4	996

(continued)

TABLE 25 (continued)

Part IIIA. Weekly and Nonweekly Reporting Member and Nonmember Banks, Fridays, 1919–21

Friday Nearest End of Month	Weekly Reporting Member Banks (1)	Nonweekly Reporting Member Banks (2)	Nonmember and Mutual Savings Banks		All Banks (5)
			Report ing (3)	Nonre porting (4)	
1919					
Aug. 1	371	208	412	6	997
Aug. 29	378	217	405	6	1006
Oct. 3	380	221	418	6	1025
Oct. 31	370	221	438	6	1035
Nov. 28	381	222	444	6	1053
1920					
Jan. 2	387	223	424	7	1041
Jan. 30	387	211	425	7	1030
Feb. 27	401	198	426	7	1032
Apr. 2	394	195	436	7	1032
Apr. 30	385	192	444	7	1028
May 28	385	204	439	7	1035
July 2	380	221	430	7	1038
July 30	388	218	419	7	1032
Sept. 3	382	215	406	6	1009
Oct. 1	377	218	396	6	997
Oct. 29	377	222	385	6	990
Dec. 3	373	250	390	6	1019
Dec. 31	318	283	407	5	1013
1921					
Jan. 28	365	252	399	5	1021
Feb. 25	355	224	391	5	975
Apr. 1	328	211	387	5	931
Apr. 29	357	201	383	4	945

(continued)

TABLE 25 (continued)

Part IIIB. Weekly and Nonweekly Reporting Member and Nonmember Banks, Wednesdays, 1921–42

Wednesday Nearest End of Month	Weekly Reporting Member Banks (1)	Nonweekly Reporting Member Banks (2)	Nonmember and Mutual Savings Banks		All Banks (5)
			Report-ing (3)	Nonre-porting (4)	
1921					
June 1	305	209	376	4	894
June 29	314	216	371	4	905
Aug. 3	301	204	352	4	861
Aug. 31	286	194	337	4	821
Sept. 28	295	196	338	4	833
Nov. 2	270	202	346	4	822
Nov. 30	265	207	352	4	828
Dec. 28	275	211	357	4	847
1922					
Feb. 1	261	229	360	4	854
Mar. 1	258	243	362	4	867
Mar. 29	273	238	363	4	878
May 3	271	219	364	4	858
May 31	269	222	365	4	860
June 28	267	226	366	4	863
Aug. 2	268	225	361	4	858
Aug. 30	271	224	356	4	855
Sept. 27	272	228	357	4	861
Nov. 1	259	241	369	4	873
Nov. 29	257	252	379	4	892
1923					
Jan. 3	265	261	389	4	919
Jan. 31	269	249	388	4	910
Feb. 28	271	237	387	4	899
Mar. 28	279	225	386	4	894
May 2	270	217	383	4	874
May 29	271	212	381	4	868
June 27	271	207	378	4	860
Aug. 1	269	226	380	4	879
Aug. 29	279	244	381	4	908
Oct. 3	278	253	386	4	921
Oct. 31	264	252	392	4	912
Nov. 28	265	251	398	4	918
1924					
Jan. 2	262	249	405	4	920
Jan. 30	267	243	403	4	917

(continued)

TABLE 25 (continued)

Wednesday Nearest End of Month	Weekly Reporting Member Banks (1)	Nonweekly Reporting Member Banks (2)	Nonmember and Mutual Savings Banks		All Banks (5)
			Report- ing (3)	Nonre- porting (4)	
1924					
Feb. 27	274	237	402	4	917
Apr. 2	266	230	400	4	900
Apr. 30	263	231	399	4	897
May 28	275	231	399	4	909
July 2	280	233	398	4	915
July 30	281	242	401	4	928
Sept. 3	277	254	404	4	939
Oct. 1	264	264	406	4	938
Oct. 29	273	267	406	4	950
Dec. 3	278	268	405	4	955
Dec. 31	262	269	404	4	939
1925					
Jan. 28	273	263	405	4	945
Feb. 25	288	257	405	4	954
Apr. 1	266	249	406	4	925
Apr. 29	276	246	407	4	933
June 3	266	243	407	4	920
July 1	267	241	407	4	919
July 29	270	241	411	4	926
Sept. 2	264	241	415	4	924
Sept. 30	276	241	418	4	939
Oct. 28	265	246	422	4	937
Dec. 2	263	251	427	4	945
Dec. 30	274	256	431	4	965
1926					
Feb. 3	268	259	431	4	962
Mar. 3	272	261	430	4	967
Mar. 31	270	263	430	4	967
Apr. 28	270	261	428	4	963
June 2	271	256	424	4	955
June 30	266	251	422	4	943
July 28	273	251	419	4	947
Sept. 1	265	251	417	4	937
Sept. 29	277	251	414	4	946
Nov. 3	280	251	411	4	946
Dec. 1	257	251	409	4	921
Dec. 29	261	251	407	3	922

(continued)

TABLE 25 (continued)

Wednesday Nearest End of Month	Weekly Reporting Member Banks (1)	Nonweekly Reporting Member Banks (2)	Nonmember and Mutual Savings Banks		All Banks (5)
			Report-ing (3)	Nonre-porting (4)	
1927					
Feb. 2	252	256	404	3	915
Mar. 2	249	261	402	3	915
Mar. 30	259	265	402	3	929
Apr. 27	258	270	406	3	937
June 1	248	276	411	3	938
June 29	258	281	414	3	956
Aug. 3	249	278	413	3	943
Aig. 31	249	276	412	3	940
Sept. 28	251	274	411	3	939
Nov. 2	239	275	411	3	928
Nov. 30	247	278	411	3	939
Dec. 28	256	281	411	3	951
1928					
Feb. 1	233	283	408	3	927
Feb. 29	237	285	406	3	931
Mar. 28	240	280	404	3	927
May 2	235	274	400	3	912
May 29	235	269	398	3	905
June 27	238	264	395	3	900
Aug. 1	231	258	398	3	890
Aug. 29	243	254	401	3	901
Oct. 3	241	249	404	3	897
Oct. 31	231	257	407	3	898
Nov. 28	240	266	410	3	919
1929					
Jan. 2	237	276	414	3	930
Jan. 30	239	270	407	3	919
Feb. 27	240	265	400	3	908
Apr. 3	238	259	393	3	893
May 1	219	258	389	3	869
May 29	232	258	386	3	879
June 26	222	257	383	3	865
July 31	233	269	386	3	891
Aug. 28	235	279	389	3	906
Oct. 2	222	292	392	3	909
Oct. 30	250	291	387	3	931
Nov. 27	237	288	381	3	909
Dec. 31	213	285	374	2	874

(continued)

TABLE 25 (continued)

Wednesday Nearest End of Month	Weekly Reporting Member Banks (1)	Nonweekly Reporting Member Banks (2)	Nonmember and Mutual Savings Banks		All Banks (5)
			Report- ing (3)	Nonre- porting (4)	
1930					
Jan. 29	227	288	371	2	888
Feb. 26	216	290	367	2	875
Apr. 2	204	292	363	2	861
Apr. 30	209	286	361	2	858
May 28	225	281	358	2	866
July 2	220	273	355	2	850
July 30	212	264	353	2	831
Sept. 3	204	251	350	2	807
Oct. 1	195	248	348	2	793
Oct. 29	201	263	350	2	816
Dec. 3	206	281	352	2	841
Dec. 31	232	296	353	2	883
1931					
Jan. 28	223	279	348	2	852
Feb. 25	220	262	343	2	827
Apr. 1	201	248	338	2	789
Apr. 29	218	258	339	2	817
June 3	206	271	340	2	819
July 1	223	281	340	2	846
July 29	218	280	339	2	839
Sept. 2	224	278	337	2	841
Sept. 30	247	277	336	2	862
Oct. 28	246	273	335	2	856
Dec. 2	211	268	334	2	815
Dec. 30	220	264	334	1	819
1932					
Feb. 3	215	262	328	1	806
Mar. 2	202	261	323	1	787
Mar. 30	212	259	319	1	791
Apr. 27	202	258	314	1	775
June 1	194	256	308	1	759
June 29	230	254	303	1	788
Aug. 3	200	245	292	1	738
Aug. 31	202	237	283	1	723
Sept. 28	200	230	274	1	705
Nov. 2	175	234	276	1	686
Nov. 30	187	239	279	1	706
Dec. 28	189	244	282	1	716

(continued)

TABLE 25 (continued)

Wednesday Nearest End of Month	Weekly Reporting Member Banks (1)	Nonweekly Reporting Member Banks (2)	Nonmember and Mutual Savings Banks		All Banks (5)
			Report- ing (3)	Nonre- porting (4)	
1933					
Feb. 1	189	241	280	1	711
Mar. 1	380	239	277	1	897
Mar. 29	275	237	274	1	787
May 3	223	234	271	1	729
May 31	212	231	268	1	712
June 28	203	229	266	1	699
Aug. 2	193	226	260	1	680
Aug. 30	217	224	256	1	698
Sept. 27	217	222	251	1	691
Nov. 1	203	223	248	1	675
Nov. 29	223	237	254	1	715
1934					
Jan. 3	218	253	260	0	731
Jan. 31	231	256	258	0	745
Feb. 28	238	260	255	0	753
Mar. 28	264	265	254	0	783
May 2	244	270	253	0	767
May 30	257	275	252	0	784
June 27	256	280	251	0	787
Aug. 1	238	275	251	0	764
Aug. 29	259	271	251	0	781
Oct. 3	263	266	251	0	780
Oct. 31	268	267	253	0	788
Nov. 28	280	274	256	0	810
1935					
Jan. 2	272	281	260	0	813
Jan. 30	297	271	261	0	829
Feb. 27	304	261	261	0	826
Apr. 3	296	268	261	0	825
May 1	278	276	261	0	815
May 29	301	285	260	0	846
July 3	305	293	260	0	858
July 31	315	283	261	0	859
Aug. 28	326	274	263	0	863
Oct. 2	308	262	265	0	835
Oct. 30	325	253	266	0	844
Nov. 27	327	265	270	0	862
Dec. 31	312	281	276	1	870

(continued)

TABLE 25 (continued)

Wednesday Nearest End of Month	Weekly Reporting Member Banks (1)	Nonweekly Reporting Member Banks (2)	Nonmember and Mutual Savings Banks		All Banks (5)
			Report-ing (3)	Nonre-porting (4)	
1936					
Jan. 29	345	276	280	1	902
Feb. 26	359	272	283	1	915
Apr. 1	356	283	288	1	928
Apr. 29	370	296	291	1	958
June 3	354	313	295	1	963
July 1	368	324	298	1	991
July 29	376	317	298	1	992
Sept. 2	363	309	300	1	973
Sept. 30	359	302	301	1	963
Oct. 28	376	295	301	1	973
Dec. 2	366	285	303	1	955
Dec. 30	367	280	304	1	952
1937					
Feb. 3	367	287	312	1	967
Mar. 3	362	292	318	1	973
Mar. 31	345	298	325	1	969
Apr. 28	343	306	324	1	974
June 2	315	315	323	1	954
June 30	288	323	323	1	935
July 28	304	317	320	1	942
Sept. 1	275	310	317	1	903
Sept. 29	307	304	315	1	927
Nov. 3	296	296	312	1	905
Dec. 1	278	290	310	1	879
Dec. 29	301	284	308	1	894
1938					
Feb. 2	271	312	314	1	898
Mar. 2	270	335	320	1	926
Mar. 30	329	336	324	1	990
Apr. 27	360	333	327	1	1021
June 1	374	329	331	1	1035
June 29	396	325	335	1	1057
Aug. 3	370	327	335	1	1033
Aug. 31	377	328	335	1	1041
Sept. 28	404	329	336	1	1070
Nov. 2	390	339	334	1	1064
Nov. 30	404	346	333	1	1084
Dec. 28	414	354	332	1	1101

(continued)

TABLE 25 (continued)

Wednesday Nearest End of Month	Weekly Reporting Member Banks (1)	Nonweekly Reporting Member Banks (2)	Nonmember and Mutual Savings Banks		All Banks (5)
			Report- ing (3)	Nonre- porting (4)	
1939					
Feb. 1	386	346	334	1	1067
Mar. 1	377	339	336	1	1053
Mar. 29	423	331	338	1	1093
May 3	397	334	338	1	1070
May 31	409	336	338	1	1084
June 28	432	339	339	1	1111
Aug. 2	414	330	339	1	1084
Aug. 30	455	321	339	1	1116
Sept. 27	461	313	339	1	1114
Nov. 1	426	344	340	1	1111
Nov. 29	460	374	341	1	1176
Dec. 27	461	404	341	1	1207
1940					
Jan. 31	448	390	349	1	1188
Feb. 28	465	376	355	1	1197
Apr. 3	452	367	363	1	1183
May 1	433	383	366	1	1183
May 29	468	399	368	1	1236
July 3	454	417	372	1	1244
July 31	468	420	371	1	1260
Aug. 28	497	422	371	1	1291
Oct. 2	460	425	371	1	1257
Oct. 30	489	427	371	1	1288
Nov. 27	492	429	371	1	1293
Dec. 31	454	432	370	1	1257
1941					
Jan. 29	515	423	379	1	1318
Feb. 26	513	414	387	1	1315
Apr. 2	491	404	397	1	1293
Apr. 30	500	422	400	1	1323
May 28	539	442	404	1	1386
July 2	541	466	408	1	1416
July 30	548	469	407	1	1425
Sept. 3	531	474	405	1	1411
Oct. 1	510	478	404	1	1393
Oct. 29	528	484	401	1	1414
Dec. 3	506	492	397	1	1396
Dec. 31	471	498	394	1	1364

(continued)

TABLE 25 (concluded)

Wednesday Nearest End of Month	Weekly Reporting Member Banks (1)	Nonweekly Reporting Member Banks (2)	Nonmember and Mutual Savings Banks		All Banks (5)
			Reporting (3)	Nonreporting (4)	
1942					
Jan. 28	540	496	396	1	1433
Feb. 25	530	494	398	1	1423
Apr. 1	491	491	400	1	1383
Apr. 29	518	507	403	1	1429
June 3	468	528	407	1	1404
July 1	451	545	410	1	1407
July 29	498	534	410	1	1443
Sept. 2	463	521	410	1	1395
Sept. 30	471	510	409	1	1391
Oct. 28	487	499	409	1	1396
Dec. 2	471	486	409	1	1367
Dec. 30	474	475	409	1	1359

Notes to Table 25

Source, by Column

Part I

1. These are seasonally adjusted sums of vault cash in clearinghouse banks of selected cities for the periods shown below. The series is discontinuous. The data come from the following sources:
   a. *Chicago, 1907—08,* from A. P. Andrew, *Statistics for the Unifed States, 1867—1909,* pp. 149—150.
   b. *St. Louis, New Orleans, San Francisco, 1907—08,* from E. W. Kemmerer, *Seasonal Variation in the Relative Demand for Money and Capital in the United States,* pp. 269, 274, 275.
   c. *Philadelphia, 1907—17,* from *The American Banker,* monthly issues.
   d. *Boston, 1907—16,* from Boston Clearing House Association, *Statement of the Associated Banks of Boston, as Returned to the Clearing House,* weekly issues.
   e. *New York, 1907—17,* from *Commercial and Financial Chronicle,* weekly issues. This source also shows data for Boston and Philadelphia.

For coverage of series, dating and seasonal adjustment, see text, Chap. 12, section 3.

2. These are residual figures for reporting banks not in the clearinghouse data of col. 1, See text, Chap. 12, section 3 for derivation.

3. Vault cash in nonreporting private banks in Mass., Penna., Md., Va., Ga., Tex., Ohio, Mich., Iowa, Mont., and Wash. was obtained at June dates from *All-Bank Statistics*, and interpolated by Method L to Wednesday nearest the end of the month.

4. Sum of cols. 1, 2, and 3.

Part II

1. These are seasonally adjusted figures for vault cash in weekly reporting member banks. The original figures come from the *Federal Reserve Bulletin*, monthly issues.

2. From the call date figures for all reporting banks, Table 24, cols. 1 plus 3, call date figures for weekly reporting member banks were deducted. For call dates that fell on a Friday, the deseasonalized Friday figure for weekly reporting member banks was used; for call dates that fell on another day of the week, a figure was interpolated by Method L to the call date between deseasonalized Friday figures for the week immediately preceding and for the week immediately following the call date. We interpolated by Method L to Friday nearest the end of the month between the call date residuals.

3. June figures, same as Part I, col. 3 were interpolated by Method L to Friday nearest the end of the month.

4. Sum of cols. 1, 2, and 3.

Part III

1. Same as Part II, col. 1, except that beginning May 1921, the figures are Wednesday data and were corrected by the Wednesday daily index. The source for the original figures, through 1941, is *Banking and Monetary Statistics*, pp. 134−162; thereafter, *Federal Reserve Bulletin*, monthly issues.

2. From the call date figures for all member banks, Table 24, Part II, col. 3, call date figures for weekly reporting member banks were deducted, as described above, for Part II, col. 2, and the residuals were interpolated by Method L to Friday nearest the end of the month, Aug. 1, 1919−Apr. 29, 1921, to Wednesday thereafter.

3. Interpolations by Method L between call date figures of Table 24, Part II, col. 1, to Friday nearest the end of the month, Aug. 1, 1919−Apr. 29, 1921, to Wednesday thereafter

4. June figures, same as Part I, col. 3, were interpolated by Method L to Friday nearest the end of the month, Aug. 1, 1919−Apr. 29, 1921, to Wednesday thereafter.

5. Sum of cols. 1, 2, 3, and 4.

We corrected the vault cash estimates for monthly seasonal movements for 1943–46 and 1947–60. The seasonally corrected Federal Reserve figures, 1943–60, are given in *A Monetary History;* [28] in this volume we do not reproduce them and do not show them for years after 1960.

4. Currency Held by the Public: at Call Dates and Monthly

Table 26 brings together the call date series for currency in circulation described in section 1 and the vault cash series described in section 2. The difference between them is the call date series of currency held by the public.

Table 27 brings together the corresponding monthly series described in sections 1 and 3.

Beginning 1943, we present seasonally adjusted Federal Reserve estimates of currency held by the public. For 1943–46 the data are for end of month. Because the period is brief, it has not been possible to correct for daily as well as monthly seasonals. Our seasonal correction is limited to the elimination of the monthly component of the seasonal variation insofar as it is distinguishable. Beginning 1947 the data are Federal Reserve seasonally adjusted monthly averages of daily figures.[29]

5. Reliability of the Estimates

The trustworthiness of our residual series cannot be measured directly. Any errors in our estimates of vault cash as well as our revisions of currency outside Treasury and Federal Reserve Banks, if not offsetting, are transmitted directly to the estimates of the currency holdings of the public. For currency in circulation we have no additional information on errors of reporting. One hypothetical source of error is the inclusion, in the reported figures, of currency which has been lost or destroyed. However, various studies of the rate of loss of currency suggest that this source of error is negligible.[30]

[28] Table A-2, col. 1, pp. 741–744.

[29] *Federal Reserve Bulletin,* monthly issues beginning Feb. 1944, for end-of-month original estimates, 1943–46; Oct. 1969, pp. 790–793, for seasonally adjusted monthly averages of daily figures, 1947–68.

[30] See *A Monetary History,* pp. 442–443, footnote 20; Robert Laurent, "Currency Transfers by Denomination," Ph.D. thesis in process, University of Chicago.

TABLE 26

*Currency in Circulation Outside Treasury and Federal Reserve
Banks, All Bank Vault Cash, and Currency Held by the Public,
National and Member Bank Call Dates, 1907–42*
(seasonally adjusted, in millions of dollars)

Call Date[a]	Currency in Circulation Outside Treasury & F. R. Banks (1)	Vault Cash, All Banks (2)	Currency Held by the Public (3)
1907			
May 20	2834	1121	1713
Aug. 22	2819	1163	1656
Dec. 3	3007	1216	1791
1908			
Feb. 14	3095	1259	1836
May 14	3087	1386	1701
July 15	3089	1354	1735
Sept. 23	3099	1445	1654
Nov. 27	3104	1424	1680
1909			
Feb. 5	3091	1409	1682
Apr. 23	3112	1429	1683
June 23	3137	1455	1682
Sept. 1	3129	1440	1689
Nov. 16	3138	1454	1684
1910			
Jan. 31	3128	1409	1719
Mar. 29	3163	1469	1694
June 30	3172	1453	1719
Sept. 1	3206	1476	1730
Nov. 10	3203	1422	1781
1911			
Jan. 7	3223	1504	1719
Mar. 7	3261	1527	1734
June 7	3300	1524	1776
Sept. 1	3293	1514	1779
Dec. 5	3305	1551	1754
1912			
Feb. 20	3326	1597	1729
Apr. 18	3325	1556	1769
June 14	3346	1524	1822
Sept. 4	3352	1514	1838
Nov. 26	3366	1542	1824

(continued)

TABLE 26 (continued)

Call Date[a]	Currency in Circulation Outside Treasury & F. R. Banks (1)	Vault Cash, All Banks (2)	Currency Held by the Public (3)
1913			
Feb. 4	3393	1554	1839
Apr. 4	3363	1529	1834
June 4	3404	1511	1893
Aug. 9	3432	1568	1864
Oct. 21	3452	1545	1907
1914			
Jan. 13	3473	1671	1802
Mar. 4	3486	1595	1891
June 30	3482	1652	1830
Sept. 12	3607	1658	1949
Oct. 31	3721	1639	2082
Dec. 31	3221	1348	1873
1915			
Mar. 4	3226	1370	1856
May 1	3298	1388	1910
June 23	3329	1446	1883
Sept. 2	3420	1547	1873
Nov. 10	3487	1536	1951
Dec. 31	3514	1540	1974
1916			
Mar. 7	3599	1585	2014
May 1	3632	1510	2122
June 30	3665	1467	2198
Sept. 12	3778	1579	2199
Nov. 17	3828	1588	2240
Dec. 27	3867	1610	2257
1917			
Mar. 5	4119	1666	2453
May 1	4198	1622	2576
June 20	4148	1482	2666
Sept. 11	4014	1124	2890
Nov. 20	4148	1113	3035
Dec. 31	4257	1092	3165
1918			
Mar. 4	4330	1064	3266
May 10	4447	1068	3379
June 29	4497	972	3525
Aug. 31	4798	904	3894

(continued)

TABLE 26 (continued)

Call Date[a]	Currency in Circulation Outside Treasury & F. R. Banks (1)	Vault Cash, All Banks (2)	Currency Held by the Public (3)
1918			
Nov. 1	5116	1010	4106
Dec. 31	5120	1012	4108
1919			
Mar. 4	4922	971	3951
May 12	4951	1016	3935
June 30	4879	992	3887
Sept. 12	4990	1032	3958
Nov. 17	5140	1066	4074
Dec. 31	5257	1040	4217
1920			
Feb. 28	5346	1032	4314
May 4	5446	1040	4406
June 30	5499	1039	4460
Sept. 8	5590	1026	4564
Nov. 15	5604	995	4609
Dec. 29	5504	1016	4488
1921			
Feb. 21	5264	975	4289
Apr. 28	5106	941	4165
June 30	4949	907	4042
Sept. 6	4755	831	3924
Dec. 31	4583	845	3738
1922			
Mar. 10	4490	882	3608
May 5	4483	858	3625
June 30	4490	868	3622
Sept. 15	4550	866	3684
Dec. 29	4699	940	3759
1923			
Apr. 3	4755	892	3863
June 30	4850	860	3990
Sept. 14	4917	927	3990
Dec. 31	4904	927	3977
1924			
Mar. 31	4879	903	3976
June 30	4860	910	3950
Oct. 10	4813	960	3853
Dec. 31	4854	939	3915

(continued)

TABLE 26 (continued)

Call Date[a]	Currency in Circulation Outside Treasury & F. R. Banks (1)	Vault Cash, All Banks (2)	Currency Held by the Public (3)
1925			
Apr. 6	4866	939	3927
June 30	4844	919	3925
Sept. 28	4847	938	3909
Dec. 31	4931	963	3968
1926			
Apr. 12	4945	979	3966
June 30	4921	942	3979
Dec. 31	4907	919	3988
1927			
Mar. 23	4931	925	4006
June 30	4907	958	3949
Oct. 10	4868	944	3924
Dec. 31	4812	943	3869
1928			
Feb. 28	4734	931	3803
June 30	4830	899	3931
Oct. 3	4766	896	3870
Dec. 31	4765	938	3827
1929			
Mar. 27	4796	896	3900
June 29	4778	869	3909
Oct. 4	4734	916	3818
Dec. 31	4674	874	3800
1930			
Mar. 27	4587	867	3720
June 30	4533	848	3685
Sept. 24	4446	795	3651
Dec. 31	4692	883	3809
1931			
Mar. 25	4648	788	3860
June 30	4839	846	3993
Sept. 29	5146	863	4283
Dec. 31	5427	816	4611
1932			
June 30	5756	786	4970
Sept. 30	5641	700	4941
Dec. 31	5546	712	4834

(continued)

TABLE 26 (continued)

Call Date[a]	Currency in Circulation Outside Treasury & F. R. Banks (1)	Vault Cash, All Banks (2)	Currency Held by the Public (3)
1933			
June 30	5642	702	4940
Oct. 25	5483	677	4806
Dec. 30	5575	739	4836
1934			
Mar. 5	5278	760	4518
June 30	5373	780	4593
Oct. 17	5392	780	4612
Dec. 31	5366	823	4543
1935			
Mar. 4	5531	816	4715
June 29	5568	862	4706
Nov. 1	5686	844	4842
Dec. 31	5749	870	4879
1936			
Mar. 4	5910	905	5005
June 30	6242	993	5249
Dec. 31	6421	948	5473
1937			
Mar. 31	6449	969	5480
June 30	6447	935	5512
Dec. 31	6416	886	5530
1938			
Mar. 1	6390	949	5441
June 30	6485	1055	5430
Sept. 28	6601	1070	5531
Dec. 31	6702	1089	5613
1939			
Mar. 29	6900	1093	5807
June 30	7062	1106	5956
Oct. 2	7257	1103	6154
Dec. 30	7426	1195	6231
1940			
Mar. 26	7589	1201	6388
June 29	7847	1259	6588
Dec. 31	8535	1257	7278
1941			
Apr. 4	9009	1300	7709
June 30	9574	1423	8151

(continued)

TABLE 26 (concluded)

Call Date[a]	Currency in Circulation Outside Treasury & F. R. Banks (1)	Vault Cash, All Banks (2)	Currency Held by the Public (3)
1941			
Sept. 24	10094	1413	8681
Dec. 31	10908	1364	9544
1942			
Apr. 4	11638	1395	10243
June 30	12457	1413	11044
Dec. 31	15123	1356	13767
1943			
June 30	17527	1564	15963
Oct. 18	18992	1608	17384
Dec. 31	20029	1563	18466
1944			
Apr. 13	21428	1772	19656
June 30	22685	1722	20963
Dec. 30	24738	1804	22934

[a]National bank call dates through 1922; national and member bank call dates thereafter.

Source by Column

1. Interpolated by Method L between the seasonally adjusted end-of-month series, given in Table 27, col. 1.
2. Table 24, Part I, col. 4, Part II, col. 4.
3. Col. 1 minus col. 2.

For bank vault cash, Table 28 shows by classes of banks the proportion of our total estimates based on reported and estimated figures. The proportion shown as reported at call dates includes nonidentically dated figures that were seasonally adjusted by us and shifted to call dates. Thus viewed, 9 per cent of our final call date results, 1907–19, and 14 per cent, 1919–42, represent interpolated values. Even a large error in our interpolation procedure will not seriously affect the reliability of our call date totals.

Thirty-six per cent of the monthly estimates represent reported figures, the remainder, interpolations by Method L between call date figures.

TABLE 27

Currency in Circulation Outside Treasury and Federal Reserve Banks,
All Bank Vault Cash, and Currency Held by the Public,
Wednesday [a]Nearest End of Month, 1907–42
(seasonally adjusted, in millions of dollars)

Wednesday Nearest End of Month	Currency in Circulation Outside Treasury & F. R. Banks (1)	Vault Cash, All Banks (2)	Currency Held by the Public (3)
1907			
May 29	2841	1126	1715
July 3	2815	1118	1697
July 31	2823	1161	1662
Aug. 28	2818	1164	1654
Oct. 2	2815	1184	1631
Oct. 30	2885	1155	1730
Nov. 27	2989	1205	1784
1908			
Jan. 1	3069	1208	1861
Jan. 29	3093	1200	1893
Feb. 26	3095	1281	1814
Apr. 1	3085	1328	1757
Apr. 29	3109	1365	1744
June 3	3060	1353	1707
July 1	3081	1362	1719
July 29	3097	1385	1712
Sept. 2	3097	1429	1668
Sept. 30	3099	1423	1676
Oct. 28	3104	1406	1698
Dec. 2	3104	1420	1684
Dec. 30	3105	1391	1714
1909			
Feb. 3	3091	1413	1678
Mar. 3	3091	1409	1682
Mar. 31	3091	1419	1672
Apr. 28	3112	1429	1683
June 2	3120	1443	1677
June 30	3143	1456	1687
July 28	3135	1463	1672
Sept. 1	3129	1442	1687
Sept. 29	3152	1444	1708
Nov. 3	3136	1432	1704
Dec. 1	3140	1437	1703
Dec. 28	3138	1429	1709

(continued)

TABLE 27 (continued)

Wednesday Nearest End of Month	Currency in Circulation Outside Treasury & F. R. Banks (1)	Vault Cash, All Banks (2)	Currency Held by the Public (3)
1910			
Feb. 2	3129	1410	1719
Mar. 2	3142	1438	1704
Mar. 30	3164	1469	1695
Apr. 27	3132	1442	1690
June 1	3155	1453	1702
June 29	3171	1455	1716
Aug. 3	3186	1476	1710
Aug. 31	3206	1478	1728
Sept. 28	3211	1453	1758
Nov. 2	3197	1423	1774
Nov. 30	3216	1473	1743
Dec. 28	3218	1484	1734
1911			
Feb. 1	3241	1506	1735
Mar. 1	3260	1530	1730
Mar. 29	3266	1523	1743
May 3	3276	1500	1776
May 31	3303	1522	1781
June 28	3282	1539	1743
Aug. 2	3260	1509	1751
Aug. 30	3292	1517	1775
Sept. 27	3283	1527	1756
Nov. 1	3286	1536	1750
Nov. 29	3306	1561	1745
1912			
Jan. 3	3298	1600	1698
Jan. 31	3316	1610	1706
Feb. 28	3330	1592	1738
Apr. 3	3314	1564	1750
May 1	3334	1547	1787
May 29	3358	1531	1827
July 3	3332	1501	1831
July 31	3352	1525	1827
Aug. 28	3353	1523	1830
Oct. 2	3345	1514	1831
Oct. 30	3375	1518	1857
Nov. 27	3365	1540	1825

(continued)

TABLE 27 (continued)

Wednesday Nearest End of Month	Currency in Circulation Outside Treasury & F. R. Banks (1)	Vault Cash, All Banks (2)	Currency Held by the Public (3)
1913			
Jan. 1	3383	1566	1817
Jan. 29	3393	1562	1831
Feb. 26	3388	1546	1842
Apr. 2	3361	1528	1833
Apr. 30	3392	1522	1870
May 28	3402	1514	1888
July 2	3415	1534	1881
July 30	3436	1567	1869
Sept. 3	3424	1552	1872
Oct. 1	3449	1553	1896
Oct. 29	3453	1544	1909
Dec. 3	3462	1576	1886
Dec. 31	3476	1606	1870
1914			
Jan. 28	3471	1624	1847
Feb. 25	3484	1613	1871
Apr. 1	3484	1630	1854
Apr. 29	3428	1664	1764
June 3	3529	1686	1843
June 30	3482	1652	1830
July 29	3473	1654	1819
Sept. 2	3539	1630	1909
Sept. 30	3728	1662	2066
Oct. 28	3722	1642	2080
Dec. 2	3343	1452	1891
Dec. 30	3225	1351	1874
1915			
Jan. 27	3250	1349	1901
Mar. 3	3225	1370	1855
Mar. 31	3260	1385	1875
Apr. 28	3295	1390	1905
June 2	3313	1426	1887
June 30	3335	1441	1894
July 28	3361	1464	1897
Sept. 1	3418	1544	1874
Sept. 29	3454	1551	1903
Nov. 3	3486	1544	1942
Dec. 1	3489	1572	1917
Dec. 28	3511	1536	1975

(continued)

TABLE 27 (continued)

Wednesday Nearest End of Month	Currency in Circulation Outside Treasury & F. R. Banks (1)	Vault Cash, All Banks (2)	Currency Held by the Public (3)
1916			
Feb. 2	3599	1554	2045
Mar. 1	3593	1579	2014
Mar. 29	3619	1558	2061
May 3	3629	1507	2122
May 31	3589	1461	2128
June 28	3660	1482	2178
Aug. 2	3692	1518	2174
Aug. 30	3760	1591	2169
Sept. 27	3798	1608	2190
Nov. 1	3835	1619	2216
Nov. 29	3822	1567	2255
1917			
Jan. 3	3887	1646	2241
Jan. 31	4012	1661	2351
Feb. 28	4108	1686	2422
Mar. 28	4169	1660	2509
May 2	4200	1618	2582
May 30	4272	1632	2640
June 27	4103	1425	2678
Aug. 1	4025	1281	2744
Aug. 29	4004	1175	2829
Oct. 3	4037	1115	2922
Oct. 31	4065	1106	2959
Nov. 28	4181	1111	3070
1918			
Jan. 2	4252	1093	3159
Feb. 1	4177	1085	3092
Mar. 1	4322	1064	3258
Mar. 29	4398	1067	3331
May 3	4451	1066	3385
May 31	4435	1013	3422
June 28	4495	972	3523
Aug. 2	4634	935	3699
Aug. 30	4792	905	3887
Sept. 27	4974	947	4027
Nov. 1	5116	1010	4106
Nov. 29	5106	1015	4091

(continued)

TABLE 27 (continued)

Wednesday Nearest End of Month	Currency in Circulation Outside Treasury & F. R. Banks (1)	Vault Cash, All Banks (2)	Currency Held by the Public (3)
1919			
Jan. 3	5104	1008	4096
Jan. 31	4959	997	3962
Feb. 28	4920	966	3954
Mar. 28	4936	992	3944
May 2	4963	1001	3962
May 29	4929	993	3936
June 27	4884	996	3888
Aug. 1	4955	997	3958
Aug. 29	4969	1006	3963
Oct. 3	5027	1025	4002
Oct. 31	5088	1035	4053
Nov. 28	5174	1053	4121
1920			
Jan. 2	5254	1041	4213
Jan. 30	5209	1030	4179
Feb. 27	5341	1032	4309
Apr. 2	5404	1032	4372
Apr. 30	5446	1028	4418
May 28	5449	1035	4414
July 2	5501	1038	4463
July 30	5532	1032	4500
Sept. 3	5583	1009	4574
Oct. 1	5621	997	4624
Oct. 29	5647	990	4657
Dec. 3	5553	1019	4534
Dec. 31	5500	1013	4487
1921			
Jan. 28	5338	1021	4317
Feb. 25	5253	975	4278
Apr. 1	5151	931	4220
Apr. 29	5105	945	4160
June 1	5023	894	4129
June 29	4952	905	4047
Aug. 3	4848	861	3987
Aug. 31	4759	821	3938
Sept. 28	4738	833	3905
Nov. 2	4627	822	3805
Nov. 30	4572	828	3744
Dec. 28	4582	847	3735

(continued)

TABLE 27 (continued)

Wednesday Nearest End of Month	Currency in Circulation Outside Treasury & F. R. Banks (1)	Vault Cash, All Banks (2)	Currency Held by the Public (3)
1922			
Feb. 1	4468	854	3614
Mar. 1	4481	867	3614
Mar. 29	4510	878	3632
May 3	4484	858	3626
May 31	4466	860	3606
June 28	4488	863	3625
Aug. 2	4466	858	3608
Aug. 30	4512	855	3657
Sept. 27	4578	861	3717
Nov. 1	4598	873	3725
Nov. 29	4634	892	3742
1923			
Jan. 3	4697	919	3778
Jan. 31	4640	910	3730
Feb. 28	4692	899	3793
Mar. 28	4748	894	3854
May 2	4768	874	3894
May 29	4824	868	3956
June 27	4848	860	3988
Aug. 1	4861	879	3982
Aug. 29	4907	908	3999
Oct. 3	4920	921	3999
Oct. 31	4878	912	3966
Nov. 28	4936	918	4018
1924			
Jan. 2	4898	920	3978
Jan. 30	4814	917	3897
Feb. 27	4872	917	3955
Apr. 2	4878	900	3978
Apr. 30	4866	897	3969
May 28	4900	909	3991
July 2	4859	915	3944
July 30	4839	928	3911
Sept. 3	4843	939	3904
Oct. 1	4792	938	3854
Oct. 29	4855	950	3905
Dec. 3	4882	955	3927
Dec. 31	4854	939	3915

(continued)

Derivation of Estimates

TABLE 27 (continued)

Wednesday Nearest End of Month	Currency in Circulation Outside Treasury & F. R. Banks (1)	Vault Cash, All Banks (2)	Currency Held by the Public (3)
1925			
Jan. 28	4875	945	3930
Feb. 25	4890	954	3936
Apr. 1	4868	925	3943
Apr. 29	4859	933	3926
June 3	4851	920	3931
July 1	4845	919	3926
July 29	4869	926	3943
Sept. 2	4841	924	3917
Sept. 30	4847	939	3908
Oct. 28	4875	937	3938
Dec. 2	4866	945	3921
Dec. 30	4929	965	3964
1926			
Feb. 3	4922	962	3960
Mar. 3	4947	967	3980
Mar. 31	4921	967	3954
Apr. 28	4977	963	4014
June 2	4927	955	3972
June 30	4921	943	3978
July 28	4971	947	4024
Sept. 1	4924	937	3987
Sept. 29	4920	946	3974
Nov. 3	4922	946	3976
Dec. 1	4876	921	3955
Dec. 29	4905	922	3983
1927			
Feb. 2	4906	915	3991
Mar. 2	4911	915	3996
Mar. 30	4937	929	4008
Apr. 27	4952	937	4015
June 1	4918	938	3980
June 29	4907	956	3951
Aug. 3	4907	943	3964
Aug. 31	4846	940	3906
Sept. 28	4881	939	3942
Nov. 2	4833	928	3905
Nov. 30	4789	939	3850
Dec. 28	4810	951	3859

(continued)

TABLE 27 (continued)

Wednesday Nearest End of Month	Currency in Circulation Outside Treasury & F. R. Banks (1)	Vault Cash, All Banks (2)	Currency Held by the Public (3)
1928			
Feb. 1	4752	927	3825
Feb. 29	4733	931	3802
Mar. 28	4798	927	3871
May 2	4790	912	3878
May 29	4780	905	3875
June 27	4825	900	3925
Aug. 1	4771	890	3881
Aug. 29	4804	901	3903
Oct. 3	4767	897	3870
Oct. 31	4717	898	3819
Nov. 28	4832	919	3913
1929			
Jan. 2	4764	930	3834
Jan. 30	4747	919	3828
Feb. 27	4757	908	3849
Apr. 3	4795	893	3902
May 1	4735	869	3866
May 29	4762	879	3883
June 26	4776	865	3911
July 31	4778	891	3887
Aug. 28	4825	906	3919
Oct. 2	4731	909	3822
Oct. 30	4763	931	3832
Nov. 27	4761	909	3852
Dec. 31	4674	874	3800
1930			
Jan. 29	4640	888	3752
Feb. 26	4623	875	3748
Apr. 2	4578	861	3717
Apr. 30	4528	858	3670
May 28	4560	866	3694
July 2	4531	850	3681
July 30	4500	831	3669
Sept. 3	4511	807	3704
Oct. 1	4427	793	3634
Oct. 29	4410	816	3594
Dec. 3	4515	841	3674
Dec. 31	4692	883	3809

(continued)

TABLE 27 (continued)

Wednesday Nearest End of Month	Currency in Circulation Outside Treasury & F. R. Banks (1)	Vault Cash, All Banks (2)	Currency Held by the Public (3)
1931			
Jan. 28	4670	852	3818
Feb. 25	4650	827	3823
Apr. 1	4650	789	3861
Apr. 29	4714	817	3897
June 3	4716	819	3897
July 1	4841	846	3995
July 29	4897	839	4058
Sept. 2	5018	841	4177
Sept. 30	5151	862	4289
Oct. 28	5393	856	4537
Dec. 2	5318	815	4503
Dec. 30	5423	819	4604
1932			
Feb. 3	5702	806	4896
Mar. 2	5611	787	4824
Mar. 30	5534	791	4743
Apr. 27	5526	775	4751
June 1	5505	759	4746
June 29	5747	788	4959
Aug. 3	5786	738	5048
Aug. 31	5711	723	4988
Sept. 28	5646	705	4941
Nov. 2	5549	686	4863
Nov. 30	5548	706	4842
Dec. 28	5546	716	4830
1933			
Feb. 1	5690	711	4979
Mar. 1	6485	897	5588
Mar. 29	6296	787	5509
May 3	5931	729	5202
May 31	5731	712	5019
June 28	5648	699	4949
Aug. 2	5566	680	4886
Aug. 30	5548	698	4850
Sept. 27	5521	691	4830
Nov. 1	5478	675	4803
Nov. 29	5559	715	4844

(continued)

TABLE 27 (continued)

Wednesday Nearest End of Month	Currency in Circulation Outside Treasury & F. R. Banks (1)	Vault Cash, All Banks (2)	Currency Held by the Public (3)
1934			
Jan. 3	5570	731	4839
Jan. 31	5236	745	4491
Feb. 28	5266	753	4513
Mar. 28	5333	783	4550
May 2	5323	767	4556
May 30	5350	784	4566
June 27	5371	787	4584
Aug. 1	5373	764	4609
Aug. 29	5409	781	4628
Oct. 3	5407	780	4627
Oct. 31	5378	788	4590
Nov. 28	5441	810	4631
1935			
Jan. 2	5372	813	4559
Jan. 30	5450	829	4621
Feb. 27	5526	826	4700
Apr. 3	5539	825	4714
May 1	5523	815	4708
May 29	5561	846	4715
July 3	5566	858	4708
July 31	5546	859	4687
Aug. 28	5615	863	4752
Oct. 2	5640	835	4805
Oct. 30	5682	844	4838
Nov. 27	5737	862	4875
Dec. 31	5749	870	4879
1936			
Jan. 29	5826	902	4924
Feb. 26	5897	915	4982
Apr. 1	5944	928	5016
Apr. 29	5963	958	5005
June 3	5993	963	5030
July 1	6241	991	5250
July 29	6214	992	5222
Sept. 2	6198	973	5225
Sept. 30	6241	963	5278
Oct. 28	6289	973	5316
Dec. 2	6333	955	5378
Dec. 30	6418	952	5466

(continued)

TABLE 27 (continued)

Wednesday Nearest End of Month	Currency in Circulation Outside Treasury & F. R. Banks (1)	Vault Cash, All Banks (2)	Currency Held by the Public (3)
1937			
Feb. 3	6436	967	5469
Mar. 3	6463	973	5490
Mar. 31	6449	969	5480
Apr. 28	6495	974	5521
June 2	6455	954	5501
June 30	6447	935	5512
July 28	6489	942	5547
Sept. 1	6519	903	5616
Sept. 29	6535	927	5608
Nov. 3	6494	905	5589
Dec. 1	6452	879	5573
Dec. 29	6418	894	5524
1938			
Feb. 2	6383	898	5485
Mar. 2	6377	926	5451
Mar. 30	6450	990	5460
Apr. 27	6454	1021	5433
June 1	6486	1035	5451
June 29	6485	1057	5428
Aug. 3	6486	1033	5453
Aug. 31	6496	1041	5455
Sept. 28	6601	1070	5531
Nov. 2	6617	1064	5553
Nov. 30	6666	1084	5582
Dec. 28	6699	1101	5598
1939			
Feb. 1	6749	1067	5682
Mar. 1	6802	1053	5749
Mar. 29	6900	1093	5807
May 3	6970	1070	5900
May 31	6988	1084	5904
June 28	7057	1111	5946
Aug. 2	7064	1084	5980
Aug. 30	7189	1116	6073
Sept. 27	7250	1114	6136
Nov. 1	7280	1111	6169
Nov. 29	7377	1176	6201
Dec. 27	7421	1207	6214

(continued)

TABLE 27 (concluded)

Wednesday Nearest End of Month	Currency in Circulation Outside Treasury & F.R. Banks (1)	Vault Cash, All Banks (2)	Currency Held by the Public (3)
1940			
Jan. 31	7479	1188	6291
Feb. 28	7556	1197	6359
Apr. 3	7597	1183	6414
May 1	7632	1183	6449
May 29	7741	1236	6505
July 3	7854	1244	6610
July 31	7924	1260	6664
Aug. 28	8039	1291	6748
Oct. 2	8098	1257	6841
Oct. 30	8254	1288	6966
Nov. 27	8362	1293	7069
Dec. 31	8535	1257	7278
1941			
Jan. 29	8719	1318	7401
Feb. 26	8876	1315	7561
Apr. 2	8998	1293	7705
Apr. 30	9153	1323	7830
May 28	9354	1386	7968
July 2	9590	1416	8174
July 30	9814	1425	8389
Sept. 3	9997	1411	8586
Oct. 1	10127	1393	8734
Oct. 29	10281	1414	8867
Dec. 3	10497	1396	9101
Dec. 31	10908	1364	9544
1942			
Jan. 28	11220	1433	9787
Feb. 25	11449	1423	10026
Apr. 1	11610	1383	10227
Apr. 29	11876	1429	10447
June 3	12146	1404	10742
July 1	12474	1407	11067
July 29	12938	1443	11495
Sept. 2	13255	1395	11860
Sept. 30	13676	1391	12285
Oct. 28	14045	1396	12649
Dec. 2	14540	1367	13173
Dec. 30	15103	1359	13744

Notes to Table 27

[a]The dating is the same as that of the monthly vault cash esti-
mates. Though described here as "Wednesday dates," Feb. 1, 1918, to
Apr. 29, 1921, dates were, in fact, Friday dates. (See Table 25, Parts
IIIA and B.)

Source, by Column

1. Published figures for end-of-month dates for the components of
   currency outside the Treasury and Federal Reserve Banks were
   corrected by us for discontinuities, summed, seasonally adjusted and shifted between the end-of-month totals by Method L
   to dates shown in this table. Before 1914, amounts outside the
   Treasury were obtained either directly, or if the stock of a component required correction, indirectly, by subtracting the amount
   in the Treasury from corrected figures of the stock. The components, their sources, and the corrections made were as
   follows.
   A. Gold coin: *May 1907,* stock of gold, from "Report of the
      Treasury," in *Annual Report* of the Secretary of the Treas-
      ury, 1909, p. 190, *minus* amount of gold reported lost in
      June 1907, from *Annual Report* of the Director of the Mint,
      1907, pp. 92 and 87, *minus* gold in Treasury, from "Report
      of the Treasurer," *loc. cit.,* 1909, p. 190; *June 1907—Dec.
      1913,* stock of gold, from *ibid.,* 1909, pp. 190 ff.; 1915, pp.
      339 ff., *minus* gold in Treasury from "Report of the Treas-
      urer," *loc. cit.,* 1909, pp. 190 ff.; 1915, pp. 339 ff; *Jan.
      1914—Dec. 1933,* gold outside Treasury and Federal Reserve
      Banks, from *Banking and Monetary Statistics,* pp. 409—412,
      plus $287 million   deducted by Federal Reserve but restored
      by us, as described in text; *Jan. 1934—Dec. 1942, ibid.,*
      pp. 412—413 and *Circulation Statement of U.S. Money.*
   B. (a) Gold certificates, (b) silver certificates, (c) silver dol-
      lars, (d) U.S. notes and currency certificates, and (e) Treas-
      ury notes of 1890: *May 1907—Dec. 1913, Circulation State-
      ment of U.S. Money; Jan. 1914—Dec. 1942, Banking and
      Monetary Statistics,* pp. 409—413 and *Circulation Statement
      of U.S. Money.*
   C. (a) Federal Reserve notes and (b) Federal Reserve Bank
      notes: *Nov. 1914—Dec. 1942, Banking and Monetary Sta-
      tistics,* pp. 409—413 and *Circulation Statement of U.S.
      Money.*
   D. Subsidiary silver: *May 1907—May 1910,* stock, from "Report
      of the Treasurer," *loc. cit.,* 1909, p. 195; 1915, p. 343,
      minus the error (interpolated monthly by Method L) reported
      to have cumulated to $9.7 million over the period, June
      1881—June 1910, in "Report of the Director of the Mint,"
      ibid., 1910, p. 290, *minus* amount in Treasury, from "Report
      of the Treasurer," *loc. cit.,* 1909, p. 194; 1915, p. 343.

Notes to Table 27 (concluded)

June 1910–Dec. 1913, Circulation Statement of U.S. Money; Jan. 1914–Dec. 1942, Banking and Monetary Statistics, pp. 409–413 and *Circulation Statement of U.S. Money.*

E. National bank notes: Same sources as for B. above, *minus* estimates of national bank notes in vaults of issuing banks and in transit, May 1907–June 1935. The estimates were derived as follows: *May 1907–June 1928, notes in vaults of issuing banks* are monthly interpolations by Method L between call date figures on circulating notes of national banks received from the Comptroller and on hand, from *Annual Report* of the Comptroller of the Currency; *notes in transit* are monthly interpolations by Method L between mid-and end-of-year estimates of the transit item, obtained by deducting national bank call date figures of national bank notes received from the Comptroller, *ibid.,* from figures on the "circulation of national bank notes secured by U.S. bonds," *ibid.,* 1918, vol. II, pp. 19–21; 1924, pp. 158–160, 1928, pp. 222–223. *July 1928–June 1935, notes in vaults of issuing banks and in transit* are monthly interpolations by Method L between mid-and end-of-year estimates, obtained by deducting national bank call date figures of national bank note liabilities, *ibid.,* annual volumes, from figures on the "circulation of national bank notes secured by U.S. bonds," *ibid.,* 1931, pp. 178–179; 1935, pp. 183–184.

F. Minor coin: *May 1907–Dec. 1913,* monthly interpolations by Method L between June figures, *Banking and Monetary Statistics,* pp. 408–409; *Jan. 1914–Dec. 1942, ibid.,* pp. 409–413 and *Circulation Statement of U.S. Money.*

The various kinds of currency itemized above were added together. This series was adjusted for seasonal in two stages: (a) Each end-of-month day was corrected by a combined daily and monthly seasonal factor; (b) Repetitive movements that still remained, May 1907–Dec. 1913, June 1924–June 1932, and June 1935–June 1941, were corrected by factors derived by the method of ratios to moving averages.

2. Table 25, Parts I and II, col. 4 (through June 1919); thereafter, Part III, col. 5.

3. Col. 1 minus col. 2.

Through 1922 call date information was available for five or six call dates annually. On the average, then, only every other monthly figure required interpolation during this period. After 1922, there were three or four member bank call dates per year, so that between two-thirds and three-fourths of the monthly figures required interpolation.

In addition to these estimation errors our estimates of currency held by the public are subject to an error of coverage during periods of panic

TABLE 28

*Reported and Interpolated Vault Cash in Various Classes of Banks
at Call Dates and End of Month as Percentages of
Total Vault Cash, 1907–42*

Class of Banks and Period Covered	Per Cent of Total Vault Cash		
	Interpolated		Total
	Reported (1)	By Method L (2)	By Method R (3)	Cols. 1+2+3 (4)

	Reported (1)	By Method L (2)	By Method R (3)	Cols. 1+2+3 (4)
Call Dates				
1907–19:				
National banks	56.0	—	—	56.0
Nonnational and				
mutual savings banks	35.0	a	9.0	44.0
Total	91.0	—	9.0	100.0
1919–42:				
Member banks	62.0	—	—	62.0
Nonmember and				
mutual savings banks	24.0	—	14.0	38.0
Total	86.0	—	14.0	100.0
Monthly				
1907–19:				
Clearinghouse banks				
in seven cities	36.0	—	—	36.0
All other banks	—	64.0	—	64.0
Total	36.0	64.0	—	100.0
1919–42:				
Weekly reporting				
member banks	32.0	—	—	32.0
Nonweekly reporting				
member banks	2.0	28.0	—	30.0
Nonmember and				
mutual savings banks	2.0	36.0	—	38.0
Total	36.0	64.0	—	100.0

aInterpolation of New York data by Method L averaged less than 0.5
per cent of total vault cash.

that have occurred at least three times since 1907: October 1907–
February 1908; August–December 1914; and February–March 1933.
In each of these periods actual or threatened suspension of payments
by banks increased the demand for currency by the public as well as the
banks. The inelasticity of the supply of legal kinds of currency led to
the creation and circulation of substitutes. In 1907 and 1914, banks
resorted to a familiar substitute for currency in settling interbank balances—the clearinghouse loan certificate. Since these clearinghouse loan
certificates did not circulate outside banks, they did not constitute an
addition to currency held by the public. Only for 1907 do we have a
detailed estimate of substitutes created for public use.[31] These substitutes included: clearinghouse loan certificates in currency denominations
to be used by banks in paying their customers; clearinghouse checks in
currency denominations; cashiers' checks in convenient denominations;
cashiers' checks drawn on New York or drafts upon reserve city banks;
negotiable certificates of deposit; pay-checks payable to bearer—a liability of the firm or corporation for whose benefit they were issued by
banks; issues of railroads, mining companies, manufacturers, and store-
keepers. Andrew estimates that in total $250 million of these substitutes
were in public circulation from the end of October 1907 until the spring
of 1908. In 1914 it is possible that addition of Aldrich-Vreeland currency to the national bank note issue eliminated the need for extralegal
currency substitutes. During the period of bank holidays in February–
March 1933 it has been estimated that probably as much as $1 billion
in substitute forms of currency were in use.[32]

Appendix to Chapter 12
DAILY AND MONTHLY SEASONAL FACTORS FOR VAULT CASH

This appendix presents the daily and monthly seasonal factors used to
correct reported national and nonnational, member and nonmember,
bank vault cash call date figures.

Table 29 lists the daily and monthly seasonal factors derived from
vault cash figures for various classes of banks for the periods shown.

[31] A. P. Andrew, "Substitutes for Cash in the Panic of 1907," *Quarterly Journal of
Economics*, Aug. 1908, pp. 497–515.
[32] H. P. Willis and J. M. Chapman, *The Banking Situation*, p. 15.

TABLE 29

Intraweekly and Monthly Seasonal Indexes, Vault Cash, Call Date Series

	Hypothetical Series			All National Banks, 1917–49	All National Banks, Aug. 1874– June 1917	State Banks and Trust Companies, New York State, 1897–1917
	Non-national Banks 1907–17	All Non-member Banks 1919–44	State Member Banks 1919–44			
Daily Indexes						
Mon.	100.0	100.8	100.7	101.2	99.6	100.7
Tues.	95.1	102.7	105.6	105.0	99.8	100.2
Wed.	103.7	102.6	103.8	106.0	102.2	99.2
Thurs.	96.4	99.9	102.0	101.3	100.3	101.7
Fri.	111.6	98.2	95.7	95.1	100.0	101.3
Sat.	93.1	95.8	92.2	91.5	98.1	97.0
Monthly Indexes						
Jan.–Feb.	100.2	(99.2)[a]	(101.2)[a]		104.3	100.1
Feb.–Mar.	103.5	96.9	98.4	94.8	100.3	98.2
Mar.–Apr.	99.0	96.7	97.6	98.5	98.6	103.4
Apr.–May	103.2	98.3	97.9	101.7	100.6	106.6
May–June	93.8	(98.0)[a]	(98.8)[a]		103.9	98.0
June–July	97.4	97.8	99.7	97.6	101.8	106.5
July–Aug.	102.8	(101.2)[a]	(103.8)[a]		99.1	101.7
Aug.–Sept.	98.6	106.2	109.5	98.5	99.6	99.5
Sept.–Oct.	89.7	97.7	100.9	100.8	96.0	97.3
Oct.–Nov.	102.6	105.9	99.7	98.9	101.1	96.1
Nov.–Dec.	103.8	95.1	88.4	101.8	95.9	92.6
Dec.–Jan.	105.3	105.5	107.9	107.4	98.8	

[a] Interpolated on basis of weekly reporting member bank data.

418

The months of the year run from the sixteenth of a calendar month to the fifteenth of the next. Nonmember and state member bank monthly indexes for months without call dates were interpolated by Method R_1, using the monthly seasonal indexes of weekly reporting member banks as the related series.

Table 30 presents the combined monthly and daily seasonal factors for vault cash in the following classes of banks:

a. Nonnational banks, 1907–17—hypothetical series
b. National banks, 1874–1917
c. State banks and trust companies in New York State, 1897–1917
d. Nonmember banks, 1919–44—hypothetical series
e. State member banks, 1919–44
f. Nonnational banks, 1919–44
g. National banks, 1917–49.

The hypothetical series for nonnational banks, 1907–17, and for nonmember banks, 1919–44, were constructed, for the sole purpose of providing estimates of seasonals, from observations dated identically with national and member bank call dates.

Weighted averages of the seasonal factors computed for vault cash in state member and nonmember banks (average vault cash over the period in each class constituting the weights), were used as the seasonal factors for vault cash in nonnational banks, 1919–44. The latter seasonals were used to adjust nonidentically dated nonnational bank figures.

No member bank seasonal indexes, as such, were computed. Adjusted state member bank data added to adjusted national bank data yielded adjusted member bank data.

TABLE 30

Combined Intraweekly and Monthly Seasonal Indexes, Vault Cash, Call Date Series

	Jan. Feb.	Feb. March	March April	April May	May June	June July	July Aug.	Aug. Sept.	Sept. Oct.	Oct. Nov.	Nov. Dec.	Dec. Jan.
Nonnational Banks, National Bank Call Dates, 1907–17 – Hypothetical												
Mon.	100.2	103.5	99.0	103.2	93.8	97.4	102.8	98.6	89.7	102.6	103.8	105.3
Tues.	95.3	98.6	94.2	98.3	88.9	92.6	97.9	93.7	84.8	97.7	98.9	100.5
Wed.	103.9	107.2	102.8	106.9	97.5	101.1	106.5	102.3	93.4	106.3	107.5	109.0
Thurs.	96.6	99.9	95.5	99.6	90.2	93.8	99.2	95.0	86.1	99.0	100.2	101.7
Fri.	111.8	115.1	110.7	114.8	105.4	109.0	114.4	110.2	101.3	114.2	115.4	116.9
Sat.	93.3	96.6	92.2	96.3	86.9	90.5	95.9	91.7	82.8	95.7	96.9	· 98.4
All National Banks, National Bank Call Dates, August 1874–June 1917												
Mon.	104.0	99.9	98.3	100.2	103.5	101.4	98.7	99.2	95.7	100.7	95.5	98.5
Tues.	104.1	100.1	98.4	100.3	103.7	101.6.	98.9	99.3	95.8	100.9	95.7	98.6
Wed.	106.5	102.5	100.8	102.8	106.1	104.0	101.3	101.8	98.2	103.3	98.1	101.0
Thurs.	104.7	100.6	99.0	100.9	104.2	102.1	99.4	99.9	96.4	101.4	96.2	99.2
Fri.	104.3	100.2	98.6	100.5	103.9	101.8	99.1	99.5	96.0	101.1	95.9	98.8
Sat.	102.4	98.3	96.7	98.6	102.0	99.9	97.2	97.6	94.1	99.2	94.0	96.9

State Banks and Trust Companies, New York State, Report Dates, 1897–1917

Mon.	100.8	104.1	107.3	98.7	107.2	102.4	100.1	98.0	96.8	93.3
Tues.	100.3	103.6	106.8	98.2	106.7	101.9	99.6	97.5	96.3	92.8
Wed.	99.3	102.6	105.8	97.2	105.6	100.9	98.6	96.5	95.3	91.8
Thurs.	101.8	105.1	108.3	99.7	108.2	103.4	101.2	99.0	97.8	94.3
Fri.	101.4	104.7	107.9	99.3	107.8	103.0	100.8	98.6	97.4	93.9
Sat.	97.1	100.4	103.6	95.0	103.4	98.7	96.4	94.3	93.1	89.6

Nonmember Banks, Member Bank Call Dates, 1919–44 – Hypothetical

Mon.	97.6	99.0	98.5	106.9	98.5	106.7	95.9	106.3
Tues.	99.6	101.0	100.5	108.9	100.4	108.6	97.9	108.2
Wed.	99.5	100.9	100.4	108.8	100.4	108.5	97.8	108.1
Thurs.	96.7	98.1	97.6	106.0	97.6	105.8	95.0	105.4
Fri.	95.1	96.5	96.0	104.4	96.0	104.1	93.4	103.8
Sat.	92.7	94.0	93.5	101.9	93.5	101.7	90.9	101.3

State Member Banks, Member Bank Call Dates, 1919–44

Mon.	99.1	98.3	98.7	100.5	101.7	110.2	100.4	89.1	108.7
Tues.	104.0	103.2	103.5	105.4	106.5	115.1	105.3	94.0	113.5
Wed.	102.2	101.3	101.7	103.5	104.7	113.2	105.5	92.2	111.7
Thurs.	100.3	99.5	99.9	101.7	102.9	111.4	101.6	90.4	109.9
Fri.	94.0	93.2	93.6	95.4	96.6	105.1	95.3	84.1	103.6
Sat.	90.6	89.8	90.1	92.0	93.2	101.7	91.9	80.6	100.2

(continued)

TABLE 30 (concluded)

	Jan. / Feb.	Feb. / March	March / April	April / May	May / June	June / July	July / Aug.	Aug. / Sept.	Sept. / Oct.	Oct. / Nov.	Nov. / Dec.	Dec. / Jan.
Nonnational Banks, 1919–44												
(Weighted average of seasonal factors for state member and nonmember banks)												
Mon.	100.6	98.2	97.8	98.9	99.0	99.2	102.8	108.1	99.6	104.5	93.6	107.1
Tues.	103.6	101.2	100.7	101.9	102.0	102.2	105.9	111.1	102.5	107.4	96.5	110.1
Wed.	102.9	100.4	100.0	101.2	101.3	101.5	105.1	110.4	101.8	106.8	95.7	109.4
Thurs.	100.5	98.0	97.6	98.8	98.9	99.1	102.7	108.0	99.5	104.4	93.4	106.9
Fri.	97.2	94.7	94.3	95.5	95.6	95.8	99.4	104.6	96.2	101.0	90.1	103.6
Sat.	94.5	92.0	91.6	92.7	92.8	93.0	96.7	101.9	93.4	98.2	87.3	100.9
All National Banks, National Bank Call Dates, 1917–49												
Mon.	96.0	99.7		102.9		98.8		99.7	102.0	100.1	103.0	108.6
Tues.	99.8	103.5		106.7		102.6		103.5	105.8	103.9	106.8	112.4
Wed.	100.9	104.5		107.8		103.6		104.5	106.9	105.0	107.8	113.4
Thurs.	96.1	99.8		103.0		98.9		99.8	102.1	100.2	103.1	108.7
Fri.	89.9	93.6		96.8		92.7		93.6	95.9	94.0	96.9	102.5
Sat.	86.3	90.0		93.2		89.1		90.0	92.3	90.4	93.3	108.9

Source: See Chap. 12, Appendix.

422

13

DEPOSITS AT COMMERCIAL BANKS:
CALL DATES

OUR CALL DATE FIGURES for all commercial banks are sums of data for national and nonnational banks, 1907–23, and for member and non-member banks, 1919–46. The national and member bank figures were obtained from the reports of the Comptroller of the Currency and the Federal Reserve System. The nonnational and nonmember bank figures are based on data from reports of state supervisory agencies in a sample of states. Our general procedure was to get the figures that are available for each state in our sample, then to construct an estimate for the United States from the figures for the sample of states.

1. Problems in Compilation of Nonnational Bank Data

In general, we used as our basic source for nonnational bank data by states the reports of the various state banking departments, supplemented by unpublished figures that certain of them sent us. As a check on these data, we relied on the annual (in some years, semiannual) returns published by the Comptroller of the Currency; state member bank figures for member bank call dates; [1] and, beginning June 1934, insured state bank figures, for mid- and end-of-year, published by the FDIC. When

---

[1] State member bank figures were compiled through Mar. 1929 from Federal Reserve Board, *Member Bank Call Report*. Thereafter they were derived as residuals: member bank figures, *ibid.*, minus national bank figures in U.S. Comptroller of the Currency, *Abstract of Reports of Condition of National Banks.*

Before Dec. 1935, postal savings redeposited in member banks are not segregated in the former source, although the item is available for national banks. Consequently, data on postal savings in state member banks, by states, are unavailable before this date.

state report figures were inconsistent with state member or state insured bank figures, we corrected the former.

Before August 24, 1917, only national banks were authorized to serve as U.S. government depositaries of the U.S. Treasury. Thereafter, state banks could also serve as depositaries. However, until recent years the returns of most state banking departments did not separate U.S. government deposits from other demand deposits. After April 1917, therefore, nonnational and nonmember bank demand deposits by states must be compiled as a total of public and government deposits. Beginning May 1, 1917, we followed the same practice in compiling totals for all commercial banks and then subtracted aggregate government deposits, independently estimated (Chapter 17), from the totals to derive the public's demand deposits at commercial banks. After November 1938, when U.S. Treasurer's time deposits, open account, came into being, the nonmember bank time deposit figures as reported are also a total of public and government deposits. Estimates of the Treasurer's time deposits were deducted.

To avoid double counting, it is necessary to subtract from the sum of demand liabilities (exclusive of interbank deposits) at each call date, by states, what is generally called the "float," i.e., cash items in process of collection, exchanges for the clearinghouse, checks on local banks or outside checks, items with Federal Reserve banks in process of collection, items in transit, and other asset items constituting duplications. This float is not, however, shown in detail in many state bank reports. Often the total shown in state reports for all nonnational banks is less than that shown for state member banks or insured banks alone in reports to the Federal Reserve System or the FDIC. When necessary, therefore, we made adjustments in the nonnational bank data.

In our compilations of time and total deposits after 1911 we excluded postal savings redeposited in banks from the individual state returns. Our tables present time deposits at nonnational and national banks and all commercial banks by states, exclusive of postal savings.[2] However, available figures for state member banks by states do not segregate

[2] Figures on postal savings redeposited in national banks are available at call dates from Nov. 26, 1912. Negligible amounts are included in our time deposit figures for earlier dates. Deduction of postal savings redeposited in nonnational banks has been possible since June 1913. Beginning June 1921 our preliminary figures for time deposits at member and nonmember banks of thirty-eight rural states and of the United States include postal savings at all state member banks. Our final figures exclude these amounts (see section 6 below).

postal savings from other time deposits until December 1935. In consequence, our figures for state member banks include postal savings. For each state these figures were deducted from the figures for nonnational banks to get figures for nonmember banks. It follows that our nonmember time deposit figures for individual states are too small by the amount of postal savings at state member banks. Further comment on this subject is reserved for the section on the compilation of member bank figures.

For the national-nonnational breakdown through June 30, 1914, we present figures for total deposits adjusted; from then on, for demand and time deposits. Before December 31, 1914, national bank reports by states as well as the reports of nonnational banks of some of the states in our sample do not provide a deposit breakdown (see appendix to Chapter 8).[3]

Until 1938, when most states adopted a form of return used by federal supervisory agencies, nonnational bank reports varied considerably in the detail given for deposit items, both among states and among report dates for any one state. Some returns gave only aggregate demand and time deposits, and the detailed constituents cannot now be determined. Some items that we would not consider deposits may have been included in these aggregates, and we cannot be sure that the breakdown into demand and time deposits as given in the banks' books is correct in detail. Some returns give only gross deposit figures, which include interbank, time, and demand deposits. New York presents a major problem in classification, since its reports prior to 1930 do not distinguish demand from time deposits.

In addition, individual deposit items in the reports, particularly for years before 1929, are occasionally difficult to classify as either demand or time deposits. Fortunately, such items are minor relative to aggregate deposits.[4] Tables of demand and time deposits for individual states in

[3] Wherever breakdowns of total deposits are available for nonnational banks, 1907–14, they are presented in the individual state tables available from the files of the National Bureau of Economic Research. The national bank breakdowns for June, Sept., and Oct. 1914 were estimated.

[4] In view of these difficulties of classification—however minor in relation to the totals involved—and the fact that the proportions of total deposits classified respectively as demand and time for the period after 1917 covered by the call date series have been partly, perhaps largely, the result of changes in banking law and practices rather than of changes in the deposit-holding desires of the public—it might be that the primary call date compilation by states and the basic monthly interpolation should have been made for total deposits.

the files of the National Bureau include a description of our procedure, state by state, and our resolution of the problems encountered in compilation.[5]

2. Report Dates

The dating of the reports of nonnational banks presents the same problem for our deposit estimates as for the estimates of bank vault cash (Chapter 12, section 2). For vault cash, we handled the problem by first correcting all observations for daily and weekly seasonals and then shifting observations for dates not identical with national or member bank call dates to those dates. For deposits we followed a different procedure, primarily because intraweekly variability, which is important for vault cash, is negligible for deposits.[6]

A variety of scattered evidence suggested that a difference in dating of deposits of as much as two weeks would not seriously affect the comparability of the data. Accordingly, we treated nonnational bank figures as comparable with national or member bank call date figures if the date of the figures was not more than two weeks distant from the national or member bank call date.[7] This involved discarding data for a small

[5] The construction of a consolidated balance sheet for all banking institutions, that includes the components of the money stock for which we compiled data (currency, demand deposits, and time deposits), and pertinent items among bank assets, would probably yield more reliable results than our technique of compilation of selected items. That is, simultaneous compilation of estimates for all important asset and liability categories would make it possible to detect inconsistencies among these estimates and to correct them. Our adjustment of deposit data for individual states was made in this way. Limited resources, however, prevented us from making simultaneous estimates for the whole United States for all asset and liability items. Deposits and vault cash are the only balance sheet items for which sample figures were used to get call date figures and for which monthly estimates were derived.

The estimates in *All-Bank Statistics, United States, 1896–1955*, Board of Governors of the Federal Reserve System, Washington, D.C., 1959, to which our estimates are keyed, were made by constructing a consolidated balance sheet.

[6] Since the public obtains currency by drawing on deposits and returns it to the banks for credit in deposit accounts, there must be intraweekly variations in deposits equal and opposite in amount to those in currency. However, an investigation of daily deposit figures of member banks in the New York Federal Reserve District by reserve classes, during 1947, revealed no appreciable intraweekly variation and an intramonthly pattern of very slight amplitude. Random and cyclical variation loomed larger than either regular intraweekly or intramonthly variation, and these were rarely significant in relation to the size of inter-call date changes.

The explanation, of course, lies in the much larger size of deposits than of vault cash, so that absolute variations that are sizable relative to vault cash are negligible relative to deposits and are swamped by other sources of variation.

[7] The choice of two weeks as the limit in admissible variation of a nonnational report date from a national or member bank call date was based on the results of tests made of the percentage changes in weekly reporting member bank deposit figures over one-,

fraction of the available report dates. However, we collected all report date figures for nonnational banks by states, and these are available in the files of the National Bureau of Economic Research.

The midyear call dates to which our estimates are keyed are called "June" call dates. However, for some years before 1919 the "June" call date is in April, May, or July. In all cases, we used for this purpose the call date closest to June 30. After 1919 this date is uniformly in June.

3. The Sample of States

At the outset, we intended to compile call date figures for nonnational banks in each of the forty-eight states and the District of Columbia. However, compilation proved so time consuming that we decided to limit the nonnational bank figures to a sample of nineteen states and the District of Columbia.

This sample was not selected in advance to provide an estimate for the country. Rather it consisted of those states for which we happened to have completed the compilation of data at the time that we decided that compilation for all states was not feasible. We therefore had to determine whether data for these states could yield reasonably accurate estimates for the United States and, if so, how best to construct such estimates. We considered two broad methods of using our sample data: first, as a unit to be "blown up" on the basis of available data for the universe for one date a year; second, as a stratification to be blown up on the basis of available data for the corresponding strata of the universe.

Considerable experimentation led us to choose the second and to classify the political units in our sample into three strata. One stratum consists of New York State by itself; a second, of nine other relatively urbanized states (states with over 60 per cent of the population in areas defined by the Census as urban) [8] and the District of Columbia; and a

two-, three-, and four-week periods. Our conclusion was that demand and time deposits are not likely to change materially within two weeks of a report date relative to the change that occurs from one report date to the next. The specific breaking point is, of course, arbitrary.

Our use of different methods for deposits and vault cash is in part no more than a reflection of the order in which various parts of the estimates were constructed. Were we beginning the process anew, we would probably treat deposits in the way that we treated vault cash rather than as we did.

[8] Ohio and Michigan in 1910 are exceptions to this statement. These states were included to maintain the formal continuity of our urbanized series. The inclusion of

TABLE 31

Percentage of Population in Urban Areas^a of Sample States Grouped Regionally, 1910–40

	Group I				Group II				Group III			
	1940	1930	1920	1910	1940	1930	1920	1910	1940	1930	1920	1910
Mid. Atl.												
N. Y.	82.8	83.6	82.7	78.9								
N. J.					81.6	82.6	79.9	76.4				
Penna.					66.5	67.8	65.1	60.4				
New Eng.												
Conn.					67.8	70.4	67.8	65.6				
Mass.					89.4	90.2	90.0	89.0				
R. I.					91.6	92.4	91.9	91.0				
E. N. Cent.												
Ill.					73.6	73.9	67.9	61.7				
Ohio					66.8	67.8	63.8	55.9				
Mich.					65.7	68.2	61.1	47.2				
Ind.									55.1	55.5	50.6	42.4
S. Atl.												
D. C.					100.0	100.0	100.0	100.0				
Del.									52.3	51.7	54.2	48.0
Fla.									55.1	51.7	36.5	29.1
Ga.									34.4	30.8	25.1	20.6
Pacific												
Calif.					71.0	73.3	67.9	61.8				
E. S. Cent.												
Ala.									30.2	28.1	21.7	17.3
W. S. Cent.												
Ark.									22.2	20.6	16.6	12.9
Mtn.												
Ariz.									34.8	34.4	36.1	31.0
Colo.									52.6	50.2	48.2	50.3
Idaho									33.7	29.1	27.6	21.5

428

third, of the nine remaining states. It happens that our first two strata coincide with the corresponding universe, since our sample includes every state in which over 60 per cent of the population is in areas defined by the Census as urban. However, we do not have data from every state for every date; consequently, some estimation is required. This explains the significance of the decision as to whether these urbanized units are treated as one stratum or divided into two, as we did. Our sample contains nine of the thirty-eight states in the remaining stratum. The data for these nine were used to construct estimates for the twenty-nine states not in the sample. The geographic location of each state and the percentage of its population in urban areas at Census years between 1907 and 1946 are given in Table 31.

Our choice of this method of constructing the estimates for the United States rests on our conclusion that the movement of deposits from call date to call date differed appreciably from one stratum to the other but either not at all, or to a much smaller extent, from state to state within the strata. We arrived at this conclusion after test calculations using the known data for member banks in the different groups of states. Our conclusion thus rests on the presumption that results for member banks can be carried over to nonnational and nonmember banks.

The precise data used in our test calculations were seasonally unad-

Ohio among relatively urbanized states in 1910 seemed justifiable since no rural state exceeded it in the percentage of total population that was urban. Michigan is clearly a borderline case in 1910, since it is exceeded in the percentage which is urban by Delaware and Colorado. During that Census decade, however, Michigan rapidly acquired an urban stamp, and therefore it seemed advisable to keep it in the relatively urbanized group over the whole period.

Notes to Table 31

[a]Urban areas, as defined by the Census, include all cities and other incorporated places having 2,500 inhabitants or more. A modification of this definition in 1930 and 1940 to include unincorporated townships and other political subdivisions which had a population of 10,000 or more and a population density of 1,000 or more per square mile made slight additions to the urban group in N. J., Penna., Conn., Calif., and N. Y., as compared with the 1920 definition. In Mass. and R. I. in 1930 and 1940 a modification of the definition resulted in a shift from the urban to the rural classification of towns that would have been counted as urban in 1920.

Source: Seventeenth Census of the United States, *Population,* Vol. I, 1950, Table 15, pp. 1-18–1-23.

justed demand deposits less duplications and time deposits at member banks in each of the nineteen states of our sample and the District of Columbia and in the remaining twenty-nine states, at member bank call dates, June 1926–June 1934. The member bank figures by states were classified in the following way:

   a. New York State
   b. Nine urban states and the District of Columbia, further broken down into two subgroups:
      1. Three urban states (Massachusetts, Michigan, New Jersey) denoted Urban I, below
      2. Six other urban states and the District of Columbia denoted Urban II, below
   c. Nine rural states in the sample
   d. Twenty-nine rural states in the nonsample

For each group, we calculated for demand and time deposits separately values of v, as defined in Chapter 10, section 5, i.e., relative deviations from inter-June trends. We then correlated the values of v for different groups, with the following results:

	Coefficients of Correlation	
Pairs Correlated	*Demand*	*Time*
1. New York, urban	+.56	+.77
2. New York, rural sample	+.11	+.66
3. Urban I, urban II	+.81	+.58
4. Urban sample, rural sample	+.08	+.74
5. Rural sample, rural nonsample	+.84	+.80

For demand deposits the results strongly support the stratification that we adopted. For time deposits, on the other hand, there is about as high a correlation between the different groups as within them. One possible explanation for this difference is that demand deposits do, but time deposits do not, have different seasonal patterns for states differing in urbanization. To test this possibility, we averaged separately the values of v for the first, second, and third inter-June call dates for each stratum. These averages suggest that (a) there are negligible seasonal movements in time deposits; (b) there are seasonal movements in the demand deposit data, but they are not large enough to account for the results. The one qualification to (b) is that New York and other urban states have opposite seasonals, hence the correlation between these two groups might be raised enough by deseasonalizing the data to eliminate any justification for our separation of New York from the other urban states. However, there would be little gain from combining these two strata because of the failure of the New York State reports before 1930 to distinguish between demand and time deposits. We therefore retained the three strata.

4. Nonnational Bank Estimates, National Bank Call Dates, 1907–23

These estimates, which were made separately for each of our strata, are given in Table 32. Part I of that table gives estimates for total adjusted deposits, 1907–14, the period for which we did not attempt separate estimates for demand and time deposits; Part II gives adjusted demand deposits, 1914–17; Part III, demand deposits less duplications, 1917–23; and Part IV, adjusted time deposits, 1914–23.

New York State. Total deposits adjusted, 1907–17, and total deposits less duplications, 1917–23, at report dates, were compiled for state banks and also for trust companies. The figures compiled for both groups of banks are gross of postal savings deposits redeposited in these banks. The series for each class of banks was corrected for seasonal. A number of series were tested for use as related series for interpolation: deposits at New York national banks, New Jersey nonnational banks, New York state member banks, New Jersey nonmember banks, and Pennsylvania nonmember banks. All test correlation coefficients were low, hence all were rejected. Instead, we interpolated by Method L between report dates to national bank call dates. Deposits of the Postal Savings System redeposited in New York nonnational banks were interpolated by Method L between June dates to call dates and subtracted from the total deposit series.

Estimates of deposits at New York private banks were added to those of state banks and trust companies. Before December 1914, call date estimates were interpolated by Method L between June figures for all private banks available in *All-Bank Statistics*. For later dates, call date figures for private banks reporting to state authorities were interpolated

TABLE 32

Deposits at All U.S. Commercial Banks, Distinguishing National from Nonnational Banks i
New York, Urbanized, and Rural States, National Bank Call Dates, 1907–23

(seasonally adjusted, in millions of dollars)

Part I. Total Adjusted Deposits and United States Government Deposits, 1907–14

	Total Adjusted Deposits					
	New York State			9 Urbanized States and D.C.		
National Bank Call Date	National Banks (1)	Nonnational Banks (2)	All Comm. Banks (3)	National Banks (4)	Nonnational Banks (5)	C(B(
1907						
May 20	654	1,430	2,085	1,762	2,487	4
Aug. 22	670	1,414	2,084	1,794	2,456	4
Dec. 3	676	1,153	1,829	1,687	2,282	3
1908						
Feb. 14	693	1,121	1,814	1,693	1,981	3
May 15	766	1,237	2,003	1,760	2,118	3
July 15	767	1,318	2,085	1,793	2,333	4
Sept. 23	794	1,376	2,170	1,844	2,352	4
Nov. 27	871	1,445	2,316	1,851	2,352	4
1909						
Feb. 5	820	1,545	2,365	1,875	2,432	4
Apr. 28	829	1,641	2,471	1,918	2,477	4
June 23	838	1,666	2,504	1,974	2,588	4
Sept. 1	836	1,697	2,533	2,010	2,601	4
Nov. 16	828	1,626	2,454	2,050	2,587	4
1910						
Jan. 31	818	1,658	2,476	2,023	2,646	4
Mar. 29	847	1,638	2,485	2,119	2,703	4
June 30	791	1,593	2,384	2,102	2,772	4
Sept. 1	822	1,595	2,416	2,109	2,746	4
Nov. 10	833	1,598	2,431	2,146	2,739	4
1911						
Jan. 7	797	1,608	2,405	2,153	2,816	4
Mar. 7	864	1,621	2,486	2,190	2,863	5
June 7	908	1,693	2,601	2,259	2,954	5
Sept. 1	911	1,706	2,617	2,266	3,017	5
Dec. 5	880	1,779	2,659	2,307	3,053	5
1912						
Feb. 20	956	1,812	2,768	2,339	3,134	5
Apr. 18	956	1,829	2,785	2,376	3,163	5

	Total Adjusted Deposits					U.S. Govt. Demand Deposits[a]
	38 Rural States			United States		United States
National Banks (7)	Nonnational Banks (8)	All Comm. Banks (9)	National Banks (10)	Nonnational Banks (11)	All Comm. Banks (12)	National Banks (13)
01	2,019	3,620	4,017	5,936	9,953	196
37	1,996	3,633	4,102	5,866	9,968	160
44	1,958	3,502	3,906	5,393	9,299	206
06	1,927	3,433	3,892	5,029	8,921	258
29	1,898	3,427	4,055	5,253	9,308	197
45	1,886	3,431	4,105	5,537	9,642	130
95	1,925	3,520	4,233	5,653	9,886	137
52	1,962	3,614	4,374	5,759	10,133	124
12	2,003	3,715	4,407	5,980	10,387	110
40	2,049	3,789	4,487	6,167	10,654	69
45	2,079	3,824	4,556	6,334	10,890	69
82	2,122	3,904	4,629	6,420	11,049	52
87	2,176	4,063	4,766	6,389	11,155	48
90	2,207	4,107	4,740	6,512	11,252	46
28	2,235	4,163	4,894	6,577	11,471	47
14	2,287	4,201	4,806	6,652	11,458	50
77	2,310	4,187	4,808	6,650	11,458	54
67	2,341	4,308	4,946	6,678	11,624	48
63	2,342	4,305	4,913	6,765	11,678	44
72	2,361	4,333	5,026	6,845	11,871	45
80	2,387	4,367	5,147	7,033	12,180	44
65	2,453	4,418	5,142	7,176	12,318	52
50	2,516	4,566	5,237	7,348	12,585	46
71	2,554	4,625	5,366	7,500	12,866	60
97	2,585	4,682	5,429	7,577	13,006	52

(continued)

TABLE 32 (continued)

	Total Adjusted Deposits					
	New York State			9 Urbanized States and D.C.		
National Bank Call Date	National Banks (1)	Nonnational Banks (2)	All Comm. Banks (3)	National Banks (4)	Nonnational Banks (5)	A Co Ba (
1912						
June 14	990	1,844	2,834	2,423	3,194	5
Sept. 4	959	1,838	2,797	2,441	3,273	5
Nov. 26	969	1,787	2,756	2,448	3,239	5
1913						
Feb. 4	975	1,761	2,735	2,466	3,336	5
Apr. 4	956	1,736	2,692	2,477	3,340	5
June 4	931	1,689	2,620	2,498	3,387	5
Aug. 9	974	1,698	2,672	2,460	3,380	5
Oct. 21	973	1,726	2,699	2,523	3,417	5
1914						
Jan. 13	964	1,768	2,732	2,533	3,416	5
Mar. 4	1,004	1,798	2,802	2,516	3,491	6
June 30	1,067	1,861	2,928	2,579	3,587	6

Part II. Adjusted Demand Deposits and United States Government Deposits, 1914–17

	Adjusted Demand Deposits					
	New York State			9 Urbanized States and D.C.		
National Bank Call Date	National Banks (1)	Nonnational Banks (2)	All Comm. Banks (3)	National Banks (4)	Nonnational Banks (5)	C E
1914						
June 30	1,005	1,580	2,585	2,087	1,679	ε
Sept. 12	1,061	1,632	2,693	2,087	1,644	ε
Oct. 31	1,055	1,681	2,736	2,056	1,570	ε
Dec. 31	1,036	1,735	2,770	2,066	1,614	ε
1915						
Mar. 4	1,044	1,795	2,839	2,131	1,670	ε
May 1	1,088	1,860	2,948	2,166	1,662	ε

			Total Adjusted Deposits			U.S. Govt. Demand Deposits[a]
	38 Rural States			United States		United States
...onal ...nks (7)	Nonnational Banks (8)	All Comm. Banks (9)	National Banks (10)	Nonnational Banks (11)	All Comm. Banks (12)	National Banks (13)
...162	2,622	4,724	5,515	7,660	13,175	54
...142	2,669	4,811	5,542	7,780	13,322	64
...233	2,739	4,972	5,650	7,765	13,415	45
...229	2,784	5,013	5,670	7,881	13,551	50
...254	2,825	5,079	5,687	7,900	13,587	45
...216	2,866	5,082	5,645	7,942	13,587	46
...174	2,885	5,059	5,608	7,963	13,571	57
...262	2,910	5,172	5,758	8,053	13,811	90
...278	2,923	5,201	5,774	8,107	13,881	81
...269	2,946	5,215	5,788	8,235	14,023	66
...16	2,971	5,287	5,962	8,419	14,381	61

			Adjusted Demand Deposits			U.S. Govt. Demand Deposits[a]
	38 Rural States			United States		United States
...ional ...nks (7)	Nonnational Banks (8)	All Comm. Banks (9)	National Banks (10)	Nonnational Banks (11)	All Comm. Banks (12)	National Banks (13)
...706	1,662	3,368	4,798	4,921	9,719	61
...656	1,642	3,298	4,804	4,918	9,722	75
...598	1,635	3,233	4,709	4,886	9,595	69
...595	1,619	3,214	4,697	4,968	9,665	62
...676	1,608	3,284	4,851	5,073	9,924	59
...669	1,597	3,266	4,924	5,119	10,043	50

(continued)

TABLE 32 (continued)

| National Bank Call Date | Adjusted Demand Deposits | | | | | |
| | New York State | | | 9 Urbanized States and D.C. | | |
	National Banks (1)	Nonnational Banks (2)	All Comm. Banks (3)	National Banks (4)	Nonnational Banks (5)	All Comm. Banks (6)
1915						
June 23	1,104	1,922	3,027	2,220	1,730	3,950
Sept. 2	1,119	1,989	3,108	2,196	1,778	3,974
Nov. 10	1,372	2,154	3,526	2,266	1,868	4,134
Dec. 31	1,366	2,313	3,679	2,348	1,853	4,200
1916						
Mar. 7	1,431	2,257	3,687	2,477	1,943	4,420
May 1	1,370	2,223	3,593	2,501	2,065	4,566
June 30	1,409	2,188	3,597	2,547	2,097	4,645
Sept. 12	1,456	2,264	3,720	2,646	2,154	4,800
Nov. 17	1,500	2,328	3,828	2,648	2,265	4,912
Dec. 27	1,378	2,364	3,742	2,763	2,382	5,145
1917						
Mar. 5	1,504	2,473	3,976	2,814	2,425	5,239
May 1	1,504	2,434	3,938	2,888	2,493	5,381
June 20	1,556	2,402	3,957	2,889	2,482	5,371

Part III. Demand Deposits Less Duplications, United States Government Demand Deposits, And Adjusted Demand Deposits, 1917–23

| National Bank Call Date | Demand Deposits Less Duplications | | | | | | | | |
| | New York State | | | 9 Urbanized States and D.C. | | | 38 Rural States | | |
	National Banks (1)	Non-national Banks (2)	All Comm. Banks (3)	National Banks (4)	Non-national Banks (5)	All Comm. Banks (6)	National Banks (7)	Non-national Banks (8)	All Comm Banks (9)
1917									
June 20	1,633	2,433	4,067	2,916	2,493	5,409	2,423	2,477	4,900
Sept. 11	1,809	2,530	4,339	3,002	2,520	5,522	2,510	2,578	5,088
Nov. 20	2,419	2,628	5,047	3,281	2,651	5,932	2,788	2,680	5,468
Dec. 31	1,957	2,617	4,574	3,185	2,593	5,778	2,752	2,742	5,494
1918									
Mar. 4	2,026	2,600	4,626	3,192	2,581	5,773	2,814	2,781	5,595
May 10	2,164	2,590	4,754	3,396	2,621	6,016	2,905	2,845	5,750

	Adjusted Demand Deposits					U. S. Govt. Demand Deposits[a]
	38 Rural States			United States		United States
ıl	Nonnational Banks (8)	All Comm. Banks (9)	National Banks (10)	Nonnational Banks (11)	All Comm. Banks (12)	National Banks (13)
	1,584	3,293	5,034	5,236	10,270	45
	1,646	3,361	5,030	5,413	10,443	48
	1,718	3,481	5,401	5,740	11,141	40
	1,762	3,600	5,551	5,928	11,479	31
	1,826	3,722	5,803	6,026	11,829	32
	1,879	3,893	5,885	6,167	12,052	37
	1,930	3,985	6,012	6,216	12,228	36
	2,039	4,202	6,265	6,457	12,722	37
	2,167	4,339	6,319	6,759	13,078	34
	2,241	4,469	6,368	6,987	13,355	30
	2,313	4,606	6,610	7,210	13,820	34
	2,394	4,706	6,704	7,321	14,025	38
	2,466	4,871	6,850	7,350	14,200	123

Demand Deposits Less Duplications			U.S. Govt. Demand Deposits			Adjusted Demand Deposits		
United States			United States			United States		
ıl	Nonnational Banks (11)	All Comm. Banks (12)	National Banks (13)	Nonnational Banks (14)	All Comm. Banks (15)	National Banks (16)	Nonnational Banks (17)	All Comm. Banks (18)
	7,403	14,376	123	53	176	6,850	7,350	14,200
	7,628	14,950	228	170	398	7,094	7,458	14,552
	7,960	16,448	1,348	1,259	2,607	7,140	6,701	13,841
	7,952	15,846	452	257	709	7,443	7,695	15,138
	7,962	15,994	683	594	1,277	7,349	7,368	14,717
	8,056	16,520	1,149	692	1,841	7,315	7,364	14,679

(continued)

TABLE 32 (continued)

| National Bank Call Date | Demand Deposits Less Duplications | | | | | | | | |
| | New York State | | | 9 Urbanized States and D.C. | | | 38 Rural States | | |
	National Banks (1)	Non-national Banks (2)	All Comm. Banks (3)	National Banks (4)	Non-national Banks (5)	All Comm. Banks (6)	National Banks (7)	Non-national Banks (8)	All Com Bank (9)
1918									
June 29	2,129	2,583	4,712	3,417	2,646	6,063	2,804	2,904	5,70
Aug. 31	2,062	2,584	4,647	3,275	2,625	5,900	2,748	3,007	5,75
Nov. 1	2,097	2,663	4,760	3,528	2,835	6,363	2,975	3,128	6,10
Dec. 31	2,041	2,712	4,754	3,430	2,819	6,249	2,967	3,184	6,15
1919									
Mar. 4	2,006	2,749	4,755	3,521	2,912	6,433	3,066	3,325	6,39
May 12	2,131	2,808	4,940	3,633	3,073	6,706	3,210	3,453	6,66
June 30	2,204	2,807	5,011	3,581	3,101	6,682	3,253	3,482	6,73
Sept. 12	2,234	2,906	5,140	3,878	3,297	7,175	3,562	3,687	7,24
Nov. 17	2,131	2,924	5,054	3,792	3,296	7,088	3,501	4,225	7,72
Dec. 31	2,159	2,936	5,094	3,798	3,416	7,214	3,703	4,050	7,75
1920									
Feb. 28	2,098	2,881	4,979	3,695	3,402	7,097	3,667	3,845	7,51
May 4	2,110	2,879	4,988	3,772	3,513	7,285	3,569	4,112	7,68
June 30	2,153	2,863	5,016	3,814	3,529	7,342	3,532	3,903	7,43
Sept. 8	2,103	2,889	4,992	3,835	3,634	7,469	3,415	3,875	7,29
Nov. 15	2,069	2,760	4,829	3,853	3,551	7,405	3,165	3,895	7,06
Dec. 29	2,059	2,815	4,874	3,689	3,564	7,254	3,095	3,587	6,68
1921									
Feb. 21	2,018	2,765	4,782	3,201	3,438	6,639	3,311	3,490	6,80
Apr. 28	2,069	2,727	4,796	3,378	3,387	6,765	2,892	3,335	6,22
June 30	2,047	2,739	4,786	3,323	3,424	6,747	2,876	3,208	6,08
Sept. 6	1,847	2,643	4,490	3,326	3,437	6,763	2,771	3,261	6,03
Dec. 31	2,001	2,676	4,677	3,281	3,357	6,638	2,764	3,163	5,92
1922									
Mar. 10	1,988	2,672	4,660	3,307	3,486	6,793	2,846	3,170	6,01
May 5	1,937	2,820	4,757	3,321	3,570	6,891	2,872	3,197	6,06
June 30	2,067	2,857	4,925	3,415	3,641	7,056	3,038	3,142	6,18
Sept. 15	2,023	2,963	4,986	3,585	3,861	7,446	3,112	3,276	6,38
Dec. 29	2,126	2,859	4,985	3,607	3,965	7,571	3,152	3,531	6,68
1923									
Apr. 3	1,947	2,953	4,900	3,597	4,113	7,711	3,242	3,520	6,76
June 30	1,810	2,924	4,733	3,756	4,097	7,853	3,225	3,409	6,63

	Demand Deposits Less Duplications United States		U.S. Govt. Demand Deposits United States			Adjusted Demand Deposits United States		
al s	Nonnational Banks (11)	All Comm. Banks (12)	National Banks (13)	Nonnational Banks (14)	All Comm. Banks (15)	National Banks (16)	Nonnational Banks (17)	All Comm. Banks (18)
	8,134	16,483	963	728	1,691	7,387	7,406	14,793
	8,217	16,303	505	423	928	7,581	7,794	15,375
	8,627	17,227	1,133	855	1,988	7,467	7,772	15,239
	8,716	17,155	273	224	497	8,165	8,492	16,657
	8,986	17,578	591	437	1,028	8,001	8,549	16,550
	9,334	18,309	575	495	1,070	8,401	8,839	17,240
	9,390	18,429	525	460	985	8,514	8,930	17,444
	9,890	19,564	563	467	1,030	9,111	9,423	18,534
	10,445	19,868	268	181	449	9,156	10,264	19,419
	10,402	20,062	392	293	685	9,267	10,109	19,377
	10,128	19,588	73	42	115	9,387	10,086	19,473
	10,504	19,955	124	105	229	9,326	10,399	19,726
	10,295	19,794	161	122	283	9,337	10,173	19,511
	10,398	19,751	56	32	88	9,297	10,366	19,663
	10,206	19,293	145	107	252	8,942	10,099	19,041
	9,966	18,809	184	150	334	8,659	9,816	18,475
	9,693	18,223	124	86	210	8,406	9,607	18,013
	9,449	17,788	171	138	309	8,169	9,311	17,479
	9,371	17,617	.'30	195	425	8,017	9,176	17,192
	9,341	17,285	'18	85	203	7,826	9,256	17,082
	9,196	17,241	163	156	319	7,883	9,040	16,922
	9,328	17,469	214	166	380	7,928	9,162	17,089
	9,588	17,717	152	115	267	7,977	9,473	17,450
	9,640	18,161	95	74	169	8,426	9,566	17,992
	10,100	18,820	156	115	271	8,564	9,985	18,549
	10,355	19,239	265	221	486	8,620	10,134	18,753
	10,586	19,373	262	188	450	8,524	10,398	18,923
	10,430	19,220	209	172	381	8,582	10,258	18,839

(continued)

Derivation of Estimates

TABLE 32 (continued)

Part IV. Adjusted Time Deposits, 1914–23

National Bank Call Date	Adjusted Time Deposits					
	New York State			9 Urbanized States and D.C.		
	National Banks (1)	Nonnational Banks (2)	All Comm. Banks (3)	National Banks (4)	Nonnational Banks (5)	A Co Ba
1914						
June 30	62	281	343	492	1,907	2,
Sept. 12	72	286	357	499	1,863	2,
Oct. 31	69	293	363	491	1,995	2,
Dec. 31	67	309	376	489	1,873	2,
1915						
Mar. 4	81	319	400	491	1,921	2,
May 1	93	332	425	509	1,920	2,
June 23	101	346	447	519	1,972	2,
Sept. 2	107	364	470	544	1,994	2,
Nov. 10	113	403	516	569	2,075	2,
Dec. 31	121	439	560	587	2,087	2,
1916						
Mar. 7	124	431	556	617	2,195	2,
May 1	141	427	569	658	2,238	2,
June 30	159	424	584	690	2,334	3,
Sept. 12	164	438	602	720	2,369	3,
Nov. 17	168	449	617	768	2,481	3,
Dec. 27	173	455	629	779	2,529	3,
1917						
Mar. 5	186	476	662	830	2,614	3,
May 1	205	466	671	867	2,639	3,
June 20	197	457	655	878	2,634	3,
Sept. 11	215	472	687	921	2,644	3,
Nov. 20	220	488	709	912	2,593	3,
Dec. 31	220	484	704	915	2,677	3,
1918						
Mar. 4	234	477	712	938	2,701	3,
May 10	226	472	697	928	2,705	3,
June 29	216	468	684	935	2,724	3,
Aug. 31	232	470	703	954	2,769	3,
Nov. 1	231	488	719	948	2,780	3,
Dec. 31	235	500	735	996	2,908	3,
1919						
Mar. 4	258	510	768	1,070	3,091	4,
May 12	265	524	788	1,046	3,167	4,
June 30	264	525	790	1,104	3,229	4,
Sept. 12	309	545	853	1,149	3,342	4,

		Adjusted Time Deposits			
	38 Rural States			United States	
:ional anks .7)	Nonnational Banks (8)	All Comm. Banks (9)	National Banks (10)	Nonnational Banks (11)	All Comm. Banks (12)
610	1,309	1,919	1,164	3,498	4,662
630	1,324	1,954	1,201	3,473	4,674
619	1,334	1,953	1,179	3,622	4,801
615	1,346	1,961	1,171	3,528	4,699
627	1,360	1,987	1,199	3,599	4,798
652	1,374	2,026	1,254	3,626	4,880
665	1,386	2,051	1,285	3,703	4,988
684	1,431	2,115	1,335	3,788	5,123
693	1,476	2,169	1,376	3,954	5,330
709	1,510	2,219	1,417	4,037	5,454
753	1,554	2,307	1,495	4,180	5,675
787	1,588	2,375	1,586	4,253	5,839
820	1,631	2,451	1,669	4,389	6,058
853	1,693	2,546	1,736	4,500	6,236
880	1,750	2,630	1,816	4,680	6,496
902	1,787	2,689	1,854	4,771	6,625
968	1,844	2,812	1,984	4,934	6,918
,006	1,892	2,898	2,078	4,996	7,074
,015	1,937	2,952	2,090	5,028	7,118
,061	1,977	3,038	2,197	5,093	7,290
,050	2,009	3,059	2,182	5,091	7,273
063	2,025	3,088	2,198	5,186	7,384
,096	2,056	3,152	2,268	5,234	7,502
,091	2,088	3,179	2,244	5,264	7,508
092	2,112	3,204	2,243	5,304	7,547
105	2,173	3,278	2,291	5,413	7,704
096	2,234	3,330	2,275	5,502	7,777
140	2,288	3,428	2,371	5,696	8,067
223	2,362	3,585	2,552	5,962	8,514
271	2,434	3,705	2,582	6,125	8,707
322	2,485	3,807	2,690	6,239	8,929
373	2,602	3.975	2,831	6,489	9,320

(continued)

TABLE 32 (concluded)

National Bank Call Date	Adjusted Time Deposits					
	New York State			9 Urbanized States and D.C.		
	National Banks (1)	Nonnational Banks (2)	All Comm. Banks (3)	National Banks (4)	Nonnational Banks (5)	A Co Bai (
1919						
Nov. 17	331	581	912	1,200	3,551	4,7
Dec. 31	340	533	874	1,235	3,541	4,7
1920						
Feb. 28	349	541	890	1,290	3,701	4,9
May 4	368	531	898	1,355	3,804	5,
June 30	371	537	907	1,399	3,889	5,2
Sept. 8	392	539	931	1,441	3,952	5,2
Nov. 15	398	524	922	1,505	3,995	5,2
Dec. 29	414	546	960	1,534	4,045	5,2
1921						
Feb. 21	416	507	923	1,599	4,046	5,1
Apr. 28	426	523	948	1,601	4,030	5,6
June 30	412	497	909	1,602	4,055	5,1
Sept. 6	407	489	896	1,611	4,007	5,6
Dec. 31	444	526	970	1,632	4,048	5,6
1922						
Mar. 10	470	566	1,036	1,671	4,097	5,7
May 5	489	565	1,054	1,693	4,162	5,8
June 30	595	677	1,272	1,742	4,262	6,0
Sept. 15	583	621	1,204	1,774	4,316	6,0
Dec. 29	609	756	1,365	1,836	4,529	6,2
1923						
Apr. 3	642	845	1,487	1,949	4,743	6,6
June 30	645	864	1,509	2,052	4,902	6,9

Notes to Table 32

Note: Detail may not add to totals, because of rounding.

[a]Only national banks were authorized depositaries of U.S. government deposits before June 1917.

[b]Includes postal savings in all state member banks.

[c]Excludes postal savings in all state member banks, deducted from sum of cols. 7 and 8, and 10 and 11.

Source, by Column

Part I

1. Total deposits excluding (a) interbank deposits, (b) float, (c) U. S. government deposits, and (d) beginning Nov. 1912, deposits of the Postal Savings System in national banks. From U. S. Comptroller of the Currency, *Abstract of Reports of Condition of National Banks,* corrected for seasonal.

			Adjusted Time Deposits		
	38 Rural States		United States		
...nal ks (7)	Nonnational Banks (8)	All Comm. Banks (9)	National Banks (10)	Nonnational Banks (11)	All Comm. Banks (12)
15	2,720	4,155	2,965	6,852	9,817
76	2,805	4,281	3,052	6,879	9,931
34	2,919	4,453	3,173	7,160	10,333
04	3,061	4,665	3,327	7,396	10,723
32	3,139	4,771	3,402	7,564	10,966
43	3,104	4,747	3,475	7,595	11,070
45	3,112	4,757	3,547	7,631	11,178
41	3,051	4,692	3,589	7,642	11,231
53	3,009	4,662	3,668	7,562	11,230
30	2,970	4,600	3,657	7,523	11,180
44	2,938	4,582	3,659	7,490	11,149
28	2,928	4,556	3,646	7,425	11,071
12	2,839[b]	4,467[c]	3,718	7,413	11,117[c]
15	2,851[b]	4,503[c]	3,806	7,514	11,308[c]
02	2,921	4,623	3,884	7,648	11,532
41	2,920	4,661	4,078	7,858	11,936
78	2,990	4,768	4,135	7,927	12,062
11	3,030[b]	4,845[c]	4,276	8,315	12,575[c]
17	3,191[b]	5,122[c]	4,538	8,779	13,300[c]
13	3,280	5,293	4,710	9,047	13,757

Notes to Table 32 (continued)

2. Total deposits excluding (a) interbank deposits, (b) float, and (c) beginning June 1913, an estimate of deposits of the Postal Savings System in New York nonnational banks. State banks and trust companies, from N. Y. State Superintendent of Banks, *Annual Report on Banks of Discount and Deposit,* corrected for seasonal; private banks from *All-Bank Statistics,* pp. 747–748.

The former source shows "nonpreferred" and "preferred" deposits and items a and b that were deducted for state banks and for trust companies at nonnational bank report dates. These figures were compared at June dates with the entries for these classes of banks in U. S. Comptroller of the Currency, *Annual Report,* and differences were reconciled.

Deposits of the Postal Savings System in New York nonnational banks at June dates were estimated by subtracting these deposits in New York national banks from Postal Savings System deposits in all New York banks (see Postal Savings System, *Statement of Operations,* annual issues). For seasonal adjustment and interpolation procedures, see text, p.562.

Notes to Table 32 (continued)

3. Col. 1 plus col. 2.

4. Same as for col. 1.   No seasonal movement was observed.

5. Annual reports of the respective state banking departments are the basic sources of report date information on total deposits adjusted. For June dates this information was checked with data for these states in U. S. Comptroller of the Currency, *Annual Report.* Differences were reconciled.

If not directly available in the state reports, deposits of the Postal Savings System in the nonnational banks of each of these ten political units were estimated for June dates by subtracting these deposits in national banks from Postal Savings System deposits in all banks of each of the units. See text, Chap. 13, section 4, for interpolation procedures. No seasonal movement was observed in the final series.

6. Col. 4 plus col. 5.

7. Col. 10 minus sum of cols. 1 and 4.

8. Figures at June dates for the thirty-eight rural states were obtained by subtracting from total deposits adjusted at all commercial banks in the United States (see *All-Bank Statistics,* pp. 36), the sum of cols. 10, 2, and 5. For nine sample states (see Table 31 for list), we obtained report date information from the annual reports of the respective state banking departments. For June dates this information was checked with data for these states in U. S. Comptroller of the Currency, *Annual Report.* Differences were reconciled.

If not directly available in the state reports, an estimate of deposits of the Postal Savings System in the nonnational banks of each of these nine states was obtained by subtracting these deposits in national banks from Postal Savings System deposits in all banks of each of the states. See text, Chap. 13, section 4, for interpolation procedures. No seasonal movement was observed in the final series.

9. Col. 7 plus col. 8.

10. The data and the source are the same as for col. 1.   No seasonal movement was observed.

11. Sum of cols. 2, 5, and 8.

12. Col. 10 plus col. 11.

13. Same source as col. 1, seasonally corrected by us.

Part II

1. The sum of (a) demand deposits, (b) dividends unpaid, (c) letters of credit and travelers' checks outstanding, (d) certified checks, (e) cashiers' checks, (f) due to Federal Reserve Banks, *minus* (g) items with Federal Reserve Banks in process of collection, (h) exchanges for clearinghouse, (i) checks on other banks in the same place, (j) outside checks and other cash items. From U. S. Comptroller of the Currency, *Abstract of Reports of Condition of National Banks,* corrected for seasonal. See text, Chap. 13, section 5, for estimates of

Notes to Table 32 (continued)

demand and time deposits at national banks, June–Oct. 1914, and for estimates of items in process of collection with Federal Reserve Banks, Nov. 1916–June 1917.

2. Total deposits adjusted at New York state banks and trust companies were compiled and corrected for seasonal, as in Part I. From these figures, time deposits adjusted at June dates, 1914, 1915 and 1021, shown in U. S. Comptroller of the Currency, *Annual Report,* were subtracted. On the assumption that time deposits had no seasonal movement, the difference gave demand deposits adjusted corrected for seasonal variation. Demand deposits were estimated at other dates by multiplying adjusted total deposits by a multiplier obtained from estimates of the ratio of demand to time deposits, interpolated as described in the text.

Estimates of demand deposits at New York private banks were added to those of state banks and trust companies. For June dates demand deposits adjusted, time deposits adjusted, and total deposits adjusted for all New York private banks are available in *All-Bank Statistics.* Beginning Dec. 1914, report date figures appear for a few private banks in the published state reports, with no breakdown of demand and time deposits until 1930 except at June dates, 1914, 1915 and 1921 and 1926–30 in *Annual Report* of the Comptroller of the Currency, as for state banks and trust companies. For June–Oct. 1914, the demand-time breakdown for private banks was derived by interpolating by Method L to call dates between the June ratios of demand to time deposits for all private banks. For Dec. 1914–June 1917, total deposits adjusted for reporting private banks were interpolated by Method L between report dates to call dates; demand-time ratios and demand deposits for these banks were estimated in the same way as for other nonnational banks. Total deposits adjusted for all private banks at June dates, less total deposits of reporting private banks, were next interpolated by Method L to call dates and were distributed between demand and time deposits according to the ratio of demand to time deposits of all private banks, interpolated by Method L to call dates. The sum of demand deposits in reporting private banks and the residual series constituted demand deposits in all private banks.

Beginning June 1917 nonnational bank figures include U.S. government demand deposits. New York's share was estimated as described in text and subtracted to get demand deposits adjusted for June 1917.

3. Col. 1 plus col. 2.

4. The data for these states, the source, and the estimation required are the same as for col. 1. The figures were corrected for seasonal variation.

5. The data for these states are demand deposits adjusted, but the sources and the estimation required are the same as described in Part I, col. 5. The figures were corrected for seasonal variation. For

Notes to Table 32 (continued)

June 1917, U. S. government deposits, estimated as described in text, were subtracted from the final figure.

6. Col. 4 plus col. 5.

7. Col. 10 minus sum of cols. 1 and 4.

8. The data for these states are demand deposits adjusted, but the sources and the estimation required are the same as described in Part I, col. 8. No seasonal movement was observed. For June 1917, U. S. government deposits, estimated as described in text, were subtracted from the final figure.

9. Col. 7 plus col. 8.

10. The data, the source, and the estimation required are the same as described in Part II, col. 1. The figures were corrected for seasonal variation.

11. Sum of cols. 2, 5, and 8.

12. Col. 10 plus col. 11.

13. Same source as Part II, col. 1, seasonally corrected by us.

Part III

1. Same data, with the addition of U. S. government deposits, and same source as described in Part II, col. 1. Figures were corrected for seasonal by us.

2. The data, the sources, and the estimation required are the same as described in Part II, col. 2, but estimates of government deposits at nonnational banks were not subtracted. Time deposits are available at June dates, 1915, 1921, and 1926 in *Annual Report* of the Comptroller of the Currency for subtracting from total deposits adjusted and for use in interpolating the demand-time ratio.

An item of float, items in process of collection with Federal Reserve Banks, although not shown in New York State bank reports, was obtained for New York state member banks, June 1919–June 1923, from *Member Bank Call Report* at member bank call dates and interpolated by Method L to national bank call dates that were not also member bank call dates. This duplicating item was deducted from reported total deposits less duplications.

3. Col. 1 plus col. 2.

4. Same data, with addition of U. S. government deposits, and same source as described in Part II, col. 1. No seasonal movement was observed.

5. The data for these states are demand deposits less duplications, but the sources, except for Pennsylvania, and the estimation required are the same as described in Part I, col. 5. For Pennsylvania additional data were obtained from unpublished statements of condition of nonnational banks furnished by the State Department of Banking.

As in Part III, col. 2, items in process of collection with Federal

Reserve Banks, reported by state member banks of these states, were deducted from demand deposits in addition to other float items reported in the state banking returns. The series was corrected for seasonal variation, 1917–18; no seasonal movement was observed thereafter.

6. Col. 4 plus col. 5.

7. Col. 10 minus sum of cols. 1 and 4.

8. The data for the sample of these states are demand deposits less duplications, but the sources, except for Delaware, and the estimation required are the same as described in Part I, col. 8. For Delaware in 1920 we used unpublished data furnished by the state bank commissioner.

As in Part III, col. 2, items in process of collection with Federal Reserve Banks reported by state member banks of these states were deducted from demand deposits in addition to other float items reported in the state banking returns. The series was corrected for seasonal variation.

9. Col. 7 plus col. 8.

10. Same data, with addition of U. S. government deposits, and same source as described in Part II, col. 1. Figures were corrected for seasonal variation.

11. Sum of cols. 2, 5, and 8.

12. Col. 10 plus col. 11.

13. Same source as Part II, col. 1, with correction for seasonal variation.

14. See source notes to Table 43, Part I, col. 5.

15. Col. 13 plus col. 14.

16–18. Cols. 10, 11, and 12 minus cols. 13, 14, and 15.

Part IV

1, 4, 10. Time deposits minus deposits of the Postal Savings System in national banks. From U. S. Comptroller of the Currency, *Abstract of Reports of Condition of National Banks;* no seasonal movement was observed. *June – Oct. 1914:* See Part II, col. 1 for a description of the breakdown of time deposits for this period.

2. See Part II, col. 2 for a description of the breakdown of time deposits.

3. Col. 1 plus col. 2.

5. The data are time deposits from the sources noted in Parts II and III for this column *minus* deposits of the Postal Savings System in nonnational banks, either shown in state reports or obtained as a residual by subtracting Postal Savings System deposits in national banks of these states from Postal Savings System deposits in all banks, shown in *Statement of Operations* of the Postal Savings System. The method of estimation used is the same as described in Part I for

this column. No seasonal movement was observed in the final series.

6. Col. 4 plus col. 5.

7. Col. 10 minus sum of cols. 1 and 4.

8. The data are time deposits from the sources noted in Parts II and III for this column excluding deposits of the Postal Savings System in nonnational banks, either shown in state reports or obtained as a residual by subtracting Postal Savings System deposits in national banks of these states from the figures for Postal Savings System deposits in all banks, shown in *Statement of Operations* of the Postal Savings System. The method of estimation used is the same as described in Part I for this column. No seasonal movement was observed in the final series.

9. Col. 7 plus col. 8.

11. Sum of cols. 2, 5, and 8.

12. Col. 10 plus col. 11.

by Method L between state report dates. Call date figures for other private banks were interpolated between the banks' June data estimated by subtracting the estimates for June dates for reporting banks from the estimates for all banks in *All-Bank Statistics*.

Before March 1930, New York State reports do not classify total deposits as demand and time. We estimated this breakdown by using the data for New York nonnational banks in the *Annual Report* of the Comptroller of the Currency at selected June dates, 1914–30. We computed the ratio of reported demand to reported time deposits at June dates for which data were available and interpolated the demand-time ratios to call dates by Method L. We did this both for 1914–23 and for 1923–March 1930 (section 6 below). The interpolation was done separately for incorporated state banks (including trust companies) and for private banks. We were particularly hesitant to resort to Method L because data on the demand-time ratio were not available for every June; consequently we had to interpolate over spans as long as five years. Nonetheless, we did resort to Method L because, despite extensive experiments, we could not find a satisfactory interpolator to use with Method R.[9]

---

[9] We tested possible interpolators for the ratio of demand to time deposits by using data for the period 1930–43, when a breakdown of demand and time deposits is presented in the state reports for many call dates. We tested interpolators by computing values of u and v as percentage deviations both from trends connecting alternate call dates, and from trends connecting June values separated by as much as five years. Both sets of tests yielded generally low correlations.

The demand-time ratios of New York national and New York state member banks were tested as possible interpolators for the demand-time ratio of New York state banks,

In April 1917 nonnational banks became authorized depositaries of the United States government. This is why we shift in 1917 from estimating adjusted deposits directly to estimating deposits less duplications. United States government deposits at nonnational banks from this date forward were estimated for the country as a whole and corrected for seasonal (see Chapter 17). For June 1917, government deposits at nonnational banks were divided among the three groups of states in the same proportion as government deposits at national banks. New York's share, estimated in this way, was subtracted from demand deposits and total deposits to get deposits adjusted at that date, the final call date for deposits in this form (Table 32, Part II). Beginning June 1917 the series is demand deposits less duplications, and government deposits are deducted from the aggregate data for all nonnational banks, not by groups of states (Table 32, Part III).

Nine Urbanized States and the District of Columbia. There are reports from all of these political units at almost every June date.[10] At call dates falling at other times in the year reports are typically available only for some of the states within the group. The problem was to estimate data for the changing number of nonreporting urbanized units. We did so by interpolating the sum of the missing observations for each call date by Method R_1. We used as the related series the totals for the maximum number of political units reporting at that call date and interpolated between June dates. This meant that the related series might differ from call date to call date even within the same June-to-June interval. This enabled us to use all reported figures. Because Method R_1 gives the same result for seasonally adjusted and unadjusted data (provided the same

New York private banks, both classes combined, New York nonmember banks, and New York loan and trust companies. Correlation coefficients were all less than +.2 except for loan and trust companies, for which the correlation with national banks was +.53, and with state member banks, +.76. However, loan and trust companies include both state member and nonmember banks, with member banks predominating. Our other results indicated that there was no significant correlation between nonmember and national banks or state member banks. The high correlation coefficients for loan and trust companies and the two interpolators must result then from the institutions' state member bank component. But we have direct data for this component from 1919 on.

Of five different series that were tested as possible interpolators of New York nonmember bank data, the highest correlation coefficient was +.38, between the ratios for New York nonmember and Illinois nonmember banks.

[10] For three states there are no figures for May 20, 1907; for two states no figures for July 15, 1908; for one state no figures for June 20, 1917, or June 30, 1919. In none of these cases is there a report dated within two weeks of the midyear date. We had a choice of interpolating the figures or of ignoring our dating rule and simply utilizing the figures for a date closest to midyear. We chose the first alternative except in 1919, when the figure for the closest date, June 2, was used.

seasonal is used for all units), we did not have to adjust the date for the separate states for seasonal.

The use of Method R_1 is equivalent to simply "blowing up" the sample. We used this method rather than the more laborious method R_2 or R_3 because the reported call date figures constituted 70 per cent, on the average, of total deposits in the nonnational banks of the nine urban states and the District of Columbia.[11]

United States government deposits were subtracted in June 1917 as described for New York nonnational banks.

Total deposits adjusted, 1907–14, demand deposits less duplications, 1919–23, and time deposits, 1907–23, showed no seasonal influences. Demand deposits adjusted and less duplications, 1914–18, required seasonal adjustment.

The Thirty-Eight Rural States. We did not obtain independent June estimates for the group of thirty-eight rural states. Instead we derived them by subtracting the estimates for the two other strata from the excess of demand and time deposits of all commercial banks in *All-Bank Statistics* over our estimates for all national banks (see section 5 below).

For inter-June dates, our estimates are the sum of the actual figures for those of the nine rural sample states for which we had reported data plus values interpolated by Method L for the rest of the thirty-eight states. We used Method L instead of Method R, with data for the sample states as the related series, because for this period our sample is so limited that it provides little information. On the average there is a report for only one state in our sample at each of the sixty inter-June call dates, 1907–23. The proportion of deposits in our sample data at these dates averaged only 5.8 per cent of the deposits estimated for the thirty-eight states.

For June 1917, we subtracted U.S. government deposits from demand deposits less duplications for this class of banks, as described for New York nonnational banks. Demand deposits less duplications were corrected for seasonal, 1918–23; total deposits adjusted and time deposits required no seasonal adjustment.

For national and nonnational banks before June 1921, the elimina-

---

[11] The percentages were obtained by averaging the ratios of the inter-June straight-line trend values of the changing sample to the inter-June straight-line trend values of the nine urbanized states and the District of Columbia.

tion of postal savings from reported time deposits presents no problem. For national banks by states the breakdown at call dates is known; for nonnational banks by states the breakdown is known or was interpolated between June data by Method L. Beginning June 1921, however, nonnational bank time deposit figures, if directly derived, are free of postal savings. If derived as a sum of nonmember and state member bank data, they are too large by the amount of postal savings held by state member banks, 1921–23. Thus, at national bank call dates that were not state member bank call dates, 1921–23, our directly derived time deposit figures for nonnational banks are accurate in respect to the exclusion of postal savings. At other dates, 1921–23, we deducted data on postal savings in all state member banks from the totals for all nonnational and all commercial banks of the thirty-eight rural states, all nonnational banks, and all commercial banks in the United States. The logic of this procedure is discussed below in the section on member bank figures.

5. National Bank Estimates, National Bank Call Dates, 1907–23

The following classes of deposits at national banks of New York, the nine other urbanized states and the District of Columbia, and at all national banks were compiled to match the call date estimates for nonnational banks: total adjusted, 1907–14; demand adjusted, 1914–17; demand less duplications, 1917–23; and time adjusted, 1914–23. From these compilations figures for national banks in the thirty-eight relatively rural states were computed as a residual.[12] Appropriate combinations of the basic series yield totals for banks for each group of states and for all forty-eight, 1907–23 (Table 32).

The published figures for national banks required special adjustments as follows:

a. For the call dates of June, September, and October 1914, the Comptroller does not present a breakdown of demand and time deposits at national banks. We estimated the breakdown at these call dates by applying to total deposits adjusted (excluding dividends unpaid, certified

---

12 National bank figures (exclusive of national banks in the Possessions) were compiled from the Comptroller of the Currency's *Abstract of Reports of Condition of National Banks.*

checks and cashiers checks, which are known at all call dates) the December 1914 ratio of demand deposits adjusted (with similar exclusions) to time deposits. Separate estimates were made for New York, the nine other urbanized states and the District of Columbia, all national banks, and the residual rural states.

b. The component of float, items in process of collection with the Federal Reserve Banks, is reported separately for national banks beginning September 11, 1917. Previously this component was combined with lawful reserve in vault and with Federal Reserve Banks. We estimated the approximate amount of items in process for call dates starting November 17, 1916, and distributed the total among banks in our three strata in the same proportion as on September 11, 1917.

Total deposits adjusted and demand deposits adjusted of New York national banks and of the national banks in the nine urbanized and the thirty-eight rural states required seasonal adjustment.

6. Nonmember Bank Estimates, Member Bank Call Dates, 1919–46

These estimates, which were made separately for each of our strata, are given in Table 33, for demand deposits in Part I and for time deposits in Parts II and III.

New York State. As noted in section 4, up to March 1930 state banking reports gave only total deposits less duplications in New York state banks and trust companies, not demand and time deposits separately. Total deposits of nonnational banks and their division between demand and time were estimated for call dates for this period as for the period 1917–23. Similar data for state member banks, available directly from the Federal Reserve, were subtracted to yield estimates of deposits at nonmember incorporated commercial banks. Estimates for private banks were also constructed in the same way as for 1917–23, separately for reporting and nonreporting private banks.

Beginning June 1930, the state reports break down total deposits of state banks and trust companies into demand and time deposits, so that it is no longer necessary to estimate these figures by interpolation, and estimates of Postal Savings System data are subtracted from time deposits instead of total deposits. Beginning March 1935, the breakdown is available in state reports for reporting private banks.

Nine Urbanized States and the District of Columbia. Method R_1, used to interpolate reported figures for nonnational banks in this group of political units (described in section 4 above), was used also to interpolate reported data for nonmember banks. On the average reported call date figures constituted 85 per cent of demand deposits and also of time deposits at nonmember banks of this stratum. Neither the estimated series for demand deposits less duplications nor that for time deposits showed seasonal movements.

The Thirty-Eight Rural States. Estimates for June dates for nonmember banks in this stratum were constructed by subtracting deposits at member banks and nonmember banks for the nine urbanized states and the District of Columbia and New York from deposits at all commercial banks, shown in *All-Bank Statistics.*

For inter-June dates our estimates are a sum of (a) directly reported data for those states in our sample of rural states for which we had such data for the particular call date (reporting sample states), and (b) interpolated estimates for the remaining rural states. The estimates for the remaining states were interpolated between June estimates by Method R_2, using as the related series deposits in the maximum number of sample states for which we had reports for the particular call dates. We tested this interpolation procedure by using data for member banks as proxies for data for nonmember banks. From these data for member banks, we also estimated the values that we assigned *b*.

One complication is the changing number of reporting sample states at different call dates. To allow for this we classified the call dates into four categories by the observed combinations of reporting sample states and others that seemed most representative:

1. Reports for essentially the whole sample (all nine states plus those sets of seven or eight sample states for which deposits in nonreporting sample states are relatively small)
2. Reports for a substantial part of the sample (six states plus those sets of seven or eight sample states for which deposits in nonreporting sample states are relatively large)
3. Reports for five states
4. Reports for three or four states.

TABLE 33

Deposits at All U.S. Commercial Banks, Distinguishing Member from Nonmember Banks in New York, Urbanized, and Rural States, Member Bank Call Dates, 1919–46

(seasonally adjusted, in millions of dollars)

Part I. Demand Deposits Less Duplications, U.S. Government Demand Deposits, and Adjusted Demand Deposits

| | Demand Deposits Less Duplications | | | | | | | | |
| | New York State | | | 9 Urbanized States & D.C. | | | 38 Rural States | | |
Member Bank Call Date	Member Banks (1)	Non-member Banks (2)	All Comm. Banks (3)	Member Banks (4)	Non-member Banks (5)	All Comm. Banks (6)	Member Banks (7)	Non-member Banks (8)	C B
1919									
June 30	4,374	638	5,011	5,003	1,679	6,682	3,752	2,983	(
Nov. 17	4,393	661	5,054	5,355	1,733	7,088	4,272	3,454	)
Dec. 31	4,441	653	5,094	5,451	1,763	7,214	4,405	3,348	(
1920									
May 4	4,305	683	4,988	5,428	1,857	7,285	4,275	3,406	)
June 30	4,315	700	5,016	5,532	1,811	7,342	4,175	3,260	)
Nov. 15	4,146	683	4,829	5,578	1,827	7,405	3,959	3,101	)
Dec. 29	4,090	784	4,874	5,347	1,906	7,254	3,744	2,938	(
1921									
Apr. 28	4,066	730	4,796	5,120	1,645	6,765	3,531	2,696	(
June 30	4,046	740	4,786	5,092	1,655	6,747	3,483	2,601	(
Dec. 31	3,967	710	4,677	5,052	1,585	6,638	3,404	2,523	!
1922									
Mar. 10	3,923	737	4,660	5,133	1,660	6,793	3,510	2,506	
June 30	4,173	751	4,925	5,382	1,674	7,056	3,698	2,482	
Dec. 29	4,207	778	4,985	5,727	1,845	7,571	3,903	2,780	
1923									
Apr. 3	4,116	784	4,900	5,784	1,927	7,711	4,019	2,743	
June 30	3,946	787	4,733	5,963	1,891	7,853	3,952	2,682	
Sept. 14	3,861	778	4,640	5,895	1,972	7,867	3,942	2,594	
Dec. 31	3,825	849	4,674	5,848	1,982	7,830	4,008	2,785	
1924									
Mar. 31	3,962	866	4,828	5,811	1,932	7,742	3,939	2,685	
June 30	4,167	882	5,049	5,981	1,995	7,977	3,900	2,702	
Oct. 10	4,571	909	5,480	6,341	2,057	8,398	4,091	2,892	
Dec. 31	4,555	980	5,536	6,308	2,120	8,428	4,209	2,881	
1925									
Apr. 6	4,528	945	5,473	6,357	2,235	8,591	4,320	3,021	
June 30	4,559	970	5,529	6,501	2,278	8,780	4,304	3,049	
Sept. 28	4,691	1,061	5,752	6,658	2,346	9,004	4,452	3,464	
Dec. 31	4,759	1,049	5,808	6,694	2,350	9,044	4,573	3,636	

and Deposits Less Duplications			U.S. Gov't. Demand Deposits			Adjusted Demand Deposits		
United States			United States			United States		
Member Banks (10)	Non-member Banks (11)	All Comm. Banks (12)	Member Banks (13)	Non-member Banks (14)˙	All Comm. Banks (15)	Member Banks (16)	Non-member Banks (17)	All Comm. Banks (18)
13,129	5,300	18,429	862	123	985	12,266	5,177	17,443
14,020	5,848	19,868	386	63	449	13,634	5,785	19,419
14,298	5,764	20,062	594	91	685	13,704	5,673	19,377
14,009	5,946	19,955	200	28	228	13,809	5,918	19,727
14,023	5,771	19,794	248	36	284	13,775	5,735	19,510
13,683	5,610	19,293	220	33	253	13,464	5,577	19,041
13,181	5,628	18,809	291	44	335	12,891	5,584	18,475
12,717	5,071	17,788	270	38	308	12,446	5,033	17,479
12,621	4,996	17,617	372	53	425	12,249	4,943	17,192
12,423	4,818	17,241	283	36	319	12,140	4,782	16,922
12,566	4,903	17,469	330	49	379	12,235	4,854	17,089
13,254	4,907	18,161	149	20	169	13,105	4,887	17,992
13,836	5,403	19,239	425	61	486	13,411	5,342	18,753
13,919	5,454	19,373	388	62	450	13,531	5,392	18,923
13,860	5,360	19,220	333	48	381	13,527	5,312	18,839
13,698	5,344	19,042	153	23	176	13,546	5,321	18,867
13,681	5,616	19,297	274	42	316	13,407	5,574	18,981
13,712	5,483	19,195	232	34	266	13,480	5,449	18,929
14,049	5,579	19,628	200	31	231	13,848	5,548	19,396
15,003	5,857	20,860	303	44	347	14,700	5,813	20,513
15,072	5,982	21,054	281	40	321	14,790	5,942	20,732
15,204	6,201	21,405	393	63	456	14,811	6,138	20,949
15,365	6,297	21,662	199	28	227	15,166	6,269	21,435
15,802	6,870	22,672	295	47	342	15,507	6,823	22,330
16,026	7,035	23,061	353	56	409	15,673	6,979	22,652

(continued)

Derivation of Estimates

TABLE 33 (continued)

| Member Bank Call Date | Demand Deposits Less Duplications | | | | | | | | |
| | New York State | | | 9 Urbanized States & D.C. | | | 38 Rural States | | |
	Member Banks (1)	Non-member Banks (2)	All Comm. Banks (3)	Member Banks (4)	Non-member Banks (5)	All Comm. Banks (6)	Member Banks (7)	Non-member Banks (8)	C B
1926									
Apr. 12	4,699	1,023	5,722	6,626	2,365	8,991	4,529	3,483	8,
June 30	4,757	978	5,734	6,754	2,356	9,110	4,470	3,127	7,
Dec. 31	4,778	1,048	5,826	6,673	2,373	9,046	4,349	3,079	7,
1927									
Mar. 23	4,951	1,069	6,020	6,777	2,312	9,088	4,396	2,957	7,
June 30	4,971	1,082	6,052	6,863	2,383	9,245	4,402	2,825	7,
Oct. 10	4,961	1,142	6,103	6,970	2,456	9,426	4,545	2,878	7,
Dec. 31	5,131	1,034	6,165	6,970	2,430	9,400	4,525	2,922	7,
1928									
Feb. 28	5,075	1,114	6,188	6,739	2,402	9,141	4,440	2,824	7,
June 30	4,965	1,087	6,052	6,905	2,449	9,354	4,485	2,750	7,
Oct. 3	4,844	1,187	6,031	6,898	2,473	9,371	4,466	2,814	7,
Dec. 31	5,008	1,206	6,214	6,966	2,544	9,511	4,562	2,886	7,
1929									
Mar. 27	5,222	1,203	6,425	6,753	2,438	9,191	4,517	2,848	7,
June 29	5,311	1,178	6,489	6,861	2,449	9,311	4,449	2,808	7,
Oct. 4	5,268	1,257	6,525	6,955	2,419	9,374	4,433	2,866	7,
Dec. 31	5,405	1,194	6,599	6,798	2,371	9,169	4,354	2,856	7,
1930									
Mar. 27	5,308	1,242	6,551	6,638	2,317	8,955	4,295	2,753	7,
June 30	5,272	1,160	6,433	6,717	2,309	9,025	4,281	2,598	6,
Sept. 24	5,280	987	6,267	6,596	2,307	8,903	4,208	2,438	6,
Dec. 31	5,313	1,031	6,344	6,629	2,124	8,753	3,967	2,200	6,
1931									
Mar. 25	5,496	905	6,401	6,529	1,961	8,489	3,993	2,137	6,
June 30	5,213	981	6,194	6,390	1,832	8,222	3,944	2,126	6,
Sept. 29	5,387	785	6,172	6,170	1,661	7,830	3,671	1,935	5,
Dec. 31	4,961	820	5,781	5,568	1,441	7,009	3,336	1,816	5,
1932									
June 30	4,694	739	5,433	4,994	1,131	6,124	3,078	1,530	4,
Sept. 30	4,972	657	5,629	5,164	1,119	6,283	2,993	1,423	4,
Dec. 31	4,912	808	5,720	5,146	1,109	6,255	2,916	1,286	4,
1933									
June 30	5,194	574	5,768	4,904	753	5,657	2,842	1,150	3,
Oct. 25	5,230	536	5,766	5,084	677	5,760	3,014	1,162	4,
Dec. 30	5,274	513	5,787	5,142	725	5,867	3,184	1,177	4,
1934									
Mar. 5	5,696	490	6,186	5,530	703	6,233	3,641	1,234	4,
June 30	6,162	445	6,607	5,961	760	6,720	3,859	1,311	5,

and Deposits Less Duplications			U.S. Gov't. Demand Deposits			Adjusted Demand Deposits		
United States			United States			United States		
ember anks (10)	Non-member Banks (11)	All Comm. Banks (12)	Member Banks (13)	Non-member Banks (14)	All Comm. Banks (15)	Member Banks (16)	Non-member Banks (17)	All Comm. Banks (18)
5,854	6,871	22,725	362	61	423	15,492	6,810	22,302
5,980	6,461	22,441	256	37	293	15,724	6,424	22,148
5,800	6,500	22,300	273	37	310	15,527	6,463	21,990
6,124	6,337	22,461	324	45	369	15,800	6,292	22,092
6,235	6,289	22,524	244	35	279	15,991	6,254	22,245
6,476	6,476	22,952	437	61	498	16,040	6,415	22,455
6,627	6,385	23,012	310	43	353	16,317	6,342	22,659
6,254	6,339	22,593	86	13	99	16,168	6,326	22,494
6,354	6,286	22,640	287	46	333	16,068	6,240	22,308
6,208	6,474	22,682	160	26	186	16,047	6,448	22,495
6,536	6,636	23,172	301	49	350	16,235	6,587	22,822
6,492	6,489	22,981	327	51	378	16,165	6,438	22,603
6,622	6,435	23,057	391	61	452	16,231	6,374	22,605
6,656	6,543	23,199	317	50	367	16,338	6,493	22,831
6,557	6,421	22,978	165	26	191	16,392	6,395	22,787
6,242	6,312	22,554	259	37	296	15,983	6,275	22,258
6,270	6,067	22,337	316	42	358	15,955	6,025	21,980
6,083	5,733	21,816	272	36	308	15,811	5,697	21,508
5,910	5,354	21,264	311	36	347	15,599	5,318	20,917
6,017	5,003	21,020	400	45	445	15,617	4,958	20,575
5,547	4,940	20,487	445	50	495	15,102	4,890	19,992
5,228	4,380	19,608	558	58	616	14,670	4,322	18,992
3,865	4,077	17,942	478	54	532	13,388	4,023	17,411
2,765	3,400	16,165	438	39	477	12,328	3,361	15,689
3,128	3,199	16,327	784	63	847	12,345	3,136	15,481
2,972	3,203	16,175	556	44	600	12,416	3,159	15,575
2,929	2,477	15,406	910	63	973	12,019	2,414	14,433
3,313	2,375	15,688	919	61	980	12,394	2,314	14,708
3,586	2,415	16,001	1,128	73	1,201	12,458	2,342	14,800
,851	2,428	17,279	1,647	83	1,730	13,204	2,345	15,549
,965	2,516	18,481	1,794	73	1,867	14,171	2,443	16,614

(continued)

Derivation of Estimates

TABLE 33 (continued)

| | Demand Deposits Less Duplications | | | | | | | | |
| | New York State | | | 9 Urbanized States & D.C. | | | 38 Rural States | | |
Member Bank Call Date	Member Banks (1)	Non-member Banks (2)	All Comm. Banks (3)	Member Banks (4)	Non-member Banks (5)	All Comm. Banks (6)	Member Banks (7)	Non-member Banks (8)	C B
1934									
Oct. 17	6,181	544	6,725	6,261	861	7,122	4,046	1,405	5
Dec. 31	6,488	612	7,101	6,548	853	7,401	4,235	1,494	5
1935									
Mar. 4	6,399	858	7,257	6,600	899	7,499	4,286	1,467	5
June 29	6,981	690	7,671	6,919	928	7,847	4,487	1,547	6
Nov. 1	6,978	792	7,770	7,448	1,021	8,469	4,754	1,551	6
Dec. 31	7,085	892	7,977	7,674	1,047	8,720	4,803	1,658	6
1936									
Mar. 4	7,230	960	8,191	7,659	1,067	8,725	4,865	1,670	6
June 30	7,732	882	8,613	8,318	1,117	9,435	5,335	1,738	7
Dec. 31	7,918	962	8,881	8,923	1,204	10,127	5,591	1,913	7
1937									
Mar. 31	7,942	968	8,909	8,297	1,151	9,448	5,520	1,885	7
June 30	7,792	937	8,729	8,684	1,160	9,843	5,620	1,889	7
Dec. 31	7,202	775	7,977	8,422	1,107	9,529	5,450	1,813	7
1938									
Mar. 7	7,469	880	8,349	8,229	1,130	9,360	5,558	1,782	7
June 30	7,504	793	8,297	8,444	1,076	9,520	5,554	1,712	7
Sept. 28	7,934	830	8,764	8,729	1,121	9,850	5,691	1,715	7
Dec. 31	8,130	904	9,034	9,036	1,141	10,177	5,816	1,881	7
1939									
Mar. 29	8,529	799	9,328	8,585	1,096	9,681	6,024	1,867	7
June 30	8,882	822	9,704	9,285	1,172	10,457	6,114	1,919	8
Oct. 2	9,589	872	10,461	9,867	1,250	11,117	6,337	1,938	8
Dec. 30	9,831	856	10,687	10,091	1,265	11,356	6,502	2,123	8
1940									
Mar. 26	10,559	850	11,409	9,941	1,245	11,186	6,686	2,056	8
June 29	11,178	955	12,133	10,646	1,213	11,859	6,765	2,056	8
Dec. 31	12,087	1,086	13,174	11,589	1,330	12,920	7,368	2,131	9
1941									
Apr. 4	12,668	1,022	13,690	11,774	1,335	13,109	7,657	2,187	9
June 30	12,676	1,255	13,930	12,688	1,352	14,041	7,933	2,182	10
Sept. 24	12,779	1,102	13,881	13,367	1,413	14,779	8,458	2,354	10
Dec. 31	12,817	1,099	13,916	13,649	1,518	15,167	8,997	2,685	11
1942									
Apr. 2	13,528	1,030	14,559	13,970	1,468	15,438	9,336	2,846	12
June 30	13,822	485	14,307	15,003	1,539	16,542	9,865	2,994	12
Dec. 31	17,705	693	18,398	19,131	1,934	21,065	13,657	4,091	17

and Deposits Less Duplications			U.S. Gov't. Demand Deposits			Adjusted Demand Deposits		
United States			United States			United States		
Member Banks (10)	Non-member Banks (11)	All Comm. Banks (12)	Member Banks (13)	Non-member Banks (14)	All Comm. Banks (15)	Member Banks (16)	Non-member Banks (17)	All Comm. Banks (18)
16,470	2,810	19,280	1,159	69	1,228	15,311	2,741	18,052
17,248	2,960	20,208	1,657	77	1,734	15,591	2,883	18,474
17,262	3,224	20,486	1,357	95	1,452	15,905	3,129	19,034
18,362	3,165	21,527	825	40	865	17,537	3,125	20,662
19,159	3,364	22,523	650	47	697	18,509	3,317	21,826
19,562	3,597	23,159	754	53	807	18,808	3,544	22,352
19,754	3,697	23,451	641	54	695	19,113	3,643	22,756
21,384	3,737	25,121	1,096	93	1,189	20,288	3,644	23,932
22,432	4,080	26,512	788	76	864	21,644	4,004	25,648
21,759	4,004	25,763	443	34	477	21,315	3,970	25,285
22,096	3,986	26,082	665	35	700	21,431	3,951	25,382
21,074	3,695	24,769	698	30	728	20,376	3,665	24,041
21,256	3,792	25,048	804	58	862	20,452	3,734	24,186
21,502	3,581	25,083	574	28	602	20,928	3,553	24,481
22,353	3,667	26,020	707	45	752	21,646	3,622	25,268
22,982	3,926	26,908	706	58	764	22,276	3,868	26,144
23,138	3,762	26,900	828	56	884	22,310	3,706	26,016
24,281	3,913	28,194	734	59	793	23,547	3,854	27,401
25,793	4,060	29,853	675	47	722	25,118	4,013	29,131
26,424	4,245	30,669	664	58	722	25,760	4,187	29,947
27,186	4,151	31,337	776	53	829	26,410	4,098	30,508
28,588	4,225	32,813	751	60	811	27,837	4,165	32,002
31,045	4,547	35,592	552	56	608	30,493	4,491	34,984
32,099	4,544	36,643	523	36	559	31,576	4,508	36,084
33,297	4,789	38,086	653	61	714	32,643	4,728	37,371
34,603	4,869	39,472	781	47	828	33,822	4,822	38,644
35,463	5,302	40,765	1,527	71	1,598	33,936	5,231	39,167
36,834	5,344	42,178	2,164	132	2,296	34,670	5,212	39,882
38,690	5,018	43,708	1,824	62	1,886	36,866	4,956	41,822
50,493	6,718	57,211	7,923	286	8,209	42,570	6,432	49,002

(continued)

TABLE 33 (continued)

Member Bank Call Date	Demand Deposits Less Duplications								
	New York State			9 Urbanized States & D.C.			38 Rural States		
	Member Banks (1)	Non-member Banks (2)	All Comm. Banks (3)	Member Banks (4)	Non-member Banks (5)	All Comm. Banks (6)	Member Banks (7)	Non-member Banks (8)	Co B.
1943									
June 30	18,175	806	18,982	22,320	2,194	24,514	15,697	4,856	20,
Oct. 18	21,450	871	22,321	26,057	2,440	28,497	18,647	5,210	23,
Dec. 31	19,318	914	20,232	24,851	2,448	27,299	17,917	5,614	23,
1944									
Apr. 13	20,120	1,492	21,613	25,772	2,359	28,131	18,832	5,880	24,
June 30	21,668	1,185	22,853	27,602	2,666	30,268	20,193	6,200	26,
Dec. 30	23,270	1,458	24,728	29,978	3,014	32,992	22,569	7,258	29,
1945									
Mar. 20	22,052	1,240	23,291	29,240	2,936	32,176	22,292	7,308	29,
June 30	25,010	1,386	26,396	32,024	3,174	35,198	24,067	7,712	31,
Dec. 31	24,968	1,443	26,411	33,951	3,498	37,449	27,444	8,998	36,
1946									
June 29	22,462	1,061	23,523	31,034	3,338	34,372	25,974	8,978	34

Part II. Adjusted Time Deposits, 1919–38

Member Bank Call Date	Adjusted Time Deposits					
	New York State			9 Urbanized States & D.C.		
	Member Banks (1)	Nonmember Banks (2)	All Comm. Banks (3)	Member Banks (4)	Nonmember Banks (5)	Co Ba
1919						
June 30	444	346	790	2,093	2,240	4
Nov. 17	606	306	912	2,484	2,267	4
Dec. 31	585	289	874	2,690	2,085	4
1920						
May 4	624	274	898	2,921	2,239	5
June 30	636	271	907	3,026	2,262	5
Nov. 15	691	230	922	3,194	2,306	5
Dec. 29	702	258	960	3,261	2,318	5
1921						
Apr. 28	733	216	948	3,392	2,239	5
June 30	700	209	909	3,424	2,234	5
Dec. 31	759	211	970	3,480	2,200	5
1922						
Mar. 10	812	224	1,036	3,609	2,160	5

and Deposits Less Duplications			U.S. Gov't. Demand Deposits			Adjusted Demand Deposits		
United States			United States			United States		
Member Banks (10)	Non-member Banks (11)	All Comm. Banks (12)	Member Banks (13)	Non-member Banks (14)	All Comm. Banks (15)	Member Banks (16)	Non-member Banks (17)	All Comm. Banks (18)
6,193	7,856	64,049	7,236	544	7,780	48,957	7,312	56,269
6,154	8,521	74,675	17,542	1,055	18,597	48,612	7,466	56,078
2,086	8,976	71,062	9,444	558	10,002	52,642	8,418	61,060
4,723	9,732	74,455	11,468	746	12,214	53,255	8,986	62,241
9,463	10,051	79,514	17,634	1,361	18,995	51,829	8,690	60,519
5,816	11,730	87,546	18,509	1,381	19,890	57,308	10,349	67,657
3,583	11,484	85,067	12,409	863	13,272	61,175	10,621	71,796
1,101	12,272	93,373	21,967	1,813	23,780	59,133	10,459	69,592
6,363	13,939	100,302	22,179	1,709	23,888	64,184	12,230	76,414
9,470	13,377	92,847	12,009	1,084	13,093	67,461	12,293	79,754

Adjusted Time Deposits					
38 Rural States			United States		
Member Banks (7)	Nonmember Banks (8)	All Comm. Banks (9)	Member Banks (10)	Nonmember Banks (11)	All Comm. Banks (12)
1,712	2,094	3,806	4,249	4,680	8,929
1,872	2,283	4,155	4,962	4,856	9,818
1,942	2,339	4,281	5,217	4,713	9,930
2,120	2,545	4,665	5,664	5,058	10,722
2,166	2,606	4,772	5,828	5,139	10,967
2,186	2,571	4,757	6,071	5,107	11,178
2,182	2,509	4,691	6,146	5,085	11,231
2,179	2,421	4,600	6,303	4,876	11,179
2,207	2,388	4,582	6,317	4,831	11,148
2,181	2,300	4,467	6,406	4,711	11,117
2,211	2,304	4,503	6,620	4,688	11,308

(continued)

TABLE 33 (continued)

| | Adjusted Time Deposits | | | | | |
| | New York State | | | 9 Urbanized States & D.C. | | |
Member Bank Call Date	Member Banks (1)	Nonmember Banks (2)	All Comm. Banks (3)	Member Banks (4)	Nonmember Banks (5)	A Co Ba (
1922						
June 30	1,034	237	1,272	3,770	2,234	6,
Dec. 29	1,106	259	1,365	4,062	2,303	6,
1923						
Apr. 3	1,219	268	1,487	4,294	2,398	6.
June 30	1,233	276	1,509	4,432	2,522	6.
Sept. 14	1,253	277	1,530	4,478	2,622	7,
Dec. 31	1,267	313	1,580	4,626	2,687	7,
1924						
Mar. 31	1,329	327	1,656	4,738	2,797	7,
June 30	1,357	341	1,698	4,963	2,810	7,
Oct. 10	1,530	365	1,895	5,129	2,849	7,
Dec. 31	1,559	411	1,969	5,266	2,855	8,
1925						
Apr. 6	1,615	410	2,025	5,465	2,887	8
June 30	1,612	440	2,053	5,669	2,955	8
Sept. 28	1,611	503	2,113	5,739	2,973	8
Dec. 31	1,669	513	2,183	5,860	3,065	8
1926						
Apr. 12	1,725	518	2,243	6,027	3,099	9
June 30	1,773	506	2,279	6,170	3,155	9
Dec. 31	1,892	514	2,406	6,336	3,179	9
1927						
Mar. 23	1,949	512	2,461	6,576	3,127	9
June 30	2,056	502	2,558	6,794	3,180	9
Oct. 10	2,135	527	2,662	6,912	3,218	10
Dec. 31	2,220	462	2,682	7,073	3,270	10
1928						
Feb. 28	2,266	502	2,768	7,147	3,336	10
June 30	2,381	481	2,862	7,462	3,334	10
Oct. 3	2,397	500	2,896	7,419	3,357	10
Dec. 31	2,470	479	2,950	7,383	3,497	10
1929						
Mar. 27	2,476	450	2,926	7,272	3,567	10
June 29	2,409	410	2,819	7,347	3,517	10
Oct. 4	2,565	470	3,034	7,234	3,726	10
Dec. 31	2,531	462	2,993	7,244	3,410	10
1930						
Mar. 27	2,664	512	3,176	7,360	3,363	10
June 30	2,792	508	3,299	7,490	3,398	10

| | Adjusted Time Deposits | | | | |
| 38 Rural States | | | United States | | |
Member Banks (7)	Nonmember Banks (8)	All Comm. Banks (9)	Member Banks (10)	Nonmember Banks (11)	All Comm. Banks (12)
2,338	2,337	4,661	7,128	4,808	11,936
2,435	2,426	4,845	7,587	4,988	12,575
2,588	2,550	5,122	8,085	5,215	13,300
2,669	2,641	5,292	8,316	5,439	13,755
2,690	2,554	5,227	8,404	5,452	13,856
2,712	2,559	5,252	8,586	5,559	14,145
2,768	2,514	5,260	8,814	5,638	14,452
2,819	2,560	5,350	9,110	5,711	14,821
2,867	2,576	5,415	9,498	5,790	15,288
2,912	2,586	5,468	9,707	5,852	15,559
2,977	2,633	5,581	10,028	5,930	15,958
3,032	2,650	5,654	10,286	6,045	16,331
3,049	2,689	5,711	10,372	6,164	16,536
3,055	2,748	5,776	10,557	6,326	16,883
3,131	2,698	5,801	10,855	6,315	17,170
3,160	2,643	5,777	11,077	6,304	17,381
3,140	2,549	5,660	11,340	6,242	17,582
3,216	2,717	5,903	11,711	6,355	18,066
3,283	2,798	6,051	12,103	6,480	18,583
3,332	2,752	6,053	12,348	6,497	18,845
3,393	2,868	6,233	12,658	6,600	19,258
3,429	2,884	6,284	12,813	6,722	19,535
3,513	2,913	6,401	13,331	6,728	20,059
3,505	2,909	6,386	13,158	6,766	19,924
3,509	2,869	6,352	13,212	6,845	20,057
3,491	2,809	6,275	13,100	6,826	19,926
3,480	2,756	6,210	13,053	6,683	19,736
3,425	2,750	6,148	12,973	6,945	19,918
3,361	2,770	6,105	12,862	6,642	19,504
3,394	2,775	6,142	13,112	6,650	19,762
3,423	2,761	6,158	13,342	6,667	20,009

(continued)

TABLE 33 (continued)

	Adjusted Time Deposits					
	New York State			9 Urbanized States & D.C.		
Member Bank Call Date	Member Banks (1)	Nonmember Banks (2)	All Comm. Banks (3)	Member Banks (4)	Nonmember Banks (5)	A Co Ba (
Sept. 24	2,758	461	3,219	7,631	3,382	11,
Dec. 31	2,493	441	2,934	7,624	3,152	10,
1931						
Mar. 25	2,498	428	2,927	7,690	3,063	10,
June 30	2,441	438	2,880	7,610	2,878	10,
Sept. 29	2,254	403	2,658	7,135	2,594	9,
Dec. 31	1,839	375	2,214	6,320	2,239	8,
1932						
June 30	1,716	352	2,068	5,888	1,989	7,
Sept. 30	1,790	329	2,119	5,785	1,927	7
Dec. 31	1,826	299	2,125	5,726	1,864	7,
1933						
June 30	1,589	276	1,865	4,781	1,260	6
Oct. 25	1,589	295	1,884	4,848	1,327	6
Dec. 30	1,534	307	1,841	4,888	1,289	6
1934						
Mar. 5	1,523	321	1,843	5,074	1,355	6
June 30	1,584	347	1,931	5,387	1,439	6
Oct. 17	1,564	345	1,909	5,446	1,364	6
Dec. 31	1,527	345	1,871	5,553	1,446	6
1935						
Mar. 4	1,520	317	1,838	5,673	1,451	7
June 29	1,482	334	1,816	5,873	1,553	7
Nov. 1	1,589	286	1,875	5,932	1,546	7
Dec. 31	1,495	362	1,857	5,975	1,592	7
1936						
Mar. 4	1,491	360	1,852	6,019	1,613	7
June 30	1,510	349	1,859	6,271	1,643	7
Dec. 31	1,613	354	1,967	6,323	1,698	8
1937						
Mar. 31	1,704	354	2,058	6,382	1,719	8
June 30	1,720	359	2,079	6,579	1,746	8
Dec. 31	1,708	413	2,121	6,647	1,807	8
1938						
Mar. 7	1,728	377	2,105	6,690	1,806	8
June 30	1,660	387	2,047	6,711	1,758	8
Sept. 28	1,652	386	2,037	6,645	1,745	8

Adjusted Time Deposits					
38 Rural States			United States		
Member Banks (7)	Nonmember Banks (8)	All Comm. Banks (9)	Member Banks (10)	Nonmember Banks (11)	All Comm. Banks (12)
3,440	2,680	6,092	13,466	6,523	19,989
3,283	2,666	5,906	13,012	6,259	19,271
3,291	2,565	5,797	13,084	6,057	19,141
3,257	2,525	5,710	12,967	5,842	18,809
3,121	2,361	5,388	12,218	5,359	17,577
2,803	2,173	4,867	10,764	4,786	15,550
2,583	1,825	4,249	9,950	4,166	14,116
2,505	1,682	4,014	9,832	3,938	13,770
2,455	1,817	4,106	9,753	3,979	13,732
2,037	1,296	3,119	8,103	2,832	10,935
2,099	1,194	3,090	8,240	2,816	11,056
2,134	1,168	3,094	8,257	2,764	11,021
2,269	1,127	3,191	8,562	2,802	11,364
2,401	1,159	3,415	9,096	2,945	12,041
2,451	1,179	3,518	9,210	2,888	12,098
2,478	1,229	3,605	9,315	3,019	12,334
2,539	1,186	3,639	9,493	2,954	12,447
2,597	1,278	3,811	9,747	3,165	12,912
2,631	1,284	3,881	9,980	3,116	13,096
2,602	1,314	3,885	10,041	3,268	13,309
2,635	1,305	3,922	10,127	3,278	13,405
2,712	1,327	4,024	10,478	3,319	13,797
2,801	1,378	4,167	10,726	3,430	14,156
2,844	1,391	4,223	10,918	3,463	14,381
2,822	1,421	4,231	11,110	3,526	14,636
2,945	1,437	4,371	11,288	3,657	14,945
2,950	1,445	4,384	11,357	3,628	14,985
2,967	1,467	4,423	11,327	3,612	14,939
2,967	1,457	4,414	11,253	3,588	14,841

(continued)

TABLE 33 (concluded)

Part III. Unadjusted Time Deposits, U.S. Government Time Deposits,
Adjusted Time Deposits, 1938–46

| | Unadjusted Time Deposits | | | | | | | | |
| | New York State | | | 9 Urbanized States & D.C. | | | 38 Rural States | | |
Member Bank Call Date	Member Banks (1)	Non-member Banks (2)	All Comm. Banks (3)	Member Banks (4)	Non-member Banks (5)	All Comm. Banks (6)	Member Banks (7)	Non-member Banks (8)	All Comm. Ba (9)
1938									
Dec. 31	1,619	400	2,019	6,712	1,749	8,461	2,989	1,445	4,
1939									
Mar. 29	1,641	344	1,985	6,755	1,796	8,552	3,024	1,442	4,
June 30	1,624	349	1,973	6,830	1,836	8,665	3,068	1,438	4,
Oct. 2	1,667	341	2,008	6,796	1,801	8,597	3,079	1,448	4,
Dec. 30	1,668	346	2,015	6,888	1,785	8,673	3,112	1,480	4,
1940									
Mar. 26	1,715	354	2,069	6,936	1,800	8,736	3,155	1,494	4,
June 29	1,701	341	2,042	7,013	1,814	8,827	3,191	1,550	4,
Dec. 31	1,761	336	2,098	7,148	1,794	8,942	3,250	1,534	4.
1941									
Apr. 4	1,793	320	2,113	7,187	1,840	9,027	3,288	1,581	4
June 30	1,764	302	2,066	7,264	1,784	9,047	3,307	1,591	4,
Sept. 24	1,816	292	2,108	7,267	1,761	9,028	3,313	1,600	4,
Dec. 31	1,789	271	2,061	7,236	1,747	8,983	3,307	1,634	4,
1942									
Apr. 4	1,732	264	1,996	6,992	1,692	8,684	3,226	1,592	4.
June 30	1,707	260	1,967	7,128	1,708	8,837	3,274	1,612	4
Dec. 31	1,757	256	2,013	7,503	1,736	9,239	3,486	1,676	5
1943									
June 30	1,860	264	2,124	8,183	1,833	10,016	3,747	1,782	5
Oct. 18	1,941	266	2,207	8,654	1,880	10,535	4,000	1,846	5
Dec. 31	2,038	267	2,305	9,036	1,950	10,986	4,190	1,886	6
1944									
Apr. 13	2,120	267	2,387	9,535	2,028	11,562	4,447	2,024	6
June 30	2,188	270	2,458	9,997	2,120	12,118	4,695	2,106	6
Dec. 30	2,461	284	2,745	11,405	2,338	13,743	5,389	2,340	7
1945									
Mar. 20	2,630	293	2,923	12,094	2,464	14,558	5,756	2,531	8
June 30	2,739	306	3,045	12,843	2,604	15,448	6,162	2,684	8
Dec. 31	3,055	301	3,357	14,238	2,830	17,068	6,914	2,982	9
1946									
June 29	3,346	316	3,663	15,333	2,975	18,308	7,433	3,201	10

		adjusted Time Deposits	U.S. Gov't. Time Deposits			Adjusted Time Deposits		
		United States	United States			United States		
	Non-member Banks (11)	All Comm. Banks (12)	Member Banks (13)	Non-member Banks (14)	All Comm. Banks (15)	Member Banks (16)	Non-member Banks (17)	All Comm. Banks (18)
09	3,595	14,904	2	0	2	11,307	3,595	14,902
13	3,582	14,995	12	0	12	11,401	3,582	14,983
18	3,623	15,141	14	0	14	11,504	3,623	15,127
39	3,590	15,129	17	0	17	11,522	3,590	15,112
35	3,611	15,276	18	0	18	11,647	3,611	15,258
03	3,648	15,451	25	0	25	11,778	3,648	15,426
01	3,705	15,606	33	0	33	11,868	3,705	15,573
6	3,664	15,820	34	0	34	12,122	3,664	15,786
35	3,741	16,006	34	0	34	12,231	3,741	15,972
3	3,676	16,009	37	0	37	12,296	3,676	15,972
4	3,653	16,047	32	0	32	12,362	3,653	16,015
1	3,652	15,983	34	0	34	12,297	3,652	15,949
9	3,548	15,497	33	0	33	11,916	3,548	15,464
7	3,580	15,687	34	0	35	12,073	3,580	15,653
6	3,668	16,414	48	0	48	12,698	3,668	16,366
8	3,880	17,668	65	0	65	13,723	3,880	17,603
5	3,992	18,587	104	1	105	14,491	3,991	18,482
3	4,103	19,366	115	2	117	15,148	4,101	19,249
0	4,319	20,419	109	2	111	15,991	4,317	20,308
0	4,496	21,376	100	2	102	16,780	4,494	21,274
5	4,962	24,217	101	2	103	19,154	4,960	24,114
9	5,288	25,767	97	2	99	20,382	5,286	25,668
4	5,595	27,339	98	2	100	21,646	5,593	27,239
7	6,114	30,321	96	3	98	24,111	6,111	30,222
1	6,493	32,604	97	5	102	26,014	6,488	32,502

Notes to Table 33

Source, by Column

Part I

1. National bank figures from U.S. Comptroller of the Currency, *Abstract of Reports of Condition of National Banks*. State member bank figures from Federal Reserve Board, *Member Bank Call Report*. The two series, separately corrected for seasonal variation, were added. *Dec. 1932–Nov. 1935:* "Deposits of other banks and trust companies (payable within 30 days but not subject to immediate withdrawal)" is not separately shown in the sources but included in demand deposits, by states (see notes to col. 10).

2. *June 1919–Mar. 1930:* Total deposits less duplications in New York state banks and trust companies, compiled at report dates from N.Y. Superintendent of Banks, *Annual Report on Banks of Discount and Deposit,* were corrected for seasonal and interpolated by Method L to member bank call dates between closest report dates. Estimates of Postal Savings System deposits in nonnational banks were deducted. (See also notes to Table 32, Parts I, II, and III, col. 2 for further detail.) From these figures time deposits adjusted, at June dates 1915, 1921, and 1926–30, shown in U.S. Comptroller of the Currency, *Annual Report,* were subtracted. On the assumption that time deposits had no seasonal movement, the difference gave demand deposits less duplications corrected for seasonal variation. Demand deposits were estimated for other dates by multiplying total deposits less duplications by a multiplier obtained from estimates of the ratio of demand to time deposits interpolated as described in Chapter 13, section 4. Estimates of demand deposits in New York private banks were added to those of state banks and trust companies. These were constructed as described in notes to Table 32, Part II, col. 2.

June 1930 – June 1946: Same as above except that the state reports break down total deposits into demand and time, so that it was no longer necessary to interpolate demand-time ratios. Estimates of Postal Savings System deposits in New York nonnational banks were subtracted from time deposits instead of total deposits.

Special problems encountered were treated as follows:

a. The Comptroller's figures for demand and time deposits at June dates 1930, 1932, and 1935–36 differed somewhat from the state report totals. We adopted the Comptroller's classification for all dates except 1930.

b. The *Annual Report* of the Superintendent of Banks was not issued in 1933–34. We obtained June data from the *Annual Report* of the Comptroller of the Currency, supplemented in 1934 by FDIC data for insured banks. At Dec. 1934 we interpolated figures for nonmember banks by Method R_1 on the basis of FDIC data for nonmember insured banks.

c. Beginning June 1934, deposits in industrial banks, shown in

Notes to Table 33 (continued)

state reports, were added to nonnational bank figures. When not given in the state reports, these deposits were estimated by Method L.

d.   From Dec. 1934 on, FDIC insured nonnational bank figures for duplicating deposits were used at end of year and at midyear in place of the state report and of the *Member Bank Call Report* figures used until that date. From Mar. 1937 on, at spring and fall call dates, the figures for items in process of collection with Federal Reserve Banks from *Member Bank Call Report* were used with an increment to raise them to the level of the midyear and end of year figures for insured nonnational banks.

For private banks the figures are a total of those reporting to the state at report dates and the remainder included in all New York private banks, as shown in *All-Bank Statistics*. For 1933–34, when the state reports were not published, the Comptroller's June data were used and interpolated by Method L to Dec. 1934. Total deposits adjusted were broken down by the demand-time ratios shown at June dates in the Comptroller's reports. Figures for the remaining private banks were obtained by subtracting total deposits adjusted of the reporting ones from those of all private banks at June dates, interpolating the differences by Method L to call dates, and applying the all-private-bank demand-time deposit ratios, likewise interpolated by Method L to call dates.

From Mar. 1935 on, state reports give demand and time deposits separately for reporting private banks, so that it is no longer necessary to depend on the Comptroller's June breakdown. Private banks did not report on Oct. 27, 1945, when state banks and trust companies were called upon to do so. Our estimate for the normally reporting private banks for that date is an interpolation by Method L.

3.   Col. 1 plus col. 2.

4,7.   *June 1919 – June 1926:*   National bank figures from U.S. Comptroller of the Currency, *Abstract of Reports of Condition of National Banks*. State member bank figures from Federal Reserve Board, *Member Bank Call Report*. The two series were added. No seasonal movement was observed in either component. *Dec. 1926 – June 1946:*   Member bank figures, obtained directly from the latter source, required no correction for seasonal variation. *Dec. 1932 – Nov. 1935:*   "Deposits of other banks and trust companies (payable within 30 days but not subject to immediate withdrawal)" is not separately shown in the source but included in demand deposits, by states (see notes to col. 10).

5.   Annual reports of the respective state banking departments are the sources of nonnational bank report date figures on demand deposits less duplications. At June dates, and beginning 1935, at certain Dec. dates also, this information was checked with data for these states in U.S. Comptroller of the Currency, *Annual Report,* and at June and Dec. dates beginning 1934 with information for insured non-

Notes to Table 33 (continued)

national banks in FDIC, *Assets and Liabilities of Operating Insured Banks*. Differences were reconciled. According to our dating rule, non-national bank figures for a report date not more than two weeks from a member bank call date may be treated as comparable to the member bank call date figures. There were reports for all states in the group within two weeks of the member bank June call date and reports from some states at each of the inter-June call dates.

From these figures demand deposits less duplications of state member banks in each state were deducted to get demand deposits less duplications in nonmember banks of each state. The reported figures at inter-June dates were interpolated as described in the text, Chap. 13, section 6. No seasonal movement was observed in the final series.

6. Col. 4 plus col. 5.

8. Figures at June dates for the thirty-eight rural states were obtained by subtracting from demand deposits less duplications in all commercial banks in the United States (see *All-Bank Statistics*, pp. 35—36) the sum of cols. 10, 2, and 5.

For nine of these states we obtained nonnational bank figures at report dates from the annual reports of the respective state banking departments. At June dates, and beginning 1935, at certain Dec. dates also, this information was checked with data for these states in U.S. Comptroller of the Currency, *Annual Report*, and at June and Dec. dates beginning 1934, with information for insured nonnational banks in FDIC, *Assets and Liabilities of Operating Insured Banks*. Differences were reconciled.

According to our dating rule, nonnational bank figures for a report date not more than two weeks from a member bank call date may be treated as comparable to the member bank call date figures. There were reports for all states in the group within two weeks of the member bank June call dates. From these figures demand deposits less duplications of state member banks in each state were deducted to get demand deposits less duplications in nonmember banks of each state in the sample. Estimates for states other than reporting sample states were interpolated for inter-June report dates by the method described in the text, Chap. 13, section 6.

9. Sum of cols. 7 and 8.

10. Sum of cols. 1, 4, and 7, minus interbank demand deposits not subject to immediate withdrawal and included in demand deposits, by states, Dec. 1932 — Nov. 1935. These interbank deposits were computed by subtracting from the sum of cols. 1, 4, and 7 the sum of demand deposits and U.S. government deposits, from *Banking and Monetary Statistics*, p. 75. No seasonal movement was observed.

11. Sum of cols. 2, 5, and 8.

12. Sum of cols. 10 and 11.

13. Same sources as col. 2; national and state member bank data, separately corrected for seasonal variations, were added.

Notes to Table 33 (concluded)

14. See source notes to Table 43, Parts I and II, col. 3.
15. Col. 13 plus col. 14.
16. Col. 10 minus col. 13.
17. Col. 11 minus col. 14.
18. Col. 16 plus col. 17.

Parts II and III

1. Same sources as for Part I, col. 1; no seasonal movement was observed. Postal savings in national banks were deducted, so data for this state are too large by the amount of postal savings in state member banks. For Oct. 1928 – Nov. 1935, interbank time deposits are not separately shown in the sources, but are included in time deposits (see notes to col. 10).

2. Same sources as for Part I, col. 2; method of estimation there described yielded time deposit estimates, which are too small by the amount of postal savings in state member banks, since Postal Savings System deposits in nonnational banks were deducted.

3. Col. 1 plus col. 2.

4,7. Same sources as for Part I, cols. 4, 7; no seasonal movement was observed. Postal savings deposits in national banks of these states were deducted, so data for these states are too large by the amount of postal savings in state member banks. For Oct. 1928 – Nov. 1935, interbank time deposits are not separately shown in the sources but are included in time deposits of each of the states (see notes to col. 10).

5. Same sources as Part I, col. 5; data are too small by the amount of postal savings in state member banks, since estimated Postal Savings System deposits in nonnational banks were deducted. The estimates were obtained by subtracting these deposits in national banks of each of the urbanized states from Postal Savings System deposits at midyear in all banks of those states. A call date series was obtained by interpolation by Method L between the annual estimates and deducted from time deposits of each state.

6. Col. 4 plus col. 5.

8. Same source as Part I, col. 8; data are too large by the amount of postal savings in state member banks in states other than the thirty-eight rural ones; method of interpolation described in text, Chap. 13, section 6.

9. Col. 7 plus col. 8, minus postal savings in all state member banks. The latter was computed by subtracting from postal savings in all member banks (*Banking and Monetary Statistics,* p. 73) postal savings in national banks.

10. Sum of cols. 1, 4, and 7, minus postal savings deposits in state member banks, June 1921 – Dec. 1946, and interbank time deposits, Oct. 1928 – Nov. 1935. The latter was computed by subtracting from the sum of cols. 1, 4, and 7 the sum of time deposits (*Banking and Monetary Statistics,* p. 75) and postal savings in national banks.

Before June 1921 time deposits are too large by the amount of postal savings in state member banks.

11. Sum of cols. 2, 5, and 8. Before June 1921 time deposits are too small by the amount of postal savings in state member banks.

12. Col. 10 plus col. 11.

13. Before Dec. 1941, government demand and time deposits (*ibid.*, p. 75), minus U.S. government time deposits *(Member Bank Call Report)*; Apr. 1942, estimated from U.S. government time deposits in national banks (U.S. Comptroller of the Currency, *Abstract of Reports of Condition of National Banks*); other call dates, from *Member Bank Call Report*.

14. Insured nonmember bank figures at June and Dec. call dates, from FDIC, *Assets and Liabilities of Operating Insured Banks;* these were interpolated to spring and fall call dates on the basis of member bank figures for those dates. Government time deposits at noninsured nonmember banks were assumed negligible.

15. Col. 13 plus col. 14.

16. Col. 10 minus col. 13.

17. Col. 11 minus col. 14.

18. Col. 16 plus col. 17.

We compiled test member bank series for four categories of reporting sample states and other states designed to correspond reasonably closely to these categories and, for each, computed test correlations between u and v, and values of b, with the following results:

RELATIONSHIP BETWEEN REPORTING SAMPLE AND OTHER RURAL STATES—
MEMBER BANKS, CALL DATES, JUNE 1926–JUNE 1934
$(n = 21)$

Category	Number of Rural States Reporting Sample	Other	Demand Deposits Less Duplications r	b	Time Deposits r	b
1	9	29	+.839	+.779	+.798	+.864
2	6	32	+.601	+.366	+.476	+.474
3	5	33	+.499	+.295	+.529	+.483
4	4	34	+.667	+.406	+.425	+.339
2,3,4 (average)				+.356		+.432

The correlation and the estimated value of b are clearly higher for the full sample than for the other categories, reflecting the greater amount of information provided by the full sample. For the other categories the differences in both r and b seemed erratic and unsystematic. Accordingly, we combined these categories and computed an average value of b for them. In actual interpolation we used the computed b's in the above table for category 1 for the call dates in that category and the computed average b's for the other call dates.

7. Reconciliation of Nonnational and Nonmember Bank Estimates, 1919–23

For 1919–23 we have nonnational as well as nonmember bank estimates. At national bank call dates that were also state member bank call dates, these two sets of estimates must be reconciled to produce the same all bank figures for (a) New York; (b) the nine urbanized states and the District of Columbia; and (c) the remaining thirty-eight states. In order to obtain this result at these call dates we did not estimate nonnational bank figures for each stratum separately; instead, we added state member bank figures for each stratum to the nonmember bank estimates for that stratum to get nonnational bank estimates.

Independent seasonal adjustment of the separate series for member and nonmember banks and national and nonnational banks would also produce inconsistencies in the two sets of aggregate figures. A problem of reconciliation arose only for demand deposits, since for none of the strata did time deposits require seasonal adjustment. In order to assure agreement between seasonally adjusted demand deposit totals for each stratum of national plus nonnational and member plus nonmember banks, we handled the three strata as follows.

New York. The problem did not arise since the nonmember bank estimates are the excess of seasonally adjusted nonnational bank estimates over seasonally adjusted state member bank estimates, and member bank figures are the sum of seasonally adjusted national bank figures plus seasonally adjusted state member bank figures.

Nine Urbanized States and the District of Columbia. Member and nonmember bank results required no seasonal adjustment. We therefore dropped the seasonal adjustment that had been made in the national and nonnational figures for 1919–23.

Thirty-Eight Rural States. Separate adjustment had been made of certain of the components of the two aggregates. We accepted the aggregate of seasonally adjusted member plus unadjusted nonmember data, subtracted the seasonally adjusted national bank figures, and used the residual as our nonnational bank estimates.

8. Member Bank Estimates, Member Bank Call Dates, 1919–46

Demand deposits less duplications and time deposits were compiled for member banks in New York, the nine other urbanized states and the District of Columbia, and in all states to match the call date estimates for nonmember banks. Estimates for member banks in the thirty-eight relatively rural states were computed as a residual.[13] These estimates are given in Table 33 together with totals for all commercial banks.

The published figures required adjustment at certain dates.

1. From December 1932 through November 1935, the *Member Bank Call Report* shows figures by states for demand deposits other than interbank which include amounts representing the item, "Deposits of other banks and trust companies (payable within 30 days but not subject to immediate withdrawal)." In the member bank call date statistics by reserve classes of banks, shown in *Banking and Monetary Statistics,* this item was deducted from demand deposits and included in interbank deposits. Since the member bank figures by groups of states in Table 33, Part I, are derived from *Member Bank Call Report,* they include the extraneous interbank deposit element; the figures for all member banks in Table 33, however, were revised in accordance with the figures in *Banking and Monetary Statistics.* From $2 million to $25 million, representing these interbank deposits, was deducted from all member bank demand deposits, December 1932–November 1935.

2. From October 1928 through November 1935, another interbank deposit item is included in time deposits of member banks by groups of states in Table 33, Part II, but has been excluded by us from the figures for all member banks. Member banks were not required to report inter-

---

[13] State member bank figures from the Federal Reserve Board's *Member Bank Call Report* were added to national bank figures, June 1919–June 1926, to get member bank figures. Thereafter, member bank figures were compiled from this source. Since Dec. 1936, call date figures of member bank demand deposits adjusted, by states, have been published in the call date reports.

bank time deposits separately before October 1928, and it is possible that the figures for time deposits for earlier call dates, for all member banks, and also by groups of states, include the interbank time deposit item. From October 1928 through November 1935 the magnitude of the item ranged from $76 million to $345 million.

3. Our decision to exclude postal savings from time deposits by states involved us in a series of adjustments, because member and state member bank data for this item are lacking for many years. Before June 1921 there are no data at all. Beginning June 1921 call date data on postal savings in all member and state member banks—but not by states—are available.[14] While postal savings data in member and state member banks by states are reported beginning December 1935, for the sake of uniformity our member bank time deposit figures by states throughout the period 1919–46 include the state member postal saving component. To get aggregate figures free of postal savings, we deducted data on postal savings in all state member banks from our preliminary figures of time deposits in all banks of thirty-eight rural states.[15]

[14] Call date data on postal savings in all state member banks are obtainable beginning June 1921 by subtracting postal savings in all national banks from postal savings in all member banks, shown in *Banking and Monetary Statistics*, p. 73.

From Dec. 1938 through Sept. 1941 the *Abstract of Reports of Condition of National Banks* combines postal savings with United States government time deposits; therefore postal savings in national banks must be estimated. For call dates through June 1942 the *Member Bank Call Report* also combines these items. A breakdown for all members as well as national and state members is, however, available for Dec. 1941 and June 1942 in FDIC, *Assets and Liabilities of Operating Insured Banks,* Dec. 1942.

[15] For our strata I (New York) and II (nine other urbanized states and the District of Columbia) we made direct estimates of deposits at national and nonnational banks, subtracting postal savings redeposited from both components. Hence, both these components and the totals for these two strata are free of postal savings redeposited in banks. However, we estimated deposits at nonmember banks in these two strata by subtracting deposits at state member banks, which include postal savings redeposited in those banks from deposits at nonnational banks. Hence, our estimates for nonmember banks in these two strata are too low by the amount of postal savings redeposited in state member banks.

For stratum III (the rural states) we estimated deposits at nonmember banks at June dates—to which our interpolations are keyed—as a residual, by subtracting our estimates of deposits at nonmember banks in strata I and II from our estimate of deposits at nonmember banks in all states. This last estimate excludes postal savings redeposited, since it is the difference between Federal Reserve estimates of time deposits at all commercial banks and at member banks, both adjusted to exclude postal savings. Since the total is correct (i.e., excludes postal savings) while amounts subtracted for strata I and II are too small, the nonmember bank residual for stratum III is too large by the amount of postal savings redeposited in state member banks in the other two strata.

For stratum III the state member bank estimates, like those for the other strata, include postal savings redeposited in state member banks of the rural states, and therefore the sum of deposits at national banks (which exclude postal savings), state member banks (which include postal savings), and nonmember banks (which are too large by postal savings in state member banks of the other two strata) is too large by the amount

Demand deposits of New York member banks through 1932 (a sum of deseasonalized national plus state member bank figures) and of the member banks in the thirty-eight rural states through 1938 were seasonally corrected.

9. All Commercial Bank Estimates of Demand and Time Deposits Adjusted, National and Member Bank Call Dates, 1907–46

Our estimates for the separate strata combine public and U.S. government deposits, because nonnational bank demand deposits, which include government deposits from 1917 on, and time deposits, which include government deposits from 1938 on, can be compiled by states only as a total of public and U.S. government deposits. To get demand and time deposits adjusted, it is necessary to deduct the U.S. government deposit component of our aggregate series for the United States as a whole.

For national and member banks this step is routine. These banks have always reported their holdings of U.S. government deposits (Table 32, Part III, column 13; Table 33, Part I, column 13). For nonnational and nonmember banks, which have been authorized depositaries of U.S. government deposits since April 1917, this item is not given sepa-

of postal savings redeposited in state member banks in all three strata. In consequence, the all-bank summation for the thirty-eight states shown in Table 33, Part II, col. 9, beginning June 1921, is the sum of cols. 7 and 8 of that table minus postal savings in all state member banks.

For June 1919–June 1921 time deposits in nonmember banks of the thirty-eight rural states are too small by the amount of postal savings in this class of banks, but time deposits of member banks in this category are too large by this amount. The all-bank figures therefore need no correction. This offsetting occurs because the all-bank time figures exclude postal savings, while the member bank figures include postal savings in state member banks. The residual nonmember figures are therefore too small by this amount. Time deposits in the categories of New York and the nine urbanized states are also too small by the amount of postal savings in state member banks in these states. The residual time deposit figures for nonmember banks in the thirty-eight rural states are therefore too small by the amount of postal savings in state member banks of these states.

It may be noted that Federal Reserve adjustments from 1921 on to eliminate postal savings redeposited in banks are subject to error because of differences between bank records and Postal Savings System records. The Federal Reserve subtrahend is the amount of postal savings redeposited in banks, according to Postal Savings System books. In 1921 and 1922 postal savings redeposited in member banks, according to bank records, are larger than postal savings redeposited in all banks, according to Postal Savings System books.

rately in most state bank reports, nor, until recently, in sources of all nonnational bank data. The procedure we used to construct the estimates given in Table 32, Part III, column 14, and Table 33, Part I, column 14, is described in Chapter 17.

Beginning November 1938, U.S. government deposits include not only demand accounts, but also Treasurer's time deposits, open account. This item is frequently combined in the sources of the data with postal savings and also with U.S. government demand deposits. Since U.S. government time deposits are almost exclusively in member banks, the problems involved in deriving a call date series for nonmember banks are less complex than for U.S. government demand deposits. The procedure we used to construct the estimates given in Table 33, Part III, column 14, is described in Chapter 17.

To get demand deposits adjusted, we subtracted U.S. government demand deposits at national banks, nonnational banks, member banks, nonmember banks, and all banks from the corresponding figures of demand deposits less duplications (Table 32, Part III, columns 16, 17, and 18, and Table 33, Part I, the same columns). Beginning December 1938, we made a similar deduction of U.S. government time deposits from the time deposit figures inclusive of these accounts (Table 33, Part III, columns 16, 17, and 18).

10. Reliability of the Call Date Estimates

Table 34 lists for each of the series described the percentage of the commercial bank series constituted by each of the components, and the percentages of the final figures based on reported data and estimated by interpolation. From three-fifths to more than four-fifths of the commercial bank figures at various dates were directly known. Of the nonnational and nonmember components we have most confidence in the category of nine urbanized states and the District of Columbia, which involved relatively little estimation. A considerable amount of estimation was required in constructing the figures for the thirty-eight rural states and for New York State. The former are less likely to differ from the true movement of the series than are the New York figures, in view of the smoother character of the series at known dates.

TABLE 34

Reported and Interpolated Deposits in Various Classes of Banks at Call Dates as Percentages of Total Deposits Adjusted, Demand Deposits Less Duplications, and Time Deposits Adjusted, 1907–46

Class of Banks and Period Covered	Per Cent of Total			
		Interpolated		Total
	Reported (1)	By Method L (2)	By Method R (3)	Cols. 1+2+3 (4)
Total Deposits Adjusted				
1907–14				
National	41.0	—	—	41.0
Nonnational				
New York	3.5	10.5	—	14.0
9 Urban	16.0	—	9.0	25.0
38 Rural	1.4	18.6	—	20.0
Total	20.9	29.1	9.0	59.0
	61.9	29.1	9.0	100.0
Demand Deposits Less Duplications[a]				
1914–23				
National	48.0	—	—	48.0
Nonnational				
New York	5.4	10.6	—	16.0
9 Urban	14.0	—	4.0	18.0
38 Rural	1.1	16.9	—	18.0
Total	20.5	27.5	4.0	52.0
	68.5	27.5	4.0	100.0

Time Deposits Adjusted[b]

1919–46					
Member	82.0		—	—	82.0
Nonmember					
New York	0.7	1.3			2.0
9 Urban	4.3	—		0.7	5.0
38 Rural	1.3	—		9.7	11.0
Total	6.3		1.3	10.4	18.0
	88.3		1.3	10.4	100.0
1914–23					
National	31.0		—	—	31.0
Nonnational					
New York	2.0	4.0			6.0
9 Urban	23.7	—		13.3	37.0
38 Rural	1.3	24.7		—	26.0
Total	27.0		28.7	13.3	69.0
	58.0		28.7	13.3	100.0
1919–46					
Member	72.0		—	—	72.0
Nonmember					
New York	1.6	0.4			2.0
9 Urban	10.4	—		2.6	13.0
38 Rural	1.0	—		12.0	13.0
Total	13.0		0.4	14.6	28.0
	85.0		0.4	14.6	100.0

Derivation of Estimates

Notes to Table 34

[a]United States government demand deposits, which are subtracted to get demand deposits adjusted, are a sum of reported figures for national banks and estimates for nonnational banks (1917–23) and of reported figures for member banks and estimates for nonmember banks (1919–46). The estimates of government demand deposits at nonnational banks are 2 per cent of demand deposits less duplications at these banks, and the corresponding estimates for nonmember banks are 5 per cent of their demand deposits less duplications.

[b]United States government time deposits, which are subtracted to get time deposits adjusted, are estimated figures for member and nonmember banks, 1938–46. The estimates of government time deposits are 0.2 per cent of time deposits adjusted at member banks and 0.1 per cent of those deposits at nonmember banks.

14

DEPOSITS AT COMMERCIAL BANKS: MONTHLY ESTIMATES

OUR MONTHLY DEPOSIT SERIES, in seasonally adjusted form only, are sums of estimates for various classes of banks for which monthly interpolators were available.

Total deposits adjusted, 1907–1914, and demand deposits adjusted and time deposits adjusted, 1914–1919, are sums of monthly estimates for: (a) New York State national banks; (b) New York State non-national banks plus all commercial banks in the nine other urbanized states and the District of Columbia; and (c) all commercial banks in the thirty-eight rural states. The estimates for (a) and (b) were interpolated between call dates by Method R_2, using as the related series monthly series derived from weekly reports of various clearinghouse banks, seasonally adjusted. The estimates for (c) were interpolated between call dates by Method L.

Demand deposits adjusted and time deposits adjusted, 1919–1945, are each sums of figures for member and nonmember banks. We processed the basic monthly member bank series that the Federal Reserve System published for various monthly dates, beginning April 1923, to conform to Wednesday dates closest to the end of the month and to our definitions of demand and time deposits adjusted. From June 1919 through March 1923, published monthly data are available only for weekly reporting member banks. We constructed estimates for non-weekly reporting member banks from regressions for 1923–28 between deposits at nonweekly reporting banks and deposits at weekly reporting member banks (for demand deposits, weekly reporting member banks outside New York City).

The monthly nonmember bank figures, 1919–45, are interpolations between the call date figures presented in Table 33, by Method L from 1919 to April 1923 and by Method R_2 from then on, using monthly changes in deposits at member banks in so-called smaller places as the related series.

From January 1946, seasonally corrected Federal Reserve monthly data for demand and time deposits adjusted carry forward our monthly series for member and nonmember banks combined.

1. Deposit Estimates, Monthly, 1907–19

To interpolate the call date figures by months, 1907–19, the classes of banks shown in Table 32 were revised by combining New York State nonnational banks with the commercial banks of the nine other urbanized states and the District of Columbia. The following data were then tested for use as interpolators of these figures and of New York national bank figures:

a. Net deposits. Net deposits are deposit liabilities subject to reserve requirements. The legal definition on the basis of which national banks computed their reserve requirements varied from time to time, but in general net deposits were defined as the excess of amounts due to banks over amounts due from banks and float, plus gross deposits including U.S. government deposits [1] but excluding amounts due to banks. We have information on net deposits of New York City banks that used the clearinghouse (some of which were and some of which were not members of the clearinghouse) and an approximation to net deposits of New York City banks that did not use the clearinghouse.[2]

---

[1] The Secretary of the Treasury abolished reserves against government deposits on Sept. 29, 1902. This exemption was extended and given formal status by the Act of May 30, 1908. The New York Clearing House Association, however, continued to include government deposits with total deposits in calculating the percentage of reserves held by its member banks. Cf. A. P. Andrew, "The Treasury and the Banks under Secretary Shaw," *Quarterly Journal of Economics,* Aug. 1907, pp. 536–539. With the creation of the Federal Reserve System, reserve requirements against U.S. government deposits were restored until Apr. 24, 1917.

[2] *Commercial and Financial Chronicle,* May 1907–Oct. 1914, presents net deposit data for banks using the New York City clearinghouse (both members and nonmembers) except for Oct. 1907–Jan. 1908 when no data are reported for nonmembers. (For the distinction between nonmembers using the clearinghouse and banks not in the clearing-

b. Net demand and net time deposits. Net demand and time deposits are those deposit liabilities subject to reserve requirements. These data are available for banks using the New York City clearinghouse.[3] Net demand deposits through April 23, 1917, were defined as the excess of demand amounts due to banks over demand amounts due from banks and cash items in process of collection, plus gross demand deposits including U.S. government deposits but excluding amounts due to banks. Beginning April 24, 1917, U.S. government deposits were exempted from reserve requirements. Net time deposits included time deposits of individuals, partnerships, corporations, states and municipalities, and postal savings redeposited in national banks.

c. Gross deposits. This category comprises all deposit liabilities of commercial banks, whether due to other banks, the U.S. government, or the public. We have information on gross deposits at clearinghouse banks (mostly national) in six cities (reserve city centers in the national banking system), and at New York City state banks and trust companies (nonnational banks) not in the clearinghouse. (The latter are the same banks for which an approximation to net deposits is available, described under item *a* above.) In addition, gross deposit data are known for New York state banks and New York trust companies and for each group for Greater New York City and for outside Greater New York City as well as for New York State as a whole.[4]

house, see J. G. Cannon, *Clearing Houses,* pp. 150–156.) Through June 1911, U.S. government deposits are separately shown though included in the net deposit figures. Net deposits of trust company members are first shown beginning July 1911; net deposits of other commercial bank members are shown separately.

This source, as well as New York State Superintendent of Banks, *Annual Report on Banks of Deposit and Discount,* 1908–1917, presents the data beginning Feb. 1908 for New York City state banks and trust companies not in the clearinghouse. Since these banks did not compute reserve requirements in the manner of national banks, net deposits could only be approximated. The approximation is presented as total deposits minus amounts due from New York City banks and trust companies (through June 1914) and amounts due from reserve city depositaries (beginning July 1914) and also less clearinghouse exchanges (beginning Oct. 1914) and U.S. government deposits (beginning July 18, 1917).

[3] *Commercial and Financial Chronicle,* beginning Dec. 1914. We copied the data through 1923 only, although they are available beyond this year. The data are given separately for members and nonmembers of the clearinghouse and also within each of these classes for members and nonmembers of the Federal Reserve System. Beginning with the end of May 1917, U.S. government deposits are shown separately from other deposits but for members and nonmembers of the clearinghouse combined.

[4] The sources and coverage of the data (after 1907) are as follows: (a) A. P. Andrew, *Statistics for the United States, 1867–1909,* pp. 149–50 [Chicago, May 1907–Dec. 1908]. (b) E. W. Kemmerer, *Seasonal Variations in the Relative Demand for Money and Capi-*

d. Other deposit series. For Boston and Philadelphia various other deposit series are available when gross deposits are no longer reported for their clearinghouse banks: [5]

	Clearinghouse Banks	
Series	*Boston*	*Philadelphia*
	Data Available Beginning	
Demand deposits less duplications	December 1914	August 1917
Demand deposits adjusted	September 1919	August 1917
Time deposits	December 1914	August 1917
Due to banks	December 1914	August 1917
U.S. government deposits	September 1919	August 1917

e. Net demand deposits and net time deposits of weekly reporting member banks. These data [6] begin in December 1917.

All these data come in the form of weekly averages, except that beginning February 1908, the net deposit figures for New York City clearinghouse member banks are also available as actual figures, dated Saturday of each week, and the weekly reporting member bank series is on a Friday basis through April 1921.

We used the averages, dating them as of Wednesday, the midpoint of the week, and constructed series in call date form, taking the figure for the weekly Wednesday date closest to a call date as the call date figure. If the underlying data changed in composition during the period for which a series was developed, discontinuities between consecutive call dates were avoided. These call date series were then seasonally corrected and tested as potential interpolators of the data in Table 32.

tal in the United States, pp. 269, 274, 275 [St. Louis, New Orleans, and San Francisco, May 1907–Dec. 1908]. (c) Boston Clearing House Association, *Statement of the Associated Banks of Boston, as returned to the Clearing House,* 1907–14 [Boston, May 1907–July 1914]. (Deposits adjusted also available.) (d) *The American Banker,* 1907–17 [Philadelphia, May 1907–June 1917]. (Due to banks also available. Beginning May 1912, exchanges for the clearinghouse are included in the figures for gross deposits but are also separately shown. Beginning August 1916, clearinghouse members are classified as national banks or trust companies.) (e) New York State Superintendent of Banks, *Annual Report on Banks of Deposit and Discount,* 1908–17 [New York, Dec. 1908–Dec. 1917]. (The data are continued in *Commercial and Financial Chronicle,* 1918–20. The series for outside Greater New York is discontinued after March 1918; the series for in Greater New York is discontinued after July 1920. The latter source, 1907–17, also presents the gross deposit data for Philadelphia and Boston and U.S. government deposits at clearinghouse banks of the latter city.)

[5] The source is the *Commercial and Financial Chronicle.* For Philadelphia clearinghouse banks a breakdown is given of national bank and trust company data.

[6] From *Federal Reserve Bulletin.*

Beginning December 1917, time deposit data for weekly reporting member banks were also tested.

To test these interpolators we computed values of u and v for the middle dates in successive overlapping triplets of call dates, and computed correlation coefficients and regression coefficients from these values. The interpolators that we selected on the basis of these tests, the test coefficients of correlation, and the regression coefficients that we used for interpolation were as follows:

Interpolator	Series to be Interpolated	Period Tested and Interpolated	r	b
1. New York City clearinghouse member banks, net deposits.	New York State national banks, total deposits adjusted.	May 1907– June 1914	+.666	.435
2. New York City banks using the clearinghouse, net demand deposits.	As above, demand deposits adjusted.	Dec. 1914– June 1923	+.630	1.242
3. As above, net time deposits.	As above, time deposits adjusted.	Dec. 1914– June 1923	+.530	.325
4. New York City nonnational (state) banks plus clearinghouse banks of a selected group of cities, gross deposits.	New York State nonnational banks plus all commercial banks in the nine urbanized states and the District of Columbia, total deposits adjusted.	May 1907– June 1914	+.562	.350
5. Boston and Philadelphia clearinghouse banks, demand deposits less duplications.	As above, demand deposits adjusted, 1914–1917; demand deposits less duplications, 1917–1923.	Dec. 1914– June 1923	+.689	.195
6. Weekly reporting member banks, time deposits.	As above, time deposits adjusted.	Dec. 1917– June 1923	+.640	.312

TABLE 35

Deposits Adjusted at All Commercial Banks, May 1907 – June 1919
(seasonally adjusted, in millions of dollars)

Part I. Total Deposits Adjusted, May 1907 – May 1914

Wednesday Nearest End of Month	National Banks of New York State (1)	Nonnational Banks of N.Y. State, and All Commercial Banks of 9 Urbanized States and D.C. (2)	All Commercial Banks	
			38 Rural States (3)	United States (4)
1907				
May	656	5,666	3,621	9,942
June	654	5,638	3,626	9,918
July	668	5,643	3,630	9,941
Aug.	663	5,610	3,625	9,898
Sept.	662	5,500	3,581	9,743
Oct.	662	5,333	3,545	9,540
Nov.	673	5,190	3,510	9,373
Dec.	674	5,034	3,475	9,183
1908				
Jan.	690	4,880	3,448	9,018
Feb.	708	4,850	3,432	8,990
Mar.	731	4,972	3,430	9,133
Apr.	749	5,050	3,428	9,227
May	757	5,199	3,428	9,384
June	756	5,317	3,430	9,503

July	769	5,419	3,449	9,637
Aug.	796	5,510	3,493	9,799
Sept.	815	5,564	3,530	9,908
Oct.	837	5,634	3,571	10,042
Nov.	861	5,740	3,621	10,221
Dec.	833	5,775	3,662	10,271
1909				
Jan.	821	5,872	3,712	10,405
Feb.	813	5,908	3,738	10,459
Mar.	814	5,971	3,764	10,549
Apr.	829	6,036	3,789	10,654
May	829	6,133	3,811	10,773
June	834	6,222	3,832	10,889
July	843	6,263	3,864	10,970
Aug.	836	6,308	3,904	11,049
Sept.	840	6,317	3,963	11,120
Oct.	825	6,318	4,036	11,179
Nov.	814	6,318	4,072	11,204
Dec.	820	6,384	4,088	11,292
1910				
Jan.	815	6,348	4,109	11,272
Feb.	828	6,391	4,136	11,355
Mar.	841	6,454	4,163	11,458
Apr.	812	6,432	4,175	11,419
May	793	6,403	4,189	11,385
June	785	6,418	4,201	11,404
July	805	6,385	4,193	11,383
Aug.	833	6,397	4,187	11,417

(continued)

TABLE 35 (continued)

Wednesday Nearest End of Month	National Banks of New York State (1)	Nonnational Banks of N.Y. State, and All Commercial Banks of 9 Urbanized States and D.C. (2)	All Commercial Banks	
			38 Rural States (3)	United States (4)
1910				
Sept.	840	6,455	4,234	11,530
Oct.	820	6,528	4,294	11,642
Nov.	826	6,573	4,307	11,706
Dec.	825	6,626	4,306	11,756
1911				
Jan.	840	6,659	4,317	11,816
Feb.	858	6,691	4,330	11,879
Mar.	873	6,717	4,341	11,931
Apr.	890	6,831	4,354	12,074
May	897	6,890	4,364	12,151
June	918	6,922	4,379	12,219
July	921	6,964	4,400	12,285
Aug.	924	6,929	4,417	12,270
Sept.	916	6,997	4,459	12,373
Oct.	901	7,113	4,513	12,527
Nov.	885	7,216	4,557	12,659
Dec.	917	7,255	4,588	12,760
1912				
Jan.	940	7,312	4,610	12,862
Feb.	957	7,323	4,633	12,913

Mar.	957	7,373	4,667	12,997
Apr.	955	7,378	4,692	13,025
May	968	7,388	4,712	13,068
June	985	7,442	4,744	13,170
July	974	7,463	4,774	13,212
Aug.	977	7,487	4,804	13,268
Sept.	961	7,479	4,865	13,305
Oct.	960	7,517	4,920	13,397
Nov.	959	7,564	4,973	13,496
Dec.	969	7,551	4,993	13,513
1913				
Jan.	971	7,574	5,009	13,553
Feb.	965	7,617	5,038	13,621
Mar.	950	7,561	5,077	13,588
Apr.	945	7,586	5,080	13,611
May	928	7,546	5,082	13,555
June	946	7,500	5,072	13,519
July	958	7,493	5,062	13,513
Aug.	977	7,566	5,098	13,641
Sept.	986	7,661	5,141	13,787
Oct.	985	7,706	5,175	13,866
Nov.	974	7,740	5,187	13,901
Dec.	979	7,773	5,197	13,949
1914				
Jan.	989	7,815	5,205	14,009
Feb.	997	7,824	5,213	14,034
Mar.	1,021	7,887	5,232	14,140
Apr.	1,041	7,938	5,249	14,228
May	1,056	8,019	5,271	14,347

(continued)

TABLE 35 (continued)

Part II. Adjusted Demand and Time Deposits, June 1914 – May 1917

Wednesday Nearest End of Month	Adjusted Demand Deposits				Adjusted Time Deposits			
	National Banks of New York State	Nonnational Banks of N.Y. State, and All Commercial Banks of 9 Urbanized States and D.C.	All Commercial Banks		National Banks of New York State	Nonnational Banks of N.Y. State, and All Commercial Banks of 9 Urbanized States and D.C.	All Commercial Banks	
			38 Rural States	United States			38 Rural States	United States
	(1)	(2)	(3)	(4)	(5)	(6)	(7)	(8)
1914								
June	998	5,308	3,367	9,674	62	2,661	1,919	4,642
July	1,015	5,314	3,341	9,670	65	2,648	1,933	4,646
Aug.	1,058	5,292	3,307	9,657	70	2,618	1,949	4,638
Sept.	1,088	5,358	3,274	9,719	73	2,702	1,954	4,728
Oct.	1,069	5,338	3,237	9,644	70	2,784	1,953	4,808
Nov.	1,059	5,417	3,223	9,699	69	2,747	1,957	4,774
Dec.	1,033	5,469	3,214	9,717	67	2,700	1,961	4,728
1915								
Jan.	1,050	5,482	3,252	9,785	73	2,730	1,975	4,778
Feb.	1,061	5,603	3,283	9,947	81	2,739	1,987	4,807
Mar.	1,072	5,627	3,276	9,975	86	2,771	2,005	4,862
Apr.	1,074	5,670	3,267	10,011	92	2,776	2,024	4,892
May	1,073	5,742	3,282	10,097	99	2,857	2,041	4,997
June	1,098	5,826	3,300	10,225	103	2,866	2,057	5,025
July	1,108	5,883	3,327	10,318	104	2,851	2,083	5,038

Aug.	1,109	5,947	3,360	10,416	107	2,845	2,114	5,066
Sept.	1,195	6,084	3,408	10,688	104	2,947	2,136	5,187
Oct.	1,381	6,318	3,469	11,168	112	3,067	2,164	5,343
Nov.	1,401	6,378	3,530	11,309	115	3,121	2,190	5,427
Dec.	1,349	6,478	3,595	11,422	127	3,240	2,217	5,584
1916								
Jan.	1,399	6,589	3,660	11,648	124	3,231	2,262	5,617
Feb.	1,468	6,696	3,711	11,875	124	3,279	2,299	5,702
Mar.	1,397	6,734	3,790	11,921	131	3,269	2,334	5,735
Apr.	1,353	6,770	3,896	12,019	141	3,347	2,378	5,866
May	1,399	6,779	3,939	12,117	149	3,447	2,413	6,009
June	1,387	6,801	3,982	12,170	159	3,395	2,449	6,003
July	1,355	6,870	4,082	12,307	179	3,466	2,495	6,138
Aug.	1,429	6,975	4,164	12,569	163	3,445	2,529	6,137
Sept.	1,453	7,101	4,233	12,786	164	3,562	2,565	6,291
Oct.	1,474	7,220	4,306	13,001	166	3,651	2,610	6,427
Nov.	1,472	7,346	4,378	13,196	171	3,780	2,648	6,599
Dec.	1,381	7,497	4,483	13,362	175	4,018	2,702	6,895
1917								
Jan.	1,502	7,591	4,540	13,633	178	4,040	2,752	6,970
Feb.	1,523	7,679	4,596	13,798	184	3,933	2,803	6,920
Mar.	1,516	7,759	4,641	13,917	191	3,967	2,847	7,005
Apr.	1,484	7,795	4,709	13,988	204	3,991	2,899	7,094
May	1,571	7,773	4,802	14,146	205	4,058	2,929	7,192

(continued)

491

Table 35 (concluded)

Part III. Demand Deposits Less Duplications, U.S. Government Deposits, Adjusted Demand Deposits, and Adjusted Time Deposits, June 1917 – June 1919

Wednesday or Friday Nearest End of Month	Demand Deposits less Duplications			U.S. Govt. Deposits	Adjusted Demand Deposits	Adjusted Time Deposits			
	National Banks of New York State	Nonnational Banks of N.Y. State, and All Commercial Banks of 9 Urbanized States and D.C.	38 Rural States	All Commercial Banks in United States	All Commercial Banks in United States	National Banks of New York State	Nonnational Banks of N.Y. State, and All Commercial Banks of 9 Urbanized States and D.C.	All Commercial Banks	
								38 Rural States	United States
	(1)	(2)	(3)	(4)	(5)	(6)	(7)	(8)	(9)
1917									
June	1,655	7,910	4,916	284	14,197	203	3,905	2,959	7,067
July	1,796	7,965	4,995	295	14,461	214	4,036	2,996	7,246
Aug.	1,809	8,053	5,059	355	14,566	215	4,003	3,025	7,242
Sept.	1,939	8,141	5,207	918	14,369	217	3,983	3,045	7,245
Oct.	2,267	8,337	5,359	1,821	14,142	221	4,130	3,053	7,404
Nov.	2,436	8,572	5,473	2,257	14,224	221	4,148	3,065	7,434
Dec.	1,927	8,364	5,497	632	15,156	221	4,111	3,090	7,422
1918									
Jan.	1,950	8,364	5,542	856	15,000	228	4,107	3,118	7,453
Feb.	2,012	8,402	5,587	1,454	14,547	233	4,117	3,147	7,497

Mar.	2,036	8,462	5,664	1,045	15,117	228	4,107	3,164	7,499
Apr.	2,128	8,502	5,729	1,218	15,141	226	4,127	3,175	7,527
May	2,104	8,612	5,734	1,951	14,499	220	4,082	3,189	7,491
June	2,055	8,561	5,710	1,562	14,764	218	4,127	3,207	7,552
July	2,133	8,500	5,723	1,506	14,850	222	4,178	3,227	7,628
Aug.	2,125	8,496	5,754	1,374	15,001	229	4,193	3,276	7,698
Sept.	2,137	8,708	5,935	990	15,790	230	4,208	3,305	7,743
Oct.	2,153	9,045	6,092	2,133	15,157	230	4,216	3,328	7,774
Nov.	2,083	8,871	6,124	1,462	15,615	238	4,291	3,372	7,901
Dec.	2,011	8,931	6,155	411	16,686	236	4,499	3,430	8,165
1919									
Jan.	2,015	9,105	6,261	991	16,390	246	4,592	3,500	8,338
Feb.	2,068	9,197	6,368	1,452	16,131	256	4,663	3,570	8,489
Mar.	2,040	9,286	6,505	989	16,843	264	4,697	3,635	8,596
Apr.	2,098	9,448	6,616	1,073	17,089	264	4,721	3,684	8,669
May	2,065	9,494	6,711	1,170	17,100	264	4,765	3,738	8,768
June	2,173	9,486	6,821	977	17,503	266	4,852	3,812	8,930

Notes to Table 35

Note: For sources of series used as interpolators, see Chap. 14, footnotes 2–6.

Source, by Column

Part I

1. These estimates were derived by interpolation by Method R_2 to Wednesday nearest end of month between the call date figures for total deposits adjusted of New York State national banks from Table 32, Part I, col. 1. Weekly average net deposits of member banks of the New York City clearinghouse served as the interpolator. This series is available in three differently constituted segments:
(a) May 20, 1907–June 7, 1911, nontrust companies exclusive of U.S. government deposits; (b) June 7, 1911–Sept. 1, 1911, nontrust companies inclusive of U.S. government deposits; (c) Sept. 1, 1911–June 30, 1914, trust companies plus other commercial banks inclusive of U.S. government deposits.

The weekly figures were attributed to Wednesday. Both a call date and a monthly series were constructed from the weekly figures, the Wednesday nearest the call date serving as the call date, the Wednesday nearest the end of month as the end of the month. Each series was separately corrected for seasonal variation. The value of *b* used was 0.435.

2. These estimates were derived by interpolating by Method R_2 to Wednesday nearest end of month between the sum of call date figures for New York State nonnational banks, from Table 32, Part I, col. 2, and for all commercial banks of nine urbanized states and D.C., from the same table, col. 6. Weekly average gross deposits of nonnational banks in New York City and of clearinghouse banks of a group of selected cities served as the interpolator. Totals of the cities reporting at each date were obtained, with two totals for dates when a change in composition or in number of cities occurred. The resulting discontinuous series of segments was linked together to make a hypothetical continuous series in both call date and monthly form, each corrected for seasonal variations. The value of *b* used was 0.350.

3. Interpolation by Method L between call date figures of Table 32, Part I, col. 9.

4. Sum of cols. 1, 2, and 3.

Part II

1. *June–Dec. 1914:* Total deposits adjusted of New York State national banks were estimated as for Part I, using segment c of the interpolator and the same value of *b*. Call date ratios of demand to

Notes to Table 35 (continued)

time deposits in these banks were computed from Table 32, Parts II and IV, col. 1, and interpolated by Method L to end of month. Time deposits equal deposits adjusted divided by the sum of the ratio and unity; demand deposits equal total deposits minus time deposits. *Jan. 1915–May 1917:* These estimates were derived by interpolating by Method R_2 to end of month between call date figures for New York State national banks, from Table 32, Part II, col. 1. Weekly average net demand deposits of New York City banks using the clearinghouse, including government deposits which are not separately reported, served as the interpolator.

A call date series and a monthly series were constructed from these data (see note to Part I, col. 1), and used for the monthly interpolation. The value of *b* used was + 1.242.

2. *June–Dec. 1914:* Total deposits adjusted of New York State nonnational and all commercial banks in nine urbanized states and D.C. were estimated using as the related series weekly average gross deposits at New York State nonnational banks and at clearinghouse banks in Philadelphia and Boston, 1914–17, and the same value of *b* as for Part I. Call date ratios of demand to time deposits at these banks were computed from Table 32, Parts II and IV, sum of cols. 2 and 6, and interpolated by Method L to end of month. Time deposits equal total deposits adjusted divided by the sum of the ratio and unity; demand deposits equal total deposits minus time deposits. *Jan. 1915–May 1917:* These estimates were derived by interpolating by Method R_2 to end of month between call date figures for New York State nonnational banks and for all commercial banks in nine urbanized states and D.C., from Table 32, Part II, col. 2 plus col. 6. Weekly average demand deposits less duplications of Boston clearinghouse banks and, beginning Sept. 1917, of Philadelphia clearinghouse banks served as the interpolator. The value of *b* was + 0.195.

3. Interpolation by Method L between call date figures of Table 32, Part II, col. 9.

4. Sum of cols. 1, 2, and 3.

5. *June–Dec. 1914:* Same as for Part II, col. 1. *Jan. 1915–May 1917:* These estimates were derived by interpolating by Method R_2 to end of month between call date figures for New York State national banks from Table 32, Part IV, col. 1. Weekly average net time deposits of New York City banks using the clearinghouse served as the interpolator. The value of *b* was + 0.325.

6. *June–Dec. 1914:* Same as for Part II, col. 2. *Jan. 1915–May 1917:* Total deposits adjusted at these banks were estimated as for Part I, col. 2, using the same value of *b*. Demand deposits adjusted of these banks as estimated in Part II, col. 2, were subtracted. The residuals are time deposits adjusted.

7. Interpolation by Method L between call date figures of Table 32, Part IV, col. 9.

8. Sum of cols. 5, 6, and 7.

Notes to Table 35 (continued)

Part III

Beginning Jan. 1918, cols. 4 and 6 dates are for Friday nearest end of month; other columns are Wednesday throughout.

1. Same as for Jan. 1915—May 1917 in col. 1 of Part II of this table, except that national bank call date figures come from Table 32, Part III, col. 1. Government deposits, which are now shown separately, were added to net demand deposits of New York City banks using the clearinghouse, the interpolator series.

2. Same as for Jan. 1915—May 1917 in col. 2 of Part II of this table, except call date figures come from Table 32, Part III, col. 2 plus col. 6.

3. Interpolation by Method L between call date figures of Table 32, Part III, col. 9.

4. *June—Nov. 1917:* A sum of government deposits in certain clearinghouse banks and estimated amounts in nonclearinghouse banks. Government deposits in banks using the New York City clearinghouse and beginning Sept. 11, 1917, the Philadelphia clearinghouse were obtained for weekly Wednesday dates nearest call dates and nearest end of month. The call date figures were subtracted from call date figures for all commercial banks from Table 32, Part III, col. 15, to obtain residuals for nonclearinghouse banks. Interpolation by Method L between the latter call date figures to end of month yielded estimates which were added to the end-of-month clearinghouse data to obtain all commercial bank figures. *Dec. 1917—June 1919:* A sum of government deposits in (a) weekly reporting member banks, (b) nonweekly reporting member banks, and (c) nonmember banks, for Friday nearest end of month.

    a. Weekly reporting member bank figures were corrected for seasonal variations, 1917—26.

    b. To get nonweekly reporting member bank figures in monthly form we first estimated call date figures for these banks and then interpolated by Method L to end of month between the call dates. The call date estimates were derived in two steps because of the high daily variability in government deposits. For example, government deposits in weekly reporting member banks at dates closest to call dates sometimes exceed reported call date deposits for all member banks. Accordingly, we first constructed a call date series for weekly reporting member banks by interpolating by Method L between two neighboring weeks to the exact call date, subtracted this series from seasonally unadjusted member bank call date figures (from *Banking and Monetary Statistics,* p. 73), and expressed the nonweekly reporting member bank residual figure as a ratio to the weekly reporting member bank figure at call dates. We applied this ratio to the seasonally adjusted weekly reporting figure for the

Notes to Table 35 (concluded)

Friday (or Wednesday) nearest to the end of each month that was closest to each call date. This gave the call date series for nonweekly reporting banks that we interpolated by Method L.

c. Interpolation by Method L between call date figures of Table 43, col. 3, were added to the member bank figures.

5. Sum of cols. 1, 2 and 3 minus col. 4.

6. Same as Jan. 1915 May 1017 for col. 5 of Part II of this table.

7. *June–Dec. 1917:* Same as Jan. 1915–May 1917 for col. 6 of Part II of this table. *Jan. 1918–June 1919:* Table 32, Part IV, cols. 2 plus 6, interpolated by Method R_2, using net time deposits of weekly reporting member banks, Friday nearest end of month, as related series. The value of b was + 0.312.

8. Interpolation by Method L between call date figures of Table 32, Part IV, col. 9.

9. Sum of cols. 6, 7, and 8.

No monthly interpolators of the call date figures for the thirty-eight rural states were tested because the call date figures are, in the main, interpolations (by Method L) between annual data.

The interpolators selected above were obtained in monthly form, corrected for seasonal. These monthly interpolator series were additional, over and above the call date series already constructed for testing purposes. The monthly series were derived from Wednesday figures closest to the end of the month (except for the weekly reporting member bank series which was on a Friday basis through April 1921). Monthly estimates were computed on the basis of the appropriate call date estimating equations. The final results, including the interpolations by Method L for the thirty-eight rural states, are given in Table 35.

For the period June 30–December 31, 1914, we lacked monthly interpolators of demand and time deposits adjusted, respectively, at New York State national banks. We therefore computed monthly total deposits adjusted, in the same way as for May 1907–June 1914 and distributed the total between demand and time deposits by using a ratio of demand to time deposits interpolated by Method L between the ratios at call dates.

For New York nonnational banks plus all commercial banks in the nine urbanized states and the District of Columbia we lacked monthly interpolators of demand and time deposits adjusted, June–December 1914, as well as a monthly interpolator of time deposits, December 1914–December 1917. Using the same interpolator as for May 1907–

June 1914, we estimated total deposits adjusted June 1914–June 1917, and total deposits less duplications, June–December 1917. Between June and December 1914 we distributed the total between demand and time deposits by using a ratio of demand to time deposits interpolated by Method L between the ratios at call dates. Beginning December 1914, we subtracted our estimates of demand deposits adjusted from the estimates of total deposits adjusted to get time deposits adjusted. Beginning June 1917, we subtracted our estimates of demand deposits less duplications from the estimates of total deposits less duplications.

Beginning June 1917, we have monthly estimates of demand deposits less duplications for each of the three classes of banks comprising our commercial bank total. To get demand deposits adjusted we deducted an estimate of U.S. government deposits (Table 35, Part III, column 4) from demand deposits less duplications. The derivation of this estimate is described in Chapter 17 below.

2. Deposits at Member Banks, Monthly, 1919–45

The monthly estimates of deposits at member banks are based on various published series available for the period 1919–45.[7] Beginning April 1923, data are available for all member banks. For earlier months, data are available only for weekly reporting member banks. The presentation of our estimates for nonweekly reporting banks and all member banks, June 1919–March 1923, will be simplified by discussing first the published all member bank series and then the earlier estimates.

Published Figures for All Member Banks, 1923 on
The published figures required adjustment on two counts: (a) their dating; and (b) their composition.

a. Dating. From April 1923 through December 1928 the monthly deposit figures were of a given Wednesday: through October 1927, either the next-to-the-last or the last of the month, thereafter, the first or the second Wednesday of the month. From January 1929 through March 1944, monthly averages of daily figures were published, there-

---

[7] Weekly reporting member bank figures, June 1919–Apr. 1923: *Banking and Monetary Statistics*, Board of Governors of the Federal Reserve System, Washington, D.C., 1943, pp. 132–136. All member bank figures, Apr. 1923–Dec. 1946: *Annual Report* of the Federal Reserve Board, *1927*, p. 108; *1928*, p. 116; *1933*, p. 168; *1934*, p. 154; *1935*, p. 153; *Banking and Monetary Statistics*, p. 42; *Federal Reserve Bulletin*, 1942–1947.

after semimonthly averages of daily figures. We adjusted these figures so that they might be considered to represent the Wednesday closest to the end of the month. This adjustment was made on the basis of weekly reporting member bank data. Because these data are available weekly, it is possible to construct a series from them dated, on the one hand, approximately like the published monthly series—the dating which is not acceptable to us—and, on the other hand, at Wednesdays nearest the end of the month—the dating we want. The deposit figures shown in the weekly reporting member bank returns are constituted exactly like those of the all member bank returns. Further, during 1923–45, demand deposits at weekly reporting banks represent about 70 per cent of all member bank demand deposits; time deposits represent about 50 per cent. We therefore used Method R_1 to interpolate between the all member bank data at monthly dates on which they were reported to the monthly dates we desired to use. For this interpolation we used deposits of weekly reporting member banks as the related series.

We compiled the series for weekly reporting member banks to be used as the interpolator dated as follows: For 1923–28, as of the Wednesday of the month exactly corresponding to the all member bank series and as of the Wednesday closest to the end of the month; for January 1929 through March 1944, as of the midpoint of the monthly averages of weekly figures and as of the Wednesday closest to the end of the month; thereafter as of the midpoint of semimonthly averages of weekly figures and as of the Wednesday closest to the end of the month.

The method was used for both demand and time deposits. It was also used to interpolate a monthly figure between the reported figures for February and April, 1933, to fill the gap in the data for all member banks that occurred in March of that year.

The member bank demand deposit series, adjusted for dating, required seasonal correction. The time deposit series did not.

b. Composition. The composition of the published monthly member bank demand and time deposit series changed, 1923–45.

The following demand deposit items were reported:

(1) Net demand deposits, April 1923–December 1935; (2) Gross demand deposits, January 1936–April 1943; (3) Demand deposits adjusted, May 1943–December 1945.

1. Net demand deposits is a legal definition on the basis of which member banks compute their reserve requirements. From April 24, 1917, through August 23, 1935, net demand deposits were defined as

the excess of demand amounts due to banks over demand amounts due from banks and cash items in process of collection, plus gross demand deposits excluding amounts due to banks and U.S. government deposits. The Banking Act of 1935 changed this definition so that net demand deposits are now the sum of all demand deposits including amounts due to banks and U.S. government deposits minus cash items in process of collection and demand balances with domestic banks.[8]

Net demand deposits are larger than demand deposits adjusted. We wanted to eliminate this excess monthly. At call dates we know the exact difference.[9] We tested various monthly interpolators of this difference, seasonally adjusted, selecting as the best the difference between amounts due to banks and balances due from banks of weekly reporting member banks, also seasonally adjusted. Values of u and v computed from the middle call dates of successive overlapping triplets of call dates for the period April 3, 1923, to December 1935 had a correlation of $+0.528$, and b had a value of 0.468. Accordingly, we estimated the difference by interpolating between the call dates by Method R_2, using as the related series weekly reporting member figures for Wednesday nearest the end of the month, and this value of b.

2. Gross demand deposits are also larger than demand deposits adjusted. The difference between gross demand deposits and demand deposits adjusted was known exactly at call dates for all member banks and weekly for all weekly reporting member banks.[10] We needed to know as well the difference for nonweekly reporting member banks at monthly dates between call dates. Ninety per cent of the difference between gross demand deposits and demand deposits adjusted of member banks was accounted for by the difference in these items of weekly reporting member banks. Both of these series were seasonally adjusted, and the data for weekly reporting member banks closest to call dates were subtracted from the member bank call date figures. We could not find a satisfactory interpolator for the call date nonweekly reporting member bank residual and therefore interpolated monthly values by Method L between call dates. The sum of the weekly reporting member bank differences and the estimated nonweekly reporting member bank

---

[8] In Apr. 1943 an amendment to the law exempted U.S. government war loan deposit accounts from reserve requirements.

[9] *Banking and Monetary Statistics*, 1943, pp. 73–75.

[10] *Banking and Monetary Statistics*, pp. 73–74, and *Member Bank Call Report*.

differences, for Wednesday closest to the end of each month, was sub-tracted from the member bank series of gross demand deposits to obtain demand deposits adjusted.

3. Beginning May 1943, the published figures corresponded with our definition of demand deposits adjusted, and after adjustment for dating no further changes in the published figures were necessary.

The published monthly Federal Reserve series of time deposits at member banks, April 1923–December 1945, represented time deposits against which reserves had to be maintained. In addition to time deposits of individuals, partnerships, corporations, states, and municipalities, the series included postal savings redeposited in member banks and, be-ginning June 1928, interbank time deposits and, beginning February or March 1939, U.S. government time deposits.[11] The latter three com-ponents of the published series are not included in time deposits under our definition of the term. We therefore made monthly estimates of the amount of these components and deducted them from the published monthly member bank data.

We know postal savings deposits in all member banks for call dates since June 1921. Beginning March 29, 1939, this item and U.S. gov-ernment time deposits were reported either as one figure or separately. Member banks were not required to distinguish between interbank de-mand and interbank time deposits until March 1939 and showed all interbank deposits as demand deposits. Weekly reporting member banks did not show postal savings separately until January 1938, and begin-ning February or March 1939, combined them with U.S. government time deposits. They did not distinguish between the two classes of inter-bank deposits until September 1934.

We were not able to discover a satisfactory monthly interpolator of the member bank call date series of postal savings, interbank, or U.S. government time deposits. Until data from weekly reporting member banks became available for these series, we interpolated monthly by Method L between the call date figures. When weekly reporting member

---

[11] Postal savings after Apr. 24, 1917, were subject to the same reserve requirements as time deposits, although by their terms they were demand deposits. The Banking Act of 1933 changed the terms under which these deposits were made to conform to the definition of time deposits.

United States Treasurer's time deposits, open account, were first established in Nov. 1938, but were not segregated from other government deposits until early 1939.

bank figures existed, we subtracted them at dates closest to call dates from the member bank call date figures and interpolated for nonweekly reporting member banks by Method L between the residual call date figures.

Estimates for All Member Banks, 1919–23

Demand Deposits. For the period before April 1923, we have net demand deposits of weekly reporting member banks but not of nonweekly reporting member banks. Weekly reporting member banks are classified according to their location in and outside New York City. An estimate of nonweekly reporting member bank deposits was made by regressing deposits of this class of banks on deposits of weekly reporting member banks outside New York City, April 1923–December 1928, both seasonally adjusted. The correlation coefficient was +.836. The estimated nonweekly reporting member bank series was added to weekly reporting member bank data for Friday closest to the end of the month, June 1919–April 1921, and Wednesday closest to the end of the month, May 1921–March 1923. From this series the difference between net demand deposits and demand deposits adjusted had to be subtracted, as for the later published data. Again the difference at call dates for all member banks was known. Data on interbank deposits and balances of weekly reporting member banks, however, were available only beginning April 1920. For all member banks we interpolated as follows: June 1919–May 4, 1920, by Method L between the call date difference series; thereafter by Method R_2, using the difference between interbank deposits and balances of the weekly reporting member banks series as the related series and a value of b of .387 based on a test correlation for 1920–23, for which the correlation coefficient was +.435.

The final monthly member bank demand deposits adjusted series is shown in Table 36, column 1.

Time Deposits. For the period before April 1923, as for net demand deposits, we know time deposits of weekly but not of nonweekly reporting member banks. The coefficient of correlation between time deposits of nonweekly and of weekly reporting member banks, April 1923–December 1928, is +.99. We therefore estimated time deposits in nonweekly reporting member banks, June 1919–March 1923, on the basis of the regression equation for 1923–28. The estimated nonweekly reporting member bank series was added to weekly reporting member

bank data for Friday closest to the end of the month, June 1919–
April 1921, and Wednesday closest to the end of the month, May 1921–
March 1923. From this series monthly values interpolated by Method L
between call date figures of postal savings in member banks were subtracted.[12] The final monthly member bank time deposits adjusted series
is shown in Table 36, column 4.

3. Deposits at Nonmember Banks, Monthly, 1919–45

For June 1919–June 1923, we estimated monthly demand deposits adjusted and time deposits for nonmember banks by interpolating by
Method L the corresponding call date series. We resorted to Method L
after testing as possible interpolators deposits at all weekly reporting
member banks and at weekly reporting member banks outside New
York City. Both gave poor results for both demand and time deposits.

For 1923–45 we estimated monthly demand deposits adjusted and
time deposits for nonmember banks by interpolating by Method R_2
between the corresponding call date series, using various monthly member bank series as interpolators. Monthly deposit series are available
not only for all member banks (these series are described in section 2
above), but also from April 1923 to December 1928, according to
the population of the city in which the member banks were located,
as follows: population less than 5,000; 5,000 to 15,000; 15,000 to
100,000; 100,000 and over. Such data are also available for the whole
period 1923–43, for the first two classes combined—described as smaller
places—and for the two remaining classes combined—described as
larger places. We tested and found satisfactory the series for smaller
places as interpolators of the call date nonmember bank figures. Before
these tests were made, the published figures for smaller places were
adjusted for changes in the classification of cities by size of population.[13]

---

[12] Before June 1921 data are available on postal savings in national but not in state
member banks.

[13] The classification of cities according to population was based on the 1920 Census
of population for 1923–31, on the 1930 Census for 1931–40, on the 1940 Census for
1940–46. Our problem was to smooth the differences introduced by the shift in the
classification of cities and towns from smaller to larger centers resulting from Census
changes. For the decadal years for which overlapping data based on the new and the
preceding Census were available, the monthly figures of deposits at banks in smaller
centers were expressed as ratios of deposits at all member banks and the ratios averaged
annually. The difference between these averages of monthly ratios may be regarded as

TABLE 36

Adjusted Demand and Time Deposits at Member, Nonmember, and All Commercial Banks, June 1919 – December 1945

(seasonally adjusted, in millions of dollars)

Wednesday Nearest End of Month[a]	Adjusted Demand Deposits			Adjusted Time Deposits		
	Member Banks (1)	Non-member Banks (2)	All Com-mercial Banks (3)	Member Banks (4)	Non-member Banks (5)	All Com-mercial Banks (6)
1919						
July	12,474	5,316	17,790	4,484	4,720	9,204
Aug.	12,633	5,438	18,071	4,594	4,755	9,349
Sept.	12,770	5,590	18,360	4,737	4,799	9,536
Oct.	13,006	5,711	18,717	5,077	4,835	9,912
Nov.	13,158	5,757	18,915	5,245	4,820	10,065
Dec.	13,574	5,673	19,247	5,323	4,719	10,042
1920						
Jan.	13,344	5,732	19,076	5,569	4,796	10,365
Feb.	13,517	5,787	19,304	5,662	4,873	10,535
Mar.	13,678	5,855	19,533	5,775	4,970	10,745
Apr.	13,455	5,910	19,365	5,833	5,047	10,880
May	13,490	5,841	19,331	5,881	5,092	10,973
June	13,397	5,735	19,132	5,977	5,139	11,116
July	13,393	5,701	19,094	5,990	5,132	11,122
Aug.	13,310	5,661	18,971	6,103	5,124	11,227
Sept.	13,255	5,629	18,884	6,151	5,117	11,268
Oct.	13,088	5,596	18,684	6,173	5,111	11,284
Nov.	12,799	5,580	18,379	6,217	5,098	11,315
Dec.	13,085	5,575	18,660	6,288	5,082	11,370
1921						
Jan.	12,710	5,446	18,156	6,407	5,033	11,440
Feb.	12,672	5,318	17,990	6,390	4,984	11,374
Mar.	12,375	5,157	17,532	6,420	4,923	11,343
Apr.	12,238	5,032	17,270	6,443	4,875	11,318
May	12,266	4,984	17,250	6,434	4,852	11,286

(continued)

TABLE 36 (continued)

Wednesday Nearest End of Month[a]	Adjusted Demand Deposits			Adjusted Time Deposits		
	Member Banks (1)	Non-member Banks (2)	All Com-mercial Banks (3)	Member Banks (4)	Non-member Banks (5)	All Com-mercial Banks (6)
1921						
June	11,964	4,944	16,908	6,425	4,832	11,257
July	11,829	4,913	16,742	6,362	4,809	11,171
Aug.	11,959	4,889	16,848	6,413	4,791	11,204
Sept.	11,781	4,864	16,645	6,413	4,772	11,185
Oct.	12,018	4,834	16,852	6,526	4,749	11,275
Nov.	12,152	4,809	16,961	6,544	4,731	11,275
Dec.	12,125	4,785	16,910	6,545	4,713	11,258
1922						
Jan.	12,021	4,815	16,836	6,512	4,700	11,212
Feb.	12,189	4,845	17,034	6,699	4,691	11,390
Mar.	12,192	4,860	17,052	6,782	4,708	11,490
Apr.	12,723	4,870	17,593	6,901	4,746	11,647
May	12,916	4,878	17,794	6,960	4,776	11,736
June	13,107	4,886	17,993	7,222	4,806	12,028
July	13,146	4,969	18,115	7,446	4,841	12,287
Aug.	13,035	5,039	18,074	7,607	4,868	12,475
Sept.	13,212	5,109	18,321	7,559	4,896	12,455
Oct.	13,204	5,197	18,401	7,680	4,931	12,611
Nov.	13,075	5,267	18,342	7,688	4,958	12,646
Dec.	13,715	5,345	19,060	7,860	5,000	12,860
1923						
Jan.	13,609	5,359	18,968	7,827	5,067	12,894
Feb.	13,621	5,374	18,995	7,908	5,134	13,042
Mar.	13,155	5,389	18,544	8,216	5,201	13,417
Apr.	13,428	5,366	18,794	8,218	5,289	13,507
May	13,525	5,340	18,865	8,278	5,360	13,638
June	13,350	5,315	18,665	8,327	5,431	13,758
July	13,334	5,318	18,652	8,297	5,448	13,745

(continued)

TABLE 36 (continued)

Wednesday Nearest End of Month[a]	Adjusted Demand Deposits			Adjusted Time Deposits		
	Member Banks (1)	Non-member Banks (2)	All Commercial Banks (3)	Member Banks (4)	Non-member Banks (5)	All Commercial Banks (6)
1923						
Aug.	13,239	5,350	18,589	8,374	5,458	13,832
Sept.	13,303	5,412	18,715	8,408	5,473	13,881
Oct.	13,383	5,468	18,851	8,463	5,508	13,971
Nov.	13,317	5,514	18,831	8,504	5,547	14,051
Dec.	13,385	5,573	18,958	8,572	5,559	14,131
1924						
Jan.	13,342	5,522	18,864	8,545	5,610	14,155
Feb.	13,252	5,482	18,734	8,733	5,622	14,355
Mar.	13,302	5,453	18,755	8,813	5,638	14,451
Apr.	13,367	5,495	18,862	8,929	5,662	14,591
May	13,489	5,517	19,006	8,954	5,680	14,634
June	13,729	5,553	19,282	9,055	5,711	14,766
July	14,012	5,602	19,614	9,170	5,741	14,911
Aug.	14,226	5,717	19,943	9,268	5,763	15,031
Sept.	14,452	5,805	20,257	9,426	5,783	15,209
Oct.	14,436	5,876	20,312	9,575	5,813	15,388
Nov.	14,770	5,909	20,679	9,640	5,840	15,480
Dec.	14,544	5,942	20,486	9,707	5,852	15,559
1925						
Jan.	14,799	5,994	20,793	9,788	5,923	15,711
Feb.	14,916	6,061	20,977	9,907	5,938	15,845
Mar.	14,760	6,097	20,857	10,040	5,935	15,975
Apr.	14,863	6,148	21,011	10,071	5,959	16,030
May	14,977	6,217	21,194	10,204	5,985	16,189
June	15,163	6,273	21,436	10,285	6,044	16,329
July	15,110	6,415	21,525	10,310	6,092	16,402
Aug.	15,364	6,660	22,024	10,384	6,132	16,516
Sept.	15,509	6,824	22,333	10,478	6,167	16,645

(continued)

TABLE 36 (continued)

Wednesday Nearest End of Month[a]	Adjusted Demand Deposits			Adjusted Time Deposits		
	Member Banks (1)	Non-member Banks (2)	All Com-mercial Banks (3)	Member Banks (4)	Non-member Banks (5)	All Com-mercial Banks (6)
1925						
Oct.	15,404	6,888	22,292	10,533	6,220	16,753
Nov.	15,304	6,917	22,221	10,584	6,272	16,856
Dec.	15,145	6,977	22,122	10,616	6,324	16,940
1926						
Jan.	15,211	6,925	22,136	10,739	6,352	17,091
Feb.	15,320	6,900	22,220	10,798	6,346	17,144
Mar.	15,329	6,821	22,150	10,831	6,332	17,163
Apr.	15,153	6,712	21,865	10,950	6,309	17,259
May	15,577	6,580	22,157	11,070	6,299	17,369
June	15,681	6,424	22,105	11,153	6,304	17,457
July	15,372	6,462	21,834	11,184	6,326	17,510
Aug.	15,493	6,488	21,981	11,266	6,325	17,591
Sept.	15,440	6,478	21,918	11,280	6,307	17,587
Oct.	15,245	6,467	21,712	11,346	6,285	17,631
Nov.	15,326	6,448	21,774	11,363	6,265	17,628
Dec.	14,995	6,461	21,456	11,330	6,243	17,573
1927						
Jan.	15,174	6,361	21,535	11,517	6,298	17,815
Feb.	15,335	6,332	21,667	11,814	6,313	18,127
Mar.	15,540	6,283	21,823	11,796	6,360	18,156
Apr.	15,423	6,286	21,709	11,896	6,386	18,282
May	15,903	6,281	22,184	12,018	6,438	18,456
June	15,593	6,252	21,845	12,111	6,477	18,588
July	15,555	6,311	21,866	12,189	6,505	18,694
Aug.	15,699	6,372	22,071	12,241	6,499	18,740
Sept.	15,443	6,437	21,880	12,341	6,483	18,824
Oct.	15,588	6,437	22,025	12,378	6,522	18,900
Nov.	16,132	6,406	22,538	12,661	6,550	19,211
Dec.	15,533	6,348	21,881	12,624	6,650	19,224

(continued)

TABLE 36 (continued)

Wednesday Nearest End of Month[a]	Adjusted Demand Deposits			Adjusted Time Deposits		
	Member Banks (1)	Non-member Banks (2)	All Com-mercial Banks (3)	Member Banks (4)	Non-member Banks (5)	All Com-mercial Banks (6)
1928						
Jan.	15,976	6,335	22,311	12,838	6,675	19,513
Feb.	16,084	6,325	22,409	12,897	6,722	19,619
Mar.	16,050	6,302	22,352	13,146	6,734	19,880
Apr.	16,411	6,290	22,701	13,238	6,731	19,969
May	16,226	6,282	22,508	13,363	6,724	20,087
June	15,594	6,242	21,836	13,370	6,730	20,100
July	15,791	6,303	22,094	13,278	6,721	19,999
Aug.	15,519	6,387	21,906	13,295	6,712	20,007
Sept.	15,723	6,448	22,171	13,177	6,766	19,943
Oct.	15,841	6,549	22,390	13,294	6,833	20,127
Nov.	15,946	6,542	22,488	13,232	6,812	20,044
Dec.	16,015	6,586	22,601	13,293	6,845	20,138
1929						
Jan.	15,736	6,544	22,280	13,213	6,867	20,080
Feb.	15,924	6,485	22,409	13,179	6,855	20,034
Mar.	15,954	6,430	22,384	13,110	6,817	19,927
Apr.	16,068	6,412	22,480	12,996	6,771	19,767
May	15,788	6,395	22,183	13,029	6,719	19,748
June	15,904	6,374	22,278	13,043	6,686	19,729
July	16,559	6,437	22,796	12,944	6,773	19,717
Aug.	16,052	6,500	22,552	12,962	6,845	19,807
Sept.	16,058	6,535	22,593	12,970	6,942	19,912
Oct.	17,947	6,485	24,432	13,028	6,863	19,891
Nov.	15,255	6,396	21,651	12,799	6,736	19,535
Dec.	16,239	6,395	22,634	12,791	6,642	19,433
1930						
Jan.	15,508	6,417	21,925	12,969	6,649	19,618
Feb.	15,842	6,348	22,190	12,869	6,651	19,520
Mar.	16,357	6,262	22,619	13,164	6,653	19,817

(continued)

TABLE 36 (continued)

Wednesday Nearest End of Month[a]	Adjusted Demand Deposits			Adjusted Time Deposits		
	Member Banks (1)	Non-member Banks (2)	All Com-mercial Banks (3)	Member Banks (4)	Non-member Banks (5)	All Com-mercial Banks (6)
1930						
Apr.	16,076	6,189	22,265	13,044	6,661	19,705
May	15,521	6,110	21,631	13,189	6,659	19,848
June	15,593	6,019	21,612	13,346	6,664	20,010
July	15,836	5,895	21,731	13,321	6,622	19,943
Aug.	15,588	5,769	21,357	13,468	6,565	20,033
Sept.	15,726	5,682	21,408	13,523	6,515	20,038
Oct.	15,789	5,603	21,392	13,603	6,465	20,068
Nov.	15,880	5,473	21,353	13,343	6,370	19,713
Dec.	15,795	5,318	21,113	12,873	6,259	19,132
1931						
Jan.	15,586	5,157	20,743	12,920	6,172	19,092
Feb.	15,843	5,047	20,890	13,116	6,113	19,229
Mar.	15,933	4,964	20,897	13,081	6,043	19,124
Apr.	15,399	4,954	20,353	13,235	5,975	19,210
May	15,083	4,910	19,993	13,135	5,891	19,026
June	15,003	4,885	19,888	12,876	5,839	18,715
July	15,019	4,725	19,744	12,771	5,737	18,508
Aug.	14,743	4,509	19,252	12,606	5,539	18,145
Sept.	14,758	4,322	19,080	12,207	5,357	17,564
Oct.	13,957	4,216	18,173	11,484	5,161	16,645
Nov.	13,731	4,121	17,852	11,130	4,969	16,099
Dec.	13,267	4,023	17,290	10,705	4,740	15,445
1932						
Jan.	12,733	3,878	16,611	10,429	4,630	15,059
Feb.	12,716	3,770	16,486	10,287	4,516	14,803
Mar.	12,689	3,678	16,367	10,220	4,432	14,652
Apr.	12,536	3,595	16,131	10,184	4,359	14,543
May	12,303	3,482	15,785	10,103	4,257	14,360

(continued)

TABLE 36 (continued)

Wednesday Nearest End of Month[a]	Adjusted Demand Deposits			Adjusted Time Deposits		
	Member Banks (1)	Non-member Banks (2)	All Com-mercial Banks (3)	Member Banks (4)	Non-member Banks (5)	All Com-mercial Banks (6)
1932						
June	12,126	3,364	15,490	9,864	4,167	14,031
July	11,856	3,248	15,104	9,899	4,080	13,979
Aug.	12,013	3,188	15,201	9,849	4,004	13,853
Sept.	12,130	3,140	15,270	9,805	3,941	13,746
Oct.	12,235	3,158	15,393	9,874	3,970	13,844
Nov.	12,551	3,162	15,713	9,778	3,978	13,756
Dec.	12,356	3,155	15,511	9,716	3,974	13,690
1933						
Jan.	12,632	3,016	15,648	9,641	3,886	13,527
Feb.	11,550	2,844	14,394	9,007	3,618	12,625
Mar.	10,915	2,628	13,543	7,789	3,129	10,918
Apr.	11,352	2,485	13,837	7,840	2,868	10,708
May	11,977	2,453	14,430	7,810	2,841	10,651
June	11,864	2,419	14,283	8,019	2,836	10,855
July	11,822	2,379	14,201	8,228	2,845	11,073
Aug.	11,923	2,342	14,265	8,240	2,837	11,077
Sept.	12,014	2,327	14,341	8,258	2,832	11,090
Oct.	12,195	2,315	14,510	8,269	2,805	11,074
Nov.	12,386	2,328	14,714	8,235	2,770	11,005
Dec.	12,585	2,335	14,920	8,290	2,758	11,048
1934						
Jan.	12,881	2,348	15,229	8,437	2,797	11,234
Feb.	13,436	2,350	15,786	8,512	2,804	11,316
Mar.	13,833	2,366	16,199	8,661	2,831	11,492
Apr.	13,932	2,393	16,325	8,818	2,873	11,691
May	14,017	2,415	16,432	8,893	2,908	11,801
June	14,043	2,442	16,485	9,061	2,944	12,005
July	14,411	2,520	16,931	9,093	2,934	12,027
Aug.	14,899	2,600	17,499	9,188	2,919	12,107

(continued)

TABLE 36 (continued)

Wednesday Nearest End of Month[a]	Adjusted Demand Deposits			Adjusted Time Deposits		
	Member Banks (1)	Non-member Banks (2)	All Com-mercial Banks (3)	Member Banks (4)	Non-member Banks (5)	All Com-mercial Banks (6)
1934						
Sept.	14,701	2,696	17,397	9,179	2,894	12,073
Oct.	15,191	2,776	17,967	9,271	2,917	12,188
Nov.	15,552	2,833	18,385	9,197	2,964	12,161
Dec.	15,323	2,890	18,213	9,272	3,015	12,287
1935						
Jan.	16,022	3,004	19,026	9,392	2,995	12,387
Feb.	16,541	3,112	19,653	9,452	2,960	12,412
Mar.	16,428	3,117	19,545	9,556	3,002	12,558
Apr.	16,752	3,126	19,878	9,730	3,061	12,791
May	16,924	3,134	20,058	9,696	3,112	12,808
June	17,364	3,127	20,491	9,688	3,162	12,850
July	17,584	3,163	20,747	9,702	3,163	12,865
Aug.	18,835	3,217	22,052	9,708	3,146	12,854
Sept.	18,288	3,288	21,576	9,846	3,125	12,971
Oct.	18,561	3,315	21,876	9,916	3,119	13,035
Nov.	18,965	3,427	22,392	9,906	3,177	13,083
Dec.	18,608	3,544	22,152	10,038	3,268	13,306
1936						
Jan.	18,643	3,484	22,127	10,041	3,284	13,325
Feb.	18,957	3,598	22,555	10,085	3,280	13,365
Mar.	18,967	3,598	22,565	10,103	3,282	13,385
Apr.	19,544	3,588	23,132	10,369	3,284	13,653
May	20,344	3,572	23,916	10,358	3,293	13,651
June	20,737	3,644	24,381	10,391	3,320	13,711
July	20,763	3,805	24,568	10,480	3,355	13,835
Aug.	20,629	3,837	24,466	10,545	3,377	13,922
Sept.	21,058	3,860	24,918	10,611	3,389	14,000
Oct.	20,930	3,912	24,842	10,648	3,404	14,052
Nov.	21,085	3,954	25,039	10,613	3,412	14,025
Dec.	21,381	4,004	25,385	10,699	3,429	14,128

(continued)

TABLE 36 (continued)

Wednesday Nearest End of Month[a]	Adjusted Demand Deposits			Adjusted Time Deposits		
	Member Banks (1)	Non-member Banks (2)	All Com-mercial Banks (3)	Member Banks (4)	Non-member Banks (5)	All Com-mercial Banks (6)
1937						
Jan.	21,128	4,004	25,132	10,780	3,450	14,230
Feb.	21,400	3,987	25,387	10,971	3,458	14,429
Mar.	21,621	3,970	25,591	10,918	3,463	14,381
Apr.	21,492	3,964	25,456	10,932	3,482	14,414
May	21,149	3,951	25,100	11,061	3,502	14,563
June	21,124	3,951	25,075	11,082	3,526	14,608
July	20,987	3,985	24,972	11,183	3,560	14,743
Aug.	20,743	3,952	24,695	11,235	3,606	14,841
Sept.	20,672	3,873	24,545	11,325	3,643	14,968
Oct.	20,184	3,790	23,974	11,298	3,655	14,953
Nov.	20,057	3,709	23,766	11,240	3,647	14,887
Dec.	19,899	3,666	23,565	11,219	3,656	14,875
1938						
Jan.	20,126	3,699	23,825	11,288	3,651	14,939
Feb.	20,351	3,711	24,062	11,370	3,631	15,001
Mar.	20,484	3,659	24,143	11,279	3,620	14,899
Apr.	20,369	3,619	23,988	11,304	3,612	14,916
May	20,022	3,584	23,606	11,270	3,611	14,881
June	20,190	3,555	23,745	11,315	3,612	14,927
July	20,429	3,597	24,026	11,234	3,604	14,838
Aug.	21,159	3,611	24,770	11,281	3,598	14,879
Sept.	21,417	3,622	25,039	11,228	3,588	14,816
Oct.	21,672	3,719	25,391	11,246	3,591	14,837
Nov.	22,171	3,789	25,960	11,182	3,587	14,769
Dec.	22,268	3,863	26,131	11,252	3,595	14,847
1939						
Jan.	22,165	3,821	25,986	11,315	3,593	14,908
Feb.	22,049	3,755	25,804	11,349	3,586	14,935

(continued)

TABLE 36 (continued)

Wednesday Nearest End of Month[a]	Adjusted Demand Deposits			Adjusted Time Deposits		
	Member Banks (1)	Non-member Banks (2)	All Commercial Banks (3)	Member Banks (4)	Non-member Banks (5)	All Commercial Banks (6)
1939						
Mar.	22,503	3,706	26,209	11,396	3,582	14,978
Apr.	22,643	3,759	26,402	11,461	3,594	15,055
May	22,778	3,803	26,581	11,441	3,601	15,042
June	22,788	3,853	26,641	11,473	3,622	15,095
July	23,545	3,930	27,475	11,505	3,614	15,119
Aug.	24,283	3,985	28,268	11,519	3,603	15,122
Sept.	24,905	4,043	28,948	11,499	3,592	15,091
Oct.	25,194	4,103	29,297	11,549	3,612	15,161
Nov.	26,044	4,148	30,192	11,507	3,617	15,124
Dec.	25,618	4,178	29,796	11,627	3,612	15,239
1940						
Jan.	26,103	4,145	30,248	11,621	3,626	15,247
Feb.	26,563	4,126	30,689	11,701	3,642	15,343
Mar.	27,051	4,097	31,148	11,823	3,652	15,475
Apr.	26,826	4,125	30,951	11,751	3,671	15,422
May	27,510	4,155	31,665	11,805	3,686	15,491
June	27,988	4,165	32,153	11,862	3,703	15,565
July	28,359	4,203	32,562	11,845	3,699	15,544
Aug.	28,389	4,245	32,634	11,890	3,698	15,588
Sept.	28,753	4,288	33,041	11,947	3,692	15,639
Oct.	29,232	4,364	33,596	11,932	3,689	15,621
Nov.	29,663	4,426	34,089	11,971	3,673	15,644
Dec.	30,142	4,491	34,633	12,101	3,664	15,765
1941						
Jan.	30,709	4,505	35,214	12,113	3,702	15,815
Feb.	31,744	4,492	36,236	12,180	3,721	15,901
Mar.	32,286	4,469	36,755	12,206	3,739	15,945
Apr.	32,288	4,553	36,841	12,285	3,729	16,014
May	32,955	4,644	37,599	12,261	3,710	15,971

(continued)

TABLE 36 (continued)

Wednesday Nearest End of Month[a]	Adjusted Demand Deposits			Adjusted Time Deposits		
	Member Banks (1)	Non-member Banks (2)	All Commercial Banks (3)	Member Banks (4)	Non-member Banks (5)	All Commercial Banks (6)
1941						
June	32,453	4,722	37,175	12,273	3,674	15,947
July	33,419	4,789	38,208	12,285	3,667	15,952
Aug.	33,311	4,809	38,120	12,326	3,655	15,981
Sept.	33,663	4,854	38,517	12,358	3,660	16,018
Oct.	33,273	4,978	38,251	12,414	3,686	16,100
Nov.	33,676	5,106	38,782	12,327	3,681	16,008
Dec.	33,383	5,231	38,614	12,276	3,652	15,928
1942						
Jan.	34,506	5,114	39,620	12,083	3,609	15,692
Feb.	35,019	5,096	40,115	11,998	3,580	15,578
Mar.	35,429	5,097	40,526	11,897	3,551	15,448
Apr.	36,392	5,105	41,497	11,948	3,542	15,490
May	37,231	5,028	42,259	11,949	3,554	15,503
June	37,361	4,954	42,315	12,037	3,579	15,616
July	38,730	5,095	43,825	12,106	3,601	15,707
Aug.	39,435	5,336	44,771	12,247	3,618	15,865
Sept.	40,026	5,674	45,700	12,347	3,641	15,988
Oct.	41,409	5,972	47,381	12,468	3,667	16,135
Nov.	41,811	6,181	47,992	12,528	3,665	16,193
Dec.	42,421	6,434	48,855	12,593	3,669	16,262
1943						
Jan.	43,695	6,598	50,293	12,943	3,699	16,642
Feb.	45,821	6,722	52,543	13,075	3,720	16,795
Mar.	47,468	6,772	54,240	13,110	3,747	16,857
Apr.	45,894	7,180	53,074	13,239	3,774	17,013
May	46,060	7,323	53,383	13,506	3,814	17,320
June	49,618	7,312	56,930	13,654	3,880	17,534
July	51,651	7,472	59,123	14,025	3,934	17,959
Aug.	54,699	7,680	62,379	14,369	3,979	18,348

(continued)

TABLE 36 (concluded)

Wednesday Nearest End of Month[a]	Adjusted Demand Deposits			Adjusted Time Deposits		
	Member Banks (1)	Non-member Banks (2)	All Commercial Banks (3)	Member Banks (4)	Non-member Banks (5)	All Commercial Banks (6)
1943						
Sept.	47,127	7,615	54,742	14,311	3,997	18,308
Oct.	47,904	7,698	55,602	14,610	4,008	18,618
Nov.	50,253	8,166	58,419	14,771	4,085	18,856
Dec.	52,838	8,415	61,253	15,038	4,102	19,140
1944						
Jan.	51,005	8,441	59,446	15,375	4,163	19,538
Feb.	51,669	8,494	60,163	15,533	4,204	19,737
Mar.	52,280	8,827	61,107	15,798	4,277	20,075
Apr.	53,359	8,959	62,318	16,182	4,358	20,540
May	54,753	9,134	63,887	16,542	4,437	20,979
June	53,628	8,705	62,333	16,750	4,494	21,244
July	54,053	8,739	62,792	17,133	4,551	21,684
Aug.	55,733	9,210	64,943	17,535	4,649	22,184
Sept.	56,544	9,664	66,208	17,977	4,752	22,729
Oct.	58,049	10,208	68,257	18,661	4,844	23,505
Nov.	59,703	10,473	70,176	18,837	4,902	23,739
Dec.	57,089	10,338	67,427	19,250	4,960	24,210
1945						
Jan.	59,710	10,358	70,068	19,563	5,091	24,654
Feb.	60,881	10,343	71,224	20,054	5,201	25,255
Mar.	62,139	10,671	72,810	20,463	5,325	25,788
Apr.	62,509	10,803	73,312	20,936	5,418	26,354
May	62,845	10,895	73,740	21,274	5,502	26,776
June	61,711	10,468	72,179	21,608	5,596	27,204
July	62,771	10,712	73,483	22,202	5,717	27,919
Aug.	63,352	11,158	74,510	22,767	5,850	28,617
Sept.	64,110	11,554	75,664	23,260	5,957	29,217
Oct.	64,299	12,013	76,312	23,694	6,045	29,739
Nov.	64,945	12,149	77,094	23,821	6,073	29,894
Dec.	63,970	12,221	76,191	24,137	6,110	30,247

Notes to Table 36

[a]Friday nearest the end of month for cols. 1 and 4 before May 1921, Wednesday in all other cases.

Source, by Column

1. Estimates were constructed for four separate subperiods.
   a. *June 1919–Mar. 1923:* (i) An estimate of net demand deposits at nonweekly reporting member banks was added to net demand deposits at weekly reporting member banks (from *Banking and Monetary Statistics*, pp. 132–136), to get totals for all member banks. The estimate for nonweekly reporting member banks was computed from the estimating equation
      $$Y = 25.0 + 0.673X,$$
      where Y = net demand deposits at weekly reporting member banks outside New York City,
      and X = net demand deposits at nonweekly reporting member banks. This equation was calculated by least squares (correlation coefficient, +0.836) from figures for Wednesday nearest end of month, Apr. 1923–Dec. 1928. For this period, net demand deposits at nonweekly reporting member banks was estimated by subtracting seasonally adjusted weekly reporting member bank figures from seasonally adjusted all member bank figures (*Annual Report* of the Federal Reserve Board, 1927, p. 108; 1928, p. 116). Net demand deposits at weekly reporting member banks outside New York City are from *Banking and Monetary Statistics,* pp. 200–205.
      (ii) Net demand deposits are larger than demand deposits adjusted. The difference was estimated by interpolating by Method L between call date differences, June 1919 to May 1920; thereafter, by Method R_2, using as the related series the difference between interbank deposits and balances at domestic banks of weekly reporting member banks. The value of b was 0.387. The difference estimates were subtracted from net demand deposits.
   b. *Apr. 1923–Dec. 1935:* (i) Net demand deposits of all member banks, monthly (from *Annual Report* of the Federal Reserve Board, 1927, p. 108; 1928, p. 116; 1933, p. 168; 1934, p. 154; 1935, p. 153), adjusted to represent the Wednesday closest to the end of the month, and also to fill the gap in the data for all member banks in Mar. 1933, by interpolation by Method R_1, using as the related series data for weekly reporting member banks adjusted as described in text. The member bank net demand deposits series adjusted for dating required seasonal correction.
      (ii) The call date differences, for all member banks, between net demand deposits and demand deposits adjusted (*Banking and Monetary Statistics,* pp. 73–75), were seasonally adjusted. The differences were interpolated to end of month by Method R_2, using as the related series seasonally adjusted interbank balances *minus* bal-

Notes to Table 36

ances with domestic banks of weekly reporting member banks, *ibid.*, pp. 136–151. The value of *b* was 0.468. In 1927 there was a change in the coverage of the related series. Through Jan. 1927 reports on amounts due to banks and balances due from banks were received from weekly reporting member banks only in the twelve Federal Reserve Bank cities; thereafter from all weekly reporting member banks. The differences between due to and due from banks shown in the source at the Wednesday nearest the call date of Dec. 31, 1926, and the following call date of Mar. 23, 1927, are therefore not comparable. The series limited to the twelve Reserve Bank cities are, however, shown together with the new all-weekly reporting data in the *Federal Reserve Bulletin* for some months after Jan. 1927. We used the twelve-city figures through Mar. 23, 1927; the Wednesday figure closest to Mar. 23, 1927, was used on the revised basis in the computation of the interpolator for the following period. In Aug. 1935 the definition of net demand deposits was changed by the Banking Act of 1935. Call date difference figures between net demand deposits and demand deposits adjusted on June 29, 1935, and Nov. 1, 1935, are therefore not comparable. We needed an estimate of net demand deposits for Nov. 1, 1935, on the old basis, to interpolate a value for July, and an estimate for June 29, 1935, on the new basis, to interpolate values for end of Aug., Sept., and Oct. For Nov. 1, 1935, we computed an estimate of net demand deposits on the old basis by adding separate computations for net demand deposits for each reserve class of member banks. Because the old definition permitted offsetting of amounts due to banks only against amounts due from banks (as well as cash items), and the reserve classes differ in respect of the preponderance of amounts due to or balances due from banks, the computation of net demand deposits, when based on aggregate figures for member banks rather than individual bank figures, should be limited to aggregates for banks in the same reserve class. If computed for all member banks as a whole, the total of net demand deposits is considerably smaller than the sum of the results for separate reserve classes. The latter in turn is smaller than the sum of individual bank net demand deposits. This is because the net due to banks that a particular bank counts as part of its net demand deposits will be offset in an aggregate by the balances due from banks of another bank for which there has not been a corresponding due to banks. See *Banking and Monetary Statistics,* p. 66. For June 30, 1935, we used a published estimate of net demand deposits on the new basis (*Federal Reserve Bulletin,* Sept. 1936, p. 700).

c. *Jan. 1936–Apr. 1943:* (i) A published monthly series of gross deposits at all member banks in the form of monthly averages of daily figures was adjusted to represent the Wednesday closest to the end of the month by the same procedure as for Jan. 1929–Dec. 1935, described above. Gross demand deposits at all member banks are

Notes to Table 36 (continued)

from *Banking and Monetary Statistics,* p. 42 and *Federal Reserve Bulletin,* monthly issues, 1942—43. Gross demand deposits at weekly reporting member banks, the sum of individual, partnership, and corporation demand deposits, certified and officers' checks, deposits of states, counties, and municipalities, due to banks, and U.S. government demand deposits, are from *Banking and Monetary Statistics,* pp. 152—163, and *Federal Reserve Bulletin,* monthly issues, 1942—43. The member bank gross demand deposits series, adjusted for dating, required seasonal correction.

(ii) Gross demand deposits are larger than demand deposits adjusted. The difference between these two measures of deposits is known for all member banks at call dates (*Banking and Monetary Statistics,* p. 75 and *Member Bank Call Report,* 1942—1943), and for weekly reporting member banks (the sources listed in (i) above). For nonweekly reporting member banks a call date series was obtained by subtracting the weekly reporting member bank differences series at Wednesday nearest call dates from the call date difference series for all member banks, both seasonally adjusted. Monthly estimates were obtained by interpolation of this call date residual difference series by Method L to Wednesday nearest the end of the month, added to the corresponding difference for weekly reporting member banks, and the total subtracted from the monthly member bank gross demand deposit series.

d. *May 1943—Dec. 1945:* Beginning May 1943 there is a published monthly series of demand deposits adjusted at all member banks. This series required adjustment only for dating and seasonal variation, not for conceptual discrepancies. The data come in the form of monthly averages of daily figures through Mar. 1944, semimonthly averages thereafter. The procedure in adjusting the dating is the same as described for Jan. 1929—Dec. 1935, above. All data are from monthly issues of the *Federal Reserve Bulletin.*

2. Estimates were constructed for four subperiods.

a. *June 1919—June 1923:* Interpolation by Method L to Wednesday nearest end of month between call date figures, Table 33, Part I, col. 17.

b. *June 1923—Dec. 1935:* The call date figures, Table 33, Part I, col. 17, were interpolated to end of month by Method R_2. The value of b was 0.627. As the related series we used net demand deposits at member banks in smaller places from the sources listed for this series at all member banks, in col. 1, above. These data were adjusted: (1) For changes in the classification of cities by size of population (see text, Chap. 14, footnote 13). (2) To shift the series to Wednesday dates nearest end of month. This was done by interpolation by Method L. (3) To estimate a missing observation for Mar. 1933. This was done by interpolation by Method L between the Feb. and Apr. adjusted estimates. (4) To allow for a change in the definition of net demand deposits in Aug. 1935. To do this we had to

Notes to Table 36 (continued)

derive estimates of net demand deposits at member banks in smaller places for June 29, 1935, on the new basis and for Nov. 1, 1935, on the old basis. The published estimate for June 1935 on the new basis for all member banks, mentioned in col. 1 above, was multiplied by the average ratio of net demand deposits at member banks in smaller places to net demand deposits at all member banks, Sept.–Dec. 1935, both on the new basis. The estimate for Nov. 1935 on the old basis for all member banks, which we constructed and which is discussed in col. 1 above, was multiplied by the ratio of net demand deposits at member banks in smaller places to net demand deposits at all member banks in June 1935, both on the old basis. (5) For seasonal.

c. *Jan. 1936–June 1943:* The call date figures, Table 33, Part I, col. 17, were interpolated to end of month by Method R_2. The value of b was 1.156. For the related series we used gross demand deposits at smaller places, from the sources listed for this series at all member banks, in col. 1, above. These data were adjusted: (1) For changes in classification of cities by size of population. (2) To shift the series to Wednesday dates nearest the end of the month. This was done by interpolation by Method L between the monthly figures closest to the desired Wednesday date. (3) To derive an estimate for the call date, Dec. 31, 1935. Since gross demand deposits at member banks in smaller places were not published for dates before Jan. 1936, the figure was derived by multiplying gross demand deposits at all member banks on that date (see the *Member Bank Call Report*) by the ratio in Jan. 1936 of gross demand deposits at member banks in smaller places to gross demand deposits at all member banks. (4) To estimate figures for gross demand deposits at member banks in smaller places after mid-Apr. 1943, when this series was discontinued. The successor series is country bank gross demand deposits excluding interbank deposits at member banks in smaller places. The interpolator used for the balance of the period through 1945 (demand deposits adjusted at country member banks) first became available in July 1943. Gross demand deposits at member banks in smaller places was therefore estimated for end of Apr., May, and June by adding estimates of interbank deposits to the figures for country member banks in smaller places. The interbank deposits estimates were derived by multiplying monthly figures for interbank deposits at country member banks by the ratio of interbank deposits at member banks in smaller centers during the last half of Apr. 1943 (from *Federal Reserve Bulletin,* 1943, p. 636) to interbank balances at country member banks in May 1943. (5) For seasonal.

d. *July 1943–Dec. 1945:* The call date figures, Table 33, Part I, col. 17, were interpolated to end of month by Method R_2, using as the related series demand deposits adjusted at country member banks (from the *Federal Reserve Bulletin,* published as monthly averages of daily figures through Mar. 1944, semimonthly averages thereafter), and interpolated by Method L to Wednesday dates nearest the end of the month. This series did not require seasonal correction. The value of *b* was 1.1252.

3. Col. 1 plus col. 2.
4. Estimates were constructed for four subperiods.
   a. *June 1919—Mar. 1923:* (i) An estimate of net time deposits at non-weekly reporting member banks was added to net time deposits at weekly reporting member banks (from *Banking and Monetary Statistics,* pp. 132—136), to get totals for all member banks. The estimate for nonweekly reporting member banks was computed from the estimating equation

   $$Y = +1219.0 + 0.777X,$$

   where Y = net time deposits at weekly reporting member banks,
   and X = net time deposits at nonweekly reporting member banks. This equation was calculated by least squares from figures for net time deposits at nonweekly reporting member banks, computed by subtracting weekly reporting member bank figures from all member bank figures (*Annual Report* of the Federal Reserve Board, 1927, p. 108; 1928, p. 116). Figures for net time deposits at weekly reporting member banks are from *Banking and Monetary Statistics,* pp. 136—140, at Wednesday nearest call dates and end of month, Apr. 1923—Dec. 1928.   The correlation coefficient was +0.99.
   (ii) Net time deposits includes Postal Savings System deposits at member banks. Monthly estimates of these deposits were deducted from net time deposits to get time deposits adjusted. Monthly estimates of postal savings at member banks were derived by Method L to end of month between call date figures (from *ibid.* p. 73). Before June 1921 the call date figures represent postal savings at national banks only; such deposits at state member banks on that date amounted to approximately $13 million, according to this source.
   b. *Apr. 1923—Aug. 1928:* (i) A published monthly series of net time deposits at all member banks, dated as of a particular day of the month, was adjusted to represent the Wednesday closest to the end of the month. See the detail for col. 1, above. No seasonal variation was observed.
   (ii) Monthly estimates of postal savings at member banks were deducted as described above for June 1919—Mar. 1923.
   c. *Sept. 1928—Sept. 1934:* (i) Same as for 1923—28 above, except that published figures are monthly averages of daily figures.
   (ii) Monthly estimates of postal savings, as above, and of interbank time deposits (now also included in net time deposits), were derived by interpolation by Method L to end of month between call date figures (from *ibid.,* p. 78). The estimates were deducted from net deposits.
   d. *Oct. 1934—Dec. 1945:* (i) Same as for 1923—28, except that published figures are monthly averages of daily figures through Mar. 1944, thereafter semimonthly averages.

Notes to Table 36 (continued)

(ii) Monthly estimates of (a) postal savings redeposited in member banks (beginning Feb. 1939, inclusive of U.S. government time deposits) and (b) interbank time deposits, were deducted from net time deposits to get time deposits adjusted. (1) For Oct. 1934–Feb. 1938 all member bank postal savings figures at end of month were derived by interpolation by Method L between call date figures (from *ibid.,* p. 75). For Mar. 1938–Dec. 1945 all member bank postal savings figures at end of month are the sum of known weekly and estimated nonweekly reporting member bank figures. From the first Wednesday in Jan. 1938 on, postal savings at weekly reporting member banks were reported (*ibid.,* pp. 157–163, and *Federal Reserve Bulletin,* monthly issues, 1942–46). The first call date for which there was a Wednesday figure no more than three days distant came on Mar. 7, 1938. Hence starting that month the weekly reporting member bank figures were used.   These figures include U.S. government time deposits beginning Feb. 1939. To get nonweekly reporting member bank figures, we subtracted the foregoing data at Wednesday nearest call dates from all member bank call date figures (from *Banking and Monetary Statistics,* p. 75, and *Member Bank Call Report,* 1942–45), and interpolated the residuals by Method L to end of month. (2) All member bank interbank time deposits at end of month are the sum of known weekly and estimated nonweekly reporting member bank figures. From the first Wednesday in Sept. 1934 through 1941 interbank time deposits at weekly reporting member banks included deposits of domestic and foreign banks (*Banking and Monetary Statistics,* pp. 149–163); and thereafter of domestic banks only (*Federal Reserve Bulletin,* monthly issues, 1942–46). In the latter source interbank deposits of foreign banks at weekly member banks are not broken down into demand and time categories, and we made no estimate of this breakdown. The first call date for which there was a Wednesday figure no more than three days distant was Oct. 17, 1934. Hence we used the weekly reporting member bank figures starting that month. These banks hold 85 per cent of interbank time deposits at all member banks. We subtracted the seasonally adjusted weekly reporting member bank figures at Wednesday nearest call dates from all member bank figures: through 1941 these included deposits of domestic and foreign banks (*Banking and Monetary Statistics,* p. 78); thereafter the member bank figures included deposits of domestic banks only (*Member Bank Call Report,* 1942–45). We then interpolated the residual series by Method L to end of month. The amount of interbank time deposits of foreign banks at all member banks not deducted from net time deposits, 1942–45, is about $12 million, at the highest.

5. Estimates were constructed for two subperiods.

a. *June 1919–June 1923:*   Interpolation by Method L to Wednesday nearest end of month between call date figures, Table 33, Part II, col. 11.

Notes to Table 36 (concluded)

b. *July, 1923—Dec. 1945:* The call date figures (Table 33, Part II, col. 11 through Apr. 4, 1942; thereafter col. 17) were interpolated by Method R2, using as the related series net time deposits at member banks in smaller places — beginning Apr. 1943, including only country member banks in smaller places — (from Federal Reserve Board, *Annual Report,* 1927, p. 108; 1928, p. 116; 1933, p. 168; 1934, p. 154; 1935, p. 153; *Banking and Monetary Statistics,* p. 42; *Federal Reserve Bulletin,* monthly issues, 1942—46). These data further described in col. 2, above, were adjusted as follows: (1) For changes in Census designations of smaller places; (2) To shift the figures to Wednesday dates nearest the end of month by interpolation by Method L between the monthly figures closest to the desired Wednesday date; and (3) To supply a figure for Mar. 1933, by interpolation by Method L between the reported figures for Feb. and Apr. No seasonal movement was observed in the final series. The value of *b* was 1.051.

6. Col. 4 plus col. 5.

After adjustment for Census changes, the monthly data were shifted to Wednesday dates nearest the end of the month by interpolation by Method L between the monthly figures closest to the desired Wednesday date. In this way also monthly figures for March 1933 were interpolated between the February and April reported figures that had been corrected for Census changes. Net demand deposits, 1923–35, and gross demand deposits, January 1936–March 1943, required seasonal corrections; time deposits, 1923–43, did not.

Beginning May 1943, the Federal Reserve breakdown of deposits at all member banks into banks in larger and smaller centers was discontinued. New series were introduced: gross demand deposits excluding interbank deposits and also time deposits at country member banks in smaller places; time deposits at all country member banks. Beginning July 1943, figures for demand deposits adjusted at all country member

the measure of accumulated change in the distribution of deposits by cities over a period starting from the midpoint of the Census year preceding and reaching its peak at the midpoint of the new Census year. Because an assistant misunderstood our instructions, the adjustment actually made was limited to the terminal five years of each decade. At the much later time when the error was discovered, we decided it was not worthwhile to recompute the adjustment from the midpoint of the prior Census year to the midpoint of the new Census year. Accordingly, the adjustment for changes in the classification of cities was as follows: The difference between the annual average ratios for the year based on the new Census and on the preceding Census was decumulated backward in equal monthly amounts until the zero point at the month that was the midpoint of the decade, 1921–31, and 1930–40; these ratio differences were then subtracted from the monthly ratios of deposits at banks in smaller centers to deposits at all member banks for corresponding months; multiplying all member bank deposit figures by these adjusted ratios yielded figures of deposits in smaller centers corrected for Census changes.

banks were shown. By interpolation by Method L of these data, published as monthly averages of daily figures, we derived series at Wednesday dates nearest the end of the month.

In order to test and use these monthly series as interpolators of our call date nonmember bank figures, we also adjusted their original dating to call dates and seasonally corrected these call date figures when necessary. We then computed values of u and v from the middle call dates of successive overlapping triplets of call dates for relevant periods. The results of these test correlations for the series we finally used and the values of b obtained are tabulated below.

Demand Deposits Adjusted at Nonmember Banks and:	*r*	*b*
Net demand deposits, member banks in small places, June 1923–December 1935	+.455	.627
Gross demand deposits, member banks in smaller places, December 1935–December 1942	+.595	1.156
Demand deposits adjusted, all country member banks, December 1942–June 1946	+.771	1.125

Time Deposits at Nonmember Banks and:		
Time deposits, member banks in smaller places, June 1923–December 1942; and country member banks in smaller places, June 1943–June 1946	+.727	1.051

We did not recognize any discontinuity in the time deposit series used as interpolator by reason of the change in its designation in April 1943. Before that date, the series covered *all* member banks in smaller places, after that date, only country member banks in smaller places.

The final monthly nonmember bank estimates for demand and time deposits adjusted, respectively, derived by using the above interpolators, are shown in Table 36, columns 2 and 5. Summations of member and nonmember bank estimates are shown in columns 3 and 6.

4. Federal Reserve Monthly Data, 1946 to Date

For the period since 1945 we made no estimates of our own but used those of the Federal Reserve. For end-of-month dates beginning December 1942 there are published Federal Reserve figures of demand and time deposits adjusted at all commercial banks. Chart 7 shows our

CHART 7

Two Estimates of Commercial Bank Demand
and Time Deposits, 1943–45

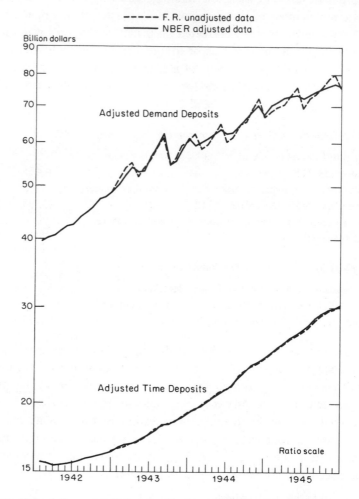

SOURCE: *Federal Reserve Bulletin,* monthly issues beginning Feb. 1944 and Table 36,
cols. 3 and 6.

series, January 1942–December 1945, for adjusted demand and adjusted time deposits, seasonally adjusted, and the Federal Reserve series,
December 1942–December 1945, for adjusted demand and adjusted
time deposits, seasonally unadjusted. The time deposit series are virtually indistinguishable on the same chart. The separate demand de-

posits series are more easily discernible. Our demand deposits series is apparently a fairly good correction of the Federal Reserve series during the period in which they overlap. The August 1943 peak in our series is higher than in the Federal Reserve series, but this may not be an overcorrection, since during this period August is not seasonally low. Accordingly, the peak movement was not smoothed.

Seasonally adjusted figures of end-of-month demand deposits adjusted were published by the Federal Reserve for monthly dates beginning January 1946.[14] We use these figures to continue our series in 1946. Since the Federal Reserve did not seasonally adjust the end-of-month adjusted time deposit series, we made the adjustment ourselves for the four years that the estimates so dated were reported.[15] We use the seasonally adjusted figures in 1946 to continue our adjusted time deposit estimates.

For the period since 1947 we use Federal Reserve seasonally adjusted monthly averages of daily figures of adjusted demand and adjusted time deposits in the latest revision available.[16]

5. Reliability of the Estimates

As a test of our member-nonmember bank estimates, we computed, for the national-nonnational breakdown, monthly estimates, 1919–22, of demand and time deposits adjusted that are similar to the estimates for the years before 1919. We compared these estimates with those constructed for the member-nonmember bank breakdown (see Chart 8). Differences in the levels of the alternative estimates are more striking than the differences in month-to-month variation. Estimates of time deposits at all commercial banks are higher when they are a summation of member and nonmember bank estimates than when they are a summation of national and nonnational bank estimates. The member-nonmember totals of demand deposits adjusted tend to be lower than the national-nonnational totals. As Table 35, Part III, shows, in order to construct demand deposits adjusted for the national-nonnational break-

14 *Federal Reserve Bulletin*, Feb. 1960, p. 135.
15 *Ibid.*, monthly issues beginning Feb. 1944 and continuing through Feb. 1947. See Chapter 8, section 4, for a review of the changes in dating of the Federal Reserve monthly estimates since 1947.
16 *Ibid.*, Oct. 1969, pp. 790–793.

CHART 8

Two Estimates of Commercial Bank Demand and Time Deposits, 1919–23

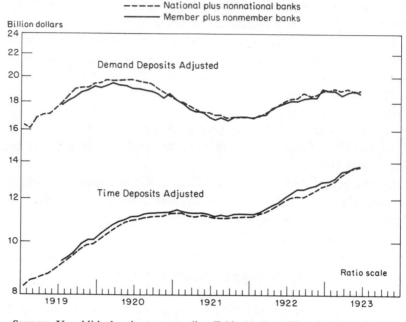

SOURCE: Unpublished estimates extending Table 35, Part III, cols. 5 and 9, and Table 36, cols. 3 and 6.

down beginning June 1917, it was necessary to deduct an estimate of government deposits from estimates of demand deposits less duplications. For the member-nonmember bank breakdown this procedure was not required. Particularly during the latter half of 1919 and 1920 there are marked discrepancies between the national-nonnational and member-nonmember bank estimates of demand deposits adjusted.

We accepted the member-nonmember summations in preference to the national-nonnational summations, 1919–23, because a much larger proportion of the former total was based on directly reported rather than interpolated data. In general, this distinction holds for the two periods 1907–19 and 1919–45 for which we present estimates. It reflects the fact that for member banks we had at the outset a basic monthly series, although it was not constituted precisely as we wished and therefore required some adjustment; for nonmember and national and non-national banks we had only call date figures and such monthly inter-polators as were available. The percentage of directly reported monthly data for national and nonnational banks separately is therefore negligible. Such data are directly reported only when a call date coincides with the end-of-month date (see Table 37). For banks in New York, the nine urbanized states, and the District of Columbia, the related series we used for interpolation impress us favorably. Although our monthly figures for all banks in the thirty-eight rural states were obtained by interpolation by Method L, the reader should bear in mind that for national banks the data are known for five or six call dates annually during the period covered. On the average then, only every other monthly figure for the national bank component had to be estimated. Deposits at national banks in the thirty-eight rural states, 1907–14, were approximately 45 per cent of deposits in all banks in those states; demand deposits, 1914–23, about the same percentage; and time deposits, 1914–23, about a third of the corresponding figures for all banks in the thirty-eight rural states. For nonnational banks in the rural group, however, we know little more than the June bench-mark data, between which we interpolated monthly estimates by Method L.

In brief, the national-nonnational bank deposit totals seem to us a good approximation, the member-nonmember bank totals, a better approximation to the true movements of the series.

TABLE 37

Reported and Interpolated Deposits in Various Classes of Banks at End of Month as Percentages of Total Deposits Adjusted, Demand Deposits Adjusted, and Time Deposits Adjusted, 1907–45

Class of Banks and Period Covered	Per Cent of Total			
	Reported (1)	Interpolated By Method L (2)	By Method R (3)	Total Cols. 1+2+3 (4)
Total Deposits Adjusted				
1907–14				
New York State national banks	–	–	7.0	7.0
New York State nonnational banks and all banks, 9 urbanized states and District of Columbia	1.0	–	55.0	56.0
All commercial banks, 38 rural states	–	37.0	–	37.0
Total	1.0	37.0	62.0	100.0
Demand Deposits Less Duplications,a or Demand Deposits Adjusted				
1914–19				
New York State national banks	0.3	–	10.7	11.0
New York State nonnational banks and all banks, 9 urbanized states and District of Columbia	1.6	–	52.4	54.0
All commercial banks, 38 rural states	1.1	33.9	–	35.0
Total	3.0	33.9	63.1	100.0

1919–23				
Member banks	47.0	—	{ 11.3[b] / 22.7[c] }	81.0
Nonmember banks	—	19.0	—	19.0
Total	47.0	19.0	34.0	100.0
1923–35				
Member banks	68.7	—	12.3	81.0
Nonmember banks	0.8	—	18.2	19.0
Total	69.5	—	30.5	100.0
1936–43				
Member banks	75.3	—	—	81.0
Nonmember banks	1.5	5.7[d]	17.5	19.0
Total	76.8	5.7	17.5	100.0
Time Deposits Adjusted				
1914–19				
New York State national banks[e]	0.1	—	3.9	4.0
New York State nonnational banks and all banks, 9 urbanized states and District of Columbia[f]	1.1	—	53.9	55.0
All commercial banks, 38 rural states	1.2	39.8	—	41.0
Total	2.4	39.8	57.8	100.0
1919–23				
Member banks	32.4	0.7[g]	38.9[h]	72.0
Nonmember banks	—	28.0	—	28.0
Total	32.4	28.7	38.9	100.0
1923–45				
Member banks	70.6	1.4	—	72.0
Nonmember banks	1.4	—	26.6	28.0
Total	72.0	1.4	26.6	100.0

Notes to Table 37

[a]U.S. government demand deposits are 0.07 per cent of demand deposits less duplications, 1917−19.

[b]Represents correction of net demand deposits to obtain demand deposits adjusted; for June 1919−Apr. 1920, the correction was made by Method L.

[c]Represents estimate of net demand deposits at nonweekly reporting member banks.

[d]Represents correction of call date differences between gross demand and demand deposits adjusted at nonweekly reporting member banks.

[e]From June to Dec. 1914, by interpolation using Method L.

[f]From June to Dec. 1914, by interpolation using Method L; from Jan. 1915 to Dec. 1917, a residual derived from two sets of estimates.

[g]Represents correction of net time deposits to obtain time deposits adjusted.

[h]Represents estimate of net time deposits at nonweekly reporting member banks.

15

DEPOSITS AT MUTUAL SAVINGS BANKS: CALL DATE AND MONTHLY ESTIMATES

THIS CHAPTER describes our estimates of deposits at mutual savings banks beginning 1907. We also constructed such estimates for 1867–75. For the intervening period, 1875–1906, estimates made by other investigators are available. Details of the construction of the estimates covering the forty-year period before 1907 are given in Chapter 11.

Mutual savings banks were in operation in eighteen states for part or all of the period 1907–46. Most of these states were in New England and the East, a few, in the Middle West and along the Pacific coast. We compiled deposit data for mutual savings banks in all eighteen states, making no distinction between demand and time deposits although small amounts of demand deposits were sometimes reported. Our series therefore represents total deposits less amounts due to banks. Our primary sources were the reports of the respective state banking departments. We checked these against the annual reports of the U.S. Comptroller of the Currency and for more recent dates, against FDIC data.

Our monthly estimates of deposits at mutual savings banks were constructed in two sections: 1907–23, when call date figures are available for a group of ten states and annual figures for the remaining states; and 1924–46, when there are available monthly figures for New York, call date figures for a group of states, and annual figures for the remaining states.

For 1907–23 we interpolated missing call date figures for the six New England states by Method R_3 and then interpolated them to the end of month by Method L. For the remaining states we interpolated monthly figures by Method L between closest reported figures—at call dates for four of the other states and annually for the rest. The final aggregate series required seasonal adjustment.

For 1924–46 we interpolated missing call date figures for nine states (six New England states and three eastern states excluding New York and Pennsylvania) by Method R_3. The resulting call date series was seasonally corrected and interpolated to end of month by Method R_2, using the deseasonalized monthly New York series as the related series. For the remaining states deposits were interpolated to end of month by Method L between closest report dates. The aggregate of deposits at all mutual savings banks, 1924–46, required further seasonal adjustment.

1. Problems of Compilation

Our sources included published and unpublished returns by state banking departments; the sections on mutual savings banks in the annual reports of the U.S. Comptroller of the Currency; and, since 1945, *Assets and Liabilities of Operating Insured Banks* of the FDIC. All demand and time deposits reported, excluding interbank deposits and postal savings redeposited in mutual savings banks, were included in our figures. The call date and annual data reported create problems because of (a) conflicts between alternative sources with respect to the number of mutual savings banks in operation or the amounts on deposit; (b) the occasional mingling of deposit items with miscellaneous liabilities; and (c) the combination of mutual savings bank with certain commercial bank—most often stock savings bank—returns. Our solutions to these problems are noted in the source notes by states in the appendix to this chapter.

The one monthly series available covers all mutual savings banks in New York State beginning January 1924. Beginning January 1935, the series represented 100 per cent coverage. For earlier years the monthly figures included some estimates. Names of banks from which reports had not been received were known. Deposits at these banks as of the latest report date were used by the compiler of the series, the Savings Bank Association of the State of New York, to get total deposits. Except at mid- and end-of-year the monthly series included only deposits in regular accounts. A small amount of deposits, of minor importance, was held in club, school-savings, and Christmas accounts in mutual savings banks. The level of the monthly series is not much affected by the exclusion of these deposits, but a characteristic seasonality imparted by these accounts is missing. At June and December dates, however, the figures included total deposits.[1]

2. Mutual Savings Bank Report Dates

The report dates of nonnational commercial banks, by states, 1907–46, tended to coincide with national and member bank call dates. This is not true for mutual savings banks, however, except for mid- and end-of-year dates. Because there was some concentration of report dates other than June and December, at end of month, we adopted the end of month as the average date of reporting. Dates falling between the sixteenth of a given month and the fifteenth of the following month were treated as the end of the given month. In monthly interpolation we treated all months as of equal duration.

For twelve states in 1907 and six states in 1908 no figure was reported at the annual bench mark. We estimated deposits at the bench-mark dates by interpolation by Method L between the closest report dates for each of these states. In the same way we estimated missing June bench-mark figures for Pennsylvania in 1917 and 1919.

Except in selected years before 1914 annual bench marks were end of June dates. The bench marks in the exceptional years are as follows:

Year	End of Month Bench Mark
1907	May
1909	April
1911	May
1912	May
1913	May

[1] Beginning 1934, the original compiler of the series used December figures for total deposits. From 1936 on, except in 1941 and 1946, the June figure of the monthly series has agreed with the figure of total deposits reported by the Superintendent of the New York State Banking Department. This may be an indication that there were only "regular" deposits at mutuals at June dates and negligible amounts of club and Christmas savings, or else that "nonregular" deposits have not been consistently excluded in the compilation of the monthly series. We might have used the published monthly figures to interpolate between the June and December figures of total deposits, but the variation between the latter and the monthly figures for those dates was too small, except at June 1941 and 1946, for the resulting monthly estimates to be substantially different from the published series.

3. Mutual Savings Bank Deposits, by States

To estimate missing call date figures, we tried to classify the states with mutual savings banks into homogeneous groups. Within each group we proposed to estimate the missing figures from deposit data for the other states by Method R_3. In order to select groups and to estimate the relevant parameters, we calculated values of v for each state with inter-June observations, taking the June bench-mark figures as the values of Y_0 and Y_2. We then computed coefficients of correlation of the v's for random pairs of states, and standard deviations of the v's for all states with a minimum of twenty-five inter-June observations over the whole period.

As the following tabulation shows, the correlation results suggested a geographical pattern in the behavior of deposits. The average correlation was $+.43$ for pairs of states in New England and the East. The corresponding average for Midwestern and Pacific states was $+.23$. Evidently there is not much relationship between the movements of deposits at mutual savings banks in the latter group of states.

Pairs	n [a]	r [b]
New England and East		
N.J., Maine	35	.550
Maine, Vt.	25	.353
N.J., Md.	36	.341
Conn., Maine	25	.595
Midwest and Pacific		
Minn., Wis.	25	.244
Ohio, Minn.	8	.054
Wis., Ore.	8	.410
Ind., Wis.	8	.147

[a] There may be more intra-annual observations for an individual state than are listed here as the number of observations on which the correlations were based. The size of n was obviously limited by the number of comparable dates for the pairs of states shown.

[b] The correlation coefficient for Connecticut and Pennsylvania (seasonally adjusted data) is $+.279$ with $n = 58$. We did not use this result. See below.

The standard deviations of the v's by states also suggest that the New England and Eastern states are different from the rest. The standard deviations are markedly higher for the Midwestern and Pacific states.

SIZE OF STANDARD DEVIATION OF v, BY STATES

	1907–23		1907–46	
	Average Deposits (millions of dollars)	*Standard Deviation*	*Average Deposits (millions of dollars)*	*Standard Deviation*
Eastern				
Md.	103	.25	175	.81
N.Y.	1,945	.96	3,912	.97
Penna.	231	1.72 (.80)[a]	433	1.44 (.78)[a]
N.J.	115	3.82	283	.87
New England				
Mass.	966	.50	1,675	.60
Maine	95	.65	121	.59
Conn.	330	.67	570	.61
Vt.	40	1.29	67	1.34
Midwestern				
Ind.			20	1.68
Minn.			57	1.93
Wis.			5	2.38
Pacific				
Wash.			57	2.22

[a] Seasonally adjusted data.

There is some tendency for the standard deviations to be high when average deposits are low, and conversely, but the relation is extremely weak. Both before and after 1924 the standard deviations seem sufficiently homogeneous for the New England states to justify treating them as equal to one another. This is also true for the Eastern states after 1924 and for New England and Eastern states combined. However, before 1924 the standard deviations for the Eastern states vary so widely that we decided there was no satisfactory way of combining them with the other states. Accordingly, before 1924 we used Method R_3 for the New England states only, thereafter for New England plus the Eastern states.

These results were based on data before seasonal adjustment. In general, mutual savings bank deposits exhibit only mild seasonal movements. For some states, however, the seasonal movements may be sufficiently pronounced to change the results if seasonally adjusted instead of original figures are used. For example, original data for Pennsylvania yield results that differ from those for other New England and Eastern states: correlations with other states are low in this group and the standard deviation is relatively high. Seasonally adjusted data, however, improve the correlation results and bring the standard deviation within the range for other Eastern states.

It may be that the low correlation results for the Midwestern and Pacific states—the observations on which these results are based are relatively small in number, even if they are for the largest number of comparable dates available for the pairs of states involved—would be raised if the data were corrected for seasonal. However, the small number of observations renders seasonal correction of the data for individual states hardly feasible. Seasonal movements present in these figures may be offsetting in the aggregates we constructed. At any rate, the seasonal corrections necessary in our final series, as described below, were slight in amplitude.

4. Scheme of Interpolation at Call Dates and Ends of Month

On the basis of the foregoing findings we divided the total period into two parts, 1907–23 and 1924–46. The steps by which we constructed final monthly series during each subperiod may be summarized as follows.

Subperiod 1907–23

1. We interpolated missing inter-June call date figures in the group of New England states only, by Method R_3, using an average of the correlation coefficients $(+.45)$ for the two pairs of states from this region shown in the tabulation in the preceding section, and assuming the standard deviation of the v's to be the same in all states. Deposits in these states represented just over 40 per cent of total mutual savings deposits.

2. The estimates or reported observations at each call date for the New England states were then summed and monthly estimates were

interpolated by Method L between the call dates (Table 38, column 1).

3. For nine other states (excluding New York and Pennsylvania) with mutual savings banks in operation for part or all of the period, we interpolated by Method L between closest reported figures to obtain end-of-month figures (Table 38, column 2). Deposits in those states approximated 9 per cent of total mutual savings deposits.

4. End-of-month estimates for Pennsylvania were interpolated by Method L between quarterly or three-times-yearly call date figures (Table 38, column 3).

5. For New York State, we interpolated monthly figures by Method L between the semiannual (or occasionally three-times-yearly) reported figures (Table 38, column 4). Deposits in New York averaged somewhat less than one-half of total mutual savings bank deposits.[2]

6. The aggregate of the separate components of our mutual savings bank deposit series was deseasonalized (Table 38, column 5).

Subperiod 1924–46

1. We interpolated missing inter-June call date figures in the combined group of New England and Eastern states (excluding New York and Pennsylvania) by Method R_3, using an average of the correlation coefficients (+.43) for the first three pairs of states from this region shown in the tabulation in the preceding section.[3] The estimates or reported observations at each call date for the group of states were then summed.

2. The resulting series was deseasonalized. Test values of u were computed for each call date between preceding and following call dates and correlated with corresponding values of v computed from the deseasonalized monthly New York series. The correlation coefficient was .77. Accordingly, monthly figures for the combined group of New England and Eastern states (excluding New York and Pennsylvania) were therefore interpolated between call dates by Method R_2 (Table 39, column 1).

[2] We investigated the possibility of transforming the semiannual New York data, 1907–23, into a quarterly series on the basis of unpublished quarterly series on amounts deposited and withdrawn and net change in amounts deposited at five New York City savings banks (in the files of the National Bureau). The exclusion of interest compounded on deposits from the potential interpolator made it impossible to use the data directly. It did not seem worthwhile to invest effort in determining the rate at which interest was paid during this period by the five banks and adjusting the series for interest payments before we could test the closeness of the relationship between the quarterly and semiannual series.

[3] The correlation coefficient for the fourth pair of states shown (New England) was computed after the interpolation for 1924–46 was completed. Had we included it, the average r would have been raised to +.45.

TABLE 38

Deposits at Mutual Savings Banks by Groups of States,
at End of Month, May 1907 – November 1923
(millions of dollars)

End of Month	All New England States (1)	Other States Excluding New York & Pennsylvania (2)	Pennsylvania (3)	New York State (4)	All States, Seasonally Adjusted (5)
1907					
May	1,214	256	158	1,389	3,019
June	1,218	257	157	1,394	3,011
July	1,221	256	157	1,392	3,017
Aug.	1,224	257	157	1,390	3,027
Sept.	1,226	257	156	1,387	3,030
Oct.	1,222	257	156	1,385	3,023
Nov.	1,223	257	156	1,383	3,021
Dec.	1,223	255	156	1,380	3,017
1908					
Jan.	1,223	255	157	1,380	3,021
Feb.	1,223	255	157	1,380	3,021
Mar.	1,223	254	158	1,379	3,018
Apr.	1,223	254	159	1,379	3,018
May	1,224	254	159	1,379	3,019
June	1,226	253	159	1,378	3,000
July	1,226	253	158	1,381	3,010
Aug.	1,227	254	158	1,384	3,024
Sept.	1,228	255	158	1,387	3,032
Oct.	1,229	257	157	1,390	3,036
Nov.	1,233	258	157	1,393	3,044
Dec.	1,238	259	159	1,396	3,055
1909					
Jan.	1,243	261	160	1,399	3,068
Feb.	1.247	263	162	1,401	3,079
Mar.	1,252	265	163	1,403	3,086
Apr.	1,256	266	165	1,406	3,096
May	1,264	267	165	1,425	3,124
June	1,271	268	165	1,445	3,133
July	1,274	269	165	1,451	3,149
Aug.	1,276	270	165	1,458	3,168
Sept.	1,278	270	165	1,464	3,181
Oct.	1,284	272	165	1,471	3,195
Nov.	1,288	273	166	1,477	3,208
Dec.	1,293	274	168	1,483	3,221

(continued)

TABLE 38 (continued)

End of Month	All New England States (1)	Other States Excluding New York & Pennsylvania (2)	Pennsylvania (3)	New York State (4)	All States, Seasonally Adjusted (5)
1910					
Jan.	1,297	276	169	1,491	3,239
Feb.	1,302	278	170	1,498	3,253
Mar.	1,306	279	171	1,505	3,265
Apr.	1,310	281	172	1,512	3,280
May	1,315	283	173	1,520	3,295
June	1,319	285	175	1,527	3,290
July	1,322	285	175	1,530	3,302
Aug.	1,326	285	175	1,532	3,318
Sept.	1,329	286	175	1,535	3,328
Oct.	1,337	286	175	1,538	3,339
Nov.	1,341	286	176	1,540	3,347
Dec.	1,345	286	178	1,543	3,356
1911					
Jan.	1,350	288	179	1,547	3,370
Feb.	1,354	290	180	1,550	3,381
Mar.	1,358	291	182	1,554	3,389
Apr.	1,362	293	183	1,558	3,400
May	1,367	295	185	1,561	3,411
June	1,372	295	185	1,594	3,429
July	1,376	295	185	1,598	3,444
Aug.	1,380	295	185	1,603	3,463
Sept.	1,384	296	185	1,607	3,474
Oct.	1,383	296	185	1,611	3,479
Nov.	1,389	296	186	1,615	3,490
Dec.	1,394	297	187	1,619	3,501
1912					
Jan.	1,399	299	189	1,622	3,516
Feb.	1,405	300	190	1,625	3,527
Mar.	1,410	302	191	1,628	3,535
Apr.	1,415	304	193	1,631	3,546
May	1,421	305	195	1,633	3,557
June	1,444	306	195	1,661	3,587
July	1,442	307	195	1,665	3,598
Aug.	1,440	308	195	1,670	3,613
Sept.	1,439	308	195	1,675	3,621
Oct.	1,445	309	195	1,680	3,633
Nov.	1,450	310	197	1,685	3,645
Dec.	1,456	311	198	1,689	3,658

(continued)

TABLE 38 (continued)

End of Month	All New England States (1)	Other States Excluding New York & Pennsylvania (2)	Pennsylvania (3)	New York State (4)	All States, Seasonally Adjusted (5)
1913					
Jan.	1,461	313	200	1,692	3,674
Feb.	1,467	316	201	1,694	3,685
Mar.	1,472	318	203	1,696	3,693
Apr.	1,478	321	205	1,698	3,704
May	1,483	323	206	1,700	3,716
June	1,497	323	207	1,725	3,732
July	1,493	323	207	1,727	3,739
Aug.	1,489	323	207	1,730	3,749
Sept.	1,496	323	207	1,733	3,763
Oct.	1,495	323	207	1,736	3,766
Nov.	1,502	323	209	1,739	3,776
Dec.	1,508	323	210	1,742	3,786
1914					
Jan.	1,514	325	211	1,747	3,805
Feb.	1,518	327	212	1,752	3,817
Mar.	1,523	329	213	1,757	3,826
Apr.	1,527	331	215	1,763	3,839
May	1,531	332	216	1,768	3,851
June	1,535	334	217	1,773	3,841
July	1,538	333	217	1,773	3,849
Aug.	1,536	331	216	1,773	3,856
Sept.	1,537	330	216	1,772	3,859
Oct.	1,538	328	215	1,772	3,858
Nov.	1,541	327	216	1,772	3,860
Dec.	1,544	326	217	1,772	3,862
1915					
Jan.	1,550	327	218	1,772	3,875
Feb.	1,553	328	219	1,772	3,879
Mar.	1,556	329	220	1,773	3,881
Apr.	1,559	330	220	1,773	3,886
May	1,562	331	221	1,774	3,891
June	1,565	332	222	1,774	3,873
July	1,571	332	222	1,782	3,895
Aug.	1,578	332	222	1,789	3,921
Sept.	1,585	332	222	1,797	3,940
Oct.	1,586	332	222	1,804	3,949
Nov.	1,595	333	223	1,812	3,967
Dec.	1,605	333	225	1,819	3,986

(continued)

TABLE 38 (continued)

End of Month	All New England States (1)	Other States Excluding New York & Pennsylvania (2)	Pennsylvania (3)	New York State (4)	All States, Seasonally Adjusted (5)
1916					
Jan.	1,614	335	227	1,830	4,013
Feb.	1,623	336	229	1,841	4,037
Mar.	1,632	338	231	1,851	4,057
Apr.	1,641	340	233	1,862	4,080
May	1,651	342	235	1,873	4,104
June	1,660	344	237	1,883	4,103
July	1,669	347	238	1,895	4,136
Aug.	1,678	350	239	1,907	4,173
Sept.	1,687	353	239	1,918	4,203
Oct.	1,699	356	240	1,930	4,230
Nov.	1,705	359	241	1,942	4,251
Dec.	1,711	363	246	1,954	4,277
1917					
Jan.	1,717	362	249	1,960	4,292
Feb.	1,723	361	253	1,966	4,299
Mar.	1,729	361	255	1,973	4,309
Apr.	1,735	361	253	1,979	4,320
May	1,741	361	252	1,985	4,331
June	1,747	361	251	1,991	4,342
July	1,749	362	250	1,991	4,347
Aug.	1,750	363	248	1,990	4,356
Sept.	1,752	370	247	1,989	4,367
Oct.	1,747	371	246	1,988	4,361
Nov.	1,746	372	244	1,987	4,359
Dec.	1,745	373	246	1,987	4,359
1918					
Jan.	1,744	373	248	1,987	4,358
Feb.	1,743	374	250	1,988	4,352
Mar.	1,742	374	254	1,989	4,351
Apr.	1,741	375	253	1,990	4,350
May	1,741	375	249	1,991	4,347
June	1,740	375	246	1,992	4,344
July	1,747	378	247	2,000	4,368
Aug.	1,755	381	248	2,008	4,397
Sept.	1,763	384	249	2,017	4,422
Oct.	1,767	387	256	2,025	4,444
Nov.	1,777	391	261	2,034	4,471
Dec.	1,787	395	266	2,042	4,498

(continued)

TABLE 38 (continued)

End of Month	All New England States (1)	Other States Excluding New York & Pennsylvania (2)	Pennsylvania (3)	New York State (4)	All States, Seasonally Adjusted (5)
1919					
Jan.	1,796	400	268	2,065	4,534
Feb.	1,806	404	270	2,088	4,564
Mar.	1,816	409	273	2,111	4,599
Apr.	1,826	414	275	2,133	4,639
May	1,836	418	277	2,156	4,678
June	1,846	422	278	2,179	4,715
July	1,857	425	279	2,194	4,750
Aug.	1,867	429	280	2,208	4,789
Sept.	1,878	433	280	2,223	4,823
Oct.	1,892	436	282	2,238	4,858
Nov.	1,906	440	283	2,253	4,892
Dec.	1,920	444	285	2,267	4,926
1920					
Jan.	1,934	448	286	2,289	4,963
Feb.	1,948	451	288	2,311	4,994
Mar.	1,962	454	289	2,333	5,029
Apr.	1,977	457	291	2,355	5,069
May	1,991	460	291	2,377	5,108
June	2,005	463	290	2,398	5,146
July	2,013	460	291	2,421	5,180
Aug.	2,022	458	291	2,443	5,220
Sept.	2,031	470	292	2,465	5,269
Oct.	2,030	473	296	2,488	5,297
Nov.	2,033	475	300	2,510	5,330
Dec.	2,036	478	305	2,533	5,362
1921					
Jan.	2,046	479	306	2,552	5,388
Feb.	2,055	480	307	2,571	5,408
Mar.	2,064	480	308	2,590	5,433
Apr.	2,065	481	307	2,610	5,452
May	2,066	482	306	2,629	5,472
June	2,067	482	305	2,648	5,492
July	2,068	481	304	2,656	5,504
Aug.	2,068	481	302	2,664	5,521
Sept.	2,069	480	301	2,672	5,533
Oct.	2,070	480	304	2,680	5,545
Nov.	2,073	479	306	2,688	5,558
Dec.	2,077	479	309	2,696	5,572

(continued)

TABLE 38 (concluded)

End of Month	All New England States (1)	Other States Excluding New York & Pennsylvania (2)	Pennsylvania (3)	New York State (4)	All States, Seasonally Adjusted (5)
1922					
Jan.	2,091	481	309	2,712	5,599
Feb.	2,105	482	310	2,728	5,619
Mar.	2,119	484	310	2,744	5,646
Apr.	2,117	485	309	2,760	5,659
May	2,114	485	308	2,775	5,671
June	2,111	485	307	2,791	5,683
July	2,124	488	306	2,808	5,720
Aug.	2,136	492	305	2,825	5,763
Sept.	2,148	495	304	2,842	5,801
Oct.	2,176	498	304	2,859	5,849
Nov.	2,186	502	310	2,876	5,885
Dec.	2,195	505	315	2,892	5,919
1923					
Jan.	2,219	509	317	2,918	5,968
Feb.	2,242	513	319	2,943	6,011
Mar.	2,266	516	322	2,968	6,060
Apr.	2,281	519	322	2,994	6,103
May	2,296	522	322	3,019	6,146
June	2,311	524	322	3,044	6,189
July	2,322	527	322	3,061	6,226
Aug.	2,334	530	322	3,077	6,270
Sept.	2,346	532	322	3,094	6,307
Oct.	2,350	535	327	3,111	6,335
Nov.	2,364	538	331	3,127	6,373

Source, by Column

1. Sums of reported and estimated figures for Conn., Me., Mass., N. H., R. I., Vt. See text, Chap. 15, Appendix, for sources and adjustments to reported figures. Missing call date figures interpolated by Method R$_3$ (r = .45, standard deviations assumed same for all six states); monthly estimates interpolated by Method L between call dates.

2. Sums of reported and estimated figures for Del., Ind., Md., Minn., N. J., Ohio, Wash. (beginning Sept. 1917), W. Va. (included through Mar. 1922), and Wis. See text for sources and adjustments to reported figures. Missing monthly estimates interpolated by Method L.

3. 4. See text for sources and adjustments to reported figures. Missing monthly estimates interpolated by Method L between the closest call dates for which there were reported figures.

5. Sum of cols., 1, 2, 3, and 4, corrected for seasonal variation.

TABLE 39

Deposits at Mutual Savings Banks by Groups of States,
at End of Month, December 1923 – December 1946

(millions of dollars)

End of Month	All New England & Selected Eastern States (1)	Other States Excluding New York & Pennsylvania (2)	Pennsylvania (3)	New York State (4)	All States, Seasonally Adjusted (5)
1923					
Dec.	2,755	175	335	3,138	6,403
1924					
Jan.	2,765	176	337	3,162	6,440
Feb.	2,772	177	338	3,173	6,460
Mar.	2,785	178	339	3,204	6,506
Apr.	2,791	179	339	3,198	6,507
May	2,804	179	338	3,212	6,534
June	2,824	180	338	3,248	6,589
July	2,837	181	337	3,270	6,625
Aug.	2,845	182	337	3,274	6,638
Sept.	2,860	184	337	3,302	6,682
Oct.	2,866	185	343	3,332	6,726
Nov.	2,886	186	347	3,358	6,778
Dec.	2,909	187	352	3,391	6,839
1925					
Jan.	2,921	188	353	3,402	6,864
Feb.	2,934	190	354	3,418	6,896
Mar.	2,947	191	356	3,431	6,924
Apr.	2,960	192	356	3,455	6,963
May	2,969	193	356	3,468	6,987
June	2,986	195	356	3,503	7,040
July	2,998	196	356	3,506	7,056
Aug.	3,012	198	356	3,517	7,083
Sept.	3,014	199	356	3,488	7,057
Oct.	3,027	201	362	3,554	7,143
Nov.	3,045	202	367	3,577	7,191
Dec.	3,064	204	372	3,600	7,240

(continued)

TABLE 39 (continued)

End of Month	All New England & Selected Eastern States (1)	Other States Excluding New York & Pennsylvania (2)	Pennsylvania (3)	New York State (4)	All States, Seasonally Adjusted (5)
1926					
Jan.	3,066	206	373	3,587	7,232
Feb.	3,084	207	374	3,625	7,290
Mar.	3,095	209	375	3,639	7,317
Apr.	3,105	210	375	3,654	7,345
May	3,117	211	376	3,672	7,376
June	3,135	212	376	3,708	7,431
July	3,147	214	377	3,726	7,464
Aug.	3,159	216	377	3,744	7,496
Sept.	3,176	217	378	3,777	7,549
Oct.	3,183	219	384	3,805	7,591
Nov.	3,216	221	389	3,868	7,694
Dec.	3,227	223	394	3,857	7,701
1927					
Jan.	3,241	224	396	3,882	7,743
Feb.	3,255	226	398	3,905	7,783
Mar.	3,272	227	400	3,940	7,839
Apr.	3,286	228	400	3,949	7,864
May	3,305	230	401	3,978	7,914
June	3,325	231	402	4,004	7,961
July	3,343	232	402	4,029	8,006
Aug.	3,361	234	402	4,051	8,047
Sept.	3,383	235	402	4,090	8,110
Oct.	3,410	237	408	4,114	8,168
Nov.	3,441	239	415	4,147	8,242
Dec.	3,467	241	422	4,160	8,289
1928					
Jan.	3,484	242	424	4,185	8,336
Feb.	3,500	244	427	4,204	8,375
Mar.	3,518	245	427	4,214	8,404
Apr.	3,540	247	427	4,245	8,459

(continued)

TABLE 39 (continued)

End of Month	All New England & Selected Eastern States (1)	Other States Excluding New York & Pennsylvania (2)	Pennsylvania (3)	New York State (4)	All States, Seasonally Adjusted (5)
1928					
May	3,558	248	427	4,257	8,490
June	3,574	249	427	4,267	8,517
July	3,586	251	429	4,287	8,553
Aug.	3,601	253	430	4,316	8,600
Sept.	3,618	255	431	4,352	8,656
Oct.	3,634	256	437	4,376	8,702
Nov.	3,650	258	442	4,387	8,738
Dec.	3,669	260	448	4,402	8,778
1929					
Jan.	3,669	260	448	4,401	8,778
Feb.	3,675	261	449	4,423	8,808
Mar.	3,677	262	449	4,426	8,813
Apr.	3,686	262	447	4,421	8,816
May	3,697	263	446	4,422	8,828
June	3,709	263	445	4,428	8,845
July	3,713	263	444	4,438	8,858
Aug.	3,715	263	444	4,444	8,866
Sept.	3,720	262	443	4,457	8,882
Oct.	3,730	262	446	4,403	8,842
Nov.	3,723	263	450	4,386	8,822
Dec.	3,721	263	454	4,382	8,820
1930					
Jan.	3,732	264	458	4,407	8,861
Feb.	3,744	265	461	4,436	8,907
Mar.	3,757	266	464	4,469	8,956
Apr.	3,770	367	464	4,489	8,990
May	3,784	267	464	4,510	9,025
June	3,797	267	465	4,530	9,059
July	3,811	267	466	4,577	9,121
Aug.	3,821	267	467	4,609	9,164

(continued)

TABLE 39 (continued)

End of Month	All New England & Selected Eastern States (1)	Other States Excluding New York & Pennsylvania (2)	Pennsylvania (3)	New York State (4)	All States, Seasonally Adjusted (5)
1930					
Sept.	3,836	266	469	4,662	9,233
Oct.	3,848	266	480	4,691	9,285
Nov.	3,849	268	490	4,723	9,330
Dec.	3,859	270	500	4,786	9,416
1931					
Jan.	3,879	271	506	4,878	9,534
Feb.	3,887	272	512	4,928	9,598
Mar.	3,893	273	517	4,973	9,655
Apr.	3,914	274	520	5,039	9,747
May	3,931	275	523	5,088	9,816
June	3,942	276	526	5,120	9,864
July	3,944	274	528	5,154	9,900
Aug.	3,948	272	530	5,194	9,944
Sept.	3,951	270	532	5,231	9,984
Oct.	3,962	268	525	5,254	10,009
Nov.	3,959	267	518	5,276	10,020
Dec.	3,943	265	511	5,251	9,970
1932					
Jan.	3,894	264	510	5,230	9,897
Feb.	3,891	262	509	5,242	9,905
Mar.	3,896	261	508	5,277	9,942
Apr.	3,885	259	508	5,273	9,924
May	3,870	258	507	5,259	9,894
June	3,862	256	506	5,266	9,890
July	3,851	255	505	5,264	9,874
Aug.	3,838	254	503	5,259	9,854
Sept.	3,832	252	502	5,277	9,863
Oct.	3,819	252	507	5,282	9,860
Nov.	3,827	251	512	5,286	9,876
Dec.	3,837	250	517	5,296	9,901

(continued)

TABLE 39 (continued)

End of Month	All New England & Selected Eastern States (1)	Other States Excluding New York & Pennsylvania (2)	Pennsylvania (3)	New York State (4)	All States, Seasonally Adjusted (5)
1933					
Jan.	3,831	247	514	5,306	9,899
Feb.	3,813	244	511	5,269	9,837
Mar.	3,787	241	508	5,204	9,740
Apr.	3,772	237	505	5,174	9,688
May	3,752	234	502	5,128	9,616
June	3,741	231	499	5,115	9,586
July	3,736	231	498	5,095	9,561
Aug.	3,731	231	497	5,074	9,534
Sept.	3,732	232	496	5,074	9,534
Oct.	3,730	232	495	5,059	9,516
Nov.	3,738	232	501	5,049	9,520
Dec.	3,748	232	506	5,046	9,532
1934					
Jan.	3,750	234	508	5,057	9,549
Feb.	3,754	236	510	5,076	9,575
Mar.	3,755	238	510	5,107	9,610
Apr.	3,766	239	510	5,107	9,622
May	3,776	240	510	5,105	9,631
June	3,776	241	511	5,120	9,648
July	3,780	242	510	5,124	9,657
Aug.	3,768	243	510	5,069	9,590
Sept.	3,790	245	510	5,140	9,684
Oct.	3,788	246	510	5,138	9,681
Nov.	3,794	247	517	5,140	9,698
Dec.	3,797	249	523	5,135	9,704
1935					
Jan.	3,805	250	524	5,132	9,710
Feb.	3,817	251	525	5,147	9,740
Mar.	3,817	252	525	5,169	9,763
Apr.	3,823	253	525	5,168	9,769

(continued)

TABLE 39 (continued)

End of Month	All New England & Selected Eastern States (1)	Other States Excluding New York & Pennsylvania (2)	Pennsylvania (3)	New York State (4)	All States, Seasonally Adjusted (5)
1935					
May	3,828	254	525	5,168	9,775
June	3,836	254	525	5,172	9,787
July	3,840	255	526	5,171	9,793
Aug.	3,844	257	527	5,168	9,796
Sept.	3,851	258	527	5,174	9,810
Oct.	3,859	259	528	5,171	9,817
Nov.	3,866	260	535	5,175	9,836
Dec.	3,870	261	542	5,168	9,841
1936					
Jan.	3,876	262	544	5,167	9,849
Feb.	3,884	263	546	5,177	9,870
Mar.	3,894	264	547	5,188	9,893
Apr.	3,900	265	548	5,185	9,897
May	3,906	265	549	5,181	9,901
June	3,916	266	550	5,196	9,928
July	3,924	267	551	5,207	9,949
Aug.	3,929	269	552	5,213	9,963
Sept.	3,934	270	553	5,218	9,976
Oct.	3,942	271	555	5,220	9,988
Nov.	3,946	272	561	5,222	10,002
Dec.	3,950	273	570	5,225	10,018
1937					
Jan.	3,963	274	572	5,234	10,042
Feb.	3,976	274	573	5,248	10,072
Mar.	3,990	274	574	5,262	10,099
Apr.	3,998	274	574	5,261	10,106
May	4,005	274	574	5,261	10,113
June	4,009	273	574	5,248	10,104
July	4,018	274	574	5,278	10,143
Aug.	4,020	274	574	5,286	10,154

(continued)

TABLE 39 (continued)

End of Month	All New England & Selected Eastern States (1)	Other States Excluding New York & Pennsylvania (2)	Pennsylvania (3)	New York State (4)	All States, Seasonally Adjusted (5)
1937					
Sept.	4,020	275	574	5,286	10,154
Oct.	4,006	276	577	5,266	10,125
Nov.	4,003	276	580	5,271	10,130
Dec.	3,998	276	583	5,271	10,129
1938					
Jan.	3,998	277	584	5,279	10,138
Feb.	4,000	277	585	5,297	10,159
Mar.	4,001	278	584	5,313	10,176
Apr.	3,998	278	582	5,314	10,172
May	3,997	278	581	5,323	10,179
June	3,991	277	580	5,316	10,165
July	3,993	278	579	5,340	10,191
Aug.	3,991	278	579	5,348	10,196
Sept.	3,989	279	578	5,357	10,202
Oct.	3,991	279	583	5,374	10,227
Nov.	3,987	280	587	5,381	10,235
Dec.	3,982	281	592	5,383	10,238
1939					
Jan.	3,991	281	593	5,406	10,271
Feb.	4,002	281	595	5,431	10,309
Mar.	4,010	281	596	5,462	10,350
Apr.	4,014	281	595	5,474	10,364
May	4,017	282	595	5,487	10,380
June	4,019	282	594	5,493	10,387
July	4,022	283	593	5,530	10,428
Aug.	4,020	284	592	5,546	10,441
Sept.	4,015	285	591	5,551	10,441
Oct.	4,024	285	595	5,563	10,467
Nov.	4,018	286	599	5,569	10,472
Dec.	4,014	287	603	5,577	10,481

(continued)

TABLE 39 (continued)

End of Month	All New England & Selected Eastern States (1)	Other States Excluding New York & Pennsylvania (2)	Pennsylvania (3)	New York State (4)	All States, Seasonally Adjusted (5)
1940					
Jan.	4,020	288	607	5,605	10,520
Feb.	4,026	289	611	5,632	10,558
Mar.	4,033	290	614	5,659	10,596
Apr.	4,038	291	613	5,671	10,612
May	4,037	291	611	5,661	10,601
June	4,035	292	610	5,647	10,584
July	4,033	292	612	5,642	10,579
Aug.	4,032	293	613	5,646	10,585
Sept.	4,033	294	615	5,651	10,593
Oct.	4,038	295	617	5,646	10,595
Nov.	4,037	295	618	5,662	10,613
Dec.	4,034	296	620	5,665	10,615
1941					
Jan.	4,043	296	620	5,653	10,613
Feb.	4,055	297	620	5,652	10,624
Mar.	4,065	297	621	5,644	10,627
Apr.	4,064	297	621	5,638	10,620
May	4,060	298	621	5,621	10,599
June	4,061	298	621	5,626	10,606
July	4,053	298	620	5,586	10,557
Aug.	4,052	298	620	5,572	10,542
Sept.	4,048	299	619	5,550	10,516
Oct.	4,041	300	622	5,565	10,528
Nov.	4,044	300	624	5,563	10,531
Dec.	4,040	301	626	5,533	10,500
1942					
Jan.	4,011	301	621	5,422	10,354
Feb.	4,007	300	616	5,401	10,325
Mar.	4,002	300	610	5,376	10,288
Apr.	4,006	300	610	5,384	10,301

(continued)

TABLE 39 (continued)

End of Month	All New England & Selected Eastern States (1)	Other States Excluding New York & Pennsylvania (2)	Pennsylvania (3)	New York State (4)	All States, Seasonally Adjusted (5)
1942					
May	4,010	301	611	5,390	10,311
June	4,021	301	611	5,421	10,354
July	4,034	304	615	5,422	10,376
Aug.	4,053	308	620	5,443	10,424
Sept.	4,067	312	624	5,444	10,446
Oct.	4,086	315	629	5,470	10,500
Nov.	4,106	319	633	5,514	10,572
Dec.	4,125	322	637	5,552	10,637
1943					
Jan.	4,149	326	642	5,583	10,700
Feb.	4,175	330	646	5,622	10,773
Mar.	4,197	334	651	5,646	10,828
Apr.	4,224	338	655	5,688	10,905
May	4,254	342	660	5,743	10,998
June	4,286	345	664	5,807	11,103
July	4,320	351	670	5,879	11,219
Aug.	4,351	356	676	5,942	11,325
Sept.	4,364	362	682	5,943	11,351
Oct.	4,406	367	685	5,994	11,452
Nov.	4,441	373	700	6,075	11,589
Dec.	4,474	379	711	6,149	11,713
1944					
Jan.	4,510	384	718	6,209	11,821
Feb.	4,542	390	724	6,258	11,914
Mar.	4,573	396	734	6,303	12,006
Apr.	4,614	401	738	6,396	12,149
May	4,654	406	746	6,483	12,288
June	4,693	411	753	6,570	12,427
July	4,732	419	764	6,636	12,551
Aug.	4,779	427	775	6,729	12,710

(continued)

TABLE 39 (concluded)

End of Month	All New England & Selected Eastern States (1)	Other States Excluding New York & Pennsylvania (2)	Pennsylvania (3)	New York State (4)	All States, Seasonally Adjusted (5)
1944					
Sept.	4,820	435	786	6,803	12,844
Oct.	4,874	442	797	6,911	13,024
Nov.	4,920	450	808	7,006	13,184
Dec.	4,966	458	818	7,094	13,337
1945					
Jan.	5,016	465	829	7,190	13,501
Feb.	5,068	473	838	7,295	13,674
Mar.	5,117	480	844	7,386	13,827
Apr.	5,179	487	855	7,515	14,036
May	5,230	495	862	7,601	14,188
June	5,288	502	870	7,714	14,374
July	5,343	510	880	7,806	14,539
Aug.	5,403	518	891	7,917	14,729
Sept.	5,455	525	901	7,995	14,876
Oct.	5,500	532	911	8,094	15,037
Nov.	5,550	540	921	8,177	15,188
Dec.	5,600	547	932	8,262	15,341
1946					
Jan.	5,650	552	939	8,343	15,484
Feb.	5,699	557	945	8,419	15,620
Mar.	5,743	562	952	8,477	15,735
Apr.	5,798	567	959	8,577	15,902
May	5,849	572	967	8,660	16,048
June	5,905	577	973	8,766	16,241
July	5,939	581	978	8,843	16,341
Aug.	5,969	585	983	8,902	16,438
Sept.	5,985	588	988	8,910	16,472
Oct.	6,026	592	994	8,976	16,589
Nov.	6,050	595	1,001	9,049	16,695
Dec.	6,078	599	1,007	9,135	16,819

3. For six other states (excluding New York and Pennsylvania) with mutual savings banks in operation for part or all of the period, end-of-month figures were interpolated by Method L between closest reported figures (Table 39, column 2).

4. For Pennsylvania, end-of-month estimates were interpolated by Method L between quarterly and three-times-yearly call date figures, as described for 1907–23 (Table 39, column 3).

5. The monthly series for New York, shown with seasonal corrections in Table 39, column 4, is described in section 1 of this chapter.

6. The aggregate of the separate components of our mutual savings bank deposit series required further seasonal correction (Table 39, column 5).

5. Federal Reserve Estimates, 1947 to Date

Beginning January 1947 we use the published monthly last-Wednesday Federal Reserve series of deposits at mutual savings banks, in seasonally adjusted form, as a continuation of our series (see Chart 9).[4] We aver-

---

[4] For the original data for 1947 see *Federal Reserve Bulletin,* Mar. 1948, p. 303, and June 1948, p. 683; for 1948–60 see *Supplement to Banking and Monetary Statistics,* Section 1, Board of Governors of the Federal Reserve System, Oct. 1962, pp. 15, 17, 19; thereafter, *Federal Reserve Bulletin,* monthly issues, table showing consolidated condition statement for banks and the monetary system, since Jan. 1968 given on p. A-17 or

---

Notes to Table 39

Source, by Column

1. Sums of reported and estimated figures for the six New England and for three Eastern states (Del., Md., and N.J.). See text, Chap. 15, for sources and adjustments to reported figures. Missing call date figures were interpolated by Method R_3 ($r = 0.43$, standard deviations assumed the same for all states). Monthly estimates were interpolated by Method R_2, using deseasonalized New York series in col. 4 as related series and a value of b of 0.367.

2. Sums of reported and estimated figures for Ind., Minn., Ohio, Ore. (beginning Jan. 1932), Wash., and Wis. See text, Chap. 15, for sources and adjustments to reported figures. Missing monthly estimates were interpolated by Method L between the closest dates for which there were reported figures.

3, 4. See text for description of these series.

5. Sum of cols. 1, 2, 3, and 4, corrected for seasonal variation.

CHART 9

Two Estimates of Mutual Savings Bank Deposits, 1943–47

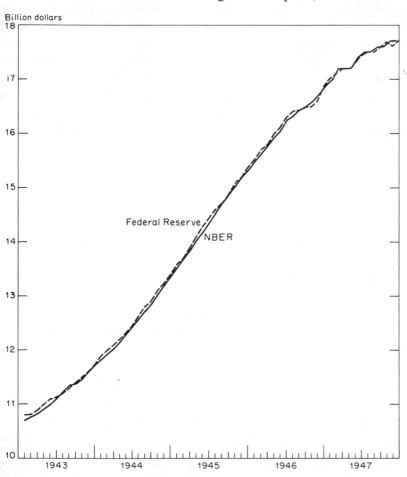

SOURCE: *Federal Reserve Bulletin,* monthly issues beginning Feb. 1944 and
Table 39, col. 5.

age pairs of the last Wednesday of the month to get figures centered at
midmonth.

A-18. A very mild seasonal movement characterizes the series. The factors we computed
are as follows:

Jan.	100.0	July	100.2
Feb.	100.0	Aug.	100.0
Mar.	100.2	Sept.	100.1
Apr.	100.1	Oct.	99.9
May	100.1	Nov.	99.2
June	100.3	Dec.	99.9

The Federal Reserve basic data for mutual savings banks for the half year January–June 1947 differ from ours in that they represent gross deposits including amounts due to banks and postal savings redeposited in mutual savings banks.[5] These items are excluded from the Federal Reserve estimates from June 30, 1947, to June 30, 1961.[6] While the items are relatively minor in amount, on an arithmetic scale the difference between the level of our series and that of the Federal Reserve is perceptible. Difference in the relative movements of the series is less marked. We do not believe that the discontinuity between the two series is appreciable enough to impair the validity of our decision to join them.

6. Reliability of the Estimates

We summarize the character of our series in Table 40. It provides information on two aspects of our procedure. First, it shows the percentage distribution of deposits at mutual savings banks among four classes of states for each of the two periods, 1907–23 and 1924–46 (column 5). Second, it presents a summary of the different constitution of the final series in the two periods (totals in columns 2, 3, and 4).

The percentages in column 5 invite no special comment. In the later period they show a slight increase in the concentration of mutual savings bank deposits in New York State and a corresponding decline elsewhere outside Pennsylvania. The most striking feature of Table 40, however, is the difference between the two periods in percentage of final monthly series obtained from direct reports. For the early period, only 19 per cent of the final series represents directly reported data; for the later

---

[5] The Federal Reserve monthly mutual savings bank deposit series may be compared at June dates with the annual series in *All-Bank Statistics, United States, 1896–1955,* Board of Governors of the Federal Reserve System, Washington, D.C., 1959, p. 48. The level of the monthly series is higher than that of the annual gross deposits series; therefore, it is possible that the monthly series includes liabilities other than deposits. The June 1947 monthly figure equals the sum of "other time," interbank, and government time deposits, given in *All-Bank Statistics* in the June 1947 breakdown. The monthly June figures, 1948–55, agree with the annual "other time" deposit figures.

[6] Through Dec. 1960 the Federal Reserve mutual savings deposit figure at June and December dates agreed with the figure for total time deposits excluding interbank time deposits given in annual reports of the FDIC for total mutual savings banks. For dates after 1960 it is not possible to determine the coverage of the Federal Reserve figure from the breakdowns given in the FDIC reports. The Federal Reserve monthly figures are described as follows in a footnote: "Beginning with June 1961 includes amounts now reported by insured mutual savings banks as demand deposits previously reported as time deposits or other liabilities" (*Federal Reserve Bulletin,* Aug. 1962, p. 1009). The change

TABLE 40

Reported and Interpolated Deposits at Mutual Savings Banks in Various States as Percentages of Aggregate Mutual Savings Bank Deposits, 1907–1946

States With Mutual Savings Banks	Por Cent of Total Mutual Savings Bank Doposito			
		Interpolated		Total
	Reported (1)	By Method L (2)	By Method R (3)	Cols. 1+2+3 (4)
1907–23				
New York	9.4	37.6	–	47.0
Pennsylvania	1.1[a]	3.9	–	5.0
New England	7.0	25.0	7.0	39.0
Other States	1.4	7.6	–	9.0
Total	18.9	74.1	7.0	100.0
1924–46				
New York	53.0	–	–	53.0
Pennsylvania	1.8[a]	4.2	–	6.0
New England and Selected Eastern States	8.7	–	29.3	38.0
Other States	0.5	2.5	–	3.0
Total	64.0	6.7	29.3	100.0

[a]The percentage of reported deposits includes a correction by Method L of under 1 per cent of the average of mutual savings bank deposits in Pennsylvania.

period the percentage is 64. The difference is almost wholly accounted for by the availability of a monthly series for New York beginning 1924.

Nearly all of the interpolation required to obtain the final series for the early period was accomplished by Method L; only a small percentage by Method R. For the later period, when 36 per cent of the final series was interpolated, we relied mostly on Method R.

in the reporting was enforced by an amendment of July 14, 1960, to the Federal Deposit Insurance Act, which authorized deductions of 16⅔ per cent of demand deposits and 1 per cent of time and savings deposits from the base on which the deposit insurance assessment was levied.

The error involved in interpolation by Method L clearly depends on the variability of a series between dates for which there are direct reports. Our examination of data for frequent report dates suggests that mutual savings deposits show little variability. We suspect that the true values of total mutual savings deposits seldom deviate more than 1 per cent from a straight-line trend between reported figures.

For this reason we believe that our monthly series for 1907–23 may be viewed with confidence despite the extensive use of interpolation by Method L. Our series for 1924–46 has of course a much smaller margin of error. It ranks high in reliability among the series we have constructed.

Appendix to Chapter 15
SOURCES OF MUTUAL SAVINGS BANK DEPOSIT DATA

Connecticut: Report of the Bank Commissioner of the State of Connecticut (Fall call dates); Connecticut Bank Department, *Quarterly Bulletin,* Nos. 5, 7, 10–14 (monthly dates, 1914–15; possibly preliminary data—October dates in this source do not agree with Bank Commissioner's *Report*); unpublished data, examined in the Office of the Director of Bank Examinations, Connecticut Banking Department (Dec. 31, 1921 and 1922; quarterly dates, 1923–45); *Annual Report* of the U.S. Comptroller of the Currency (June dates).

Delaware: Delaware Insurance Department, *Banks and Banking* (estimates shown for mutual savings banks deposits, June 1909, combined with deposits of other banks in this source); *Annual Report* of the Comptroller of the Currency and of the State Bank Commissioner of Delaware.

Indiana: Auditor of Indiana, *Report of the Bank Department* (in the *Indiana Year Book*), 1917–20; *Annual Report* of the Department of Banking of Indiana; *Annual Report* of the Department of Financial Institutions of Indiana; *Annual Report* of the U.S. Comptroller of the Currency.

Maine: Annual Report of the Bank Commissioner, Banking Department, Maine (call dates), and unpublished data, 1920–46, from the Bank Commissioner's Office (quarterly dates); *Annual Report* of the U.S. Comptroller of the Currency.

Maryland: Annual Report of the Bank Commissioner, Banking Department, Maryland (December dates); unpublished June data, 1910, 1913–16, and 1934, obtained from the Federal Reserve Board; *Annual Report* of the U.S. Comptroller of the Currency (other June dates).

Massachusetts: Annual Report of the Commissioner of Banks of Massachusetts; also mimeographed "Comparative Statement of Condition of All Savings Banks," issued by the Commissioner of Banks; *Annual Report* of the U.S. Comptroller of the Currency.

Minnesota: Annual Report of Minnesota Banking Department; *Abstract of Reports of Condition of Minnesota Banks* (available to us beginning 1917); *Annual Report* of the U.S. Comptroller of the Currency. At report dates other than June 1917–28, estimated deposits at stock savings banks were deducted from published figures for mutual and stock savings banks combined.

New Hampshire: Annual Report of the New Hampshire Bank Commissioner; *Annual Report* of the Comptroller of the Currency, 1909, 1911–13, 1915, 1944–46. Deposits at guaranty savings banks were deducted from reported figures for mutual and guaranty savings banks combined.

New Jersey: Annual Report of the Commissioner of Banking and Insurance of New Jersey; unpublished data, 1927–46, from the State of New Jersey Department of Banking and Insurance; *Annual Report* of the Comptroller of the Currency (June figures through 1941). At midyear dates, 1907–08 and 1919–20, estimated amounts of deposits at the Paterson Savings Institution, a stock savings bank, were deducted. The state reports present December data for all savings banks combined, but also include returns from individual banks. By subtracting the figures for the Paterson Savings Institution from the state report aggregate for all savings banks, it was possible to obtain December figures for deposits at mutual savings banks.

Unpublished state figures for mutual savings banks only are available for all call dates beginning 1927. For June dates, 1942–46, this was the source of our figures. At December dates, 1941–44, the Comptroller's figures are slightly larger than the state report figures; in December 1946, $100,000 smaller. We used the Comptroller's figures in cases of disagreement.

Beginning December 1936, figures for two associations—institutions possessing the characteristics of both a savings bank and a building and loan association, in that all of the deposits are invested in bonds and mortgages and each depositor has the privilege of making a mortgage loan—must be added to the savings bank aggregate in the state reports. (The Comptroller includes these associations in mutual savings bank data throughout the period.)

New York: Annual Report, Part II, of New York State Superintendent of Banks and of U.S. Comptroller of the Currency; FDIC, *Assets and Liabilities of Operating Insured Banks,* 1945–46. The State report figure for July 1, 1914, is not in agreement with the Comptroller's figures for June 30, 1914. We used the former. Monthly figures for dates other than June and December, beginning January 1924, were obtained from *Survey of Current Business Supplement, 1932,* pp. 76–77; *1936,* p. 47; *1938,* p. 56; *1940,* p. 52; *1942,* p. 65; *1947,* p. 75, and deseasonalized by us.

Ohio: Annual Report of U.S. Comptroller of the Currency and FDIC, *Assets and Liabilities of Operating Insured Banks,* June 1946. The State Division of Banks publishes abstracts of the condition of mutual savings and commercial banks combined.

Oregon: Annual Report of the Oregon Banking Department and U.S. Comptroller of the Currency. The first Oregon mutual savings bank was chartered October 1931.

Pennsylvania: Annual Report of Commissioner of Banking of Pennsylvania and of U.S. Comptroller of the Currency; unpublished data, 1918–46, from Pennsylvania Department of Banking. Figures exclude deposits at a stock savings bank, from unpublished Federal Reserve data at midyear dates, from *Annual Report* of U.S. Comptroller of the Currency at December dates, 1936–46, and from interpolation by Method L at other dates.

Rhode Island: Annual Report of: the Bank Commissioner; the Chief of Division of Banking and Insurance, Division of Banking, Department of Taxation and Regulation; and the Banking Bureau, Department of Business Regulation, State of Rhode Island. *Annual Report* of the U.S. Comptroller of the Currency. In 1918–19 the Comptroller properly classified subscriptions to United States Liberty Loan bonds as deposits —shown as "other liabilities" in the State reports. In 1925 the Comptroller includes an item, "reserved for depositors' interest" in deposits. Because this classification does not seem defensible, we followed the state report in this instance.

Vermont: Annual Report of the Commissioner of Banking and Insurance of Vermont and of U.S. Comptroller of the Currency; unpublished data received from the Commissioner's Office (1920–46); and FDIC, *Assets and Liabilities of Operating Insured Banks.* State report for June 1907 shows two totals for mutual savings deposits, and discrepancy cannot now be correctly explained; we accepted the version selected by the Federal Reserve Board. Comptroller's data, June 1914 and 1935, are preliminary figures; state report figures for these years are final. FDIC figures were used, June 1941 and 1943.

Washington: Annual Report of the State Banking Supervisor, Division of Banks, Washington, and of U.S. Comptroller of the Currency; and FDIC, *Assets and Liabilities of Operating Insured Banks.* The first Washington mutual savings bank was formed on September 12, 1917.

West Virginia: Annual Report of Bank Commissioner of West Virginia and of U.S. Comptroller of the Currency. The latter source, 1918 and 1921, disagrees with the state report, but according to the Federal Reserve Board, U.S. Comptroller figures agreed with reports on file for these years submitted and signed by the cashier of the single mutual savings bank trust company in April 1922.

Wisconsin: Annual Report of Wisconsin Commissioner of Banking (Fall dates) and of U.S. Comptroller of the Currency (midyear dates). Quarterly reports available for all Wisconsin banks combined do not segregate mutual savings banks returns.

16

DEPOSITS WITH THE POSTAL SAVINGS SYSTEM

THE POSTAL SAVINGS SYSTEM was established by an Act of Congress in 1910 and went into operation January 3, 1911, with the opening of postal savings banks in each state. Depositors' balances including outstanding principal and unclaimed deposits, but excluding accrued interest outstanding and postal savings stamps (which were sold until September 1942), were compiled by us from the *Annual Report of Operations of the Postal Savings System* for monthly dates beginning January 1911. Beginning 1914, annual figures are available on depositors' balances in the Possessions. We obtained a monthly series by interpolating by Method L between the annual figures. We deducted the monthly series from the balances to the credit of all depositors of postal savings. The residual series, which was seasonally adjusted, January 1913–July 1930, therefore represents all postal savings deposits to the credit of depositors in the continental United States.

The government did not keep funds received on deposit on hand but transferred them back to the banks throughout the United States and the Possessions, or alternatively invested them in government securities. Up to 90 per cent of postal savings were redeposited in banks through 1932; thereafter the proportion redeposited dwindled, as the payment of the 2½ per cent interest required by the government became burdensome to the banks. We excluded amounts redeposited in banks from our figures of time deposits at all banks in the United States, and present total deposits with the Postal Savings System, including both amounts redeposited in banks and amounts not so redeposited, minus amounts deposited in the Possessions. Small differences between our series and the published Federal Reserve postal savings series—end of the month, 1943–46, last Wednesday of month thereafter—are attributable to Federal Reserve exclusion of amounts redeposited in banks outside the continental United States rather than amounts to the credit of depositors there.[1] Beginning November 1955, we show Federal Reserve figures in Table 1. The Postal Savings System was discontinued on April 27, 1966, by the Act of March 28, 1966. Entries for Postal Savings System deposits were given in the *Federal Reserve Bulletin* on a preliminary basis through September 27, 1967; entries on a revised basis were eliminated after June 30, 1967.

[1] See Chapter 15, footnote 4, for sources of the Federal Reserve postal savings series.

17

UNITED STATES GOVERNMENT
BALANCES

THE U.S. GOVERNMENT holds cash balances in a number of different forms: (1) At the Treasury in Washington and mint and assay offices in the form of currency, notes in process of retirement, and gold and silver bullion in excess of specific liabilities against them; (2) at other government departments and bureaus in the form of currency; (3) at commercial and mutual savings banks in the form of demand or time deposits to the credit of the U.S. Treasurer or other government officers; (4) at Federal Reserve Banks in the form of demand deposits to the credit of the U.S. Treasurer.

Government deposits at commercial and mutual savings banks (item 3) are not for the most part drawn upon directly by the Treasury for disbursements to the public. The bulk of these deposits is held in so-called special depositaries. When the government wishes to draw on its deposits, it instructs the banks in question to transfer stated amounts to the U.S. Treasurer's account at each of the Federal Reserve Banks (item 4). These deposits at the Federal Reserve Banks (and its branches) are the checking accounts of the government from which nearly all payments to the public are made.

Government deposits included in item 3 are also maintained in classes of depositaries other than special depositaries. A relatively insignificant fraction of government payments is made by checks drawn on accounts in these depositaries by postmasters, clerks of U.S. courts, and other government officers.

We include item 2 in our estimates of the public's currency holdings because we regard these as balances held by the federal government in its role as one of the agencies cooperating in the production and distribution of goods and services—a role comparable to that played by states and municipalities—rather than in its role as the ultimate monetary authority. We exclude item 1 from the public's currency holdings because we treat these as balances held by the federal government in its role as an ultimate monetary authority, and hence as amounts that it could arbitrarily change, e.g., by printing and holding currency it is authorized to print or by destroying currency on hand, without any effects on the rest of the economy.

We exclude both items 3 and 4 from the public's deposit holdings for the same reasons that we exclude item 1 from the public's currency holdings. This is not fully justified since some part of the government's deposits are clearly held in its role as an operating agency and should be treated on a par with the deposits of states and municipalities, which are included in full in our deposit estimates. However, we have been able to find no way to distinguish operating balances from monetary balances. We have therefore excluded the whole of government deposits as a lesser evil than including them.

In view of our treatment of these various components of Treasury balances, we needed separate estimates for items 1, 3, and 4. For these items our final estimates are given in Table A-3 of *A Monetary History*. They are for annual and semiannual dates, 1867–1907, and monthly thereafter. Call date figures from 1907 on, used in constructing the call date estimates of the public's holdings of currency and deposits presented in earlier chapters, are given in Table 41.

Items 1 and 4 are readily available (section 1). Item 3 requires extensive estimation, especially after 1917 (sections 2 to 4).

Until 1917 only national banks were eligible depositaries of government funds. Hence, call date figures on the amounts of government deposits can be taken directly from the balance sheets of these banks and require no further discussion. A monthly series was derived by adding monthly data for government deposits in clearinghouse banks of various cities to deposits in nonclearinghouse banks. Deposits in nonclearinghouse banks were estimated at call dates by subtracting deposits in clearinghouse banks from deposits at all national banks. These call date figures were interpolated by Method L to end of month (section 4). Beginning April 1917, we needed estimates for nonnational banks, since direct bank record information on government demand deposits in non-

TABLE 41

United States Government Balances,
Call Dates, 1907–46
(seasonally adjusted, in millions of dollars)

| | | U. S. Government Balances | |
| | | At Commercial and | At Federal |
Call Date[a]	Treasury Cash (1)	Savings Banks (2)	Reserve Banks (3)
1907			
May 20	340	196	
Aug. 22	327	160	
Dec. 3	262	206	
1908			
Feb. 14	297	258	
May 14	332	197	
July 15	330	130	
Sept. 23	306	137	
Nov. 27	279	124	
1909			
Feb. 5	314	110	
Apr. 28	315	69	
June 23	303	69	
Sept. 1	304	52	
Nov. 16	304	48	
1910			
Jan. 31	310	46	
Mar. 29	302	47	
June 30	312	50	
Sept. 1	301	54	
Nov. 10	313	48	
1911			
Jan. 7	315	44	
Mar. 7	309	45	
June 7	318	44	
Sept. 1	352	52	
Dec. 5	348	46	
1912			
Feb. 20	344	60	
Apr. 18	343	52	
June 14	362	54	
Sept. 4	362	64	
Nov. 26	371	45	

(continued)

TABLE 41 (continued)

| Call Date[a] | U. S. Government Balances | | |
	Treasury Cash (1)	At Commercial and Savings Banks (2)	At Federal Reserve Banks (3)
1913			
Feb. 4	369	50	
Apr. 4	358	45	
June 4	365	46	
Aug. 9	351	57	
Oct. 21	345	90	
1914			
Jan. 13	328	81	
Mar. 4	324	66	
June 30	323	61	
Sept. 12	339	75	
Oct. 31	347	69	
Dec. 31	425	62	
1915			
Mar. 4	409	59	
May 1	385	50	
June 23	359	45	
Sept. 2	333	48	
Nov. 10	296	40	15
Dec. 31	297	31	17
1916			
Mar. 7	280	32	10
May 1	288	37	41
June 30	299	36	101
Sept. 12	322	37	42
Nov. 17	307	34	25
Dec. 27	292	30	29
1917			
Mar. 5	241	34	13
May 1	252	38	57
June 20	242	176	429
Sept. 11	256	398	29
Nov. 20	221	2,607	206
Dec. 31	230	709	101
1918			
Mar. 4	274	1,277	110
May 10	275	1,841	139
June 29	292	1,691	91

(continued)

TABLE 41 (continued)

		U. S. Government Balances	
Call Date[a]	Treasury Cash (1)	At Commercial and Savings Banks (2)	At Federal Reserve Banks (3)
1918			
Aug. 31	264	928	76
Nov. 1	262	1,988	249
Dec. 31	294	497	51
1919			
Mar. 4	356	1,028	202
May 12	368	1,070	131
June 30	393	985	51
Sept. 12	399	1,030	34
Nov. 17	416	449	89
Dec. 31	393	685	31
1920			
Feb. 28	333	115	127
May 4	256	229	29
June 30	242	284	25
Sept. 8	214	88	41
Nov. 15	225	253	15
Dec. 29	224	335	27
1921			
Feb. 21	218	210	62
Apr. 28	240	309	34
June 30	205	425	43
Sept. 6	207	203	59
Dec. 31	219	319	96
1922			
Mar. 10	217	379	22
May 5	223	267	64
June 30	224	169	33
Sept. 15	219	271	44
Dec. 29	229	486	9
1923			
Apr. 3	223	450	76
June 30	212	381	34
Sept. 14	213	176	39
Dec. 31	214	316	38
1924			
Mar. 31	227	266	100
June 30	223	231	43

(continued)

TABLE 41 (continued)

| Call Date[a] | U. S. Government | | |
	Treasury Cash (1)	At Commercial and Savings Banks (2)	At Federal Reserve Banks (3)
1924			
Oct. 10	232	347	45
Dec. 31	212	321	51
1925			
Apr. 6	209	456	25
June 30	207	227	25
Sept. 28	207	342	32
Dec. 31	204	409	16
1926			
Apr. 12	228	423	48
June 30	204	293	11
Dec. 31	202	310	17
1927			
Mar. 23	198	369	6
June 30	214	279	31
Oct. 10	207	498	20
Dec. 31	209	353	18
1928			
Feb. 28	205	99	28
June 30	203	333	24
Oct. 3	208	186	33
Dec. 31	203	350	23
1929			
Mar. 27	201	378	23
June 29	207	452	36
Oct. 4	215	367	38
Dec. 31	217	191	29
1930			
Mar. 27	211	296	24
June 30	213	358	27
Sept. 24	210	308	43
Dec. 31	212	347	19
1931			
Mar. 25	210	445	51
June 30	228	495	47
Sept. 29	223	616	22
Dec. 31	223	532	54

(continued)

TABLE 41 (continued)

| | | U. S. Government Balances | |
Call Date[a]	Treasury Cash (1)	At Commercial and Savings Banks (2)	At Federal Reserve Banks (3)
1932			
June 30	222	477	4
Sept. 30	261	847	51
Dec. 31	274	600	8
1933			
June 30	268	973	35
Oct. 25	277	980	28
Dec. 31	286	1,201	10
1934			
Mar. 5	3,282	1,730	38
June 30	2,999	1,867	64
Oct. 17	2,947	1,228	53
Dec. 31	3,047	1,734	121
1935			
Mar. 4	2,895	1,452	91
June 29	2,913	865	102
Nov. 1	2,603	697	54
Dec. 31	2,581	807	544
1936			
Mar. 4	2,506	695	379
June 30	2,538	1,189	690
Dec. 31	2,390	864	244
1937			
Mar. 31	2,739	477	311
June 30	3,501	700	93
Dec. 31	3,641	728	142
1938			
Mar. 7	3,549	862	182
June 30	2,340	602	860
Sept. 28	2,783	752	864
Dec. 31	2,722	766	923
1939			
Mar. 29	2,708	896	1,201
June 30	2,605	808	944
Oct. 2	2,272	738	507
Dec. 30	2,424	739	634

(continued)

TABLE 41 (concluded)

| Call Date[a] | U. S. Government Balances | | |
	Treasury Cash (1)	At Commercial and Savings Banks (2)	At Federal Reserve Banks (3)
1940			
Mar. 26	2,369	853	701
June 29	2,222	844	250
Dec. 31	2,226	642	368
1941			
Apr. 4	2,219	595	979
June 30	2,312	751	980
Sept. 24	2,322	860	379
Dec. 31	2,228	1,631	867
1942			
Apr. 4	2,147	2,329	289
June 30	2,223	1,921	290
Dec. 31	2,206	8,251	799
1943			
June 30	2,305	7,849	455
Oct. 18	2,308	18,698	487
Dec. 31	2,317	10,110	579
1944			
Apr. 13	2,287	12,323	264
June 30	2,333	19,106	650
Dec. 30	2,389	19,975	440
1945			
Mar. 20	2,349	13,376	120
June 30	2,316	23,892	599
Dec. 31	2,301	23,960	977
1946			
June 29	2,288	13,202	833

[a]For national banks through 1922; for member banks thereafter.

Source, by Column

1. *May 1907—Oct. 1914:* Interpolated by Method L between seasonally adjusted sums of first-of-month data — for cash, excluding minor coin (from *Circulation Statement of U. S. Money*), and for minor coin, (from the Treasury *Daily Statement*), here dated as of end of the preceding month. *Dec. 1914—Dec. 1921:* Interpolated by Method L between

national or nonmember banks is unavailable. We made call date estimates by using equations relating the ratio of demand deposits adjusted
to government deposits at nonnational or nonmember banks to the corresponding ratio for national banks. We estimated these equations from
data for insured nonnational, insured nonmember banks, and national
banks, 1934–46 (sections 2 and 3). A monthly series was derived by
adding monthly figures for government deposits in weekly reporting
banks to deposits in nonweekly reporting banks, members and nonmembers. Deposits in nonweekly reporting banks were estimated at call dates
by subtracting deposits at weekly reporting member banks from our
estimates of deposits at all banks. These call date figures were interpolated by Method L to end of month (section 4).

1. Treasury Cash and Government Deposits at Federal Reserve Banks, Call Dates, 1907–46

Treasury cash holdings are reported in the monthly *Circulation Statement of United States Money*.[1] Before 1914 this source omits minor
coin. We added the amount of minor coin in Treasury on the date of the
Circulation Statement (first of the month) as shown in the Treasury

---

[1] Published under this title from Mar. 1887 through Dec. 1965 (Fiscal Service, Treasurer of the United States, Treasury Dept.). The title was changed on Jan. 31, 1966, to
Statement of United States Currency and Coin.

---

seasonally adjusted end-of-month figures (from *Banking and Monetary
Statistics*, pp. 373–374). *Apr. 1922–June 1946* (call dates not coincident with weekly report dates): Interpolated by Method L between
data for neighboring weeks (from *ibid.,* pp. 378 ff. and *Federal Reserve
Bulletin,* monthly issues).

    2. Table 32, Parts I and II, col. 13, and Part III, col. 15; Table 33,
Part I, col. 15; and beginning Dec. 1938, plus Table 33, Part III, col.
15.

    3. Call dates, other than end of month, not coincident with weekly
report dates: Interpolated by Method L between data (rounded to
thousands of dollars) for neighboring weeks (from *Federal Reserve
Bulletin,* monthly issues, and *Commercial and Financial Chronicle*).
Dec. 31 dates, 1914–41: *Banking and Monetary Statistics,* pp. 330–
332; 1942–46, *Federal Reserve Bulletin.* Other end-of-month dates:
Federal Reserve Bulletin.

Daily Statement.[2] Beginning 1914, our source is *Banking and Monetary Statistics,* Board of Governors of the Federal Reserve System, Washington, D.C., 1943, for end-of-month and Wednesday data;[3] beginning 1942, the *Federal Reserve Bulletin.*

The call date figures for Treasury cash, 1907–21, are seasonally adjusted end-of-month data for coincidental call dates and interpolations by Method L between the seasonally adjusted end-of-month data for other call dates. Thereafter actual figures were obtained for Treasury cash at call dates falling on weekly report dates or coinciding with the end of the month. For other call dates Treasury cash was interpolated by Method L between weekly data preceding and following the call date. This series was then deseasonalized.

Government deposits at Federal Reserve Banks are reported on Federal Reserve Bank balance sheets, shown weekly and monthly in the *Federal Reserve Bulletin* and *Banking and Monetary Statistics.*[4] Actual figures are shown in Table 41 for deposits at Federal Reserve Banks at call dates falling on weekly report dates or coinciding with the end of the month. For other call dates deposits were interpolated by Method L between weekly data preceding and following the call date. The series was not adjusted for seasonal because we could not make a satisfactory seasonal adjustment.

2. Government Demand Deposits, Call Dates, 1917–46

For the period 1917–46 most state bank reports and other sources of all nonnational bank data include government deposits with other deposits without showing them as a separate item. We do have estimates of (a) total government deposits (at special depositaries and at national and nonnational bank general depositaries) from the Treasury *Daily Statement,* and (b) government deposits at national and member banks at national and member bank call dates. Hence our first idea was to estimate government deposits at nonnational and nonmember banks

[2] Available in printed form for every Treasury business day since Jan. 3, 1895.

[3] Pages 373–374, for end-of-month figures, Nov. 1914–Dec. 1921, seasonally adjusted by us; pp. 378 ff., through Dec. 1941 for Wednesday figures nearest end of month, seasonally adjusted by us through 1933.

[4] Sources of the original monthly figures are the same as for Treasury cash (see preceding footnote).

at call dates by subtracting (b) from (a). However, extensive experimentation persuaded us that this was not possible, primarily because Treasury records and bank records differ in the dates on which they record various transactions. This difference is wide and irregular, hence we were unable to reconcile Treasury and bank records satisfactorily. Accordingly, we decided to rely wholly on bank records and to estimate missing information for some classes of banks by using available information for other classes.

Problems of Reconciling Treasury and Bank Records

United States government deposits at all banks may be classified according to their origin, as follows: (1) deposits of federal officers, i.e., U.S. postmasters, clerks of U.S. District Courts, etc.; (2) deposits arising from sales of government securities; and (3) tax deposits by individuals, partnerships, and corporations.

Originally, only national banks were eligible depositaries for deposits of the first kind, but more recently any bank that is a member of the FDIC has become eligible for designation by the Secretary of the Treasury as a regular depositary and financial agent of the federal government. Until November 15, 1944, the Treasury *Daily Statement* distinguished between deposits to the credit of the Treasurer of the United States and to the credit of other government officers. Since that date the Treasury *Daily Statement* has discontinued reporting amounts credited to government officers other than the Treasurer.

Deposits of the second kind, originally termed "War Loan deposit accounts" and now known as "Treasury tax and loan accounts," have been held at banks that qualify as special depositaries. The system of special depositaries was created during World War I. The First Liberty Loan Act of April 24, 1917, authorized banks purchasing government securities issued under the terms of that act, for their own or their customers' accounts, to make payment by crediting the amount of the subscription to special accounts, designated "War Loan accounts." Since that date, Treasury circulars announcing a projected offer of bills, bonds, notes, or certificates of indebtedness have always indicated whether payment by credit to War Loan accounts for accepted tenders may be made by qualified depositaries. Upon pledging certain specified securities as collateral and upon recommendation of the Federal Reserve Bank in its district, any incorporated bank or trust company and occasionally mutual savings bank or dealer in government securities may be designated by the Secretary of the Treasury as a special depositary.

During 1918, income and excess-profits-tax deposits were carried with special depositaries. Special depositaries have also credited to Tax and Loan Accounts receipts of withholding taxes since 1948; Social Security taxes since 1950; and other tax receipts as of most recently.

Every depositary bank notifies the Federal Reserve Bank of its district daily of changes in the various classes of government deposits on its books. The Federal Reserve Banks maintain records of the account of each tax and loan depositary and they in turn notify the Treasury of the aggregate net change in government deposits with depositary banks as far as known to them. The information compiled from the reports of the twelve Federal Reserve Banks is published in the Treasury *Daily Statement*.

Four factors account for the failure of deposits reported on Treasury records as of a particular date to correspond in amount with the deposits reported on bank records for the same date.

1. War loan deposit figures as reported in the Treasury *Daily Statement* have included, since 1932, balances in one or more nondeposit banking corporations that are not included in commercial bank statistics. These corporations are investment companies, including dealers in government securities, under the supervision of the Banking Department of the State of New York, which have been authorized to act as financial agents and depositaries of public money of the United States.

In addition, Federal Land Banks and mutual savings banks have from time to time served as U.S. depositaries. Their holdings must also be deducted from the Treasury *Daily Statement* totals of deposits in banks to derive a figure comparable to the total on commercial bank books.

The Treasury *Daily Statement* also includes U.S. government deposits in banks in the Possessions. Since our deposit series is limited to commercial banks in the continental United States, deposits in the Possessions must be deducted from the Treasury series if the series is to be used in conjunction with data for the continental United States.

2. On November 15, 1944, as noted, the Treasury *Daily Statement* discontinued reporting the item "Deposits in national and other bank depositaries of Government officers other than the Treasurer of the United States." No comparable change was made in instructions to com-

mercial banks. Instructions to member banks for reporting deposits of the U.S. government have been for many years substantially as follows: "This term should include all deposits of public moneys made by or for the account of the United States or of some department, bureau, or official thereof. Deposits of United States postmasters of Government funds other than postal savings funds, which have come into their possession by virtue of their official position, should be classified as United States Government deposits."

3. Treasury figures combine U.S. government demand and time deposits. Many banks have also combined these classes of government deposits on their books. For our purpose, a breakdown is required whether we use Treasury figures or bank records.

4. The most serious differences between the Treasury and commercial bank records of U.S. government deposits arise from two factors: The first is Federal Reserve Bank notification of the Treasury by mail rather than by wire of changes in the various classes of U.S. government deposits on depositary bank books. Until March 23, 1918, all reports to the Treasury were on a mail advice basis. Since then, war loan deposits have been published in the Treasury *Daily Statement* on an actual date basis from wire advices received from the Federal Reserve Banks. The item, "In special depositaries—income and excess profits tax deposits," which appeared in the Treasury *Daily Statement* from June 14 through August 4, 1918, was apparently on a mail advice basis. Obviously discrepancies would exist between Treasury and bank record data due to lags corresponding to the length of time it took mail to reach Washington from the various district banks.

The second factor is differences in the dates on which entries in government accounts are made by depositary banks and by the Federal Reserve Bank of the district to which the depositary banks report. There are several reasons for such discrepanies. A Treasury circular on a given date announcing an issue of government securities specifies a subsequent date on which payment is due. The bulk of the issue is generally disposed of on the day of the announcement of the tender, substantially smaller amounts being taken during the next few days. Remittances by credit to war loan accounts for the bulk of the offering will appear on the books of the depositary banks on the announcement day. The Reserve Bank entries in such accounts, however, will be made subsequently upon receipt of advice from the banks. On the Reserve Bank books the sales appear to be spread over several days after the announcement day, not concentrated on that day. As a result, if a tender occurs on or about a member bank call date, there are likely to be substantial differences between depositary bank records of U.S. government deposits and Federal Reserve Bank records, i.e., the figures shown in the Treasury *Daily Statement*. On June 30, 1944, and June 30, 1945, during the peak of the large war loan drives, there were discrepancies of over $1,000 million and $1,300 million, respectively, between member bank figures of war loan deposits and the figures reported to the Treasury by the Federal Reserve Banks for this item. Similarly, data supplied to the Federal Reserve System by the Treasury Department for war loan account balances of nondeposit banking corporations do not agree with the data, purporting to refer to the same dates, supplied us directly by these corporations.

It is not only the record of sales of government securities that do not synchronize on depositary bank and Federal Reserve Bank books. Records of withdrawals from war loan accounts also do not always synchronize. From time to time the Treasury makes calls on its war loan accounts with special depositaries, specifying a future date when a percentage of the total balances on the announcement date is to be withdrawn. Member banks sometimes record withdrawals from war loan accounts on the day the announcement is made by the Treasury, whereas the Federal Reserve Banks record the withdrawals on the withdrawal date specified in the announcement.

It is possible to eliminate reasonably satisfactorily discrepancies between Treasury and bank records due to items 1, 2, and 3. It is not possible to do so for those due to item 4.

Estimates from Bank Records

Government demand deposits, demand deposits adjusted, and, of course, their sum, demand deposits less duplications, are available for all national bank call dates. In addition, from 1917, these deposits are available for national banks, state member banks, and all member banks, for all member bank call dates. Since 1934, this information is also available semiannually for insured nonnational and nonmember banks from FDIC figures. Throughout the period, except for some call dates in the 1940's, only demand deposits less duplications is known for all nonnational and nonmember banks.

The available series were seasonally adjusted. The data were then expressed in the form of ratios of demand deposits adjusted to government deposits. The ratios for June and December dates for 1934–46 were then plotted as scatter diagrams on double logarithmic paper for various subdivisions of all insured banks. Excellent linear relationships, with the indicated correlation coefficients between the logarithms of the ratios, were found for the following pairs of classes of banks.

	Correlation Coefficient
a. Insured nonnational and national banks	+.988
b. Insured nonmember and national banks	+.929
c. Insured nonmember and state member banks	+.882
d. Insured nonmember and all member banks	+.915

In view of the higher correlations for (a) and (b) than for (c) and (d), we decided to use the data for national banks to estimate government deposits at both nonmember banks and nonnational banks. Accordingly, we computed, for the first two pairs, the regressions connecting the variables:

$$\text{(a)} \quad \log Y = -.138 + 1.193 \log X$$

$$\text{(b)} \quad \log Y = .360 + 1.045 \log X$$

We used equation a to estimate government deposits at nonnational banks at those national bank call dates for 1917–22 that were not also member bank call dates. We used equation b to estimate government deposits at nonmember banks at all member bank call dates from 1917 through March 1938 and at all call dates other than the June and December dates thereafter.

In order to use equation b to estimate government deposits at nonmember banks for 1917–19, we first had to estimate demand deposits less duplications in nonmember banks at member bank call dates, since the call date nonmember series in Table 33 does not begin until June 1919. These estimates are given in Table 42.

The procedure was simply to compute log X from data for national banks for the relevant date, substitute in (a) or (b) according as the date was a national bank call date only or a member bank call date, compute log Y, take its antilogarithm, and divide demand deposits less

TABLE 42

Derivation of Demand Deposits Less Duplications, Nonmember Banks, Member Bank Call Dates, 1917–19

(millions of dollars)

Member Bank Call Date	Demand Deposits Less Duplications, All Banks (1)	Demand Deposits Adjusted		U. S. Government Demand Deposits		Demand Deposits Less Duplications, Nonmember Banks (6)
		National Banks (2)	State Member Banks (3)	National Banks (4)	State Member Banks (5)	
1917						
June 20	14,376	6,850	370	123	8	7,025
Dec. 31	15,846	7,443	2,444	452	135	5,373
1918						
May 10	16,520	7,315	2,759	1,149	402	4,895
June 29	16,483	7,387	2,744	963	486	4,904
Nov. 1	17,227	7,467	3,131	1,133	573	4,923
Dec. 31	17,155	8,165	3,412	273	160	5,144
1919						
Mar. 4	17,578	8,001	3,598	591	295	5,093

duplications for the relevant group of banks and date by unity plus the estimated Y. The final estimates are given in Table 43, columns 3 and 5.

For national bank call dates that were not member bank call dates, this procedure gave an estimate only for all nonnational banks with no breakdown between state member and nonmember banks. For member bank call dates the estimate derived in this way for nonmember banks was added to the reported figure for state member banks to get deposits at all nonnational banks.[5]

At June dates, 1934–46, and December dates, 1934–45, when U.S. deposits at insured nonmember banks are known, we had to estimate only deposits at noninsured nonmember banks. We did so by using equation b to estimate the ratio of demand deposits adjusted to U.S. government demand deposits at all nonmember banks and then assuming that this same ratio could be used for noninsured nonmember banks. In order to apply this procedure, we needed estimates of demand deposits less duplications at June and December dates for noninsured nonmember banks. These estimates are given in Table 44.

For these dates the estimates of government deposits for all nonmember banks (Table 43, Part II, column 3) are the sums of the directly reported figures for insured nonmember banks (column 4) and the estimates for noninsured nonmember banks (column 5).

How reliable are our call date estimates of U.S. government demand

---

[5] The Federal Reserve has discarded the aggregate data for U.S. deposits in state member banks as of June 1918, because the individual bank reports, by states, for this call date, among others, have been destroyed. The figures nonetheless seem to us subject to a smaller margin of error than new estimates. We have therefore retained them.

Notes to Table 42

Source, by Column

    1. Table 32, Part III, col. 12.

    2. Table 32, Part III, col. 16.

    3, 5. *June 1917:* member bank figures in *Banking and Monetary Statistics*, p. 73 (corrected to exclude letters of credit—erroneously included despite statement to the contrary, p. 69 – and estimated collection items with Federal Reserve Banks) less national bank data; *thereafter: Member Bank Call Report.*

    4. Table 32, Part III, col. 13.

    6. Col. 1 minus sum of cols. 2, 3, 4, and 5.

deposits at nonnational and nonmember banks? For insured nonnational banks, the regression plus and minus one standard error of estimate yields a range from 85 per cent of the value given by the regression to 118 per cent. For insured nonmember banks, the percentage range for the same standard error range is 69 to 144. Clearly, the estimates are subject to substantial error. However, the magnitudes involved are so small that even a large error is tolerable. In addition, the estimates are superior to the only available alternative, the Treasury *Daily Statement* figures, according to which government deposits at nonnational and nonmember banks at some call dates are negative.

3. Government Time Deposits, Call Dates, 1938–46

Beginning November 1938, U.S. government deposits include not only demand accounts, but also Treasurer's time deposits, open account. Two problems are presented by the reported figures. First, Federal Reserve data for government deposits at all banks, June and December dates, combine demand and time deposits; and second, national and member bank call date reports, December 1938 through September 1941, show combined Postal Savings System and government time deposits.

Since almost all U.S. time deposits are at member banks, and since the changes in this item from call date to call date are relatively small, we combined figures for member banks with FDIC figures for insured nonmember banks at June and December dates and interpolated by Method L to other call dates (Table 45).

We estimated call date series of government time deposits at member banks, December 1938–September 1941, by subtracting government demand deposits, shown separately in the *Member Bank Call Report,* from combined government demand and time deposits shown in *Banking and Monetary Statistics.* Thereafter, except for April 1942, call date figures of government time deposits at member banks are shown in *Member Bank Call Report.* The figure for April 1942 is an estimate based on national bank government time deposits.

TABLE 43

Derivation of United States Government Demand Deposits, at Call Dates, in *Nonnational Banks*, 1917–23, and in *Nonmember Banks*, 1917–46

(all dollar figures in millions)

Part I. June 1917 – March 1934

National and Member Bank Call Date	Nonmember Banks		U.S. Government Demand Deposits			Nonnational Banks	
	Demand Deposits Less Duplications (1)	Ratio of Demand Deposits Adjusted to U.S. Government Demand Deposits (2)	Nonmember Banks (3)	State Member Banks (4)	Nonnational Banks (5)	Demand Deposits Less Duplications (6)	Ratio of Demand Deposits Adjusted to U.S. Government Demand Deposits (7)
1917							
June 20	7,025	152.53	45	8	53	7,628	43.93
Sept. 11					170	7,960	5.32
Nov. 20	5,373	42.87	122	135	1,259		
Dec. 31					257		
1918							
Mar. 4					594	7,962	12.40
Mar. 10	4,895	15.87	290	402	692		
June 29	4,904	19.28	242	486	728		
Aug. 31					423	8,217	18.42
Nov. 1	4,923	16.45	282	573	855		
Dec. 31	5,144	79.88	64	160	224		
1919							
Mar. 4	5,093	34.89	142	295	437		

May 12					495	9,334	17.85
June 30	5,300	42.17	123	337	460	9,890	20.16
Sept. 12	5,848	91.93	63	118	467		
Nov. 17	5,764	62.46	91	202	181		
Dec. 31					293		
1920							
Feb. 28	5,946	210.41	28	77	42	10,128	237.81
May 4	5,771	159.29	36	86	105		
June 30					122		
Sept. 8					32	10,398	323.70
Nov. 15	5,610	170.10	33	74	107		
Dec. 29	5,628	128.09	44	106	150		
1921							
Feb. 21	5,071	130.77	38	100	86	9,693	111.74
Apr. 28	4,996	93.81	53	142	138		
June 30					195		
Sept. 6	4,818	132.00	36	120	85	9,341	108.53
Dec. 31					156		
1922							
Mar. 10	4,903	100.07	49	117	166		
May 5	4,907	249.59	20	54	115		
June 30					74	9,583	82.02
Sept. 15	5,403	87.27	61	160	115	10,100	86.69
Dec. 29					221		
1923							
Apr. 3	5,454	87.24	62	126	188		
June 30	5,360	111.35	48	124	172		
Sept. 14	5,344	232.56	23				
Dec. 31	5,616	133.03	42				

(continued)

TABLE 43 (continued)

National and Member Bank Call Date	Nonmember Banks		U.S. Government Demand Deposits			Nonnational Banks	
	Demand Deposits Less Duplications (1)	Ratio of Demand Deposits Adjusted to U.S. Government Demand Deposits (2)	Nonmember Banks (3)	State Member Banks (4)	Nonnational Banks (5)	Demand Deposits Less Duplications (6)	Ratio of Demand Deposits Adjusted to U.S. Government Demand Deposits (7)
1924							
Mar. 3	5,483	162.66	34				
June 30	5,579	180.47	31				
Oct. 10	5,857	130.86	44				
Dec. 31	5,982	149.49	40				
1925							
Apr. 6	6,201	97.87	63				
June 30	6,297	225.69	28				
Sept. 28	6,870	146.19	47				
Dec. 31	7,035	125.16	56				
1926							
Apr. 12	6,871	112.03	61				
June 30	6,461	171.86	37				
Dec. 31	6,500	173.48	37				
1927							
Mar. 23	6,337	140.60	45				
June 30	6,289	180.27	35				
Oct. 10	6,476	104.81	61				
Dec. 31	6,385	148.80	43				

1928			
Feb. 28	6,339	482.11	13
June 30	6,286	135.91	46
Oct. 3	6,474	249.38	26
Dec. 31	6,636	135.62	49
1929			
Mar. 27	6,489	127.23	51
June 29	6,435	105.35	61
Oct. 4	6,543	129.15	50
Dec. 31	6,421	244.10	26
1930			
Mar. 27	6,312	169.98	37
June 30	6,067	144.38	42
Sept. 24	5,733	159.64	36
Dec. 31	5,354	146.53	36
1931			
Mar. 25	5,003	109.00	45
June 30	4,940	98.15	50
Sept. 29	4,380	73.91	58
Dec. 31	4,077	74.69	54
1932			
June 30	3,400	85.36	39
Sept. 30	3,199	49.64	63
Dec. 31	3,203	72.02	44
1933			
June 30	2,477	38.59	63
Oct. 25	2,375	37.75	61
Dec. 30	2,415	21.93	73
1934			
Mar. 5	2,428	28.15	83

(continued)

TABLE 43 (concluded)

Part II. June 1934 – June 1946

National and Member Bank Call Date	All Nonmember Banks		U.S. Government Demand Deposits			Noninsured Nonmember Banks	
	Demand Deposits Less Duplications (1)	Ratio of Demand Deposits Adjusted to U.S. Government Demand Deposits (2)	Nonmember Banks (3)	Insured Nonmember Banks (4)	Noninsured Nonmember Banks (5)	Demand Deposits Less Duplications (6)	Ratio of Demand Deposits Adjusted to U.S. Government Demand Deposits (7)
1934							
June 30			73	54	19	461	22.81
Oct. 17	2,810	39.81	69	48	29	752	24.98
Dec. 31			77				
1935							
Mar. 4	3,224	33.08	95	28	12	763	62.73
June 29			40				
Nov. 1	3,364	69.96	47	35	18	1,063	59.45
Dec. 31			53				
1936							
Mar. 4	3,697	67.80	54	74	19	888	45.00
June 30			93	61	15	1,067	71.16
Dec. 31			76				
1937							
Mar. 31	4,004	115.46	34	25	10	941	91.56
June 30			35	19	11	866	76.61
Dec. 31			30				
1938							
Mar. 7	3,792	64.78	58	19	9	768	85.34
June 30			28				
Sept. 28	3,667	80.89	45	45	13	1,047	78.34
Dec. 31			58				

Date							
1939							
Mar. 29	3,762		56	48	11	882	76.17
June 30		66.19	59				
Oct. 2	4,060		47	45	13	1,126	88.50
Dec. 30		86.29	58				
1940							
Mar. 26	4,151		53	48	12	1,026	84.92
June 29			60	47	9	1,191	124.64
Dec. 31		76.89	56				
1941							
Apr. 4	4,544		36	50	11	1,155	106.14
June 30		123.76	61				
Sept. 24	4,869	102.89	47				
Dec. 31			71	50	21	1,260	57.79
1942							
Apr. 4	5,344		132	50	12	600	50.82
June 30		39.34	62				
Dec. 31			286	229	57	973	15.95
1943							
June 30			544	495	49	870	16.60
Oct. 18	8,521	7.08	1,055				
Dec. 31			558	477	81	1,395	16.32
1944							
Apr. 13	9,732		746	1,207	154	1,266	7.23
June 30		12.04	1,361				
Dec. 30			1,381	1,175	206	2,104	9.20
1945							
Mar. 20	11,484	12.30	863				
June 30			1,813	1,620	193	1,485	6.70
Dec. 31			1,709	1,470	239	2,183	8.13
1946							
June 29			1,084	999	85	1,255	13.77

Notes to Table 43

Source, by Column

Part I

1. Through Mar. 4, 1919, from Table 42, col. 6; thereafter, Table 33, Part I, col. 11.
   2. Estimated from the equation: $\log Y = .360 + 1.045 \log X$,
      where X = ratio of demand deposits adjusted to U.S. government
      demand deposits, seasonally corrected, at national
      banks,
   and Y = the same ratio at nonmember banks.
Demand deposits adjusted and U.S. government deposits in national banks (through June 1923 from Table 32, Part III, cols. 16 and 13; thereafter from Comptroller of the Currency, *Abstract of Reports of Condition of National Banks*) were seasonally corrected by us.
   3. Col. 1 divided by col. 2 plus 1.00.
   4. *Member Bank Call Report*.
   5. At national bank call dates that were also member bank call dates, sum of cols. 3 and 4; at national bank call dates that were not also member banks call dates, col. 6 divided by col. 7 plus 1.00.
   6. Table 32, Part III, col. 11.
   7. Estimated from the equation: $\log Y = -.138 + 1.193 \log X$,
      where X = ratio of demand deposits adjusted to U.S. government
      demand deposits, seasonally corrected, at national
      banks,
   and Y = the same ratio at nonnational banks.
The sources of the data and the procedure are the same as described for col. 2 above.

Part II

1. Same as Part I, col. 1.
   2. Same as Part I, col. 2.
   3. Sum of cols. 4 and 5, at June and Dec. dates; at other dates, col. 1 divided by col. 2 plus 1.00.
   4. FDIC, *Assets and Liabilities of Operating Insured Banks,* 1934–46.
   5. Col. 6 divided by col. 7 plus 1.00.
   6. Table 44, col. 3.
   7. Same as Part I, col. 2.

TABLE 44

Demand Deposits Less Duplications at Noninsured
Nonmember Banks, June and December 1934 – June 1946
(seasonally adjusted, in millions of dollars)

| Call
Date | Demand Deposits Less Duplications at
Nonmember Banks | | |
	All (1)	Insured (2)	Noninsured (3)
1934			
June	2,516	2,055	461
Dec.	2,960	2,208	752
1935			
June	3,165	2,402	763
Dec.	3,597	2,534	1,063
1936			
June	3,737	2,849	888
Dec.	4,080	3,013	1,067
1937			
June	3,986	3,045	941
Dec.	3,695	2,829	866
1938			
June	3,581	2,813	768
Dec.	3,926	2,879	1,047
1939			
June	3,913	3,031	882
Dec.	4,245	3,119	1,126
1940			
June	4,225	3,199	1,026
Dec.	4,547	3,356	1,191
1941			
June	4,789	3,634	1,155
Dec.	5,302	4,042	1,260
1942			
June	5,018	4,418	600
Dec.	6,718	5,745	973
1943			
June	7,856	6,985	871
Dec.	8,976	7,581	1,395
1944			
June	10,051	8,785	1,266
Dec.	11,730	9,626	2,104
1945			
June	12,272	10,786	1,486
Dec.	13,939	11,756	2,183
1946			
June	13,377	12,122	1,255

4. Total Government Deposits at Commercial and Mutual Savings Banks, Monthly, 1907–42

Our monthly series before December 1917 is dated as of Wednesday nearest the end of the month and is based on data for government deposits at clearinghouse banks of New York, Philadelphia, and Boston, whenever reported. At call dates the sum of the seasonally adjusted clearinghouse data was subtracted from seasonally adjusted government deposits at all banks, May 20, 1907–February 5, 1909; June 20, 1917–March 4, 1918. Residual figures for nonclearinghouse banks were interpolated monthly by Method L between call dates and added to the monthly estimates for clearinghouse banks to get the monthly estimates of total government deposits at all banks during these intervals (Table 46, Parts I and II). From February 5, 1909, through June 20, 1917, when data available on government deposits in clearinghouse banks represented a negligible percentage of the total, the monthly estimates are interpolations by Method L between the seasonally adjusted national bank call date figures (see *A Monetary History*, pp. 750–752, Table A-3, column 2).

Although government deposits in clearinghouse banks are reported after 1917, we used weekly reporting member figures instead, since a larger percentage of total government deposits was on deposit with the latter banks. Our monthly series beginning December 1917 is a sum of deseasonalized monthly data for weekly reporting member banks and estimates for nonweekly reporting member banks and nonmember banks, obtained by interpolating by Method L between call dates (Table 46, Part III). The series is dated as of Friday nearest the end of month through April 1921, Wednesday thereafter.

The chief problem posed by these data was the derivation of the non-

---

Notes to Table 44

Source, by Column

1. Table 33, Part I, col. 11.
2. Compiled from FDIC, *Assets and Liabilities of Operating Insured Banks,* and seasonally adjusted.
3. Col. 1 minus col. 2.

TABLE 45

United States Government Time Deposits at All Banks, at Call Dates, 1938–46

(thousands of dollars)

Member Bank Call Date	U. S. Government Time Deposits		
	Member Banks (1)	Nonmember Banks (2)	All Banks (3)
1938			
Dec. 31	1,790	—	1,790
1939			
Mar. 29	12,000	—	12,000
June 30	14,140	—	14,140
Oct. 2	17,000	—	17,000
Dec. 30	18,050	—	18,050
1940			
Mar. 26	24,000	—	24,000
June 29	32,755	—	32,755
Dec. 31	34,425	—	34,425
1941			
Apr. 4	36,425	—	36,425
June 30	36,650	—	36,650
Sept. 24	32,480	—	32,480
Dec. 31	34,120	—	34,120
1942			
Apr. 4	33,000	—	33,000
June 30	34,465	50	34,515
Dec. 31	47,675	200	47,875
1943			
June 30	64,965	300	65,265
Oct. 18	103,600	1,000	104,600
Dec. 31	115,465	1,737	117,202
1944			
Apr. 13	108,667	2,000	110,667
June 30	99,596	2,257	101,853
Dec. 30	101,121	2,054	103,175
1945			
Mar. 20	97,421	2,064	99,485
June 30	97,889	2,074	99,963
Dec. 31	95,742	2,535	98,277
1946			
June 29	97,413	4,510	101,923

weekly reporting member bank series. For other kinds of deposits the difference in dating—never more than three days—between weekly reporting member bank reports and call date reports may be ignored and the residual figures may be considered to measure the condition of nonweekly reporting member banks. However, government deposits show such large variations that this difference in dating may result in substantial errors. For example, there are occasional negative residuals when weekly reporting data closest to call dates are subtracted from call date figures. We circumvented this difficulty by interpolating by Method L weekly reporting member data between two neighboring weeks to the exact call date (Table 47, column 2). We expressed the residual non-weekly reporting member bank figure as a ratio of the weekly reporting series at call dates (column 4) and applied this percentage to the final weekly reporting figure (seasonally adjusted, Wednesday nearest end of month) that was nearest the call date. Interpolation by Method L between the resulting figures gave monthly estimates to be added to the weekly reporting monthly data and the nonmember monthly data (Table 46, Part III). Beginning December 1938, monthly interpolations by Method L between the call date figures of government time deposits (Table 45, column 3) were added to get total government deposits (Table 46, Part IV).

Notes to Table 45

Source, by Column

1. *Through Dec. 1941:* U. S. government demand and time deposits (from *Banking and Monetary Statistics,* p. 75), *minus* U. S. government demand deposits (from *Member Bank Call Report*). *Apr. 1942:* estimate based on U. S. government time deposits in national banks (from Comptroller of the Currency, *Abstract of Reports of Condition of National Banks*). *June 1942–June 1946: Member Bank Call Report.*
2. June and Dec. dates: either (a) data for all nonnational banks (from Comptroller of the Currency, *Annual Report),* minus state member bank data (derived by deducting national bank data from all member bank data), or (b) estimated from data for insured nonmember banks (from FDIC, *Assets and Liabilities of Operating Insured Banks).* Other call dates were interpolated by Method L.
3. Col. 1 plus col. 2.

5. Federal Reserve Estimates of Government Deposits, Monthly, December 1942 to Date

Beginning December 1942, we shift to Federal Reserve estimates of government deposits. Through December 1946, these are end-of-month estimates covering government demand and time deposits at commercial and mutual savings banks.[6] The estimates beginning January 1947 refer to the last Wednesday of the month.[7]

In 1960 the Federal Reserve introduced a new series of government demand deposits at member banks with data back to 1947 in the form of semimonthly averages of daily figures.[8] This series was continued through June 1961. It was then superseded by a series of government demand deposits at all commercial banks, also given as semimonthly averages of daily figures, with data back to 1947.[9] Current figures have since been shown as monthly averages of daily figures.[10] For government time deposits, only the total at all banks as of the last Wednesday of each month back to 1947 is available in unpublished form from the Federal Reserve.

[6] *Federal Reserve Bulletin,* monthly issues, beginning Feb. 1944.

[7] Currently shown, on p. A-18 of the *Federal Reserve Bulletin,* 1968 issues, as part of the table, "Consolidated Condition Statement, Details of Deposits and Currency."

[8] *Federal Reserve Bulletin,* Oct. 1960, pp. 1116–1121. In *A Monetary History,* Table A-3, we combined this series, which we seasonally adjusted, and monthly estimates that we constructed from call dates estimates of government demand deposits at all other banks and of all government time deposits. We consider that Table A-3, col. 2, is superseded from 1947 on by the Federal Reserve estimates of government demand deposits at commercial banks in the form of monthly averages of daily figures.

[9] *Federal Reserve Bulletin,* Aug. 1961, p. 1001. The member bank series is still available (*ibid.,* 1968 issues, table, "Aggregate Reserves and Member Bank Deposits," either p. A-16 or p. A-17). Since Oct. 1966, seasonally adjusted as well as unadjusted data have been available back to 1947.

[10] *Federal Reserve Bulletin,* 1968 issues, either p. A-16 or p. A-17, table on "Money Supply and Related Data," shows the seasonally unadjusted U.S. government demand deposits at commercial banks.

Derivation of Estimates

TABLE 46
United States Government Deposits at All Banks, Monthly,
1907–08; 1917–42
(millions of dollars)
Part I. May 1907–December 1908

National Bank Call Date	Wednesday Nearest End of Month	United States Government Deposits		
		Clearing-house Banks (1)	Nonclearing-house Banks (2)	All Banks (3)
	1907			
May 20		39	156	196
	May 29	36	154	190
	July 3	35	144	179
	July 31	31	136	167
Aug. 22		30	130	160
	Aug. 28	31	130	161
	Oct. 2	37	132	169
	Oct. 30	65	133	198
	Nov. 27	77	134	211
Dec. 3		72	134	206
	1908			
	Jan. 1	83	154	237
	Jan. 29	67	174	241
Feb. 14		73	185	258
	Feb. 26	62	181	243
	Apr. 1	48	171	219
	Apr. 29	46	163	209
May 14		39	158	197
	June 3	22	145	168
	July 1	21	127	148
July 15		12	118	130
	July 29	11	119	130
	Sept. 2	11	123	134
Sept. 23		12	125	137
	Sept. 30	11	124	135
	Oct. 28	11	119	130
Nov. 27		10	113	124
	Dec. 2	10	113	123
	Dec. 30	10	109	120
	1909			
Feb. 5		5	105	110

(continued)

TABLE 46 (continued)

Part II. June 1917–November 1917

National Bank Call Date	Wednesday[c] Nearest End of Month	United States Government Deposits		
		Clearing-house Banks (1)	Nonclearing-house Banks (2)	All Banks (3)
	1917			
June 20		<u>125</u>	<u>51</u>	<u>176</u>
	June 27	218	66	284
	Aug. 1	154	141	295
	Aug. 29	154	201	355
Sept. 11		169[a] <u>175</u>[b]	229 <u>223</u>	<u>398</u>
	Oct. 3	248	670	918
	Oct. 31	582	1,239	1,821
Nov. 20		<u>961</u>	<u>1,646</u>	<u>2,607</u>
	Nov. 28	848	1,409	2,257
Dec. 31		<u>279</u>	<u>430</u>	<u>709</u>

Part III. December 1917–November 1938

Wednesday[c] Nearest End of Month	United States Government Deposits			
	Nonmember Banks (1)	Weekly Reporting Member Banks (2)	Nonweekly Reporting Member Banks (3)	All Banks (4)
1917				
Dec.	121	452	59	632
1918				
Jan.	163	538	155	856
Feb.	200	1,021	233	1,454
Mar.	236	499	310	1,045
Apr.	281	591	406	1,218
May	270	1,326	355	1,951
June	244	1,014	304	1,562
July	254	906	346	1,506
Aug.	263	731	380	1,374
Sept.	272	304	414	990
Oct.	283	1,393	457	2,133
Nov.	180	1,021	261	1,462
Dec.	67	328	16	411

(continued)

TABLE 46 (continued)

Wednesday[c] Nearest End of Month	United States Government Deposits			
	Nonmember Banks (1)	Weekly Reporting Member Banks (2)	Nonweekly Reporting Member Banks (3)	All Banks (4)
1919				
Jan.	101	672	218	991
Feb.	136	895	421	1,452
Mar.	138	482	369	989
Apr.	132	638	303	1,073
May	128	789	253	1,170
June	123	655	199	977
July	109	560	188	859
Aug.	97	699	179	975
Sept.	82	422	167	671
Oct.	70	385	158	613
Nov.	70	319	149	538
Dec.	90	477	26	593
1920				
Jan.	76	299	29	407
Feb.	62	55	32	149
Mar.	44	96	35	175
Apr.	30	131	38	199
May	31	111	50	192
June	36	90	64	190
July	35	125	78	238
Aug.	35	83	96	214
Sept.	34	192	111	337
Oct.	33	88	125	246
Nov.	38	31	68	137
Dec.	44	199	22	263
1921				
Jan.	42	141	21	204
Feb.	41	161	21	223
Mar.	39	258	20	317
Apr.	38	220	19	277
May	46	108	14	168
June	53	324	10	387
July	50	423	15	488
Aug.	47	223	19	289
Sept.	45	382	24	451
Oct.	41	280	29	350
Nov.	39	223	33	295
Dec.	36	195	37	268

(continued)

TABLE 46 (continued)

| Wednesday Nearest End of Month | United States Government Deposits | | | |
	Nonmember Banks (1)	Weekly Reporting Member Banks (2)	Nonweekly Reporting Member Banks (3)	All Banks (4)
1922				
Jan.	42	339	65	446
Feb.	47	369	87	503
Mar.	44	157	73	274
Apr.	35	166	56	257
May	28	193	42	263
June	21	104	28	153
July	27	213	26	266
Aug.	34	237	24	295
Sept.	40	102	22	164
Oct.	48	241	19	308
Nov.	54	298	17	369
Dec.	61	266	15	342
1923				
Jan.	61	145	29	235
Feb.	62	132	42	236
Mar.	62	267	56	385
Apr.	57	220	53	330
May	53	280	50	383
June	48	214	48	310
July	37	159	26	222
Aug.	28	163	8	199
Sept.	26	165	19	210
Oct.	31	106	28	165
Nov.	36	85	38	159
Dec.	42	124	49	215
1924				
Jan.	38	135	47	220
Feb.	35	163	45	243
Mar.	34	188	43	265
Apr.	33	181	43	257
May	32	130	42	204
June	31	108	42	181
July	35	104	46	185
Aug.	39	115	51	205
Sept.	43	163	55	261
Oct.	43	216	56	315
Nov.	41	230	57	328
Dec.	40	127	58	225

(continued)

Derivation of Estimates

TABLE 46 (continued)

Wednesday Nearest End of Month	United States Government Deposits			
	Nonmember Banks (1)	Weekly Reporting Member Banks (2)	Nonweekly Reporting Member Banks (3)	All Banks (4)
1925				
Jan.	47	132	67	246
Feb.	53	149	76	278
Mar.	62	252	87	401
Apr.	54	183	77	314
May	39	201	64	304
June	28	98	54	180
July	34	78	56	168
Aug.	42	68	59	169
Sept.	47	133	61	241
Oct.	50	93	61	204
Nov.	53	78	61	192
Dec.	56	171	61	288
1926				
Jan.	58	195	64	317
Feb.	59	265	66	390
Mar.	60	234	68	362
Apr.	56	211	63	330
May	46	276	58	380
June	37	137	53	227
July	37	155	53	245
Aug.	37	112	54	203
Sept.	37	183	55	275
Oct.	37	147	55	239
Nov.	37	129	56	222
Dec.	37	124	56	217
1927				
Jan.	40	161	51	252
Feb.	43	189	47	279
Mar.	44	142	43	229
Apr.	41	141	42	224
May	38	123	42	203
June	35	108	41	184
July	44	110	49	203
Aug.	51	133	56	240
Sept.	60	213	62	335
Oct.	56	190	65	311
Nov.	50	39	68	157
Dec.	44	147	71	262

(continued)

TABLE 46 (continued)

Wednesday Nearest End of Month	United States Government Deposits			
	Nonmember Banks (1)	Weekly Reporting Member Banks (2)	Nonweekly Reporting Member Banks (3)	All Banks (4)
1928				
Jan.	27	104	84	215
Feb.	13	62	95	170
Mar.	21	132	86	239
Apr.	30	92	74	196
May	37	62	65	164
June	45	135	55	235
July	39	307	48	394
Aug.	33	392	43	468
Sept.	26	60	36	122
Oct.	33	143	44	220
Nov.	40	189	52	281
Dec.	49	127	62	238
1929				
Jan.	50	113	57	220
Feb.	50	66	53	169
Mar.	52	135	47	234
Apr.	55	121	61	237
May	58	165	74	297
June	61	173	88	322
July	57	106	77	240
Aug.	54	123	68	245
Sept.	50	137	57	244
Oct.	43	138	54	235
Nov.	35	175	51	261
Dec.	26	63	47	136
1930				
Jan.	30	48	44	122
Feb.	33	9	42	84
Mar.	37	102	39	178
Apr.	37	81	44	164
May	40	85	48	173
June	41	129	54	224
July	40	136	51	227
Aug.	37	53	48	138
Sept.	36	109	45	190
Oct.	36	120	46	202
Nov.	36	2	47	85
Dec.	36	156	48	240

(continued)

TABLE 46 (continued)

| Wednesday Nearest End of Month | United States Government Deposits | | | |
	Nonmember Banks (1)	Weekly Reporting Member Banks (2)	Nonweekly Reporting Member Banks (3)	All Banks (4)
1931				
Jan.	39	125	45	209
Feb.	42	105	41	188
Mar.	45	162	37	244
Apr.	47	191	43	281
May	49	15	51	115
June	50	206	57	313
July	53	238	66	357
Aug.	56	139	78	273
Sept.	58	227	87	372
Oct.	57	171	77	305
Nov.	55	200	63	318
Dec.	54	269	53	376
1932				
Jan.	51	446	56	553
Feb.	49	244	58	351
Mar.	47	409	61	517
Apr.	44	198	63	305
May	41	302	66	409
June	39	323	68	430
July	48	375	86	509
Aug.	55	184	100	339
Sept.	62	515	114	691
Oct.	56	509	109	674
Nov.	50	464	106	620
Dec.	45	359	102	506
1933				
Jan.	47	296	110	453
Feb.	50	98	117	265
Mar.	53	268	124	445
Apr.	57	307	132	496
May	60	278	139	477
June	63	628	146	837
July	62	610	164	836
Aug.	62	918	179	1,159
Sept.	61	766	194	1,021
Oct.	62	1,005	212	1,279
Nov.	67	934	174	1,175
Dec.	74	672	126	872

(continued)

TABLE 46 (continued)

Wednesday Nearest End of Month	United States Government Deposits			
	Nonmember Banks (1)	Weekly Reporting Member Banks (2)	Nonweekly Reporting Member Banks (3)	All Banks (4)
1934				
Jan.	78	1,020	174	1,272
Feb.	82	1,688	221	1,991
Mar.	81	1,352	216	1,649
Apr.	78	1,246	210	1,534
May	76	1,255	206	1,537
June	73	1,374	201	1,648
July	72	1,440	179	1,691
Aug.	71	1,302	161	1,534
Sept.	70	997	140	1,207
Oct.	70	871	122	1,063
Nov.	73	879	147	1,099
Dec.	78	1,293	179	1,550
1935				
Jan.	86	1,291	185	1,562
Feb.	94	1,191	190	1,475
Mar.	81	991	201	1,273
Apr.	68	1,139	210	1,417
May	55	965	219	1,239
June	41	687	228	956
July	42	574	192	808
Aug.	43	563	164	770
Sept.	45	612	128	785
Oct.	47	522	99	668
Nov.	50	552	113	715
Dec.	53	631	129	813
1936				
Jan.	53	595	112	760
Feb.	54	553	96	703
Mar.	63	700	121	884
Apr.	73	839	142	1,054
May	84	926	167	1,177
June	93	796	187	1,076
July	90	856	183	1,129
Aug.	87	830	178	1,095
Sept.	84	718	175	977
Oct.	82	671	171	924
Nov.	79	492	166	737
Dec.	76	632	162	870

(continued)

TABLE 46 (continued)

Wednesday Nearest End of Month	United States Government Deposits			
	Nonmember Banks (1)	Weekly Reporting Member Banks (2)	Nonweekly Reporting Member Banks (3)	All Banks (4)
1937				
Jan.	60	469	121	650
Feb.	47	369	89	505
Mar.	34	319	56	409
Apr.	34	304	62	400
May	35	176	71	282
June	35	519	77	631
July	34	447	78	559
Aug.	33	598	79	710
Sept.	33	546	81	660
Oct.	32	426	82	540
Nov.	31	456	83	570
Dec.	30	622	84	736
1938				
Jan.	44	630	70	744
Feb.	56	730	58	844
Mar.	52	630	62	744
Apr.	45	653	66	764
May	36	662	70	768
June	28	441	74	543
July	34	453	87	574
Aug.	40	416	97	553
Sept.	45	492	107	644
Oct.	50	515	120	685
Nov.	54	585	131	770

(continued)

TABLE 46 (continued)

Part IV. December 1938—November 1942

Wednesday Nearest End of Month	United States Government Deposits				
	Demand			Time, All Banks (4)	Demand and Time, All Banks (5)
	Nonmember Banks (1)	Weekly Reporting Member Banks (2)	Nonweekly Reporting Member Banks (3)		
1938					
Dec.	58	573	141	2	774
1939					
Jan.	57	622	140	6	825
Feb.	56	682	140	9	887
Mar.	56	562	139	12	769
Apr.	57	679	139	13	888
May	58	684	140	13	895
June	59	518	140	14	731
July	55	558	134	15	762
Aug.	51	534	129	16	730
Sept.	48	447	124	17	636
Oct.	51	501	135	17	704
Nov.	54	573	144	18	789
Dec.	58	517	155	18	748
1940					
Jan.	56	553	153	20	782
Feb.	55	606	152	22	835
Mar.	54	509	150	25	738
Apr.	56	625	156	27	864
May	58	695	162	30	945
June	60	531	168	33	792
July	59	525	164	33	781
Aug.	59	512	162	33	766
Sept.	58	431	158	34	681
Oct.	57	483	155	34	729
Nov.	57	558	152	34	801
Dec.	56	406	149	34	645
1941					
Jan.	50	164	142	35	391
Feb.	44	299	135	36	514
Mar.	36	389	127	36	588
Apr.	43	383	133	36	595
May	52	449	139	37	677
June	61	433	147	37	678

(continued)

TABLE 46 (concluded)

Wednesday Nearest End of Month	United States Government Deposits				
		Demand			Demand and Time, All Banks (5)
	Nonmember Banks (1)	Weekly Reporting Member Banks (2)	Nonweekly Reporting Member Banks (3)	Time, All Banks (4)	
1941					
July	56	472	164	35	727
Aug.	50	701	186	33	970
Sept.	49	712	203	33	997
Oct.	56	729	199	33	1,017
Nov.	64	988	193	34	1,279
Dec.	71	1,194	189	34	1,488
1942					
Jan.	88	1,111	243	34	1,476
Feb.	107	1,507	297	33	1,944
Mar.	130	1,835	365	33	2,363
Apr.	112	1,494	376	33	2,015
May	84	1,497	390	34	2,005
June	63	1,349	401	35	1,848
July	97	1,790	485	37	2,409
Aug.	140	1,792	590	39	2,561
Sept.	174	2,477	673	41	3,365
Oct.	208	3,009	757	43	4,017
Nov.	251	3,700	862	46	4,859

Note: National bank call date entries underlined.
[a]Excludes Philadelphia clearinghouse banks.
[b]Includes Philadelphia clearinghouse banks.
[c]Fridays, June 1917–April 1921, Wednesdays thereafter.

Source, by Column

Part I

1. Sum of government deposits at clearinghouse banks of New York City (from *Commercial and Financial Chronicle*), and of Boston

(from Boston Clearing House Assn., *Statement of the Associated Banks of Boston, as Returned to the Clearing House*). The data are weekly averages, which we attributed to Wednesday. The figure for Wednesday nearest the call date was taken as the call date figure. The call date series was adjusted for seasonal by the same seasonal index that was applied to government deposits at all national banks, 1907–22. Wednesday data closest to the end of the month constitute the monthly series. Attempts to deseasonalize the monthly data, 1907–11, failed.

2. Call date figures are col. 3 minus col. 1. The call date residuals were interpolated by Method L to the Wednesday nearest the end of each month.

3. Call date figures come from Table 32, Part I, col. 13. Other figures are sums of cols. 1 and 2.

Part II

1. Through Sept. 11, 1917, same as Part I, col. 1. Beginning Sept. 11, 1917, government deposits in clearinghouse banks of Philadelphia (from the *American Banker*) are included.

2. Same as Part I, col. 2.

3. Call date figures come from Table 32, Part III, col. 15. Other figures are sums of cols. 1 and 2.

Part III

1. Interpolated by Method L between call date figures of Table 43, col. 3.

2. *Banking and Monetary Statistics,* pp. 132 ff. and monthly issues of *Federal Reserve Bulletin*. Seasonally adjusted in four periods: 1917–26; 1927–31; 1932–40; 1941–47.

3. Interpolated by Method L between figures of Table 47, col. 6.

4. Sum of cols. 1, 2, and 3.

Part IV

1., 2., 3. Same as Part III.

4. Interpolated by Method L between call date figures of Table 45, col. 3.

5. Sum of cols. 1, 2, 3, and 4.

TABLE 47

United States Government Demand Deposits at Nonweekly Reporting Member Banks, at Monthly Dates Nearest Member Bank Call Dates, 1917–42

(dollar amounts in millions)

Member Bank Call Date	All Member Banks (1)	United States Government Demand Deposits — Unadjusted Data			United States Government Demand Deposits — Seasonally Adjusted Data		Monthly Date Nearest Call Date
		Weekly Reporting Member Banks (2)	Nonweekly Reporting Member Banks (3)	Col. 3 as Per Cent of Col. 2 (4)	Weekly Reporting Member Banks (5)	Nonweekly Reporting Member Banks (6)	(7)
1917							1917
Dec. 31	649	574	75	13.07	452	59	Dec. 28
1918							1918
May 10	1,459	827	632	76.42	531	406	May 3
June 29	1,521	1,170	351	30.00	1,014	304	June 28
Nov. 1	1,708	1,286	422	32.81	1,393	457	Nov. 1
							1919
Dec. 31	472	450	22	4.89	328	16	Jan. 3
1919							
Mar. 4	884	601	283	47.09	895	421	Feb. 28
June 30	902	692	210	30.35	655	199	June 27
Nov. 17	386	263	123	46.77	319	149	Nov. 28
							1920
Dec. 31	649	615	34	5.53	477	26	Jan. 2

Date								Date
1920								
May 4	190	147	43	29.25	131	38		Apr. 30
June 30	260	152	108	71.05	90	64		July 2
Nov. 15	220	91	129	141.76	88	125		Oct. 29
Dec. 29	316	285	31	10.88	199	22		Dec. 31
1921								**1921**
Apr. 28	273	251	22	8.76	220	19		Apr. 29
June 30	390	378	12	3.17	324	10		June 29
Dec. 31	306	257	49	19.07	195	37		Dec. 28
1922								**1922**
Mar. 10	330	267	63	23.60	369	87		Mar. 1
June 30	156	123	33	26.83	104	28		June 28
1923								**1923**
Dec. 29	462	437	25	5.72	266	15		Jan. 3
1923								
Apr. 3	404	334	70	20.96	267	56		Mar. 28
June 30	296	242	54	22.31	214	48		June 27
Sept. 14	144	137	7	5.11	163	8		Aug. 29
								1924
Dec. 31	237	170	67	39.41	124	49		Jan. 2
1924								
Mar. 31	292	238	54	22.69	188	43		Apr. 2
June 30	179	129	50	38.76	108	42		July 2
Oct. 10	302	226	76	33.63	163	55		Oct. 1
Dec. 31	242	166	76	45.78	127	58		Dec. 31
1925								**1925**
Apr. 6	412	306	106	34.64	252	87		Apr. 1
June 30	177	114	63	55.26	98	54		July 1
Sept. 28	278	191	87	45.55	133	61		Sept. 30
Dec. 31	304	224	80	35.71	171	61		Dec. 30

(continued)

TABLE 47 (continued)

Member Bank Call Date	United States Goverment Demand Deposits						Monthly Date Nearest Call Date (7)
	Unadjusted Data				Seasonally Adjusted Data		
	All Member Banks (1)	Weekly Reporting Member Banks (2)	Nonweekly Reporting Member Banks (3)	Col. 3 as Per Cent of Col. 2 (4)	Weekly Reporting Member Banks (5)	Nonweekly Reporting Member Banks (6)	
1926							1926
Apr. 12	379	294	85	28.91	234	68	Mar. 31
June 30	228	164	64	39.02	137	53	June 30
Dec. 31	234	161	73	45.34	124	56	Dec. 29
1927							1927
Mar. 23	407	313	94	30.03	142	43	Mar. 30
June 30	218	158	60	37.97	108	41	June 29
Oct. 10	435	337	98	29.08	213	62	Sept. 28
Dec. 31	267	180	87	48.33	147	71	Dec. 28
1928							1928
Feb. 28	86	34	52	152.94	62	95	Feb. 29
June 30	257	183	74	40.44	135	55	June 27
Oct. 3	159	99	60	60.61	60	36	Oct. 3
							1929
Dec. 31	262	176	86	48.86	127	62	Jan. 2
1929							
Mar. 27	411	305	106	34.75	135	47	Apr. 3
June 29	348	231	117	50.65	173	88	June 26
Oct. 4	315	222	93	41.89	137	57	Oct. 2
Dec. 31	143	82	61	74.39	63	47	Dec. 31

1930						**1930**	
Mar. 27	325	235	90	38.30	102	Apr. 2	39
June 30	281	198	83	41.92	129	July 2	54
Sept. 24	257	182	75	41.21	109	Oct. 1	45
Dec. 31	267	204	63	30.88	156	Dec. 31	48
1931						**1931**	
Mar. 25	502	408	94	23.04	162	Apr. 1	37
June 30	395	309	86	27.83	206	July 1	57
Sept. 29	526	380	146	38.42	227	Sept. 30	87
Dec. 31	412	344	68	19.77	269	Dec. 30	53
1932						**1932**	
June 30	387	320	67	20.94	323	June 29	68
Sept. 30	738	604	134	22.19	515	Sept. 28	114
Dec. 31	475	370	105	28.38	359	Dec. 28	102
1933						**1933**	
June 30	806	654	152	23.24	628	June 28	146
Oct. 25	918	758	160	21.11	1,005	Nov. 1	212
Dec. 30	967	814	153	18.80	672	**1934** Jan. 3	126
1934							
Mar. 3	1,790	1,583	207	13.08	1,688	Feb. 28	221
June 30	1,658	1,446	212	14.66	1,374	June 27	201
Oct. 17	1,143	1,003	140	13.96	871	Oct. 31	122
Dec. 31	1,636	1,437	199	13.85	1,293	**1935** Jan. 2	179
1935							
Mar. 4	1,270	1,095	175	15.98	1,191	Feb. 27	190
June 29	779	585	194	33.16	687	June 26	228
Nov. 1	650	546	104	19.05	522	Oct. 30	99
Dec. 31	844	701	143	20.40	631	Dec. 31	129

(continued)

TABLE 47 (continued)

| Member Bank Call Date | United States Government Demand Deposits | | | | | | Monthly Date Nearest Call Date (7) |
| | Unadjusted Data | | | | Seasonally Adjusted Data | | |
	All Member Banks (1)	Weekly Reporting Member Banks (2)	Nonweekly Reporting Member Banks (3)	Col. 3 as Per Cent of Col. 2 (4)	Weekly Reporting Member Banks (5)	Nonweekly Reporting Member Banks (6)	
1936							**1936**
Mar. 4	600	511	89	17.42	553	96	Feb. 26
June 30	1,037	840	197	23.45	796	187	July 1
Dec. 31	882	702	180	25.64	632	162	Dec. 30
1937							**1937**
Mar. 31	415	353	62	17.56	319	56	Mar. 31
June 30	628	547	81	14.81	519	77	June 30
Dec. 31	781	688	93	13.52	622	84	Dec. 29
1938							**1938**
Mar. 7	752	697	55	7.89	730	58	Mar. 2
June 30	543	465	78	16.77	441	74	June 29
Sept. 28	707	581	126	21.69	492	107	Sept. 28
Dec. 31	790	634	156	24.61	573	141	Dec. 28
1939							**1939**
Mar. 29	775	621	154	24.80	562	139	Mar. 29
June 30	694	546	148	27.11	518	140	June 28
Oct. 2	675	528	147	27.84	447	124	Sept. 27
							1940
Dec. 30	743	572	171	29.90	517	155	Jan. 3

	1	2	3	4	5	6	
1940							
Mar. 26	725	560	165	29.46	509	150	Apr. 3
June 29	711	540	171	31.67	531	168	June 26
Dec. 31	616	451	165	36.59	406	149	Dec. 31
1941							**1941**
Apr. 4	523	394	129	32.74	389	127	Apr. 2
June 30	619	462	157	33.98	433	147	July 2
Sept. 24	781	608	173	28.45	712	203	Oct. 1
Dec. 31	1,709	1,475	234	15.86	1,194	189	Dec. 31
1942							**1942**
Apr. 4	2,164	1,805	359	19.89	1,835	365	Apr. 1
June 30	1,724	1,329	395	29.72	1,349	401	July 1
Dec. 31	7,923	6,755	1,168	17.29	5,471	946	Dec. 30

Source, by Column

1. *Member Bank Call Report.*
2. Estimates at exact member bank call dates were obtained by interpolating by Method L between data for neighboring weeks (from *Banking and Monetary Statistics*, pp. 132 ff. and *Federal Reserve Bulletin*, monthly issues).

3. Col. 1 minus col. 2.
5. Table 46, Parts III and IV, col. 2, for dates shown in col. 7 of this table.
6. Col. 4 times col. 5.

Author Index

Andrew, A. Piatt, 88, 206, 209, 265, 274–280, 284, 286, 301, 316, 356, 370, 417, 482–483

Angell, James W., 105, 108, 261, 268, 272, 303

Ashley, William J., 96

Axilrod, Stephen H., 131

Barnett, George E., 209, 263, 268

Baumol, William J., 108

Blodget, Samuel, Jr., 2, 214, 233–234, 244, 249–250

Blumberg, Aryeh, 74

Bollman, Erick, 101

Bonar, James, 95

Brainard, William C., 135

Brechling, Frank P. R., 128

Brill, Daniel H., 131

Broida, Arthur L., 129–130

Brunner, Karl, 185–186

Burns, Joseph M., 134

Cagan, Phillip, 60, 108, 156

Campbell, Colin D., 108

Cannan, Edwin, 97–99, 103

Cannon, James G., 377, 482–483

Cantillon, Richard, 95

Carson, Deane, 124

Chapman, John M., 417

Chase, Samuel B., Jr., 110, 123–126, 135

Chau, L. C., 131

Chetty, V. Karuppan, 152–153, 188

Christ, Carl F., 128

Cohen, Morris, 131–132

Cole, Arthur H., 241–242

Courchene, Thomas J., 128

Cox, Albert H., Jr., 168

Crawford, William H., 202, 214, 237–240, 244, 262

Currie, Lauchlin, 261, 267–271

Davis, Andrew M., 101

Dewey, Davis R., 93

Dobb, Maurice H., 98

Duesenberry, James, 132

Dunbar, Charles F., 101–102

Elliott, Roy, 152–153, 178–180

Fand, David, 78, 128, 334, 336–338

Feige, Edgar L., 128, 180–182, 184

Fisher, Irving, 98, 202, 260, 262, 264–267, 270, 275

Ford, James L., 152

Fortson, James, 152, 180

Friedman, Milton, 75–76, 106, 108, 112, 115, 162, 177, 179, 187–188, 297, 321

Fullarton, James, 95–96

Gainsbrugh, Martin R., 132

Gallatin, Albert, 101, 202, 234–236, 244, 249–250, 253, 262

Galper, Harvey, 184–185

Gibson, William, 187

Goldberger, Arthur S., 131

Goldsmith, Raymond, 56

Gouge, William M., 201, 236, 241

Gramley, Lyle E., 110, 123–126, 135

Gras, Norman S. B., 93

Griliches, Zvi, 131

Grunfeld, Yehuda, 132

Gurley, John G., 88, 126–128, 152, 182, 185, 215, 253–254, 258–259

Guthrie, Harold W., 130–131

Hamburger, Michael J., 184–185

Hamilton, Alexander, 93, 247

Hamilton, Earl J., 93, 99, 101

Hansen, Alvin, 101–102

Harrod, Roy, 127

Hart, Albert G., 56, 133

Hawtrey, Ralph G., 101–102

Hepburn, A. Barton, 260

Hester, Donald, 180–181

Hicks, Earl, 59–60

Hicks, John R., 129

Hill, C. H., 99

Horvitz, Paul M., 168

Huang, D. S., 131
Hume, David, 95

Johnson, Harry G., 88, 106
Jung, Allen F., 169

Kane, Edward J., 152
Kaufman, George G., 187
Kemmerer, Edwin W., 202, 209, 260, 262, 264, 270, 370, 483
Kessel, Reuben A., 175
Keyes, Emerson W., 336
Keynes, John M., 101–103, 106, 118–119, 127, 133, 135
Kindahl, James K., 78, 334–336
King, Willford, I., 261, 267–268
Kinley, David, 209
Klein, Benjamin, 117
Klein, Lawrence R., 131
Klopstock, Fred H., 74
Knapp, Georg F., 95
Kosobud, Richard F., 130
Kreinin, Mordechai E., 130–131
Kuh, Edwin, 132
Kvasnicka, Joseph G., 74–75

Laidler, David, 186–187
Latané, Henry A., 88, 105, 261
Laumas, Gurcharan S., 180
Laurent, Robert, 395
Law, John, 93, 99–101
Lee, Tong Hun, 128, 180–185
Leijonhufvud, Alex, 133
Leong, Yau Sing, 261, 267–268, 309
Lipsey, Richard G., 128
Little, Jane S., 75
Lucas, R., 131

McCulloch, John R., 98
Macesich, George, 215, 242–243, 254–255, 258–259
MacLeod, Henry D., 101
Maddala, G. S., 131
Marshall, Alfred, 98, 103, 123
Martin, David A., 258
Meiselman, David, 177, 187–188
Meltzer, Allan H., 98, 128, 185–186
Meyer, John R., 132
Mill, James, 95–96

Mill, John Stuart, 95–96
Miller, Merton H., 108
Mitchell, Wesley C., 101–102, 215, 243, 251, 260–261, 263–268, 270–271, 275, 280–281
Morgan, James N., 130
Muhleman, Maurice L., 260

Newcomb, Simon, 101
Newlyn, Walter T., 88, 110, 118–124, 127
Noble, Robert, 153
Norman, George W., 98
Norton, Frank E., 132

Oliver, Elma, 360
Orr, Daniel, 108

Pesek, Boris P., 88, 94, 110–118, 123–124, 145, 152
Petty, Sir William, 99
Pigou, Arthur C., 101–102
Pugh, Olin S., 169

Rathbun, Daniel B., 132
Reierson, Roy, 74
Ricardo, David, 97–98
Rist, Charles, 95–96, 103
Robertson, Dennis H., 101–103
Rodkey, Robert G., 76

Samuelson, Paul A., 105
Saving, Thomas R., 88, 94, 110–118, 123–124, 145, 152
Sayers, Richard S., 127, 129, 135
Schumpeter, Joseph A., 95, 99–100
Schwartz, Anna J., 179, 360
Seaman, Ezra, 203, 214, 235–236, 262
Selden, Richard T., 162
Shapiro, Harold T., 128
Shaw, Edward S., 88, 126–128, 182, 185, 215, 253–254, 258–259
Sidgwick, Henry, 101
Smith, Adam, 97
Smith, Paul E., 108
Smith, Thomas, 95–96
Smith, Walter B., 241–242
Snyder, Carl, 261, 267
Sparks, Gordon R., 132

Sraffa, Piero, 98
Stark, T., 152
Steuart, Sir James, 101
Suits, Daniel B., 131–132

Teigen, Ronald L., 108
Temin, Peter, 215, 255–256, 258–259
Thornton, Henry, 98
Timberlake, Richard H., Jr., 152, 180, 257
Tobin, James, 108, 124, 135
Tooke, Thomas, 95–96, 103
Tullock, Gordon C., 108
Twain, Mark, 105

van Dillen, J. G., 93
Van Fenstermaker, J., 240, 256
Viner, Jacob, 96

Walker, Amasa, 201
Walker, Frank A., 98
Wallace, Neil, 131
Walters, Raymond, Jr., 236
Warburton, Clark, 215, 237, 241, 244, 250–254, 258–259
Wernette, John P., 252
Wettereau, James O., 237
White, William H., 128
Willett, Thomas D., 255
Williamson, Jeffrey G., 254–255
Willis, H. Parker, 95–96, 417
Wood, Oliver G., Jr., 169

Yeager, Leland, 60, 88, 110, 118, 121, 123–124

Zellner, Arnold, 131

Subject Index

American Express Company, travelers' checks, 60, 136
no legal reserve requirements against, 60*n*
question of money characteristics, 60*n*, 118*n*, 121
See also Travelers' checks
Andrew, A. Piatt, breakdown of deposits by, 265, 278–279
accuracy of, 279–280, 285
compared with 1909 data, 279–280
Angell, James W., money estimates of, 270–271
compared with ours, 303–309
Assets, nominal value, 2, 89
liquid:
as definition of money, 126–127
as joint products, 116–117
as low capital risk, 133
as short-dated, 132–134
as weighted aggregate, 134*n*
conceptual problems in measuring aggregate, 128–130
double-counting, 134*n*
nonpecuniary services, 112*n*, 117*n*
restrictive vs. comprehensive totals, 132*n*
substitutability among, 127–128, 180–184
various measures of, 130–132
vs. overdraft facilities, 149
money:
as demand determined, 123–126
as limited to debt-discharge, 105–110
as liquid assets, 126–130
as noninterest-bearing net wealth, 110–118
as sum of various components, 92
as weighted aggregate, 92
effect on loan market, 118–123
lack of definite theoretical specification, 90–91, 137–138
meaning in past usage, 93–102
near-money, 2, 89, 105; relation to money supply, 123*n*

nonliquid, 2
seven categories of, 148
characteristics of, 149–150

Bank charters:
effect on net worth if number restricted, 110–111
effect of free entry and interest paid on deposits, 113
Bank notes:
distinction between bank and public holdings, 202–203
regarded as claims to money, 105, 201
treated as form of credit by metallists, 95*n*
Bank of the United States:
First, 208, 237
Second, 208, 235, 237, 241*n*
Banking School, opposition to bank note limitation, 95
definition of money, 94
Banks, all:
defined, 75, 332
nonreporting, 211–212, 241*n*, 262–270, 273–274, 359, 370
Banks, commercial:
as financial intermediaries, 111, 124*n*
as government depositaries, 332–333, 424
as part of public re: time deposit business, 83
as producers of deposits, 111
capital of, 233–234, 237–240
checking deposit controversy, 111, 113
classes of, 75, 317–318
clearinghouse, data for, used in interpolation, 79, 370, 377–378, 481–485, 590
defined, 75, 332
member, 332, 357, 359
net worth, 110–111, 113
nonmember, 332, 357, 359, 369
nonnational, 269, 275, 332
number of, 233, 317

private, 287n, 288n, 332
reports, accuracy of, 330
state member, 269, 332, 357, 359
weekly reporting, data used in inter-
    polation, 268, 378–379, 498–503,
    590–592
Banks, mutual savings:
defined, 75, 332
geographical coverage, 175, 531
    coverage in more developed areas,
        193
    preference for time deposits in de-
        veloped areas, 176n, 193
Banque Générale, 100
Barter economy, features of, 106, 119n
Bills of exchange as means of payment,
    93, 98n, 105n
Blodget, Samuel, Jr., estimates of bank
    notes and specie, 233–234
Building societies, 120–121, 127

Call dates:
definition of, 79
frequency of, 1921–22, 79
meaning of "June," 319, 427
Central banks:
effect of nonbank financial intermedi-
    ary liabilities on monetary con-
    trol, 127
open market operations, 125
Certificates of deposit:
before 1914, no uniform classifica-
    tion, 264, 275–280, 284, 294–
    295
in 1920's:
    demand, considered time by An-
        gell, 270
    so treated by Currie, 269
since 1961:
    time, large negotiable, 80–81, 148,
        170–171
    ceiling interest rates, 169n
    comparable to market instru-
        ments, 81, 148n
    data on, 151n
    excluded by us from M₂, 81, 151
Checks in process of collection:
excluded from deposit estimates, 57
procedure questioned, 59n

with clearinghouses, 265n
with F. R. Banks, 424, 450
    See also Float
Checks, postdated, as medium of ex-
    change, 105n
Complementarity in demand, currency
    denominations, 141–142
opposed to substitutability in demand,
    144
Comptroller of the Currency, U.S.:
reports from national banks, 208
    deposit classes in, 265
    savings deposits in:
        as demand deposits, 263n
        Comptroller's doubts on accu-
            racy, 281–282
        meaning of, 278
        variations in, 280–281
        when first shown, 279
reports from state banks, 208–209,
    286
    incompleteness of, 208, 280n
Crawford, William H., monetary esti-
    mates of, 237–240
Currency:
data on, 207–208
    American Express travelers' checks
        excluded, 60
    held by banks. See Vault cash
    held by public, 57, 208, 336–337, 339,
        395
    coin:
        complementarity of notes, 141–
            143
        premium on and demand for,
            143n
        commercial bank deposits as sub-
            stitutes, 144
    defined, 333
    estimates by us:
        commercial bank, monetary au-
            thority holdings excluded, 82
        correct only for M₂ money defi-
            nition, 83
        dating of, 157
        derivation, 76, 335–395
        foreigners' holdings included, 60
        inclusion of some U.S. govern-
            ment holdings, 60, 564–565

Currency (cont.)
  held by public (cont.)
    estimates by us (cont.)
      monthly and quarterly, 57–58, 395
      mutual savings bank holdings, 86n
      reliability, 401, 415, 417
      Treasury holdings excluded, 565
    estimates by F.R., 57, 83, 85n, 395
    individual vs. business, size of holdings, 107, 109
    notes, denominations:
      size of, and inflation, 143n
      substitution of, in supply, 142–143
    slow recognition of concept, 202–203
    substitutes in panics, 60n, 415, 417
    types of, substitution in demand, 141
  held by Treasury. See Treasury cash
  outside Treasury and F.R. Banks, 76, 336–337, 339, 352–357
    at call dates, 79, 357
    composition, 353
    defined, 333
    lost, 395
    monthly, 79, 357
    pre-Civil War series defective, 249–250
    quarterly, 339–351
    revisions of basic data, 353–357
    seasonal adjustment, 357
  stock, 2
    before 1789, 257n
    commodity vs. fiduciary, 89
    data, 205–209, 352–357
    denominations over \$100 discontinued, 105n
Currency School, definition of money, 94
  support of bank note limitation, 95
Currie, Lauchlin, money stock estimates of, 268–269

Deposits, commercial bank:
  data on, a by-product of regulation, 2, 150, 201

include bank-issued travelers' checks, 74
large fraction unclassified, before 1914, 76–77, 264–265
demand less duplications, defined, 233
gross, defined, 483
individual, classes of, 264
  Andrew's data, 265
  in Comptroller's Report, 265n
  "not classified," 264–266
interbank, excluded for money defined as M_2, 83–84
long distinguished from public's, 202
part held for time, should be in money defined as M_1, 85n
misleadingly termed, 59
net, defined, 482–483, 499–500
restrictions on convertibility of, 81
taxes on, post-Civil War, 78, 335, 337
Deposits, commercial bank, adjusted demand and time:
  change in supply conditions, 155, 163, 166–167, 170
  common percentage decline, 1929–33, 167
  dating, 1867–1968, 58
  difference in reserve requirements, 156
  differential growth rates, 156
  division before 1914 questioned, 154–155, 274, 330
  estimates by F.R. before 1914, 76–77
    conceptually different from later, 76–77, 153, 275, 302
    inadequate data, 275, 425
    possible errors, 274–275, 285–286, 301–302
  estimates by F.R., 1946–68, 57–58, 522–525
  estimates by us, 1914–45, 78–79
    at call dates, 79, 432–445, 454–471
      member, 474–476
      national, 451–452
      nonmember, method of interpolation, 453, 473–474; recon-

ciled with nonnational, 473–474

nonnational, compilation problems, 423–426; problem of discrepant dating, 426–427

nonnational, interpolators used, 431, 446–451; sample of states, 427–431

reliability, 477–480

subtraction of redeposited postal savings, 423–424, 475–476

subtraction of U.S. deposits, 476–477

monthly, 481

by groups of states, 1914–19, 486–487

member, how estimated, 1919–23, 502–503; published data adjusted, 1923–45, 498–501

nonmember, interpolators used, 1919–45, 503, 522–523

reliability, 525–527

subtraction of U.S. deposits, 498

quarterly, 58

exclude bank and Treasury holdings, 57

exclude U.S. holders' dollar deposits abroad, 74

holder vs. bank records, 150

homogeneity, 155

ignore mail float, 59

include foreigners' and foreign commercial bank holdings, 74

include foreign institutional holdings at F.R. Banks, 74

interest payments on, average rates, 158–159

declining differential, 1933–45, 167

postwar widening differential, 168

shift in favor of time, 1914–29, 159

once treated as claims to money, 95, 201

pecuniary vs. nonpecuniary returns, 159–160

debits as measure of nonpecuniary returns, 158–161

same total returns, demand and time, 161

per capita, correlated with income, compared with broader deposit totals, 177–178

quantity as measure of net wealth, 110

ratio of demand to time, changes and supply conditions, 170

erratic since 1946, 170

substitutability in supply, 142, 163

Feige's evidence, 180

for currency, 144

Deposits, commercial bank, demand adjusted:

bank services, 168, 172

business holdings, 107, 109

greater than personal, 109, 141

index of business money balances, 142

response to yield on savings and loan shares, 183

components, 263n

defined, 233, 269

interest payments, and moneyness, 116

and marginal nonpecuniary services, as free good, 113

before 1914, 77

interpreted as money-debt, 111

legal prohibition since 1933, 165–167; evaded, 117n

services on, 168n, 172

no bank incentive to distinguish from time (pre-1914), 77

per capita, correlated with income, 177, 193

personal holdings, attributable to asset motives, 109

response to yield on savings and loan shares, 183

service charges, 163

since 1933, only class transferable by check, 81

subject to check, a component of, 263

total debits, 109n

transactions services, zero marginal, positive average yield, 114

vs. dominant money, 114–115

Deposits, commercial bank, time adjusted:
  a misnomer, 81
  elasticity of response to yields on savings and loan shares, 183
  holdings, geographical concentration, 176
    mainly by individuals, 107, 141–142
    number of accounts, 141–142n
  interest payments on:
    ceiling rates payable, 148n, 165, 169n
    decline and excess reserves, 1933–40, 165
    services substituted for, 131n
  growth rate, since 1945, 169
  meaning different after 1914, 77
  moneyness of, 175
  per capita, correlated with income, by states, 177, 193
  See also Certificates of deposit
Deposits, commercial bank, total adjusted:
  defined, 333
  estimates:
    aggregate:
      annual, 1867–1906, 335–339
      monthly, 1907–14, 486–497
      quarterly, 1867–1907, 342–343
    national, 337–339
    nonnational:
      by Fand, 1875–96, 78, 337–338
      by F.R., 1896–1955, 76–77, 273–274
      by Kindahl, 1867–75, 78, 335–336
      by us, 1907–23, 423–431
    reasons for, before 1914, 76–77, 138
  velocity, whether lower than that of bank notes or coin, 97
Deposits, Federal Reserve:
  commercial bank:
    held against time, should be in M_1, 84, 85n
    not subtracted from monetary totals, 83

other financial institutions, 84n
Treasury, 565–566, 573
Deposits, mutual savings bank:
  estimates, 1867–1946, 336–339, 538–554
    compilation problems, 532–553
    discrepant dating, 533
    reliability, 548–558
    sample of states, 534–536
    scheme of interpolation, 530–531, 537
    sources of data and revisions, 558–561
  estimates by F.R., 1947–68, 58, 554, 556
  seasonal adjustment, 555n
  moneyness, 116–117, 152–153
  pecuniary and nonpecuniary returns, 175
  compared with commercial time, 172
  ratio to commercial demand, by states:
    higher than in nonmutual savings states, 189
    substitutability for commercial time, 176
    vs. ratio of commercial time to demand, 176
  reasons not defined by us as money:
    cyclical behavior, 178
    per capita correlations with income, 177, 193
    ratios to commercial demand, 189
  rise in, 1929–33, 163
  substitutability for currency and commercial demand and time, 144, 176
Diamond-water paradox, 112–113

Economic theory:
  no precise definition of money in, 91, 94
  price vs. monetary theory, 90
Elliott, Roy, on weighting assets by moneyness, 152n
Euro-dollar deposits:
  fraction held by U.S. public, 74n

not in U.S. estimates of public's deposits, 74n
reserve ratio, 74n
size of market, 74n

Fand, David, monetary estimates by, 337–338
Federal Deposit Insurance Corporation:
all-bank series, 209
insured bank reports, 209, 316, 576
Federal Reserve Bank of St. Louis, evidence on definition of money, 116
failure to consolidate accounts, 85n
Federal Reserve System:
liquid asset surveys, 130n, 131n
monetary estimates—
adjusted demand and time deposits:
1896–1913 (annual), 76–77, 261–262, 274; arbitrary division of deposits, 77, 302; national bank error, 275–286, 302; nonnational bank error, 286–294, 297–298, 301–302
1946–68 (monthly), 57–58, 482, 522–523
1943–45, compared with ours, 524–525
all-bank, 1896–1955, 212, 261
excellent coverage of, 317
individual state data, dating inconsistent, 315n
currency held by public, 1943–68, 57, 395
development, 272–274
failure to consolidate accounts, 85n
member bank reports, 209
mutual savings bank deposits, 58, 523–525, 554, 556
1943–47, compared with ours, 555–556
seasonal adjustment, 555n
Postal Savings System deposits, 562
reasons for former inclusion of mutual and postal savings deposits in money, 81n, 82n
U.S. government deposits, 593
vault cash, 379, 395

Feige, Edgar L., re: substitution in demand for demand and time deposits:
criticized by Hester, 180n, 181n
criticized by Lee, 181–182
validity of prewar findings questioned, 180
Financial intermediaries:
commercial banks, 59n, 113, 124n
net worth as wealth, 112, 118
nonbank liabilities, 126–127
as money substitutes, 128
elasticity of substitution in demand questioned, 128, 181–184, 185n
offsetting changes in money, 127
vs. public, 134
Fisher, Irving:
monetary estimates, 262–263, 265–266
on definition of money, 98n
on float, 265n
tests of quantity of money equation, 264
Float:
bank, 59n, 426
data on, 426, 452
development of concept, 203
Fisher's role, 265n
holder vs. bank records, 59n, 60n
mail, 59n, 60n
Flow-of-funds accounts, measure of demand deposits, 59n, 60n

Gallatin, Albert:
monetary estimates, 234–235
on definition of money, 101n
Gold stock, revisions of published data, 353–354
See also Specie
Government:
debt as wealth, 135
inconvertible paper money, "forced" issue, 94, 95n, 96n, 331
Gramley and Chase, alleged new view, 123–125
absence of empirical evidence, 126n
Gurley and Shaw:
definitions of money, 126n

Gurley and Shaw (cont.)
  liquidity as essential feature of money, 126
  money stock estimates, 253–254
  theses re: financial intermediary liabilities, 126–127
  tests of, 127–128

Hester, Donald, criticism of Feige's findings, 180n, 181n
High-powered money, as definition of money:
  implied by recent criteria for money, 118, 122, 124, 136
  in nineteenth century, 84, 118
  possibly Fisher's, 98n
  as exogenous variable, 124
  distinct from other assets in supply of money analysis, 124n

Instant purchase clause, legal enforcement unnecessary, 114n, 115n
Interest rates:
  as only variable reconciling asset demand and supply, 135
  changes in level due to liquidity shifts, 133, 135
    presumed effects on spending, 133, 135
  rise in, with term to maturity, and savings deposits as money, 175
  short-dated assets, presumed large changes in quantities held, 133–135
  size of adjustment due to open market operations, short- and long-run equilibrium, 125
Interpolation procedures, general approach, 321
  Method L (straight line), 322, 330
    effect on amplitudes, 330
    special case of Method R, 324
  Method R (related series), 323–326
    estimating relevant parameters, 326–327
  Method S (step method), 328
  more accurate with seasonally adjusted data, 76, 322

Kemmerer, Edwin W.:
  currency estimates, 262
  tests of quantity equation, 264
Keynes, John M.:
  asset motives for money-holding stressed, 102
  bank notes as "small change," 127
  definition of money, 106n, 118n, 119n
    pragmatic approach, 103
    referring to short-dated assets, 132
  rigid price assumption, 132n, 135n
Kindahl, James K., deposit and vault cash estimates, 335–336
King, Willford I., monetary estimates, 267

Law, John:
  career of, 100n, 101n
  definition of money, 99–100
Lee, Tong Hun, on substitution in demand for various nominal value assets:
  criticism of Feige's findings, 181–182
  his findings criticized, 183–184
Leijonhufvud, Alex, on Keynes' view of money as short-dated assets, 133n
Leong, Yau Sing, monetary estimates, 267–268
  compared with ours, 309
Life insurance policies, cash surrender value, 132n, 148
Liquidity:
  ambiguity of meaning, 129
  as essential feature of money, 90, 102, 128–129
    advocated by minority of economists, 95n
    antecedent of current view, 95n
    implications of approach, 129–130
    effects on spending of shifts in total, 132–133
    price level a datum, 135, 137
    shifting portfolio composition vs. sticky yields, 132
    stress on demand conditions, 135, 137
  diverse usage of term, 129, 136
  See also Assets, nominal value

Macesich, George, money stock estimates, 254–255
compared with Temin's, 258
Market equilibrium (Marshallian), constant quantities and large price
adjustment, 124–125
Gramley-Chase analysis limited to,
123–124
Medium of exchange:
as essential feature of money, 105–
106, 128–129, 136
implications of approach:
nominal and real values distinguished, 137
supply conditions stressed, 136
unacceptable as money definition,
110, 137
generally, currency, demand deposits,
and travelers' checks, 106
importance of, for money economy,
granted, 110
Pesek-Saving assumptions, 111–112,
112n
Metallists, economists classified as, 95
theoretical vs. practical, 95n, 99n
vs. cartalists, 95n
Minor coin, 356–357
Mitchell, Wesley C.:
currency estimates, 1860–66, 251;
1896–1911, 263
cyclical analysis of deposits, 264
estimates of deposits subject to check,
265–266
Monetary:
authorities, consolidated accounts of,
57n
control of real quantity of money,
Keynesian assumption, 135n
money balances, 57, 563
mingled with Treasury operating
balances, 60
not combined with public's by
us, 57n
data:
by-products of regulation, 150, 201
problems concerning:
dating, 212–213
errors, 329–331
intraweekly movements, 213

nonreporting banks, 211
unclassified deposits, 212
window-dressing, 212–213
reported by issuers of currency and
deposits, 59, 138, 150, 201
sources of:
on currency, 207–208
on deposits, 208–209
on specie, 205–207
estimates:
compendium of, before 1867, 8,
214–259
defects, 9, 75; compared with other
economic magnitudes, 9
differences among, 215, 257–259,
303–312, 523–525, 554–556
exclusion of American Express
travelers' checks, 60
of official agencies, 201, 237–251,
272–302, 379, 523–524, 554–
556, 562, 593
of private scholars, 233–237, 251–
256, 260, 271, 335–338
ours:
annual, 336, 338–339
call date, 357–370, 423–474,
536–537, 572, 589
monthly, 370–395, 481–523,
536–537, 562, 590–592; based
on F.R. annual estimates, 317;
why they begin in 1907, 315
original, not consolidated, 86n
quarterly, 339–342
reliability, 80, 329–330, 395,
477–480, 525–530, 556–557
semi-annual, 337–338
totals, alternatives:
currency only, 89
currency plus time deposits, 141–
142, 151
demand deposits only, 89, 141–
142, 151
M_1, evidence for, 80, 151, 180, 182
M_2, money for us, 1867–1960,
153–154
evidence against, 92, 180–181,
185–187
evidence for, 92, 178–180, 185–
188

Monetary (cont.)
  totals (cont.)
    M$_2$ (cont.)
      more homogeneous than M$_1$,
        151, 171
      M$_2$-CD's, money for us, 1961–68,
        81, 148, 150, 170–171
      economically more continuous
        with earlier M$_2$, 81, 147, 170
    M$_3$, 81, 151, 171
      1929–33 more continuous with
        earlier years than M$_2$, 165
      no recent evidence on, 179
      possible geographical bias, 175–
        176
    M$_4$, 82, 151, 171
      no recent evidence, 179
      selected in test, 178
    broader than M$_4$, 89, 187n
  totals:
    a recent development, 201–202
    before 1867, 215
    criterion for choosing among, 177
    need for:
      to avoid dealing with individual
        assets, 89
      to distinguish money from near-
        money, 89
      to sum items more influenced by
        supply than demand, 139–140
    problems of estimating, 211–212
      based on unweighted sums, vs.
        weighted by moneyness, 92
      consolidated vs. combined sums,
        83–85, 284n, 285n
    substitution in demand, vs. in sup-
      ply, as condition for, 142–143
Money:
  as a medium of exchange, 90, 104,
    106–107
    no explanation of size of balances,
      107
    problems with approach, 105–107,
      136
  as characterized by liquidity, 90, 126
    advocated by a minority, 102–103
    antecedent of current view, 95n
    emphasized since 1945, 102
  as high-powered money, 104, 145
  as joint product, 147, 151–152

  as net wealth, 94–95, 110, 117
  as temporary abode of purchasing
    power, 106
    emphasized by Cambridge cash-
      balances approach, 106
    illustrations of, 107, 141
    not identical with medium of ex-
      change, 107
    vs. savings deposits' abode, 175
  as weighted sum of assets, 2, 126,
    147, 151, 188
  asset function of, 104
  balances, substitution in supply of
    currency and deposits, 144
    business, size of:
      consistent with transactions
        needs, 109
      demand deposits as index, 141–
        142, 150
      negligible savings and loan share
        holdings, 183
    personal, size of, 109, 141
      currency and time deposits as
        index, 141–142, 151
      larger than transactions needs,
        107n
      response to yield on savings and
        loan shares, 183
    ratio to transactions, 109
    size of, on inventory theoretic
      analysis:
        during hyperinflations, 107–108
        smaller than actual, 108
    transactions services, zero price vs.
      zero quantity, 114
  commodity, 110
  definition of, 118
    acknowledges a distinctive asset
      subtotal, 89–90
    a priori approaches:
      monetary effects on interest rates
        (Gramley-Chase), 110
      net wealth (Pesek-Saving), 110–
        116
      neutrality (Newlyn-Yeager),
        119–121
      stress on medium of exchange,
        106
      suggestive but misleading, 90

basis for, nominal vs. real, 138–139
empirical approach, 2, 104, 118, 137, 198
Keynes' influence on broadening, 102
may vary for different countries and periods, 1, 91
not crucial to conclusions, 2, 92, 198
not specified precisely by theory, 91
relevant factors for, 138, 141
subject to change with growth of knowledge, 91
three coexisting since 1800, 94
excluding bank money, 95–97, 145
excluding bank notes, 83
including deposits, 97, 102
See also Monetary totals
demand for:
determinants, 139–140
different definitions, 197
less variable than supply, 139
responsive to change in high-powered money, 204
simple function attainable, 139
stability of, 197–198
diverse usage of term, 94
dominant, 110, 113–115
economy, features of, 106, 119n, 120n, 125
fiat, 111
fiduciary, 113
government paper, 94, 95n, 96n, 331
nonpecuniary services, 110, 112n, 114n
relation to other economic magnitudes, 90
supply:
determinants, 139
high-powered vs. other assets, 124n
no simple function for, 139
types, 93
velocity, 95
contrasted with that of vault cash by metallists, 95n, 96
effect of claims to money on, 97
trend, 1914–29, 1929–33, 162n, 163
vs. circulating medium, 94
Moneyness, 92
defined by Pesek-Saving, 111
demand deposits vs. currency, 152–153
deposit categories, 114n, 115n, 115–117, 145
weighted averages of assets with, 147, 151–153

National bank notes, revisions of circulation data, 355–356
National Monetary Commission, 263–264, 286
1909 survey of U.S. banks, 209, 275
definition of savings, 275–278
on individual deposit classes, 263–264
Net worth, banks, 110, 113
elimination through free entry, interest on deposits, 112–113
vs. that of other financial intermediaries, 112, 118
vs. that of radio and TV stations, 112, 118
Neutrality:
as applied by Yeager, 121
criterion of assets labeled money, 119–120
defined by Newlyn, 119
satisfied by high-powered money, 121–122
Newlyn, Walter T.:
currency and deposits as neutral, 120
definition of money, neutrality as criterion, 119
high-powered money implicit, 122–123
unstated assumption of, 120
New York State:
deposit estimates for, 3
demand-time breakdown, 448
member banks, 474–476
mutual savings banks, 532–533, 537, 554
national banks, 481, 497
nonmember banks, 452–453
nonnational banks, 427–431

New York State (cont.)
  deposit estimates for (cont.)
    reliability, 477–480
  postal savings in banks, 475n
  vault cash estimates for, 359, 361,
    367
Nominal vs. real magnitudes, 135n, 138

Open market operations:
  initial effect on interest rates, reduced
    by effect on quantity of money,
    125
  money demand responsive to, 123–
    124
  sequence of adjustments to, 125
Overdraft facilities, not asset, 149–150

Personal income, decline in variability
    among states with smaller varia-
    tion in deposit-holding, 196
Pesek-Saving:
  definition of money, 110–118
    as net wealth and medium of ex-
      change, 110
      nonpayment of interest on de-
        mand deposits, as condition
        for, invalid, 116–117
      price level effects, 114–115
      high-powered money implicit, 117–
        118
    medium of exchange function
      taken for granted, 111–112
  on instant repurchase clause, 115n,
    116n
  on joint products of money-debt, 116
  on transactions services of money;
    confusion of zero price and zero
    quantity, 114
Petty, Sir William, definition of money,
    99n
Postal Savings System, 3
  deposits, 560
    pecuniary and nonpecuniary re-
      turns compared with commercial
      time, 171–172, 175
    discontinued, 1966, 148, 149n, 561
  redeposits in banks:
    data, combined with time, 424–425
      in member and national, 423n,
        424n, 424–425, 475, 501, 503

estimates of:
  in nonmember banks, 452–453,
    475
  in nonnational banks, 431, 451,
    475
  reserve requirements against, 501n
Price level, distinction between nominal
    and real quantity of money, 138–
    139
  in Keynesian analysis, 135
Public, 57
  defined ideally, 58–59
  departures from ideal definition, 60,
    331

Quantity of money. *See* Monetary totals
Quantity of money equation:
  Cambridge cash-balances version,
    emphasis on money as abode of
    purchasing power, 106
  transactions version, tested with no
    single money total, 202, 264
Quasi-money, 119–122
  See also Assets, near-money

Radcliffe Committee, 127–128
  on liquidity: no settled concept or
    measure, 130n
Regulation Q, 148n, 165
Reserve requirements against deposits:
  demand vs. time:
    distinction important after 1914, 77
    member, by classes of banks, 156,
      158
      difference in time deposit growth,
        156, 158
      role of difference in 1930's,
        165–167
    nonmember, ratio of time to de-
      mand growth vs. member, 156,
      158
    not distinguished before 1914, 154–
      155
    state laws governing, 76n
  government:
    Act of 1908 exempting, 480n
    in Banking Act of 1935, 498
    in F.R. Act, 481
    Treasury exemption of, 1902–08,
      482n

redeposited postal savings, 501*n*
Risk, types of capital, 133–134
Rural states:
  deposit estimates, 451–453, 472–476, 481, 497
  reliability, 477–480
  sample, 427–431

Savings and loan associations, 3
  not regarded as banks, 318
  shares, 57
    as quasi-money, 120
    data for, 58
      seasonal factors, 56, 76
      elasticity of response to, 75–76, 145
      own yield, 183
        own yield and that of other assets combined, 184–185
        yield on other assets, 183
    holdings:
      by business, 183
      geographical concentration, 176
    pecuniary and nonpecuniary returns, 171–172
      compared with commercial bank time, 172
      quarterly advertised rates, 184*n*
      per capita, correlated with personal income, 177, 193
Sayers, Richard S., on liquid assets as superseding money, 126–127, 129
Schumpeter, Joseph A., on theoretical vs. practical metallists, 95*n*
  on Law as theoretical, 98*n*, 99*n*
Seaman, Ezra C., monetary estimates of, 235–236
Seasonal movements, methods of adjustment, 320–321
  in currency outside Treasury and F.R. Banks, 357
  in deposits:
    commercial bank, 430–431, 450–452, 473–474, 476, 484, 497, 499, 524–525
    government, 577, 592
    mutual savings bank, 532, 536–537, 554, 555*n*
    postal savings, 562
  in savings and loan shares, 56

in Treasury cash, 573
in vault cash, 360–362, 377–378, 417–422
Silver:
  certificates, premium on and effect on demand, 143
  subsidiary coin, revision of data, 355
Smith, Adam, bank notes as displacing specie, 97*n*
Specie:
  defined, 205
  held by public, 207, 211
  in banks, 211
    as duplicating notes and deposits, 203
  stock of, estimates, 6, 205–207, 243–244
    Blodget's, 233–234
    definition of, 206*n*
    reliability, 210–211
    Seaman's, 235–236
  vs. bank notes for discharge of debts, 105
  See also Gold
Substitution effect in demand:
  different for firms and individuals, 142
  of currency items, 140
  of deposits:
    and savings and loan shares, 177–184
      own- vs. cross-elasticity, 184–185
      statistical results, descriptive differences, 182, 183*n*
    demand and business currency, 141
    time and personal currency, 141–142
    vs. complementarity in demand, 144
    vs. substitution in supply at fixed exchange rates, 142–143
Substitution effect in supply:
  of categories of deposits, 144–145
    changing terms, 145, 155
    increased by bank services, postwar, 168
    near-perfect elasticity of demand, time, pre-1914, 155
  of currency:
    and deposits, 144

Substitution effect in supply (cont.)
  of currency (cont.)
    denominations, 142–143
    types of, 140

Temin, Peter, money stock estimates,
    255–256
  compared with Macesich's, 258
Tobin, James, banks as financial inter-
    mediaries, 124n
Trade credit, 128n, 134
Travelers' checks, as currency, 148
  as medium of exchange, 60n, 136
  to be included in money estimates, 75
  See also American Express Com-
    pany
Treasury Department, U.S.:
  balances, 333
  banking data compiled by, 208, 236,
    240–243
  cash assets, 207–208, 564–565, 572–
    573
    composition of, 245–248
  currency issues of, 207
  currency receivable by, 247–248
  Deposit Act and, 247
  deposits at commercial banks, 572–
    573
    Bank of the U.S., 246–247
    Daily Statement vs. bank records,
      574–577
    estimates:
      call date, 449–450, 476–477,
        577–580
      monthly, 590–592
      reliability, 580–581
    not always reported separately,
      317, 426
    only at national before 1917, 565,
      573–574
    state banks, 209
    time combined with redeposited
      postal savings, 501
  deposits at F.R. Banks, 573
  distribution of surplus, 244
  government depositaries, selection of,
    246–247, 424
  specie, data on, post-Civil War, 206–
    207

  defective series, 244–245
  specie holdings, pre-Civil War, 207,
    211, 244

Urbanized states:
  deposit estimates for, 427–431, 449–
    453, 474–476, 481, 483, 485,
    497–498
  reliability, 477–480
  redeposited postal savings in banks,
    475n

Vault cash:
  defined, 333
  estimates:
    all-bank annual, quarterly, 78, 335–
      339, 342–343
    all-bank call date, data compilation,
      357–359
      discrepant dating, 359–360, 363–
        364, 426
      methods of interpolation, 364–
        367
      reliability, 367, 369
      seasonal adjustment, 64, 360–
        363, 417–419
    all-bank monthly, 370–379
      clearinghouse and other, 370,
        377–378
      weekly reporting and other, 378–
        379
      reliability, 401, 415
    commercial bank, 57, 86n
  public monetary asset, if money cur-
    rency only, 83
  velocity of, 95
    contrasted with money, 96n
    metallists' view, 95n
Viner, Jacob, on definition of money by
    Currency and Banking Schools,
    96n

Warburton, Clark, money stock esti-
    mates, 250n, 251–253
Wealth:
  holders, short vs. long-run control by,
    in liquidity approach, 140
  holders, ultimate, 141–142

nonhuman:
  measured by marginal utility, 112–114
  money, a subtotal of, 90, 94
    commodity and fiat, 110
  net worth of financial intermediaries, radio, TV stations, 111–112, 118
  real, plus high-powered money, 135
    government debt, question of inclusion, 135

Wildcat banking, 115n

Yeager, Leland:
  on definition of money, 121
  on monetary authorities and neutrality, 121–122
  on public's ability to affect monetary totals, 123–124
  on supply of money and near-money, 123n
  on travelers' checks, 60n, 121